Grenada and Soviet/Cuban Policy

Other Titles of Interest from Westview Press

Revolution and Intervention in Grenada: The New Jewel Movement, the United States, and the Caribbean, Kai P. Schoenhals and Richard A. Melanson

American Intervention in Grenada: The Implications of Operation "Urgent Fury," edited by Peter M. Dunn and Bruce W. Watson

†*Latin American Politics and Development,* edited by Howard J. Wiarda and Harvey F. Kline

†*U.S. Policy Toward Latin America: From Regionalism to Globalism,* Harold Molineu

Revolution or Order? The Politics of Change and Institutional Development in the Caribbean Basin, Marvin Will

†*The Caribbean Challenge: U.S. Policy in a Volatile Region,* edited by H. Michael Erisman

†*Revolution and Counterrevolution in Central America and the Caribbean,* edited by Donald E. Schulz and Douglas H. Graham

Other Titles Published Under the Auspices of the Naval Postgraduate School and the Kennan Institute for Advanced Russian Studies

Naval Postgraduate School

†*Eurocommunism Between East and West,* edited by Vernon Aspaturian, Jiri Valenta, and David Burke

†*Soviet Intervention in Czechoslovakia, 1968: Anatomy of a Decision,* Jiri Valenta

†*Soviet Decisionmaking for National Security,* edited by Jiri Valenta and William C. Potter

Kennan Institute for Advanced Russian Studies

Scholars' Guide to Washington, D.C., for Russian/Soviet Studies, Steven A. Grant, revised edition by Bradford P. Johnson and Mark H. Teeter

Industrial Labor in the USSR, Arcadius Kahan and Blair Ruble

Soviet/Cuban Strategy in the Third World After Grenada: Toward Prevention of Future Grenadas, a Conference Report by the Woodrow Wilson International Center for Scholars

Transcaucasia: Nationalism and Social Change, edited by Ronald G. Suny

†Available in hardcover and paperback.

About the Book and Editors

The 1983 invasion of Grenada by U.S. and East Caribbean forces focused wide attention on the importance of radical regimes with claims to Marxist-Leninist legitimacy throughout the Third World. The government and party documents captured during and after the invasion provide an unprecedented view into the inner workings of a radical faction bent on usurping power in a small state, shaping an effective vanguard party with an ideology based on its understanding of Marxist-Leninist doctrine, and applying it to a situation for which it had not been designed. The contributors to this volume use the documents to analyze Grenada's internal crisis and the dilemma it posed for Soviet and Cuban policy. The questions they seek to answer include: What are the problems that such a situation creates for U.S. policy—particularly policy in the Caribbean? What do the documents say about intentions and policy options of both the Soviet Union and Cuba? What was the basis for the timing and the intensity of actual U.S. reactions, and what are its options for long-range strategic planning? This is the first major compilation of analytical papers written by eminent American strategic thinkers to deal with the documents found by the U.S. forces in Grenada.

Jiri Valenta is professor of political science and director of Soviet, East European, and Strategic Studies at the Graduate School of International Studies, the University of Miami, Coral Gables. His publications include *Soviet Decisionmaking for National Security* (with W. Potter, 1984), *Soviet Intervention in Czechoslovakia: Anatomy of a Decision* (1979), and *Eurocommunism Between East and West* (with V. Aspaturian and D. Burke, 1980). **Herbert J. Ellison** is head of the Kennan Institute for Advanced Russian Studies, the Woodrow Wilson International Center for Scholars, Washington, D.C. He is the editor of *Soviet Policy Toward Western Europe: Implications for the Atlantic Alliance* (1983) and *The Sino-Soviet Conflict: A Global Perspective* (1982).

Published under the auspices of the
Kennan Institute for Advanced Russian Studies,
Woodrow Wilson International Center for Scholars, Washington, D.C.,
and the Program of Soviet and East European Studies,
Department of National Security,
Naval Postgraduate School, Monterey, California

STUDIES OF THE
KENNAN INSTITUTE
FOR
ADVANCED RUSSIAN STUDIES

THE WILSON CENTER

Grenada and Soviet/Cuban Policy: Internal Crisis and U.S./OECS Intervention

edited by Jiri Valenta and Herbert J. Ellison

A Special Study of the Kennan Institute for Advanced Russian Studies
The Wilson Center

Routledge
Taylor & Francis Group
LONDON AND NEW YORK

First published 1986 by Westview Press, Inc.

Published 2018 by Routledge
52 Vanderbilt Avenue, New York, NY 10017
2 Park Square, Milton Park, Abingdon, Oxon OX14 4RN

Routledge is an imprint of the Taylor & Francis Group, an informa business

Library of Congress Cataloging-in-Publication Data
Grenada and Soviet/Cuban policy.
(A Special study of the Kennan Institute for Advanced Russian Studies, the Wilson Center)
1. Grenada—History—American invasion, 1983—Influence—Addresses, essays, lectures. 2. Communism—Grenada—Addresses, essays, lectures. 3. Grenada—Foreign relations—Communist countries—Addresses, essays, lectures. 4. Communist countries—Foreign relations—Grenada—Addresses, essays, lectures. 5. United States—Foreign relations—Caribbean Area—Addresses, essays, lectures. 6. Caribbean Area—Foreign relations—United States—Addresses, essays, lectures. I. Valenta, Jiri. II. Ellison, Herbert J. III. Series.
F2056.8.G754 1986 972.98'45 85-22741

ISBN 13: 978-0-367-00627-3 (hbk)
ISBN 13: 978-0-367-15614-5 (pbk)

Grenada and Soviet/Cuban Policy:
Internal Crisis and U.S./OECS Intervention
edited by Jiri Valenta and Herbert J. Ellison

ERRATA

Pages 340 and 341 should be transposed.

Pages 469–472 should follow page 458 (Document 22 should consist only of pages 468 and 473).

The document below was erroneously omitted. It should follow page 320.

EMBASSY OF GRENADA IN THE USSR

Dobruninskaya Ulitsa 7
Apartment 221
Moscow
USSR

Telephone
237-25-41
237-[illegible]

Course name: WCM - World Communist Movement
SPP - Social Psychology and Propaganda
- Historic Experience of the CPSU

<u>Names of Students</u>

<u>School name</u>	<u>Real name</u>
Fear Achebe	Derrick James
David Gill	Sam Braithwaite
Justin Lorainey	Fabian Cutram
Bill Jordan	Anselm DeBourg
Francis Che	Glen Noel
Bernadine Peters	Rita Joseph
David Allen	Ian Lambert
Dave Gordon	Andre Mc. Queen
John Franklyn	Ronnie Spooner
-	William St. Louis
-	Gordon Raeburn
-	Roy Cooper
-	Patrick Superville
-	Fred Burris

Contents

Illustrations

MAPS

PHOTOS

Foreword

The turmoil in the Caribbean and Central America does not have a single cause; it results from both indigenous factors and outside intervention. Some liberals see revolution as the result of poverty and injustice, and ignore the East-West security dimensions of the problem, the role of Leninist ideology, and the actions of the Soviet Union and its allies. Some conservatives point to the evil machinations of the Kremlin and its proxies to explain revolution and ignore the economic, social, and political roots of discontent. In reality, however, causes of revolution are both internal and external.

One cannot specify which dimension of the conflict in the Caribbean Basin deserves the most urgent attention from the United States because the various aspects of the problem form a seamless web. Accordingly, the National Bipartisan Commission on Central America set forth three key aims of U.S. policy in Central America: democratic self-determination, social and economic progress, and cooperation in meeting security threats to the region. Without advances on the first two, there can be no security. Without an adequate security shield, there can be no progress on the other fronts. If U.S policy is to succeed in Central America, the problem must be attacked at all levels and treated as a whole. It is unfortunate that both liberals and conservatives have emphasized those aspects of the report with which they agree while attacking the other provisions. To emphasize economic advance, political development, or security measures in isolation guarantees failure.

As a matter of necessity as well as humanity, military aid to El Salvador should be conditioned on progress toward human rights. This was the view of the Bipartisan Commission on Central America, but three members qualified their position in a footnote to the report. They generally endorsed this approach, but said it should not be pursued in a manner that would lead to a Leninist takeover. The only way the United States can give leaders like Jose Duarte enough leverage to make progress on human rights may be to use the ultimate threat of cessation of foreign aid, but applied sensitively, and measured in terms of progress, not instant solutions. While

---

Winston Lord is the President of the Council on Foreign Relations, New York, NY, and was a Senior Counselor to the National Bipartisan Commission on Central America.

this strategy is risky, the United States must make clear the need to control the violent right as well as the left. This is important not only on moral grounds but also because no viable solution is possible if the right as well as the left crushes the center. There has been progress since Duarte's election, and consequently increased support both in this country and abroad, especially in Western Europe.

In El Salvador, the Commission's preference for elections as opposed to power-sharing arrangements is the best—and democratic—way ultimately to end the conflict. The guerrillas propose to scrap the present government and military structure in El Salvador, and instead they hope to install a mixed provisional government by fiat—a classic Leninist approach. Precedents strongly suggest that this would be only a prelude to the elimination of the moderate elements of the coalition. On the other hand, the left cannot be asked to take part in elections without security guarantees. Once Duarte's position is more consolidated, it is possible that true security eventually can be provided. Duarte has been forging an alliance with the sane right and the center before making serious overtures to the left. Perhaps he can split off some relatively moderate elements of the left if he keeps up military pressure on the guerrillas, further solidifies his political position, and offers amnesty and genuine participation in the democratic process.

With regard to Nicaragua, the United States should not rely exclusively on military pressures or on negotiations with the Sandinistas. Both are needed. The fatuous notion that force and diplomacy can be compartmentalized neatly should be rejected. If the United States relaxed its pressures on Nicaragua, the Sandinistas would be much less prone to negotiate.

Just as in El Salvador, the left is more likely to reach for a political solution if it cannot count on a military victory; indeed this is why the Nicaraguans began sounding somewhat more reasonable in the fall of 1984. Sandinista rhetoric became more conciliatory after U.S. naval deployments in Central America, military exercises in Honduras, and the Grenada rescue mission. U.S. aid to the Nicaraguans opposing the Sandinista regime could be used as a bargaining chip in future negotiations in exchange for genuine political participation by democratic forces.

Finally, containment should not be the ultimate goal of the United States in Nicaragua; internal reforms should be stressed as well. This is also the clear preference of the nations of Central America and the Contadora group. It would be a blatant double standard to insist on progress toward democracy in El Salvador, but not in Nicaragua. In short, the U.S. must press the Sandinistas to move toward greater pluralism and openness in their society as part of any package deal, which must also include an end to exporting revolution and a scaling down of the Soviet/Cuban presence. These were some of the issues discussed in an innovative and stimulating conference held at the Naval Postgraduate School in Monterey, California on August 15–18, 1984. As at the Council on Foreign Relations, where he was a visiting fellow from 1981–1982, Dr. Jiri Valenta demonstrated scholarship and organizational talent in setting up the institutional groundwork for a bipartisan approach toward controversial topics. He and his cochairman, Dr. Herbert Ellison of the Kennan Institute, did a splendid job in cochairing the conference. The purposes of the meeting were (1) to generate scholarly examination of documents captured during the U.S./East Caribbean forces' intervention in Grenada in October 1983, so as to determine the causes of the bloody coup in Grenada and the impact of the intervention on Soviet/Cuban politics in the Caribbean Basin and other areas of the Third World; and (2), to examine in bipartisan fashion U.S. options for countering Soviet/Cuban adventurism.

Both objectives were met. The resulting volume book tells much more about Soviet/Cuban strategy and tactics in the Third World than was known before. It also provides a useful corollary to recommendations put forward by the Bipartisan Commission. For all of these reasons, this work should be read not only by scholars, but also by policymakers, analysts, and all discerning readers who care about America's role in the world.

Winston Lord
New York, NY

Preface

The United States/Organization of East Caribbean States intervention in Grenada on October 26, 1983 focused attention on the problems of radical regimes in the Third World in general, and on the Caribbean Basin in particular. The intervention also brought into focus Soviet and Cuban strategy and tactics in the Third World. Most importantly, the intervention marked the first reversal of Soviet-backed Cuban military activism in a decade. Cuban activism reached its height during Soviet/ Cuban interventions in Angola during 1976–1977 and in Ethiopia from 1977–1978. This activism subsequently extended to new revolutionary clients in close proximity to the United States such as Nicaragua, El Salvador, and Grenada. The discovery of voluminous secret files during and following the intervention in Grenada provided a unique opportunity to examine not only the inner workings of a radical Third World regime, but also the rudiments of Soviet/Cuban strategy in the Third World both before and after the U.S./OECS intervention.

The idea of a conference on Grenada was conceived by the conference chairs in 1983–1984 at the Woodrow Wilson International Center for Scholars, Washington, D.C. Jiri Valenta and Herbert Ellison sensed a feeling of urgency in undertaking an interdisciplinary examination of the serious political and economic issues facing the Third World, particularly in the Caribbean Basin. It was clear that Soviet and Cuban policies *vis-à-vis* radical Third World forces and the latter's genesis of revolution were having a substantial impact on Third World development. Thus it was resolved to address these issues by eliciting bipartisan interaction among specialists on the Soviet Union, the Third World, and Cuba, in both the scholarly community and government areas.

In the fall of 1983, scholars at the Woodrow Wilson International Center initiated a dialogue among specialists on the USSR, Latin America, and other Third World nations. This exchange was stimulated in part by the work of the Bipartisan Commission on Central America which had invited several Wilson Fellows to testify at its hearings. The ongoing need to generate a multidisciplinary inquiry culminated in a conference organized by the Soviet and East European Studies Program of the Department of National Security Affairs at the Naval Postgraduate School, and cosponsored by the Wilson Center's Kennan Institute, the Office of the Secretary of Defense, and the National Strategy Information Center, Inc.

The conference group included prominent specialists with varying political perspectives, representing the United States Government, the media, American universities, and several research institutions. Many of the participants had served as leading consultants or witnesses for the Bipartisan Commission on Central America. As a product of the interaction of this diverse mix of specialists, analysts, and policymakers, the conference report neglected neither the East-West nor the North-South dimensions of the problems of revolution in the Third World, specifically in Latin America.

The specific objectives to be met by convening the conference were:

— to generate a scholarly examination of documents captured during the U.S./East Caribbean forces' intervention in Grenada in October, 1983 with a view toward analyzing the causes of the bloody coup in Grenada and the impact of the intervention on Soviet/Cuban strategy and tactics in the Caribbean Basin and other areas of the Third World, and

— to examine, in bipartisan fashion, U.S. options for countering Soviet/Cuban strategy and tactics in the Third World.

Participants asked to write papers addressed a set of questions posed by the cochair of the conference, Dr. Jiri Valenta. The conferees were not held to a rigid frame of reference, nor did they represent a single point of view. As a result, many differing interpretations were provided, both by authors of papers and by discussants. The common starting point was an invitation to study the Grenada documents, and to consider a number of questions regarding the Grenada revolution and Soviet/Cuban strategy that had been raised in an article published by Jiri and Virginia Valenta recently in *Problems of Communism* (July-August 1984).

Dr. Valenta's "recommendations" at the end of this volume do not reflect a unanimity of opinion on the part of conference participants or the viewpoints of the organizations they represent. Rather, they are based on the exchange of ideas that took place during the conference.

BACKGROUND

Though highly uneven, the documents captured during the Grenada intervention provide an unprecedented glimpse into the inner workings of an aspiring Third World Leninist regime. They clearly illuminate Bernard Coard and his faction's drive toward the Leninist transformation of the New Jewel Movement (NJM). In 1983, this trend climaxed in a violent factional struggle that led to the death of Prime Minister Maurice Bishop and precipitated the U.S./East Caribbean forces' intervention.

The Grenada documents provide new insights into Soviet and Cuban policies *vis-à-vis* radical Third World regimes, particularly as compared to

Soviet literature on the subject. A key Soviet/Cuban strategic objective in the Third World is to aid in the selective building of socialist-oriented, revolutionary, anti-U.S. regimes. The most advanced such regimes are those with evolving Leninist vanguard parties structured on the principle of democratic centralism (Afghanistan, Ethiopia, Angola, South Yemen, and perhaps Nicaragua) and guided by cadres trained in the USSR and other communist countries, or at least well-connected with Soviet bureaucracies. The Soviet objective in Grenada—a country not very high on the Soviet list of priorities, yet with a potentially important strategic location—was to help create an advanced type of socialist-oriented nation that eventually could serve as a bridge between the Soviets and Cubans and other revolutionary forces in the region. A foothold in the region also could be of benefit to the Soviet Union by preoccupying the United States in its own strategic hinterland. Therefore, the Soviets accorded special status to the New Jewel Movement in an ideological agreement with the Communist Party of the Soviet Union (CPSU); they also concluded several "top-secret" arms transfer agreements, and provided for military assistance and increasing advisory assistance. The leadership of the NJM aspired to become a revolutionary bridge to other nations in the region and institutionalize Leninism following the Cuban example. Both were essential preconditions for continued and improved Soviet support, and the Coard faction hoped its compliance eventually would lead to Soviet recognition of the NJM as a proper communist party.

The Grenada documents also highlight the increasing sophistication of the Soviet Union's methods for furthering its strategic objectives in the Third World, especially regarding its utilization of the auxiliary capacities of junior allies such as Cuba, North Korea, Libya, and some Warsaw Treaty Organization (WTO) nations. By backing up the actions of its junior allies, the Soviet Union is able to further its global interests while deflecting attendant costs and risks that otherwise might prove damaging to its international relations. On the other hand, when a regime such as Cuba acts as a broker between the Soviets and other radical regimes, serious tactical disagreements can arise and precipitate crises such as the one that occurred in Grenada.

The absence of Soviet military support during the Grenada intervention had an adverse, though uneven, impact on the Soviet alliance system, and on some radical Third World regimes, particularly in the Caribbean Basin. It helped put Nicaragua on the defensive and temporarily increased pressure for a negotiated settlement in El Salvador. Its effects were also seen in Suriname and possibly in Angola and Ethiopia. Above all, the Grenada experience demonstrated that the USSR avoids contracting military alliances with vulnerable communist and Third World radical nations—particularly those adjacent to the U.S. periphery, where Washington is willing to protect its interests with military force. Grenada created much concern in Cuba and raised the perceived costs and risks of Soviet and Cuban support for radical Third World regimes, especially in the Caribbean Basin. In its net effect, however, Grenada represented only a temporary setback for Soviet and Cuban policies. The long term impact of the intervention should not be exaggerated, especially in the absence of an American consensus regarding the need for long-term polices aimed at curbing Soviet/Cuban military activism in the Third World.

RECOMMENDATIONS

While there was no conclusive evidence of an immediate threat to U.S. security interests in Grenada, circumstances prior to the intervention (e.g., the murder of Prime Minister Bishop, the threat to U.S. citizens, and the violent and unpredictable nature of the situation) made the U.S. and East Caribbean security forces' intervention an extraordinary yet necessary measure. In the long run, the probable negative consequences of U.S. inaction far outweighed the immediate costs of intervention. In spite of reservations held by some conferees, there was a strong consensus on this issue. Although there was no unanimity of opinion, the following policy recommendations were made by conference participants.

— Top priority should be given to long-term strategic planning toward prevention of superpower confrontation and escalation of conflict in the Third World.
— U.S. policymakers must anticipate long-term challenges in the Caribbean Basin, Central and South America, and other parts of the Third World. The Caribbean Basin is especially important to the United States; therefore, the U.S. should be attuned to Soviet/Cuban "security linkages" with nations in this region. Studies are needed on Soviet and Cuban perceptions and policies regarding the Third World and their existing ties with radical forces.
— In Grenada, the priority effort should be to influence political and economic stability, and to prevent a return of left or right dictatorships by encouraging a coalition of democratic forces.
— Bipartisan support should be given to long-term economic assistance programs to Third World nations, particularly in the Caribbean Basin, and on a higher level than presently contemplated.
— The National Endowment for Democracy should be encouraged to initiate programs of education and research in the area of Soviet/Cuban Third World strategy.
— As an immediate measure, the U.S. should continue to exert a high degree of pressure to eliminate "death squad" tactics, and to support democratic processes and institutions in El Salvador and elsewhere in the Western Hemisphere.
— The U.S. should be open to possibilities for negotiation with Cuba and Nicaragua. More caution should be exercised in the classification of Third World radical regimes.

— The U.S. should increase political and economic aid to each Caribbean Basin nation as its capacity permits; it should strengthen existing ties with these states and cultivate ties with both ruling and opposition parties through diplomatic exchange programs; and it should post credible, dynamic, and linguistically qualified U.S. diplomatic representatives in these nations.
— In the Caribbean Basin, much more emphasis should be given to the development of technical infrastructures (roads, ports, communications), advice on planning and budgeting, and education of economists and financial experts. Funding should come from both private and public sectors.
— The U.S. should be prepared to offer all forms of security assistance in accordance with the needs of developing nations in the Caribbean Basin, taking into account each nation's record on human rights.
— Section 660 of the Foreign Assistance Act, which prohibits police training, should be critically reviewed and amended for countries where governments exhibit respect for human rights.
— U.S. policy should distinguish between Soviet/Cuban sponsored strife and indigenous revolutionary situations. Where appropriate and warranted by the circumstances, the U.S. should consider aid to democratic forces combatting oppressive governments.
— A counterstrategy should be developed to intensify constraints on Soviet/Cuban acquisition and use of surrogates. U.S. policy should capitalize on differences between the Soviet Union and its junior allies.
— U.S. negotiations with Cuba and Nicaragua should be based on reciprocity, verifiable agreements, and monitoring. Soviet and Cuban military ties with Nicaragua or other radical regimes in the Caribbean Basin should be nonnegotiable.
— The U.S. must continue to be prepared to combine diplomacy and, if necessary, force (direct or indirect) to further its foreign policy objectives and protect U.S. security interests in the Caribbean Basin. The most preferable use of force is indirect; its direct use should be reserved only for extraordinary circumstances, comparable to those that existed in Grenada in October 1983.
— The U.S. should encourage its allies to cooperate in efforts to increase constraints on the military activities of the Soviet Union, Cuba, and other Soviet client states in the Third World.
— The specific elements of a bipartisan policy toward the Caribbean Basin (as contained in the Kissinger report) should be institutionalized by legislation and promptly implemented.
— A bipartisan consensus regarding U.S. policy toward the Third World is essential. An extensive program should be adopted to increase public awareness of Soviet/Cuban policies in the Third World by founding new research centers, by promoting more extensive cooperation between the U.S. Government and academic institutions, and through

better use of the public media. American policymakers should become vigorously involved in this effort.

Jiri Valenta
Monterey, CA

Herbert J. Ellison
Washington, D.C.

Acknowledgments

The Grenada conference, the proceedings of which provided the materials for this volume, required a comprehensive organizational and scholarly effort. Above all, thanks to Virginia Valenta, who conducted extensive interviews during three field trips to Grenada and helped with the preparation of the conference.

The Valentas are very grateful to Robert Dickerman of the USIA in Bridgetown, Barbados. He helped arrange the Valentas' two speaking tours in the East Caribbean and was extremely helpful to the Valentas' research efforts. The Valentas would like to thank the acting U.S. Chargé d' Affaires in Grenada, Ray Haverkamp, Richard Tierney of the U.S. Embassy, and Jack Barton of the USIA for their encouragement and assistance. The Valentas are also indebted for interviews with Alistair Hughes, a distinguished Grenadian journalist, Leslie Pierre, editor-in-chief of *The Grenadian Voice* (St. George's), three surviving members of the Maurice Bishop faction of the NJM leadership (George Louison, Einstein Louison, and Kenrick Radix), and a number of high officials of the governments of Grenada, Barbados, and Dominica.

A dedicated group of officers of all services contributed time and talent to the conference while pursuing full-time graduate studies in the Soviet and East European Studies Program, Department of National Security Affairs at the Naval Postgraduate School, Monterey, California. In many ways the conference was their conference. This group of officers was directed by LT Fred Shaheen, USN, who helped Dr. Valenta to orchestrate all aspects of the preparation and execution of the four-day event during which he also served as a conference rapporteur. Special thanks go to LCDR Steve Harris, USN, and LT Jay Wilkins, USN, for their enthusiastic assistance.

We are also grateful to Bradford Johnson of the Kennan Institute for his part in planning and coordinating the conference from Washington and for serving as a conference rapporteur. Thanks go to Evan A. Raynes for editing the conference materials, and to Larry McLellan, Gladys Clearwaters, and Phyllis McClellan for their technical support on the conference report.

For their assistance and encouragement on this project, we are especially grateful to Nestor Sanchez, Ambassador Sally Shelton, Hugh McGowan, Walter Raymond, Constantine Menges, Abraham Lowenthal, Charles Fairbanks, Jr., Kay Stephenson, Dov Zakheim, Anthony Gray, COL George Thompson (USAF), RADM Robert H. Shumaker (USN), Provost David Schrady, Dean Kneale Marshall, James Billington, the entire staff of the Kennan Institute at the Woodrow Wilson International Center for Scholars, and Moira McLeod of the Graduate School of International Studies, University of Miami.

Jiri Valenta
Monterey, CA

Herbert J. Ellison
Washington, D.C.

Grenada and Soviet/Cuban Policy

GRENADA

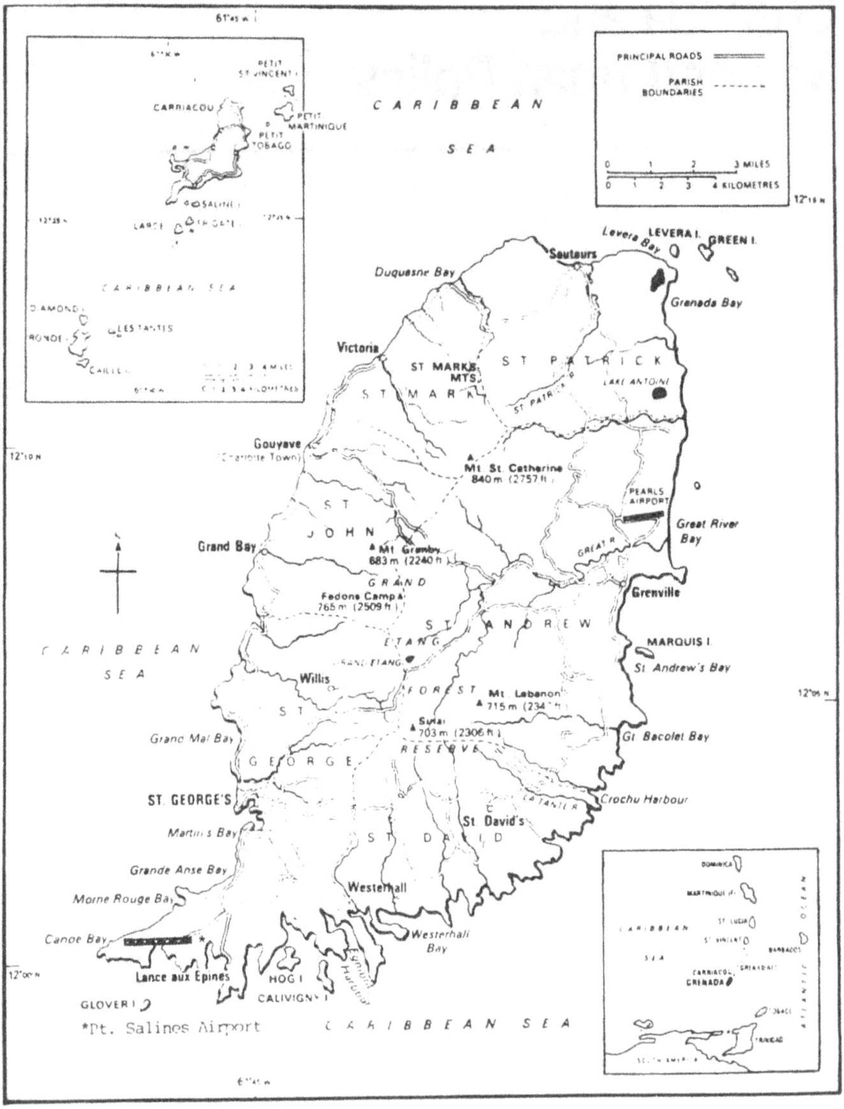

(Graphics and cartography by James French Crispelle.)

Part I
Revolution in Grenada: The USSR, Cuba, and Eastern Europe

JIRI VALENTA
VIRGINIA VALENTA

Leninism in Grenada

The U.S. and East Caribbean forces' intervention in Grenada on October 26, 1983 focused attention on the problems of the Caribbean Basin. The factors contributing to the Grenadian revolution of 1979 and to its downfall four years later will long occupy analysts, whose initial interpretations of the nature of Grenada's government exhibited striking variation. Some argued that Maurice Bishop's New Jewel Movement (NJM) was a typical Third World radical regime; others emphasized the regime's Marxist-Leninist character. There was further disagreement about the authenticity of the latter, but by now it is difficult to deny either the NJM's inclinations toward Leninism[1] or its extensive political, ideological, and above all military ties with the Soviet Union and Cuba. Both are richly documented in the voluminous secret files discovered in Grenada after the invasion.[2] Regardless of one's opinions about the intervention, these documents are a windfall for scholars in providing an unprecedented glimpse into the inner workings of an aspiring Third World Leninist regime and its relations with more established radical regimes elsewhere.[3]

The authors of this study used the Grenada documents and the authors' interviews in Grenada and Barbados with business and labor leaders, journalists, and politicians (including former NJM officials) to analyze the NJM revolutionary regime, its relationships with other communist countries, and its dissolution. The following questions were addressed: (1) What factors contributed to the emergence of the New Jewel Movement, and how did it assume power? (2) How did the movement regard itself, and how did it go about the socialist transformation of society; what new structures and policies did it introduce? (3) To what extent did the New Jewel Movement become a Leninist party? (4) What were the NJM's connections to the USSR and Cuba and to other communist states? (5) How did the internal power struggle and the October 1983 anti-Bishop coup develop; what role did the Soviets and Cubans play in these events; and what were the consequences? (6) What are the lessons of Grenada for other radical regimes in the developing world, and for Soviet and Cuban policies toward them?

ESTABLISHMENT OF THE NJM REGIME

Grenada's size, history, and socioeconomic conditions provided a rich medium for revolution. Because of its miniscule size (only 133 square miles), the island easily could be taken over by a small but well-organized and disciplined force—which is precisely what happened in March 1979 when about 40 armed men launched the coup that overthrew the government of Prime Minister Eric Gairy. Economically, Grenada is blessed with a tropical climate and fertile soil though it has less infrastructure and fewer public services than, for example, neighboring Barbados. In the social sphere, the predominantly rural population of the country, made up primarily of descendants of African slaves and of indentured laborers from the West Indies, was characterized by a rigid stratification of classes based on color and education. It was extremely difficult for blacks to cross the line separating them from the lighter-skinned and better-educated elite.[4]

Class rigidity, coupled with a Spanish/French/British colonial heritage and plantation economy, conditioned an authoritarian political culture in which democratic traditions never became entrenched among the politically unaware, impoverished masses. History and social organization have accustomed the people of Grenada to entrust government to leaders possessing the dual qualities of "boss man" and savior.[5] In the past few decades, they looked first to the black politician Gairy, and later to the lighter-skinned, London-educated Maurice Bishop to fill this role.

More than anyone else, Gairy created the conditions that made the revolution possible. Although he and Bishop were to become political antagonists throughout the 1970s, Bishop and the younger Gairy of the 1950s had much in common. At that time, Gairy was a radical politician who set up a rurally-based trade union, and like Bishop at a later stage, he organized island-wide strikes and demonstrations. As a result of these disturbances, the British Navy intervened in the capital of St. George's in 1951 to restore order, and Gairy was arrested.

After 1951 Gairy gave up violent tactics and switched to electoral politics. Subsequently, his Grenadian United Labor Party won six consecutive elections.[6] When Grenada acquired full rights of internal self-government in 1967, Gairy became Prime Minister. Once in power, however, he reverted to political violence and intimidation. His brutal reign, often likened to that of "Papa Doc" Duvalier in Haiti, was perpetuated by a paramilitary group known as the Mongoose Gang.[7] Nevertheless, even under such repressive rule, important socioeconomic changes were occurring, such as the replacement of the old "plantocracy" by farmers of small and medium-sized estates.[8] Eventually, Gairy's oppressive rule and bizarre behavior antagonized most of his following in the rural areas. Worsening socioeconomic conditions set the stage for the popularly supported NJM to take over in 1979.

The leftist New Jewel Movement came into being in 1973 when two radical groups, the Joint Endeavor for Welfare, Education, and Liberation (JEWEL) and the Movement for the Assemblies of People, merged and adopted a socialist manifesto.[9] The manifesto, an interesting amalgam of various socialist theories (with large doses of Tanzanian Christian socialism), proclaimed "People's Assemblies as the new form of government."[10] Gairy's secret police and night ambush squads forcibly suppressed strikes organized by the NJM, and in 1973 NJM leader Maurice Bishop was severely beaten. The following year, in a demonstration known as Bloody Monday, Bishop's father, Rupert, was killed.

After Grenada was granted independence on February 7, 1974, the NJM concluded a tactical electoral coalition (the People's Alliance) with the conservative Grenadian National Party and the United People's Party. In general elections held in 1976, the People's Alliance won 48.5 percent of the vote, and six seats in parliament out of a total of 15. Three of those seats went to NJM leaders: future Prime Minister Bishop; Unison Whiteman, future Minister of Foreign Affairs; and a relative newcomer to the NJM, Bernard Coard.

Dissatisfied with Gairy's presumed manipulation of the 1976 elections, the NJM organized a number of trade unions, and some leaders began to push for radicalization of the movement. Coard, in particular, advocated a shift to scientific socialism and Leninization of the party. To promote this goal, he organized a study group (the Organization for Revolutionary Education and Liberation—OREL) which constituted almost a separate branch of the party. As early as 1977, some of the NJM's founding members sensed a bid by Coard to take over the party, and some actually left the party because of a subsequent trend toward Leninization. A solid enough core remained, however, to mount a successful takeover of the capital on March 13, 1979.

While Gairy was out of the country, the NJM seized the True Blue army headquarters and the only radio station in Grenada according to an expertly executed plan. Bishop himself was already a friend and admirer of Fidel Castro, and it is possible that the NJM revolutionaries were assisted or trained either by Cubans or by Cuban-trained comrades from Guyana.[11] Most Grenadians were probably unconcerned about this connection. Having long since become dissatisfied with Gairy, they wholeheartedly embraced the charismatic Bishop. As the distinguished Grenadian journalist Alistair Hughes put it, the people "went Bishop, not Socialist."[12]

The NJM leadership aspired to Leninism in both the institutional and ideological sense. This emerges clearly from documents in which members of the Politburo, including both Bishop and Coard, reaffirm their Leninist credentials on many occasions as a way of legitimizing their actions or rebutting their critics—a type of esoteric communication typical of both aspiring and mature Leninist regimes. The documents also suggest that

Grenadian leaders hoped (and were encouraged by the Soviets and Cubans) to model their revolution on those of other communist countries (such as Cuba) that had successfully completed the transformation to Leninism and joined the "socialist commonwealth." Despite serious tactical differences, and later a fierce power struggle, members of both the Bishop and Coard factions shared this commitment, concurring that it was necessary to initiate the socialist transformation of Grenada.

Cultural and historical differences notwithstanding, Grenada during 1979–1983, like Cuba during 1962–1969 and Eastern Europe during 1945–1953, underwent an analogous first stage of socialist transformation in which the main task of its aspiring Leninist party was to eliminate "reactionary" political and economic forces decisively. From the available documents, it is clear the NJM leadership saw itself engaged in a heroic struggle against such forces. To be successful, they believed their party had to build new Leninist structures in a hierarchy of command able to respond to unexpected challenges from both external and internal enemies of the revolution. During this period, party-created and party-directed mass organizations typically assumed key roles in the political mobilization of the population. The premium was on ideological consciousness, moral incentives, and mobilization of large strata of the population to join the struggle. Such institutions of coercion as the secret police and armed forces became symbols of "vigilance" against real and imaginary forms of internal and external subversion. In addition, "fraternal assistance" was solicited from like-minded foreign parties and governments in the struggle. Thus, according to Bishop, the NJM had three objectives for Grenada: (1) to build a socialist society; (2) to build a vanguard party around Leninism's hierarchical ruling principle of democratic centralism; and (3) to adhere to proletarian internationalism—ideological shorthand for alignment with the USSR, Cuba, and other communist countries.[13] (Appendix A, Document 1)

SOCIALIST TRANSFORMATION

Although the NJM had a radical program from the start, several factors contributed to the regime's further radicalization. One such factor may have been a lack of tact on the part of some U.S. diplomats dealing with the new Bishop government in early 1979. The pace and extent of socialist transformation were also influenced by some Grenadian leaders, especially the doctrinaire Coard, who wanted to accelerate the process. Nevertheless, the change proved to be slow and laborious because of difficult local conditions, and probably also because the NJM leadership had learned from the experience of Cuba and other communist countries that too rapid a disengagement from capitalism could strain the economy and burden allies abroad.

The economic bases of Grenada are tourism, agriculture, and some agro-industry, particularly the traditional export of cocoa, bananas, nutmeg, and mace, which are the largest earners of foreign currency (35%). Agricultural laborers, who number approximately 6,000 out of 90,000–100,000 inhabitants, were supposed to become the labor force of agro-industrial plants still on the drawing board. The Grenadian economy was to be diversified, but in the words of one NJM Central Committee resolution, "the development and modernization of agriculture hold the key to winning the peasantry to socialism and the transformation of the countryside along Socialist lines."[14]

Accordingly, new jingles in the style of socialist realism extolled the role of the People's Revolutionary Government (PRG) in socialized agriculture:

> To get manure
> Is now quite easy
> Since the PRG has provided subsidy.

Contrary to the provisions of the NJM's 1973 manifesto on decentralized village assemblies, newly established mass organizations such as the Agriculture and General Workers' Union and the Production Farmers' Union were created to assure centralized party supervision over agricultural production. Meanwhile, nationalization of fisheries and the cocoa industry was hampered by mismanagement, the poor quality of some equipment donated by communist countries, and the need to keep the island financially afloat from month to month.

Tourism was another source of foreign currency. Unlike Eastern Europe during the late 1940s and early 1950s, tourism was not curtailed, but rather encouraged. In part, the controversial new airport under construction at Point Salines was meant to encourage a greater influx of tourists to what Bishop hoped would become a "socialist paradise" in the Caribbean. However, while some tourists continued to come to the beautiful beaches of Grenada, there was a decline in the number of long term visitors from Western nations. As for trade with the communist world, the large increase expected from the establishment of a State Trading Corporation had not materialized as of 1983—in part because of high transportation costs, and also because of Soviet and East European economic difficulties.

Although Grenada kept a mixed economy, the state sector became dominant. The central government's planning and allocation role increased gradually but consistently throughout all sectors of the economy via the newly established Marketing and National Import Board, and after July 1983, the new Ministry of State Enterprises. Other such organizations included the state-controlled National Commercial Bank (established to regulate financial institutions) and the Grenada Resorts Corporation (in charge of the island's various hotels). To expedite the transformation process, pressure was exerted on private industry and commerce through seizures, taxation, and various laws. Although increasingly embattled, the private sector was tolerated as long as it served the revolution. Had the NJM remained in power, in time it probably would have established a state monopoly on foreign trade, nationalized most private industry, and collectivized the bulk of agricultural production.

Grenadian Church. The Grenadian Interior Ministry, under the leadership of chief of counterintelligence Keith Roberts, monitored "key middle class elements" with ties to foreign diplomats and all foreign visitors who remained in Grenada longer than four weeks, including all students at the medical school in St. George's, as well as the "mood and movement of the school hierarchy and professors."[18] (Appendix A, Documents 2 and 3)

The first to incur the wrath of the revolution were Gairy's supporters. Next came NJM supporters or members opposed to the Leninization process, along with other "anti-socialist elements" such as the Rastafarians, who were originally tolerated. Last to be accused of counterrevolutionary tendencies were Bishop himself and his faction in the Central Committee, which came under "heavy manners" in the extreme—illustrating the proposition that revolutionaries tend to devour their own.

Surely there was great naivete, confusion, and ineptitude in the Grenadian leadership. Nevertheless, as surviving Politburo member George Louison told the authors, all of the leaders of the New Jewel Movement were constantly learning from the experience of "fraternal parties" during their travels in Cuba, the USSR, Eastern Europe, and North Korea. The recorded discussions of NJM leaders in the Politburo and Central Committee confirm that they studied the examples of other communist parties and radical developing countries, and skillfully wielded those examples in their debates. Indeed, they used esoteric Leninist vocabulary and ideological justifications not only in conducting party business, but at times even in private settings.

To some NJM leaders like Bishop, the Leninist vocabulary may have seemed a bit alien, at least for a time; to others, it appeared to be the only mode of political communication. Originally, Bishop's speeches were devoid of the class analysis and similar rhetoric found in speeches by Coard and his supporters. There was rather an emphasis on the rights of women, children, the peasantry (not the working class), and the need for food, housing and health care. However, even Bishop's speeches acquired a more ideological ring after mid-1981.[19] (Appendix A, Document 1)

Just as Bishop's addresses at times seemed to avoid Leninist code words and formulae, so his behavior showed a degree of disregard for democratic centralism. Certainly Bishop's opponents accused him of violating this principle when he opposed the majority CC decision to divide leadership responsibilities with Coard, whereby Bishop would continue as Prime Minister and Coard would assume the role of Chairman of the Central Committee.

A crucial resolution of the PRAF branch of the New Jewel Movement that passed on October 12, several days before Bishop's death, unambiguously stated that "based on the fundamental Leninist principle of democratic centralism," the decisions of the NJM Central Committee "have the force of law and form the basis of [the] activity and conduct of all party bodies and every single party member." (Appendix A, Document 4) Members further pledged that they would never allow "cultism, egoism, the unreasonable and unprincipled desires of one man or a minority to be imposed on our Party."[20] (Appendix A, Document 4) As one of Bishop's opponents stated, "the only problem at the CC was that Maurice would not conform to democratic centralism."[21] Another opponent asked:

> Will we institute democratic centralism for all? Will the Minority submit to the Majority? Will there be one discipline binding on all or will it be for everyone except the leader? Will we practice criticism and self-criticism frankly and openly as demanded by Comrade Lenin, or will the CC be intimidated by one man?[22]

When Bishop refused to go along with the reorganization of the party leadership proposed by the Central Committee, his opponents insisted on "cold-bloodedness" and "Bolshevik staunchness."

PROLETARIAN INTERNATIONALISM

The Bishop regime's interest in cultivating close ties with foreign communist states was fully reciprocated by the Soviet Union. The documents captured in Grenada clearly show that in spite of the country's miniscule size and repeated Soviet statements that the Caribbean Basin was "very distant" and not a "priority area,"[23] (Appendix A, Document 5) Soviet and Cuban involvement in Grenada was gradually increased, and in some areas went far beyond what was indicated in published Soviet, Cuban, Grenadian, and other Caribbean sources. Soviet ties with Grenada served three types of objectives: political-ideological, military-security, and to a much lesser extent, economic.

Ideology and Politics. The Soviet Union's most important objective in the Caribbean Basin is political, namely, to encourage and support "anti-imperialist" (i.e., anti-American) forces. The most vigorous forms of support are given to those regimes classified as revolutionary, i.e., fully developed Leninist regimes such as Cuba, or those following the path toward socialism such as Grenada (before October 1983) and Nicaragua. The growth of political-ideological ties between Grenada and the Soviet Union and its allies was manifest in the relatively large number of officials and intelligence operatives from the USSR and other communist nations discovered in Grenada at the time of the U.S./East Caribbean forces' intervention—including 47 Soviets. Taking into account that the Soviet Embassy had been set up only in November 1981 when the Soviet Ambassador Gennadiy Sazhenev arrived and wire services were installed by the Soviet news agency TASS, this is a considerable number.

As early as 1981, the Soviet press spoke of Grenada's "progressive social transformation" and referred to the NJM as the "political vanguard."[24] Yet exercising their usual caution, Soviet spokesman referred to the regime (along with those in Nicaragua, Angola, Ethiopia, and Afghanistan) as "progressive," "anti-imperialist," "national-democratic," or at most on the path toward "socialist-orientation"—that is, not yet fully Leninist. One Soviet analyst went a step further in describing both Grenada and Nicaragua in terms of a *novaya revoliutsionnaya narodno-demokraticheskaya gosudarstvennost* (new revolutionary popular democratic statehood),[25] an expression akin to those utilized by the Soviets in the late 1940s to describe East European regimes that soon became Leninist. The generally cautious terminology probably reflected Moscow's guarded expectations—conditioned by unpleasant experiences with other radical Third World regimes, and by Cuba's arduous path toward Leninism—and the desire to set apart the regimes that embody Leninism's most mature form, described as "developed socialism:" the USSR itself, the nations of Eastern Europe, Mongolia, Vietnam, and Cuba. But even if Grenada was not yet considered part of the socialist commonwealth, by 1982 some Soviet officials had begun to treat the New Jewel Movement as a fraternal (Marxist-Leninist) party. Some lower level officials in Moscow even called the NJM a "communist party" in conversations with Grenadian Ambassador W. Richard Jacobs and Counselor Bernard Bourne.[26] (Appendix A, Document 6)

While informally the NJM was considered a fraternal party, it was not accorded the same treatment as the Nicaraguan junta. The Soviets often adopted a protective attitude toward Grenadian diplomats in Moscow, explaining that Soviet relations with the NJM should not be conducted on the highest level so as not to provide the United States with a pretext to "further squeeze Grenada." According to Soviet officials, since Nicaragua was already under attack from the United States, it was necessary to express Soviet support for Nicaragua on a higher political level. Grenadian diplomats perceived this was also due to Grenada's smaller size and lesser importance relative to Nicaragua, and perhaps some residual confusion on the part of CPSU officials about the ideological orientation of the NJM. For example, Soviet officials could not understand the NJM's continued membership in the Socialist International.[27] (Appendix A, Document 7)

Formal relations between the NJM and CPSU began with the visit of Deputy Prime Minister Coard to the USSR during May-June 1980 in the wake of supportive lobbying by the Communist Party of Cuba and the Workers' Party of Jamaica.[28] (Appendix A, Document 6) After gathering considerable information about the NJM and observing indications that the revolution was taking hold, the Soviets decided to make a formal commitment to Grenada during Prime Minister Bishop's visit to the USSR in July 1982. According to the important secret agreement of July 27, 1982 the CPSU and NJM agreed to cooperate in ways similar to those pursued by the Soviets in dealing with other anti-imperialist, socialist-oriented countries in the Third World. In line with a "common commitment . . . to socialism," the agreement stated that "inter-party cooperation is a most important basis" for the development of relations between Grenada and the USSR. According to six of the seven main points in this accord, Soviet relations with Grenada would be handled primarily through party channels, although the agreement also provided for the "all around development of interstate relations and ties between mass organizations." The agreement required the CPSU and the NJM to "extend and deepen" cooperation "at all levels," and to "exchange experience in party work and party guidance" in the social, economic, and cultural development of their respective countries, "including regular exchange of information." It also provided for "consultation and exchanges of opinion on international matters."[29] (Appendix A, Document 8) Subsequently, Soviet-Grenadian relations were conducted primarily on a party-to-party basis and Bishop and other NJM officials held unofficial talks with high-level Soviet officials during visits and stopovers in the USSR in 1982 and 1983.

According to the CPSU-NJM accord, both parties agreed to cooperate in "training party and government cadres," and to develop contacts between party press organs and other mass media. The Soviets, who were originally bewildered that no work had begun on construction of a party headquarters for the NJM, were to assist in building one. This transaction, in which the Soviets were to reimburse the Cubans for material and technical support, offers a good example of close Soviet/Cuban cooperation in Grenada.[30] The Soviets agreed to supply office equipment and cars as well. They also "pressed" the NJM into accepting a number of scholarships for Grenadian party officials (15 in 1982 alone). (Appendix A, Document 7) NJM members "with a higher cultural level" were to study at the Higher Party School of the CPSU Institute of Social Sciences along with their counterparts from other revolutionary parties in the Third World. Fourteen Grenadians were enrolled there in May 1983.[31] Soviet officials also recommended that the NJM should think seriously about sending teacher trainees to the USSR and consider establishing its own party school as a "top priority" (as Afghanistan, Angola, Mozambique, South Yemen, and Ethiopia have done).[32] (Appendix A, Document 9)

Still other Grenadians were trained in Cuba, where the course of study included propaganda and foreign relations, particularly regarding other Caribbean nations. In 1983 Cuba was scheduled to receive 18 Grenadian party cadres for study and training in political indoctrination and propaganda techniques. Those selected for such training represented but a small fraction of dozens of Grenadians said to be studying in Cuba at the time of the U.S./Organization of Eastern Caribbean States (OECS) intervention. Finally, according to NJM agreements on cooperation with the East German Socialist Unity Party (SED) and the Bulgarian Communist Party, other Grenadians studied at the Karl Marx Party College in East Berlin, and ten were enrolled at the Academy of Social Sciences of the Central Committee in Sofia.

As provided by the work plan of the NJM's propaganda department, the propaganda organs of the USSR and other communist nations began to distribute "progressive materials" in Grenada for the purpose of deepening "the internationalist spirit and socialist consciousness of the Grenadian masses." Among other things, this was aimed at exposing "the evil and war-mongering policies of imperialism," promoting "the life of people under socialism," and highlighting "activities of progressive and revolutionary parties" in the Caribbean region.[33] There were, in addition, a number of Soviet civilian consultants and advisers attached to various Grenadian ministries (e.g., the Ministry of Education) and other agencies.[34] A Grenadian/Soviet friendship society was formed.

The Soviets established still other organizational ties with the NJM through the newly founded Grenada Peace Council (GPC), which became an integral part of the World Peace Council (WPC)—an organization supervised by the International Department of the Central Committee of the CPSU. GPC representatives participated in a number of WPC meetings, during 1982–1983, including preparations for "A Week in Solidarity with Nicaragua" (December 1982), and the International Preparatory Committee of the World Assembly for Peace and Life [and] Against Nuclear War convened in Prague (June 1983). Although the Soviet Peace Fund subsidized the travel of Grenadian officials on Aeroflot and the Cuban airline Cubana, the Soviets apparently desired that travel between Grenada and Havana should be paid for by the Grenadian Government.[35] Thus the NJM's participation in the activities of the WPC was limited by Grenada's geographic remoteness and continuing financial difficulties. In fact, the Grenadian Peace Council was criticized at the WPC meeting in Lisbon on November 2, 1982 for insufficient "flow of information," and a continuously low level of activity. WPC Regional Secretary Hill Arboleda of Panama made the point that because of the paucity of information emanating from Grenada, the WPC-controlled media were not yet able to publish an article on the Grenadian revolution.

In 1983, the NJM concluded various new agreements with the Communist Party of Cuba providing for closer and more regular cooperation between the two parties than between the NJM and the CPSU, including "regular meetings and exchange of experience between the different departments and secretaries of both parties." According to one secret agreement, the PCC and the NJM were to "coordinate the positions of the governments of Cuba and Grenada at international events, conferences, and agencies where they participate, in attention to the political, economic, and social interests of both Parties."[36] (Appendix A, Document 10) Bilateral relations were also advanced by the Grenada/Cuba Friendship Society. The NJM, which saw itself as a bridge between the PCC and leftist parties in the English-speaking Caribbean, participated in other antiimperialist projects with Cuban party officials, such as hosting meetings (partly funded by Havana) of representatives from nonaligned nations. The NJM even took part in (and was appointed to the secretariat of) the Libyan General Congress of the World Center for Resistance against Imperialism, Zionism, Racism, and Reaction.[37]

Security. Another objective of the Soviet Union in the Caribbean Basin is to enhance its military and intelligence-gathering capabilities. Moscow seeks to develop military ties with revolutionary regimes in the region so as to accomplish what former Chief of the Soviet General Staff Marshal Nikolay Ogarkov described in a 1983 conversation with his Grenadian counterpart, Major Einstein Louison, as "raising the combat readiness and preparedness" of progressive forces facing a threat from imperialism. Ogarkov specified the conditions favorable to this goal: "Over two decades ago there was only Cuba in Latin America; today there are Nicaragua and Grenada, and a serious battle is going on in El Salvador."[38] (Appendix A, Document 11) Although the Soviets proceeded very cautiously in order not to provoke the United States, in the long run they probably desire to secure access elsewhere in the Caribbean to military and intelligence facilities of the sort they now have in Cuba.

The captured documents demonstrate that the Soviets gradually upgraded Soviet military aid to Grenada. Indeed, military aid actually preceded ideological recognition of the NJM. Even before the first formal arms agreement signed in Havana on October 27, 1980 the Soviet Union and Cuba provided 1,000 automatic rifles, and Nicaragua provided 2,000 uniforms. The top secret 1980 Agreement between the Government of the USSR and the Government of Grenada on Deliveries of Special and other Equipment "free of charge of delivery," was valued at 4.4 million rubles.[39] (Appendix A, Document 12) (Interestingly, this agreement was concluded before the U.S. presidential election, suggesting that the choice of leaders in Washington was not the critical issue for either the Soviets or the Grenadians.) Cuba was to act as the intermediary in the Soviet arms transfers. Although two Soviet Coast Guard boats were to be sent directly to Grenada, in 1983 weapons and ammunition were sent almost exclusively through Cuba. The Soviets delivered their wares by sea to Cuban ports where they were transported on Cuban ships to Grenada. Once at their final destination, the arms were delivered at night to hidden depots throughout the island during planned power outages.[40]

The "special equipment" listed in the 1980 agreement included 12 mortars, 24 antitank grenade launchers, 54 machine guns, 1,000 submachine guns, 18 antiaircraft mounts, and other weapons, communication devices, ammunition, logistical equipment, and spare parts. Article 3 of the agreement called for the training of Grenadian servicemen in the USSR to ensure their mastery of the equipment. There was also a stipulation that Grenada would not sell or transfer arms to third parties without Soviet consent. The agreement further obligated Grenada to preserve the secrecy of the terms and implementation of the accord.

A second top secret Soviet military aid agreement was signed in Havana on February 9, 1981 constituted a Protocol to the 1980 agreement. It called for arms shipments to take place between 1981 and 1983. The Soviets again used the euphemism "special and other equipment,"[41] the value of which went up this time to five million rubles. The agreement provided for delivery of eight armored personnel carriers, two armored reconnaissance and patrol vehicles, 1,000 submachine guns, a variety of armaments and munitions, and engineering, communications, and transport equipment. Included were 12,600 complete sets of uniforms, apparently designed for an army of 6,300 men. Also included were spare parts and training and auxiliary equipment valued at nearly one million rubles.

A third top secret arms agreement worth ten million rubles[42] was concluded in Moscow on July 27, 1982 for the period 1982–1985. (Appendix A,

Document 13) Included were an additional 50 armored personnel carriers, 60 mortars, 30 antitank and other heavy guns, 50 portable rocket launchers, 50 light antitank grenade launchers, 2,000 submachine guns, small arms, communications and engineering workshops, and other equipment. Unlike the others, the 1982 agreement also included "civilian" equipment for Grenada's expanding Ministry of the Interior. The Ministry and the Peoples' Militia were to receive 20 light antitank rocket launchers and 50 submachine guns, plus "special instruments" such as infrared viewers, videotape recorders, tape recorders, cameras, PTU-47 television systems, and other equipment designed for clandestine intelligence gathering. The Grenadians also requested mini-microphones and accessories for bugging purposes.

Another interesting feature of the 1982 agreement was that it provided not only for the training of Grenadian servicemen at Soviet military schools, but also (in Article 3) for their training in Grenada by Soviet military and security "specialists and interpreters." At their own expense, the Grenadians were to provide Soviet personnel with "comfortable living accommodations," "municipal utilities, medical services, and transport facilities for the execution of their duties," and "meals at reasonable prices at the places of their residence," without "any taxes and duties." No such privileges were provided for Grenadian military personnel in the USSR.

Future plans for greater Soviet military involvement in Grenada are suggested by Article 4 of the 1982 agreement. According to this section, the USSR would periodically send a group of Soviet advisers to Grenada to plan technical assistance for an equipment and vehicle repair shop, a command-staff school, and storage facilities and roads. An additional agreement was reached in November 1982 to send a team of Soviet specialists to Grenada for 15 days to assist with these tasks. According to Marshal Ogarkov, the Soviet Union was going to send a team of military experts to Grenada in 1983 to "conduct studies related to the construction of military projects." Ogarkov also indicated that although Grenada's additional request for military aid beyond the 1982 agreement was officially handled by the Soviet Ministry of Foreign Trade, the Ministry of Defense "would exercise some control on the solution."[43] (Appendix A, Document 11) U.S. forces found yet another secret agreement, still unsigned and dated 1983, for the delivery of "special and other equipment" valued at 5.4 million rubles for the period 1984–1986. Included were two patrol gunboats, spare parts, tools and accessories, 3,000 uniforms, and 12,000 rounds of ammunition.[44]

In accordance with the above agreements, Grenadian officers were sent for military training in the USSR. In late 1982 there were 15 Grenadians studying at Soviet military schools, and an additional 20 were expected to arrive in 1983. Some officials of the Ministry of the Interior were also trained in the USSR in intelligence and counterintelligence. The decision to train the latter group resulted from a discussion between Defense Minister General Hudson Austin and Vladimir Klimentov, very likely the Soviet KGB chief in Jamaica, and a followup request to then KGB chairman, Yuri

Andropov. Two other influential senior officers trained in the Soviet Union, Colonels Liam James and Ewert Layne, later would be key players along with General Austin in the anti-Bishop conspiracy.[45]

Like the USSR, Cuba granted training scholarships to Grenadian military personnel (12 in 1982). In accordance with a secret written agreement, Cuba maintained 27 permanent military advisers in Grenada supervised by a Cuban working inside the Grenadian Ministry of Defense (with access to communications facilities), plus a dozen or so additional advisers sent for short terms of two to four months. Unlike the Soviets, the Cubans did not insist on special living arrangements; they specified only "fresh foodstuffs," "necessary transport means," "means of personal hygiene," and a "small stipend" for each advisor.[46] (Appendix A, Document 14) By 1982 the Cuban presence in Grenada consisted of a small contingent of military advisers, a number of overt and covert agents and civilian workers, and several hundred construction workers (many of them armed) building the runway at Point Salines.

There is no evidence that the controversial airport was planned primarily as a military base. It was designed mainly for tourism. But the nearby double-fenced facilities occupied by the Cubans, called "Little Havana" by some, was operated like a military camp. The complex, containing oil and water storage tanks, barracks stocked with guns and ammunition, and a hospital, had direct access to the airport. Plans for a second "Little Havana" were in the making. Grenadians were not allowed inside the complex, contributing to resentment among Grenadian workers.[47] It appears the airport was to have some military purpose after its official opening, scheduled for March 13, 1984. This is suggested, amidst other evidence, by an entry in the diary of Liam James. As early as March 1980 he recorded that the "airport will be used for Cuban and Soviet military."[48] Initially it probably would have served as a facility for Soviet reconnaissance aircraft, and as a refueling stop for Soviet and Cuban transports bound for Angola.

The captured documents show that Moscow was eager to have the Grenadians begin work on another project in 1983—a Soviet-sponsored satellite station. Like the airport, the station was designed mainly for civilian use, but it also could have served military purposes. However, the Grenadians wanted to postpone the project until 1984 because of concern that it might interfere with completion of the airport.[49]

There was a division of labor in communist security assistance to Grenada following the pattern established earlier in Africa. The Cubans donated the manpower; the East Germans provided technical and military or internal security equipment and highly qualified technicians; and the Czechoslovaks supplied explosives, ammunition, and automatic rifles. The East Germans also upgraded Grenada's telephone system. After Bishop's trip to Pyongyang in April 1983, North Korea agreed to supply arms worth $12 million, including thousands of rifles, 50 rocket launchers, two coast guard boats, and uniforms. There was also a military agreement with Bulgaria, and even Vietnam concluded an agreement with Grenada to train 20 military officers.

(The Grenadian students had to delay their departure until September 1982, since Vietnam was unwilling to provide transportation and the Grenadian government could not afford to send them earlier.)

The documents suggest that in addition to the potential access to Grenadian officers and facilities it provided the donors, communist military aid was designed for a more immediate military purpose: to build a sizable Grenadian armed force of four regular and 14 reservist battalions by 1985.[50] Since arms transfers were scheduled through 1986, U.S. forces recovered fewer arms than indicated in the agreements. The weapons recovered in Grenada, however, were already sufficient to equip about 10,000 men.

Economics. Economic objectives played a minor role in Soviet strategy in the Caribbean Basin. Soviet-Grenadian economic cooperation progressed between 1979 and 1983, but not as rapidly as military-security relations. Economic aid to Grenada was not proportionate to the aid given Cuba, and was aimed primarily at reinforcing Soviet political objectives.

Still, Grenadian officials consulted frequently with Soviet Gosplan (State Planning Committee) officials and Council for Mutual Economic Assistance (CMEA) experts on various aspects of economic cooperation. Gosplan offered a training course to several NJM officials, led by a permanent secretary of the Grenadian Ministry of Construction, Michael Prime. The NJM, for its part, actively sought long-term markets in CMEA nations. The Soviet Union, East Germany, and Bulgaria agreed to purchase, at stable prices and steady intervals, such vital Grenadian export commodities as cocoa, nutmeg, and bananas. The Soviets also granted Grenada several million dollars worth of foodstuffs and construction materials, and supplied dozens of vehicles and machines on deferred payment terms. In addition, they offered miscellaneous credits and donations, and upgraded Radio Grenada from a one-kilowatt to a 75-kilowatt station capable of broadcasting to foreign audiences. A Soviet AN-26 transport aircraft was to be outfitted in 1983 for the special use of the Grenadian leadership, with spare parts stored in Cuba under the supervision of Soviet specialists in that country.[51] (Appendix A, Documents 6 and 15) East Germans delivered dozens of trucks and other vehicles to Grenada, mainly for use by various government ministries. Although most assistance from North Korea was military, they also agreed to provide assistance with agricultural equipment and fishing boats, and to construct a national sports stadium for 15,000 people. North Korean advisers were supposed to begin work in Grenada by the end of 1983.

The utility of some of the equipment received from communist sources was affected by poor quality or Grenadian mismanagement. For example, of the ten fishing boats donated by Cuba, Bishop reported that only two were working, and that even those could "collapse at any time." As a result, the National Fishing Company "lost about 60 percent of its revenue."[52]

There is no evidence that the Soviets provided funding for the controversial Point Salines airport complex. In part, this may have been for tactical political reasons. According to Frederick Kissoon (a friend of Bishop and Unison Whiteman and a foreign affairs advisor on Third World affairs in the NJM leadership), the Soviets advised the NJM in early 1981 that it would be in Grenada's interest if Moscow maintained a low profile in the construction of the airport. After all, the Grenadian leaders were cautioned, a conspicuous hand by the USSR could cause unnecessary pressures on the People's Republic of Grenada, or even sabotage the project.

Most of the grants and loans for the airport and several other public works projects came from Libya, Cuba, Canada, Iraq, Syria, the OPEC fund, and the European Economic Community. Colonel Qadhafi was personally addressed by Bishop in a September 1983 letter as "the last remaining hope for providing the necessary financing to complete the international airport" in time for its scheduled opening in March 1984.[53] Likewise, there was no indication that Moscow would fully finance water supply or seaport development projects recommended by Soviet technicians. Nor, apparently, did the Soviets commit themselves to supply 20,000 tons of free fertilizer, as the Grenadians requested.[54] (Appendix A, Document 15) Thus, the USSR was unable, or unwilling, to provide much help in transforming Grenada into a socialist paradise in the Caribbean.

In fact, the meetings of Grenada's Committee of Economic Ministers often were spent haggling about the scarcity of money and the need for short-term loans from OPEC banks.[55] The gravity of Grenada's financial situation was suggested by the government's aforementioned inability even to pay for the travel requirements of midlevel NJM officials. Facing overall liquidity problems, in the summer of 1983 Bishop proposed that Grenada copy the example of Cuba and Suriname "in keeping two sets of records in the banks." Subsequently, the Grenadian Politburo decided to invite Cuban and Nicaraguan experts to train Grenadians "in the readjustment of the books."[56]

By mid-1983, the Soviet Union and its allies had accumulated a substantial political and security, if not economic, investment in Grenada. When it then appeared that this investment might be jeopardized by leadership rivalries and policy shifts on the island, the Soviets—though apparently not the Cubans—began to maneuver to protect their position in the developing Grenadian power struggle. The violent outcome seemed briefly to work in Moscow's favor until it was forcibly reversed by the joint intervention of the United States and Grenada's immediate neighbors. An understanding of this dramatic sequence of events requires a closer look at the internal dynamics of the island's bitter factional contest, and at Soviet and Cuban policies during the approaching revolutionary dénouement.

INTERNAL POWER STRUGGLE

It was against a backdrop of political uncertainty and serious economic problems that high-level internal tensions began to surface in Grenada in September 1983. There seems to have been no single issue that precipitated the factional conflict. Rather, the documents suggest it was the generally shared feeling in the NJM Politburo that the revolution was failing, coupled with the personal ambition of Bernard Coard, that triggered the power struggle.

The NJM leadership had begun to worry about a looming crisis in the summer of 1983. The reports of the Central Committee plenary sessions of July 13–19, 1983 expressed concern about "the slow pace of party development along Leninist lines."[57] The minutes of another, extraordinary CC meeting held a month later suggest that a number of Politburo members had concluded that the revolution in Grenada was facing a dangerous crisis. Among those who commented were General Austin, who claimed that the masses were in a "state of demoralization." Selwyn Strachan, Politburo member in charge of ideology and propaganda and Minister of National Mobilization in charge of propaganda, who believed that "sections of the party had begun to rebel against the higher organs," and that this "silent rebellion" could turn into "open rebellion" unless drastic measures were taken. Liam James added that this was "*the beginning of the disintegration of the party.*" [Emphasis in original.] Complaints from Cuban and East German party officials along these lines were also mentioned.[58] Even Bishop agreed that the party faced the "threat of disintegration."[59]

The systemic crisis in Grenada was accompanied by a factional struggle between Bishop and Coard. Both men possessed loyal followings. On one level, the Bishop-Coard conflict was one of personalities—the spontaneous and charismatic Bishop versus the calculating and ascetic Coard. Coard, in obvious reference to Bishop, would speak about Politburo members coming to CC meetings with "hands and minds swinging." While Coard apparently was able to impress NJM and fraternal country bureaucrats (as well as some visiting American scholars), Bishop retained his immense appeal to broad segments of the Grenadian masses in spite of the mounting crisis.

On another level, the NJM power struggle was ideological and political. Coard and his supporters were impatient with the pace of Grenada's socialist transformation. Apparently, Bishop, Unison Whiteman, and George Louison, with long-term objectives similar to Coard's, favored a more gradual approach. (One might recall that Bishop and Whiteman were the founders of the NJM, which in the early 1970s was socialist, but not Leninist.) The Bishop-Coard relationship worsened after October 1982, when Coard resigned from the Politburo and the CC.[60] He was, however, able to arrange the ouster of Bishop's Politburo allies Vincent Noel and Kenrick Radix. Coard also retained his important job as Deputy Prime Minister in charge of the economy and finances. He or one of his deputies supervised the payrolls of the PRAF and the Ministry of the Interior. As the political struggle mounted in late 1983, Coard's manipulation of PRAF salaries, amounting to bribery, is said to have accounted, at least in part, for his success in coopting the officer corps to act against Bishop.[61]

Three officers played conspicuous roles in the political assault on Bishop at NJM Central Committee meetings in September 1983: Lt. Colonel Layne, a political supervisor of the armed forces; Lt. Colonel James, Minister of the Interior in charge of police and intelligence operations; and Major Leon

Cornwall, a former chairman of the National Youth Organization who belonged to Coard's secret "educational" cell. Cornwall, significantly, had just returned from an ambassadorial post in Cuba, where he was treated rather shabbily.[62] The Cubans apparently preferred to deal directly with Bishop and other more senior NJM leaders. Cornwall's return from Cuba, and subsequent secret appointment as chief of the Main Political Department of the Armed Forces, were integral parts of the anti-Bishop plot. The mastermind behind the operation, however, was Coard himself. Coard's Jamaican-born wife Phyllis, who was said to be as brilliant and as doctrinaire as her husband, was another major conspirator.

The minutes of the Central Committee's fateful sessions of September 14–16 show that the anti-Bishop coalition (actually a majority of the Politburo) accused him of vacillating between "petit bourgeois-opportunist" and Leninist policies. All agreed that there was a deep crisis in the party, although they disagreed sharply about how to resolve it. However, the Coard faction rapidly turned the session into an anti-Bishop cabal that showed every sign of having been orchestrated in advance.

The attack on Bishop began with James' proposal to alter the agenda. As the agenda was shifted to the "state of the party and revolution," Layne led a carefully prepared attack on Bishop that was strongly supported by Politburo members Cornwall, James, Strachan, and Chalkie Ventour. The basic charges were that Bishop was guilty of (1) "right opportunism"—i.e., allowing the party to deteriorate into a "social democratic" party instead of fashioning it into a "Marxist-Leninist vanguard," and (2) an inability to "tighten" Grenadian relations "with the World Socialist Movement, especially Cuba, the USSR, and the GDR." Layne, who perhaps knew something Bishop did not, argued that Grenada's relations with these countries were "becoming more and more complex."[63] (Appendix A, Document 16) Cornwall was somewhat more specific. According to him, the NJM had to explain its internal problems to fraternal parties because "they already knew the problems that we experience now;" silence only would cause others to see NJM leaders "jokers," he argued. In fact, as Cornwall revealed, the fraternal parties were already "accusing [the NJM leadership] of instability."[64] (Appendix A, Document 16) "Sister Phyllis" phrased the problem in Leninist jargon: "The international support of the working class is lessening."[65] (Appendix A, Document 16) She also criticized the leadership's "idealism" and "voluntarism."

The solution proposed by Cornwall was that the Grenadian party should be built by "drawing [on] the experience of other countries;" Grenadians should "start working on a party constitution" and "develop commissions for different areas of work." In particular, he stressed the recommendations of a commission entrusted with studying the experience of the Soviet Union and Cuba. Strachan supported James and Layne by arguing the need to transform the NJM along Leninist lines, and pinpointed "ideological development as key to the development of the party." James added that the Central Committee and the whole party must study the work of Brutents (presumably Karen N. Brutents, a leading Soviet International Department ideologist on, and liaison official with, the Third World).[66] (Appendix A, Document 16) This proposal was strongly seconded by Phyllis Coard.

The turning point came when James proposed remedying NJM difficulties by creating a collective leadership. The Prime Minister's functions would be divided, with Bishop continuing his work among the masses and the militia, and Coard taking responsibility for party work (including chairmanship of the Organizational Commission of the Central Committee). This was an old trick that James may have learned from his Soviet contacts, or from study of Soviet and East European politics, where division of responsibilities often precedes demotion. The plan was thus for an incremental erosion of Bishop's power.

The other members of the conspiracy quickly assented to James' proposal, supporting their position with analogies from communist countries. Strachan claimed that the unitary leadership of Fidel Castro (with whom Bishop was often compared) was unique because the Cuban leader was "always reflecting and thinking,"[67] the obvious implication being that Bishop was lacking in these qualities. James extolled the collective leadership of the Nicaraguan junta, and Cornwall used the same example. Layne also supported the proposal, referring to the East German example of two parties (presumably the communists and social democrats) joining, under Soviet tutelage, in the Socialist Workers' Party (SED) in 1946—a poor model, indeed, but nobody protested. Later, Layne invoked yet another example supporting the switch to a "scientifically decided" form of leadership—the division of labor between political commissars and military officers in the USSR. According to Layne, this system worked and helped to defeat the counterrevolution. James pointedly warned that failure to implement the plan for dividing responsibilities between Coard and Bishop would be tantamount to "right opportunism."[68] (Appendix A, Document 16) Given their ready recourse to Leninist terminology and historical data, it is possible that both Layne and James had reviewed the Soviet and East European experience with Coard, if not with their Soviet bloc contacts, before the meeting. Indeed, during the meeting, Bishop noted—perhaps sarcastically—that he was struck "by the levels of thought and preparation of comrades as evident in their various contributions."[69] (Appendix A, Document 16)

By this time, a few Politburo members had heard enough. Minister of Agriculture George Louison defended Bishop, observing that the Central Committee was "still capable of leading." Accused by anti-Bishop conspirators of disturbing the proceedings for "opportunistic reasons," Louison characterized the argument about his own "right opportunism" with a scatological expletive.[70] (Appendix, Document 16) He failed to see how joint leadership could benefit the NJM. Louison then argued, correctly, that in other communist states in which one person heads the government, and another directs the party, the former is normally subordinate to the latter—the clear implication being that the proposal for collective leadership was a ruse designed to subordinate Bishop to Coard. Another Politburo member,

Minister of External Affairs Unison Whiteman, also disagreed with the joint leadership model and suggested a compromise whereby Coard would become Bishop's deputy.

In response to his critics, Bishop cited the example of the CPSU, but drew a different lesson, reminding his colleagues that they must be careful in applying ideological labels too quickly. He warned about disunity, and asked his colleagues for more time to reflect on the operational aspects of the proposed joint leadership (and perhaps also to devise some countermeasures). When it came time to vote, Bishop abstained along with Whiteman and union leader Fitzroy Bain; Louison voted against the proposal; and the remaining nine members voted in favor. (Austin arrived late and did not vote.) Bishop was in the minority, much as Nikita Khrushchev had been during the Soviet leadership crisis of June 1957. The question now was whether, like the Soviet leader, Bishop could outmaneuver his opponents at the Central Committee level and transform a hostile Politburo majority into what Khrushchev had called a mere "arithmetical majority."

The next few weeks provided the answer, and it was not in Bishop's favor. Unfortunately for Bishop, the Central Committee in Grenada seems to have had only nine members in addition to the eight who were on the Politburo, and the majority in both groups were now opposed to Bishop. Bishop's actual removal from power probably was prepared in early October when he and his closest Politburo supporters, Louison and Whiteman, were in Hungary and Czechoslovakia negotiating for economic aid. Leaving the country while the power struggle was unresolved was a crucial tactical error on Bishop's part. While abroad, Bishop was able to negotiate a deal for three electrical generators and a hydroelectric power station from Czechoslovakia, and some agricultural aid from Hungary. However, apparently he was unable to regain the confidence of the Soviets.

During and just after his trip, when he was said to be under the strong influence of Louison (who was "poisoning his mind," according to Coard's faction), Bishop became convinced that the proposal for joint leadership was actually a plot. His authority at home had visibly declined. This became obvious on October 8, when only one Politburo member was on hand to greet him at the airport. A record of their conversations indicates that Bishop and his supporters had begun to worry about the "mood in the party for blood"—what Coard supporters, such as Politburo member Chalkie Ventour, were referring to as the "Afghan solution" or "Afghan line"[71] should Bishop reject joint leadership. The reference, of course, was to the bloody December 1979 coup in Afghanistan in which President Hafizullah Amin was killed. Such a solution was all the more ironic since Bishop's regime was one of the few that had voted in 1980 against UN condemnation of the original, Soviet-sponsored "Afghan solution."

Bishop lost the second round of the fray when he unsuccessfully argued his case at a Central Committee meeting on October 12 during which some members kept brandishing their weapons. Bishop's opponents accused him of showing contempt for the Leninist principle of democratic centralism in his unwillingness to submit to joint leadership. Layne quoted a long passage from an ideological pamphlet to demonstrate that Lenin would have disapproved of Bishop's behavior. The Central Committee adopted a formal resolution in favor of restructuring the party leadership that would have effectively sealed Coard's control over the party machinery. On the same day, the PRAF branch of the NJM, controlled by James, Layne, and Cornwall, adopted an anti-Bishop resolution. (Appendix A, Document 4) Unlike Khrushchev, who was able to reverse the Politburo decision at the Central Committee level with the help of the military and security elites, Bishop had lost his power base among these two vital groups now allied with Coard. Attempts by Bishop's supporters failed to mobilize elements of the People's Militia and rally support for him in the PRAF. That night, according to witnesses, the emotionally strained Bishop was unable to sleep as tension mounted between both factions on the island.[72]

On October 15, 1983 another CC meeting was held and James again led the attack on Bishop, citing his continued defiance. Bishop was expelled from the party, disarmed, and confined to his house without access to a telephone. Bishop supporters George Louison and Kenrick Radix were confined at Richmond Hill Prison. This was followed on October 17 by Strachan's public denunciation of Bishop and announcement that Coard would succeed him as prime minister. However, this measure was postponed because of the manifest displeasure of the large crowds listening to Strachan's announcement.

Thus, while the majority of the Central Committee had turned against Bishop, the masses had not. On October 19, "Bloody Wednesday," a mob of at least 10,000 people (about one-tenth of the population) led by Bishop's loyal friend, Politburo member Unison Whiteman, liberated Bishop and several of his supporters. Some in the crowd took the exhausted Bishop (who had refused to eat for fear of being poisoned) to Fort Rupert, while others waited for him to make an appearance at Market Square. At the fort, the crowd would have had access to radio equipment, telephones, and arms, so the Coard coalition faced the prospect of an armed popular uprising in support of Bishop. Indeed, if the socialist transformation of 1979–1983 was a revolution from above, this appeared to be a revolution from below: the leader and the masses versus the Coard clique and the officer corps; the populist versus the totalitarian Leninist regime; the people versus the party.

At this point, in the opinion of the winning anti-Bishop coalition, the crisis called for "casting all emotions aside." In other words, violence if need be. Coard and his followers obviously meant to follow the example of fraternal parties in dealing with counterrevolutionaries. Even Austin, who had joined the Coard conspiracy only in late September, apparently saw the conflict as a continuation of the constant struggle of Leninist forces against "right opportunists" during 1903–1924 in Russia, 1921 in Mongolia, 1956 in Hungary, 1968 in Czechoslovakia, and 1980–1981 in Poland.[73] Coard, whom Louison described as "always ready to go for the jugular," then ordered the PRAF to attack Fort Rupert with all three of its Soviet-supplied armored personnel carriers. Bishop and his followers could have tried to defend their position, but by this point the physically weakened and emotionally strained Bishop had no heart for an all-out civil war.

In the unresisted attack—Bishop reportedly told his people not to fire—many demonstrators were killed. Bishop and some of his supporters, including Whiteman, Bain, and Bishop's companion Jacqueline Creft (Minister of Education, Youth and Social Affairs) were allegedly lined up against a mural depicting Che Guevara and shot.[74] Louison, who was in prison at the time, was told that orders to kill them were given by Coard's supporters in the Central Committee. As Bishop and his comrades were shot, a white flare was fired from Fort Rupert as a signal to Coard, who was in his residence on another promontory on the opposite side of the city. Meanwhile, Layne was heard to chant, "Central Committee's order given; Central Committee's order obeyed."[75] The reign of terror that ensued lasted until October 25 when the intervention occurred. (A large number of Grenadians were treated by the intervention forces or American medical students for wounds received during that riotous week.)

PRAF conspirators Cornwall, James, Layne, and Erstwhile "Bishop-worshipper" Austin played a prominent role in the new leadership. Coard, the mastermind of the anti-Bishop conspiracy, kept out of sight and allowed Austin, who was extremely popular in the armed forces, to appear as the main actor. Coard apparently calculated that this would prompt the masses to follow. He probably also anticipated some support from the Soviet Union, for there are indications that Moscow was not unhappy about the latest turn of events.

An "Afghan Line?" There is still no clear evidence about the extent of Soviet or Cuban involvement in the NJM power struggle of September-October 1983. Crucial NJM documents are available, but not the archives of the CPSU or the PCC. Nevertheless, the available evidence suggests that Soviet officials knew about the Bishop-Coard rivalry and, unlike the Cubans, probably sought to aid the anti-Bishop conspirators in their efforts to demote him. At any rate, they made no move to help the embattled Bishop. The Soviets probably were suspicious of Bishop's independence, suggested by his belated attempts (apparently not coordinated with Moscow) at rapprochement with the United States, and his poor Leninist credentials, suggested by his unwillingness to abide by the NJM Central Committee decision to impose collective leadership. Surely the Soviets would have felt more at ease with the ideologically more compatible *apparatchik*, Bernard Coard.

As past masters of factional politics and close observers of the power struggle on the island, the Soviets generally prefer to deal with various cliques in a collective leadership rather than charismatic or headstrong individual communist leaders such as Josef Tito, Enver Hoxha, Mao Zedong, Hafizullah Amin, and perhaps at times even Fidel Castro. Typically, Soviet control is maintained by playing off competing groups against one another or, if necessary, even by keeping them at each other's throats. Although analogies with Grenada (like all analogies) are necessarily imperfect, rival leadership factions frequently have been manipulated to Soviet advantage, as demonstrated during the crisis situations in Hungary in 1956, Czechoslovakia in 1968, Afghanistan in 1979, and Poland in 1980–1981.

In the Grenadian case, circumstantial evidence suggests that the Soviets had established a "back channel" to Coard's faction quite early. Coard's own personal relationship with Moscow is suggested by the fact that it was he who led the first two high-level NJM visits to the USSR in 1979 and 1980. He also attended the 26th CPSU Congress in 1981 and the funeral of Leonid Brezhnev in 1982. Furthermore, when the Soviet leadership agreed to receive five members of the NJM leadership for a vacation in the USSR, it was Coard with his wife and their three children who apparently went in the summer of 1983.[76] (Appendix A, Documents 16 and 19) Phyllis Coard is said to have been friendly with the wives of Soviet advisers in Grenada. In addition, of the three military officers most actively involved in the struggle against Bishop, Layne and James had both studied in the Soviet Union, and Cornwall reportedly maintained extensive contacts with his Soviet counterparts. Austin, too, had close ties with Soviet military and security officials, and had led a high-level Grenadian delegation to Moscow in November 1981. The Soviets most probably shared the Coard faction's hostile attitude toward right-opportunistic tendencies in the NJM.

As noted above, it is likely that the Soviets had become disenchanted with Bishop for another related reason. The turning point in Bishop's relations with Moscow appeared to be June 1983, when he visited the United States with a delegation that included members of the Grenadian private sector. Afterward, Bishop admitted that he had tried to convince some U.S. officials of the "need to normalize diplomatic and state-to-state relations,"[77] and vowed that he would continue to strive toward that goal. The captured NJM briefing notes and memorandum concerning Bishop's meeting with National Security Advisor William Clarke and Deputy Secretary of State Kenneth Dam likewise refer to a Grenadian proposal to establish diplomatic relations in 1983 (Appendix A, Document 17). Bishop subsequently remarked that he and senior American officials had agreed that the content of their meeting should "remain secret," and that therefore he was not "at liberty to disclose the details."[78] Apparently there was a second, off-the-record secret meeting between Bishop and U.S. officials.[79]

At least one Soviet foreign ministry official, Chief of the First Latin American Countries Department Vladimir Kazimirov, hinted that the Soviets were displeased that they had not been properly informed by Grenadian diplomats about the Bishop visit. When Kazimirov asked about the nature of Bishop's meeting with Clarke, he was told by the Grenadian Ambassador that "thus far the results are confidential." Kazimirov implied that it would have been courteous to inform the Soviets about the intention of the visit.[80] (Appendix A, Document 6) The Soviets were probably similarly disturbed by Bishop's effort to conduct a dialogue with neighboring capitalist Caribbean states. Given the traditional Soviet paranoia about the loyalty and orthodoxy of its socialist allies, the Soviet leadership had sufficient reason to lose confidence in Bishop.

Soviet reservations about Bishop were clearly apparent during his last foreign tour, a month before the coup. Reports about the unexpected cancellation of a visit to Moscow were later denied by Louison, who noted that Bishop stopped briefly in Moscow for a change of planes and unofficial consultations with Soviet officials at Vnukovo Airport.[81] By then, the Soviets must have known about the mounting power struggle in Grenada. Had they really wanted to help Bishop, they would have scheduled an official visit or extended him some other dramatic form of political or economic support. Whether or not Soviet officials were actively involved in the anti-Bishop coup a few weeks later remains a matter of speculation.

When the coup took place, the Soviets, unlike the Cubans, did not eulogize Bishop and his supporters. The official Soviet account in the CPSU's leading theoretical journal *Kommunist* talked vaguely about a "tragic turn of events" caused by "the differences within the party." Not only did the Soviets fail to admonish Coard—they still have not admitted Bishop's death was the result of a conspiracy, attributing it rather to "an armed clash in one of the districts of St. George's."[82] Later, the Soviet newspaper *Izvestiya* published a letter from Cornwall (dated November 18, 1983), ostensibly smuggled out of his jail cell in St. George's. The letter refers to Coard and other members of the anti-Bishop faction as "Grenadian patriots" awaiting execution.[83] Apart from its propaganda value, such unusual publicity might indicate Moscow's true sympathies.

In contrast, it appears that Castro tried to boost Bishop's prestige and morale en route to Grenada after his foreign tour in September 1983. After receiving a cold shoulder in Moscow, Bishop reportedly was warmly received in Havana where he made an unscheduled stop on his way home. Bishop was said to have spent two extra days in Cuba, during which the Cubans gave him a reception attended by no fewer than eight Cuban Politburo members.[84] This angered the Coard faction, who charged that Bishop had taken internal NJM business to Cuba in an attempt to use his friendship with Castro to retain power. For his part, the Cuban leader seems to have viewed Grenada's internal conflict mainly as an unfortunate clash of personalities. Indeed, Castro probably favored Bishop partly for personal reasons; the two were friends and shared a certain charismatic approach to leadership. Still, it would be wrong to exaggerate Soviet/Cuban tactical differences over the handling of the October 1983 crisis in Grenada. There is no record of a sustained Cuban attempt to intervene on Bishop's behalf during the final phase of the coup.

Once the anti-Bishop coup took place, Castro endeavored to save the life of his counterpart, imploring "generosity" in a letter to the NJM Central Committee on October 15. Castro described Bishop as the "central figure" of the Grenadian revolution, and "the object of great sympathies and respect," and warned that "even explaining the events to our people will not be easy."[85] (Appendix A, Document 18) The Cuban leader also reportedly put through a last-minute telephone call to Austin in a futile effort to prevent Bishop's execution. On October 19, Castro promptly lamented the death of Bishop and his followers, whom he described as "dignified and honest" leaders. As one of Coard's supporters complained, the Cubans took "a personal and not a class approach," and thereby helped create "an atmosphere for speedy imperialist intervention."[86]

In fact, Castro's mistrust of the new leaders may have been one reason for the largely symbolic nature of Cuba's military assistance to Grenada following Bishop's death. More compelling reasons centered around reports in the American media that a U.S. naval task force originally destined for Lebanon had been diverted toward Grenada.[87] That the Cubans were aware of this is supported by Castro's public statement advising Austin and Layne about the naval maneuver in a message to Cuban personnel in Grenada. He noted that the Cuban presence on the island was "too small to be taken as a factor of military importance in the face of a large-scale invasion." In Grenada, as opposed to Angola or Ethiopia, the idea of sending reinforcements was "unthinkable" because "the U.S. squadrons and aircraft carriers were moving," and Cuba had "no means of transportation to send reinforcements." The Soviet Union was unwilling to repeat an airlift of Cuban troops of the sort it had undertaken in Africa. Nevertheless, as Castro explained, no matter how many reinforcements he sent, "they could not compare to the naval and air forces deployed by the United States."[88]

Castro sent Colonel Pedro Tortolo Comas and some 150–200 seasoned Cuban soldiers (possibly disguised as construction workers) to command the symbolic resistance of the Cubans stationed in Grenada. The last-minute transfer could account for the American failure to estimate correctly the number of Cubans on the island. The original estimate was 250–300, but by the time of the invasion there were over 700 Cubans in Grenada. Some may have arrived on the ship *Vietnam Heroico*, which remained outside St. George's harbor during the critical week to serve as a communications link, as it had in Angola. While the Cubans thus were prepared for a possible intervention, they did not anticipate its exact timing.[89] The airstrip at Point Salines was blocked by trucks, and other obstacles, suggesting that the Cubans might not have been expecting reinforcements. But the Soviets were in no position—for logistical as well as cautionary reasons—to back up a Cuban effort, or to uphold the post-coup regime themselves. Instead, the Soviet response was limited chiefly to a display of anti-American sentiment during the October revolution anniversary parade in Moscow.[90]

POSTSCRIPT

Unlike the Cuban missile crisis of 1962, Soviet and Cuban involvement in Grenada did not present an immediate threat to U.S. interests; nor is there conclusive evidence that Grenada had become a depot for large concentrations of Soviet arms designed for future use in Latin America.

Nevertheless, in the years ahead, such threats could have become a reality, at which time it would have been much more difficult to affect a reversal. The Soviets made a significant though guarded commitment to Grenada. They accorded it a special revolutionary status and promised to send a considerable number of weapons to strengthen the NJM against internal and external threats.

The resulting arsenal made the Grenadian armed forces a factor to be reckoned with in the West Indian environment. Grenada's army could have threatened the country's small neighbors, and indeed this was the overwhelming consensus of the OECS. Some of the countries in question have no armed forces at all, while others have armies of less than a few hundred. Even Jamaica has a smaller army than the one that was being trained and equipped in Grenada although the former's population is 20 times larger. Furthermore, although Grenada did not have Soviet military bases at the time of the U.S./OECS intervention, one cannot exclude the possibility that it might have become a component of Soviet military planning and a bridge to revolutionary forces elsewhere in the region as Cuba has been during the last quarter-century.

The NJM crisis of October 1983 derived initially from internal problems. Newly installed Leninist regimes, with their emphasis on military power, ideological mobilization, economic controls, democratic centralism, and Bolshevik staunchness, tend to produce the kind of popular disenchantment and factional bloodshed witnessed in Grenada. The Leninist experiment introduced in Grenada was also a poor fit for local conditions. To some observers, the attempt to introduce a Leninist regime into the unlikely environment of the Caribbean appeared theatrical and absurd. However, they overlook the equally incongruous transplant of Leninist structures into such seemingly inhospitable environments as Catholic Poland, democratic Czechoslovakia, and most importantly, Caribbean Cuba.

Of course, the communist regimes of East Europe might not have survived were it not for the continuous threat of Soviet military intervention to keep orthodoxy on track. In the case of Grenada, however, "proletarian internationalist" ties with the USSR and Cuba were unable to contain the internal crisis and subsequent power struggle. On the contrary, arms supplied by the USSR and other communist countries became a destabilizing factor, serving not to defend the revolution's original leaders, but rather to destroy them.

The Grenadian episode thus demonstrates that Third World leaders dependent upon the USSR, much like leaders of communist countries on the Soviet periphery, cannot be assured of continuing Soviet support. Deviation or perceived offense can be the pretext for removal. Moreover, outside the immediate Soviet sphere, even a mortal challenge from imperialism does not ensure Moscow's automatic protection. What happened in Grenada has troubling implications for Nicaragua and even for Cuba. In the final analysis, Castro could count only on his own forces to defend revolutionaries elsewhere in the Caribbean Basin. He may now be wondering about Soviet backing for Nicaragua (or for Cuba itself) in the event of a direct conflict with the United States. In contrast to its behavior in Eastern Europe and remote African regions, the USSR now seems much less willing to support pro-Soviet regimes in America's backyard—particularly when Washington is willing to protect its interests with military force.

The key players in the Grenadian power struggle of September-October 1983 consisted of the anti-Bishop Coalition and the pro-Bishop Minority.

The Anti-Bishop Coalition

1. Bernard Coard, Politburo member (until October 1982) and Deputy Prime Minister.
2. Lt. Colonel Liam James, Politburo member and Minister of the Interior.
3. Lt. Colonel Ewert Layne, Politburo member and party supervisor of the armed forces.
4. Leon Cornwall, chief of the armed forces' Main Political Administration; previously Ambassador to Cuba.
5. Phyllis Coard, wife of Bernard Coard and head of the National Women's Organization.
6. Selwyn Strachan, Politburo member in charge of ideology and propaganda.
7. Chalkie Ventour, Politburo member.
8. General Hudson Austin, Politburo member, Minister of Defense, and Minister of Construction (joined anti-Bishop group in the fall of 1983).

The Pro-Bishop Minority

1. Maurice Bishop, Politburo member, Central Committee chairman, and Prime Minister.
2. Unison Whiteman, Politburo member and Minister of External Affairs.
3. George Louison, Politburo member and Minister of Agriculture.
4. Fitzroy Bain, Politburo member and leader of Union of Agricultural Workers.

NOTES

Documentary sources: As of April 1984, the U.S. Government has released several series of documents captured in Grenada, cited here as the Grenada Documents. Each series, consisting of NJM Political Bureau and Central Committee minutes, secret agreements with communist countries, letters, diaries, personal papers, and reports from the Grenadian Embassy in Moscow, is indexed in dozens of "logs." Unfortunately, the packets are not yet properly sorted; some are unnumbered, and a few are not entirely legible.

Poster printed by the surviving leaders of the pro-Bishop NJM faction organized as the October 19th Martyrs Foundation after the carnage of October 1983. The victims pictured include Politburo members, Maurice Bishop, Unison Whiteman, Fitzroy Bain, and NJM officials, Vincent Noel and Jacqueline Craft (Bishop's girlfriend). Many other Grenadians killed still have not been identified. (Courtesy of Jiri and Virginia Valenta.)

A preliminary evaluation of some of the documents was published by the U.S. Department of State and Department of Defense on December 16, 1983 under the title "Grenada: A Preliminary Report." Michael Ledeen and Herbert Romerstein, both of Washington, D.C., are compiling and editing another volume of documents soon to be published.

1. The term Leninism is used as opposed to Marxism-Leninism. It was Lenin,

not Marx, who developed the concepts of vanguard party, dictatorship of the proletariat, democratic centralism, and proletarian internationalism that are the building blocks of the political system adhered to and propagated by the Soviet Union.

2. The documents thus refute the view that Moscow was providing mainly moral support to revolutionary regimes in the Latin America such as Grenada. For an example of this view, see Cole Blasier, "Comment," in Alan Adelman and Reid Reading (eds.), *Confrontation in the Caribbean Basin: International Perspectives on Security, Sovereignty, and Survival* (Pittsburgh, PA: University of Pittsburgh Press, 1984), pp. 268–274.

3. Only twice before have Western scholars had access to comparable sets of documents. Merle Fainsod analyzed Soviet decisionmaking based on a unique collection of original materials captured by German troops in Smolensk. Later, based partly on documents of the Central Committee of the Czechoslovak Communist Party, several scholars analyzed Czechoslovak internal politics and Soviet decisionmaking during the crisis of 1968. See Merle Fainsod, *Smolensk under Soviet Rule* (Cambridge, MA: Harvard University Press, 1958); H. Gordon Skilling, *Czechoslovakia's Interrupted Revolution* (Princeton, NJ: Princeton University Press, 1976); Galia Golan, *The Czechoslovak Reform Movement: Communism in Crisis, 1962–68* (Cambridge, England: Cambridge University Press, 1971); and Jiri Valenta, *Soviet Intervention in Czechoslovakia, 1968: Anatomy of a Decision* (Baltimore, MD: The Johns Hopkins University Press, 1979).

4. Michael G. Smith, *Stratification in Grenada* (Berkeley, CA: University of California Press, 1965). *See also* the excellent analysis of Aaron Segal, "Background to Grenada: When the Social Scientists Invaded," *Caribbean Review*, Miami, FL, Fall 1983, pp. 40–44.

5. See "The Grenada Document: The Bitter, Epic Struggle for the Isle of Spice," special supplement to the Barbados newspaper *Nation*, Bridgetown, February 1984. The analyses of the *Nation* between 1979 and 1983 are indispensible for any student of the Grenadian revolution.

6. For a detailed discussion, see Archie Singham, *The Hero and the Crowd in a Colonial Polity* (New Haven, CT: Yale University Press, 1968). Interviews conducted in Grenada reinforced the authors' views.

7. "The Grenada Document," supplement to the *Nation*, loc. cit., p. 9.

8. *See* the excellent analysis of Anthony P. Maingot, "Options for Grenada: The Need to be Cautious," *Caribbean Review*, Fall 1983, pp. 24, 28.

9. For background on the NJM, *see* ibid., pp. 25–26; and V.S. Naipaul, "An Island Betrayed," *Harper's*, New York, March 1984, pp. 61–72.

10. Manifesto of the New Jewel Movement, Grenada Documents, undated; see also Maingot, loc. cit., p. 26.

11. Authors' interviews in Barbados and Grenada, February 23–27, 1984.

12. Authors' interview with Alistair Hughes in St. George's, February 24, 1984.

13. *See* the most significant and comprehensive Bishop speech: Line of March for the Party, Presented by Maurice Bishop, Chairman Central Committee, General Meeting of Party, September 13, 1982, Grenada Documents, unnumbered.

14. Central Committee Resolution on Agriculture, Grenada Documents, undated, Log No. 100310; and position paper On Possible Establishment of a State Trading

Corporation for Effecting Grenada's Trade with the Socialist Countries, ibid., undated, Log. 100310.

15. "What We Must Do," by Garvin Stuart, and "More Food," by Haleem Abdulwali, Renalph Gebon (ed.), *Tongues of the New Dawn: An Anthology of Poems*, St. George's, Festival of the Revolution, March 10–13, 1981, pp. 33–34 and 54–55.

16. Authors' interview with George Louison, St. George's, February 26, 1984.

17. Secret area-by-area report on the Political Situation in Grenada, undated, Grenada Documents, Log No. 102604.

18. Excerpts from Restricted Report of the Delegation Sent to Grenada by the Americas Department with the Aim of Gathering of Sources for the Characterization of the Religious Situations in the Country, and the Contacts for Further Cooperation between the PCC and the NJM Regarding the Question, August 13–24, 1982, ibid., Log No. Il; and Plan of C.I. Operations [Counter intelligence], undated, ibid., Log No. 104968.

19. See Line of March of Party, op. cit.

20. Resolution of the People's Revolutionary Armed Forces Branch of the New Jewel Movement, October 12, 1983, Grenada Documents, Log No. 100103.

21. See the third installment of a letter written by Grenadian trade union leader and Bishop's friend, Vincent Noel, to members of the NJM Central Committee two days before the murder of Noel and Bishop, *The Grenadian Voice*, St. George's, February 11, 1984. This newspaper came into being in its present form after the U.S./OECS intervention. We are indebted to the editor, Leslie Pierre, who shared many insights with us during several interviews in Grenada.

22. Minutes of the Extraordinary General Meeting of Full Members of the NJM, September 25, 1983, ibid., Log No. 102645.

23. Confidential Report from the Grenadian Embassy in Moscow on the NJM's Relations with the CPSU, undated (but sometime after December 1981) ibid., Log No. 102329.

24. See, for example, K. Kochaturov, "Changes on the Island of Spices," *Pravda*, Moscow, August 17, 1981.

25. A.I. Stroganov, *Latinskaya Amerika* (Moscow, May 1983), p. 134.

26. Confidential Report on Grenada's Relations with the USSR from Grenadian Ambassador to Moscow, W. Richard Jacobs, to Foreign Minister Unison Whiteman, Prime Minister Bishop, Deputy Prime Minister Coard, and Politburo Ewert Layne, July 11, 1983, Grenada Documents, Log No. W.

27. Memo from Comrade Bernard Bourne [Minister-Councellor of the Grenadian Embassy in Moscow] to Comrade Maurice Bishop, Chairman of the Central Committee of the New Jewel Movement, June 30, 1982, ibid., Log No. 109242. (Also listed as Log No. 104262.)

28. On Cuba's role as "a champion" of Grenada's case in Moscow, *see* Grenada's Relations with the USSR, July 11, 1983, loc. cit. For a Jamaican Workers' Party offer of assistance in this regard, *see* Trever Munroe's letter to Bishop dated October 16, 1979, ibid., Log No. 104729.

29. Agreement on Cooperation between the New Jewel Movement of Grenada and the Communist Party of the Soviet Union, July 27, 1982, ibid., Log No. 102318. Also in Russian.

30. Handwritten notes from meeting between Hudson Austin and the Cuban Minister of Construction, 1983, ibid., Log No. 100003.

31. Memo from Bernard Bourne to Prime Minister Bishop, op. cit.; Report of Bernard Bourne on the Work of the NJM Party Branch in Moscow, ibid., May 10, 1983, Log No. L; and Minutes of Organizing Committee, April 18, 1983, ibid., Log No. 100718.

32. Report of Meeting with Acting Rector of the CPSU Party School, Gaidum, Oleg P. (by W. Richard Jacobs), May 23, 1983, ibid., Log No. 103672.

33. Work Plan and Guidelines for the NJM's Propaganda Department, ibid., unnumbered.

34. *See* recollections of V. Alikperov, senior scientific associate of the Azerbaydzhan Scientific Research Institute of Pedagogical Sciences in Baku, in N. Barskiy, "They Returned to Baku from Grenada," *Bakinskiy Rabochiy* (Baku, November 15, 1983). Alikperov had worked earlier in Ethiopia.

35. Memo from Bernard Bourne to the Grenadian Peace Council, Grenada Documents, November 6, 1982, Log No. 102640.

36. Secret Cooperation and Exchange Plan between the Communist Party of Cuba and the New Jewel Movement of Grenada for the 1983 Period, June 29, 1983, ibid., Log No. 100016.

37. Report on the General Congress of the World Center for the Resistance of Imperialism, Zionism, Racism, and Reaction, ibid., Log No. 103025.

38. Memorandum of Meeting between Chiefs of the General Staff of the Soviet Armed Forces and People's Revolutionary Armed Forces of Grenada [Marshal Nikolay Ogarkov and Major Einstein Louison] March 10, 1983, ibid., Log No. 100008. Louison was in the Soviet Union for training at the time.

39. Top Secret Agreement between the Government of Grenada and the Government of the Union of Soviet Socialist Republics on Deliveries from the Union of SSR to Grenada of Special and Other Equipment, October 27, 1980, ibid., Log No. 000190. Also in Russian.

40. Authors' interview with an official of the East Caribbean Security Forces.

41. Protocol to the October 27, 1980 Grenada-USSR Agreement on Arms Deliveries, February 9, 1981, Grenada Documents, Log No. 000193.

42. Top Secret Agreement between the Government of Grenada and the Government of the Union of Soviet Socialist Republics on Deliveries from the Union of SSR to Grenada of Special and Other equipment, October 27, 1982, ibid.

43. Meeting between Chiefs of General Staff of Soviet Armed Forces and People's Revolutionary Armed Forces of Grenada, March 10, 1983, op. cit.

44. Agreement between the Government of the Union of Soviet Socialist Republics and the Government of Grenada on Deliveries from the Soviet Union to Grenada of Special and Other Equipment, Moscow, dated 1983, ibid., Log No. 103866.

45. Austin, a Bishop supporter until shortly before the October 1983 coup, was warden at Richmond Hill Prison under Gairy. After he was fired by Gairy, he joined the NJM, and during the March 1979 coup, he personally commanded the successful raid on the army barracks. Austin subsequently became a member of the NJM Politburo and Minister of Defense. In the latter capacity, like his nominal subordinates James and Layne, he developed a close working relationship with various Soviet officials.

46. Secret Protocol of Military Collaboration between the Government of the Republic of Cuba and Peoples' Revolutionary Government of Grenada, undated, Grenada Documents, Log No. 000194. *See also* the analysis of Nestor D. Sanchez in *Caribbean Review*, Fall 1983, pp. 21–23 and 59.

47. Authors' interviews in St. George's, and Minutes of the Political-Economic Bureau, August 10, 1983, Grenada Documents, Log No. 100282.

48. Entry from James' diary for March 22, 1980, ibid., Log No. Y. It is instructive to recall that during the Soviet/Cuban airlift to Angola in 1975, Barbados served as a refueling stop for two weeks after which vociferous complaints in the Miami press resulted in rerouting through Guyana.

49. Handwritten notes from a meeting between Hudson Austin and the Cuban Minister of Construction, op. cit.

50. Request for Military Assistance to the PRA Forces of Grenada from the USSR Armed Forces, July 2, 1982 (unsigned), Grenada Documents, Log No. 102174.

51. For data on Soviet economic aid for 1983–1985, *see* Summary of Prime Minister's meeting with Soviet Ambassador, May 24, 1983, ibid., Log No. 103913; and Economic and Technical Cooperation Agreement between Grenada and the USSR, May 1980, ibid., Log No. 103866. On aid to Grenada, see Nazim Burke's *aide memoire* on the Visit to Grenada of the GDR Delegation (August 13–20, 1982), ibid., Log No. F; and Grenada's Relations with the USSR, July 11, 1983, op. cit.

52. Minutes of Politburo meeting, September 15, 1982, Grenada Documents, Log No. GG.

53. Letter from Maurice Bishop to Mummar Qadhafi, September 26, 1983, ibid., Log No. R.

54. Summary of Prime Minister's meeting with Soviet Ambassador, May 24, 1983, op. cit.

55. Minutes of Committee of Economic Ministers Meeting, May 9, 1983, Grenada Documents, Log No. 100719.

56. Minutes of Political-Economic Bureau Meeting, August 3, 1983, ibid., Log No. 100283.

57. Central Committee Report on First Plenary Session, July 13–19, 1983, ibid., Log No. 100243.

58. Minutes of Emergency Meeting of NJM Central Committee, August 26, 1983, ibid., Log No. 100319.

59. Ibid.

60. Apparently Coard resigned because he felt that was his only real choice at the time. The alternatives would have been either to tolerate the "slackness," which was unacceptable, or to introduce "Leninist measures," which would have precipitated "personality clashes" with Bishop. *See* Minutes of Meeting of the Central Committee, October 15, 1982, ibid., Log No. Q1. After being deposed, Bishop reportedly believed that Coard was contemplating suicide; Bishop's stated reason for requesting that Chief of Counterintelligence Keith Roberts follow Coard was to ensure Coard's own safety. *See* the second installment of a letter by Vincent Noel to the members of the Central Committee of the NJM, *The Grenadian Voice*, February 4, 1984.

61. Authors' interviews in Bridgetown, Barbados, and St. George's, Grenada, February 1984.

62. From the documents it appears that on at least one occasion, Cornwall's residence telephone and the telephones, telex, and electricity at the Grenadian Embassy in Havana were disconnected after Cornwall failed to pay his phone bill. Minutes of the Politburo Meeting, June 22, 1983, Grenada Documents, Log No. 100291.

63. Extraordinary Meeting of the Central Committee NJM, September 14–17, 1983, ibid., Log No. 000123, pp. 3–4.

64. Ibid., p. 28.

65. Ibid., pp. 9 and 16.

66. Ibid., pp. 20–1, 25.

67. Ibid., p. 18.

68. Ibid., pp. 27–30, 33.

69. Ibid., p. 10.

70. Ibid., p. 33; and authors' interview with George Louison, February 26, 1984.

71. References to the "Afghan line" are in Noel's letter to the Central Committee as published in *The Grenadian Voice*, February 4, 1984; and in a report on Meeting of the Politburo and Central Committee, October 12, 1983, Grenada Documents, Log No. 000149. This was confirmed by authors' interviews.

72. Noel's letter to the Central Committee, loc. cit.; authors' interview with Louison in Grenada, February 26, 1984.

73. Report on Meeting of the Politburo and Central Committee, October 12, 1983, loc. cit.; *see also* report on the Meeting of the Politburo and Central Committee, September 26, 1983 (portions illegible).

74. Authors' interviews in St. George's, February 1984. Anthony Maingot's interview sources suggest, however, that Bishop and his comrades were shot in a jeep on the way to the hospital. Private communication to the authors.

75. Interview with George Louison by Bernard Diederich, *Caribbean Review*, Fall 1983, pp. 17–18.

76. Reference to the Coard family's vacation in the Soviet Union in Summary of Prime Minister's meeting with Soviet Ambassador, op. cit.; *see also* Foreign Relations Report, undated (but probably published in 1981), ibid., Log No. 105757 for references to earlier travel by Coard to the USSR and Eastern Europe.

77. Report on a press conference of Maurice Bishop in Prague, *Rude Pravo*, October 6, 1983, p. 2.

78. CANA, Bridgetown, June 9, 1983, transcribed in Foreign Broadcast Information Service, *Daily Report: Latin America* [hereafter FBIS-LAM], Washington, DC, June 10, 1983, p. S/5.

79. Handwritten notes that appear to be memoranda of the meeting between Bishop, U.S. National Security Advisor William Clarke and Deputy Secretary of State Kenneth Dam, Grenada Documents, Log No. A; and Briefing Notes on Meeting with Judge William Clarke, Chairman of the N.S.C., undated, ibid., Log No. 105300.

80. Grenada's Relations with the USSR, July 11, 1983, op. cit. So far the available evidence suggests that while Bishop did not consult Moscow about his visit to Washington, he was advised on how to deal with the press and various U.S. organizations by Gail Reed, wife of Cuban Ambassador Julian Torres Rizo. *See* her undated letter, ibid., Log No. DD.

81. Authors' interview with George Louison in Grenada, February 26, 1984.

82. D. Murav'yev, "Grenada—Victim of U.S. Imperialist Aggression," *Kommunist* (Moscow), No. 16 (November 1983), pp. 109–111.

83. *Izvestiya*, Moscow, January 12, 1984.

84. Reported by Strachan to Noel; *see* third installment of Noel's letter to the Central Committee, *The Grenadian Voice*, February 11, 1984. Louison, in an interview with the authors, and Castro, in From Fidel Castro Ruz to the Central Committee, New Jewel Movement, October 15, 1983, Grenada Documents, Log No. T, denied that Bishop had discussed Grenada's internal situation. However, the evidence suggests otherwise.

85. Letter from Fidel Castro Ruz to Central Committee, New Jewel Movement, October 15, 1983, Grenada Documents, Log No. T.

86. *See* handwritten note on Cuba's Response, written by one of Coard's supporters, October 1, 1983, Grenada Documents, unnumbered.

87. *See*, for example, "U.S. Marines, Ships on Way to Grenada," *Virginian-Pilot* (Norfolk), October 22, 1983.

88. *See* Castro's press conference about Grenada, Havana television, October 26, 1983, FBIS-LAM, October 26, 1983, pp. Q/1-14.

89. Authors' interviews in Barbados and Grenada, February 1984.

90. There were, however, unconfirmed reports that the Soviets did provide some token assistance to the Grenadian armed forces. For example, the third-ranking Soviet official on the island was said to have been apprehended as he was chauffeured about in an air-conditioned Mercedes, pinpointing U.S positions at the airport during the early stage of the invasion; there were also reports of antiaircraft fire from the Soviet Embassy during those first hours.

RICHARD PIPES

Comments

There is something comic-opera about dealing with a country as miniscule as Grenada—in which we find documents written by semi-literate people who give themselves airs about being revolutionary leaders. At the same time, however, the Grenada experience sheds important light on Soviet policy in the Third World.

The Grenadian revolution was striking because communist ways of thinking were superimposed on a totally unprepared society with apparent ease. It is similar to a big company like Bechtel transferring modern technology to countries like Saudi Arabia or Libya, or any other place. It is as if entire "modules" are readymade to be provided and transplanted into underdeveloped nations. Once transplanted, they do not work as well as they did at their point of origin; just as gigantic industrial projects in Third World countries tend to collapse and rot in rust, so do many Marxist ideas.

Why did the Soviet Union and Cuba pick Grenada? One must consider this question in light of the tremendous strains on the Soviet economy and the high cost of Soviet imperial expenditures. In recent years it has become clear that the Soviet economy cannot sustain an imperial drive of the dimensions of the 1970s; Soviet resources simply will not stretch any further. In several open sources, Soviet specialists on the Third World are increasingly advising their comrades in the Third World not to rush with nationalization of industries, not to rush with socialism, to maintain good relations with their own middle classes and the United States, and in some cases they are brazenly advising the building of socialism with capitalist money. Such advice was given specifically to Nicaragua.

In considering Soviet expansionism over the last several years, it is apparent that there is a great effort to concentrate on smaller, relatively inexpensive countries that will not impose a great strain on the Soviet economy, but which have great strategic value. The Soviets are shying away from long-term policies aimed at transforming Third World countries in feudal or prefeudal conditions into socialist nations. The former option has proven to be extremely expensive. It is beyond the means of the Soviet

Union, and has often led to tremendous disappointment. As a result, the Soviets are concentrating on seizing naval and air bases which are relatively cheap. From this point of view, Grenada was an ideal target. It sits athwart an important naval and commercial route to the United States, and could have been used to disrupt American oil supplies and other imports.

Grenada was not a fully structured communist society. It rather fits into what was once called a "national democracy" in the 1960s, or what is now called a socialist-oriented society. According to Soviet theorists, this is a society which makes the transition from feudalism to socialism without going through capitalism. They have formulated elaborate ways and means by which this can be accomplished. The elements mentioned in Jiri and Virginia Valenta's paper "Leninism in Grenada" are proof that the country had gone communist, or would seem to be proof that the country had become a society of a socialist-oriented type rather than officially communist.

Accordingly, the American liberation of Grenada was not so much a violation of the Brezhnev doctrine, nor the loss of a "communist" state the Soviets would find intolerable. Rather, it should be categorized as a socialist-oriented country that went wrong—of which there are many examples. The only difference between Grenada and other such cases is that Grenada was "lost" by force of arms. This is something very new; it must have had a profound effect on Soviet thinking.

When President Reagan took office, Soviet specialists on the United States were divided about the "Reagan phenomenon." On one side there was a group associated with Giorgi Arbatov that argued, partly in self-defense, that Reagan was really nothing very new. He was just like Nixon—an anti-communist for electoral purposes—and once he got settled into office, one could make a deal with him.

Another school ably represented by Aleksandr Bovin argued that Reagan represents a new tidal wave of American nationalism. He is serious, and one should take his anticommunism seriously. The Bovin school now says that anticommunism has become American militarism—something new that deserves close attention. This position has probably gained the upper hand as a result of the invasion of Grenada.

In regard to the Grenadian power struggle, one thing the Soviets have learned over the past 20 years of expansion into the Third World is that while popular, charismatic leaders are useful in paving the way for a socialist-oriented type of government, they are unreliable once in power because they are basically nationalist rather than communist in character. (This goes back to the Chiang Kai-shek experience of the 1920s.) They cannot be played with for long; they should be quickly replaced with internationalists—essentially people of no local stature—who owe their allegiance entirely to those they depend upon for their political power. The evidence suggests that this is what the Soviets have done in South Yemen, where a more popular leader was replaced with a less popular leader. They did so in Afghanistan, and possibly in Angola, where it is not clear whether or not Neto died a natural death. In Grenada, Coard was clearly an internationalist.

He had no mass base of support, and he was not a charismatic figure. Had he succeeded, he would have been totally dependent upon Moscow. The evidence also suggests that Castro prefers charismatic nationalist leaders because the more of these that exist in the Third World, the stronger his leverage with the Soviets.

Jiri and Virginia Valenta argue that Third World leaders dependent upon the USSR cannot be assured of continuing Soviet support, but we did not need Grenada to tell us that. Soviet officials have stressed time and again—and Western bankers would not listen—that they would not bail out any friendly country that went bankrupt, and that the "umbrella theory" was invalid. Moreover, they proved in action that they had meant what they said. In addition, they have said repeatedly that countries far from the periphery of the Soviet Union would have to defend themselves, and that the Soviet Union would not be able to do so. The fact that they have never given ironclad guarantees to Cuba is evidence of this. Thus there exist severe limits on Soviet imperial ventures, for much of the Soviet empire is very vulnerable.

After reading the Grenada documents, it is difficult to hold the position that the problem in Central and Latin America is not the Soviet Union, but rather poverty. I do not deny that poverty is a problem 90% of the world, but the real problem is the Soviet Union.

The problem in Grenada was not poverty. The primary product of Grenada is nutmeg, which is mainly used in eggnog. Nevertheless, it did not give the impression of being a poor country. Grenada was communized, not because of internal problems, but because of external pressures. In essence, a group with a power-base attitude came into authority and enforced a system. It therefore seems very specious to argue that the Soviet Union is not a problem. Statements to this effect resemble theories that ascribe crime to social problems, not to criminals. It can be argued that police are not needed because they are unable to eliminate crime. But no one makes this diagnosis when it comes to protecting his own interests and protecting his home from burglars. Then a police force is quite useful, even vital.

The same is true of Central America, where there are social problems and there is poverty. Yet these problems become international problems and a threat to American security when the Soviet Union moves in. Because they focus on a miniscule example of this problem, the Grenada Documents are very useful. They are proof that the Soviet Union is the prime mover of revolution in this area, and that the real problems are not social, economic, nor even historic, but the result of a foreign power bent on isolating the United States and exploiting identifiable instabilities and animosities to create regimes hostile and dangerous to American interests. Those who hold liberal views on Latin America should reconsider their premises on the basis of the evidence.

VERNON V. ASPATURIAN

The Impact of the Grenada Events on the Soviet Alliance System

Any forceful assertion or action by the United States that affects Soviet interests and ambitions is bound to leave its impact upon the Soviet alliance system, here defined as the complex network of obligations which the Soviet Union has assumed or contracted toward its allies, clients, and friends in the international system. These obligations are not only military in character: they are political, ideological, economic, and diplomatic as well. Some Soviet obligations are contractually assumed by treaties and agreements and are mutual; others are unilaterally undertaken by the Soviet Union for political, ideological, strategic, or other reasons; some are implicit in the character of Soviet relations with certain countries, or are inferred by its allies and clients; and still others are assumed by the targets and adversaries of the Soviet Union in the absence of explicit or public Soviet commitment.

The Soviet alliance system corresponds roughly with what might be characterized as the Soviet imperial system or Soviet empire—terms which some observers find objectionable or inappropriate largely because of the unique character of the origins and evolution of the network of allies, clients, and dependencies that make up the Soviet alliance system.[1] The nature, intensity, and credibility of Soviet obligations and commitments are diverse, uneven, and not entirely predictable. They vary in accordance with the status and character of the dependency, its importance to Soviet interests and ambitions, and the risks, costs, and benefits of fulfilling such obligations.

The unexpected invasion of Grenada, a small speck of land in the Caribbean, induced disturbing though uneven reverberations throughout the entire Soviet alliance system. The impact of the invasion was highly uneven. Some commitments were weakened; some were intensified and reinvigorated; and some were probably affected only minimally. Aside from the impact of Grenada upon Soviet commitments, we must also consider Grenada's impact upon the complex problem of perceptions concerning the credibility of Soviet commitments.

The perceptual problem exists at several levels. First, there is the Soviet perception of what the impact has been in terms of its own assessment of its obligations and risks, and the corresponding reordering of priorities it may have induced. Second, there are the perceptions of individual Soviet allies and client states concerning the impact on Soviet commitments with respect to themselves. Where do they now stand in the Soviet scale of priorities, and how credible are Soviet commitments under the new circumstances? Third, what is the perception of the United States with respect to Grenada's impact on Soviet commitments? And finally, what is the Soviet perception of how Grenada affected the perception of its allies, clients, and third parties, especially China and the United States?

The answers to these questions may not correspond to one another. Consequently, if the Kremlin draws one set of lessons, its allies and clients draw different ones, and the United States draws still others, the likelihood that misjudgment, miscalculation, and confusion will result is considerable. It should be noted that the allies and clients of the Soviet Union do not share identical concerns relating to the credibility and viability of Soviet commitments. For the most part, allied and client states on the Soviet periphery will probably welcome any erosion of the Soviet commitment to military intervention, whereas distant client states in the Third World, which can afford the luxury of Soviet "fraternal" or "internationalist" assistance without the corresponding risk of Soviet domination, are likely to be concerned about any weakening of already tenuous Soviet commitments. Hence, whereas the invasion of Grenada created anxieties in Cuba and Nicaragua, the consequences were probably more welcome in Eastern Europe. It is likely that both tendencies were further aggravated by the second post-Brezhnev succession which followed soon after the invasion. The intersection of these two events may have given the leaders of East Germany and Bulgaria the impression in the fall of 1984 that they could go ahead with official visits to West Germany, even in the face of public displays of Soviet displeasure. Both East Germany and Bulgaria eventually cancelled their plans under Soviet pressure, but East Germany did so only after several months of oblique, but unmistakable, Soviet condemnation of the planned visit.

THE CHARACTER AND SIGNIFICANCE OF THE GRENADA DOCUMENTS

The captured Grenada documents represent a treasure trove of new information which illuminates the genesis, evolution, and reliability of Soviet commitments to its dependencies. Furthermore, they provide additional insights as to how accurately Soviet obligations are perceived by Soviet allies and clients, and how Soviet reliability is assessed under varying conditions and circumstances. Nevertheless, these documents must be approached with due care, for no matter how important they may be, there are certain inherent limits to their usefulness and dependability having nothing to do with their provenance or authenticity.

The documents cannot be characterized as a professional historian's ideal model of what constitutes definitive evidentiary material. They are highly uneven in character, and cannot be considered as a comprehensive or reliable sample of the entire universe of Grenadian documents which are inaccessible or unobtainable because of destruction or official policy. The documents represent a mixture of reports, memos, letters, drafts, notes, minutes, proceedings, agreements, contracts, and miscellaneous papers of varying degrees of definitiveness and authoritativeness.

Furthermore, they are almost entirely drawn from Grenada, with virtually no counterpart documents from the Soviets or Cubans. The documents include letters to Soviet leaders, and Grenadian assessments of Soviet behavior, but there are neither letters from the Soviets in response, nor Soviet evaluations of Grenada or Soviet-Grenadian relations. Thus there is no way that Grenadian assessments can be compared with Soviet perceptions and evaluations. The Grenada documents may represent authentic Grenadian views, but the documents themselves are scant indication of whether they are accurate or correspond to Soviet views. The information contained in the documents cannot rise above the competence, perceptiveness, general reliability, and accuracy of the source. Some of the documents themselves complain of errors, incompleteness, and partiality in various records and reports. Valuable though the documents might be, they represent *ex parte* evidence which may be often self-serving or inaccurate. For definitive Soviet views, we must await the examination of counterpart Soviet documents—i.e., Soviet memos, letters, diplomatic correspondence, party correspondence, etc.—if they ever become accessible.

In the meantime, Grenadian perceptions of Soviet views and reactions can be compared with views expressed in open-source Soviet publications. Of course this will lack the flavor of empirical specificity and operational application (to say nothing of the distinctive spice of confidential communications) that the Grenada documents so vividly provide. This is not to denigrate their importance or saliency in illuminating Soviet behavior, however.

The Grenadian documents graphically demonstrate how the leaders of certain Third World Soviet clients react to Soviet behavior. They expose the innermost thoughts, ruminations, anxieties, and expectations of Grenadian leaders in dealing with Moscow, and cast new light on the manner in which the Soviet Union seeks to establish multiple channels of influence and penetration in the process of acquiring new client states. As revealed in the documents, Grenadian leaders were obsessively concerned with state and party protocol, the operational significance of party-state relations, channels of communication in the Soviet alliance system and how Grenadian channels should be shaped, and the Soviet perceptions of the New Jewel Movement's stage of development in the Marxist-Leninist scheme of things. Thus by knowing what the Grenadians felt was important, we are provided with valuable information and new insights as to the character and nature of Soviet operational behavior. For the most part such aspects of Soviet behavior have been shrouded in secrecy and confidentiality.

THE SIGNIFICANCE OF THE GRENADA EVENTS AS A CASE STUDY OR PRECEDENT

The impact of the Grenada events on Soviet obligations, policies, and behavior should be neither over nor underestimated; nor should we exaggerate or downgrade the relevance of the Grenada documents. Grenada was not recognized by Moscow as a "socialist" state, or a member of the "socialist community" or "world socialist system." (The terms "socialist" and "communist" are used interchangeably in this paper, since the former corresponds to Soviet terminology and the latter to common Western usage.)

The political and ideological obligations that the Soviet Union has assumed with reference to Eastern Europe did not apply to Grenada—to say nothing of military obligations in the absence of treaty commitments. Furthermore, as the Grenadians themselves repeatedly lamented, the Soviets "regard Grenada as a small, distant country, and they are prepared only to make commitments to the extent of their capacity to fulfill, and if necessary defend, their commitment"—an observation that applies to an entire class of Soviet dependencies throughout the world.[2] (Appendix A, Document 6)

Grenada As a Possible Soviet Global Asset: Regional Proxy of the USSR

Grenada was not high on the Soviet list of priorities because of its rather insigificant size, remote location, viability, and vulnerability to "imperialism" (i.e., American power), but it may have rated higher on the Soviet list of priorities than the Grenadians themselves believed because of its potentially strategic location. Global and regional concerns are paramount in Soviet calculations, and the relative importance of a given dependency varies with the changes in that context as the Grenadian Ambassador to Moscow, W. Richard Jacobs, quickly recognized. Accordingly, he plotted the alteration of the context within which Grenada was situated in order to escalate its value in the Soviet scale of priorities.

> By itself, Grenada's distance from the USSR, and its small size, would mean that we would figure in a very minute way in the USSR's global relationships. Our revolution has to be viewed as a worldwide process with its original roots in the Great October Revolution. For Grenada to assume a position of increasingly greater importance, we have to be seen as influencing at least regional events. We have to establish ourselves as the authority on events in at least the English-speaking Caribbean, and be the sponsor of revolutionary activity and progressive developments in this region at least.[3] (Appendix A, Document 6)

Aside from strategic considerations, the ideological character of the Grenadian regime is important in our understanding Soviet expectations and anticipatory commitments to "socialist-oriented" regimes such as Nicaragua. To enhance Grenada's importance in Soviet eyes, Ambassador Jacobs suggests in the above passage that Grenada should assume the role of a Soviet proxy in the hope that Moscow will reward it accordingly. Thus, Ambassador Jacobs continues his report by citing possible "recruits" for the Soviet Union.

> Of all the regional possibilities, the most likely candidate for special attention is Surinam. If we can be an overwhelming influence on Surinam's international behaviour, then our importance in the Soviet scheme of things will be greatly enhanced. To the extent that we can take credit for bringing any other country into the progressive fold, our prestige and influence would be greatly enhanced. Another candidate is Belize. I think we need to do some more work in that country.[4] (Appendix A, Document 6)

What immediately springs to mind when reading these words are the following questions. To what extent were the Grenadians pursuing a course which would indeed find favor with Moscow or at least coincide with Soviet ambitions; to what extent were they modeling their behavior on the Cuban example (after all, Cuba "recruited" Grenada); and to what degree is Nicaragua pursuing the same goals in Central America, particularly with respect to El Salvador? In a sense, the Grenadian documents appear to unveil a hitherto unnoticed Soviet strategy for the proliferation of client or communist states. They impart new meaning to the concept of "exporting revolution" and cast doubt on the credibility of Soviet statements that deny engaging in such activities. If proxies are executing the dirty work of "exporting revolution" on their own initiative, can one appropriately target Moscow as the culprit?

This issue has arisen earlier in somewhat different form. The relationship of Tito's Yugoslavia to the Greek communist uprising in 1947 and the role of China and Hanoi in the Vietcong rebellion in South Vietnam come to mind. The real question that emerges is whether responsibility lies only with the direct "exporters of revolution" or whether those who support and accept a supporting role are equally culpable. The answer is that even if Moscow originally opposed the export of revolution by its clients, once it supports its clients' efforts, it must bear responsibility since it has the option to disavow and condemn such activity openly. Covert opposition is insufficient to negate culpability.

Soviet open-source literature, although in tortured and turgid verbiage, confirms the Grenadian assessment that the value of future client states in the Soviet Union's global calculations determines the nature and level of Soviet commitments. According to one important Soviet exegesis:

> Now that the U.S. and its allies are intensifying their economic expansion into developing countries, joint measures by the CMEA members to help the liberated countries strengthen their independence are a top priority. Even if these measures do not produce an immediate effect, they help to strengthen the positions of real socialism's [i.e., the USSR's] natural allies and force

imperialism to take countermeasures that are often substantially "costlier" in a political and economic sense. We think this is the standpoint from which the socialist countries should decide on what sort of aid they are going to provide to their allies among the liberated states and should assess the domestic and international impact of this aid.[5]

Grenada As a Model Socialist-Oriented Country: Intensifying the Soviet Connection

Aside from the value of potential clients to Soviet global aspirations, the nature and character of sociopolitical and economic structures and possibilities are also important calculations in the Soviet decision to accept or recruit client states and determine the extent and intensity of Soviet commitments and obligations. Apparently, the precondition for recruitment as a client is a "national-democratic, anti-imperialist" stage of "socialist orientation." That is, the candidate nation must have a regime or charismatic leader committed to pursue a pro-Soviet foreign policy and a program of socioeconomic and sociopolitical transformation. Both of these preconditions are perceived as necessary in order to assure progress toward the next stage of "socialist orientation." The linkage of these prerequisites also provides Moscow with both domestic and foreign policy control mechanisms on future client states. According to an authoritative Soviet theoretician on these matters, K.N. Brutents, who serves as a deputy in the International Department of the CPSU Central Committee in charge of contacts with the Third World:

> The cornerstone of socialist orientation is naturally the direction of domestic development. But experience has shown that a progressive, anti-imperialist foreign policy is also an essential component. These two aspects are organically linked. . . . Socialist orientation is impossible without close friendship and cooperation with the socialist world; it is even less possible on the basis of hostility towards it.[6]

Given the limited resources of the USSR, Moscow must be careful as to how it apportions its assistance to Third World countries and extends preference to "socialist-oriented" countries.

> In deciding to provide direct political and moral support and material assistance, the Soviet Union and other socialist countries give preference to countries that are carrying out progressive socio-political, social and economic transformations, have embarked on a noncapitalist path of development, and have a socialist orientation.[7]

Soviet assistance to such countries is designed as the first step in consolidating the dependency status of socialist-oriented regimes. The next step is to interlock the economic development of socialist-oriented countries with the economies of the communist world. In the guise of aiding their development, the goal is to convert these nations into sources of raw materials and food for the Soviet bloc in return for low-quality manufactured goods. This strategy has been discussed openly in Soviet publications.

> Anticipating the possibility of aid from the socialist countries . . . revolutionary forces . . . often try to unduly accelerate progressive socio-political, social and economic transformations . . . [and] usually disregard the extent to which the socialist states are able to provide them with aid. . . . Today the cost of immediate industrialization is often too high . . . for the socialist countries that are helping them. . . . Given the international division of labor that is developing within the world of socialist systems and the food problem that exists in a number of socialist countries, there is another way for the young socialist-oriented states to eliminate their backwardness: by intensifying their traditional agricultural production and obtaining machinery and equipment through cooperative arrangements with the developed socialist countries. . . . [This] is a complex process that entails, among other things, the creation of a certain degree of complementariness between the two groups' economies.[8]

According to its ambassador in Moscow, by July 1983 Grenada was considered to be what will be called in this discussion a Type I "socialist-oriented" country on the verge of becoming a Type II version—i.e., one with a Leninist vanguard party which would move it closer to becoming part of the "world socialist system." In the words of Ambassador Jacobs:

> Grenada is regarded as being on the path of Socialist orientation. There is general acceptance among Soviet authorities that we are at the national democratic, anti-imperialist stage of Socialist orientation. The USSR assigns a special place to these types of countries in its foreign policy. This is, of course, also the case with other Socialist countries. In terms of their priority, the countries of Socialist orientation come right after the Socialist community.[9] (Appendix A, Document 6, for notes 9–10)

Jacobs further emphasized that it was "absolutely imperative" to maintain this assessment of Grenada's stage of development because of "the very high priority that is placed on the consistency of analysis here." He maintained that the NJM was considered to be on the verge of becoming a "communist" or "Marxist-Leninist" party and that this would enhance Grenada's status in Soviet calculations and priorities, although it would still rate relatively low in the hierarchy of socialist-oriented nations.

> The comrades responsible for Grenada in the International Section have told me that they operate on the basis that the NJM is a "Communist Party." Given the relatively low level of these comrades . . . one is not sure about the authoritativeness of this statement, though I doubt that they would make a statement like that without the necessary authority. In any event, my clear impression is that we are being treated as a fraternal party—i.e., a M-L Party. . . . Although we are regarded as a fraternal party, we are not in the "inner group," i.e., members of the Socialist community.[10]

Thus the intrinsic importance and significance of Grenada as a precedent is less important than its perceived ideological character, which shifts the point of reference from Grenada's resemblance to other socialist countries, to Grenada as a precedent for other "socialist-oriented" countries at a similar stage of development. It should be noted that the Soviet preoccupation with the ideological character of the NJM played an important role in triggering the factional conflict in the NJM leadership. In their zeal to meet the Soviet criteria of a vanguard party, the dominant faction of the NJM voted to accelerate the revolutionary process, purge the party, and restructure it in accordance with Leninist principles.[11] (Appendix A, Document 16) What is of significance here is that there is considerable evidence to support the view that the relationship between the Soviet Union and Grenada on this score was an accurate reflection of Moscow's relationship with other socialist-oriented countries deemed to be in a similar stage of development.

An analysis of the discussions and debates that took place in the Grenadian Politbureau and Central Committee leaves no doubt that some Grenadian leaders had done their ideological homework and were obsessed with the goal of warping the NJM into the abstract Soviet mold cast for socialist-oriented countries.[12]

Socialist-Oriented Countries and the Correlation of Forces: The Lessons of Grenada

Soviet commitments to socialist-oriented countries are deliberately designed to be simultaneously ambivalent and open-ended. Soviet Third World clients such as Grenada are largely self-declared Marxist-Leninist regimes, seeking association, assistance and protection from the Soviet Union. As the Grenadian documents indicate, self-appointed prospective clients must often take energetic measures to elicit Soviet interest, to say nothing of long-term support. But once the Soviets "adopt" these states, they must demonstrate their value as instruments of Soviet policy and transform their domestic political, social, and economic structures to conform with Soviet specifications. Such transformations in turn create structural and institutional opportunities for Soviet penetration and control. Moreover, the commitment of the client states must be absolute, whereas the reciprocal Soviet commitment remains both provisional and optional. This allows the Soviets the option of unilateral disengagement while reducing opportunities for client states to do so. Because of the vulnerability of most Soviet clients, the Soviet option of unilateral disengagement is imperative, but the geographical remoteness of these states renders it difficult to ensure that they cannot opt for unilateral disengagement. Hence the emphasis on maximizing the channels and levels of Soviet penetration, and the importance Moscow places on the creation of Leninist vanguard parties, and the indoctrination of leaders and students in Soviet ideology at Soviet institutions.

While the Grenada experience is not applicable to all Soviet dependencies, it is probably representative of several. The point of reference is not necessarily Grenada's size or importance, but its character as a socialist-oriented regime in transition. The issue is not only what the Soviet Union will do if such a regime comes under assault, but also: (1) how Moscow relates to these regimes, (2) what strategies will be pursued in determining their policies, and (3) what will be the evolution and reaction of such regimes to Soviet demands (implied, inferred, or overt).

Cuba and Nicaragua have indicated, by both word and deed, that the Grenada precedent is too close for comfort for their tranquillity. Although Cuba is considered to be a socialist country and part of both the "socialist community" and the "world socialist system," the Soviet Union has no formal treaty obligation to come to its defense. The Soviet commitment to Cuba is ideological and unilaterally assumed, i.e., Cuba is covered by the "socialist commonwealth," or "Brezhnev doctrine," whereas Nicaragua is covered at best only by the unilateral Soviet "obligation" to provide military assistance if requested (as was the case in Afghanistan). In any event, Moscow decides whether such obligations will be observed. For example, nations that are highly vulnerable such as Cuba and Nicaragua cannot reasonably expect the Soviet Union to risk a war with the United States over their fate.

There is strong evidence to suggest that Moscow and its dependencies have misjudged the possible range of U.S. behavior; in essence, they believed that the "correlation of forces" had effectively precluded the possibility of armed intervention in the Caribbean and the Third World in general. Indeed, Moscow apparently was on the verge of thinking that U.S. credibility had evaporated with respect to NATO and Western Europe as well. Apparently neither Bishop, Cuba, nor Moscow thought that the United States would intercede in Grenada. According to one Soviet source, Bishop related "that Reagan preferred to use a cat's paw, and would not dare to attack Grenada."[13]

Certainly, the Grenadians arrived at this judgment largely because they were influenced by repeated Soviet claims that the correlation of forces had shifted in favor of world socialism. This was emphasized by one of the Grenadian documents entitled "Foreign Relations Report." This extravagant report, with observations and intentions worthy of a global power, confidently asserts:

> One of the main characteristics of the present international conjuncture is the changing balance of forces. Previously imperialism led by the USA held unchallenged sway over mankind. Now the Socialist community is strong and growing still. The USSR is the equal, at least, of the USA. Other poles of power have developed. . . . The point is that U.S. imperialism no longer holds sway over mankind. Though it remains powerful, U.S. imperialism is on the decline. . . . Thus Grenada's foreign policy *must* be cognizant of and reflect this change in the balance of forces.[14] (Appendix A, Document 19)

Almost certainly, the tepid response of the Carter administration to events in Iran constituted a watershed in Soviet assessments of the American capacity or willingness to use force in defense of its interests. Thus, according to one influential Soviet source:

> Understandably, the United States reacted violently to the collapse of the Shah's regime, and there were plans for massive intervention in Iran. Why the United States did not dare put them into action is largely explained by the appropriate Soviet warning, and by the general international situation marked by a shift in the balance of forces of the two socioeconomic systems in favor of socialism.[15]

With specific reference to the overthrow of Somoza in Nicaragua, the same source observed:

> Another eloquent example is the popular revolution in Nicaragua. Since the time the Monroe Doctrine was proclaimed, U.S. imperialism has looked on Latin America, and especially the Caribbean, as its own private domain. It has repeatedly resorted to armed intervention in the region. . . . It is significant that the last incident of intervention in the mid-1900s when the American troops invaded the Dominican Republic, was not repeated in 1980, following the overthrow of the dictator Somoza. . . . The fact that U.S. imperialism did not dare to drown the Nicaraguan revolution in blood proves that the world situation has changed and that the Socialist countries' solidarity with the liberation movement is of paramount importance.[16]

To be sure, Soviet assertions that the United States was effectively deterred from using force to intervene in the Western Hemisphere did not constitute an explicit promise to provide military assistance to socialist-oriented regimes whose existence is threatened by the United States. However, it would not be unreasonable to assume that many Soviet dependencies may have inferred a Soviet willingness to do so. It should be noted that Moscow has carefully limited its explicit promises of military support only to those countries with which it has formal alliance commitments; everything else is assumed, implied, or inferred.

The Grenada events have shed new light on the credibility of Soviet assessments of the military balance and of the resolve of the United States. A certain erosion in the credibility of Soviet support for socialist-oriented countries has also taken place. This is clearly appreciated by Moscow, whose representatives have noted that arresting and reversing developments in these countries undermines both the reliability and credibility of the Soviet connection:

> The socialist-oriented countries are subjected to imperialism's mounting pressure. . . . In its effort to defeat the trend of social development represented by these countries, imperialism hopes to minimize the prestige of socialism . . . [and] to undermine or to weaken in this way the alliance and cooperation of these countries with the socialist world.[17]

Nevertheless, one can forgive the misjudgment of the Grenadians in view of the reassuring assessment of the world situation that the Soviet Chief of Staff, Marshal Ogarkov, gave to his anxious Grenadian counterpart.

> About the situation in the world, Marshal Ogarkov pointed out that the United States would try now and in the future to make things difficult for progressive changes in all regions and continents. The Marshal said that over two decades ago, there was only Cuba in Latin America. Today there are Nicaragua, Grenada, and a serious battle is going on in El Salvador. The Marshal of the Soviet Union then stressed that United States imperialism would try to prevent progress, but that there were no prospects for imperialism to turn back history.[18] (Apppendix A, Document 11)

THE SOVIET ALLIANCE SYSTEM: LAYERS OF OBLIGATION

The Nature of Soviet Commitments

The Soviet-sponsored network of patron-client dependency relationships reflects a variety of levels of obligation, explicit and implicit, unilateral and multilateral, juridical and ideological, military and nonmilitary. The nature and intensity of Soviet commitments vary not so much from state to state as they do according to different categories or classes of states. The most intense commitment is formalized by traditional military treaty alliances, with the multilateral Warsaw Treaty Organization demanding the most intense set of mutual obligations. Generally speaking, lower levels of obligation are subsumed by higher levels. The least intense Soviet commitment is the informal patron-client relationship in which the Soviet obligation is essentially rhetorical and diplomatic in character. Sometimes these unilateral declarations of commitment appear to promise more than reasonably can be expected and thus represent a future intention or capability rather than current reality. This is apparently reflected in a somewhat extravagant statement by former Defense Minister Marshal Grechko in 1974.

> At the present stage, the historic function of the Soviet Armed Forces is not restricted to their function in defending our motherland and other socialist countries. In its foreign policy activity the Soviet state purposefully opposes the export of counter-revolution and the policy of oppression, supports the national liberation struggle, and resolutely resists imperialists' aggression in whatever distant region of our planet it may appear.[19]

A further step in expanding the range of unilateral Soviet commitments to its various allies and dependencies is contained in a chapter on foreign policy in the 1977 constitution in which purely ideological commitments are transformed into state obligations. According to Article 28, the goals of Soviet foreign policy include "Consolidating the positions of world socialism, supporting the struggles of peoples for national liberation and social progress, [and] preventing wars or aggression."[20]

But unilateral obligations are simply that. They are obligations that the Soviet Union may choose to implement or not, depending on the given situation. Most importantly, they provide the Soviets with a pretext for action for which they do not have to make any prior commitments. This category of obligation has been the most seriously damaged by the Grenada precedent. It represents both the widest and shallowest form of obligation. For most socialist-oriented countries, it represents the weakest form of unilateral obligation, but for nations on the Soviet periphery, such as Afghanistan, it can be quite powerful.

Conversely, the Grenada events have had least impact upon the most formal Soviet commitments, namely those contracted through the Warsaw Pact and the individual bilateral alliances that Moscow maintains with each member state and Mongolia. These are nations on the Soviet periphery within easy reach of Soviet military power. Formal military alliance commitments are further reinforced by the unilaterally declared Soviet "socialist commonwealth" or "Brezhnev doctrine," which commits Moscow to preserve the socialist character of communist states against domestic as well as external threats. In addition, there exists a smaller group of socialist states that are not covered by formal military alliance obligations. These consist of North Korea, Vietnam (and Laos and Cambodia), and Cuba. Hypothetically they are covered by the Brezhnev doctrine, and all three nations have contracted a number of nonmilitary treaties with Moscow. The Soviet Union is their sole source of military equipment and supplies, and this constitutes the principal manner in which the Soviet Union discharges its obligations to these states.

As a general rule, the Soviet Union is reluctant to provide ironclad military obligations to vulnerable, divided, or territorially distant states whether they are communist or noncommunist. It does not wish to be drawn inadvertently into an East-West conflict because of its allies' vulnerability or uncontrollable adventurism. Vietnam is vulnerable to China and the United States; Cuba is exposed to American power; and North Korea's obsession with the eventual absorption of South Korea involves a continuous risk of conflict with the United States. It should be recalled that the Soviet Union involved itself in neither the Korean War nor the conflict in Indochina, and it allowed neither to interfere with its normal relations with the United States. Significantly, the Soviets never went beyond providing equipment and supplies.

One must assume that the Grenada events served to erode the Soviet commitment to this group of states, but more importantly it served to arrest any movement toward closer ties that may have been in the offing. The perceived erosion of Soviet commitments by these states is important in itself.

The least intensive Soviet commitment is to the broad class of less developed states characterized as socialist-oriented countries. Until relatively recently, the concept of a socialist-oriented country was somewhat elastic and amorphous, but in recent years the concept has been formalized and subjected to extensive theoretical development. Socialist-oriented countries, now recognized in two varieties according to Soviet categorization, include some 20 states with an aggregate population of 220 million people.[21] In Africa and Asia alone, according to Soviet sources, socialist-oriented countries account for 12 million square miles and 150 million people. It is not always possible to secure an up-to-date list of Soviet approved socialist-oriented countries, but the following list, divided into two categories designated by their formal official names, appears to be complete.

Type I "National Revolutionary" Socialist-Oriented Countries

Algerian People's Democratic Republic
Revolutionary People's Republic of Guinea
United Republic of Tanzania
Democratic Republic of Madagascar
Syrian Arab Republic
Republic of Equatorial Guinea
Republic of Zimbabwe

Type II Vanguard Party ("Revolutionary-Democratic") Socialist-Oriented Countries

Socialist Ethiopia
Democratic Republic of Afghanistan
People's Republic of Angola
Democratic Republic of Yemen
People's Republic of Mozambique
People's Republic of the Congo
People's Republic of Benin
Republic of Guinea-Bissau
Grenada (before October 1983)
Nicaragua

Both Grenada and Nicaragua were viewed as being in a state of transition from Type I to Type II, but Grenada's transition was arrested by invasion and Nicaragua's transition is now in a stage of suspension for tactical reasons. The residually amorphous nature of the concept of transition is reflected by a number of states that move in and out of the Type I socialist-oriented category. Somalia and Iraq are examples of socialist-oriented countries currently in bad standing. Syria has moved from type I to II several times. Egypt under Nasser was classified as a Type I nation, as was Ghana under Nkhrumah and Mali from time to time. On the other hand, Laos and Cambodia are now apparently classified as socialist states, whereas Afghanistan, which is close to being a part of the Soviet Union without formal incorporation, is still classified as a socialist-oriented country. At the same

Maps Showing the Location of ''Socialist-oriented'' Countries, by Type

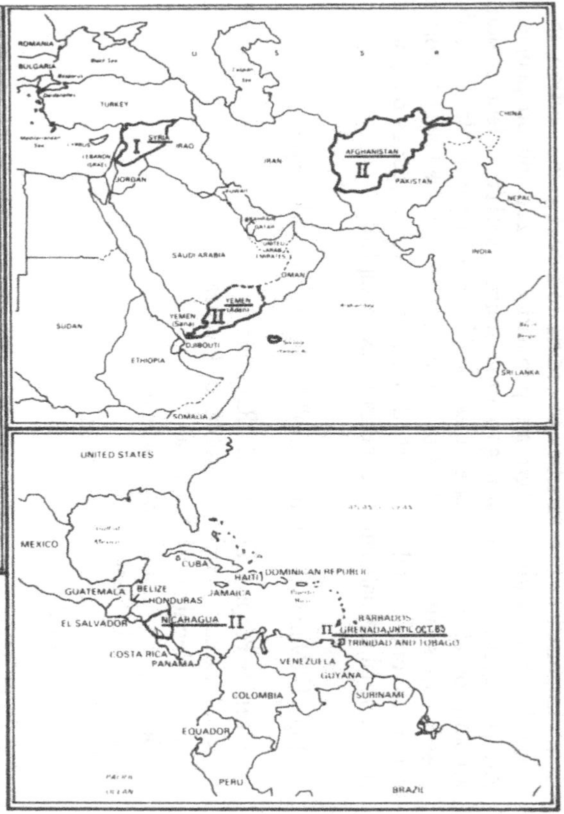

Type regime is illustrated by roman numeral. Type I: National-Revolutionary. Type II: Vanguard Party (Revolutionary Democratic Regimes).

Source: Hosmer & Wolfe, *Soviet Policy and Practice Toward Third World Conflicts*, pp. 2, 10, 57. (Constructed by Captain Mark A. Fassio, USAF; graphics and cartography by James French Crispelle.)

time, Soviet responses to events in Afghanistan and Grenada represent two poles between which the Soviet commitment to socialist-oriented regimes oscillates. Grenada represented a maximum risk of confrontation and minimal loss of assets, whereas Afghanistan represented a minimal risk of confrontation and the possible loss of a valuable asset in the absence of a Soviet intervention.

Current Soviet conceptualizations of Types I and II countries are based on the definition provided by Brezhnev at the 26th Communist Party Congress of the Soviet Union in 1981:

> These include gradual elimination of the positions of imperialist monopolies, of the local big bourgeousie and feudal elements, and restriction of foreign capital. They include the securing by the people's state of commanding heights in the economy and transition to planned development of the productive forces, and encouragement of the cooperative movement in the countryside. They include enhancing the role of the working masses in social life, and gradually reinforcing the state apparatus with national personnel faithful to the people. They include anti-imperialist foreign policy, revolutionary parties expressing the interests of the broad mass of the working people which are growing stronger there.[22]

Without going into extensive discussion concerning the specific characteristics of the various kinds of subcategories of socialist-oriented countries and modes of transition from Type I to Type II, suffice it to say that the Soviet Union prefers the "vanguard party" type, toward which it encourages movement in various ways. Grenada imagined itself as a possible model of the quintessential vanguard party regime and offered itself as a spokesman for all socialist-oriented countries in dealing with Moscow. Jacobs perceptively notes:

> In order to elevate our priority in the socialist scheme of things . . . we have to raise and discuss with the highest authorities, *global and regional* issues rather than parochial or national issues. In other words, our legitimate begging [?] operations have to be cast in the larger world context. We have in fact done this in the past quite successfully, linking our national requests to a global analysis. What we need to do now, it seems to me, is to become the spokesman for a broader constituency—perhaps the countries of socialist orientation.[23] (Appendix A, Document 6)

As the Grenada documents suggest, Moscow is very careful in making commitments to less developed countries, especially non-vanguard party nations which are viewed as socially unstable and subject to changes in ideological orientation. As one of the Grenada documents perceptively notes:

> The Soviets have been burnt quite often in the past by giving support to governments which have either squandered that support, or turned around and become agents of imperialism, or lost power. One is reminded of Egypt, Somalia, Ghana, and Peru. They are therefore very careful, and for us sometimes

> maddeningly slow in making up their minds about who to support.[24] (Appendix A, Document 6)

In the end, the Soviets were "burned" once again in Grenada, and as a consequence, they are apt to be even more careful in committing themselves in similar situations, just as other socialist-oriented countries may have lessened confidence in repeated Soviet assurances that imperialism cannot reverse the historical process.

The Issue of Historical Reversibility: Grenada as a Precedent

In this connection, it should be noted that reversibility of the historical process in socialist-oriented countries is not ruled out according to the Soviet theory. This amounts to a form of ideological self-defense, since the Soviet Union wishes to protect the precedent that no socialist system has ever been overturned in order to preserve what might be called "cognitive credibility." Once the Soviet Union recognizes a country as authentically socialist—part of the world socialist system—Moscow is committed to its survival. This is why the Soviet Union has been reluctant to categorize states as socialist that are remote from other socialist states. Cuba remains the only socialist country that is not contiguous to another communist state and hence it remains the most vulnerable to reversibility. The possibility of reversal of the historical process in socialist-oriented countries, however, remains a constant danger.

> Imperialism is aware of historical experience, which had shown that the ultimate choice of the direction of social development . . . may be a long time in the making . . . which may zigzag, and that socialist orientation in itself does not guarantee the victory of socialism and does not rule out backtracking and returning to capitalism.[25]

The vanguard party type of socialist-oriented country is presumably less susceptible to reversibility because it is organized along Leninist lines and has passed the point of greatest danger in the internal class struggle. Soviet writers have warned that the period of transition from a Type I to Type II socialist-oriented country represents a special time of vulnerability to imperialist intervention as social elements slated for extinction seek external support.[26] According to the Grenada documents, Grenada was precisely at such a point in its evolution at the time it was invaded.

The vanguard party type socialist-oriented country is described in Soviet writing as essentially an inferior, premature type of socialist society which becomes a dependency of the Soviet Union since there has been a burning of bridges to the capitalist world insofar as its domestic structures are concerned. According to Soviet sources, the vanguard party is defined as follows:

> In Soviet and foreign Marxist historical science, the term "vanguard revolutionary parties of the working people" refers to parties in transition from revolutionary-democratic to Marxist-Leninist parties. Vanguard parties have a number of classical features in common with Marxist-Leninist parties. They acknowledge Marxism-Leninism as their ideological basis, build their activity on the principles of democratic centralism, and add to their ranks by individually selecting the best representatives of the working class, the peasantry and other working strata of the population. The above features determine the vanguard nature of these parties, which in a way are prototypes of Marxist-Leninist parties.[27]

Once a vanguard party takes over, the socialist-oriented country in question in effect becomes a "subjective" socialist country, although its socio-economic order retains residual capitalist elements. Deepening relations with the Soviet Union and increasing institutionalization of state, party, and social structures maximizes its possibilities of surviving and developing a socialist society along noncapitalist lines of development. Mongolia's development and relationship to the USSR is constantly held up as the model to emulate. It should be noted that Mongolia has been on the "noncapitalist" path of development toward socialism for nearly 60 years—and remains light years away from reaching it. In general, the dependency relationship between the Soviet Union and socialist-oriented countries is only thinly disguised by official Soviet analyses:

> The forms of international cooperation between the Communist Party of the Soviet Union and revolutionary-democratic parties are exceedingly rich and diverse in character. They include constructive conversations at the highest party and government levels, the conclusion of agreements on cooperation among parties, exchange of party delegations, mutual participation in each other's party congresses, and other important governmental and political undertakings, exchanges of experience in party organizational and ideological work, coordination of action in international organization, and, as has already been noted above, cooperation in the training of party-government and administrative-management cadres.[28]

SOME PRELIMINARY CONCLUSIONS

During the 1970s, the United States was perceived as self-deterred by Vietnam and Watergate, and by the growth of Soviet power. This enhanced Soviet "cognitive confidence," that is, confidence in the accuracy and validity of Marxist-Leninist analytical forecasts. But the rising self-confidence and assertive foreign policy of the Reagan administration, which reached a climax in the successful Grenada operation, cannot but serve to undermine the reliability and accuracy of the cognitive apparatus of Soviet leaders. More importantly it undermines the blind faith that socialist-oriented regimes tend to place on the infallibility of Marxist-Leninist analytical categories.

In operational terms, this means that for Soviet leaders the level of risk involved in the further expansion of the Soviet empire has increased, and for socialist-oriented countries the level of risk involved in offering themselves as instruments of Soviet policy has also risen. Correspondingly, the intensity of the Soviet Union's already weak commitment to socialist-oriented countries has been further diminished, and the attractiveness of alignment with the Soviet Union has been reduced in the eyes of several Third World countries. Thus the Grenada events have served to raise both the risks and the costs of assembling and maintaining a Soviet empire or affiliating with the Soviet alliance system if this is perceived as inimical to U.S. interests.

In terms of Soviet commitments to socialist states, there has been a serious erosion in the credibility of those commitments to North Korea, Vietnam, and Cuba (especially the latter). The fact that these nations perceive a lessened Soviet commitment will serve to dampen North Korean adventurism with respect to South Korea and probably impel Cuba to act more gingerly and prudently in its international relations. With sizable contingents of troops in Africa, Cuba is particularly vulnerable, and thus Castro must recalculate the value and risks of deepening involvement in pursuing Soviet global policies. The situation with respect to Vietnam is more ambiguous, since it is vulnerable to Chinese rather than American power. The context is different, but the Soviet indifference to Grenada's fate must have surely unsettled Hanoi to some degree.

The Grenada operation has served to raise the risks of Soviet expansion, but it has also raised the risks incurred by small nations which become involved in the East-West rivalry. The more proximate and vulnerable to American power, the more risky and costly their affiliation with the Soviet Union. For both the Sandinista regime in Nicaragua and the rebels in El Salvador, the lesson of Grenada is that the only real restraint on the exercise of American power in the region is not so much Soviet power as the lack of domestic consensus in the United States. Accordingly, these forces are beginning to realize that their fate will be decided more by the domestic political context in the United States than by a favorable evolution of the global correlation of forces in favor of the Soviet Union. Some of the Grenada documents suggest that some Grenadian leaders had already begun to see this and emphasized the importance of the American press and public opinion as a restraint on U.S. behavior.[29]

In this regard, the Soviet cognitive apparatus may be counterproductive for both Moscow and its dependencies, since it can result in both "cognitive optimism" and "cognitive pessimism," depending upon the direction of perceived events. The Grenada documents demonstrate clearly and vividly the tremendous faith that socialist-oriented leaders tend to place in the global "correlation of forces."

Although Grenada is little more than a speck on the rim of the Caribbean, Grenadian leaders were obsessed with the overall global rivalry between Washington and Moscow, and it profoundly influenced their perceptions, policies and behavior. A number of the Grenada documents exhibit uninhibited glee with respect to what was considered a favorable shift in the correlation of forces toward the Soviet Union.[30] (Appendix A, Documents 6 and 19) As a result of the invasion of Grenada, socialist-oriented leaders who previously experienced optimism with regard to favorable shifts in the correlation of forces can only feel pessimistic because of the post-Grenada shift.

Perceived unfavorable changes in the correlation of forces can also affect Soviet commitments to socialist nations on the Soviet periphery. At the very least, such changes encourage anti-Soviet sentiment in socialist states and raise the perceived risks of Soviet military intervention. Once it became clear that the Carter administration might be replaced by a Reagan administration, the course of Soviet behavior in both Poland and Afghanistan was strongly influenced by the prospect of a more assertive American foreign policy. Although it cannot be proven, the advent of the Reagan administration may have served to dampen whatever sentiment may have existed in the Soviet leadership to intervene militarily in Poland or to escalate the war in Afghanistan. There appears to be little question that the strong rhetoric of the Reagan administation has had a visible impact on Soviet behavior, which has been remarkably prudent during the past three years. The unsettled leadership situation in Moscow undoubtedly accounts for much of this restraint, but even succession questions may have been influenced by the assertive rhetoric and military buildup of the Reagan administration. The Grenada operation served to complement this rhetoric and military buildup with action, which is always the most important factor for the Soviet leadership in determining the intentions of the United States and its readiness to employ force in the defense of its national interests.

The Grenada events once again raise to the forefront the issue of the "reversibility" of historical processes and Soviet faith in the permanence of socialist systems. As noted above, the Soviet leadership maintains an ideological safety valve in preserving the distinction between socialist and socialist-oriented regimes, with the former considered irreversible and the latter subject to dissolution. For socialist states within the immediate range of Soviet military power, "historical permanence" is ensured by the Warsaw Pact, bilateral alliances, the Brezhnev doctrine, and a proven record of Soviet military intervention. Afghanistan, considered a socialist-oriented regime rather than a socialist country, was blessed with Soviet military intervention in accordance with a variant of the Brezhnev doctrine whereby the Soviet Union reserves the option to supply military assistance in the form of intervention upon the request of the country involved. This is a Soviet option rather than commitment, as the Grenada events have demonstrated.

As noted earlier, Cuba, Vietnam, and North Korea, while considered full members of the socialist community, are actually in a "gray area" as to the issue of reversibility. The Soviet Union is obligated to provide military assistance in the form of military intervention under the Brezhnev doctrine, but this guarantee is rendered somewhat moot with regard to Vietnam and

Cuba because of its lack of practical applicability in areas distant from the Soviet Union. North Korea shares a border with the Soviet Union, but falls into another category, inasmuch as Soviet intervention is likely only under circumstances that rule out the possibility of confrontation with the United States—both of which are highly unlikely. Any immediate threat to North Korea's socialist system is in any event non-existent.

The threat to Vietnam does not exist not because of its socialist system but rather because of its orientation. The principal threat to Vietnam comes from China, which implies at worst a changeover from a pro-Soviet orientation to a pro-Chinese one. Laos and Cambodia are in an even grayer area since their "socialist" credentials have not been finalized. They are no longer categorized as socialist-oriented countries, but neither are they considered "socialist." Their reversibility is therefore still an open question, and it is questionable whether Moscow would risk a confrontation with China to preserve their rather flimsy socialist character. The character of their socialist systems will depend more upon Vietnamese than upon Soviet guarantees. Thus, the immediate threat to Vietnam is more a "conversion" from one socialist system to another rather than a "reversal" of the historical process.

The supreme conundrum for Castro is if Moscow is committed to Cuba's irreversibility. There is little question that Cuba is the Soviet Union's most important ally vulnerable to American power, and this is recognized by both Castro and Moscow. As for historical precedents aside from Grenada, it should be recalled that during the Vietnam war, the United States escalated action against North Vietnam in the face of strong Soviet and Chinese threats, but no military countermeasures ever materialized. The United States did not press the ultimate test by seeking to overthrow the Hanoi regime, but even such an action would have risked Chinese rather than Soviet intervention.

Although the Korean War occurred more than three decades ago when the overall global balance was different, it is noteworthy that North Korea was under virtually complete U.S. military occupation, and for a brief moment no longer existed, but even this did not trigger Soviet military intervention. The Chinese intervened and North Korea's "socialist" future was reinsured. It appears, however, that Moscow was ready to accept the extinction of the North Korean regime rather than risk a war with the United States.

None of these precedents, although they are not entirely compelling, is reassuring for Castro. The conclusion is that Moscow is not likely to run undue risks to preserve Cuba's socialist character, even though the possible "reversal" of Cuban socialism constitutes a serious threat to one of the most fundamental tenets of Soviet ideology—one that supports the entire structure of Soviet cognitive infallibility, upon which rests the legitimacy of the entire Soviet enterprise. Reversals would undermine "infallibility," which in turn would undermine the doctrine of inevitability. For the Soviet leadership this would be the equivalent of a pious Christian losing faith in "The Last Judgment."

NOTES

1. For the author's approach to this subject, see Vernon V. Aspaturian, "The Anatomy of Soviet Empire: Vulnerabilities and Strengths," in K. Dunn and W. Staudenmaier (eds.), *Military Strategy in Transition: Defense and Deterrence in the 1980s* (Boulder: Westview Press, 1984).

2. Confidential report on Grenada's Relations with the USSR, from Grenadian Ambassador to Moscow, W. Richard Jacobs, to Foreign Minister Unison Whiteman, Prime Minister Bishop, Deputy Prime Minister Coard, and Politburo Member Ewert Layne, July 11, 1983, Grenada Documents, Log No. W.

3. Ibid.

4. Ibid., p. 5.

5. Yu. S. Novopashin, "The Influence of Real Socialism on the World Revolutionary Process: Methodological Problems," *Voprosy Filosofii*, August 1982.

6. Karen Brutents, *The Newly Freed Countries in the Seventies* (Moscow: Progress Publishers, 1983), pp. 79–80.

7. Novopashin, op. cit.

8. Ibid.

9. Grenada's Relations with the USSR, op. cit.

10. Ibid.

11. Minutes of the Extraordinary Meeting of the Central Committee, NJM, September 14–16; ibid, Log No. 000123.

12. For recent authoritative Soviet literature on "socialist-oriented" countries, see the following: Karen Brutents, op. cit.; Anatoly Gromyko (ed.), *African Countries' Foreign Policy* (Moscow: Progress Publishers, 1983); Y.S. Novopashin, op. cit., pp. 3–16; G. Kim, "The USSR and National State Construction in Developing Countries," *International Affairs* (Moscow), January 1983, pp. 35–44; V.E. Chirkin, "Lenin's Theory of Revolutionary Democratic Power and the Contemporary World," *Voprosy Filosofii* (1982 No. 9), pp. 22–25; V.F. Li, "The Political Superstructure in Societies of Socialist Orientation," *Voprosy Filosofii* (1981 No. 9); and Yu. V. Irkhin, "Vanguard Revolutionary Parties of the Working People in Newly Independent Countries," *Voprosy Istorii* (April 1982), pp. 55–67.

13. Yu. Alexandrov (ed.), *Grenada: U.S. Terrorism in Action* (Moscow: Novosh Press, 1983), p. 13.

14. Foreign Relations Report, Grenada Documents, undated, Log No. 105757.

15. K. Brutents, op. cit., pp. 273–74.

16. Ibid., p. 275.

17. Ibid., pp. 104–05

18. Memorandum of Meeting Between Chiefs of General Staff of Soviet Armed Forces and People's Revolutionary Armed Forces of Grenada [Marshal Nikolay V. Ogarkov and Major Einstein Louison], March 10, 1983, Grenada Documents, Log No. 100008.

19. As cited by H. and W. Scott, *The Soviet Armed Forces*, 2nd edition (Praeger, 1981), p. 67.

20. *Constitution of the USSR* (Moscow, 1977), Chapter 28.

21. Yu. S. Novopashin, op. cit., pp. 3–16. Other calculations refer to socialist-oriented countries in Africa and Asia comprising two million square kilometers and 150 million people. A. Gromyko, op. cit., p. 51.

22. Cited in Brutents, op. cit., p. 79.

23. Grenada's Relations with the USSR, July 11, 1983, op. cit., p. 7.

24. Ibid., p. 2.

25. Brutents, op. cit., pp. 105–106. Egypt from Nasser to Sadat is repeatedly and at length cited as the prime illustration of reversal from socialist orientation to capitalist orientation.

26. Brutents, op. cit., pp. 75–108.

27. Yu. V. Irkhin, op. cit..

28. V.F. Li, op. cit.

29. Report to the NJM Politburo from Foreign Minister Unison Whiteman, Interim Report on NJM American Resistance Programme, March 29, 1983, Grenada Documents. Among the most important objectives of this "North American Resistance Programme" was "to mobilize public opinion (including in the U.S. Congress) to restrain the U.S. Government from attacking Grenada militarily." Apparently the program failed. *See also* Select Agenda For Discussion with Prime Minister Maurice Bishop, undated. According to this document, articles in the *Washington Post* by various journalists "begin to compile a strong and convincing anti-Reagan position which objectively serves Grenada's interest. The stark reality now is that the PRG needs to clearly and masterfully formulate a programme designed to cash in liberal and left support. Such a programme must be linked to (a) the 1984 Presidential elections . . . and (c) the serious and wide spread disenchantment in the U.S. over Reagan, and especially his foreign policy in Central America."

30. "Grenada's foreign policy *must* be cognizant of and reflect this change in the balance of forces. A foreign policy which is not mindful of the international conjuncture is doomed to failure., Grenada's Relations with the USSR, op. cit. [Italics in original.]

JACK F. MATLOCK, JR.

Comments

Professor Aspaturian has provided a thorough and, in my opinion, very sound analysis of the light that the Grenada documents cast on the Soviet alliance system. In reading his paper and pondering the message of the Grenada documents, several broader questions came to mind, and I would like to use Professor Aspaturian's study as a springboard to present some of them.

The first relates to the old but persistent question of whether the Soviet Union is a traditional great power or a revolutionary communist power. Another way of putting this is to ask how important ideology is to Soviet decisionmakers.

The Grenada documents present the Grenadian view almost exclusively. But one is struck when reading them by the depth of the Grenadian conviction that ideological appearances were extremely important to the Soviets. The Grenadians could have been mistaken, of course, but if we think about Soviet categorizations of Third World states, which Professor Aspaturian describes so lucidly, we immediately recognize that these categories are based largely on ideological factors. Thus the Grenadians do not seem to have been totally misled on this point.

This suggests that when we deal with the Soviet Union, we are dealing with a country different in nature from a traditional expansionist great power. At the same time, it is clear that one does not adequately define the Soviet Union's foreign policy by saying that it is "ideological." Ideology has its place in our definition, but if we go beyond the Grenada documents and look at the record of Soviet foreign policy, it is evident that many of the characteristics of imperial Russian foreign policy have been fused with Leninist concepts.

For this reason, the debate over whether the Soviet Union is an ideological or traditional power seems sterile. Surely the answer is that the Soviet Union is both—not an incoherent mixture, but an amalgam. The Grenada documents reflect the ideological element more clearly, but even from a traditional Russian point of view, there would seem to be value—ideology entirely aside—in having a potential base, or at least an irritant, close to the United States so long as it is considered a principal adversary.

The second question is, if ideology is important to the Soviet Union, does it represent anything more than a post hoc rationalization? In other words, is the real motivation geopolitical and ideological and only something like icing applied to a cake?

The question is relevant because most of us who have spent time in the Soviet Union find that one of the rarest commodities in that scarcity-ridden society is a person who really believes in communist ideology. Most Soviet citizens seem totally cynical, about both the ideology itself and the motivations of those charged with purveying it. As a whole, dialectical materialism (diamat) and Marxist-Leninist ideology probably comprise the most taught and least learned subject in educational curriculums. Diamat seems to be treated with derision by most students—an obligatory waste of time, useful only as raw material for bitter jokes. Even Soviet officials do not give the impression that they personally put great stock in ideology. In short, one senses none of the revolutionary élan today that observers described in the 1920s and 1930s.

The loss of revolutionary fervor is not the whole story, however. The simple fact is that those who run the system cannot give up the ideology, whether they believe in it or not. This would be impossible, for ideology provides the sole source of their legitimacy as rulers. Their power does not stem from constitutional processes; it can be justified only on ideological grounds, both to the Soviet people and to the world at large. When so much at home seems to be either unsuccessful or inconsistent with established ideology, it becomes important for Soviet leaders to claim ideological victories, thus proving the superiority of communism. Such claims have a legitimizing impact; they contribute an important element to Soviet objectives that were absent from the motivations of monarchs and today are absent from those of real (as opposed to pseudo) constitutional republics.

Yet Leninist ideology has struck deeper roots than observed patterns of cynical manipulations would seem to indicate. The fact is that so much Soviet discourse has been forced into the mold of Leninist reasoning that it affects the thinking even of those who would privately profess disbelief in its fundamental tenets. Entirely aside from its use as a propaganda tool, Leninist ideology provides a framework for looking at the world and analyzing political developments. While ideology does not often answer concrete policy questions in a clear-cut fashion—indeed it is often manipulated to justify inconsistent policy decisions—it serves to define options and to channel decisions in certain directions.

The way in which the Soviets define their alliance system provides a good example of how ideology can be applied toward geopolitical ends. Professor Aspaturian has provided a clear description of the categories the Soviets use to define various gradations in their alliance system. These gradations rest on ideology but have important geopolitical implications. When the Soviets speak of the "irreversibility of socialist gains," they are using a code expression for the Brezhnev doctrine, which applies to those nations described as "socialist" or part of the "socialist commonwealth" bordering on the Soviet Union. In these cases the ultimate guarantee of "irreversibility" is the Soviet army.

Irreversibility can be looked at in other ways as well. If one examines the sort of changes the Soviets encourage in those countries that are soliciting Soviet support or trying to become members of the "socialist camp"—obviously the aim of the Grenadian leaders—we see pressure for internal changes that tend to become irreversible if fully implemented. The Soviets tend to push for two goals: the formation of a "vanguard party," and the socialization of capitalist economies.

The Soviets distrust charismatic leaders, though they often make use of such figures. This is because charismatic leaders are hard to control; if they get into domestic trouble or lose power, socialist gains are lost or "reversed." The Soviet experience with Sukarno, Nasser, Nkrumah and others has led to a cautious attitude concerning heavy investments in support of left-leaning charismatic leaders.

From a Soviet point of view, it is most desirable to rely on a "vanguard party" that is highly bureaucratized and in control of all significant sources of power. Such a party is much more difficult to topple than a charismatic individual, and the very idea of such a party can be sold to charismatic leaders as a reliable mechanism for remaining in power. Recent events in Ethiopia provide a classic example of how the Soviets pressure their clients to build vanguard parties.

Economic socialization is closely associated with the establishment of a vanguard party, although pressures to move in this direction sometimes might be delayed for tactical reasons. Several Soviet "experiments" in economic socialization ran aground in the 1960s and tended to be extremely expensive. When the proper time comes, however, the Soviets always push for increasing economic socialization. Perhaps this is not merely a drive for ideological consistency. If we assume that the Soviets want to build irreversibility into the revolutionary process, there are good reasons for such efforts. The fact is that when the economy of a country is socialized, many groups which normally compete for power or influence over policy are destroyed. If they are not destroyed, they can threaten the emerging totalitarian system.

If we look at countries that have undergone this process for a few years, we find that many changes in fact are irreversible. A country that has gone through a period of socialization and centralization of economic decision-making has great difficulty in turning the clock back to a pluralistic system even if there are drastic political changes. Foreign investors have been chased out and usually cannot be brought back without offending local nationalism, which can serve as a powerful barrier to the reversal of socialist regimes. If the local middle class has been eliminated or seriously weakened, it is extremely difficult to reinstate an indigenous private sector. Thus the successors to communist regimes have limited possibilities of becoming Third World success stories in the mold of South Korea, Singapore, Taiwan and the Ivory Coast. These countries have made spectacular gains in economic development, and none has followed the path of socialist development.

Soviet ideology has little to do in practice with Marxism aside from its rhetorical content. It has almost everything to do with Leninism. Certainly Leninism is an outgrowth of Marxism, but it is a variant that many Marxists would not recognize as legitimate. Eduard Bernstein and Rosa Luxemburg did not, and in view of his later writings, one can argue that Friedrich Engels would not either. Indeed, we make a real mistake if we uncritically adopt the Soviet term "Marxist-Leninist" as if the two were synonymous. To do so leads to confused thinking about real issues.

The point is that Leninism is an ideology that is particularly useful to leaders having trouble retaining power. Buttressed with military hardware and free mercenaries, Leninism is what the Soviets offer to Third World leaders who wish to strengthen their domestic positions. It is not a formula for economic development or solving social problems; indeed, it exacerbates such problems. It remains a formula for staying in power no matter how other national interests suffer. Sometimes this option is foreclosed by military coups or rebellions. However, if enough Cuban troops are present, such risks are minimized, as the events in Congo-Brazzaville demonstrated.

The Marxist side of the Soviet ideology—the socioeconomic theory—is largely propaganda. It is domestically useful until people see that reality does not correspond to theory. It is also of use internationally with groups such as the Socialist International that are inclined to see kinship between "Marxists" of various types. In reality, however, such kinship does not exist.

Pondering how to deal with the Soviet Union and in analyzing Soviet foreign policy, we do ourselves a disservice if we carry on our debate in terms of "left" and "right." Is there any legitimate reason for a liberal and a conservative in the democratic tradition to disagree on the nature of Soviet power? Or for a European Social Democrat and a Christian Democrat to do so? The nature of Soviet power has nothing to do with the left-right distinction as it is usually defined. The proper distinction is rather a matter of totalitarian and nontotalitarian systems. If a system is totalitarian, it makes little difference whether it claims antecedents on the left or right extreme of the political spectrum. In either case, it is the antithesis of democracy and should be seen as such by all those who espouse democracy. We should abandon modes of thought based on faulty preconceptions, look at the facts as they are, and conduct our policy debates on the basis of reality rather than catchwords such as "left" and "right."

MARK FALCOFF

Bishop's Cuba, Castro's Grenada: Notes Toward an Inner History

The capture of several thousand documents pertaining to the brief rule of the New Jewel Movement (NJM) in Grenada (1979–1983) is without doubt one of the most important scholarly windfalls since World War II. Apart from the fact that these papers afford us an intimate view of a Leninist state in the making, they allow us to chart the currents of Soviet, East bloc, Cuban, and Third World influence, in which Grenada was for more than three years a peculiar and in many ways improbable point of convergence. They are of particular interest for students of the Cuban role in the circum-Caribbean because Cuba—by the frequent admission of the NJM leadership—was the most important country in the Grenadian revolutionary process.[1] (Appendix A, Document 16) This chapter will attempt to draw upon the Grenada documents to measure the dimensions of that relationship, to characterize the nature of Soviet-Cuban strategic cooperation there, and to identify some of the implications that the Grenadian episode poses for Cuba, Cuban-Soviet relations, and U.S. policymakers who must respond to both.

CUBA'S REVOLUTIONARY FOREIGN POLICY

Almost since its inception, the Castro regime has been actively engaged in the export of revolution as a means of historical and ideological self-justification, as a substitute for economic success at home, and as an extension of Castro's oversized ego. But the theaters of opportunity—both real and perceived—have shifted several times since 1959. Initially, Cuba sought to replicate its experience of rural guerrilla warfare in other Latin American countries (whether dictatorships or democracies) convinced that they were ripe for overthrow. Such efforts did not, however, include the English-speaking Caribbean. After several failures, including a particularly grievous setback in Bolivia, Havana shifted course and sought normal state-to-state relations with the proximate governments it formerly had sought to overthrow. This policy eventually led Colombia, Venezuela, and Costa Rica to propose to the Organization of American States (OAS) in 1975 that members be permitted to lift the embargo on Cuba that they had commonly agreed to a decade before.

At the same time, Cuba combined "ideological pluralism" with a pragmatic search for targets of opportunity in Africa, the Middle East, and the Caribbean Basin. By the end of the 1970s, Cuban "advisors" were at work in an astonishing number of nations, not all of whose governments could strictly speaking qualify as Marxist. Moreover, in the English-speaking Caribbean, the Cubans succeeded in surmounting linguistic and cultural barriers to become an important presence in Jamaica and Guyana, with diplomatic missions which presided over "an ever-increasing network of . . . activities in health, education, construction, agriculture, tourism, sports, and some would maintain, politics."[2] These activities did not significantly alter the nature of the recipient governments, whose policies toward Cuba were very clearly—if cynically—conceived to outflank leftist elements at home, and to put the fear of God into reluctant sources of economic largesse in Washington, London, and elsewhere. They did, however, indicate the degree of flexibility the Cubans were prepared to bring to their international policies, still officially denominated by the quaint term "proletarian internationalism."

CUBA AND THE NEW JEWEL REVOLUTION

Cuba's relationship to the English-speaking Caribbean entered an entirely new phase in 1979 when the New Jewel Movement seized power in Grenada through a coup d'etat—the first in West Indian history. From Havana's perspective, what was particularly significant about this event was the emergence—again, for the first time in that region—of a Leninist regime committed to transforming itself along classical Soviet lines and becoming a full partner in the Soviet international alliance. Amost immediately, the Cubans were called upon to provide Maurice Bishop's People's Revolutionary Government (PRG) with the economic and political assistance to make this possible, and they did so in amounts which were incongruous to the small size of the island, its limited resources, and doubtful strategic value.

As in Guyana, Suriname, and Jamaica (during the rule of Michael Manley), the Cuban presence in Grenada was most visible in the area of economic cooperation and assistance. This took the form of outright donations of equipment (ten fishing boats which almost immediately became inoperative), skilled construction labor, construction materials, and some technical and engineering expertise.[3] The Cubans also reportedly provided "tremendous and invaluable assistance" in agriculture, education and health projects.[4] (Appendix A, Document 19) The largest focus of Cuban activity was at Port Salines, the site of a new international airport, where there were so many Cuban workers living in a special compound that serious tensions arose and several incidents involving Grenadian workers were reported.[5]

The ostensible purpose of the Port Salines airport was to generate foreign exchange by developing a new source of tourism from Western Europe. While it doubtless would have lent itself to such use, enough evidence has surfaced to suggest that its construction might have served other ends as well. Eric Gairy originally conceived the project for the same reasons by Eric Gairy, and the New Jewel Movement (then, of course, in opposition) opposed it on the grounds that a massive wave of affluent tourists would corrupt the morals and cultural integrity of the Grenadian people. After 1979, however, it suddenly became—as Maurice Bishop explained to Libyan dictator Muammar Qadhafi—"of extreme importance to our revolutionary process."[6] The Cubans apparently shared this view, as evidenced by the high priority assigned to the airport in their own assistance program. One of the Grenada documents—excerpted from the notebook of an NJM Central Committee member—explicitly notes, "airport to be used by Cuban and Soviet military."[7] This was certainly the perception of local laborers at the site. As the Special Branch assigned to look into Grenadian-Cuban tensions reported, the Grenadian workers in Port Salines regarded "the Cubans as building a military base for their own benefit."[8]

Before 1979, there was nothing about the Cuban relationship with Grenada that set it apart from Castro's links to other English Caribbean governments which by no stretch of the imagination could be regarded as Marxist-Leninist.[9] After the Grenadian revolution, however, the interpretation of "fraternal cooperation" went far beyond that which existed elsewhere in the region (with the possible exception of Nicaragua). For example, a secret agreement between the Cuban Communist Party (PCC) and the New Jewel Movement projected joint plans for 1983 and called for the exchange of delegations for "mutual consultation and study." In the same accord, the Cubans offered to share the experience and expertise of such organizations as the Workers' Central Union, the Cuban Women's Federation (FMC), the Association of Small Farmers, and the Young Communists. The Cubans also promised to send technical advisers skilled at organizing public meetings and propaganda.[10] (Appendix A, Document 10)

The Cubans were active in assisting the Grenadians to achieve what in other contexts has been called *Gleichschaltung*—that is, the subordination of all elements of society to the purposes of the state. The NJM seriously studied the possibility of copying a version of Cuba's Labor Army for their system of National Service;[11] the Cubans agreed to maintain military specialists in Grenada; and they granted Grenadian soldiers and officers scholarships at Cuban military institutions.[12] (Appendix A, Document 14)

Of particular interest were Cuban efforts to assist the Bishop government in its efforts to counteract the opposition of Grenada's churches. For example, the joint party agreement cited above called for the Grenadians to receive a specialist in 1983 to help "in the work with the religious people for exchange of experiences in the work of the Party in this sector."[13] (Appendix A, Document 10) The churches must have posed a problem almost from the beginning, for as early as 1981 NJM officials were discussing the subject with the PCC.[14] Eventually, in the fall of 1982, a special delegation from the Americas Department of the PCC was sent to Grenada to survey the situation and render a full report. It concluded by recommending (1) installation of a full-time NJM member to deal with the religious question, (2) collation and consultation of factual information on Grenada's religious institutions and their activities, (3) promotion of contacts among clergy and laity from Nicaragua and other Latin American circles linked to the theology of liberation, (4) familiarization visits by selected Grenadian Protestant pastors to the Matanzas Evangelical Seminary, and (5) formation of "a reciprocal information link and an exchange of criteria on the strategy and tactics of the Church and the mechanisms of prevention and response."[15] (Appendix A, Document 2)

However, the Cubans' most valuable contribution to the Bishop regime was in the international sphere. In the first place, they acted as a guide to world politics, particularly the labyrinth of Third World and Soviet international front organizations. For example, when three Grenadian women were scheduled to attend the World Conference of Women in Prague in 1981, they stopped first in Havana to receive a briefing from the International Secretary of the Federation of Cuban Women (FMC), Esther Véliz. The discussion reportedly centered on "what Cuba sees as a difference in emphasis between the European organizations and those of the underdeveloped world. . . . The FMC felt that the European organizations emphasize peace at the expense of National Liberation Struggles."[16] When NJM official Don Rojas went to Angola on an orientation visit, he stopped in Cuba to coordinate with the Casa de las Américas on a forthcoming conference of the Caribbean Committee of Intellectual Workers.[17] The PCC and the NJM also worked closely within the context of the Socialist International, where the New Jewel Movement had the status of an observer party. The Cubans provided the Grenadians with their own confidential assessments of various socialist leaders, some of which make quite piquant reading,[18] and the Grenadians agreed in the 1983 Joint Party Accord to provide the Cubans with "two comrades linked to the work of the Socialist International for exchanging experiences and criteria on this aspect."[19] (Appendix A, Document 10) The American wife of the Cuban Ambassador to Grenada was invited to coach Maurice Bishop on how he should conduct an upcoming visit to the United States. On the subject of specific meetings, she wrote that "[Ramón Sánchez] Parodi from the Cuban Interests Section [of the Czech Embassy in Washington] will be the single most clear person on this whole question."[20] Apparently the Cubans were also prepared to assist the Grenadians in financing and hosting a meeting of the nonaligned movement.[21]

Second, Cuba became an international entrepot through which the Soviets and other members of the Eastern bloc funneled both economic and military aid. For example, at a meeting between Bishop and the Soviet ambassador in May 1983, the latter promised armored carriers, 14.5 mm shells, and spare parts—all to be shipped through Cuba. At the same time, the Soviets promised Bishop an airplane (apparently to be used between Havana and St. George's) that would be shipped in parts and assembled in Cuba. ("They will prefer Cuban pilots use it.")[22] (Appendix A, Document 15) The Cubans also acted as a conduit for the German Democratic Republic (GDR). It was from the Ministry of Interior in Havana that Colonel Liam James, Grenadian Director of Security and Internal Order, learned that a grant of military equipment and small arms was to be provided by the GDR.[23]

Cuba's role as an intermediary was determined largely by the fact that the port and storage facilities of Havana harbor were far superior to those in Grenada, but in all probability it also responded to a deeply-felt Soviet need to maintain a low profile in the Caribbean, a region where—according to the Grenadian ambassador in Moscow—they were interested "in reducing areas of conflict with the USA."[24] (Appendix A, Document 5) On another occasion the same Grenadian diplomat wrote:

> If we meet at too high a level [in the context of party-to-party contacts between the NJM and the CPSU], the USA would use this as an excuse to further squeeze Grenada. (This is one of the explanations as to why the Prime Minister did not meet with Andropov in April.)[25] (Appendix A, Document 6)

Third, the Cubans became the most important source of guidance for the NJM in its dealings with the Soviet Union. This was true on matters both large and small. When Bishop decided to send a military delegation to Moscow to request additional assistance, he first sent its leader, General Hudson Austin (together with the Cuban military attaché), to Havana. As Bishop explained in a letter to Raúl Castro, chief of the Cuban armed forces (FAR), "I hope that during this period you or Cde. Senen Casas may be able to find time to hold discussions with him, and offer your advice and suggestions on the best ways to present this document to the Soviets."[26] When the Grenadian government was exploring the possibility of installing a satellite dish linking the island to InterSputnik, the Soviet international telecommunications organization, they met with officials of the Cuban Ministry of Communications, who explained the capabilities of the system and offered to provide technicians familiar with the equipment to install telephonic centrals manufactured in the GDR.[27]

Most importantly, the Cubans acted as an advocate for the Grenadians in the highest circles in Moscow. Judging from the lengthy reports of W. Richard Jacobs, Bishop's ambassador to the Soviet Union, the Soviets were reluctant to make commitments to Grenada beyond their power to fulfil and defend those commitments if necessary. They responded to Grenada's requests, he wrote, only "because Cuba has strongly championed our case."[28] (Appendix A, Document 6) It would appear, in fact, that the Soviets regarded Grenada as Cuba's "project," to which they would lend assistance on a provisional basis, pending additional evidence of (1) the stability of its government, (2) its relative immunity from U.S. intervention, and above all, (3) the durability of its professed "socialist orientation," i.e., pro-Soviet orientation. Put another way, Grenada's relationship to Cuba was roughly congruent to Cuba's relationship to the Soviet Union. This suggests a kind of subcontracting of Soviet influence in certain areas of the Third World where Moscow lacks experience, knowledge, and geographical proximity, but possesses a reliable surrogate. It is a tactic designed to explore the possibilities for expanded influence without risking future Egypts or Somalias (or Ghanas or Perus).

This was a frustrating situation for the Bishop government—all the more so, Jacobs reported, because "the comrades responsible for Grenada in the International Department [of the CPSU] have told me that they operate on the basis that the NJM is a 'communist party.'"[29] (Appendix A, Document 6) The ambassador gave some thought as to how Grenada might coax the Soviets into a higher profile and upgrade Soviet-Grenadian relations. In one particularly interesting dispatch in mid-1983, Jacobs speculated that Grenada could assume a position of "increasingly greater importance" only if "seen as influencing regional events."

> We have to establish ourselves as the authority on events at least in the English-speaking Caribbean, and be the sponsor of revolutionary activities and progressive developments in this region at least.[30] (Appendix A, Document 6)

To this end, he proposed semiannual meetings "with progressive and revolutionary" parties of the region "critical to the development of closer relations with the USSR." Perhaps, he suggested, someone on the Central Committee of the NJM could "pay a visit to the USSR after one of these meetings [for information purposes]. We must be sure, though, that we become the principal point of access to the USSR even to the point of having our Embassy serve as their representative while in the USSR." This was a formula for engaging in pro-Soviet activities in the Caribbean along racial-cultural and linguistic lines so that Grenada would stand to the ministates of the region as Cuba stood to the revolutionary left in the Dominican Republic, Puerto Rico, and Central America. It would also raise Grenada's stature in Soviet eyes and eventually allow the New Jewel Movement to bypass their Cuban sponsors to a certain degree.

IMPLICATIONS FOR FUTURE CUBAN POLICY

The PRG of Grenada is now history, but what impact does that history have on its principal foreign sponsor? In the first place, it seems doubtful that Cuba will again so unreservedly support a revolutionary government in the Eastern Caribbean purely on the basis of a personal friendship with its leader. That this was the operative consideration in Grenada is beyond doubt. A Central Committee document drafted after the palace coup which deposed Bishop referred to "the deep personal friendship between Fidel and Maurice which," it noted with some irritation, "caused the Cuban leadership to take a *personal* and not a *class* approach to developments in Grenada." However, Castro told Bishop's successors, "in our country, the Grenadian revolution and Cde. Bishop as its central figure were the object of great sympathy and respect. Even explaining the event to our people will not be easy."[31] (Appendix A, Document 18) Of course, the PRG dissolved in much the same fashion as it had formed in the first place, which raises further questions—for the Cubans at least—as to the viability of fundamentally personalistic, self-styled revolutionaries in the Eastern Caribbean behind whom there rests no substantial organized popular movement. In this sense, Grenada can be seen as Cuba's "Egypt" or "Peru."

Second, the joint intervention undertaken by the United States and the Organization of Eastern Caribbean States (OECS) has forced the Cuban leadership to revise its views on the political feasibility of U.S. military operations in the Caribbean Basin. In Cuba as in the United States itself, the conventional wisdom before the intervention was that the use of force anywhere in the region would meet with such overwhelming congressional and public opposition as to discard the option. It is now clear that such is not the case where military force can be marshalled effectively and quickly. In particular, the ministates of the Eastern Caribbean offer far more vulnerable targets than the nations on the Central American mainland or Cuba. These countries operate within a different cultural world than the Hispanic-American left, and for that reason they may prove less amenable to revolutionary transformations. All of this may well presage a long period of "malign neglect" in the English-speaking Caribbean as Cuba rededicates its efforts on behalf of revolutionary forces in El Salvador and Guatemala, and toward shoring up the Sandinista regime in Nicaragua.

Third, the capacity of the Cubans to leverage aid from the Soviet Union for its clients (at least those in the Caribbean Basin) might have been seriously damaged—not that it appears that such leverage was very great in the first place. For example, the Soviets sent Grenada elsewhere to find resources to complete its airport;[32] they virtually steered the Grenadians into the arms of the International Monetary Fund;[33] and apart from arms transfers and scholarships to CPSU party schools and Soviet military institutions, the Soviets were remarkably unresponsive to pleas for large-scale assistance. Thus, what is Cuban leverage now? As with Allende's fall in Chile, Cuba's failure to impose its purposes within its own sphere of influence may well lead Soviets strategists to rethink the reliability of Havana's intelligence capabilities and the perspicacity of its political leaders.

IMPLICATIONS FOR FUTURE U.S. POLICY

The most significant contribution that the Grenada documents make to our understanding of the Soviet Union is to further illuminate the nature of the Cuban-Soviet alliance. Therein we find confirmation that while the Cubans cannot (and therefore do not) differ from the Soviets on any major international issue, they have considerable freedom to pursue their own goals, particularly within the Caribbean.[34] This is gradually becoming something of a scholarly consensus. Moreover, in service of these objectives, the Cubans can draw upon a wide range of Soviet-bloc contacts and sources of assistance. Hence, except on issues which directly affect U.S.-Soviet relations (such as the placement of offensive missiles in Cuba), the U.S. cannot logically expect to negotiate the parameters of Cuban international conduct with Moscow, particularly in areas that might be of minor interest to the Soviet Union, but are of major interest to both Cuba and the United States.

Second, the collapse of the NJM regime in Grenada and the subsequent willingness of the United States (and the OECS) to reestablish order and expel the Cuban influence have inflicted serious damage on Castro's credibility throughout the Eastern Caribbean. Before 1983, among leftist parties and forces in the Caribbean, it was widely assumed that Cubans rode "the wave of the future" and represented "the forces of history." It is now clear that the "future" can be cancelled, and "history" can be turned about. Conversely, the credibility of the United States as a regional hegemonist has been significantly advanced. It is difficult to exaggerate the importance of such symbolism, for it seems to have become an independent variable in relations between the superpowers and the small states on their immediate periphery.

Finally, Grenada illustrates the often displayed willingness of the Soviets and Cubans to allow client states to draw upon Western sources of aid. Although one school of foreign policy thinking holds that such aid can be used to wean Marxist regimes away from the Soviet Union, this is not what the Soviets and Cubans believe. They regard the political order as utterly fundamental to the ideological identity of a given regime. Hence the disproportionate attention given to training Grenadian party cadres and military personnel, and the dispatch of intelligence and police operatives. Economic assistance was to be obtained where it could be found, even if this required the anomaly of quasi-membership in such apparently incompatible organizations as the Socialist International. Such terms as "normalization of relations" or "ideological pluralism" mask a careful understanding of the sources of political power. This indicates a lesson for U.S.-Cuban relations as important as any that could have been derived from the brief episode of Leninism in Grenada.

NOTES

1. Minutes of the Extraordinary Meeting of the Central Committee, NJM, September 14–16, 1983, Grenada Documents, Log No. 000123.

2. Anthony Maingot, "Cuba and the Commonwealth Caribbean: Playing the Cuban Card," in Barry B. Levine (ed.), *The New Cuban Presence in the Caribbean* (Boulder, CO: Westview Press, 1983).

3. Minutes of Politburo Meeting, September 15, 1982, Grenada Documents, Log No. GG1.

4 "Foreign Relations Report " undated (probably 1981), ibid., Log No. 105757.

5. Minutes of Politburo Meeting, April 7, 1982, ibid., Log No. 105657; Report from Head of the Special Branch to Minister of National Security, July 14, 1981, ibid., Log No. 103890; Minutes of the Political-Economic Bureau Meeting, August 10, 1983, ibid., Log No. 100282.

6. Letter from Maurice Bishop to Muammar Qadhafi, September 26, 1983, ibid., Log No. R1/100.

7. Excerpt from Liam James' Notebook, ibid., Log No. Y1.

8. Ibid., Log No. 103890.

9. Maingot, "Cuba and the Commonwealth Caribbean," op. cit.

10. Cooperation and Exchange Plan between the Communist Party of Cuba and the New Jewel Movement for 1983, June 29, 1983, Grenada Documents, Log No. 100016.

11. Progress Report on Commission No. 5, ibid., Log No. 102602.

12. Secret Protocol of Military Cooperation between the Government of the Republic of Cuba and the People's Revolutionary Government of Grenada, ibid., Log No. 000194.

13. Secret Cooperation and Exchange Plan between the Communist Party of Cuba and the New Jewel Movement for the 1983 Period, ibid., Log No. 100016.

14. Minutes of the Politburo Meeting, May 20, 1981, ibid., Log No. H48.

15. Excerpts from Restricted Report of the Delegation Sent to Grenada by the Americas Department with the Aim of Starting the Gathering of Sources for the Characterization of the Religious Situation in the Country and the Contacts for Further Cooperation between the PCC and the NJM Regarding the Question, August 13–14, 1982, ibid., Log No. II-1.

16. Report to the NJM Politburo on the World Conference of Women and WDIF Congress, Prague, and Visit to Bulgaria by Sisters P. Coard, R. Joseph, and E. Calliste, October 3–30, 1981, ibid., Log No. 105656.

17. Report to Prime Minister Maurice Bishop on Trip to Angola, February 10, 1983, ibid., Log No. EE1.

18. Report of Manuel Pinero Losada of the Americas Department of the Cuban Communist Party on the Meeting of the Socialist International's Committee for the Defense of the Nicaraguan Revolution, ibid., Log No. PP1; and unsigned, undated Report of the Bonn Meeting of the Socialist International, ibid., Log No. NN1.

19. Secret Cooperation and Exchange Plan between the Communist Party of Cuba and the New Jewel Movement for the 1983 Period, June 29, 1983, op. cit.

20. Letter from Gail Reed to Maurice Bishop, ibid., Log No. DD1. *See also* Minutes of the Politburo meeting, June 17, 1981, ibid., Log No. L51, in which George Louison was sent to get a briefing from the Cubans before taking an official delegation to Mexico.

21. Minutes of the Politburo Meeting, January 5, 1983, ibid., Log No. 100270; and Minutes of the Politburo Meeting, December 29, 1982, ibid., Log No. 103448.

22. Summary of the Prime Minister's Meeting with Soviet Ambassador, May 24, 1983, ibid., Log No. 103913.

23. Letter from the Cuban Minister of the Interior to Colonel Liam James, Director of Security and Internal Order, undated, ibid., Log No. 102644.

24. Confidential report from the Grenadian Embassy in Moscow on the NJM's Relations with the CPSU, undated (but sometime after December 1981), ibid., Log No. 102329.

25. Confidential report on Grenada's Relations with the USSR, from Grenadian Ambassador to Moscow, W. Richard Jacobs, to Foreign Minister Unison Whiteman, Prime Minister Bishop, Deputy Prime Minister Coard, and Politburo Ewet Layne, July 11, 1983, ibid, Log No. W.

26. Letter from Maurice Bishop to Raul Castro, November 14, 1981, ibid., Log No. 102647.

27. Minutes of Meeting at the Ministry of Communications in Havana, November 9, 1982, ibid., Log No. 102517.

28. Grenada's Relations with the USSR, op. cit.

29. Ibid.

30. Cuba's Response to the Issue, ibid., Log No. 000015.

31. Letter from Fidel Castro Ruz to the Central Committee, New Jewel Movement, October 15, 1983, ibid., Log No. T1.

32. Letter from Bishop to President Hussein of Iraq, asking, *inter alia*, for funds to help complete the airport, ibid., Log No. 103861; and Log No. 103860 chronicles an agreement for such assistance from Libya.

33. Minutes of Politburo Meeting, May 27, 1981, ibid., Log No. 103448.

34. Robert Pastor, "Cuba and the Soviet Union: Does Cuba Act Alone?," in Levine (ed.), *The New Cuban Presence in the Caribbean*, op. cit.

JORGE I. DOMINGUEZ

Report to the Political Bureau, Central Committee, Communist Party of Cuba, from the Special Task Force on the U.S. Imperialist Aggression Against Grenada

This is a work of social science fiction. This report is not known to exist. I have imagined it as a plausible, though fictional, reconstruction of the views of the Cuban leadership. However, it is very faithful to available documentation concerning Cuba's relations with Grenada. Frequent citations are made to pertinent documents. In short, I have not allowed my imagination to roam unrestrained beyond what the documents support.

I adopted this approach in order to complement Mark Falcoff's article because I believe that the scholarly use of "imaginary realism" is a constructive but neglected way to think about the future. The future of Soviet/Cuban strategy in light of the Grenada events indeed was the mandate for this volume and the conference that preceded it[1]—and thus the usefulness of my approach, which of course is a "cousin" of role playing and simulation exercises.

REPORT ON THE INVASION OF GRENADA

The Obvious Lessons

The U.S. imperialist aggression against Grenada requires our party and government to examine our policy toward what befell the New Jewel Movement (NJM) and the Grenadian government. This section of our report summarizes some lessons concerning Cuban foreign policy toward Grenada.

The United States can crush a revolution if it commits necessary military and political resources to that end. We have known this since the beginning of our revolution. Our necessary response has been to arm ourselves and to raise the cost of a U.S. invasion so that aggression against Cuba would be highly unlikely unless there is general or all-out war. From this perspective, the U.S. invasion of Grenada teaches us nothing that we did not know previously.

However, this obvious lesson had not been learned by the Grenadian leadership. Their 1981 report on foreign relations contained their views on the balance of forces in the world, featuring phrases such as "The USSR is the equal, at least, of the USA," and "U.S. imperialism no long holds sway over mankind. Though it remains powerful, U.S. imperialism is on the decline."[2] (Appendix A, Document 19)

There are important truths in that particular report. The global correlation of forces has shifted to favor the socialist countries in comparison to a generation ago. But our Grenadian comrades overestimated that shift, especially with regard to the Western hemisphere. Hence, they let their guard down. The minutes of the NJM Central Committee for August 26, 1983 featured pervasive complaints that military preparedness was extremely low and declining. One parish report's comment on the militia stated: "It does not seem that imperialism exists anymore."[3]

We have learned the lesson of imperialism's continuing power. But we must also make certain that other revolutionaries, especially the Sandinistas, do not miscalculate the global correlation of forces.

There are other lessons to be drawn from the imperialist aggression against Grenada. The United States does not feel bound by international law. This utterly lawless invasion was a naked display of power to achieve the aims of imperialism. Again, this is nothing new. Recall only the assassination plots against Fidel Castro that even a U.S. congressional committee documented.

Grenada's leadership did not only make mistakes; it also followed some prudent policies. For example, Grenada was not subverting its neighbors. It had a militant revolutionary government, but not a stupid one. It had excellent relations with fraternal and other progressive opposition parties in the Caribbean,[4] and played an important leadership role among them.[5] Essentially, this was not different from the good political relations maintained between kindred parties in the Socialist International and the World Union of Christian Democrats. The NJM knew, however, that it had to be cautious in the conduct of these political relations in order not to present imperialism with an excuse to attack. Consequently, the Grenadian leadership limited its direct support of revolutionary forces both geographically and ideologically.

First, they had to maintain good government-to-government relations with the nations of the Eastern Caribbean. There is evidence of such an effort. Grenada joined and worked well in the Organization of Eastern Caribbean States (the OECS was eventually used by the imperialists to give a veneer of legality to their naked aggression). Grenada was also an active and constructive participant in the Caribbean Community and Common Market (CARICOM). Grenada had offered scholarships at its fisheries school to other Caribbean states. It had even extradited some political enemies of other Caribbean governments caught on Grenadian territory (as in the case of Bumba Charles, a leader in the seizure of Union Island from the government of St. Vincent and the Grenadines).[6] Second, beyond the Eastern Caribbean, the NJM made principled ideological distinctions between various armed groups. It did not support everyone who claimed to be a revolutionary. For example, it wisely gave no response to a request from Colombia's M-19 guerrillas "to develop best possible links" with the NJM.[7]

This analysis might leave the erroneous impression that the Grenadian government did not support national liberation efforts. That is, of course, incorrect. Beyond the Eastern Caribbean, the NJM supported such struggles to the extent of its capabilities. Impoverished Grenada contributed no less than 50,000 East Caribbean dollars to the struggle of the South West African Peoples Organization (SWAPO) against South Africa over Namibia.[8] It worked with us and others to support the Salvadoran revolution.[9] (Appendix A, Document 24)

Implications for Nicaragua and Other Friendly Nations

Some have suggested that as a consequence of the new aggressiveness of imperialism, Cuba will exercise greater restraint in its relations with revolutionary forces in order to avoid provoking imperialist aggression. We firmly reject this assumption. This would amount to our surrender to imperialism. We are aware that close relationships with friendly governments, especially in this hemisphere, are dangerous to our friends, and we should be frank and candid about this danger. But we should not fail to pursue policies that serve our own interests. We recommend no major foreign policy change as a result of the Grenada events.

Others have said that Cuba should have augmented its forces on Grenada to fight the U.S. invasion. We firmly reject this position. As President Fidel Castro told the Coard-Austin group on October 22, three days before the aggression, "Cuba cannot send reinforcements . . . because of the overwhelming U.S. air and naval superiority in the area."[10]

Thus we must clearly tell the Sandinistas that Cuba will not be able to send reinforcements if Nicaragua is invaded because of overwhelming U.S. military superiority in the Central American theater. We should also reassure the Sandinistas that our personnel on the ground will fight, if they have to. We must tell our African allies that they should distinguish between the circumstances surrounding the Grenada events on the one hand, and conditions in Angola and Ethiopia on the other. Imperialism was fully engaged in Grenada. The United States, in contrast, never committed its military might in Angola or Ethiopia. Cuban assistance is possible only when imperialism has not made a fullscale military commitment.

This raises several hypothetical questions. Should Cuba have sent reinforcements if only OECS countries had invaded Grenada? We think not because that surely would have provoked U.S. intervention. As President Fidel Castro told the Coard-Austin group on October 22, "Jamaica, St. Lucia, and Barbados have no forces to invade Grenada and, in that case they [the Grenadian armed forces] could defeat them with their own forces without greater difficulties."[11] Accordingly, we should convey to Nicaragua and other friendly states that Cuba will not send reinforcements if the national armed forces can defeat aggressors on their own. But we should reassure them that Cuban personnel in place will fight. This is prudent and should make a U.S. invasion less likely.

Another hypothetical question is whether Cuba should have sent reinforcements to Grenada—independent of the question of U.S. military power—given the execution of Maurice Bishop and other evidence of the decomposition of the Grenadian revolution. We think not, and as President Fidel Castro told the Coard-Austin group on October 22, "the unfortunate developments in Grenada render the useless sacrifice entailed in the dispatching of reinforcements in a struggle against the United States morally impossible before our people and the world."[12]

The Coard-Austin group, however, has made serious charges against Cuba. In October 1983, they stated that the "deep personal friendship between Fidel and Maurice which [sic] has caused the Cuban leadership to take a *personal* and not a *class* approach to the developments in Grenada." [Emphasis in original.] They also thought that it was "clear that the Cubans' position creates an atmosphere for speedy imperialist intervention."[13]

This charge is rank slander. As President Fidel Castro explained on October 15 to the NJM Central Committee, Cuba regarded Maurice Bishop as the central figure of the Grenadian revolution. The NJM itself supported Bishop as party and government leader. Cuba did not invent Bishop's central role. The President's letter went on to say that the Grenadian revolution, led by Bishop, had Cuba's great sympathies and respect. He pledged Cuba's "strictest attention to the principles of not interfering in the slightest in the internal affairs of Grenada, fulfilling the promises made in the field of cooperation. *Our promises are not to men. They are to the peoples and to principle*" (emphasis added).[14] (Appendix A, Document 18)

Therefore Cuba's views should be communicated, albeit with subtlety, to the Sandinistas and other revolutionaries to give them incentives to preserve revolutionary unity. This should give Cuba additional leverage to deal with its allies. Cuba will not defend thugs masquerading as revolutionaries because Cuba's fundamental commitment is to revolution itself.

Do the Grenada events prove that Cuba is an unreliable ally that created the necessary preconditions for the imperialist invasion of Grenada? This is impossible. We have explained the concrete reasons that distinguish Grenada from Angola and Ethiopia, and the problems posed by the internal decomposition of the Grenadian revolution. The world knows, moreover, that Cuban reservists in Grenada fought more bravely and more ably against impossible odds than Grenada's own regular troops. The world knows, too, that Cubans were the only foreigners who shed their blood for Grenada. We were loyal and reliable allies of a revolution that committed suicide.

Problems of Cuban-Grenadian Cooperation

Several serious problems developed between Cuba and Grenada during the course of the Grenadian revolution. At times, interpersonal relations between Cubans and Grenadians were not good. Problems also arose stemming from the objective conditions of underdevelopment in both countries as well as from our insensitivity in handling some government-to-government and party-to-party relations. However, these problems pale in comparison to the fatal flaw of our insufficient information about internal splits within the NJM.

President Fidel Castro has described how Maurice Bishop had "very close and affectionate links with our party's leadership." In contrast, "Coard's group never had such relations or such intimacy and trust with us. Actually, we did not even know that group existed."[15] Fidel Castro wrote to the NJM Central Committee on October 15: "Everything which happened was for us a surprise and disagreeable." He went on to warn: "In my opinion, the divisions and problems which have emerged will result in considerable damage to the image of the Grenadian revolution, as much within as outside the country."[16] (Appendix A, Document 18)

Our lack of accurate intelligence data is inexcusable, but the dimensions of our failure should not be exaggerated. Although Bishop was in Cuba a few days before he was deposed and killed, he did not tell us about the NJM's internal problems.[17] (Appendix A, Document 18) But still we knew that all was not well in Grenada. As early as the summer of 1983, Manuel Pineiro (Head of the American Department of the Central Committee) told Grenadian Ambassador Cornwall on the basis of reports from our personnel in Grenada that the state of NJM party and government work was poor. In addition, our personnel in Grenada raised the matter directly with members of the NJM Central Committee.[18]

Consequently, the Cuban armed forces, intelligence services, and the Ministry of the Interior should improve our intelligence capabilities even in friendly countries, with special attention to possible splits with leadership circles.

The Dimensions of Cuban Policy Toward Grenada

Cuban policies toward Grenada were summarized in bilateral agreements between Cuba and Grenada. There are certain principles that we believe should be emphasized, however.

We believe it prudent to retain the principle that military agreements should be secret as stipulated by Article XII of the Cuban-Grenadian agreement covering 1982–1984.[19] (Appendix A, Document 14) Host governments should continue to be expected to provide food, transportation, and health services as well as "a small stipendium for the personal expenses of every member equivalent to 30 U.S. dollars."[20] Host governments should incur some expenses to demonstrate their good faith.

We are especially proud of our ability to respond promptly to the military needs of the Grenadian revolution. In April 1979, within days of revolutionary victory in Grenada, we transferred a substantial inventory of weapons to Grenada.[21] As General Hudson Austin wrote to Division General Arnaldo Ochoa concerning the followup on Ochoa's visit to Grenada, our military relations were excellent.[22]

On the day of the invasion, there were 784 Cubans in Grenada, including diplomatic personnel with their children and other relatives; 636 were construction workers, with the balance in many other fields, including 65 from our armed forces and Interior Ministry.[23]

Aside from formal economic and military agreements, we believe Cuba's central contribution to the Grenadian revolution was to serve as a broker between Grenada and other socialist countries. As Grenada's ambassador to the Soviet Union wrote, the Soviets are "very careful, and for us sometimes maddingly slow, in making up their minds about who to support. They have decided to support us for two main reasons. Cuba has strongly championed our cause," and the Soviets are impressed with the internal development of the Grenadian revolution.[24] (Appendix A, Document 6)

The fundamental importance of our intermediary role cannot be underestimated. It had many practical aspects, derived from Grenada's poor transportation and communication links with the outside world and its relative political unimportance. For example, the 1982 Soviet-Grenadian agreement stipulated that the final shipment point for Soviet supplies destined for Grenada would be the port of Havana.[25] (Appendix A, Document 13) Whenever appropriate, we even provided the Grenadians with Cuban technical personnel to help them in their negotiations with the Soviets.[26] Similarly, Grenada and Vietnam made preliminary contact in Havana.[27] Havana was also the final shipment point for sending of Czechoslovakian rockets and warheads to Grenada.[28] (Appendix A, Document 20)

Our intermediary role had other political features as well. For example, Cuba provided the principal guidance for Grenadian and other Caribbean delegates to the General Congress of the World Center for the Resistance of Imperialism, Zionism, Racism and Reaction, which was hosted by Libya. Manuel Pineiro briefed the delegates on what to support and what to oppose. So close were Cuban-Grenadian relations that "there was a line that Cuba was using Grenada to influence other Caribbean parties and organizations."[29] Our collaboration with Grenada enabled us to rally several delegations to cool off support for Libya's ambitions. As Pineiro said to the Grenadian and Caribbean delegates, "we should avoid giving support to the idea of Libya being the center of the world anti-imperialist struggle."[30]

This illustrates how Grenada in fact helped us on several occasions. Cuba might have rallied other Caribbean delegations on its own, but it was easier with Grenadian help. Grenada also helped Cuba in the Socialist International (SI), of which the NJM was a member. We exchanged information and met in secret with several SI members to coordinate strategy between the progressive forces in the SI. We should continue to caucus with the following friendly members: the radical party of Chile, the Jamaican People's National Party, El Salvador's Nationalist Revolutionary Movement, and what remains of the NJM.[31] (Appendix A, Document 24)

The Soviet Union, Cuba, and Grenada

We have already alluded to Cuba's role as a broker between Grenada and the Soviet Union and other socialist nations. In this section, we wish to discuss two issues. Was the Soviet Union too slow in responding to Grenada's needs in early stages of the Grenadian revolution, and was there a pro-Soviet and an anti-Cuban edge to the factional struggle within the NJM? We believe that the answer to both questions, with certain qualifications, is no.

We have noted how the Soviets characteristically displayed caution in responding to the Grenadian revolution. The imperialists describe our role as that of a Soviet proxy, but they have the relationship exactly backward. We took the lead in building Grenada's link to the socialist world. As late as the end of 1982, the Grenadian Embassy in Moscow plaintively reported, "the Caribbean—as they [the Soviets] repeatedly state—is very distant from them. It is, quite frankly, not one of their priority areas."[32] (Appendix A, Document 5) On one occasion the Grenadian ambassador to the Soviet Union asked the Cuban ambassador to the USSR about the quality of the Soviet-Grenadian relationship. Vice President Carlos Rafael Rodriguez was consulted and replied "that Cuba had taken fifteen years to establish close PB [Political Bureau]-to-PB relations and we [Grenadians] must work at it with patience and determination."[33] A good summary of the triangular relationship concludes the Grenadian ambassador's report to the Grenadian leadership: "we have to work on the Soviets for some considerable time before we reach the stage of relationship that, for example, we have with the Cubans."[34] (Appendix A, Document 5)

In short, the Soviets were cautious and slow, but no more than usual. From 1980 onward, the second year of the Grenadian revolution, they were providing considerable military and economic assistance.[35-36] Of course, we hope that the Soviets will become involved in our endeavors when we need their assistance, but experience teaches us that this is not likely. Their early relationship with Grenada was as good as or better than past history would give us reason to expect.

Some members of the Coard-Austin group may have had anti-Cuban attitudes. Central Committee member Leon Cornwall had been the Grenadian ambassador to Cuba, but he encountered several difficulties in his work—some of which we must accept the blame for. He mentioned his problems serving in Cuba during the period when the leadership struggle was developing in Grenada, but he never linked his attitude toward Bishop to his problems in Cuba.[37] (Appendix A, Document 16)

Bernard Coard told the NJM Central Committee in the discussions of September 1983 that "for the record he had personally raised a number of times with the Cuban comrades the need for advisors in party building, organization and ideological work. . . . However, there has not been a positive response so far."[38] That was said in the context of discussing NJM political problems, not foreign relations, and Coard did not in fact link his anti-Bishop views to anti-Cuban sentiments. In fact, the substance of Coard's remarks suggests that he sought Cuban aid.

The Soviets knew Coard better than they knew Bishop. Coard had taken the initiative to travel to Eastern Europe or the Soviet Union every year since 1979 to develop links with the socialist community.[39] (Appendix A, Documents 15 and 19) He was more self-consciously Leninist than Bishop. It is likely that the Soviets felt more comfortable with Coard than with Bishop, but there is no evidence they did much to help him.

The Soviets had reason to be upset with Bishop, especially concerning the circumstances of his trip to the United States in June 1983. We worked with Bishop on the preparation of his visit to the United States,[40] but Bishop did not inform the USSR of his trip. When the Director of the First Latin American Department of the Soviet Foreign Ministry asked the Grenadian ambassador for a briefing about Bishop's meeting with U.S. National Security Advisor William Clarke, he was told that "the results are confidential." The Soviet official made the point that it would have been courteous to inform Moscow of the intention of the visit given the nature of U.S.-Soviet-Grenadian relations.[41] (Appendix A, Document 6) For these reasons, the Soviets were unlikely to oppose Bishop's replacement by Coard, but we have found no evidence that they actively supported it. Given their low level of information about Grenada, the low-profile policy the Soviets adopted toward Grenada was prudent and acceptable to us.

In short, there is no significant evidence of anti-Cuban views among the members of the Coard group, much less of any link between such views and the overthrow of Bishop. Nor is there any evidence of a Soviet role in the events that led to Bishop's overthrow. There are, however, two differences between the Cuban and Soviet responses to the events of October 1983. We condemned Bishop's overthrow and death while the Soviets remained silent. We fought and died for the Grenadian revolution while the Soviets only protested the invasion. The Soviets made no move to help or hinder any of the factions in the struggle, and they had far fewer personnel in Grenada than ourselves. This low profile was consistent with Soviet policy toward Grenada since 1979.

Conclusions

The destruction of the Grenadian revolution, at the hands of the Coard-Austin group and the imperialists, was a tragedy. We have all learned from it, and earlier lessons have been reinforced as well. We believe our party, government and people should be proud of our actions in Grenada, but we should learn from our mistakes so they do not recur. Above all, we believe that in due course this setback will be turned into a victory as the revolutionaries of "Our America" become more skillful and more committed to the courageous struggle that will culminate in the defeat of imperialism.

We are confident that the march of history will lead to successful revolutions by the peoples of this hemisphere. *Patria o muerte! Venceremos!*

NOTES

1. An earlier, longer version of this paper was presented at the conference on "Soviet-Cuban Strategy in the Third World after Grenada" sponsored by the Kennan Institute for Advanced Russian Studies and the Naval Postgraduate School, Monterey, CA, August 15–17, 1984.

2. Foreign Relations Report, undated (but probably published in 1981), Grenada Documents, Log No. 105757.

3. Minutes of Emergency Meeting of NJM Central Committee, August 26, 1983, undated, ibid.

4. Draft Workplan of the NJM International Relations Committee for 1983, undated, ibid.

5. Report on the General Congress of the World Center for the Resistance of Imperialism, Zionism, Racism and Reaction, June 26, 1982, ibid.

6. Foreign Relations Report, op. cit.

7. Minutes of the Politburo Meeting, December 29, 1982, Grenada Documents.

8. Minutes of the Politburo Meeting, December 9, 1981, ibid.

9. *See* Report on Meeting of Secret Regional Caucus of SI [Socialist International] Held in Managua, January 6–7, 1983, ibid., Log No. 100446.

10. Documents made available by the Cuban Interests Section to the United States [hereafter CIS], Statement by the Cuban Communist Party and Government on the Imperialist Intervention in Grenada, October 25, 1983.

11. CIS, ibid.

12. CIS, ibid.

13. On Cuba's Response to the Issue, October 21, 1983, ibid.

14. Letter from Fidel Castro Ruz to the Central Committee NJM, October 15, 1983, ibid., Log No. T.

15. Fidel Castro, Farewell Address in Funeral Homage to the Heroes Fallen in Unequal Combat against Yankee Imperialism in Grenada, November 14, 1983, CIS.

16. Letter from Castro, op. cit.

17. Ibid.

18. Minutes of Emergency Meeting of NJM Central Committee, August 26, 1983, Grenada Documents.

19. Secret Protocol of Military Collaboration between the Government of the Republic of Cuba and the People's Revolutionary Government of Grenada, undated, ibid., Log No. 000194.

20. Protocol of the Military Collaboration about the Material Means, Service and Assuring Personnel, Annex No. 2, undated, ibid.

21. Material Means Received from Foreign Countries within the Period 1979–1981, undated (probably late 1981), ibid.

22. Letter from General Hudson Austin to Division General Arnaldo Ochoa, May 16, 1982, ibid.

23. *Granma Weekly Review*, November 6, 1983.

24. Confidential report on Grenada's Relations with the USSR, from Grenadian Ambassador to Moscow, W. Richard Jacobs, to Foreign Minister Unison Whiteman, Prime Minister Bishop, Deputy Prime Minister Coard, and Politburo Member Ewert Layne, July 11, 1983, Grenada Documents, Log No. W.

25. Top Secret Agreement between the Government of Grenada and the Government of the Union of Soviet Socialist Republics on Deliveries from the Union of SSR on deliveries Grenada of Special and Other Equipment, July 27, 1982, ibid. *See* Article 2.

26. Meeting of the Ministry of Communications, November 9, 1982, ibid.

27. *Embajada de Grenada en Cuba*, February 18, 1982, ibid.

28. Bill of Lading from Czechoslovak Ocean Shipping for 1,250 Cases of Explosive Ammunition (Warheads, Rockets) on Order of Grenadian Embassy in Havana, undated, Grenada Documents, Log No. 102951.

29. Report on the General Congress, ibid.

30. Ibid.

31. Report of Meeting of Secret Regional Caucus of SI Held in Managua, op. cit.

32. Confidential report from the Grenadian Embassy in Moscow on the NJM's Relations with the CPSU, undated (but sometime after December 1981), ibid.

33. Ibid.

34. Ibid.

35. *See*, for example, Protocol to the October 27, 1980 Agreement between the Government of Grenada and the Government of the Union of Soviet Socialist Republics on Deliveries from the Union of SSR to Grenada of Special and Other Equipment, February 9, 1981, ibid.; *see also* Annex.

36. Agreements Concluded between the Government of the USSR and the Government of Grenada, May 29, 1982, ibid.

37. Extraordinary General Meeting of Full Members, September 25, 1983, op cit.

38. Undated and untitled handwritten notes of the Plenary Meetings of the NJM Central Committee, February 1983, ibid.

39. Foreign Relations Report, undated, op. cit.; and Summary of Prime Minister's Meeting with Soviet Ambassador, May 24, 1983, ibid.

40. See letter from wife of Cuban Ambassador to Grenada to Maurice Bishop discussing trip preparations, undated, ibid.

41. Grenada's Relations with the USSR, op. cit.

CHARLES GATI

Fraternal Assistance: Eastern Europe in Grenada

The secret documents found by United States military forces in Grenada in 1983 raise three questions with regard to the Soviet Union's Warsaw Pact allies in Eastern Europe.

(1) What was the scope of East European involvement in the attempted Sovietization of Grenada in the early 1980s? Do the documents shed new light on East European involvement in the Third World, or do they enrich our knowledge by providing documentary evidence that merely affirms what is already known?

(2) Do the documents challenge our conception of Soviet-East European relations? Much that has been written in recent years about the changing attitudes and expectations of the Soviet Union regarding Eastern Europe points to the replacement of a "satellite" relationship by a "tutelary" relationship.[1] According to the prevailing consensus, the communist states of Eastern Europe have been increasingly allowed to assert their individuality, albeit in a cautious manner. Is this change in Soviet-East European relations confirmed or contradicted by the Grenada documents?

(3) What do the Grenada documents imply for Western and especially American policy toward Moscow's junior allies? Do the documents confirm or contradict the wisdom of the policy of selective treatment—the policy of "differentiation"—which for over two decades has sought to treat each Warsaw Pact state differently? For over two decades, the communist nations of Eastern Europe have been judged by two criteria: the distance they maintain from the Soviet Union on matters of foreign policy, and their degree of domestic political and economic liberalization. Do the documents suggest that differences within the Warsaw Pact are more apparent than real—that all East European states are merely surrogates of the Soviet Union? If so, should Western nations replace "differentiation" with a uniform policy toward *all* East European states—a policy essentially similar to Western

policy toward the Soviet Union itself? Hopefully, the following discussion will shed some light on these questions.

THE SCOPE OF EAST EUROPEAN INVOLVEMENT IN GRENADA

Aside from insignificant trade activities, East European involvement in the Third World began in 1955 when Czechoslovakia agreed to sell arms to Nasser's Egypt. The deal was substantial, involving the sale of 300 tanks, 200 jet fighters, 100 artillery pieces, and 60 heavy bombers.[2] It was widely assumed that Prague acted at Moscow's behest and that this was primarily a political rather than purely a commercial transaction. Clearly, the deal marked the beginning of East European support for the Soviet Union's strategic objectives in the Third World. At a minimum, the Soviet Union seeks to reduce Western influence in selected Third World countries, and at most it hopes to replace Western influence by a growing Soviet or Soviet-bloc presence.

In the 1950s, the five key countries in which the Soviet Union sought influence were Egypt, Iran, Iraq, India, and Indonesia. Since those meager beginnings in the mid-1950s, however, Soviet and Warsaw Pact involvement in the Third World has grown significantly. No longer focusing on the above countries, Moscow has established diplomatic ties, expanded commercial relations, offered military assistance, and indeed established its presence in dozens of countries in Asia, Latin America, and Africa. Needless to say, the communist nations of Eastern Europe have followed suit.[3] Aside from the special case of Romania, the five loyal Warsaw Pact states—Poland, Czechoslovakia, the German Democratic Republic (GDR), Hungary and Bulgaria—have helped in the implementation of Soviet objectives in the Third World and at the same time have sought to reap economic benefits for themselves. Generally short of raw materials readily available in the Third World, desirous of selling their finished or semifinished goods which frequently do not meet Western standards, and hopeful of reducing their reliance on Soviet energy, the East Europeans have found certain Third World countries to be ideal trading partners.

Yet the evolving pattern of East European-Third World trade clearly reflects political preferences as well as a measure of coordination within the Warsaw Pact. The sudden expansion of East European economic activity with Mozambique, Angola, and Nicaragua in the 1970s was far from accidental. That it happened at Moscow's request or insistence is beyond dispute. But the East Europeans still had choices to make. As a former insider, a high-ranking Hungarian foreign policy official who subsequently defected, put it:

> . . . it would be an oversimplification and certainly misleading to argue that the Five [East European Warsaw Pact states excluding Romania] had no room for maneuver. It would be equally misleading to state that Soviet decisionmakers

> always asked for unconditional collaboration from their East European allies. An unwritten law presupposed the understanding that Eastern Europeans had freedom of action to the extent that such freedom served, or at any rate did not counter, Soviet national interests. This "law" also presumed that the Kremlin would give some operative consideration to Eastern European interests.[4]

Accordingly, the East European regimes have been guided by several often conflicting considerations in their relations with the Third World. One was to satisfy Soviet foreign policy interests. Another was to make economic gains. A third was to act in such a way as to signal distance and hence a measure of independence from Moscow in order to keep Western connections, particularly economic connections, intact. Finally, the East Europeans have sought to make their commitments modest because of pressing economic needs and popular grumblings about Third World assistance programs. The result of these four types of pressures has been a series of significantly differentiated East European policies toward the Third World, ranging from Czechoslovakian activism to Hungary's and Poland's largely symbolic performance. Clearly these differences have never been solely a function of each nation's relationship with the Soviet Union, but of each country's capabilities and domestic circumstances as well.

Indeed, one need not deny the existence of ideological affinity among Warsaw Pact regimes concerning their internationalist obligation to help Third World countries in the "anti-imperialist" struggle to recognize that there are substantial differences in their actual commitment to that struggle. True, the relative global share of East European trade with the Third World (approximately 6–8% of the total) has remained fairly constant over the years.[5] In addition, all of the five loyal Warsaw Pact members—including Hungary and Poland—have assisted or trained radical forces in the Third World, and all have sold military equipment to the Third World.[6] But the scope and range of this involvement has varied greatly. The GDR has long specialized in establishing little "Red Gestapos" (political police forces) in selected countries such as Angola, South Yemen, Nicaragua, and elsewhere—a rather curious preference for a German state. Czechoslovakia and to a lesser extent Bulgaria have long been major arms suppliers to Third World countries and reportedly to various terrorist organizations as well. Hungary and Poland have reportedly trained the Palestine Liberation Organization (PLO) and perhaps other national liberation forces as well. They have also transferred arms to certain Third World countries, though their assistance programs stress trade and technical assistance.

In Grenada, the pattern of East European involvement, as revealed by the documents captured by U.S./OECS forces, reflects past patterns. The documents indicate that certain Warsaw Pact states, most notably Czechoslovakia, became quite active in Grenada.

There is evidence of a military accord with Czechoslovakia (and Bulgaria) and the delivery of Czechoslovakian military equipment through Cuba.[7] The same report identifies a Czechoslovakian arms shipment—free of charge—of 3,000 automatic rifles with 30 boxes of spare parts and one million cartridges, and 30 bazookas with five boxes of spare parts and 5,000 shells. Another document records the delivery of 1,250 cases of "explosive ammunition" (warheads and rockets) via Havana.[8] (Appendix A, Document 20) A trade agreement between Czechoslovakia and Grenada lists goods to be delivered by Grenada: 80 tons of nutmeg every year from 1984 through 1988 and fresh vegetables ("quantities to be mutually agreed upon").[9] There is evidence of Grenadian requests for economic and technical assistance from Czechoslovakia (June 1980) asking for qualified personnel to prepare feasibility studies concerning projects in agriculture, hydro-power, construction, and garment production, etc. In June 1982, an extensive 5,000–6,000 word study was actually submitted by a certain Jiri Cerhonek of Czechoslovakia entitled "A Project for Grenada's Economic Development in the Period 1983–85."[10] The introduction states that "this study should be used as the first step to create a development programme in the years 1983–85 as the basis of working out the three-year state economic programme, from which the one-year plans will be derived." In addition, Czechoslovakia signed a Protocol on Cooperation between Radio Free Grenada and Czechoslovak Radio in December 1980 that provided for the exchange of programs and correspondents as well as for the training of two editors from Grenada to participate in Czechoslovak Radio's "training seminars."[11] The Grenada documents also include a copy of an air transport agreement between the two countries[12] and an offer of 14 scholarships at Czechoslovakian institutions.[13]

Conversely, there is little documentary evidence of Bulgarian involvement in Grenada. Aside from a reference to the military accord cited above, the documents included an "Agreement for Cooperation between the Bulgarian Communist Party and the New Jewel Movement of Grenada for the Period 1982–83."[14] (Appendix A, Document 21) It provided for the exchange of two-member delegations to make one-week visits per year and the training of 10 Grenadian "cadres" at the Bulgarian Party's Academy of Social Sciences and Management, a rather high-level political training school. It is also known that three of the 900 foreigners expelled from Grenada after the U.S./OECS intervention were Bulgarians.[15]

The only other Soviet bloc nationals found in Grenada were ten East Germans (and about 800 Cubans). Why the American government's preliminary report on the Grenada documents claims that "East Germany was the most heavily involved of the Soviet bloc countries" is not clear.[16] The available documents on GDR involvement suggest that East Germany was somewhat less active than Czechoslovakia. In any case, one report describes a meeting held in Moscow on May 20, 1983 between the Chairman of the Council of Ministers of the GDR and Grenada's Ambassador to the Soviet Union. The East German official was reported to have "assured the Ambassador that the GDR will do everything necessary to fulfill all agreements reached between the GDR and Grenada and would, to the extent of its capacity, give further aid. He said that, in [the] view of the GDR, Cuba, Nicaragua and Grenada were the countries of greatest hope in the Caribbean region." Another East German official, Deputy Minister of Foreign Affairs V. Neugebanck stated that it was the policy of the GDR to concentrate its attention on Grenada, Nicaragua, and Cuba in the Caribbean region, and that his government would do everything in its capacity to assist in the development and consolidation of the Grenadian revolution.[17] (Appendix A, Document 22)

Another document involving East Germany was a party-to-party agreement signed in Berlin on June 10, 1982. It provided for 11 Grenadian "comrades" to study or vacation in the GDR and for four East Germans to do likewise in Grenada. In also called for a "temporary adviser" from the GDR to help Grenada "on questions of building up the Party (duration of stay to be agreed)," and for continued East German assistance "in the operation of the New Jewel Movement's printing press and the training of personnel in this area."[18] (Appendix A, Document 23)

Hungary and Poland figure in the Grenada documents only in passing. There were public reports that high-level Grenadian officials visited Budapest, and Grenada had nothing critical to say about the declaration of martial law in Poland in 1981. Moreover, Prime Minister Bishop concluded an economic agreement with Hungary shortly before his death in October 1983. Hungarian and Polish officials expressed solidarity with the "struggling masses" of Grenada, coupled with statements about their own economic problems. The documents provide no evidence of Hungarian or Polish assistance to Grenada—neither of the usual type (arms, medicine, hospitals) nor the more bizarre type (e.g., visiting gypsy orchestras or soccer teams) that these nations sometimes sent to Third World countries.

It therefore seems that Grenada was primarily a Soviet-Cuban project to which Czechoslovakia, and to a lesser extent the GDR and Bulgaria, made a contribution. The captured documents discussing the role of the Soviet Union and Cuba leave no doubt about their desire to exploit the opportunity offered by the Grenadian revolution and to transform this tiny island into a Leninist dictatorship. Indeed, much Soviet and Cuban aid was designed to support the emerging ruling class of this dictatorship: the extensive weaponry, the buildup of propaganda machinery, the airplane intended for exclusive use of the leadership, the holiday visits, the cars—and even the four guillotines supplied by Moscow.[19] But there is simply no evidence of comparable "fraternal assistance" extended by Moscow's East European allies.

The documents also suggest a degree of similarity between the processes of takeover in Grenada and the postwar Sovietization of Eastern Europe. Between 1945 and 1948, the communization of Eastern Europe was engineered by the Soviet Union against the political preferences of most East Europeans. In Grenada, it was Cuba but also the Soviet Union and its junior allies that engineered the process. The similarities are striking. Control over the police was a primary goal in both Eastern Europe and Grenada, and a network of informers was formed quickly in both cases. Also in both cases, local communists were extremely attentive to Western opinion and skillfully sought to manipulate it. Indeed, in order to mislead and divide Western opinion, Sovietization is invariably characterized by a gap between public posturing and behind-the-scenes maneuvering. For public consumption, local communists are portrayed as democrats and reformers committed to social and economic equality and political pluralism. To make that posture believable, they claim they will build churches and even tolerate a measure of dissent, for the time being at least. Yet over a period of months or a few years, gradually, step-by-step, they keep moving closer to the goal of one-party hegemony; they seek to divide their noncommunist partners, gather strength and power, and find that even the appearance of pluralism stands in the way of complete control. And despite all the promises, when the revolution fails to deliver economic and other benefits, they always blame their failure on Western machinations. It is amazing how easily Westerners seem to forget that communist parties almost always hide their ultimate objectives in the beginning because they prefer the incremental road to power in true Leninist fashion.

IMPLICATIONS ABOUT SOVIET-EAST EUROPEAN RELATIONS

There is also a great deal to be learned about Soviet-East European relations by considering what the Grenada documents do not contain. In none of the documents is there any indication of close Soviet coordination with other Warsaw Pact countries. The strategic role of Cuba as a major actor, a surrogate, and a place for the transfer of all goods shipped to Grenada is clear. But if Moscow agreed on a division of labor with its East European allies, such an agreement is neither stated nor implied. Some of these secret discussions were such that a Soviet participant could have been quoted as saying something to the effect that "we will discuss your request with our allies," "we will ask our allies to help you because we can't," "we'll tell our comrades in Eastern Europe to shape up and give you what you need," or even "our East European comrades occasionally have to be reminded of their internationalist duties, but they need cheap energy from us and so they'll come around to helping you."

The apparent absence of both extensive East European support for Grenada and a division of labor among Warsaw Pact states should not be surprising. After all, most of them have done as little as possible to assist General Jaruzelski's Poland. The fact is that even as they shared a common view of the importance of Grenada (public statements indicate as much), and even as they presumably exchanged information about Grenada,[20] most East European states regard themselves as minor players in the East-West conflict outside continental Europe. Most of them are politically and/or economically weak, and they are primarily interested in their own political survival. Even within Europe, some have been flirting with the idea of a continuation or revival of European détente, implying that today's tense international atmosphere reflects poor relations between the United States and the Soviet Union, not between East and West. Once Moscow's staunchest ally and still its leading trading partner, the GDR has been the subject of barely veiled Soviet criticism for having taken this position. And the Hungarians, who in recent months have hosted West German, British, Italian, and American leaders in an unprecedented series of summits, published an authoritative statement earlier this year upholding the right of Warsaw Pact nations to pursue their national interests, at times even at the expense of their internationalist obligations.[21]

How the leaders of each East European state interpret the conflict between their national interests and internationalist obligations is the key to understanding their choices and policies. Without access to their deliberations, we have to rely on public statements and actual behavior. Judging them in this manner, it appears that Czechoslovakia, living in self-imposed isolation from the West, has the most to gain from supporting even internationalist (i.e., Soviet) causes. As suggested by the Grenada documents, the GDR, whose population is most exposed to Western information and values, seems to be drawing back from the role it played in the 1970s as Moscow's main surrogate in the Third World. There is little doubt of Soviet irritation with GDR foreign policy,[22] although so far it stems primarily from East German policy toward the Federal Republic of Germany (FRG), not the Third World. Bulgaria, a loyal supporter of internationalist fraternal assistance, lacks the resources to be of much help to the Soviet Union, and indeed its foreign policy posture in the Balkans suggests the possibility that even Sofia may be capable of fresh, if not independent, initiatives. For several decades, Poland and especially Hungary have done as little as possible in the Third World without risking Soviet reprisals.

None of this is meant to imply that Moscow has "lost" Eastern Europe, that East European leaders are not pro-Soviet, or that they are bad communists who have forgotten their duty to assist in the struggle against U.S. imperialism by strengthening the forces supposedly upholding the causes of peace, justice, and socialism. On the contrary, it is possible they would like to do more, if only they had adequate resources, if only they did not have to cope with the popular belief at home that assistance to the Third World drains their economies, and if only their Third World activities did not damage their dealings with the West. But given these constraints, internationalist duties take second place to their national interests (obviously less so in Czechoslovakia than in Hungary or Poland).

In the final analysis, the Grenada documents offer fresh evidence confirming the reluctance of East European communist regimes except Czechoslovakia and the GDR to support distant Soviet foreign policy objectives. Their support indicates that they cannot stay afloat without Soviet backing; hence the ever-present threat of Soviet intervention keeps them in line. On the other hand, their reluctance means that continued dependence on Moscow does not translate into the obligation to support the Soviet Union on all issues. The Soviet reluctance to rely on military intervention to keep the Warsaw Pact in line provides Moscow's junior allies with considerable room for maneuver. Further, the more Soviet leaders find themselves preoccupied with succession struggles of their own, the more the East Europeans have room to pursue their national interests. Similarly, the less important the issue for which Moscow requests support, the more likely it is that the East Europeans will do as little as possible. In Grenada, some East European regimes took advantage of these factors, and others followed the Soviet lead. Obvious differences in their levels of involvement indicate that the East Europeans can cautiously assert their individuality in the 1980s, provided they assess their national interests rationally and balance conflicting interests—and then walk on what amounts to a political tightrope.

IMPLICATIONS FOR U.S. FOREIGN POLICY

Public rhetoric during presidential elections notwithstanding, the United States has long pursued limited objectives toward the Warsaw Pact states of Eastern Europe. As shown in NSC 58,[23] the United States developed a policy in 1949 aimed at the encouragement of "national communism" in the Soviet sphere of influence. Unable to "free" Eastern Europe or introduce political pluralism in the region, U.S. policy has sought to weaken the ties that bind Eastern Europe to the Soviet Union. Without saying so explicitly, the United States has tried to drive a wedge between Moscow and its junior allies.

The technique by which this limited objective has been pursued is known as "differentiation."[24] It signifies an attempt to reward some communist states and penalize others according to two criteria: the distance they maintain from Soviet foreign policy and their degree of domestic economic and political liberalization, for example as regards human rights issues. Using one or the other of these criteria, the United States has for some years favored Romania, Hungary, and Poland (prior to 1981) with some economic benefits, high-level visits, and other gestures of diplomatic support. Much less has been done for Czechoslovakia, the GDR, and Bulgaria. (Yugoslavia, highly courted by the United States, is in a different category altogether.)

Although such a "ranking" system seems justified by the evidence regarding East European involvement in Grenada, the United States probably should not draw major conclusions about Eastern Europe on the basis of the Grenada documents alone. Yet to the extent that the documents confirm existing differences within the Warsaw Pact, the United States should exploit such differences and compete for influence in Moscow's front yard. Grenada is a timely reminder of the Soviet Union's attempt to overcome "geopolitical realities" in Central America. The United States, relying on peaceful diplomatic and economic instruments of policy, should continue to seek no less in Eastern Europe.

NOTES

1. Recent works on Soviet-East European relations include Sarah M. Terry (ed.), *Soviet Policy in East Europe* (New Haven: Yale University Press, 1984); Robert L.

Hutchings, *Soviet-East European Relations: Consolidation and Conflict, 1968–1980* (Madison: University of Wisconsin Press, 1983); Karen Dawisha and Philip Hanson (eds.), *Soviet-East European Dilemmas: Coercion, Competition, and Consent* (London: Royal Institute of International Relations, 1981); and Christopher D. Jones, *Soviet Influence in Eastern Europe: Political Autonomy and the Warsaw Pact* (New York: Praeger, 1981).

2. Vratislav Pechota, "Czechoslovakia and the Third World," in Michael Radu (ed.), *Eastern Europe and the Third World: East vs. South* (New York: Praeger, 1981), pp. 77–105.

3. Radu, op. cit.

4. Janos Radvanyi, "Policy Patterns of Eastern European Socialist Countries Toward the Third World," in Radu, op. cit., pp. 333–344.

5. Roger Kanet, "Patterns of Eastern European Economic Involvement in the Third World," in Radu, op. cit., pp. 303–332.

6. Roger Kanet, "Soviet and East European Arms Transfers," in NATO Economics Directorate, *External Economic Relations of CMEA Countries: Their Significance and Impact in a Global Perspective* (Norfolk, U.K.: Thetford Press, 1968), pp. 171–194.

7. Grenada Documents, Log No. 102169.

8. Bill of Lading from Czechoslovak Ocean Shipping for 1,250 Cases of Explosive Ammunition (Warheads, Rockets) on Order of Grenadian Embassy in Havana, May 18, 1982, ibid., Log No. 102951.

9. Ibid., Log No. 103858.

10. A Project for Grenada's Economic Development in the Period 1983–1985, ibid., number illegible.

11. Protocol on Cooperation of Radio Free Grenada and Czechoslovak Radio, ibid., Log No. 103909.

12. Ibid., Log No. 103958.

13. Ibid., Log No. 102331.

14. Agreement for Cooperation between the Bulgarian Communist Party and the New Jewel Movement of Grenada for the Period 1982–1983, undated, ibid., Log No. 103676. Furthermore, in what may be the most most interesting of all the Grenada documents, the Grenadian Ambassador to the USSR W. Richard Jacobs reported from Moscow of "a very frank and friendly discussion" he had had with Boyko Dimitrov, director of the Bulgarian Communist Party's Institute of International Relations and a former Bulgarian Ambassador to Grenada. When Jacobs apparently complained that he had encountered difficulties arranging sufficiently high-level meetings with Soviet officials, Dimitrov told him that "even Bulgaria sometimes faces this problem and that it is a question of size, distance and priorities. I think he is correct. But then we have to deal with these realities. In order to elevate our priority in the socialist scheme of things . . . we have to raise and discuss with the highest [Soviet] authorities global or regional issues. In other words, *our begging operations have to be cast in the larger world context.*" (Appendix A, Document 6) Jacobs also observes: "We have a very sympathetic hearing in Bulgaria with Boyko Dimitrov and we should perhaps draw ever closer to the Bulgarian party. In the GDR, we also have made a good impression and there is great sympathy there for the NJM. Four comrades will be coming for rest and recreation in 1983." Confidential report on Grenada's Relations with the USSR, from Grenadian Ambassador to

Moscow, W. Richard Jacobs, to Foreign Minister Unison Whiteman, Prime Minister Bishop, Deputy Prime Minister Coard, and Politburo Member Ewert Layne, July 11, 1983, ibid., Log No. W.

15. *Grenada: A Preliminary Report* (Washington: Department of State and Department of Defense, December 16, 1983), p. 2.

16. Ibid., p. 24.

17. Meeting with Deputy Minister of Foreign Affairs (Latin America and Caribbean) V. Neugebanck, May 18, 1985, Grenada Documents, Log No. 102855.

18. Agreement on Cooperation between the New Jewel Movement of Grenada and the Socialist Unity Party of Germany for the Years 1982 to 1985, June 10, 1982, ibid., Log No. 103896. There exists an additional important document prepared in Havana in which Cuba officially informs Grenada of a gift from the GDR intended "to strengthen the operative capacity of the Security Bodies of your country." The list of items given to Grenada was not particularly long. Ibid., Log No. 102644.

19. Ibid., October 4, 1982, unnumbered.

20. Confidential report on Grenada's Relations with the USSR, op. cit. Ambassador Jacobs reported from Moscow that Warsaw Pact states tended to exchange information about Grenadian developments. But then he added, "In any event, I have not formed the impression that there is [a] generalized view within the community."

21. Charles Gati, "East Europe's Communists Are Tugging at Russia's Leash," *Washington Post*, Outlook section, July 8, 1984. Also see F. Stephen Larrabee and R.G. Livingston, "Rethinking Policy on East Germany," *New York Times*, Op-ed page, August 22, 1984.

22. *Pravda*, July 27, 1984 and August 1, 1984; "Encourage Honecker, Quietly," *The Economist*, August 4, 1984; and Serge Schmemann, "Chill in Bloc: Soviet Chides Germans," *New York Times*, August 6, 1984.

23. "NSC 58: United States Policy Toward the Soviet Satellite States in Eastern Europe, September 14, 1949," in Thomas N. Etzold and John Lewis Gaddis (eds.), *Containment: Documents on American Policy and Strategy, 1945–1950* (New York: Columbia University Press, 1976), pp. 211–223.

24. On the policy of differentiation, *see* Charles Gati, "Polish Futures, Western Options," *Foreign Affairs*, Vol. 61, No. 2 (Winter 1982/83), pp. 292–308.

CONDOLEEZA RICE

Comments

Since the 1955 Czechoslovakian-Egyptian arms deal, scholars have sought to understand the role of Eastern Europe in the Soviet Union's effort to extend socialist power into the Third World. Charles Gati's analysis of the Grenada documents suggests that students of this question have been correct in holding that the contributions of Eastern Europe vary both in scope and intensity. This diversity can be explained, in part, by the political distance that the member states of the Warsaw Pact wish to and are able to maintain from Moscow.

Even the casual observer can see that there are limits to East European autonomy. One can surmise that East European states would hardly figure in a discussion of Grenada were it not for their association with the Soviet Union. The broad outlines of East European policy, Romania excepted, are set by Moscow. But within these parameters there is room for maneuver. The "don'ts" are very clear for the East Europeans. Their policies must never be in direct conflict with those of the Soviet Union and should be at least nominally supportive. On the other hand, the contributions that the Soviets expect from Eastern Europe are far less clear. East European contributions range from Hungary's limited economic assistance to the very active military activities of the GDR.

Clearly, the East Europeans have to assess the costs and benefits of involvement in the Third World and tailor their activities accordingly. Perhaps the most difficult issue is how the East Europeans view benefits which are not readily apparent, for example a sense of socialist duty and allegiance to the Soviet Union. The Grenada documents are helpful in assessing this issue.

It is easy to understand why complementary trade relations are sought by the East Europeans. Markets for East European finished goods are limited and there is a pronounced need to find sources of raw materials. Technical assistance agreements through long term credit programs also create beneficial and lasting economic arrangements. These are the activities which all East European states, including Hungary and Poland, have sought. In the Grenada documents, there is no evidence of Polish and Hungarian activity. However, the documents show that Czechoslovakia, the GDR, and Bulgaria sought economic ties with Grenada. The Czechs, for example, prepared a report on Grenada's economic development that clearly indicated how Grenada's import/export structure was considered potentially complementary to Czechoslovakia's.[1] Other documents show the Czech interest in exporting machine tools and equipment to Grenada—products that have limited markets outside the Eastern bloc.[2]

Interestingly, there is a provision in one document that states that balance of payment deficits could be settled, at the request of the creditor, in convertible currency.[3] These arrangements were apparently long-term. Grenada was studying ways to achieve greater compatibility between its economy and that of the Soviet bloc.[4] To a large degree, this diminished the ability of the United States to exert economic pressure on Grenada. A number of industrial and agricultural technical assistance arrangements were undoubtedly intended to cement Grenada's economic relationship with the socialist world.

The political calculus for the Bulgarians, East Germans and Czechs in Grenada was clearly more complicated than "rational" economic motives would suggest. There were activities where economic benefits, even in the long term, were dubious. East bloc-Grenadian military assistance agreements cause us to wonder how Grenada, with a serious balance of payments problem, was planning to pay for the large quantity of weapons it was importing. During the 1970s, Czechoslovakia found a growth industry in the arms trade. Its favorite customers were oil-rich Arabs. There is not enough detail to know what East bloc expectations for payment were, but it is likely that the arrangement in Grenada was similar to the one in Ethiopia, where arms were supplied on very long-term credit or as outright grants. There was, however, at least one case to the contrary. The Grenada documents indicate a shipment of Czech ammunition through Cuba that was marked "prepaid."[5] (Appendix A, Document 20)

Other activities were even less profitable and must be placed under the heading "fraternal assistance." East Germany and Czechoslovakia attempted to help Grenada develop broadcast facilities and train journalists. There is also, for the first time, evidence that East Europeans trained party cadres.[6] Bulgaria and East Germany were scheduled to tutor the New Jewel Movement (NJM) in the experience of socialist construction.[7] (Appendix A, Documents 21 and 23) Such Bulgarian and East German activities seem to confirm the impression of many scholars that the East German and Bulgarian role in the Third World has grown and diversified in recent years (see Appendix A, Documents 21, 22, and 23).

On the other hand, the activities of the GDR were not as pervasive as one might expect given the recent history of East German involvement in the Third World. The GDR once sought involvement in the Third World to gain a national "identity" and compete with the Federal Republic of Germany (FRG) on the world stage. There was also an undeniable link with Moscow as the Honecker government sought special favor with the Soviet leadership. Since 1955 the Soviets have enjoyed a junior ally in the Third World that is willing to give freely of its resources and act as a surrogate when necessary. In contrast to other Warsaw Pact members, the GDR seemed willing and able to go to any remote place in support of Moscow's goals. From 1955 until 1970 Czechoslovakia performed this role. But after the events of 1968 and the malaise that followed, Prague's role was usurped by the more trusted GDR.

While by no means absent in Grenada, the GDR was much less in evidence than one might expect. It is always possible that relevant documentation is missing or that East German activities were such that they were subject to higher classification and greater protection. Charles Gati suggests that the GDR was actually less involved than Czechoslovakia in Grenada. But this does not necessarily mean, as he argues, that the GDR's role in Grenada was linked to Honecker's rapprochement with West Germany. The GDR might simply have been overextended concentrating its efforts on Africa, and Grenada might simply have been a low priority for both the Soviet Union and the GDR. One might even argue the counter case, that Honecker sought to "buy" room for maneuver in Europe with active support of Soviet activities in the Third World and that Grenada is a special case. The Grenada documents simply do not provide enough definitive evidence to answer the questions raised by East Germany's circumscribed role in Grenada.

Perhaps it should not be surprising that Bulgaria, Czechoslovakia and the GDR were heavily involved in Grenada. They are Moscow's most trusted allies, and the GDR and Czechoslovakia share difficulties in forging legitimacy and support at home. Czechoslovakia has been particularly ineffective in creating support since the Soviet invasion of 1968. The line between loyalty to Moscow and popular legitimacy at home is a fine one. Those who have failed to walk that line successfully are those who are most actively seeking Moscow's approval in the Third World.

As important as the approval of the Soviet Union might be, other factors that drive Czechoslovakian, East German, and Bulgarian activity in the Third World should not be ignored. It is possible these states take seriously their commitment to the socialist bloc and consider it imperative to aid young revolutions in the Third World. Moreover, foreign policy initiatives in support of Moscow are better than no foreign policy initiatives at all. There is some pride to be found in an active foreign policy outside the European theater. The Poles and Hungarians seek similar gratification as well, but do so in an East-West rather than an East-South context.

Nevertheless, East European activity in the Third World has not been without its costs. The East Europeans risk the creation of beneficial ties that can easily be dismantled if relations sour between the Third World states and the Soviet Union. Czechoslovakian interests, for example, were damaged in Egypt where ties established over almost 20 years were suddenly severed when the Soviets fell out of favor. The prospect of tying long-term economic relations to Soviet policies over which they have little control must be troubling. The losses were not very grave in Grenada, but the financially strapped East Europeans can hardly afford lost revenue. The risks are presumably greater when they support policies in regions where Cuba rather than the Soviet Union is the primary sponsor.

The potential costs also include the specter of soured relations with the West. Economically progressive Hungary and economically depressed Poland cannot afford tensions with the West, and their foreign policies are probably constrained by this fact. Gati's assertion that the GDR has begun to reassess its role as its ties with the West deepen bears watching, for it is much too early to tell if this is a long-term trend. Czechoslovakia and Bulgaria, already isolated from the West, arguably have little to lose in casting their lot more firmly with Moscow.

The picture that emerges, then, is hardly one of a well-coordinated division of labor in the Third World among the Warsaw Pact states. Documents are not available that could support the existence of central direction from Moscow. This does not mean that they do not exist. But the great variation in the contributions of the East Europeans supports Gati's contention that there exists a loose association of donors rather than a coordinated effort. When searching for policy coordination, it is wise to remember that the Warsaw Pact has encountered problems in achieving satisfactory integration and division of labor in Europe itself, for example in weapons production. If coordination in this key area is imperfect, it would be surprising to find it in the Third World.

One might go further and ask whether tight coordination and a division of labor are even necessary. A division of labor can take place naturally with the East Europeans contributing according to their comparative advantages and abilities. When a coordination was needed among the Soviets, East Germans, and Cubans in the Ethiopian airlift operation, it was achieved. Nothing approximating that level of coordination was apparent in Grenada. On the contrary, the Grenada documents support the trend to which we have grown accustomed in the Third World: the Soviets and their allies tend to act on the basis of bilateral rather than multilateral ties. Most activities are not undertaken through the Warsaw Pact which carries with it binding responsibilities and duties. Instead, some states do their socialist duty as cheaply as possible, while others are inclined to perform more enthusiastically. Apparently, the Soviets are not willing to force the issue.

Thus the U.S. policy of differentiation toward Eastern Europe on the basis of distance from Moscow and domestic liberalization seems to be well-founded. The two dimensions of differentiation should be taken together, however, because they do not always go hand in hand. Romania's foreign policy independence has won great favor in the United States in spite of an extremely repressive system at home. On the other hand, Hungary's tacit support for Moscow's foreign policy line has seemingly blinded American policymakers to the considerable domestic liberalization which Kadar has undertaken. American policy must not confuse the two sides of differentiation, for it stands as the West's only hope of encouraging the evolution of East European regimes toward popular legitimacy and diminished reliance on Moscow. If Grenada can be taken as an example, such a trend might produce East European policies in the Third World less supportive of the anti-Western policies of their Soviet sponsor.

NOTES

1. A Project for Grenada's Economic Development in the Period 1983-85, by Jiri Cerhonek of the Czechoslovak Socialist Republic, June 1982, Grenada Documents.
2. Draft Proposal of Protocol between the People's Revolutionary Government of Grenada and the Government of the Czechoslovak Socialist Republic on Delivery of Goods, undated, ibid.
3. Ibid., Article VI.
4. On the Possible Establishment of a State Trading Corporation for Effecting Grenada's Trade with Socialist Countries, undated, ibid.
5. Memorandum to Chief of Staff Major E. Louison from Chief of Logistics K. Fraser, October 9, 1982, ibid.
6. Protocol on Cooperation between Radio Free Grenada and Czechoslovak Radio, and Meeting with GDR State Committee for Sound Broadcasting, May 19, 1983, ibid.
7. *See*, for example, Agreement on Cooperation between the New Jewel Movement of Grenada and the Socialist Unity Party of Germany for the Years 1982-85, June 10, 1982, ibid., Log No. 103896, and Agreement for Cooperation between the Bulgarian Communist Party and the New Jewel Movement of Grenada for the Period 1982-83, undated, Log No. 103676.

Part II
The Impact of the Grenada Events on Soviet/Cuban Policies in Central America, the Caribbean Basin, and Africa

HOWARD J. WIARDA

The Impact of Grenada in Central America

There seem to be two senses in which the Grenada intervention of October 1983 has not yet faded, or has not been permitted to fade, from our television screens and consciousness. The first, most apparent, and probably most ephemeral reason is that Grenada became a campaign issue in the 1984 election, with the Democrats charging the intervention was another sign of the Reagan administration's "reckless adventurism" in foreign affairs, and the Republicans using films from the intervention to demonstrate administration firmness, decisiveness, and willingness to employ force to prevent Soviet/Cuban expansionism in the American sphere of influence.

The second, more lasting reason for Grenada's continuing importance is the treasure trove of documents captured on Grenada by U.S./OECS forces. These documents, which are so extensive they can be measured most easily in cubic feet and whose authenticity cannot be doubted, show in excruciating detail a Marxist-Leninist revolution in progress. They are crucial to our understanding of the internal dynamics of the Grenadian revolution and its external ties and relations with Cuba, Czechoslovakia, the Soviet Union, Bulgaria, East Germany, Nicaragua, the Salvadoran rebels, European socialist parties and governments, as well as the Socialist International, and various support groups in the United States. The Grenada documents provide the first clear mapping of a revolution *en marche* in both its domestic and, now all-important, international relations. Without hyperbole it may be said that they do for our understanding of these international linkages what the documents made available to Harvard Professor Merle Fainsod after World War II did for our understanding of the internal dynamics of Soviet rule.[1]

The purposes of this paper are to comment on the rising Soviet/Cuban presence in Central America and the Caribbean Basin, to discuss preliminarily what the Grenada documents reveal about the international aspects of the revolutionary process in the area, to focus on the impact of the U.S.

intervention on revolutionary prospects in Central America and Suriname, and to offer some conclusions concerning the impact of Grenada on changing Soviet/Cuban strategy in the region and what this implies for U.S. policy.

THE RISING SOVIET/CUBAN PRESENCE IN CENTRAL AMERICA AND THE CARIBBEAN BASIN

In another paper,[2] the author has analyzed the rising presence of the Soviet Union and Cuba in Central America and the Caribbean Basin. Overall, the Soviets have considerably increased their presence and capabilities in the region during the last two decades—diplomatically, politically, commercially, militarily, culturally, and in terms of Soviet prestige and power. Moreover, the strategies and tactics pursued by the Soviet Union and its allies are now considerably more sophisticated than they were 20 years ago. Nevertheless, the paper also emphasized the severe constraints—having to do with distance, logistics, the difficulties the Soviets face operating in the Latin American context, and the domestic conditions of the Soviet Union itself—that serve to limit the Soviet role and presence in the area.

Hence, while Soviet capabilities in Latin America have increased, and while its tactics and strategy have become more sophisticated, there are also severe restraints operating on Soviet initiatives in the Western Hemisphere. It seems unlikely that we shall soon see a much larger and direct Soviet presence in Latin America. Rather what we will probably see is the Soviet Union attempting to continue to take advantage of revolutionary situations and anti-American sentiments that already exist in the area to gain advantage for itself and to frustrate and embarrass the United States. That is what Soviet machinations with regard to Cuba, Nicaragua, and Grenada—the three Marxist-Leninist regimes that have come to power in Latin America—are all about.

WHAT THE GRENADA DOCUMENTS REVEAL[3]

In light of recent events in Central America and Grenada, the question arises as to whether the Soviet Union has a timetable for expansion in Latin America. Is there a master plan or a blueprint for the conquest of the Western Hemisphere, like Hitler's plan to build a European empire?[4]

The information we have points toward negative answers to these questions. There appears to be no timetable, no master plan, no blueprint. But perhaps we are asking the wrong set of questions. If we ask instead, does the Soviet Union have a set of global goals, strategies, and tactics, the answer is yes. To date, these goals include protecting the Soviet strategic superstructure, expanding Soviet influence and prestige worldwide, embarrassing and weakening the United States, and strengthening the Soviet state and military. The tactics are to take advantage of opportunities as they present themselves, even to hurry them along if possible. This implies that Soviet foreign policy focusing on the Third World, and more specifically on Central America and the Caribbean Basin, is driven more by opportunities than by a master plan. This is true of Soviet policy in general, and the Grenada documents seem to confirm the assertion.

Under Khrushchev, the Soviet Union sought to expand its ties with the Third World left in general, not just with orthodox communist regimes and parties as under Stalin. But early tactics produced a mixed set of results. Arms transfers did not seem to gain the Soviets much mileage. Sometimes overly close relations were established with a charismatic leader (e.g., Sadat), and when they changed their minds the Soviets sometimes lost all. The Soviets posited these regimes would gradually evolve toward Marxism-Leninism, but it seldom worked out that way and few orthodox communists were produced. Growing disillusionment set in within the Soviet leadership regarding the Third World, and in the late 1960s and early 1970s there was a certain retreat from several Third World commitments.

More recently, the Soviets have reassessed their attitudes toward the Third World. When Nicaragua, rather like Cuba, gravitated unexpectedly into the Soviet camp, the conclusion became obvious that with relatively little commitment, opportunities could be seized upon and important gains could be made. Soviet strategy became a matter of focusing on long-term possibilities rather than scoring short-term advantages.[5] This is a forumula for assistance to broad-based popular-front and "anti-imperialist" forces in revolutionary contexts, and even in some democratic countries. But there are currently more "quality controls" built into Soviet foreign policy in Latin America than during earlier Soviet forays into the Third World. These include the following:

1. Greater selectivity in terms of the quality and reliability of the client.
2. Greater willingness by the Soviets to involve themselves in the internal affairs of their clients.
3. Greater use of proxy forces (e.g., the Cubans).
4. Greater use of local intermediaries who presumably know more about local conditions than the Soviets (again the Cubans).
5. Greater control over local internal policy and security forces, with special assistance provided by the East Germans.
6. Greater support for local communist parties in directing and leading more broadly-based revolutions.
7. Greater centralization of political control over revolutionary insurrections, including the forging of unity among otherwise disparate groups as in Nicaragua and El Salvador.
8. Greater concern for Third World collective security arrangements for mutual support of revolutionary regimes using the GDR for security training, Bulgaria for intelligence work, and Cuba for the direct supply of troops when necessary.

Planning, Coordination, and Tactics

The above background discussion provides us with a sense of the general orientation and strategies pursued by the Soviets in dealing with the Third

World. However, with regard to more specific tactics and orientations, the Grenada documents are most revealing. What follows is a listing of some of the important points that stand out in the documents. Other investigators might well be impressed by additional features or give different emphases to the same points.

1. From 1979 onward, the Soviet Union appeared to keep a certain distance from the Grenadian revolution and the New Jewel Movement (NJM). The NJM was considered a "fraternal party," but it was not treated on the same level as other communist parties. The Grenadian ambassador in Moscow labored to increase the Soviet involvement in Grenada, but the Soviets were often reluctant. There was not a high degree of Soviet attention to day-to-day events in Grenada. The Soviets were involved in and supportive of the Grenadian revolution, but they appeared to refrain from "micro-managing" Grenadian affairs. Thus the Soviet role in Grenada was limited.[6] (Appendix A, Document 6)

Perhaps two dozen Grenadians were given training in the Soviet Union, but they were unhappy in the "American" division in Moscow where they were in the same study group as the *gringos* and the Canadians. The documents also show that the Soviets wanted the Grenadians to serve as intermediaries to other English-speaking groups in the Caribbean and to bring another country into the communist fold. Moscow suggested either Suriname or Belize, but it recognized the latter might take some time. The documents further show that Cuba, Nicaragua, and Grenada were already thought of as securely ensconced in the Soviet camp, and that El Salvador would be the next battleground. But the Soviets did not press too hard and apparently they had modest expectations of the Grenadian revolution. One senses from the documents a certain skepticism on the part of the Soviets as to the stablity and the trustworthiness of their Grenadian client. The coup against Bishop might in fact demonstrate a Soviet willingness to dump unorthodox Marxist leaders of whom it disapproves, but Soviet complicity in Bishop's overthrow and violent death is not indicated in the documents.

2. Instead of becoming directly involved in everyday Grenadian affairs, the Soviet Union chose to operate through Cuba. A fascinating question, not fully resolved by the documents, is the degree to which there is a central direction from Moscow versus autonomy on the part of Soviet proxies. The documents seem to show that the Cubans had considerable autonomy, though ultimate authority was lodged in Moscow.[7] (Appendix A, Document 7) In this sense, the Soviets had the best of all possible worlds. They could claim credit for all successes, wash their hands of failures and blame them on the Cubans, and embarrass the United States in its own backyard without actually provoking the U.S. by becoming directly involved in its backyard.

3. This analysis, however, does not do full justice to the Cuban role in Grenada. The documents show the Cubans were pivotal to a degree not realized before. They were involved in all aspects of the Grenadian revolution.

Grenada was Cuba's "project" or "client," just as Cuba is a client of the Soviet Union. Cuba was the go-between in the Soviet-Grenadian relationship. Cuban technicians not only helped build the famous Port Salines airport, but also provided doctors, medical assistance, and several teachers. Cubans sometimes sat in on meetings of the Central Committee and Politburo of the NJM. Grenadian leaders were frequently shuttled to Havana for advice and counsel. There was a cooperation and exchange agreement between the Cuban Communist Party and the NJM, as well as between the NJM and the Communist Party of the Soviet Union (CPSU). (Appendix A, Documents 8 and 10) One gets the impression that the Grenadians did practically nothing without consulting with the Cubans first, certainly on important matters.[8]

4. The Grenadian revolution was much more planned, sophisticated, and serious than commonly believed. In the Western media, Grenada has been generally pictured as "comic opera." A revolution on a small island whose population is only 100,000 and whose chief export is nutmeg is not taken seriously. But in fact the Grenadian revolution was very serious. It had its comic opera aspects, and these sometimes have been seized upon even by those who have examined the documents (which are full of misspellings, amusing anecdotes, personal foibles, amateurism and misbegotten encounters of various sorts); but a closer reading reveals a serious revolution, with serious leaders, serious issues, serious debates, wrenching decisions, and finally, a horrendous dénouement in the events leading to the murder of Maurice Bishop and his followers. This is serious business, not the stuff of *opéra bouffe*.

5. Related to the seriousness of the Grenadian revolution is the fact that it was considerably more Marxist-Leninist than previously thought. Reading only the popular press accounts prior to the intervention, one had the image of a carefree and relaxed revolution, led by romantic socialists, a merry band of Robin Hoods, and a revolution calmed by cool island breezes and shaded by lazy palm trees. On the contrary, the detailed minutes of Politburo meetings show a dedicated Marxist-Leninist leadership unequivocably committed to embarrassing the United States and strengthening its ties with Cuba and the Soviet Union. This was not a group of somewhat fuzzy-headed reformers, but a dedicated cadre of Marxist-Leninists with clear aims and goals.[9] (Appendix A, Document 8)

6. Equally impressive is the degree of coordination among the international actors involved in the Grenadian revolution. Again, Cuba provided the key. But the East Germans, Czechoslovakians, Bulgarians, and Soviets were also intimately involved. Jamaican Prime Minister Michael Manley lent support and occasionally was useful to the above revolutionary coalition. The division of labor among the communist countries aiding Grenada was quite impressive. The Soviet Union provided overall guidance and direction; the East Germans were involved in security and police training; Czechoslovakia sent weapons; and Cuba provided trainers, construction crews, and technicians. Not all Eastern European nations were involved in or even interested in Grenada,

but among those communist states involved in the Caribbean, the planning and coordination has increased markedly over the years.[10] (Appendix A, Documents 5, 10, and 22) The popular image of the Grenadian revolution is one of haphazardness, disorganization, and general sloppiness. But the reality revealed in the Grenada documents is one of coordination, a rather efficient and quite rational division of labor, and a level of sophistication and communist cooperation that is both unexpected and impressive.

7. Some of the most revealing documents deal with the Socialist International (SI). The Grenadians and their allies made strenuous efforts to manipulate the SI—to turn it into an anti-American organ, and use it to gain support and legitimacy for the revolution.[11] The documents reveal a sophisticated understanding of the SI and its divisions. Particularly singled out for disapproval by the Grenadians and Cubans were former Venezuelan President Carlos Andres Pérez, Portuguese Prime Minister Mario Soares, and Spanish Prime Minister Felipe González—all of whom had reservations about the Nicaraguan revolution and the purity of purpose of the Salvadoran guerrillas, and insisted on coupling condemnations of U.S. military machinations in Central America with a call for the removal of "all" (presumably Cuban as well as American) military forces from the area. Particularly singled out for praise were former West German Chancellor Willy Brandt and Dutch and Scandinavian socialist and social-democratic parties who were more sympathetic to Cuban, Nicaraguan, and Grenadian points of view. The SI has long been a major worldwide voice in support of democracy and human rights, but that should not blind us to the divisions within its ranks that are being manipulated by elements whose agendas are not at all democratic. The Grenada documents even suggest that certain revolutionary states were planning a secret coalition within the Socialist International.

8. Finally, the Grenada documents indicate an effort by the Soviets, Cubans, Nicaraguans, and Grenadians to influence domestic opinion in the United States (and also Canada).[12] Various church groups, human rights agencies, newspapers, university groups, and congressmen are singled out as avenues for spreading propaganda, disinformation, and favorable publicity about the Grenadian revolution. One of the more extraordinary documents in the collection is a letter from Gail Reed, the American wife of the Cuban Ambassador to Grenada Julian Torres Rizo, to Maurice Bishop prior to his visit to the United States. Among other things, Bishop is advised on how to deal with the American media: "In the absence of violence . . . controversy will do."[13]

Grenada's Ties with Nicaragua Prior to the U.S. Intervention

Other authors in this volume are focusing their analyses on Grenada's ties with revolutionary Cuba. As the documents reveal, Cuba is the linchpin in revolutionary operations in the Caribbean—the essential hub from which other activities radiate. In a manner of speaking, Nicaragua is one of the "spokes" in the Cuban "wheel," and Grenada was yet another. Cuba was the center, but there were also direct ties between Grenada and Nicaragua.

These ties were not extensive, and the barriers of language, political culture, and the absence of direct transportation further added to the difficulty of maintaining close relations. Nevertheless, the documents reveal some interesting ties.

Grenada signed a mutual health assistance pact with Nicaragua. Two Grenadian teachers (out of 12 originally scheduled to go) were sent to Nicaragua to assist in its literacy program. Indicative of the limited ties between the two countries, and also the way in which relations among revolutionary countries in the Caribbean were coordinated, travel arrangements for these teachers had to be made through the Nicaraguan ambassador to Havana.[14]

Grenadian representatives were sent to a secret regional caucus held in Managua to plan strategy for influencing the Socialist International.[15] (Appendix A, Document 24) This was not a meeting of the SI itself, but only of revolutionary countries making plans for an upcoming meeting. Grenada professed its solidarity with the Nicaraguan revolution and with the Salvadoran guerrillas on many occasions. It registered its protest against the U.S.-supported *contras* in Nicaragua, but there are documents that speak of Grenadians being sent to the Nicaraguan-Honduran front as a symbol of solidarity with the Nicaraguan militia.[16] There are also letters from Nicaraguan commanders to their Grenadian counterparts wishing their revolution well. So far as material aid, however, the documents only reveal that Nicaragua sent 2,000 militia uniforms to Grenada and the material for 2,000 more.[17] (Appendix A, Document 25)

Grenada and Nicaragua had virtually no relations whatsoever prior to 1979, and even after their respective revolutions, Grenadian-Nicaraguan relations remained quite limited. Relations were confined for the most part to symbolic expressions of sympathy and solidarity. The real impact of Grenada on Nicaragua came in the wake of the U.S./OECS intervention, not before.

THE U.S. INTERVENTION AND ITS EFFECTS

The U.S./OECS intervention in Grenada in October 1983 may have been a watershed. From the point of view of the Reagan administration, the Grenada intervention showed both the efficiency of U.S. military actions, and perhaps more importantly, a willingness to use force in defense of American interests, thus demonstrating that the United States had finally overcome its guilt complex over Vietnam. Perhaps the major effect of the intervention, however, was felt by Grenada's revolutionary neighbors: Suriname, the rebels in El Salvador, and Nicaragua.

The impact of the intervention in Grenada was felt most immediately in Suriname. On the night of October 25, only hours after the Grenada U.S. intervention, Lt. Colonel Daysie Bouterse, chief of the Surinamese army and head of the government since February 1980, announced on national television that Cuban Ambassador Oscar Osvaldo Cárdenas had been given six days to leave the country. Cuba was asked to reduce its diplomatic relations to the *chargé d'affaires* level. Bouterse announced further that a cultural and economic agreement with Havana had been suspended. In addition, 25 Cuban diplomats and 80 advisers were asked to leave the country, leaving the Cuban Embassy in Paramaribo with only minimum personnel.[18]

Bouterse's rule in Suriname had become increasingly brutal over the years. His relations with Cuba had once been warm, and the Cubans had been energetically cultivating ties with Suriname at several levels. They had given training to the leaders of Suriname's 3,000 man militia. The Cubans were suspected of being behind some of the moves toward greater totalitarianism that characterized Bouterse's rule, and they had sought to increase their influence within the army.[19]

The expulsion of the Cuban ambassador and other actions to reduce Cuban influence in Suriname were directly related to the events in Grenada, albeit not entirely in sequence and for the precise reasons that one might expect. Bouterse had become increasingly resentful of the Cubans' interference in his country. In 1983, he sought to mend relations with the United States. Suriname army officials felt the Cubans were partly responsible for the bloody developments in Grenada and feared the same might happen in their country. Some military officers were also resentful of Cuban efforts to interfere in army affairs, and hence they put pressure on Bouterse to remove the Cubans. Bouterse apparently feared he might meet the same fate as Maurice Bishop. Finally, there are reports that Brazil, which lies on Suriname's southern border and is fearful of any Cuban or leftist presence nearby, exercised pressure on Paramaribo.[20]

Although Bouterse's actions coincided with the U.S. intervention and were doubtless influenced by it, the decision to reduce the Cuban presence was actually made before the invasion. The intervention accelerated the process and gave it particular immediacy, but the process was already underway. Partly for economic reasons, the Surinamese had been trying to improve ties with Washington so as to qualify for economic assistance and better trade relations. Apparently, the Cubans had been trying to influence key Surinamese groups to oppose this policy—a strategy that produced resentment toward the Cubans, especially from inside the army. Suriname also tried to obtain aid from the Dutch to improve its failing economy, but the Dutch said there would be no renewed assistance until progress had been made to restore democracy and improve human rights.[21] Thus a considerable variety of motives lay behind Suriname's strong actions against the Cubans. But while the Grenada intervention was not the sole cause of Suriname's change of policy, it certainly helped accelerate the decision.

The impact of the U.S./OECS intervention was also felt strongly but somewhat ambiguously by the guerrillas in El Salvador. In general, the U.S. action was seen as a blow to revolutionary hopes and aspirations throughout the hemisphere.[22] For the Salvadoran guerrillas, it meant that the U.S. was willing to use force to prevent their coming to power. With the strong

U.S. military buildup in Central America over the last four years, this did not come entirely as a surprise. Rather than representing a break with the past, the Salvadoran guerrilla leadership saw the invasion of Grenada as merely one more, albeit dramatic, military escalation in a process that had been long underway. Nevertheless, the invasion forced a major reassessment of guerrilla policies.

For the rank-and-file in the Salvadoran guerrilla movement, there were no additional calls for patriotism, heroism, or the need for a long struggle. Whether such admonitions would have been acceptable to the peasants who make up the guerrilla ranks was questionable. Fighting a corrupt and incompetent El Salvadoran army is one thing, but the prospect of fighting the well-equipped Americans is quite another. The possibility of defeat or death began to loom large, and the guerrillas began to have trouble filling their ranks. The election of a legitimate, democratic president in 1984 added further to these fears, and the guerrillas increasingly turned to forced impressment to fill their ranks.[23]

One conclusion reached by the guerrilla leadership was that the Reagan administration was willing to employ any means, including armed intervention, to prevent a guerrilla victory. Thus, in contrast to the high expectations of some guerrilla leaders for a quick victory, others began to feel that final victory might be a long way off. A second conclusion, flowing from the logic of the first, was that the guerrillas should try to remove President Reagan from office. If Mr. Reagan was willing to go so far as to use force in the region, perhaps a Democratic president would not be so inclined. With the Soviet Union similarly disinclined to see a second Reagan administration and Cubans providing the arms, the guerrillas began preparing for a fall offensive. Rather like the Tet offensive in Vietnam, the guerrillas hoped to raise the costs of continuing American support for El Salvador by launching a bloody offensive just prior to the U.S. election. Aimed chiefly at influencing U.S. voters, the offensive was designed 1) to raise the level of carnage and violence seen on U.S. television screens and kill as many as possible in the process (which might have an effect similar to the October 1983 killing of the 241 servicemen in Lebanon that led to an American withdrawal); 2) to provoke right wing death squads into further undisciplined and indiscriminate slaughters (thus stimulating U.S. outcries similar to those which followed the killing of the four church women in December 1980); and 3) to make the cost of "staying the course" in El Salvador so high that the American public—notoriously impatient with murky and protracted guerrilla wars—would force the administration to withdraw or elect a new administration. The wheels and mechanisms were thus put in place to affect the U.S. elections.[24] But the offensive was never launched, and President Reagan was reelected.

An alternative conclusion, also stemming from the logic of the first, was that the guerrillas should increase pressures for a negotiated solution while simultaneously continuing the guerrilla struggle. Some guerrilla leaders feel that because the United States will not let them win, it is prudent to opt for a negotiated settlement that brings them into a position of power and gives them the opportunity to regroup and continue their struggle by other means. Indeed, it is current guerrilla strategy to increase pressure in El Salvador and the United States for a negotiated settlement, and the guerrillas are presently engaged in talks with the El Salvadoran government. Among some guerrilla leaders, a negotiated settlement is now viewed as preferable to a guerrilla victory because the latter, à la Grenada, will only invite U.S. armed intervention.[25]

Once again, it is Cuba at least as much as the Salvadoran guerrillas who have formulated these plans. But the high-level of coordination and centralization of tactics among revolutionary groups and countries is a phenomenon that was well underway before the invasion of Grenada. It is Cuba (and obviously by extension the Soviet Union) that insisted on a Tet-like offensive to affect U.S. public opinion. Deputy Foreign Minister Ricardo Alarcon set forth the logic for such an offensive, and Vice President Carlos Rafael Rodríguez, plainly speaking for Fidel Castro, has provided the logic for a negotiated settlement. According to Mr. Rodríguez, "A military victory by the guerrillas now in El Salvador could provoke an immediate U.S. reaction. We of course believe the guerrillas can win but that through negotiations we can avoid what might occur if they do."[26]

Such "advice" has not been always appreciated by the guerrillas in El Salvador. Some guerrilla leaders still believe they can win the war and that the threat of U.S. intervention is exaggerated. Having struggled in the bush for so long, they harbor a certain resentment toward the Cubans for trying to run their revolution. They remain convinced, perhaps rightly, that the United States will eventually tire of the war, pack its bags, and go home. Then their moment of triumph will have arrived.

The impact of the Grenada intervention on El Salvador therefore might have been temporary. There was much soul-searching among the guerrillas, but now they have a new strategy. They know that the present heavy U.S. commitment to Central America will not allow a quick victory. They hope that a new offensive can affect U.S. public opinion. Guerrilla leader Joaquín Villalobos has a long history of sacrificing his men for the sake of impacting U.S. elections. But even if this strategy fails, the guerrillas are prepared for a long struggle.

Initially, the strongest effects of the invasion of Grenada were felt in Nicaragua. To the point of paranoia, the Nicaraguans were absolutely convinced that they were next. Of course the Sandinistas have long felt that a U.S. invasion was imminent. Even while fighting during 1977–1979, they kept looking up at the sky waiting for the 82nd Airborne to drop down upon them. They were surprised when the expected invasion never occurred and the revolution succeeded. Some analysts believe that this partially explains the chaos and confusion in the present Nicaraguan regime. It is possible that the Sandinistas never expected to win and that they still don't know what to do with power they have gained.

The Grenada intervention unquestionably added to the paranoia of the Sandinista regime. In the first blush of the intervention, the Sandinistas were absolutely certain they would be invaded. These fears were fanned further by the American media's reaction to the intervention, which suggested that Grenada was a "dress rehearsal" or "warm-up" for invading Nicaragua. Even columnists such as Tom Wicker of the *New York Times* and Mary McGrory of the *Washington Post* made these claims.[27] They attempted to sway U.S. public opinion against such an invasion, but the effect of their columns was to fan the flames of paranoia in Managua.

The Reagan administration was not averse to seeing the Sandinistas squirm and added further pressures with its studied ambiguity. When asked if Grenada was a prelude to Nicaragua, President Reagan refused to say that it was not and he dropped several strong hints that it might be. The Nicaraguans had long been fearful that the "cowboy" in the White House might be "crazy" enough to consider invading them, but now they were certain of his intentions. Other administration officials were equally vague when asked similar questions about an invasion of Nicaragua. Meanwhile, adding further to the Sandinistas' fears, the U.S. military buildup in the Caribbean and Central America continued; the U.S.-sponsored *contras* stepped up their raids; and the Central American Defense Council (CONDECA), which like the Organization of East Caribbean States (OECS) might help legitimize and provide multilateral cover for a U.S. intervention, was revived.

Nicaragua's erstwhile allies were not always helpful. The Soviet Union advised the Sandinistas that in the event of an invasion, they could not count on Soviet military assistance. The Soviets said plainly they would write no blank checks for economic assistance and that Soviet military involvement was out of the question. The Cubans also told the Nicaraguans that Cuba would not be able to defend them in the event of an American invasion. This left Nicaragua alone and isolated to face the "Colossus of the North." In addition, it was known that Cuban "workers" in Grenada had been instructed to "fight to the death" to show the United States how bloody and difficult it would be if the United States invaded Nicaragua or Cuba. However, the Cubans did not fight to the death for Grenada—a fact that was not lost on the Sandinista leadership. Playing the "Cuba card" was looking less and less attractive to the revolutionary governments of Suriname and Nicaragua. The already powerful sense of paranoia in Managua was strengthened when the Cubans announced plans to pull some of their advisers out of Nicaragua and to reduce their military presence and training programs. This partially removed one of the possible provocations for an American intervention, but left Nicaragua to fend for itself.[28]

These feelings of defeatism, impending doom, and paranoia on the part of the Nicaraguan leadership eventually gave way to more reasoned assessments. The fear of a U.S. invasion was (and is) still present, but paralysis was replaced by preparations. The elements in the Sandinista plans to resist an American invasion include the following:[29]

1. Use the American threat as a means to rally Nicaraguan public opinion, unify the population behind the revolution, and call for greater popular efforts and sacrifices to repel a possible invasion.
2. Build up Nicaragua's defense forces by further increasing the size of the armed forces and the militia (which are already the largest and best equipped in Central America), and strengthen centralized and concentrated political controls.
3. Let the United States know how costly an intervention would be by stressing how stiff the resistance will be. To this end, the Nicaraguans revealed some of their defensive strategies. In addition, they emphasized their intention to fight to the bitter end, the fact that Nicaragua is much stronger and more heavily armed than Grenada had been, and that U.S. intervention would be bloody and prolonged—as opposed to the quick, surgical strike in Grenada. Their intention was to convince the United States that an invasion of Nicaragua would require far more patience and commitment on the part of American public opinion than is likely to be forthcoming.
4. Step up the propaganda war internationally with special emphasis on the United States. This includes reestablishing good relations with the Socialist International (which had become disillusioned with Nicaragua) and activating the revolution's friends and supporters in the United States to write letters, sway public opinion, and support alternative peace plans which, if adopted, would at least allow the revolution to survive.
5. Avoid antagonizing the United States. This message was conveyed forcefully to the Sandinistas by Castro himself, i.e., maintain a low profile for the time being. As a result, a substantial number of Cubans were removed from Nicaragua. Such a strategy would seem to indicate that the Sandinistas should become more conciliatory and allow a certain degree of domestic liberalization. The problem, as both the Sandinistas and the Americans know, is that these steps might produce an independent dynamic of their own that could undermine the revolution and its leadership—and still not satisfy the Americans.

There can be no doubt that the Grenada intervention greatly increased U.S. pressure on Nicaragua. It gave the United States an immense amount of renewed leverage in determining the fate and ultimate direction of the Nicaraguan revolution. Essentially, the Nicaraguan response has been to augment preparations for a possible invasion and to step up its propaganda war while seeking to avoid provocation. The Nicaraguans have reassessed their situation. The early effect of the intervention was very sobering, but the shock has worn off. There is still fear of a U.S.-sponsored invasion in one of several forms—directly, by the *contras*, with CONDECA, or a combination of all three—but several members of the Sandinista leadership are no longer certain of an intervention. They are perfectly aware that U.S. public opinion will not support a foreign quagmire such as Vietnam or Lebanon for a long period of time (as distinct from the "quick and clean" operation in Grenada). They know that Congress and U.S. foreign policy agencies are divided, and they know that the U.S. Department of Defense is extremely reluctant to become involved in another imbroglio where goals are not clearly defined, the public is not supportive, and becoming bogged down would reflect adversely on the military itself.

Nevertheless, a certain sense of fatalism and despair has set in among the Nicaraguan leadership. The revolution has not produced the glorious results expected. The economy is a disaster; the country is beginning to fragment and polarize; the opposition is growing; and the Americans might well strangle the revolution. Policy has reached a dead-end. Many Sandinistas have decided they were far happier as triumphant guerrillas than with the far more complex, less glorious, even boring task of governing. No matter what they do, the revolution does not seem to be working. They are damned if they liberalize and open up the country, and damned if they go further toward full-fledged Marxism-Leninism of the Cuban variety. Tomas Borge of the Sandanista junta has said privately that no matter what they do, the Americans will not allow their revolution to survive. In short, the Sandinistas are convinced that their revolution is in grave trouble.[30]

CONCLUSIONS AND IMPLICATIONS

The fact that Grenada has faded from the American news and public consciousness does not mean it has been forgotten by foreign policy analysts. Throughout the world—particularly in Central America and the Caribbean, the Soviet bloc, and the United States—analyses of the implications of Grenada are ongoing. My own assessment is that the Grenada intervention had far greater implications internationally than the small size or importance of that particular island would seem to indicate.

However, it is not likely that Grenada was a watershed in the sense that some enthusiasts have written. I do not believe that Grenada shows that the United States has definitely overcome the Vietnam syndrome, that it has surmounted its foreign policy divisions, or that it will now be prepared to act decisively in other areas where its basic interests are affected. There is some truth in these claims, but it is not likely that things have changed all that much.

Similarly, we must distinguish between interventions in small islands and interventions in mainland countries. These might be designated as "models." The first the "Santo Domingo model," and the second is the "Vietnam model" (after the two major U.S. military interventions of the 1960s). In the first paradigm, of which Grenada is a recent illustration, it is possible to move in quickly, isolate and defeat the resistance, form a provisional government, and withdraw quickly, all of which are elements of a "successful" intervention. But in a mainland country such as Vietnam or Nicaragua, matters are not so easy. Guerrilla forces cannot be isolated and pinned down so easily. Rather than face defeat they may flee into a neighboring country, and the invading forces would then have to bomb their sanctuaries, etc. In this event, the United States would have a "second Vietnam" on its hands. The distinction between Santo Domingo and Vietnam, or between Grenada and Nicaragua, is carefully kept in mind in Department of Defense contingency planning. This is why we should not expect Grenada-like invasions on the mainland of Central America—although that possibility cannot be ruled out entirely.

We must further distinguish between countries. In Nicaragua, which displayed an acute sense of paranoia and had long expected a U.S. invasion, the effect of Grenada was electric. In Cuba, which has been living with the threat of American intervention for a full quarter century, the invasion of Grenada undoubtedly has caused fears, but the Cuban leadership probably does not believe it will be invaded in the foreseeable future. The Grenada intervention had a galvanizing effect on Suriname, and while it had little immediate effect on the guerrillas in El Salvador, it did prompt a change in tactics.

Nevertheless, there are considerable clues that the Grenada intervention had significant long-term implications for guerrilla and revolutionary forces in Central America and the Caribbean Basin. The evidence is still fragmentary, but it seems to point to the following implications which add up in an especially significant manner.

1. Though the immediate effects on El Salvador were not marked, the Grenada intervention appears to have prompted the guerrillas into a long-term reassessment. The guerrillas now appear to realize that they underestimated the strength of the Salvadoran army, underestimated the resiliency of Salvadoran society, overestimated the degree of support for their cause by the Salvadoran people, underestimated the will and staying power of the United States, underestimated Mr. Duarte and the importance of elections and a legitimated Salvadoran government, and overestimated their own possibilities. Hence they are "hunkered" in for a long struggle which they may not win, and which might lead to a certain atrophy and isolation of their struggle.[31]
2. Cuba is also taking stock. Although there is much rhetorical flourish to the contrary, some reports indicate that Castro has concluded that socialism will not soon triumph anywhere else in Central America and that he has already begun to pull back his forces.[32] If this is so, Cuba might begin to look elsewhere for the furtherance of "proletarian internationalism."
3. The Nicaraguan revolution has become somewhat immobilized in a bunker mentality and is facing frustration or defeat on all sides. This might well lead to diminished Nicaraguan (and Cuban) support for the guerrillas in El Salvador and significantly reduced efforts to spread the Nicaraguan revolution to other countries.[33]
4. There are signs that the Soviet Union is reassessing its options as well. Historically, Latin America has not been a high-priority area for the Soviets. At little or no cost, they have made gains by catching plums that fall into their lap. But aside from their close relationship with Cuba, they have not been willing to commit major resources to the region. The Soviets are not looking for a major confrontation with the United States in the Caribbean. The invasion of Grenada coupled with the U.S. military buildup in the area might influence the Soviets to look elsewhere for targets of opportunity. This would be consistent with Leninist principles concerning the need to constantly probe for soft spots, a long history of cautious Soviet involvement

> in the Third World, and a quiet assessment of what they can reasonably expect to accomplish.[34]

It is not entirely clear that the Grenada intervention was an unadulterated defeat for the Soviet Union. The Soviets and Cubans have reaped some propaganda advantages from the invasion. Moreover, the Soviets do not suffer long from pique or guilt. They will reassess and try again. In this sense, Grenada might be seen as only a temporary setback for the Soviets. It also might lead the Soviets to conclude that the United States has raised the costs of Soviet adventurism in Central America and the Caribbean to a level they are unwilling to pay. Hence they might opt to look to other areas for opportunities to expand their influence. The Grenada intervention might have been a significant triumph for American foreign policy in the Western Hemisphere, but it did not in any significant way reduce the overall strength and reach of the Soviet Union or its capacity to look for advantages in other areas where the United States seems less heavily committed.

NOTES

1. Merle Fainsod, *Smolensk Under Soviet Rule* (Cambridge: Harvard University Press, 1958); Fainsod, *How Russia is Ruled* (Cambridge: Harvard University Press, 1953).

2. Howard Wiarda, "Soviet Policy in the Caribbean and Central America: Opportunities and Constraints." Paper presented at a conference on Soviet Foreign Policy, The Kennan Institute of Advanced Russian Studies, Woodrow Wilson International Center for Scholars, and the United States Information Agency, Washington, D.C., March 2, 1984; forthcoming in a volume entitled *Soviet Foreign Policy*, edited by Helmut Sonnenfeldt. This paper contains considerably greater detail on each of the themes mentioned—Soviet capabilities, tactics, and constraints.

3. As of April 1984, the U.S. Government had released several series of documents captured in Grenada cited here as the Grenada Documents. The documents consist of New Jewel Movement Politbureau and Central Committee minutes, secret agreements with communist countries, letters, diaries, personal papers, and letters from the Grenadian embassies in Moscow and Havana, etc. Most of the documents have been logged but not necessarily properly sorted. Some are unnumbered and others are illegible; others have yet to be released.

A preliminary evaluation was published by the Departments of State and Defense on December 16, 1983 entitled *Grenada: A Preliminary Report*. Michael Ledeen of the Georgetown University Center for Strategic and International Studies is editing another volume of documents soon to be published.

4. The information in this part of the paper derives from a conference on "The Orchestration of Soviet Proxy Assets: The Case of Latin America and the Caribbean," The Hoover Institution, Washington, D.C., June 13, 1984, the presentations and papers of which are forthcoming in a book to be published by the Hoover Institution.

5. The best analysis is Ernest Evans, "Revolutionary Movements in Central America: The Development of a New Strategy," in Howard J. Wiarda (ed.), *Rift and Revolution: The Central American Imbroglio* (Washington, D.C.: American Enterprise Institute for Public Policy Research, 1984), pp. 167–193.

6. Jiri and Virginia Valenta, "Leninism in Grenada," *Problems of Communism* (July-August 1984); *see also* Confidential report on Grenada's Relations with the USSR, July 11, 1983, Grenada Documents, Log No. W.

7. Memo from Bernard Bourne [Minister-Counsellor of the Grenadian Embassy in Moscow] to Comrade Maurice Bishop, Chairman of the Central Committee of the New Jewel Movement, June 30, 1982, Grenada Documents, Log. No. 104262; *see also* Jorge Dominguez, "Cuba's Relations with Caribbean and Central American Countries" in Alan Adelman and Reid Reading (eds.), *Confrontation in the Caribbean Basin* (Pittsburgh: Center for Latin American Studies, University of Pittsburgh, 1984), pp. 165–202.

8. The full impact of Cuba's role can only be appreciated by a full reading of the Grenada documents. See especially the minutes of NJM Politburo and Central Committee meetings.

9. *See,* for example, Top Secret Agreement on Cooperation between the New Jewel Movement of Grenada and the Communist Party of the Soviet Union, July 27, 1982, Grenada Documents, Log No. 102318; and Henry Feuer, "Was Bishop a Social Democrat?" *Caribbean Review* (March 1974), pp. 37–39.

10. Confidential report from the Grenadian Embassy in Moscow on the NJM's Relations with the CPSU, undated (but sometime after December 1981), Grenada Documents, Log No. 012329; handwritten notes from meeting between Hudson Austin and the Cuban Minister of Construction, ibid., Log No. 10003; Secret Cooperation and Exchange Plan between the Communist Party of Cuba and the New Jewel Movement of Grenada for the 1983 Period, ibid., Log No. 100016; and Meeting with [East German] Deputy Minister of Foreign Affairs (Latin America and Caribbean) V. Neugebanck, May 18, 1983, ibid., Log No. 102855.

11. Emergency SI [Socialist International] Meeting in Panama, memo from Unison Whiteman to NJM leadership of March 3, 1981, ibid., Log No. NM; unsigned analysis of SI Presidium Meetings in Bonn, April 1–2, 1982, ibid., Log No. NN; and Report on Meeting of SI held in Bonn, April 1–2, 1982, by Ferris Augustine, High Commissioner, to Foreign Minister Unison Whiteman, ibid., Log No. OO.

12. Report to the Politburo Meeting, March 29, 1983, from Unison Whiteman on attempts to influence U.S., British, and Canadian public opinion, ibid., Log No. 2.

13. Letter headed "Dear Maurice" from Gail Reed advising Bishop on tactics to use with the press and other organizations during his visit to the United States, ibid., Log No. DD.

14. Minutes of the Politburo meeting of October 21, 1981, ibid., Log No. B.

15. Unsigned, untitled report on the SI from a Leninist perspective, ibid., Log No. UU. Report on Meeting of Secret Regional Caucus of SI [Socialist International] Held in Managua, January 6–7, 1983, ibid., Log No. 100446.

16. Portion of a handwritten note from Major Roberts concerning observers to be sent to the Nicaraguan war, ibid., undated, Log No. 000084.

17. Letter from Nicaraguan Minister of Defense Humberto Ortega Saavadera to Comrade Maurice Bishop, February 19, 1981, ibid., Log. No. X.

18. *Foreign Broadcast Information Service*, October 28, 1983; and *The New York Times*, October 27, 1983.

19. FBIS, *Defense and Foreign Affairs Daily*, October 28, 1983, 46–47.

20. FBIS, *Defense and Foreign Affairs Daily*, October 21, 1983. Note that this report is dated *before* the Grenada intervention.

21. FBIS, *Latin American Index*, July 15, 1984; and *FBIS*, October 28, 1983.

22. *The Washington Post*, March 31, 1984; and *Los Angeles Times*, October 28, 1983.

23. The material in this section was based in part on interviews with U.S. intelligence officials; also see the papers prepared as part of the Hoover Institution study mentioned in note 4.

24. Based on press accounts of interviews with the guerrillas, for example, *Washington Post*, October 31, 1983, and May 14, 1984.

25. *See* especially the report from Havana by Edward Cody, *Washington Post*, March 18, 1984. The strongest case for a negotiated settlement is Robert Leiken's Introduction in *Central America: Anatomy of Conflict* (New York: Pergamon Press, 1984). This position was set forth by Leiken before it became, for other reasons, the strategy of the guerrillas. For the problems and traps in such a policy see the discussion in U.S. Congress, House, Committee on Foreign Affairs, Foreign Assistance Legislation for Fiscal Year 1985 (Part 6): Hearings and Markup before the Committee on Foreign Affairs and its Subcommittee on Western Hemisphere Affairs. *Review of Proposed Economic and Security Assistance Requests for Latin America and the Caribbean; Recommendations of the National Bipartisan Commission on Central America* (Washington, D.C.: Government Printing Office, 1984) pp. 213–214.

26. Quoted in Cody, op. cit. The same position was set forth by Fidel Castro in his interview with Tad Szulc, *Parade*, April 1, 1984.

27. See Ms. McGrory's column in the *Washington Post*, November 28, 1983.

28. *Soviet World Outlook* (November 15, 1983); *International Outlook* (November 28, 1983).

29. Based on Reports from Nicaragua in the *Washington Post*, October 27, 1983, October 31, 1983, November 12, 1983, and in *The New York Times*, November 10, 1983, November 24, 1983, and November 25, 1983.

30. Based on interviews by U.S. Department of State officials with the Sandanista leadership in April-May 1984.

31. Based on interviews by the author with U.S. intelligence officials during June-July 1984.

32. *Washington Post*, October 30, 1983 and March 18, 1984; *Economist*, January 14, 1984; *World Press Review*, March 1984; and *El Pais*, December 5, 1983.

33. This is one of the bargaining chips Nicaragua has in its renewed efforts to open negotiations with the United States.

34. W. Raymond Duncan, "Soviet Interests in Latin America: New Opportunities and Old Constraints," *Journal of Interamerican Studies and World Affairs*, May 1984; R. Osgood, "Central America in U.S. Containment Policy," in A.F. Lowenthal

and S.F. Wells (eds.), *Working Papers*, (Washington, D.C.: Latin American Program, Wilson Center, 1983; and *Washington Post*, May 28, 1984.

The author would like to acknowledge the assistance of Janine T. Perfit who aided enormously with the research. Dr. Iêda Siqueira Wiarda and Professor Richard M. Millett offered useful comments on an earlier version. Some of the analyses in this paper were based on classified materials made available on a not-for-direct-attribution basis, and on interviews with U.S. intelligence officers, also on a not-for-attribution basis.

RICHARD L. MILLETT

Comments

Before 1979, considering the impact of events in Grenada on Central America would have been an absurdity. Ties between the islands of the Caribbean and Central America were almost nonexistant. The major point of contact, Belize, only served to emphasize the differences between the two regions. Yet in July 1980, two of the three heads of state present at Nicaragua's celebration of the first anniversary of the Sandinista revolution were from Caribbean Community and Common Market (CARICOM) nations: George Price of Belize and Maurice Bishop of Grenada. Prime Minister Bishop played a major role in establishing contacts between Central America and the Caribbean, but the actual significance of this development and the impact of the intervention on Central American-Caribbean relations remains difficult to assess.[1]

In examining the links between Grenada and Central America, a few basic facts should be kept in mind. The New Jewel Movement (NJM) took power in Grenada over four months before the Sandinista triumph in Nicaragua. Grenada was the second nation to grant diplomatic recognition to the Sandinista provisional government and it played a leading role in advocating the Sandinista cause at the June 1979 emergency meeting of the Organization of American States (OAS) on the Nicaraguan crisis. The role of most CARICOM nations at this meeting was relatively muted, although Jamaica also sympathized with the Sandinistas. Finally, Cuba assisted the Grenadians by serving as a major source of information on Central America; it helped Grenada to establish contacts with its neighbors to the West, and acted as something of a guide to the thicket of Central American politics.

For both the NJM and the Sandinistas, relations with Cuba were of central importance. Cuba served as a link between Nicaragua and Grenada and helped shape Grenada's attitudes toward events throughout Central America. Some of Grenada's relations in the region were personal, such as those between Bishop and Fidel Castro. Grenada's ties to Nicaragua, however, were more historic, dating back to Castro's support for the nascent Sandinista National Liberation Front (FSLN) in the early 1960s and the training that many Nicaraguan commanders received in Cuba. In both Grenada and Nicaragua, there was a marked tendency to look to Cuba for leadership in foreign affairs, to support Cuban foreign policy initiatives in international forums, and to praise Cuban accomplishments in domestic speeches and publications.[2]

Grenada, Nicaragua, and Cuba also shared a common perception that the United States was their principal external enemy. This sentiment existed during the Carter administration, but was strengthened considerably after the election of Ronald Reagan. American support for counterrevolutionary activities in Nicaragua and the Reagan administration's repeated verbal attacks on Cuban and Soviet influence in Grenada convinced Grenada that the United States was plotting its overthrow. This stimulated somewhat closer ties with both Cuba and Nicaragua and a renewed emphasis on the threat posed by "U.S. imperialism." In a July 1981 letter to Daniel Ortega, Bishop stressed that the United States had "decided to make an all-out onslaught on our two revolutions." He added that "the propaganda war, the economic aggression, the political and industrial destabilization and the threat of mercenary invasion all lead to the unmistakeable conclusion that imperialism has decided to attempt to overthrow our popular revolutions this year."[3]

Both Grenada and Nicaragua tried to use the American media to portray a favorable image of their revolutions. At the same time, they used their own medias to portray the United States as responsible for virtually all domestic problems, and to rally the population against the threat of direct intervention. Grenada clearly had less success than Nicaragua in both areas. The American media had little interest in a small island that most of the U.S. population could not have located on a map. Internally, Grenada lacked the past history of U.S. intervention and national resistance that influenced Nicaraguan opinion so heavily. Furthermore, no matter how they tried, the NJM leadership could never prove that there were ties between the former Grenadian dictatorship and the United States such as those that existed between the Somoza dictatorship and the United States.

Grenadian-Nicaraguan relations excepted, direct Grenadian ties with Central America were very limited. Diplomatic relations were maintained with Panama through the Grenadian Ambassador to Cuba, and there were limited ties with Belize.[4] (Appendix A, Document 19) Most of the other Central American nations were included in a list of "countries with which Grenada does not wish to develop close relations."[5] (Appendix A, Document 19) There was little trade or other direct contact with these nations, and as a result, most of Grenada's relations with Central America were conducted through international bodies such as the United Nations, the OAS, and the Socialist International (SI). The NJM placed considerable stress on the correctness of its verbal and voting position with these bodies. It characterized the El Salvador government as "a genocidal regime backed solely by U.S. imperialism and devoid of any internal base," and declared that "the true and authentic representative of the Salvadoran people is the Frente Democrático Revolucionario (FDR)."[6] (Appendix A, Document 19) This simplistic formulation reflects Grenada's isolation from Central American realities, the influence of Cuba, Nicaragua, and the USSR on its foreign policy, and its almost desperate need to demonstrate its revolutionary credentials. The latter was probably most important to the NJM, for Grenada's attitude on questions such as the civil war in El Salvador would have a greater impact on Soviet and Cuban perceptions of Grenada than on the actual course of events in Central America.

While Grenada's direct links with Central America were few, the history of the Grenadian revolution as revealed in the documents captured in Grenada sheds important light on the internal processes of revolutionary groups in Central America and on Cuban and Soviet policies towards such movements. There are limits to this approach, however. Grenada is not Central America. The NJM did not come to power through a long guerrilla struggle, nor did it develop and cultivate an extensive international support network before the revolution. It also never faced the necessity of incorporating numerous, diverse non-Leninist elements into its leadership as the Sandinistas were compelled to do in Nicaragua. Finally, although beset by deep internal divisions, the NJM never had to contend with the coalition problems faced by the guerrillas in El Salvador or Guatemala who are divided into organizationally distinct bodies, united only through a loose and frequently strained coordinating body.

Grenada's international contest was also different. Despite strains, it never had the problems with its Caribbean neighbors that Nicaragua experienced in Central America. Indeed, efforts by the United States to separate Grenada from the rest of the English-speaking Caribbean were strongly resisted within the region and met with little success. The lack of contiguous borders, the absence of active counterrevolutionary groups in neighboring nations, and the good fortune of not having to deal with the Central American tradition of seeking to subvert nearby governments with differing ideologies made Grenada's international context quite distinct from that of Nicaragua or El Salvador.

The Grenada documents provide useful insights into the efforts of revolutionary groups to influence international organizations such as the Socialist International. Most revealing in this regard is the report of the Secret Regional Caucus of revolutionary groups held in Managua in January 1983 with the avowed purpose of manipulating the SI. The attendees classified the leaders of the SI into friends and enemies, and their efforts to avoid any criticism of the Soviet Union and Cuba demonstrate the fact that revolutionary groups such as the NJM and the Sandinistas have limited ideological affinity for democratic socialism and give a much greater allegiance to revolutionary Leninism.[7] (Appendix A, Document 24)

The documents also reveal how the Soviets deal with new Third World revolutionary governments and, conversely, how such governments seek to influence Soviet policies and curry Soviet favor. What emerges from many of these documents is a picture of the NJM seeking to involve the relatively cautious Soviets more deeply in Grenadian affairs by using every opportunity to demonstrate its ideological reliability and international utility. The prevailing image is that Grenada sought more military equipment than even the Soviets were willing to provide; it attempted to establish even closer party-to-party and state-to-state ties with the socialist community; and ultimately it was concerned with its orthodoxy and acceptability to the communist world.[8] (Appendix A, Document 6) While direct evidence is lacking, it is quite possible that Nicaragua pursued a somewhat similar course. This would help explain, for example, the growing Nicaraguan desire for advanced fighter aircraft in the face of obvious Soviet and Cuban reluctance to proceed with such deliveries. It would also explain Nicaraguan voting behavior at various international forums and the constant visits of high-ranking Nicaraguan officials to the Soviet Union and other East bloc nations.

Another fact that emerges from the documents is the tendency of revolutionary governments to have an exaggerated vision of their own importance and to compete with similar governments for prestige and influence. Grenada's ability to compete on a world scale was severely limited, and therefore it placed its emphasis on regional politics, especially in the Caribbean. Grenada saw itself as a regional leader shaping OAS policy toward the Caribbean, countering U.S. policy and eventually even exercising influence on Belize and Suriname in order to bring them more into line with Soviet/Cuban objectives.[9] (Appendix A, Document 6)

The Grenada documents also provide confirmation of the preoccupation of Leninist regimes with securing armaments. The Soviets and their allies seemed much more able and willing to supply weapons and uniforms to Grenada than any form of viable economic assistance. While the NJM had only minimal impact on Central America during its rule, its overthrow had a far greater impact. Critics of Reagan administration policies were often quick to draw parallels between events in Grenada and those in Central America, seeing the Grenada invasion as a "dress rehearsal" for similar events in Nicaragua or El Salvador.[10] More temperate critics refrained from predicting an imminent invasion, but declared that the intervention reflected preference for military solutions in Central America.[11] However, there have not been any U.S. actions in Central America similar to the Grenada intervention since October 1983. It has become increasingly obvious that military intervention in Central America is not likely, for conditions in Central America and the Caribbean Basin are quite distinct. Intervention in Nicaragua or El Salvador would be far more difficult than it was in Grenada. It would cost more lives and arouse much greater opposition both domestically and from the international community.[12] The post-Grenada debates in the UN and the OAS demonstrated that Latin American sensitivities to American military actions remain very high. Accordingly, it is highly unlikely that the OAS would ever provide a legitimizing cover for U.S. military actions in Central America as the Organization of East Caribbean States (OECS) did in Grenada.

While the United States has undertaken no Grenada-like operation in Central America since October 1983, the effect of the invasion has been significant in certain nations. In Nicaragua, it produced considerable confusion in the Sandinista leadership and discredited the position allegedly advocated by Foreign Minister Miguel D'Escoto that the U.S. was too internally divided and too paralyzed by memories of Vietnam to intervene in the region.[13] It also made clear the inability and unwillingness of Cuba and the Soviet Union to protect Nicaragua from U.S. intervention. In their messages of congratulations on the fifth anniversary of the Sandinista revolution, both the USSR and Cuba pointedly omitted any commitment of support for Nicaragua. Instead, they stressed the need to avoid unnecessarily antagonizing the United States, thus depriving it of an excuse for military intervention. Following the Grenada intervention, Nicaragua adopted a somewhat more conciliatory approach to the Contadora process. It sped up its timetable for domestic elections, and took great pains to deny the existence of Soviet or Cuban military bases on Nicaraguan territory.

In El Salvador, the most notable effect of the invasion was a much greater emphasis in guerrilla propaganda about the threat of direct U.S. military intervention and the need for protracted fighting before victory could be achieved. This may have been a serious tactical error on the guerrilla's part since it is not the approach one should take to persuade peasants to join guerrilla ranks; nor does it actually encourage faith in ultimate victory. Whether or not Grenada had any impact on the guerrilla's decision to accept President Duarte's offer to meet with them in October 1984 is virtually impossible to determine.

At least as important as the reaction of the Central American left to the invasion of Grenada was the reaction of those on the center and the right. The Grenada intervention raised their hopes that the United States would overthrow the Sandinistas and bring them to power. This exaggerated their already strong tendency to look for salvation from the United States, to strive to make themselves acceptable to the White House (more than to their own people), and to emphasize and exaggerate the Soviet-Cuban presence in Nicaragua and the extent of domestic opposition to the Sandinistas.[14] The net effect of these tendencies has been harmful to both their own interests and those of the United States.

Among the armed forces of Honduras, El Salvador, and Guatemala, the Grenada intervention increased confidence in the reliability of the United States as an ally and reinforced the belief that a military solution was possible in Central America.[15] For those involved in efforts to find a peaceful solution in Central America through the Contadora process, the invasion gave them a greater sense of urgency—sense that time might be running out on efforts to avert a regional conflict.[16]

No final assessment of the impact of the Grenada events is yet possible. There have been some positive results in Central America such as increased American credibility, a lessened fear of Cuban and Soviet power in the region, and at least the possibility of greater flexibility on the part of leftist forces to negotiate political solutions. On the other hand, the invasion might have increased the tendency of many groups, most notably the Nicaraguan opposition, to rely too heavily on the United States. The invasion also might have produced a mood of increased intransigence among elements on the far right, and it is possible it convinced extremist elements among the Sandinistas and the Salvadoran left that armed conflict with the United States is inevitable.

The United States must be careful in assessing the impact of Grenada on Central America. We have a tendency to hear what we want to hear from such regions. We emphasize increased regional confidence in the United States and filter out related messages of increased dependency and a growing tendency by some regional actors to see their major task as promoting a Grenada-style U.S. involvement in Central America. Signs of increased flexibility on the left are easily exaggerated, while contrary efforts to mobilize conflict and seek closer military ties with Cuba and the USSR are not given sufficient weight. It is often hard to distinguish changes in tactics from changes in basic strategy on the part of the left.

In the aftermath of the Grenada intervention, the United States must determine the message it wants to send to Central America and distinguish it from the messages that are being perceived in the region. Care must be taken not to confuse our reliability as an ally with any desire to produce client states. It must be clear that the United States has no interest in supporting one minority faction against another and that the fervent embrace of a variety of U.S. policy goals is not the sole criteria for American support and assistance. In this regard, a true hands-off approach to the governance of Grenada would have a most positive impact. It must be clear that the United States will support regional self-defense efforts. However, the Reagan administration should also make it clear that U.S. support should not be considered a substitute for such efforts, and that American policy is designed to supplement not minimize local costs for defense. Finally, it must be clear that the military option is neither desired by the United States, nor inevitable. If a military solution in Central America is perceived as desired U.S. policy, then the right will do everything possible to bring it about. Likewise, if conflict is perceived as inevitable, then the left has no incentive to reach a political solution. Naturally, such perceptions have a great deal to do with how the invasion of Grenada is perceived in Central America, and in the long run they will have a far greater impact on the region than the actual invasion itself.

NOTES

1. For a study of ties between Central America and the CARICOM nations, see Richard Millett, "Central America and the Caribbean: An Emerging Relationship," in Ulrich Fanger, et al. (eds.), *Problems of Caribbean Development* (Munich: Wilhelm Fink Verlag, 1982), pp. 77–90.

2. For an example of Grenadian dependence on Cuba in international forums *see* Report on the General Congress of the World Center for the Resistance of Imperialism, Zionism, Racism and Reaction, Grenada Documents, Log. No. 103025.

3. Letter from Maurice Bishop to Daniel Ortega, July 17, 1981, ibid., Log. No. C-1.

4. Foreign Relations Report and List of Countries with which Grenada Does Not Wish to Develop Close Relations, ibid., undated (but probably published in 1981) Log No. 105757.

5. Ibid.

6. Ibid.

7. Report on Meeting of Secret Regional Caucus of SI [Socialist International] Held in Managua, January 6–7, 1983, ibid., Log No. 100446; Report on SI Committee for Latin America and the Caribbean, August 1983, ibid., Log. No. 104403; Report on Meeting of SI Committee for the Defense of the Nicaraguan Revolution, June 1981, ibid., Log No. 105352; and Foreign Minister Unison Whiteman to NJM Leadership, March 3, 1981, ibid., Log No. MM.

8. Examples abound in the Grenada documents. *See* Confidential report on Grenada's Relations with the USSR, from Grenadian Ambassador to Moscow, W. Richard Jacobs, to Foreign Minister Unison Whiteman, Prime Minister Bishop, Deputy Prime Minister Coard, and Politburo Member Ewert Layne, July 11, 1983, ibid., Log No. W; and Confidential report from the Grenadian Embassy in Moscow on the NJM's Relations with the CPSU, undated (but probably sometime after December 1981), ibid., Log No. 102329.

9. Foreign Relations Report, op. cit.; and Grenada's Relations with the USSR, op. cit.

10. For example see the full page advertisement in *The New York Times* headed "Grenada Was a Dress Rehearsal," *The New York Times* November 13, 1983, p. 33.

11. Wayne S. Smith, "The Grenada Complex in Central America," *Caribbean Review* (Fall, 1983), pp. 34–35.

12. For a detailed study of the costs of a U.S. intervention in Central America, see Theodore Moran, "The Cost of Alternative U.S. Policies Toward El Salvador," in Robert Leiken, *Central America: Anatomy of a Conflict* (New York: Pergamon Press, 1984), pp. 153–172.

13. Interviews in Mexico and Nicaragua, March 1984, and in Honduras and Costa Rica, July 1984.

14. Ibid.

15. Interviews with Honduran, Salvadoran, and Guatemalan military officers between November 1983 and July 1984.

16. Interviews in Mexico, March 1984, and in Colombia, August 1984.

ANTHONY P. MAINGOT

Grenada and the Caribbean: Mutual Linkages and Influences

On March 13, 1979 a group of 45 men took power on the island of Grenada. The active phase of the "Glorious Grenadian Revolution" lasted four hours and took the lives of two of former Prime Minister Gairy's defenders. According to Fidel Castro, it was "a big revolution in a small island."

In early 1979 the nature of the new regime was not defined. In Prime Minister Bishop's first address to the nation on March 13, he assured the people that "all democratic freedoms, including freedom of elections, religious and political opinion" would be restored.[1] The movement against Gairy had been broad-based and popular.[2] Three months after the coup, an experienced Caribbean observer reported that the new leadership had done nothing to dispel the notion that there would be a slow but definite return to democracy. He also reported on the Cuban and Guyanan arms and advisors already on the island. But even the Barbadian Prime Minister Tom Adams expressed relief that Grenada was "being run apparently without recourse to unnecessary ideology or in the interests of a foreign power." British and Canadian diplomats and Grenadian businessmen seemed to share this sanguine view of the future.[3]

On the other hand, Bishop's August 19, 1977 interview in the Cuban magazine *Bohemia* admitted that the New Jewel Movement (NJM) "began to develop along Marxist lines in 1974 when we began to study the theory of scientific socialism." He said that he and his followers had gone beyond the influence of U.S.-style Black Power to Third Worldism, to understanding the Cuban experience, and that the experiences of Guyana and Jamaica convinced them that socialism was "the only solution to our problem." This was about the time that the Trinidad branch of the NJM led by University of the West Indies lecturers Bernard Coard and Richard Jacobs, became an integral part of the movement. In university circles, both men generally were regarded as Marxist-Leninists.[4]

When U.S. Ambassador Frank Ortiz issued a warning on April 10, 1979 that the U.S. would "view with displeasure any tendency on the part of Grenada to develop closer ties with Cuba," the Bishop regime responded, "We would sooner give up our lives before we compromise, sell out, or betray our sovereignty."[5]

Without changing his nationalist tone, Bishop's speeches thereafter took on a strident anti-American flavor. In early June, after praising the help of Guyana, Jamaica, and his friends in Dominica and St. Lucia, his statement that the "internationalist approach that our country will increasingly be taking over the next few months and years"[6] was somewhat revealing. In July, he compared Grenada's struggles in education to the national liberation movements of Angola, Mozambique, and Guinea-Bissau.[7] Then came the Sandinista victory in Nicaragua, and from that point on, Bishop would refer to the Nicaraguan revolution as having had the greatest impact and influence on the island's revolutionary struggle.[8]

In February 1980, a group of Surinamese army sergeants brought parliamentary politics to an end, and their leader, Major Daysie Bouterse, soon began making radical leftist statements. Bourtese in fact described Bishop's Grenada as the best example of a true revolutionary regime.

On March 13, 1980 Grenadians celebrated the first anniversary of their revolution by hosting some 1,000 guests from 42 countries, with Jamaica's Michael Manley and Nicaragua's Daniel Ortega as honored guests.[9] Manley set the tone for the festivities by singling out for special praise and "a special place in the heart of every Caribbean man and woman who cherishes freedom, the incomparable Fidel Castro." Bishop followed by calling the Cuban leader a "living legend," a source of inspiration to all people "struggling for freedom and justice."[10] He proclaimed, "If there had been no Cuban revolution in 1959, there could have been no Grenadian revolution in 1979." The celebration ended with a rally headed by 15 speakers representing left and broadly-based progressive groups throughout the Caribbean, including representatives from Haiti, Puerto Rico, Guyana, Trinidad, Tobago, Jamaica, Barbados, Antigua, Dominica, St. Lucia, and St. Vincent.

The tone and direction of the People's Revolutionary Government (PRG) had been set, and their allies in the Caribbean identified with their cause. Bishop spoke of the coming nature of the political system when he described a future democracy that would be more than "putting an 'X'" for five seconds, every five years.

Those in the Caribbean who understood the nature of Leninist leadership—and there were few—appeared to have deciphered the nature of the PRG. In February 1979, the Bishop government intercepted a letter drawn up by British Dominican priests in Trinidad that was signed by Dominicans based in Grenada. The letter to fellow Dominicans in England, who had been in the forefront of the Christian-Marxist dialogue for the past 20 years, was an invitation to come to Grenada. "Many among you," the letter states, "are better read in Marxist ideology than any member of the People's Revolutionary Government."[11] They said the island was a "tiny but significant field of experiment to test their theories." The invitation was to "cooperate and assist" in the experiment since in the future they would have to "live and work in an increasingly Marxist Caribbean."

Whatever the role that the theology of liberation might have in Third World societies, it was clear from Bishop's response that his regime wanted none of it. He expressed himself as "shocked and disgusted" at these "carefully laid counterrevolutionary plans to sabotage the revolution." The clergy, he warned, should stick to their "traditional and perfectly acceptable role of Ministers of Religion."

The incident was a major indication of a central aspect of the new Grenadian elite's approach to revolution. They took their ideology very seriously; they had long prepared for their revolution, carefully planned its course, and were not about to engage in philosophical debates outside the inner circles of the party.

The central premise of this paper is that while the revolutionary process was fueled and initially sustained by a nationalistic and righteously indignant populace, the PRG elite was broadly Marxist with an inner core of determined Leninists.[12] (Appendix A, Document 1) State power and tactics dictated their actions, not Grenada's political culture and social structure. It was their intention to use the state to bring about social change in a society that they increasingly described as recalcitrantly conservative and petty bourgeois. They sincerely believed that their friends abroad would be of critical assistance in this enterprise.

The result was that national and international concerns and interests became intimately interrelated in the elite's beliefs and actions. They needed not merely formal relations—which they enjoyed with their neighbors from the beginning—but special "fraternal" relationships. The most central of these of course was to be with Cuba. Bishop made this clear for Grenada and others in an early speech in Havana: "We look to the people of Cuba, we look to your revolution and your leadership to ensure that the revolutionary process in the Caribbean and Central American region continues to go forward with strength."[13] From the very beginning, the NJM portrayed events in Grenada as part of a much wider process in the Caribbean. Therefore, Guyana and Jamaica were crucial to Grenada for material and moral support. Grenada in turn would serve as a model to the Eastern Caribbean. Hindsight reveals just how badly the Grenadians judged their society. The following will attempt to show how badly they judged the region as well.

GUYANA AND JAMAICA

In the early 1970s, Guyana took the leadership in many radical reforms in the Caribbean Basin. Its nationalization in July 1971 of the Demerara Bauxite Co. (DEMBA), a subsidiary of the Aluminum Company of Canada (ALCAN), contributed to legitimizing the idea of state ownership in the British Caribbean. "In that sense," a sympathetic Caribbean scholar wrote in 1974, "the nationalization signaled the initiation of a new wave of economic nationalism that is now sweeping the region from one end to the other."[14]

There were other signs that tended to show that Guyana was making a strong turn to the left. For one, it was Burnham who had taken the lead in the joint West Indian recognition of Cuba in 1971 and again in emphasizing a Third World, nonaligned stance. He was rewarded with visits by Castro, who heaped praise on his performance in the region, and with invitations to the USSR.

From a constitutional point of view, Burnham's shift was quite dramatic. The 1970 constitution contained very traditional and standard provisions on rights and responsibilities—and a reference to "reverence for the Deity"—while the 1980 Cooperative Republic Constitution declared the state to be "secular" and "in transition from capitalism to socialism." As stated in Chapter II, Article 15(1):

> The economy will develop in accordance with the economic laws of socialism on the foundation of socialist relations of production and development of the production forces.

All these changes were encouraging to those radicals who believed in state-directed change as the only way to transform basically unrevolutionary societies. This was precisely why such groups jumped at the Soviet approach to Third World development—the "noncapitalist path"[15]—that became the message of the Caribbean as stated in June 1975 at the Havana Conference of Communist and Workers' Parties of Latin America and the Caribbean. The Havana Declaration, wrote the influential Guyanese Marxist, Clive Y. Thomas, "virtually underwrites all the major proposition of the theory of non-capitalist development" and marks "a definite shift in emphasis in the struggle for decolonization and socialism in the Third World."[16] It accepts "national democracy" as a legitimate phase, both operationally and theoretically, in the transition to socialism and the dictatorship of the proletariat. Broad alliances of "progressive forces" rather than the leadership of "vanguard" parties were now acceptable, since the priority was no longer to enthrone socialism, but rather to engage in anti-feudal, anti-imperialist, and national democratic struggles.

This theory is so obviously political, so broad and flexible, it can serve multiple political purposes and parties, and this is precisely what happened in the Caribbean. The NJM, which previously cast its 1973 Manifesto as a progressive "nationalist" document, became eager to claim *post facto* that the noncapitalist path is precisely the objective that they sought to achieve in the 1973 Manifesto.[17]

This theory is exactly what Burnham needed, especially in preparation for his move against the powerful English Booker interests. He had not been getting support from Cheddi Jagan's pro-Soviet party. The People's Progressive Party (PPP) had been boycotting Parliament for two years, and radical intellectuals were organizing what would become the Workers' and People's Alliance.

In August 1975, Jagan and the PPP announced their stance of "critical support." Although charging that the People's National Congress (PNC) electoral victory was "stolen," and that "many evils like Booker's monopoly, erosion of fundamental rights, absence of democracy, discrimination, corruption, and squandermania still persist," Jagan concluded that the PNC's recent policies had weakened imperialism, and that the PPP should put an end to its boycott of Parliament. It was now Jagan's turn to shift positions:

> The situation now, therefore, demands a more flexible approach on the part of the PPP. . . . Our political line should be changed from non-cooperation and civil resistence to critical support. This can lay the basis for a political solution in our country.[18]

This "critical support" was the indicated political strategy of the "noncapitalistic path." It became a Caribbean-wide phenomenon.

Whatever the Grenadian reasons for using the noncapitalist model, it was clear that it could not have been a response to the same objective conditions that were present in Guyana. Guyana, as distinct from Grenada, had not one, but three "vanguard" parties. It was the Burnham and PNC's constant preoccupation to use every trick in the book to outmaneuver the others. Conversely, during the mid-1970s the charismatic Bishop had virtually no organized opposition.

With the PNC calling itself a vanguard party, with Burnham snugly entrenched as a major Third World leader enjoying the friendship of the Soviet Union and Cuba, with 80% of the economy in state hands, and with a new and convenient Constitution and no successful challenges to an electoral system that secured Burnham two-thirds majorities without fail, Jagan and the PPP seemed outmaneuvered and outwitted. When Burnham refused to proceed with major parts of the noncapitalist model and the creation of a National Front, Jagan decided that it was time to move to a more radical stance.

In an April 1977 meeting of the Caribbean communist parties that the PPP called a "turning point in the struggle of the region," the West Indian representatives cited events in Vietnam, Angola, Mozambique, Cambodia, and Guinea-Bissau as evidence that the correlation of forces in the world had changed. They now were in the epoch of transition from capitalism to socialism. Again, as was the case with the nationalizations of 1971, Guyana seemed to serve as a rallying point for West Indian Marxists. Again, the international machinery was brought into play to make up for the lack of a national movement. This was typical of the "transferrals" to be seen in Grenada as well.

National immobility is insignificant in the face of global developments. "We come here," noted Jamaica's Trevor Munroe, "under the inspiration, the guidance, the initiative of the PPP. We look to the Communist Movement in Guyana, for the movement of Marxism in Guyana has shown us how to fight."[19] It remained, of course, quite unclear exactly who they were going to fight. Burnham was visibly unperturbed and, if anything, politically more in control than ever.[20] But a leader like Burnham is not one to want enemies on all flanks, and soon thereafter the New Jewel Movement's coup in Grenada relieved him of considerable pressure.

Certainly, there was no love lost between Burnham and Gairy, but this personal antipathy was secondary to the benefits derived from a friendly Grenadian regime—one eagerly welcomed by Cuba and the radical network in the area. Given the political nature of this network, it was logical that every element of the Caribbean left harbored hopes of deriving specific benefits from the NJM's victory and rule. In Burnham's case, it was not simply a matter of keeping Cheddi Jagan in reign; he had already managed that quite adequately and consistently. It was the Workers' and People's Alliance (WPA)—the other vanguard party—that was worrisome. As Burnham's luck would have it, the WPA was virtually a carbon copy of the early NJM.

Fundamentally an intellectual movement which began in Jamaica and then gravitated to the University of Guyana, the WPA was rapidly developing into the main threat to Burnham's rule. Not only were they drawing on youth of the cities, they were also building an Indian-creole alliance not seen since the early days of the Jagan-Burnham coalition.[21]

The WPA's leadership was theoretically "collective," but its leader was indisputably Walter Rodney. Originally a radical Black Power advocate, Rodney's ideas evolved to incorporate virtually anything that challenged white capitalism. As he noted, he was "extending the definition of Black Power by indicating the nature of its opposite, 'White Power'." He illustrated this idea by citing Cuba as the only country in the West Indies and the Western hemisphere that had broken with white capitalism. He agreed with Stokely Carmichael that Fidel Castro was one of the blackest men in the Americas. "Other West Indian leaders on the other hand qualify as 'white'."[22]

Rodney had discovered and proven that race, not class or ideology, was the route to mass protest and action, and the initial spark now known as the "Rodney affair" perhaps can be considered the critical watershed of the 1960s and 1970s. Whatever the rationalization about being black or white, radical groups of every inclination began to utilize the approach throughout the Caribbean. Journals such as *Abeng* in Jamaica, *Moko* in Trinidad, and *Ratoon* in Guyana had similar styles and focuses though different ideological underpinnings.

Burnham's speedy move to assist the NJM—first with weapons and advisors, donations, rice, and then with diplomatic support—was a means of buying some protection. The point is, of course, that for the NJM elite, the situation in Guyana was profitable in other terms as well. The NJM utilized Burnham for the links he provided to the CARICOM states and to the nonaligned movement; they used Jagan for the links he provided to the socialist bloc; and they used both Burnham and Jagan to reinforce their ties with Cuba, which was in both the nonaligned and the socialist bloc. As cozy as this mutual exchange of benefits might have been, it was not devoid of contradictions. (Nothing in Caribbean politics ever has been.)

For one, there was the terrible dilemma that to the WPA, Burnham was the Gairy of Guyana. Part of its broad appeal had been similar to that of the pre-1979 New Jewel Movement in Grenada (e.g., the call for free and fair elections). As one of the WPA's leaders put it, "To us a socialism that is not democratic in content as well as form is not socialism at all. . . ." The call was for the right to strike, to publish, to assemble to hold free and fair elections"[23]—everything which by that time the New Jewel Movement had discarded as "bourgeois democracy." The contradictions between these two otherwise similar movements took a tragic turn when Walter Rodney died in a mysterious bomb explosion, pointing to a state-directed plot. With the area's radicals now vehemently anti-Burnham, the NJM kept a low profile and attempted to convert any occasion noting Rodney's death into an anti-imperialist statement.[24]

These conditions created an opportunistic and instrumental association—not the kind of cohesion necessary for region-wide concerted action. The reality is that the Caribbean always has been obfuscated by a veritable deluge of international rhetoric. Jamaica demonstrates this pattern as well.

If Burnham in Guyana and Eric Williams in Trinidad knew how to play the game of political survival with skill,[25] they were in strong competition with Jamaica's Michael Manley, a true virtuoso in what Rexford Tugwell once called the "art of politics." Though Manley received his political start by leading a "moderate" trade union movement during the early 1950s, he had been anything but politically predictable either in actions or in thought.

Under pressure from the "radical" wing of his People's National Party (PNP) which showed increased strength in the 1976 elections, Manley began radicalizing his rhetoric. The role of Cuba in that rhetoric was noticeable. As early as July 1975, his speeches not only had a strident pro-Cuban and anticapitalist tone, but an anti-American one as well. The United States, Manley told the Cubans, now finds itself "morally isolated."[26] Yet not two months after his return from Cuba in 1975, Manley lectured the National Executive Council of the PNP on the "vital matter of the difference between communism and socialism," noting that the two ideologies had "totally different" perspectives on a wide range of subjects and that the PNP was decidedly in favor of "democratic socialism."[27] When addressing North American audiences his tone was considerably more conciliatory, especially after mid-1977.[28]

Pushed on the left by one of the Caribbean's most important Marxist-Leninist theoreticians and leaders, Dr. Trevor Munroe, Manley managed to emerge from each confrontation within his party more radical but stronger. He had learned to assert and reassert the West Indian tradition of "one leader," which the masses believed was being challenged by the radicals. Never did Manley toy with anything as risky as "collective leadership." "Comrade Leader" Manley continually upheld what Archie Singham called the "hero and the crowd" characteristics of Jamaican and West Indian political culture.

It is precisely this characteristic that allowed Manley to carry out a virtually independent foreign policy with radical overtones even as he was keeping his party's left wing under "heavy manners," as West Indians would say. Like Burnham, however, Manley was not one to underestimate his opponents, and accordingly the goodwill of both Cuba and Grenada came in very handy. Even as he was expelling presumed communists from the PNP, he was extolling their virtues abroad. This ability to play both sides of the Cuban and Grenadian card was especially convenient since the Cubans did not seem to be put off by it (at least not publicly). Much less put off were the Grenadians, who were highly dependent on Manley, as they were to Burnham. Thus, the PNP—and by implication the system within which it functioned—continued to enjoy the support of the Cubans and Grenadians regardless of which way it played its cards.

Cuba's policy was to support friendly regimes no matter how these are opposed by domestic Marxist forces. In Cuban eyes, Jamaica and Guyana are no different from Spain, Peru, or Mexico in this regard. In exchange for this support, the Cubans hoped to benefit from Jamaica's and Manley's very real prestige in Third World circles and several developed nations as well. The Cubans have learned that it pays to support friendly noncommunist regimes rather than putting all their bets on small communist parties with little chance of coming to power. The theory of the noncapitalist stage of development provides a very adequate basis for such international flexibility. It is precisely this strategy of ideological and operational flexibility that the Grenadians benefitted from so royally.

To the Grenadians, Manley represented a respectability which, interestingly enough, stemmed to a large degree from the fact that he was a democratically-elected statesman. This status gave him standing with the Socialist International (of which he was a vice president) and among Latin American and North American democrats in general. Manley's prestige was such that his support for the Grenadian regime, his secret meetings in Managua on ways to influence the Socialist International[29] (Appendix A, Document 24), and his constant praising of Castro and Cuba as paragons of freedom did not seem to affect his international standing. But the contradictions and ironies of politics were bound to catch up with one even so skillful as Manley. On May 25, 1983 the Grenadian government announced the appointment of Jamaican Richard Hart as attorney general and director of public prosecutions.[30] He was also made Chairman of the New Constitution Commission (along with radical Trinidadian lawyer Allan Alexander). He was one of a rather large group of Jamaicans working for the PRG, and more specifically, say some, for the Leninist Coard faction. Their recognized leader was Trevor Munroe.[31] It appeared that Manley had an exposed flank, but strangely enough, it was in Grenada not Jamaica—a fact that one cannot take lightly given the West Indian sense of subtle and not so subtle historical ironies. The idea of Manley providing legitimacy to a regime that hires one of his old political (and presumably "class") enemies to write its constitution was regarded as a not so subtle irony to some, and poetic justice to others.

To a strict ideologue, and in terms of Marxist-Leninist theory, with its carefully delineated ontology of "stages," of party structures and world correlations, the broader Caribbean must have seemed a bewildering and chaotic scene. A Jamaican Social Democrat (and his national opponents), a Guyanese "cooperative" socialist (and his national enemies), and a Cuban communist all served as the pillars of a movement that was speedily admitted as a full member of the Socialist International. But even as handy a conceptual framework as the noncapitalist path of development could not long cover up the international and national tensions that naturally resulted from the above contradictions.

The Eastern Caribbean

West Indian scholars are apt to say that all the above is well and good, but what about the Eastern Caribbean which, after all, was the NJM's primary area of concern? Most importantly, do the countries of the Eastern Caribbean share a distinct political culture which naturally made the Grenada revolution a powerful model? The answer is both yes and no. There are strong cultural similarities between the countries of the Eastern Caribbean, but there is no evidence that they behaved any differently than other nations with regard to Grenada. The same factors of ideological commitment and instrumental support operate in the Eastern Caribbean as they do elsewhere.

By mid-1979, the leaders of the NJM were firmly in power, friend Fidel Castro was hosting the sixth summit conference of the nonaligned movement, and things seemed to be going their way. Certainly to Maurice Bishop, with solid support at home and flanked by his friends from Guyana and Jamaica, all indications were that they were living in a "changing world."[32] This was especially so as concerned the Caribbean. "We know," he told the Havana gathering, "that the balance of forces in the world is changing. We know that today there is being built a new Caribbean—Jamaica, Guyana, a new Grenada, Dominica, [etc.]. . . ." It is also correct that by mid-1979 the islands of the Eastern Caribbean had joined the ideological-political fray. What was not clear, however, was who was benefiting from these developments.

The May 1979 Memorandum on Economic Cooperation between Trinidad and Barbados demonstrated how these two islands perceived trends in the Eastern Caribbean. It called for close cooperation between oil-rich Trinidad and fast-growing Barbados in defense and security matters, in support of the University of the West Indies, and in energy. This was an obvious step to counter the activities of the radicals in the Eastern Caribbean who had been on the move for a decade. The radicals did not delay long in responding. The July 1979 Declaration of St. Georges (Grenada) signed by the Prime Ministers of Grenada, Dominica, and St. Lucia was supposed to herald a dramatic shift in the ideological orientation of the Eastern Caribbean. Bishop played the stellar role, closely followed by Deputy Prime Minister George Odlum of St. Lucia. The distant third was Oliver Seraphin of Dominica. Bishop and Odlum had previously revealed that they had met in the mid-1970s on Rat Island, off St. Lucia, to plan a revolutionary strategy for the Eastern Caribbean. This was a meeting of Marxists among which Trevor Munroe of Jamaica was the most influential.[33] Out of that meeting came the various "forums" (i.e., Marxist discussion groups) that operated in each island. From his position at the University of the West Indies and his "loyal opposition" to Manley's government, Munroe established himself as the preeminent theoretician of the left in the area. He continued as something of a mentor to the Grenadian Leninists to the bitter end, but publicly it was the signatories of the Declaration of St. Georges that stole the limelight.

The first test of their powers came in St. Vincent where the aging veterans of the decolonization process were pitted against the young middle-class radical intelligentsia. The election was originally judged a toss-up between divided traditional forces—Milton Cato's St. Vincent Labour Party, "Son" Mitchell's New Democratic Party (NDP), and Ebenezer Joshua's People's Political Party (all three figures were past premiers of the island)—and the radical forces recently united under the banner of the United People's Movement (UPM). This coalition joined a social democratic party (People's Democratic Movement) with two others professing "scientific socialism," ARWEE and YULIMO.

YULIMO was led by a white Vincentian, Dr. Ralph Gonsalves, of the University of the West Indies campus in Barbados. An intense and attractive public speaker, Gonsalves projected the values and ideology of the new middle class radicals of the region. They were impatient with parliamentary structures and procedures, moved by a profound conviction that they could provide better leadership than the old guard, and convinced that history was on their side.

The election results, however, indicated that Vincentians were not yet ready for what Dr. Gonsalves called "a broad theoretical programme of socialist orientation." Cato's Labour Party won 11 of 13 seats, and ex-Premier "Son" Mitchell's NDP won the remaining two. Moreover, Cato had campaigned on virtually one theme: "Stem the leftist tide." It paid off—and not merely electorally. Immediately after the Cato victory, an incident took place which held great significance for the future of the Eastern Caribbean. An uprising of Rastafarians on one of St. Vincent's Grenadine islands (Union Island) occasioned the intervention of a contingent of Barbadian police. Cato had requested them, fearing that it was a diversion from an impending coup attempt in St. Vincent. The first intra-Caribbean intervention in history had taken place.

Events in the other islands also showed that the euphoria surrounding the St. George's Declaration was already on the wane. In Dominica, Prime Minister Seraphin began to moderate his statements and court U.S. investments. In St. Lucia, there developed a most promising prospect for the left—a real split between Prime Minister Louisy and Deputy Prime Minister

Odlum. On the surface the split had to do with the Louisy government's harder line toward the Rastafarians and other dissident groups, but in fact it was a power struggle, with Louisy apparently refusing to turn over the government to the radical wing per a secret but widely known understanding.

The defeat of Odlum and the radical wing in St. Lucia illustrated the complexities of West Indian societies, and the difficulties of revolutionary transformation in the Caribbean. There is good evidence that Odlum attempted to gain support among the youth by displaying strong support for St. Lucia's Rastafarians. Unfortunately for Odlum, his Grenadian allies were just then launching an offensive against their own Rastafarians and this cost him dearly.[34] Beginning in mid-1981, the documents of the NJM's International Relations Committee (IRC) repeatedly mentioned the hardening of attitudes among what they always referred to as the "reactionary" governments of the area.[35]

By August 1981, Bishop told the Central Committee that "We have lost the propaganda fight on the regional front."[36] He blamed this on U.S. efforts to isolate Grenada, but there were internal problems as well. For example, in October 1982 the International Relations Committee of the NJM was found to be very deficient in its regional work as most of its members were continually absent.[37] Clearly things were not going well for the NJM. Each of the new anticommunist governments in the area began to dismantle the array of arrangements made by their predecessors. That the radical euphoria was evanescing was indicated when a large number of party-to-party scholarships for study in Cuba were rescinded in all but Grenada's case.[38]

To be sure, radical groups continued to look on Grenada as having an important leadership role. Note the minutes of the Politburo meeting of December 29, 1982:

> Dr. Ralph Gonsalves of St. Vincent had broken with the UPM and formed a new Marxist-Leninist party, the Movement for National Unity. He wanted to come to Grenada to discuss the situation and establish "fraternal links" with the NJM. Comrade Strachan (in charge of ideology and agitprop) was put in charge of the Gonsalves visit. Colombia's M-19 guerrilla movement sent a letter requesting "the best possible links with our Party." Letter was filed without reply.

Both cases reflected the realities of international relations at the time. Gonsalves represented nothing but a splinter of a splinter group; Grenada was just then negotiating a trade agreement with Colombia,[39] so any contact with the M-19 guerrillas would have been embarrassing, to say the least.

Contacts with the Caribbean continued apace, but there is evidence that the PRG had decided on a dual strategy by mid-1981: (1) to strengthen the "institutional" position at home through a series of military treaties with the Cubans and Soviets, and (2) to maximize the material benefits of contacts with the West.

In late 1980, the NJM was admitted to full membership in the Socialist International, and on July 24, 1981 Brent Carlsson, general secretary of the

SI, and Ron Haywood, general secretary of the British Labour Party, sent a telegram to various governments calling for full support for Grenada. "Together with the Government of National Reconstruction in Nicaragua," read the telegram, "it offers a beacon of hope and social justice in Central America and the Caribbean."[40] The material benefits to be derived from such contacts (e.g., free milk, butter oil, food, and agricultural assistance in general) were many.

But the big "market" was the United States, and it is quite conceivable that the failure to make significant inroads in the Caribbean provided part of the impetus for the NJM to explore contacts with the U.S. Government. There were many aspects to Grenada's failure in the Caribbean that would tend to justify the NJM's pessimism about radical changes in the area and the need to be more pragmatic about building socialism in one island.

The data in Table 1 (see page 142) clearly demonstrates the total lack of electoral support for those groups in the region most closely associated with revolutionary Grenada. Grenada's Leninist experiment obviously had not advanced the cause among these groups. Groups friendly to the NJM, such as the PNC in Guyana and the PNP in Jamaica, had their own internal reasons for offering their support.

Perhaps no sector of the Caribbean working class had dealt the NJM and Bishop a greater blow than the working class of Suriname, which in 1982 gave Bishop his greatest embarrassment in foreign affairs by cutting off all electricity and services during his state visit. The murders carried out by the Bouterse regime became a source of deep shame in a region hardly accustomed to such deeds.[41] In short, there seemed to be a "Latin-Americanizing" of the area—not a welcome thought for societies still deeply conservative according to the NJM's own analyses. On the other hand, the trip of Ian Jacobs to the United States during March-April 1983 was, according to his report, a smashing success. His targets were black American groups, and much of his itinerary appeared to be arranged by Angela Davis and the U.S. Communist Party.[42] There was talk of buying a building in New York, and even a radio station.

This trip set the stage for Bishop's own tour of the United States, and in a sense, his appeal to race and ethnicity took him back to his first entry into politics—the 1970 Black Power demonstrations in Trinidad. The NJM was rediscovering the region-wide power of racism apparently even in the United States, as evidenced by the list of U.S. support groups aiding Grenada. But this approach was bound to have unwanted results *vis-à-vis* the Leninist Coard faction of the NJM. In a fundamental manner, Bishop's America policy was deviationism, especially after Coard and his followers passed a resolution in October 1983 calling for "stringent Leninist measures" in the leadership.

It now seems evident that even as Bishop and his few friends in the Central Committee decided to pursue the U.S. tack in mid-1983, the split in the party was so deep and bitter that it was a doomed enterprise. It is good to remember, however, that Bishop's string of defeats began in the

Table 1. Caribbean Parties with Close Links to NJM

Country	Party	Leader (Percentage of Vote in Own Constituency)	Overall Electoral Performance
Antigua	ACLM	Tim Hector (1980: 2.8%)	1980: 1.2%
Bahamas	Vanguard	Lionel Clark	NC
Barbados	Monali		NC
Dominica	DLMA	Bill Riviere (1980: 21.8%)	1980: 8.4%
St. Lucia	PDP	George Odlum (1982: 46.2%) Mike Pilgrim (1982: 35.6%)	As PLP 1982: 27.1%
St. Vincent	UPM	Simeon Greene (1979: 16.8%) Ralph Gonsalves (1979: 19.1%)	1979: 13.6%
Jamaica	WPJ	Trevor Munroe	NC
	PNP	Michael Manley (1980: 55%)	1980: 42.3%
Guyana	PPP	Cheddi Jagan	1980: 19.0%*
	WPA	Collective Leadership	Boycott
	PNC	Forbes Burnham	1980: 77.0%*

NC = Did not contest election.

*Electoral manipulations render these figures mere estimates. Sources: Patrick A. M. Emmanuel, *General Elections in the Eastern Caribbean: A Handbook*, (Cave Hill, Barbados, 1979); and Douglas Midgett, *Eastern Caribbean Elections, 1950–1982*, (Iowa City: University of Iowa, n.d.).

Caribbean. The movement toward Western capitalist states came as a result of the closing of options in the Caribbean. In that sense the Coard faction was analytically correct in fearing a "right opportunistic" turn in the revolution. But they (and their Leninist advisors from Jamaica, Guyana, and Trinidad) were objectively wrong in assuming that a harder line would stop its erosion. Neither the objective nor the subjective conditions were present, and in the face of growing public discontent, no amount of foreign advisors could stem the tide.[43] As Max Weber predicted, in times of systemic crisis, charismatic authority becomes supreme. The mass slogan, "No Bishop, no Revo!" was proof of that.

Conclusions

The tragic end of the NJM regime in Grenada is now a matter of history. Yet there is already a certain predictability to post-invasion developments in the Caribbean. This can be illustrated by the First Advisory Meeting of the Anti-imperialist Forces of the Caribbean and Central America which was held in Havana in mid-June 1984. Thirty-one parties and delegations were represented, and among the representatives was Trevor Munroe of Jamaica's WPJ, who accepted Cuba's version of the October events in Grenada, as distinct from his initial analysis which sided with the Coard group. There were delegates from the "vanguard" PPP and the "vanguard" PNC in Guyana, both of whom signed the declaration which calls for defense against imperialist destabilization of Guyana, Cuba, and Nicaragua. Representing Grenada were Kendrick Radix, expelled in early 1983 from the Central Committee as "indisciplined" and "petty bourgeois," and Don Rojas, Bishop's Press Secretary who had to hide for his life in October 1983. They now lead a group called the Maurice Bishop Patriotic Movement. In other words, the same actors, the same resolutions, the same instrumental political-strategic compromises couched in the language of historical "laws" and "inevitability" are present. Such inevitability is doubtful, however, in light of recent political compromises.

On July 12, 1984 the Caribbean news service CANA reported from Georgetown that the "vanguard" WPA had decided to drop its pledge to overthrow the Burnham dictatorship. Since the WPA felt that after Grenada "there can't be any dreams of revolution by force of arms or any such things," it was decided that they would have to consider for the first time a "struggle for free and fair elections."[44] In Marxist-Leninist ontological terms, this is clearly a step backwards. But beyond theory and praxis, there is the human story to be told about the WPA's change of tactics. Significantly, the spokesman for this strategy is Euzi Kawayna, formerly a close advisor to Burnham and now co-leader of the WPA. In a sense he represents an entire generation of West Indians. He emerged from the Black Power movement promising socialist revolution, thereby confirming a historical progression that had long been expounded by West Indian Marxists—first a racial revolution then socialism. To fully understand what Grenada has meant for this vision, one has to turn to views "from the inside," so to speak, not to international meetings in Havana or Georgetown. In this respect, no one has analyzed the meaning of the invasion of Grenada more poignantly than Tim Hector, the leader of Antigua's Liberation Movement. Noting that Bishop in the end was "shocked" by the views and sentiments of his colleagues, he reminisces:

> Between Euzi Kawayna of Guyana, Maurice Bishop, and I, there is and has been, a peculiar and unbreakable bond. We were all forged in the same crucible, Black Power, and socialism was but a logical extension of that banner.[45]

With these credentials, Hector's verdict on Bishop's murder is significant. "History will absolve his right-wing detractors, but not his unexpected left-wing enemies."

Here, then, is at least one important lesson to be learned from Grenada. Grenada represented the death of a dream that tragically went in two different directions. The dream was born of a generation's moral indignation about prevailing social conditions, and a belief in socialism's regenerative promises. Unfortunately, it was pursued in terms of a model born in Russia, elaborated in Cuba, and promoted by an international network of theorists and advisors. The consequence was a fundamentally un-Marxian approach to development. The more the people resisted, the more tenacious and repressive the state machinery became. The approach was Leninist in conception, Stalinist in practice, and brutal in its ultimate results. Clearly, it did not benefit the people. Indeed, the resistance of the Grenadian people was a major factor contributing to the crisis that brought their country's Leninist experiment to an end.

NOTES

1. Speech, March 13, 1979, *Maurice Bishop Speaks* (NewYork: Pathfinder Press, 1983), p. 25.

2. Anthony P. Maingot, "A Critique," *Independence for Grenada: Myth or Reality*, Institute of International Relations, St. Augustine, Trinidad, 1974.

3. *The Miami Herald*, June 27, 1979.

4. This author held the Chair of Latin American Studies at the Institute of International Relations, Trinidad. Coard was a visiting lecturer there from 1972–1974.

5. Speech, April 13, 1979, *op. cit.*, pp. 26–31.

6. Speech June 15, 1979, ibid., pp. 42–47.

7. Speech, July 2, 1979, ibid., p. 45.

8. At the Sixth Summit Conference of the Nonaligned Movement, Havana, Bishop included Iran with Nicaragua as being the most important of such examples. Speech, September 6, 1979, *op. cit.*, ibid., p. 48.

9. The only West Indian Head of Government to attend. Neither Trinidad, St. Vincent, nor Antigua were represented.

10. Speech, March 13, 1980, *Bishop Speaks*, *op. cit.* p. 23.

11. Speech, February 15, 1980, ibid., pp. 60–69; *Caribbean Bulletin*, January-February 1980, pp. 21–22; and *Grenadian Newsletter*, February 1980.

12. The assertion that Bishop and the leadership were already Marxist is based on their own admission. *See* Line of March for the Party presented by Maurice Bishop, Chairman, Central Committee, to General Meeting of Party, September 13,

1982, pp. 37–39; and Bishop's and Unison Whiteman's interview in *Bohemia*, August 19, 1977.

13. Speech, May 1, 1980, op. cit., p. 100.

14. Norman Girvan, *Corporate Imperialism: Conflict and Expropriation* (White Plains, NY, 1976), p. 184.

15. Calling it a Soviet approach is in keeping with the analyses of Jiri and Virginia Valenta, "Leninism in Grenada," *Problems of Communism*, July-August 1984; and Vernon V. Aspaturian's chapter in this volume.

16. Clive Y. Thomas, "The Havana Declaration of June 1975," paper presented to the Conference on Contemporary Trends and Issues in Caribbean International Affairs, May 23–27, 1977, Trinidad, p. 2.

17. W. Richard Jacobs and Ian Jacobs, *Grenada: The Route to Revolution* (Havana: Casa de las Américas, 1980), p. 78. The authors cite Soviet scholars V. Solodovnikov and V. Bogoslovsky, *Non-Capitalist Development* (Moscow, 1975) as their authority.

18. Cheddi Jagan on Critical Support, address to the 25th Anniversary Conference of the PPP, August 3, 1975, p. 12.

19. *The Mirror* (Overseas Edition), April 1977, pp. 3–4.

20. Even the formerly antagonistic U.S. administration now seemed to mellow to the inevitability of Burnham's rule. In June 1977, for example, Assistant Secretary of State Terrence Todman told the House Subcommittee on Inter-American Affairs, "Guyana is seeking a different path to social and economic development, one with which we have no quarrel and which we have no reason for fear. Despite its different political philosphy, and our differences in the past, Guyana looks to us for understanding and cooperation." U.S. Congress, House, U.S. Policy Towards the Caribbean, Hearings, House Subcommittee on Inter-American Affairs, June 28, 1977, p. 30. Hereafter cited at Hearings, SIAA.

21. John Hearne provides an excellent analysis of the WPA's role in *The Jamaican Weekly Gleaner*, August 4, 18, 25, and September 1, 8, and 15, 1980.

22. Rodney, Walter, *The Groundings with My Brothers* (London: Bogle-L'Ouverture Publications, 1969), p. 31.

23. Thomas, Clive, "The Current Crisis in Guyana," *Guyana Forum*, October 1981.

24. The internal contradictions in leftist circles were evident when one understands that it was the editor of *Caribbean Contact*, Rickey Singh, who requested Bishop's involvement. Singh, a Guyanese radical, was a political opponent of Burnham. *See* Minutes of Politburo Meeting, May 13, 1981, Grenada Documents. When the statement was drafted, the Politburo turned it down as being "too rough" and ordered a redrafting emphasizing "anti-imperialism." Minutes of Politburo Meeting, June 10, 1981, ibid.

25. For an analysis of the Trinidad case see Anthony P. Maingot, "Cuba and the English-Speaking Caribbean," in Barry B. Levine (ed.), *The New Cuban Presence in the Caribbean* (Boulder: Westview Press, 1983), pp. 19–42.

26. Excerpts from Address to Cuban Workers, July 12, 1975, in Hearne (ed.), *The Search for Solutions*, pp. 205–206. For an example of party rhetoric, see the speech by Minister of Foreign Affairs Dudley Thompson to the Second Socialist International Meeting, Caracas, May 25, 1976. (Ottawa: Maple House Publishing Co., 1976)

27. Hearne, op. cit., pp. 169–171.

28. See "Jamaica's Manley," *The Tropic Magazine*, April 11, 1976, p. 24; and "Michael Manley, Jamaica and the U.S.," *The New York Times*, January 21, 1978.

29. At this meeting in early January 1983, the following organizations were represented: Nicaragua's FSLN; El Salvador's MNR; Chile's RP; Jamaica's PNP; Cuba's CC; and Grenada's NJM. Three new Caribbean parties were seen as strengthening the "progressive forces" in the SI by gaining consultative observer status: Puerto Rico's PIP, Guyana's WPA, and St. Lucia's PLP. The agenda appeared to be more Leninist than social democratic as it called for making the Secret Regional Caucus an ongoing organ, purging social democrats, a bank account in the Bahamas, and support for the Bouterse regime in Suriname. Report on Meeting of Secret Regional Caucus of SI [Socialist International] Held in Managua, January 6–7, 1983, Grenada Documents Log No. 100446.

30. Hart was one of the so-called "4-H's" expelled in 1952 by Norman Manley in his purge of the Marxist "caucus" within the PNP. The Marxists established the People's Freedom Movement which soon proved to have little leadership cohesion and even less popular support. In 1963 he moved to Guyana to edit the PPP's *Mirror*, but left for England two years later.

31. These observations are based on interviews in Grenada and Trinidad, April 13–17, 1984.

32. Speech, September 6, 1979, op. cit., p. 56.

33. Tony Thorndike, "Revolutionary Political Culture: The Case of Grenada," Caribbean Studies Association (CSA), May 30, 1984, St. Kitts.

34. The issue of the Rastafarian opposition to the NJM regime was an especially sensitive one given its symbolic links with antiestablishment and Black Power groups in the region. The hardliners wanted 300 Rastafarians "picked up" and their locks shaved. Bishop opposed this, as did Cuban Ambassador Rizo who was consulted as to tactics. Finally, only major leaders were arrested. *See* Minutes of Central Committee Meeting, June 24, 1981, Grenada Documents. Not surprisingly the Stalinists within the Central Committee (such as Phyllis Coard) wanted to handle the situation with "heavy manners," i.e., forcefully, with internment camps and what was called "a rigid programme" (possibly psychiatric reprogramming). Minutes of Central Committee Meeting, June 24, 1981.

35. Symptomatic of an anticommunist "fear" which was gaining strength throughout the area, St. Lucia's most important newspaper, the *Voice*, editorialized on April 5, 1981 that it was clear that the radicals (Odlum and Pilgrim) had "penetrated" the traditional St. Lucia Labour Party but had failed to achieve their goals.

36. Minutes of Central Committee Meeting, August 19, 1981, Grenada Documents.

37. Analysis by CC of IRC work, October 12, 1982, ibid.

38. By September 1980, the numbers were as follows: Grenada, 40; St. Lucia, 12; Dominica, 6; St. Vincent, 2; Antigua, 2. *Caribbean Bulletin*, September-October, 1980.

39. *Caribbean Bulletin*, May-June, 1982.

40. *Caribbean Bulletin*, September 1981.

41. The leader of the nation-wide strike which happened to coincide (or was planned to coincide) with Bishop's state visit in late October 1982 was Cyril Daal

of the Moederbond, a general association of 36 trade unions. Daal would be one of the 15 prominent leaders murdered by the government soon thereafter.

42. Ian Jacobs, March 23–April 21, 1983. Even in Miami the tour was successful, arranged it appears, by the pro-Castro group, La Casa.

43. Much attention has been placed on the Cuban presence during the tragic October 1983 events. Equally important was the sizable number of Trinidadian, Guyanese, and especially Jamaican "advisors" who supported the Coard faction.

44. Reported in the *Jamaican Weekly Gleaner*, July 24, 1984, p. 9.

45. *The Outlets* (St. Johns, Antigua), October 21, 1983, p. 1.

GEORGES A. FAURIOL

Comments

If judged solely on the basis of its geopolitical attributes, Grenada would be an unlikely candidate for a significant global or even regional role. Reflecting an understanding of this reality, most lesser states in the world have combined moments of activity in the international community—a speech at the United Nations, for example—with long periods of invisibility.

Maurice Bishop's Grenada played a different tune, however, and in a most telling manner acquired a new ideological constituency abroad. Even if Bishop was perceived to have emphasized a necessary political approach related to the needs of Grenadian development, a floundering domestic ideological environment and a precarious sense of diplomatic maneuverability brought to the fore the worst by-products of radical aspirations: authoritarian opportunism, an acrimonious domestic political stalemate, and an incoherent ideological posture. Grenada was not a comic opera, but the documents captured by U.S. forces in October 1983 confirm many of the abuses inherent in revolutionary situations and the colossal absurdity of misguided ideologues. The Grenada documents also underline the degree to which internal agitation transformed the almost spontaneous popularity of Bishop's early rhetoric into stifling communist orthodoxy.

The internal dynamics of the Grenadian revolution and their relevance to present and future trends in the Caribbean Basin constitute Tony Maingot's core agenda in the preceding paper. He correctly notes these trends are uncertain. On one hand, the bases of modern Caribbean political culture are anchored in Fabian politics and the advances of the area's trade union movement. To a certain extent, Maurice Bishop was representative of a highly politicized and cultured generation of leaders that succeeded the aging political aristocracy of Norman Manley of Jamaica, his son Michael, Forbes Burnham of Guyana, and many others. It could be argued that Marxist undercurrents have been part of the political scenery of this generation. Its kinship with the political traditions of British Labour values has deep personal and philosophical roots. Maingot implies that Grenadian Marxism brings about a mix of ideologies not native to the Eastern Caribbean, but this perhaps overlooks the very conducive environment that exists for radicalism in the region.

On the other hand, the unique circumstances of the Grenada experience generate some appropriate skepticism regarding its applicability to other countries in the region. Maingot points out how the failure of the New Jewel Movement (NJM) might have been linked to Bishop's eleventh-hour search for contacts with the United States, thus illustrating the degree to which Grenada had deviated from Caribbean norms. Whether this linkage actually existed is questionable, but the nature of Bishop's approach to Washington was symptomatic of how far removed his leadership was from both Caribbean and other regional realities.

Bishop's appeal to an activist black American constituency paralleled the NJM's appeal to radical groups cultivated by Grenada in the Caribbean. Not to underestimate their hazardous nature, both constituencies operated on the fringes of the polity, and by 1982 there was a clear electoral trend in the region away from groups most closely associated with revolutionary Grenada in Dominica, Jamaica, and Barbados, etc.

One must also take note of the unique tone of the political culture of the Eastern Caribbean. This stems from British ideological influences and has manifested itself in the form of an imperfect but operational version of parliamentary politics. Flexibility is a key aspect of the region's political culture. This can be seen in the somewhat opportunistic behavior of many Caribbean leaders over the past 30 years. It suggested a tendency toward political pragmatism, but clearly there was not flexibility present in Grenada.

Yet pragmatism can be taken too far with detrimental results. The flexibility of Burnham's foreign policy—a mish-mash of nonaligned rhetoric—resulted in an ultimately meaningless diplomacy and an unfavorable domestic environment in Guyana. Furthermore, Bishop's and Manley's loose operational definition of social democracy ultimately generated weak rather than flexible regimes. Such failures are striking and ironic in comparison with another form of flexibility: the fundamentally pragmatic approach of Cuban policy in the Caribbean, i.e., Havana's ability to shift its positions, and to appear to be occasionally concilliatory in its relations with non-Marxist parties in the region. This constitutes flexibility by political design—a dangerous although probably effective approach. In the final analysis, political pragmatism in the English-speaking Caribbean is sometimes considered a sign of weakness in that it might represent an inability to articulate a meaningful ideology relevant to domestic needs or the strategic reality of the region.

Maingot's analysis deals only with the English-speaking Caribbean, and concludes with a number of overgeneralizations regarding U.S. foreign policy. The policy of the United States should not be fictionalized. It is misleading to characterize U.S. foreign policy as either "flexible" (implying ineffectiveness during the Carter years) or "hard line" (implying a sterile interest in pressure and force since 1980). One cannot be reassured by the possibility that U.S. policy toward the Caribbean might be considered of "secondary" importance in the region because of the consolidation of a political culture in the Eastern Caribbean "with a preference for parliamentary pluralism." If nothing else, the Grenadian episode (and Michael Manley's Jamaica) underlines the thin margin of safety within which the countries of the Eastern Caribbean operate. Thus American policy toward the area is both salient and relevant to the future of the region.

American policy toward Grenada suffered for reasons connected to the broader scope of U.S.-Latin American relations in general. American foreign policy toward Latin America and the Caribbean has been embroiled in a domestic controversy stemming from the historical use of "gunboat diplomacy" and the haunting specter of Vietnam. A form of isolationism and collective guilt was manifest during the 1970s. The result was not a coherent policy, but rather an illusion that all was well in the region except for American meddling.

Unlike the retrenchment of the 1920s when the United States viewed itself as being too good for the world, during the 1970s there was a strong temptation to suggest that the United States should not involve itself in Latin America because it no longer had a moral justification for doing so. A distorted product of the philosophical bases of the American republic, to this day there is an extraordinary sentiment that seems to shape public impressions regarding the Caribbean in a manner generally removed from other foreign policy concerns. Many feel that the United States must exact strenuous moral perfection from itself and its friends before being worthy of pursuing its interests and objectives in the region. However, this standard is not often applied to the opponents of the United States in the region, and therefore it is self-defeating.

American policy toward Latin America and the Caribbean Basin is obscured by crude and imperfect expressions of historical reality. The result infused into public thinking an extraordinary degree of misinformation and *mea culpa* reasoning. This is compounded by a tendency to confuse day-to-day issues with more important trends currently shaping the region. In policymaking terms, this has led to an unfortunate absence of strategic logic, quixotic estimates of the sociopolitical forces at play in the region, and ultimately to an inclination to confuse the normal shortcomings of U.S. policy with excessive pragmatism on one hand, and intransigent grudges on the other.

Some insist that the objective of U.S. policy in the Western Hemisphere is war while others feel that any retreat from current policy will result in serious damage to vital American interests. These views have permeated the debate over Central America to an alarming degree. Democrats reach for negotiated political solutions and support regional peacemaking efforts such as the Contadora process. Some liberal Democrats even appear ready to argue that neither geographical proximity nor ideological incompatibility are factors particularly relevant to American interests in Latin America and the Caribbean Basin. Conservative thinking publicly rejects the notion that the United States should accept the institutionalization of leftist regimes in the area, and several moderate Democrats and Republicans share the belief that future military interventions are likely in the region. But each of these strains of thought fails to address the implications of a policy failure in the region.

Radicalism is alive and well in the Eastern Caribbean. The Grenadian intervention should not mislead observers into assuming that Soviet influence or Leninist radicalism has disappeared from the region. The question is not the degree to which Grenadan radicalism influenced other states in the region, but rather whether the region is likely to produce future Grenadas. Tony Maingot might be overly optimistic in suggesting that the buffer to extremism in the Caribbean is not U.S. power but rather the political culture of the region. There is no doubt that the latter represents an extraordinary strategic asset and a unique indication of local political preferences. But the countries of the Eastern Caribbean remain vulnerable to violent subversion, and thus both they and the United States will have to be vigilant for the forseeable future.

COLIN LEGUM

Grenada: Linkage and Impact on the Third World

THIRD WORLD REACTIONS TO THE INVASION OF GRENADA

The American and Asian components of the Third World feel themselves physically and politically remote from the Caribbean region, and even from much of Latin America. Except for countries like Guyana, Jamaica, Cuba, Brazil, and Chile, there are relatively few political points of contact between these two poles of the developing world. Only when some major political event occurs, or a singular political figure appears on the Caribbean-Latin American scene, is any special notice paid to events in the Western Hemisphere by the Afro-Asian world. The U.S./OECS military intervention in Grenada was such an event, but previously the murdered Grenadan Prime Minister, Maurice Bishop, was not seen as a singularly important Third World figure.

Unlike the older established leaders of the Caribbean, such as Forbes Burnham of Guyana and Michael Manley of Jamaica, Bishop had no close contact with African leaders. It is difficult to find any references to Bishop's New Jewel Movement (NJM) in the African media, government statements, or diplomatic exchanges. Although there were some references in the Grenada documents to the Ethiopian experience in socialist orientation, there is absolutely no evidence of political links between the NJM and even the most radical African regimes, such as Ethiopia, Angola, Mozambique, and Libya.[1] (Appendix A, Document 16) Nor is it possible to discover whether Bishop had even ever visited any of these countries. If he did, his visits received no publicity and remain, so far as can be established, unrecorded. Bishop avoided attending the summit meetings of the Commonwealth of Nations where he could have had contact with many Third World leaders. He chose instead to be represented by deputies, and at none of the summits did the NJM play a significant role. Bishop's only contacts with Third World leaders outside the Caribbean region (where his closest official contact was with Burnham) were at the two nonaligned summit meetings that he attended.

Overall, it seems fairly clear that there was no significant political linkage between the NJM and radical regimes in Africa. However, in a statement issued on 26 October, the Angolan Central Committee referred "with consternation" to the murder "of our great friend, Maurice Bishop," and expressed "admiration for the people of Grenada and the Cuban solidarity workers in that country."

Other African reactions to the invasion of Grenada were standard, with little essential difference between the views of those assignedly moderate and radical leaders. The sole exception was Libya's Gadhafi who took an apocalyptic view of the results of American intervention. In a message sent to the chairman of the UN Security Council and the UN Secretary-General on 25 October, he said:

> What is happening now in Grenada has not only killed the freedom of Grenada, but also the civilization of the 20th century. . . . The only thing that can rescue humanity and civilization which are now being buried, is an international alliance to invade the United States itself and impose the principles of humanity, freedom and justice, as well as to purge the spirit of evil Nazism in the U.S., which has become a threat to the freedom of all the smaller nations and world peace.

The particular dottiness of the Libyan Leader is idiosyncratic and it elicited no response from other Third World leaders, who nevertheless reacted in a uniformly tough manner as indicated by the speeches of their representatives in the UN Security Council debate on Grenada.

Reflecting the official position of Angola's ruling party (the Popular Movement for the Liberation of Angola), the Angolan Ambassador to the United Nations, Elisio de Figeiredo, told the Security Council, "the intervention in sovereign Grenada once again shows the essence of the imperialist policy of the United States, whether it be in Africa or Latin America."[2] He went on to link U.S. actions in Grenada with its "criminal cooperation with racist South Africa, complicity in acts of sabotage against the "frontline states," and the creation of military bases on the African continent"—all links, he said, in a single strategy based on U.S. interests "for the attainment of which Washington was prepared even to use force."

Speaking in a similar vein, though in more temperate language, Tanzania's ambassador to the United Nations, Paul Milyango, expressed a view reflective of a broad range of Third World opinion: "Today Grenada is the victim of the U.S.; tomorrow the victim could be any other underdeveloped country." Tanzania's Foreign Ministry described Bishop's murder and the American intervention as "equally repulsive."[3] This was also the position taken by Zambia's Foreign Ministry which "unreservedly condemned the invasion of Grenada just as it had strongly condemned the callous murder of its Prime Minister."[4]

The Ethiopian reaction also was stated in less extreme terms than that of the Angolans. Its Foreign Ministry described the invasion of Grenada as "unprovoked and premeditated; to claim otherwise is pathetic." The Ethiopians, however, seemed to have been much more concerned with the American invasion of Grenada than with Bishop's fate.[5] The reaction of Zimbabwe's Prime Minister Robert Mugabe was somewhat sharper, but still less harsh than the Angolan indictment. He described the invasion "by the joint forces of the U.S. and its Carribbean allies" as an "act of wanton aggression carried out in complete defiance of the UN Charter and the sovereign right of the people of Grenada."[6] Nigeria described the U.S./ OECS intervention as "deplorable, unjustified, and a violation of the UN Charter" and added that it denounced "the frequent threats of the superpowers to topple governments they did not like."[7]

There was no evidence of any change in Soviet and Cuban policies toward its closest allies in Africa as a result of developments in Grenada. The happenings in that "distant little country" were undoubtedly useful for the Soviet/Cuban propaganda onslaught against "American imperialism" and to defuse Third World criticism of its military offensive in Aghanistan. But the changes in Soviet relations with Angola and Mozambique at the end of 1983 were concerned not with Grenada, but with the détente that was begining to develop between those countries and South Africa.

Cuban troop reinforcements in Angola were reported in the last quarter of 1983, but that can be seen to have been in direct response to the ongoing South African military offensive deep into Angola. The introduction of fresh combat troops seems to have come directly from Cuba. If so, they were only indirectly replaced by the withdrawal of Cuban troops from Ethiopia, first in evidence in mid-1983, months before the invasion of Grenada.

Much of the strongest opposition to the invasion of Grenada centered on the claim that a superpower had used military force to "occupy" a Third World country. Many nonaligned leaders drew parallels between their opposition to the Grenada intervention, the Soviet invasion of Afghanistan, and Vietnam's invasion of Kampuchea. This view was exemplified in the following statement by Robert Mugabe:

> We are agreed with the others [in the Commonwealth] that regional situations of conflicts must be ameliorated, that the situations of Grenada, Afghanistan, Kampuchea require the same solution. There has been a violation in respect of the situations of international law and the principle that requires that we respect the territorial integrity of other nations, and that the only remedy we see is that the forces that invaded these countries must withdraw. This position Zimbabwe holds very, very firmly indeed. We hold it in respect of Afghanistan, and we have had our views pronounced on that issue, not only in the Commonwealth but also in the forum of the Non-aligned Movement and at the United Nations as well. And similarly we hold that the invasion in Grenada was wrong. We took a firm position in the Security Council and we take a firm position here. We are glad that the Commonwealth recognizes

> the need for the withdrawal of the forces from Grenada, as indeed we recognize that there must be withdrawal of those forces which invaded Afghanistan and Kampuchea.[8]

Much opposition was also levied against the use of military force. Concomitantly, support was expressed for regional action to deal with the possible political fallout of such crises. This view, propounded by the Prime Minister of Trinidad and Tobago, carried the endorsement of all the Caribbean countries except for Jamaica, Barbados, Dominica, Antigua, and Barbuda. They declared that (1) any solution for problems like Grenada should be regional in nature, (2) such solutions should not be military and should not include external intervention of any sort, and (3) they should not be in breach of the U.N. Charter or international law in general.[9]

Many Third World leaders expressed an abiding suspicion or fear that in the aftermath of its victory in Grenada, the United States was likely to resort to the use of force to protect its perceived interests, especially in the Western Hemisphere. When asked whether he felt his country was threatened by the United States, President Burnham of Guyana answered:

> Of course I do. As a matter of fact so do most small countries whose microeconomic policies do not appeal to the American concept of what they should be . . . The late Maurice Bishop pointed out in 1981 that there was an exercise on the part of the American military entitled Amba and in 1982 he told us about an exercise called Ambreed. The details which he gave us in respect of Ambreed coincide almost exactly with the real exercise that took place on the 25th of October 1983. It seems passing strange that there should be this coincidence of details.[10]

Burnham, like many other nonaligned leaders, saw the invasion of Grenada as falling within the pattern of American intervention in Nicaragua and El Salvador, and earlier in Chile. Linked to the accusation that the United States undermines regimes considered to be a threat to its security, is a widespread belief in the Third World that, irrespective of administration, Washington is obsessed about the role of Cuba and the Soviet Union in the real or imagined support they give to opposition movements or governments in Central and South America and the Caribbean Basin. This perception of Washington's behavior almost automatically guarantees nonaligned support for Cuba in any situation where declared American policy is to counter Cuban/Soviet actions. For the most part, American and Third World views on this issue are irreconcilably antagonistic. Thus, once Washington identified the hand of Havana and Moscow in Grenada, the guaranteed reaction from much of the Third World was condemnatory of the intervention. Washington's subsequent claim, though well-substantiated, that U.S. forces were acting in response to appeals from Grenadian leaders as well as from Barbados, Dominica, and several smaller East Caribbean governments was widely treated as a pretext for a military operation that was believed to have been planned long before the actual intervention.

The fact that the members of the OECS genuinely felt themselves to be threatened by developments in Grenada was heavily overshadowed by the presupposition that the United States wished to use its military muscle to assert its power, irrespective of whether it was acting at the invitation of local actors involved in the conflict. In the course of an appeal he made to fellow delegates at the Commonweath summit meeting in New Delhi in November 1983, Antigua and Barbuda's Prime Minister Lester Bird declared:

> Delegations here must understand that we live in a region where a neighbour is hostile to the constiutional, political and economic arrangements within some countries. To say we are fearful of this would be an understatement; to say we feel threatened by this would underrate our real concern.[11]

The Prime Minister of Dominica, Ms. Mary Eugenia Charles, who as chairperson of OECS delivered the request for U.S. military assistance, made a formidable impact on Commonwealth leaders by her uncompromising tough defence of her action:

> Within the last three years, we were a bit concerned about the building up of arms in Grenada. We knew that there were colossal amounts of arms, far in excess of that any country could require in this area. And we were concerned about that. We were also concerned because we knew that the dissident forces in our islands, in each of the islands, had a little grouping. . . . [The killings in Grenada] made us realize that if we did not take steps now we will all be under the control of a small group of thugs in Grenada. And this we did not want in our country. And therefore we had no compunction deciding that we must go in and make sure that the Grenadian people got what they wanted and make sure that we didn't get what we didn't want in our country. We looked down and looked at the fact that we did not have the means to do what we wanted to do. . . . Quite frankly I can tell you that if the circumstances arose exactly the same again, I would take exactly the same action, in spite of the fact that many people in this room have blamed us for doing it. We are sure that we were right in what we did.

Prime Minister Charles took a view directly opposite to that of President Burnham about the threat of the United States to smaller countries in the hemisphere. She asserted, "I am quite sure that this fear that the whole world has of a great mighty big America taking us over and submerging us is completely unfounded."[12]

There are also particularist reasons for some countries' hostility to the United States military intervention in Grenada. Nonaligned countries are constantly wary of how the actions of superpowers in one part of the globe might affect developments in their own regions. In the case of Grenada, a number of African countries—especially the frontline states[13]—perceived a danger of South Africa advancing reasons similar to those of the United States to justify military intervention in countries close to their borders. This concern, which colored much of the debate in Africa after the Grenada affair, was expressed by Zimbabwe's Prime Minister Mugabe at the New Delhi Commonwealth meeting:

> If legitimacy is accorded the invasion in Grenada, it could act as a basis on which South Africa can claim legitimacy for its own acts of aggression against us. An invader is an invader whether he be your brother or sister, who lives next door and comes to interfere with the running of your own affairs, and begins to give orders to you and your family as to how the affairs should be run. We condemned the invasion in Grenada and did so not just because of the principles of the United Nations Charter, but also because of a possible analogy that could exist between it and the acts of aggression by South Africa. South Africa is currently occupying the southern part of Angola as you are aware, and if we conceded that this invasion by the countries of the Caribbean . . . is justified because of reasons given, namely that Grenada had become a threat to them, that the system in Grenada was not in accordance with the other systems of the area and because of the presence of the Cubans, South Africa would feel justified; it would actually say it is fighting for the cause of Western democracy, fighting against a system that would seek to bring about a change in the area, and that it [is] fighting against communism . . .[14]

This theme was also developed by President Burnham who said,

> The argument that justifies the American lawlessness in the invasion of Grenada justifies South African incursions also. They continue incursions into the Front-Line States and the invasion of countries like Mozambique, Angola and Lesotho.[15]

LIKELY THIRD WORLD REACTIONS TO THE DOCUMENTARY EVIDENCE CAPTURED IN GRENADA

Is it possible that Third World attitudes toward the invasion of Grenada are likely to change in light of the Grenada documents? My own opinion is that while the evidence will be received with interest, it will not change fundamental Third World attitudes toward the American intervention for the following reasons.

1. Cuban and Soviet involvement in Grenada simply repeats similar conditions in other Third World countries (e.g., Angola, Ethiopia, and South Yemen), and the doctrine of nonalignment positively affirms the sovereign right of every country to enter into foreign relations with any country of its own government's choosing.
2. The documentary evidence of Soviet military supplies and Cuban military assistance to the New Jewel Movement (NJM) is not likely to be very different from what exists in the archives of many nonaligned nations. It is not likely to prove to be either shocking or revealing except among those governments hostile to the Soviet Union and Cuba.

3. The true nature of the NJM will not cause most nonaligned leaders to change their views about the intervention because movements such as the NJM are known to exist in other parts of the Third World and are not necessarily thought of as being a threat to their neighbors even though they might disapprove. Compared, for example, with the current situation in Ethiopia, where the Leninist Ethiopian Workers' Party was recently launched, "revelations" about the nature of the NJM are small fare. Third World leaders are likely to be unimpressed by the true nature of the NJM because other Grenada-like developments have been contained or transformed by purely domestic forces, or as a result of regional influences. This was the case in Zanzibar, the Seychelles, and Mauritius after the sweeping victory of the Mauritian Militant Movement (MMM).

4. While the Grenada documents clearly show that the NJM was hiding its true intentions, they also show that the initiative for involving the Cubans and Soviets in Grenadian affairs came from the NJM itself. (Appendix A, Document 6) There is no evidence that the NJM was coerced by its allies.

5. Finally, the documents do not provide evidence that the NJM intended to allow Grenada to be used as a military or political base for the Cubans or Soviets to expand their influence in the region even though the NJM might have entertained grandiose ambitions about its ability, with Cuban and Soviet help, to "export its revolutionary ideas" to its neighbors. On the whole, nonaligned leaders pour scorn on the idea that revolutions are exportable. Many will argue that there is no supportive evidence for such "exports" since the birth of the Third World.

Most influential leaders in the nonaligned movement are likely to remain unsympathetic to American military intervention anywhere in the Western Hemisphere. They will continue to look with sympathy on the Castro regime, though not necessarily toward its ambitions. They will hold to their line that military intervention in the Third World by either superpower is equally unacceptable, and they will continue to assert their view that military force should be used only when it is not in breach of the U.N. Charter, or to rescue citizens who may be in danger (which is not generally held as the case with the American students in Grenada).

MILITARY INTERVENTION: GRENADA AND THE FALKLAND ISLANDS

Third World reactions to the use of force in the Falkland Islands and Grenada were strikingly different. In the case of the Falklands, support for British military intervention was overwhelming. The notable dissenters were those nations that normally can be expected to hew Moscow's line (e.g., Cuba, Vietnam, Afghanistan, South Yemen and Ethiopia), those who for their own reasons do not wish to offend Moscow (e.g., Angola, Mozambique, Congo, Benin, Syria, and Libya), and those in Latin America who identified with Argentina's case. Third World backing for Britain was reflected in the rare unanimity of all Commonwealth members, including prominent nonaligned countries such as India, Tanzania, Guyana, and Zimbabwe.

The two reasons most frequently advanced by nonaligned governments for their stand in support of Britain were the right of the Falkland Islanders to self-determination, and opposition to armed force as a means of settling territorial disputes. Britain was adjudged to have acted justly in defense of both of these principles. However, it was also felt at a fairly early stage of the conflict that Prime Minister Thatcher was wrong in refusing to refer the dispute to the United Nations for a negotiated settlement.

In the case of Grenada, almost the exact opposite reaction was forthcoming. Except for nations normally supportive of American positions and the six East Caribbean states that requested American military assistance, almost the entire Third World condemned the United States for the Grenada intervention.

THE PROBLEM OF REGIONAL SECURITY FOR SMALL STATES

Beyond the immediate arguments in the Third World over the rights and wrongs of America's decision to intervene militarily in Grenada, there looms the larger, perennial question of how to provide for the security of the smaller and weaker states of the world. This is a major issue in all of the forums of the nonaligned nations. In Southeast Asia, Indonesia, Malaysia, the Philippines, Singapore, and Thailand have formed a regional security organization called the Association of South-East Asian Nations (ASEAN). Similar moves in this direction have been made—but so far without great success—in Southern Africa by the frontline states. In West Africa, Nigeria, Togo, Benin, and Ghana are currently engaged in trying to implement a decision by the 14-nation Economic Community of West African States (ECOWAS) to establish a mutual security system. At the New Delhi Commonwealth summit meeting, sharp divisions of opinion over Grenada were bridged by an agreement that the Commonwealth should assist the members of OECS in setting up a regional security system. The first meeting to implement this idea was held recently in London.

Regional security organizations have so far met with little practical success. This is partly because the countries of most regions are seldom politically homogeneous and often quite hostile to each other. Moreover, unless at least one of the countries concerned has a significant military potential of its own, it is not feasible to create a credible security system especially if the perceived threat is from a powerful nation as is the case with South Africa in Southern Africa, or Israel in the Middle East. Therefore, for practical reasons, small nations that feel themselves threatened usually find it expedient—however much they dislike the idea—to adopt a strong external power, as a strategic ally. But even such strategic allies have their limitations as Arab nations have discovered in the Middle East, and as Mozambique and Angola recently discovered when the Soviet Union was unable or unwilling to provide them with protection from attacks by South Africa. On the other hand, Cuba and Syria both have benefitted from their strategic alliance with Moscow.

By and large, major military powers have been reluctant to tie themselves too closely to developing nations with specific security guarantees. There are exceptions, of course, such as France's role in some of its former African colonies, Britain's security guarantees to Belize, and Soviet and American involvement in their respective spheres of influence. In cases such as Belize and Djibouti, the presence of small garrison forces has succeeded in acting as a deterrent to predatory neighbors. But, as Colonel Jonathan Alford, Deputy Director of the International Institute of Strategic Studies, has pointed out:

> The reason why small states that feel themselves under threat seek the reassurance of stationed forces is precisely because there is the hope of invoking much greater forces from the external guarantor power. The guarantor is forced to think about his exposed and potentially vulnerable garrison which will give an urgency to reinforcement plans which would otherwise be absent. This, of course, is precisely why large states are reluctant to enter into security relationships with small states and seem to spend most of their time trying to wriggle out of them.[16]

Undoubtedly, the best solution would be to encourage and support the establishment of balanced regional defense forces, as is currently envisaged in the Eastern Caribbean. At a minimum, such locally sanctioned and supported forces would be in a good position to deal with military coups felt to be a threat by nations in the region. The risk, of course, is that these forces could be used to support an unpopular regime against the will of its people. A promising example of regional intervention is offered by Senegal's effective support of Gambia, whose government was saved from a 1981 coup attempt that was not popularly supported. Another example is the support that Egypt has given to the Nimeiri regime in Sudan on several occasions.

The problem of providing for the security of small states was highlighted by the crisis in Grenada but calls for much more serious study than it has so far received either in the Third World or the West. A useful starting point for such studies is offered by Colonel Alford in his work *The Security Dilemmas of Small States*.[17] Some of his major conclusions are as follows:

The external security problems of microstates are generally manageable, but where a threat is palpable, stationed forces may be a permanent necessity, whether from a regional grouping under regional security arrangements—such as CARICOM in the Caribbean or the Gulf Cooperation Council (GCC) in the Persian Gulf—or from a former colonial power (e.g., Britain or France). The United Nations and the Commonwealth must be at least theoretical candidates, but agreement in the Security Council may be hard to obtain and the Commonwealth is a very far-flung organization.

Another set of conclusions relate to domestic crises with which small states usually cannot cope. An almost infinite variety of circumstances might be envisaged, but domestic forces hostile to legitimate regimes can easily become unmanageable. This is the greatest danger faced by small states.

I would argue that the most appropriate response is additional policing, and that something concrete must be done in this area. Soldiers do not make very good policemen, but violence easily can reach the point where armed insurrection rather than extensive disorder is at issue. My preference, then, is for military action by a single power, even if some window-dressing or legitimization by small regional contingents is necessary. After all, Anguilla, the New Hebrides, and Grenada all "worked." After the immediate crisis has been defused, it is certainly possible and probably desirable for regional forces to hold the ring, but I would remain extremely skeptical about forceful regional solutions to major internal security problems unless an unusually high degree of regional homogeneity exists, as perhaps in the Eastern Caribbean or the GCC.

Finally, Alford describes an idea called steady-state security assistance. Small states are unlikely to provide much or any of the logistics, training, intelligence, information, or infrastructure normally associated with internal or external security. To the extent that these are sought by a legitimate regime, others must try to provide such assistance in a consistent and steady fashion.

My own view is that such assistance, if properly regulated, can be just as much help to Third World countries as aid and trade. "Nothing has ever been made until the soldier has made safe the field where the building shall be built; and the soldier is the scaffolding until it has been built, and the soldier gets no reward but honour."

NOTES

1. Minutes of the Extraordinary Meeting of the Central Committee NJM, September 14–16, 1983, Grenada Documents, Log No. 000123, p. 20.
2. Angola Press Agency (ANGOP), London, November 1, 1983.
3. Radio Dar-es-Salaam, October 26, 1983.
4. Radio Lusaka, October 26, 1983.
5. Radio Addis Ababa, October 26, 1983.
6. Radio Harare, October 27, 1983.
7. Radio Lagos, October 31, 1983.
8. Prime Minister Robert Mugabe, statement made at a press conference in New Delhi, November 29, 1983.
9. A consensus resolution adopted at a meeting in Port of Spain attended by Trinidad, Guyana, St. Vincent, the Bahamas, and Belize, October 22, 1983.
10. President Forbes Burnham, statement made at a press conference in New Delhi, November 25, 1983.
11. The Honorable Lester Bird, speech to the Commonwealth summit meeting in New Delhi, November 25, 1983.

12. Prime Minister Eugenia Charles, statement at press conference in New Delhi, November 25, 1983.

13. The frontline states are Tanzania, Angola, Botswana, Mozambique, Zambia, and Zimbabwe.

14. Mugabe, *op cit*.

15. Forbes Burnham, *op cit*.

16. Colonel Jonathan Alford; "The Security Dilemmas of Small States," *The World Today* (London: Royal Institute of International Affairs), August and September 1984.

17. *Ibid*.

MICHAEL CLOUGH

Comments

Was the American intervention in Grenada a success? There are two different grounds upon which this question can be answered. The operation can be judged a success if it accomplished specific objectives set forth by President Reagan and his advisors at the time they announced the decision to intervene, namely to rescue American medical students on the island and eliminate a potential threat to the countries of the Eastern Caribbean. In the immediate aftermath of the operation, the President and his supporters declared the operation a success primarily on the ground that these goals were accomplished. In the months following the intervention, however, they began to declare more and more frequently that the action was a success on the ground that by demonstrating renewed resolve it enhanced American standing in the world. This claim was echoed repeatedly at the August 1984 Republican national convention in Dallas. The Republican Party platform declared:

> Grenada is small, and its people few; but we believe the principle established there—that freedom is worth defending—is of monumental importance. It challenges the Brezhnev doctrine. It is an example to the world.[1]

Similiarly, Vice President George Bush told the assembled delegates, "Because President Reagan stood firm in defense of freedom [in Grenada], America has regained respect throughout the world."[2] In more specific terms, Constantine Menges, special assistant to the President for Latin American affairs argued:

> Grenada was a key factor in demonstrating the will and capacity [of the United States] to help its friends to resist [indirect] aggression. It increased the morale of all the friends of democracy in the region, and I think around the world. And it destroyed the myth of irreversibility of pro-Soviet dictatorships—regimes that have moved into the Soviet orbit.[3]

This essay assesses the validity of such claims regarding the nature of the Grenada intervention with regard to the Third World in general, and Africa in particular. (It would be implausible to assert that the intervention in Grenada had any unique affect on Africa, but Africa provides a useful laboratory in which to explore Grenada's affect on American interests throughout the Third World.) Before examining specific claims that have been made concerning the international impact of the Grenada operation, several general observations should be made.

First, it is important to recognize the existence of several dynamics which incline policymakers and analysts to overestimate the long-term effects of dramatic events such as Grenada, the bombing of the Marine compound in Lebanon, and the 1979 Iranian hostage crisis. One such dynamic is a subtle cognitive tendency to believe that the more dramatic an event, the more likely it is to have significance. Thus, Grenada tends to be seen as a potential watershed in large part because it captures our immediate attention—not the reverse. Wishful thinking almost certainly plays a role in causing policymakers to exaggerate the effects of certain events. Hoping that the invasion of Grenada would enhance American credibility abroad, officials are more likely to believe that it had such an effect.

Tendencies to exaggerate the significance of individual dramatic events are reinforced by the news media. One of the main functions of editorial pages and news analysis programs such as "Nightline," the "McNeil-Lehrer Report," and "Washington Week in Review" is to explain the larger significance of current events. In such forums, commentators generally emphasize the importance of the events being discussed. They do so, at least in part, because of a subconscious tendency to believe that if those events lacked a broader significance they would not be worthy topics of discussion.

The highly competitive and partisan nature of our political system also tends to cause political leaders to exaggerate the importance of Grenadas and Lebanons.[4] To extract maximum political capital from "successes," presidents and their supporters often seek to amplify their magnitude and portray small local victories as major international triumphs. Conversely, their political adversaries feel impelled to present events in the worst possible light and depict relatively minor developments as global setbacks.

No matter how dramatic, individual events rarely result in significant changes in the world situation or foreign images of American foreign policy. Paradoxically, while many analysts overestimate the impact of events such as Grenada on others' images of the world, such events seldom cause them to alter their own images of the world.[5] The Reagan administration's action in Grenada might have had a long term effect on how others see the United States, but whether in fact it will depends more on the overall pattern of American foreign policy than on the Grenada intervention.

Second, it must be recognized that the effects of the invasion of Grenada on American standing in the Third World (to the extent that there are any) is not dependent on how Americans believe others will or ought to perceive that action, but rather on how the Third World perceives it. An important corollary of this point is that the way in which both foreign and domestic groups perceive the Grenada intervention depends heavily on the beliefs they held before the intervention.[6]

Both conservatives and liberals are guilty of projecting their beliefs into the minds of foreign elites. Given the core presupposition of most conservatives that shows of force are the best way to earn the respect of allies and adversaries, the tendency is to believe that Grenada will enhance American standing in the world. Conversely, liberals who believe that aggressive displays of military power invariably reinforce negative stereotypes of American foreign policy quickly concluded that the global perception of the invasion can only be negative. The conclusions that others reach about the broad significance of American actions will depend on the context in which such actions occur. But before any conclusion about the international effect of the Grenada intervention can be made, it is necessary to know more about how the intervention is being presented to the world.

Over the course of the year following President Reagan's decision to intervene, administration officials and other commentators have given less and less attention to the rather unique set of circumstances that made it possible for the United States to act so decisively in October 1983. There is an obvious reason for their deemphasis of context. The more contextually determined the decision to intervene, the less plausible are the claims quoted above that the Grenada operation can be read as a signal of America's will to act forcefully in the Third World. Initially, both President Reagan and Secretary of State Shultz strongly emphasized contextual factors in their justifications of the intervention. In a question-and-answer session on November 3, 1983 the President was asked whether the success of Grenada meant that he might be able to use military force in similiar situations elsewhere. The President replied:

> No, I can't foresee any situation that has exactly the same thing that this one had. It had exactly what we announced in the beginning—the need to protect the lives and the safety and the freedom of about 1,000 Americans, most of them students down there in medical school, and in answer to a request on the part of the other nations bound by treaty together in the East Caribbean that we lend our support to them in freeing this up because they lacked the strength and capability of doing it. . . . if all the conditions were the same, I don't see why our reason would be any different. But I don't foresee any similiar situation on the horizon.[7]

Similiarly, in a news conference on the first day of the operation, Secretary Schultz emphatically denied that the action was intended as a signal to the Soviets or Cubans.[8] Obviously, it is possible that both the President and his Secretary of State were being disingenuous in these statements. Even if that were the case, however, the fact that they made them served to reduce the likelihood that foreign leaders would view the Grenada intervention as an indicator of how the United States would act in other areas of the Third World. By emphasizing the uniqueness of the Grenada context, the administration made it easier for observers who were not predisposed to view the action as a signal of American resolve to discount its broader significance. Moreover, the fact that Reagan and Shultz felt it necessary to emphasize the objective of protecting the medical students and deny that the intervention was motivated even in part by a desire to demonstrate resolve indirectly confirms the continuing existence of strong domestic political limits on the president's ability to use force.

What conclusions, then, can we draw about the effects of the Grenada intervention on American standing in the Third World? This question is best answered by examining the specific contentions of those who argue that the effects have been positive.

Impact on Soviet Policy

According to some administration officials, the use of force in Grenada caused Soviet leaders to reassess the risks of expansive policies in the Third World. This might be especially true with regard to the Caribbean Basin and Central America.[9] However, it is unlikely that Grenada had a positive effect on Soviet policy toward Africa. It is likely that the "success" of the Grenada intervention has made Moscow intent on avoiding embarrassing reversals in America's back yard, but this is probably not the case in distant Africa.

The differences between the military environment that American forces confronted in Grenada and the situation they would face in a similar operation in Africa are patently obvious. Military intervention in Africa would be vastly more difficult to initiate and sustain. It would be far more risky, the probable outcome would be much less predictable, and the Soviet Union would be in a much better position to assist embattled allies on that continent than it was to aid the shortlived Coard regime. Given these differences, it is hard to believe that Soviet military planners would base projections of American policy toward Angola, Libya, or Ethiopia (the three countries where it is believed the Reagan administration would most like to see a change of regime) on decisions taken in easy-win cases such as Grenada or the Gulf of Sidra incident.

Arguments to the effect that by demonstrating American resolve, the Grenada operation will serve to deter Soviet expansion elsewhere in the Third World rest in large part on a misreading of recent developments in Africa. Contrary to conservative mythology, Soviet "successes" in Angola (1975–1976) and Ethiopia (1977–1978) were primarily the result of situational advantages rather than a lack of American resolve.[10] Such factors are likely to continue to be the best predictor of Soviet behavior.

One respect in which the Grenada events may have caused the Soviets to adopt a tougher stance in some African situations stems from the fact that Soviet leaders are at least as concerned as their American counterparts with projecting an image of resolve. Consequently, a predictable Soviet response to Grenada might be to seek opportunities that would repair the damage done to the credibility of their position in the Third World. Paradoxically, the likelihood of such a response is increased by repeated American claims (such as those quoted above) that Grenada represented a major defeat for the Soviet Union.

One case where Grenada might have had such an effect is Angola. Shortly after the intervention, the Soviets sent South Africa and the United States a number of signals that they would not allow the MPLA regime in Angola to be overthrown by South African-backed guerrillas under the leadership of Jonas Savimbi. These signals included direct communications with South Africa, an increase in the Cuban military presence in Angola, and new transfers of sophisticated military equipment. Although it is unlikely that Grenada was solely responsible for causing the Soviets to take these actions (indications that Savimbi's forces might threaten Luanda were almost certainly more important), it might have led Soviet leaders to upwardly revise their estimates of the possible international costs of a defeat of their Angolan allies. Similiarly, the outcome in Grenada may have caused both the Cubans and the Soviets to increase pressure on MPLA leaders to resist any deal with the United States or South Africa that would appear to reduce their presence in Angola. In sum, if the Grenada intervention had any effects on Soviet activity in Africa, they were probably negative.

IMPACT ON SOVIET ALLIES

Some officials claim that the Grenada events caused radically inclined Third World states to reassess their ties with the Soviet Union. This claim rests on two propositions: (1) that Grenada demonstrated that the Soviet Union cannot protect its clients and is therefore not a reliable ally; and (2) that it evidenced a new American willingness to raise the costs of alliance with the Soviet Union. Some Third World states appear to have recently reassessed the value of close relations with the Soviet Union. But in the one region where this appears to have occurred—Southern Africa—the process began well before President Reagan took office, and for reasons much more complex than the American show of force in Grenada.[11]

Soviet influence in Southern Africa has declined over the past five years for three reasons. First, by 1980 African leaders had concluded that the Soviet Union was not able to provide the kinds of economic and technical assistance necessary for long-term development. Second, a steady escalation of insurgencies in Angola and Mozambique convinced leaders in those countries—and in the newly independent state of Zimbabwe—that a military relationship with the Soviet Union and Cuba was not a guarantee of security. These two developments were necessary but not sufficient to cause a foreign policy realignment. Also required was a third factor: the willingness of Western governments to offer these countries an alternative to reliance on the Soviets.

The Lancaster House settlement of 1979 was critical in this respect. By rejecting the advice of conservatives that they side with the internal parties in Rhodesia/Zimbabwe, Prime Minister Margaret Thatcher and President Jimmy Carter convinced key African figures (especially President Samora Machel of Mozambique) that cooperation with the West was possible. Without such a development, it is doubtful that Zimbabwe would have chosen to ignore the Soviet Union and rely instead on Western support, or that Machel would have pressured Mugabe to accept British demands.[12]

Mozambique's recent rapprochement with South Africa provides further evidence of the importance of a nonideological approach that recognizes and respects the vital interests of governments that it seeks to influence, and skillfully uses inducements as well as threats. Immediately after the Reagan administration took office, relations with Mozambique deteriorated sharply. A major reason for this occurrence was Mozambique's fear that the United States under Reagan would align itself with South Africa and support efforts to destabilize radical regimes in the region. Relations improved only after President Machel and his advisors came to believe that it would be possible to get the United States to use its influence in Pretoria to facilitate an agreement that would not threaten the survival of their regime.[13] Until they reached that conclusion, Mozambique could not afford to risk a break with Moscow. Moreover, had Assistant Secretary of State Chester Crocker and South Africans made unrealistic demands for internal political changes in Mozambique (as the Reagan administration has done in Nicaragua), increased pressure on the regime would have almost certainly led to greater Mozambican reliance on the Soviet Union and Cuba.[14]

Similiarly, the tentative progress that has been made in discussions between Washington and Luanda concerning the Cuban presence in Angola began to occur only after the United States began to downplay its threat to support National Union for the Total Independence of Angola (UNITA) insurgents[15] and acknowledged that any agreement must satisfy legitimate Angolan security concerns.

Outside of Southern Africa there is no evidence that Third World countries with substantial ties to the Soviet Union have changed their orientation since 1981. If anything, the reverse has occurred. The Soviet military presence in Syria is far more extensive than it was in 1981.[16] In September 1984, Ethiopia formally created a vanguard party, thus solidifying its ideological links with Moscow.[17] Libya under Qadhafi remains Libya under Qadhafi, and Vietnam is still closely tied to the Eastern bloc both economically and militarily.

Grenada and the resolute policy it is said to symbolize might have caused some states to conclude that ties with the Soviet Union and Cuba are now more likely to lead to conflict with the United States. But this does not mean that having come to that conclusion those states will choose to loosen their ties with Moscow. If states like Ethiopia and Libya believe that Washington is irreversibly committed to their demise (as conservative rhetoric concerning the principles involved in the Grenada intervention suggests), their only option is to prepare for the eventual confrontation. Inevitably, this will lead to closer military relations with the only other big power in the neighborhood—the Soviet Union. For the reasons discussed above, there is a good chance they will succeed.

IMPACT ON "FRIENDLY" REGIMES

A final claim advanced by some officials is that by responding to the request of the Organization of Eastern Caribbean States (OECS) to intervene in Grenada, the Reagan administration enhanced the credibility of American commitments to its friends and allies throughout the Third World. This claim suffers from all the problems cited at the beginning of this essay: the tendency to exaggerate the effects of single events, the tendency to project our beliefs into the minds of others, and the tendency to ignore the specific context of Grenada. Notwithstanding, it is probably true that the Reagan administration policies have increased the confidence of friendly regimes that they can count on American support. In the abstract, this would seem a positive development. Before we accept this easy conclusion, however, there are two issues that need to be raised.

First, I think we need to rethink the notion of "friendly" regimes as it applies to the Third World. The term "friend" implies that there is a common bond or affective tie involved in a relationship which goes beyond a mere complementarity or coincidence of interests. This is almost certainly true of our relations with nations such as Canada, Great Britain, and France. In our relations with Third World countries, however, this is only very rarely the case. As I have argued elsewhere with regard to Africa, the foreign policies of almost all Third World regimes involve a near incessant drive to ensure security.[18] Commitments to abstract notions like the "Free World" are luxuries such regimes can ill afford. This argument has several implications. It suggests that "standing up for democracy" in Grenada is likely to earn us few rewards in the Third World. More importantly, it means that our relations with Third World countries are almost certain to remain impermanent, resting as they do on relatively short-term calculations of the benefits they confer to individual regimes. Given these circumstances, the only credibility that the United States should be concerned about is the credibility of its commitment to defend American interests—and in the Third World there are very few situations where our long-term interests require that we ensure the survival of particular regimes.[19]

Secondly, we must recognize that commitments to friendly regimes are not without costs. Ironically, one cost is a loss of influence over the regimes to which we are committed. As we have discovered with Mobutu's Zaire, once a leader believes that the United States views his regime's survival as critical to its interests and credibility, he is less likely to take seriously threats to reduce or cut off aid if he chooses not to respond to our suggestions and demands.[20] A related cost is the possibility that friendly regimes will begin to overrely on our security guaranteees, and as a consequence fail to make needed internal reforms or promote accommodations essential to regional peace.[21] This may be occurring in the Sudan. Finally, commitments to specific regimes make it more likely that regional rivals, with whom we might otherwise develop an entirely workable relationship, will begin to define us as the enemy.

In short, before we applaud the Reagan administration for sending a reassuring signal to "friendly" regimes around the world, we need to consider more carefully what the actual impact of the Grenada intervention will be both on their behavior and, more importantly, on American interests.

NOTES

1. *The New York Times*, Aug 22, 1984,
2. Ibid., Aug 23, 1984.
3. Remarks presented at conference on Soviet/Cuban Strategy in the Third World After Grenada, August 15–18, 1984, cosponsored by the Kennan Institute for Advanced Russian Studies, and the and Naval Postgraduate School, Monterey, CA.
4. For an insightful discussion of the effects of partisan politics on the discussion of foreign policy debate, *see* I. M. Destler, Leslie Gelb, and Anthony Lake, *Our Own Worst Enemy* (Simon & Schuster, 1984).
5. On the cognitive dynamics of "learning" and attitude change in international relations, see Robert Jervis, *Perception and Misperception in International Relations* (Princeton University Press, 1976, especially Part II).
6. For general evidence on this point, see Ibid., pp. 143–154.
7. Department of State Bulletin, December 1983, p. 78.
8. Ibid., p. 70.
9. *See* chapters in this volume by Howard Wiarda and Richard Millett.
10. On Ethiopia, *see* Marina Ottaway, *Soviet and American Influence in the Horn of Africa* (Praeger, 1982); and Tom J. Farer, *War Clouds on the Horn of Africa*, 2nd ed. (Carnegie Endowment for International Peace, 1979). On Angola, *see* John Marcum, *The Angolan Revolution*, Vol. II (MIT Press, 1978).
11. Singleton, Seth, "The Natural Ally: Soviet Policy in Southern Africa," in Michael Clough (ed.), *Changing Realities in Southern Africa* (Berkeley: Institute of International Studies, 1982).
12. Michael Clough, "From Rhodesia to Zimbabwe," ibid.
13. Michael Clough, "United States Policy in Southern Africa," *Current History*, Mar 1984.
14. Michael Clough, "Mozambique: American Policy Options," *Africa Report*, November-December 1982.
15. Michael Clough, "United States Policy in Southern Africa," op. cit.; and Helen Kitchen and Michael Clough, *The United States and South Africa: Realities and Red Herrings* (Washington, D.C.: Center for Strategic and International Studies, 1984).
16. Anthony Cordesman, "Syrian-Israeli C^3I: The West's Third Front," *Armed Forces Journal International*, March 1984, pp. 87–90.

17. David Ottaway, "Ethiopia Forms its First Party," *The Washington Post*, September 11, 1984.

18. Michael Clough, "The Foreign Policies of African States: Images, Determinants, and Patterns," paper presented at Soviet-American conference on Sub-Saharan Africa, Moscow, June 26–29, 1984.

19. Richard Feinberg, *The Intemperate Zone* (W. W. Norton & Co., 1983); and Tom J. Farer, "Searching for Defeat," *Foreign Policy*, Fall 1980.

20. On the problems of the United States has had dealing with Mobutu, *see* Johathan Kwitny, *Endless Enemies* (Congdon & Weed, Inc., 1984); and M. Crawford Young, "Zaire in the International Arena," paper presented at conference on Continuity and Change in Africa, May 1982, the Naval Postgraduate School, Monterey, CA.

21. An interesting argument to this effect concerning Ethiopia is made by Fred Halliday and Maxine Molynex, *The Ethiopian Revolution* (London: Verso Editions, 1981), pp. 214–225.

Part III
Grenada and East-West Relations

DOV S. ZAKHEIM

The Grenada Operation and Superpower Relations: A Perspective from the Pentagon

PRELIMINARY OBSERVATIONS

Evaluating Soviet motivations and actions from the perspective of the present, or near present, affords an analyst little in the way of hard documentation upon which to base his or her analysis. The Soviet Union remains a closed society. Indeed, it is probably more closed today than in the 1930s when defectors and show trials provided evidence of the inner workings of a brutal totalitarian regime. It is more closed than in the 1950s, when Nikita Khrushchev for his own reasons, lifted the veil over Stalinist excesses and allowed some literary liberalization. And it is more closed than in the 1960s when Brezhnev solidified his hold on the party and state apparatus.

Recently the Soviet Union was led by a true faceless bureaucrat about whom little was known (Konstantin Chernenko). Until his surprising reemergence as a political force during the final declining months of his predecessor, Yuri Andropov, he had been written off as a lackey of the Brezhnev regime. The tenuous leadership situation in the Soviet Union today is a unique turn of events in Soviet history that has spewed forth the fastest turnover of Soviet/Russian leaders since Lvov gave way to Kerensky, who preceded Lenin.

In a country whose apparatchiks are notorious for their conservatism and slavish cleaving to what they perceive to be the party line, there is great reluctance among the middle level bureaucracy to voice opinions or observations that might cost them their jobs the next day. Nevertheless, one cannot analyze superpower relations without speculating about Soviet motives and perceptions. Otherwise, all one is left with are official Soviet and American statements, and the imbalance that arises between what Raymond Aron described as a West that speaks with many voices and a Soviet Union that speaks with one.[1]

THE VALUE OF GRENADA TO THE SOVIETS: WHAT ARE SOVIET GOALS?

To examine the impact of Grenada intervention on superpower relations is to presume that Grenada meant something to the Soviets. How much it meant derives from several factors. Grenada's value to the Soviet Union was partly a function of actions taken by the Grenadian leadership. It was also a function of Soviet policies in the brief period from 1980–1983 when Moscow responded to the enthusiastic embrace of Leninism evinced by the New Jewel Movement (NJM). However, any evaluation of Grenada's importance to the Soviets necessarily reflects the way in which Soviet geopolitical are assessed.

There exist at least three different views of the motivations that propel the international behavior of the Soviet Union. One view holds that the Soviet Union is prompted by an expansionist ideology that will not rest until it has swallowed, by force or other means, the remainder of the world. Within this view there are variations. Some contend that Soviets have a "master plan," while others see Soviet foreign policy as more oriented toward strategic objectives and the seizing of opportunities as they present themselves, but nevertheless fixed on the belief that communism will one day triumph worldwide.[2]

A second view acknowledges that communist ideology has fashioned the Soviet state in a manner fundamentally different from others. This view nevertheless posits that *qua state*, the Soviet Union can be expected to act like all other states within the international system.[3] It will, of course, act to its own advantage. Nevertheless, it will recognize that as a member of the international community, its shares much in common with that community. Therefore, its behavior will be rational, and its leadership can be relied on to behave in a manner similar to the leadership of other states, according to the accepted norms of statecraft.

The third view holds that ideology fits neatly into the historic expansionist impulses that drove imperial Russia, and that it might not be the prime motivating factor behind Soviet foreign policy. Thus the Soviet leadership might not be blinded by ideology or prone to irrational behavior, and could well be cautious about expansion. The expansionist impulse will never be far from the surface, however, and opportunities to nourish it will be continually exploited by Moscow.[4]

An assessment of the impact of Grenada based on either the first or third view will be clearly different from one based on the second. To those who view the Soviet Union as just another state with a different form of government, the Grenada intervention was as much a sideshow of U.S.-Soviet relations as was Soviet involvement in the first place. It was "opportune" for the Soviets to have a government in the Caribbean that considered itself "fraternal." It would have been equally opportune if that government had been located elsewhere, and the fall of that government made little difference. Soviet concerns were centered elsewhere, and its relationship with the United States focused on other issues. It is noteworthy in this regard, that the International Institute for Strategic Studies, *Strategic Survey* for 1983–84 does not even mention Grenada in the context of its discussion of superpower relations.[5] The Strategic Arms Reductions Talks (START), intermediate-range nuclear forces (INF), and anti-satellite (ASAT) weapons were viewed by the authors of that volume as central to U.S.-Soviet relations, while Grenada was merely a local affair of some significance for Central America and U.S.-Cuban relations, but not much else.

What did Grenada offer the Soviets? Only if one assumes an aggressive, expansionist thrust to Soviet foreign policy does Grenada's value—and loss—appear important for the Soviets. It would seem that despite being a tiny, relatively poor island with a large proportion of its population chronically unemployed, Grenada provided the Soviets with certain gains.

For the ideologues in the Kremlin (and there is no evidence that this breed has passed away or that the Soviets have given up trying to win the minds of those in the Third World and elsewhere who display an ideological bent), Grenada was a promising development. It was a showpiece example of the spread of Marxism-Leninism. To be sure, there were local peculiarities. Yet what local conditions can be said to be ideal for any Leninist state beginning with Tsarist Russia itself?

Grenada was an example of what Gavin Kennedy has described as an armed-party state, as opposed to a one-party state with an army.[6] As in other communist regimes, and unlike in other authoritarian governments, the military, as well as other state elements, derived its authority from the party. Moreover, whatever the motivations of Grenadian leaders, there can be no denying the degree to which they absorbed the political lexicon, culture, and structural norms of Marxism-Leninism. The creation of a Central Committee, the efforts to organize Soviet-like structures within the framework of the old Anglo-Caribbean parish system, and the ties to fraternal communist parties and states all reflected a slavish, almost childlike mimicry of the Soviet Union.[7] (Appendix A, Document 16)

But Grenada was not merely a boon to the ideologues. Those who are concerned primarily with realpolitik had much to gain from Grenada as well. Grenada was another input to what Brezhnev constantly referred to as the "correlation of forces" in the world—that great balance sheet that assessed the relative standing of East and West in terms of an index of military, political, geographic, economic, and cultural factors (the relative values of which were never specified). Perhaps most importantly, Grenada represented another successful effort to find holes in the Monroe Doctrine, an objective that Nikita Khrushchev articulated in his memoirs.[8] Together with Michael Manley's Jamaica, Grenada represented a break with the British parliamentary tradition. It embodied a clear reversion from democratic

Potential Security Implications of Aircraft Based in Cuba, Nicaragua, and Grenada (MIG-23 Flogger Combat Radius-560m, 1″ = 1,000m)

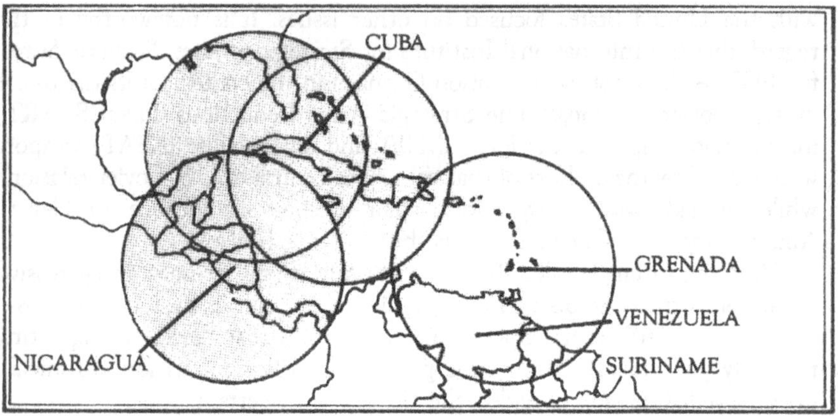

"If Cuban fighters were to stage out of Central America (i.e., Nicaragua) or Caribbean airfields, i.e., Grenada), and those in Cuba, they could strike all of Central America, the Caribbean Islands, parts of southeastern United States (highly unlikely), and oil fields located in Mexico (Veracruz) and Venezuela." U.S. Joint Chiefs of Staff, in Military Posture for FY-83. (Constructed by Lieutenant Jeff Johnson, USAF: graphics and cartography by James French Crispelle.)

institutions to those of Marxism-Leninism. One does not have to be an ideologue to appreciate the significance of this transformation.

In addition, Grenada was of potential military utility to the Soviets. It presented a problem for American military planners, who had to allow for the possibility that the island could be used as a base for Soviet long-range bombers or reconnaissance aircraft, or for Cuban fighter aircraft targeting petroleum facilities in the nearby Dutch Antilles and Venezuela, or oil tanker routes to Europe.[9] It mattered little whether the Point Salines airport would be used primarily as a tourist facility as claimed. It was the *potential* that the airport offered to Soviet military and logistical requirements that worried American analysts. Moreover, Grenada was a way-station in another respect. It represented a potential storehouse for equipment to support insurgencies elsewhere in the region. Documents captured after the October intervention reveal the extent to which planned supplies, as well as those found warehoused on the island, far exceeded Grenada's needs.[10] (Appendix A, Documents 12 and 13.)

From a variety of perspectives, Grenada was a useful asset to the Soviet Union. Its loss, therefore, must be viewed as a blow to the efforts of the Soviet Union to expand its foothold in the Western Hemisphere. In addition, unless one assumes no connection between Soviet and Cuban policy, the Grenada intervention resulted in further blows to Soviet efforts aimed at creating "progressive" gains at the expense of "reactionary" powers. Most notable in this regard were the expulsion of Cuban advisors from Suriname and Castro's admission of his inability to come to the aid of revolutionary regimes in the Western Hemisphere. It is arguable, however, that the greatest blow that the Grenada operation dealt to the Soviets was in terms of the Soviet Union's perception of its long-term relationship with the United States. To understand the nature of this blow it is necessary to turn to American perceptions of the invasion of Grenada.

GRENADA AND AMERICA'S SELF-IMAGE

The Grenada intervention was exceedingly popular in the United States. No less than 60% of the population appeared to support the president's action.[11] This support was widespread despite howls of "foul" from the press because it was excluded from the initial landings. Public enthusiasm was buttressed by images of American medical students kissing the ground after their rescue and cheering Grenadians welcoming American troops. It was further fueled by the televised sight of the ascerbic Dominican Prime Minister Eugenia Charles insisting to her interlocutors that the United States had intervened at the very urgent and necessary request of the Organization of Eastern Caribbean States (OECS), whose member nations were incapable of coping by themselves with what they perceived to be a threat to their security.

Moreover, the Grenada intervention may have signalled a major step toward recovery from the Vietnam syndrome.[12] The characteristics of this syndrome, as manifested in public attitudes and governmental behavior during the latter part of the 1970s were (1) an inward-looking mentality, and in some quarters, a somewhat isolationist view of the U.S. role in the world, (2) a fatalistic resignation to the "fact" of America's limited ability to influence world events, (3) a *mea culpa* attitude to the world's troubles (this being somewhat inconsistent with the preceding attitudinal patterns), (4) the implicit and sometimes explicit acceptance of the notion that America was a reactionary power that had to come to terms with progressive developments taking place in the Third World, and (5) suspicion about American military modernization programs in light of the preceding tendencies.

But beginning in 1980, with the election of a president who had campaigned on the basis of a need to revive the nation's defenses, it appeared that the American public was beginning to emerge from the psychological cocoon spun by Vietnam. The shooting down of two Libyan aircraft on August 19, 1982, seemed to confirm American resolve. There was little criticism and much applause for those who had reasserted America's freedom to navigate in international waters. Furthermore, the Reagan administration successfully persuaded Congress to support a significant buildup of America's military resources, thus demonstrating a readiness to deploy U.S. forces in support of commitments to friends and allies.

In 1983 alone, U.S. military force deployments included (1) operations in the Middle East as part of a multinational contingent without whose presence the Gemayel government in Lebanon would most surely have fallen, (2) the use of naval and air forces to deter Libyan moves against the Sudan, (3) extensive military exercises to demonstrate America's commitment to the free states of Central America, and (4) the redeployment of AWACS aircraft and F-15 fighters to assist Chad in its war with Libyan-backed insurgents. But all of these efforts except the show of force in the Eastern Mediterranean were relatively small scale, and none involved sustained and organized military operations against U.S. forces (the attacks on U.S. forces in Lebanon tended to be costly, but rather sporadic).

The Grenada operation went further, however. It was not only a "rescue mission," but a decisive use of U.S. military capabilities in support of U.S. foreign policy objectives. Grenada was a combined operation, incorporating all branches of the U.S. military. The operation involved nearly 2,000 personnel on the first day and nearly 8,000 military by mid-November. It encountered organized opposition from the Grenadian People's Revolutionary Army (PRA), and many of the approximately 650 Cubans on the island who clearly served as more than mere advisors or construction workers. That the United States public did not flinch from supporting an operation of this size indicates that when the cause is perceived as just, the American public and administration act as one.

The Grenada intervention was militarily significant, for although it was relatively undemanding compared to the types of opposition that might be expected in a conflagration in Southwest Asia or Europe, it nevertheless imposed a variety of strenuous demands on U.S. forces. These included rapid and coordinated planning among the services, the redeployment of units from their usual patterns of peacetime operation, and the establishment of adequate communication and support networks. Most importantly, the operation was successful in minimizing the danger to U.S. citizens on the island and limited the damage inflicted on the local population. The spectre of an Iranian hostage crisis hung over the operation, and indeed, as Secretary of State Shultz indicated, this was a prime factor motivating its initiation. "Mission accomplished" therefore meant more than merely routing the Grenadian and Cuban resistance.

The cumulative impact of Grenada on America's self-image should not be underestimated. It represented a clearcut military success—something that the American public had not witnessed since before Vietnam. It marked the expression of American vigor in foreign policy, and signified an understanding of the role of force as a vehicle for the support of U.S. foreign policy objectives when all other options are closed except passive resignation to the whims of fate. Since 1980, President Reagan has spoken of a determination to restore the United States to its role as a world leader and stand up to those who threaten American interests. Perhaps more than any other action since he has come to office, the invasion of Grenada has lent substance to such goals.

GRENADA AND THE SOVIET IMAGE OF THE UNITED STATES

The 1970s witnessed a remarkable expansion of both the capabilities and uses of Soviet military power. During the last decade the Soviet Union underwent a major modernization of its armed forces that led to capabilities to undertake new missions. At the same time, the United States debated whether to increase military spending in real terms, allowed crucial modernization programs to be delayed, and permitted its overall military readiness to decline. In the strategic realm, the Soviet Union achieved nuclear parity with the United States and appeared to be on the verge of obtaining superiority in certain force capabilities. In addition, Moscow revived its competition with the United States regarding intermediate-range nuclear forces with the deployment of hundreds of SS-20 missiles.

Soviet advances in the conventional realm were no less notable. In fact, Soviet conventional forces were put to frequent use during the latter half of the 1970s. The Soviet army evolved into a highly maneuverable combat force whose hallmarks were speed and firepower. The navy continued its transformation from a coastal defensive unit designed to protect against amphibious attack, to a deep-water fleet with the capability to interpose itself between Western naval forces and distant insurgencies. The air force, originally designed to defend against bomber attacks, greatly extended its combat and logistical capacity. Finally, Soviet mobile units, formerly with little range or load bearing capacity, extended their reach and payload to intercontinental range.

The results of this transformation were first seen in 1974 when a Soviet airlift of Cuban forces coupled with a small naval show of force—a signal to outsiders to keep away—enabled the outnumbered MPLA to sieze power in Angola. The 1977–1978 Ethiopian-Somali war signaled a new stage in Soviet operations in the Third World. An even larger airlift of Cuban forces was accompanied by a lift of Soviet equipment and the presence of several Soviet generals advising the Ethiopians. Then came Afghanistan, where for the past four years the Soviets have deployed over 100,000 troops supported by airmobile strike operations.[13] In addition, the Soviets and their allies are supporting the Sandinista regime in a similar manner to which they supported Cuba during the 1960s.[14] Thus by 1980 the Soviets had completely transformed their armed forces and demonstrated a readiness to use them in limited situations, while the United States appeared reluctant to enter the fray. As that reluctance was indeed manifest, there was nothing to stop Soviet intervention in the Third World.

But all this has changed since 1980. The Soviets continue to battle the Islamic resistance in Afghanistan, but have yet to score the major victory they anticipated nearly five years ago. Indeed, they have scaled down their presence in Ethiopia, and their sometime Libyan associates are presently relatively quiescent.

This turn of events is due as much to the changing nature of American self-confidence and diplomacy as it is to leadership struggles in the Kremlin. Superpower relations form a seamless worldwide web. Soviet and American leaders closely watch each other to assess the impact of the other's actions on bilateral relations. This is why a confident United States is in a very different bargaining position than an introspective, uncertain America. A confident United States that demonstrates a willingness to heed the call of weak friends and allies is unlikely to allow its alliances to crumble or its friendships to dissipate. It is able to ensure the deployment of its missiles on the territories of its European allies in the face of pressures from the Soviet Union. It is able to marshal European nations to deploy their forces in the Middle East for the first time in decades. It is able to strengthen its bonds in Asia not merely with Japan, but with the ASEAN states as well. Finally it is able to demonstrate its reliability to those African countries unfortunate enough to share boundaries with Qadhafi's Libya.

As the Soviet Union is beset with economic troubles and unrest among its allies in Poland and East Berlin, the resurgence of the United States can only prompt an agonizing reappraisal of its foreign policy. Such a reappraisal certainly will be influenced by the increasingly powerful Soviet military establishment which is reputed to be a force for conservatism. Thus the impetus for an accommodation with the United States could well come from those whose training is more in matters of Mars than Marx. For the Soviet military establishment, ideology is likely to be far less important than a realistic and rigorous definition of Soviet security interests and requirements.

For the present, however, the Soviets appear to be in the midst of an uncertain phase. They clearly never expected the reflowering of American patriotism or the coming to power of a vigorous administration so soon after the Vietnam War. To a nation as influenced by history as the Soviet Union, all that has happened to America in recent years is rather alien. It has come too soon. Soviet uncertainty has manifested itself in a number of ways. Most notable are the naked attempts to bully NATO into rejecting the deployment of American intermediate-range missiles, the walkout on START and INF talks, and the Olympic boycott. Yet each time Soviet policy has backfired. Cruise missiles are being deployed in Europe; the U.S. position on START—a product of a Congressional bipartisan effort and the findings of an independent commission—has resulted in the stilling of voices calling for a unilateral nuclear freeze; and the Olympic boycott did not dampen the spirit of the Los Angeles games—it rather demonstrated a lack of worldwide support for Soviet propaganda ploys.

Grenada's input to these events may not have been obvious, but it was nonetheless present. As an American writer put it, "Men hate to be pushed around. . . . When this happens . . . they begin to think in terms of a punch in the nose. And this is exactly what Reagan administered to the Soviets and their surrogates in Grenada."[15] Moreover, there is reason to believe the Soviets are beginning to realize this.

GRENADA AND A STRATEGY TO COUNTER THE EAST

Grenada was an expression of American capabilities, not a model for repeated military excursions. It was a unique response to a unique situation. American citizens seemed threatened in an atmosphere characterized by lawlessness and the absence either of legitimate government or other sources of succor. It all seemed like a flashback to Iran in 1979. Most importantly, the United States received an appeal from an established regional organization to come to its assistance. It responded, and did so successfully. To be sure, the United States did not escape criticism from some nervous Latin American states, or even from most of its NATO alies. But as *Strategic Survey* and others have noted, this criticism was far less harsh than some (for example the Soviets) might have wished.[16] With respect to NATO there was no impact at all on the schedule for deploying intermediate-range missiles to Europe. In fact, for all the criticism of the intervention, there was an acknowledgement that the United States had acted in its national interest as it might have been expected to do prior to the 1970s.

The gains that democracy has made in Grenada will not be preserved without a struggle, however. And on the fortune of democracy rides the credibility of the United States. The liberation of Grenada was political, not economic. Unemployment is rampant, and as long as it remains high, agitators will find ready listeners. Despite graffiti along Grenadian roads describing NJM leaders as "crooks,"[17] those who would seek to undermine a return to parliamentary government could resurface if given the opportunity. Grenada will continue to need economic assistance specific to its immediate needs and within the more general context of the administration's Caribbean Basin Initiative. The October 1983 military campaign was the initial blow for democracy in Grenada. An economic campaign is the only way to preserve it.

To date, the U.S. has disbursed or allocated 57.2 million dollars to Grenada for budget assistance, development projects, and completion of the Point Salines airport complex. This is in addition to security assistance and PKO (Peace Keeping Operation) funding used to support the Caribbean Peacekeeping Force and train and equip the Grenadian police force.

THE MESSAGE OF GRENADA

It is important to recognize that the situation in Nicaragua is quite different from the one that existed in Grenada. The United States has recognized the Sandinista regime and has exchanged ambassadors with Nicaragua. It has sought, thus far without success, to convince the Sandinistas not to export their revolution to other countries in the region. However faint the dialogue with Managua, a dialogue nevertheless exists. In the final weeks of October 1983, there was no government on the island of Grenada with which any reasonable dialogue could have been conducted.

There is another fundamental difference. The Grenada events were internal to that state. The current crisis in Central America affects several nations (as did Grenada). However, the United States has acted on the proposition voiced by Nicaragua's neighbors that Central American governments are best suited to cope with the insurgencies that threaten them, and that the United States can best assist them through the provision of training and support. These governments have not issued an OECS-like call for aid. They have stated that they do not want U.S. intervention, and as the Reagan administration has stated on many occasions, the United States does not want to intervene.

The message of Grenada, perhaps already assimilated by the Soviet Union, reiterates the basic tenets of U.S. national security policy. The "message" is that the United States does not intend to remain a passive observer on the international scene; it is determined to be a credible ally and friend; it recognizes the need to carry on relations with the Soviet Union in a business-like manner and that arms negotiations are central to those relations; and it acknowledges, as Raymond Aron observed in *Peace and War*, that the West recognizes the primacy of peace while Marxism-Leninism adheres to the primacy of conflict. Peaceful coexistence must be seen in this light,[18] but nevertheless, the United States will continue to assume that the Soviet Union shares its interest in peace although it of course will remain vigilant in the event that this is not the case. The final message of Grenada is that after the wrenching decade of the Vietnam era, the American people are again prepared to support a vigorous foreign policy that protects and underscores American interests throughout the world.

NOTES

1. Raymond Aron, *Peace and War: A Theory of International Relations* (New York: Doubleday, 1966), p. 62.
2. See for example, Jiri and Virginia Valenta, "Soviet Strategy and Policies in the Caribbean Basin," in Howard J. Wiarda (ed.), *Rift and Revolution: The Central American Imbroglio* (Washington, D.C.: American Enterprise Institute, 1984).
3. See "Containment: Indispensable Yet Unsatisfactory" and "The Soviet System" in Aaron Wildavsky (ed.), *Beyond Containment* (San Francisco, California, Institute for Contemporary Studies, 1983).
4. Aron discusses the plausibility of a universal empire under Russian control in *Peace and War*, pp. 759–760; *see also* Charles Wolf, Jr. "Extended Containment," in *Beyond Containment*, pp. 147–168.
5. "U.S.-Soviet Relations: The Euromissile Contest," *Strategic Survey 1983–1984* (London: 1984), pp. 36–41.
6. Gavin Kennedy, *The Military in the Third World* (London: Duckworth, 1974), p. 19.
7. Extraordinary Meeting of the Central Committee NJM, September 14–16, 1983, Grenada Documents, Log No. 000123.

8. Nikita Khrushchev, *Khrushchev Remembers* (London: Little Brown, 1971), pp. 449–463.

9. See Wallace Nutting's remarks in, "How Oil Fueled the Invasion of Grenada," *Business Week* (November 7, 1983), p. 42.

10. Top Secret Agreement between the Government of Grenada and the Government of the Union of Soviet Socialist Republics on Deliveries from the Union of the SSR to Grenada of Special and other Equipment, October 27, 1980, ibid., Log No. 000190; and Top Secret Agreement between the Government of Grenada and the Government of the Union of Soviet Socialist Republics on Deliveries from the Union of SSR to Grenada of Special and Other Equipment, July 27, 1982, ibid. These documents are reproduced in "Documents Pertaining to Relations Between Grenada, the USSR and Cuba," op. cit. *See also* Nestor D. Sanchez, "What Was Uncovered in Grenada: The Weapons and Documents," *Caribbean Review*, 1983, pp. 21–28 and 59; and *Soviet Military Power, 1984* (Washington, D.C.: Government Printing Office, 1984), p. 128.

11. Gallup Poll findings of November 18–21, 1983 on percentage approving "the way President Reagan is handling the situation in Grenada."

12. For a similar but foreign perspective, see Oakland Ross, "Grenada: Tonic for U.S. Image, a Setback for Cuba," *Toronto Globe and Mail*, November 25, 1983, p. 7.

13. For additional discussion, *see Soviet Military Power, 1984*, op. cit., p. 132.

14. Ibid., pp. 121–123, *passim*.

15. Dinesh D'Souza, *The Washington Post*, Outlook section, August 12, 1984.

16. "The United States: Foreign Policy Dilemmas," *Strategic Survey 1983–84*, p. 43.

17. Such graffiti were clearly visible along Grenada's main roads during the author's visit to the island in May 1984.

18. Aron, op. cit., pp. 672–673.

In addition, the author would like to thank Mark Forman for his valuable assistance.

CHARLES W. MAYNES

COMMENTS

Dov Zakheim's paper seems designed less as an analysis of the American Grenada intervention than as a campaign document for the 1984 elections aimed at proving that the world has radically changed for the better since the election of Ronald Reagan in 1980. To this end he strives to paint an unrelieved picture of American decline throughout the 1970s, which he claims "all" changed after 1980. Having portrayed the landscape he moves on to depict the Grenada intervention as perhaps the crowning achievement in a master plan by the administration to end the decline of U.S. power, wipe away the memory of America's failure in Vietnam, and regain the respect of allies and enemies alike. Unfortunately, to avoid marring his picture, Zakheim is forced to leave out evidence both before and after 1980 that would complicate his artistic effort.

He states that prior to 1980 the United States was slow in the modernization of its forces and allowed their readiness to decline. However, analysts such as Alton Frye—one of the principal authors of the "build-down" proposal that the administration itself has adopted—have pointed out many times that the truth is quite the opposite. Between 1970 and 1975, 550 Minuteman III missiles with 1,650 warheads were deployed in addition to 304 Poseidon sea-based missiles with 3,040 warheads. Moreover, in the late 1970s new guidance systems and warheads were installed on 300 missiles. Trident missiles began to enter service in 1979 and are still in production. In addition, the U.S. defense system soon will consist of 264 bombers with 2,112 weapons.

For the period after 1980, Zakheim does not so much misrepresent the facts as he overlooks them. In his recitation of American victories under the firm hand of the Reagan administration, it is significant that nowhere does he mention that the humiliating slaughter of the Marine contingent in Beirut was taking place at precisely the same time that the president was deciding to move against Grenada.

In fact, the coincidence of these two events brings us to the real meaning of the Grenada intervention. It was not a decisive and favorable turning point in American foreign policy after our defeat in Vietnam. As the *Economist* has pointed out, the President made his decision to invade Grenada within a day of news of the numbing truck bombing in Beirut.

The administration had earlier argued that an American withdrawal from Lebanon would adversely affect the American position throughout the world. In effect, the administration was trapped by its own rhetoric. Having grotesquely overstated the stakes involved in Lebanon and irresponsibly underestimating the price of staying there, it found that when the U.S. military presence was jeopardized, it had to do something to restore American credibility. Unfortunately for the leaders of the thug-like faction that seized power from Maurice Bishop in Grenada, their timing was wrong, and they provided a heaven-sent opportunity for the Reagan administration to look tough at a cheap price in one part of the world while it was looking weak at a tragic price in another.

This explanation of the Grenada intervention does not necessarily mean that the decision to intervene was a mistake. Great powers must worry about their credibility *vis-à-vis* both allies and adversaries. The new rulers of Grenada had little to commend them, and neighboring states seemed genuinely alarmed by the course of events in Grenada. The invasion served to redress both these concerns. But the final accounting for the Grenada intervention is not yet in.

Throughout the world, grave damage was done to the image of the United States as a law-abiding nation. The left in Latin America and West Europe has been given a new rallying cry for the anti-American campaigns that periodically sweep both areas. Furthermore, the United States has taken on a responsibility in Grenada that it might find it cannot handle. As Dr. Zakheim points out at the end of his paper, the hardest battles in Grenada lie ahead in the economic realm. If the United States cannot lower the Grenadian unemployment rate and preserve democratic rule in the country, many who now applaud the invasion will begin to denounce it.

My personal view is that the invasion was a wash. It enabled the United States to achieve some important political objectives, but at a cost the administration conveniently wishes to forget. In a few years, after the effects of the invasion work their way through the international system, we will be able to form a more definitive picture of the significance of the Grenada intervention.

Meanwhile, it behooves us not to exaggerate the impact of the conquest of a small island thousands of miles from the Soviet Union. Grenada may have been "another input" into Brezhnev's determination of the "correlation of forces" in the world, but if so, it was a raindrop in a swimming pool. During the decade of disaster that Dr. Zakheim denounces, there was indeed a shift in the correlation of the forces in the world, but not in the direction he identifies. From the Soviet point of view, the decisive shift occurred in Asia and the Middle East as China and Egypt (the most important political powers in these regions) moved into a strategic relationship with the United States. The Soviet Union has been trying frantically ever since to encourage compensating developments, but nothing comparable has been found, certainly not in Grenada.

The fact that China has entered into a strategic relationship with the United States serves to refute a neoconservative canard often embraced by administration officials. Many neoconservatives find great significance in the Grenada intervention because they accept Ambassador Jeane Kirkpatrick's contention that once a country turns communist, it is lost to the free world forever. But the Kirkpatrick thesis confuses diplomacy and ideology and is couched in bad history. In Eastern Europe the history of the last 40 years attests to nothing else if not the inability of communist regimes to implant communist ideology on entire nations. Only the Soviet army has prevented counterrevolutionary movements from succeeding in Eastern Europe.

But even if communist nations could never cease to be communist, it remains questionable whether this is a threat to American security. At issue is the external behavior of a given state, not its internal politics. As China has demonstrated, it is possible that a nation with an internal order no American would embrace can have a foreign policy of which the United States would approve. The Soviets understand this reality even if neoconservatives in the United States do not. Indeed, this is why the Soviet Politburo probably follows the Reagan administration's relatively successful China policy with greater concern than it followed events in Grenada.

Dr. Zakheim argues that the Soviet Union viewed Grenada as a hole in the Monroe Doctrine. This might be true, but the Grenada documents do not prove this. On the contrary, they suggest a small government desperate to lure the Soviet Union into playing a larger role in Grenadian affairs.

Dr. Zakheim's statements to the contrary, it is far from clear that the United States had exhausted all other options before it decided to invade Grenada. Much about the origins of the intervention remains surrounded in ambiguity. Key to the official American position regarding the legality of the intervention is the alleged call for assistance from the Governor General of Grenada, Sir Paul Scoon. It is interesting that a House of Commons commission recently released a study of the events leading to the invasion and noted that commission members, after their visit to Grenada and the United States, were unable to determine whether such a request was ever made. "Both the timing and nature of this request, which is said by the U.S. Government to have been a critical factor in providing a legal justification for their decision to act, remain shrouded in some mystery, and it is evidently the intention of the parties directly involved that the mystery should not be dispelled."

In addition, it is not settled that the U.S./OECS intervention marked a "clearcut military success." Months before the intervention the President declared that events in Grenada represented a threat to the national security of the United States. Nevertheless, American troops hit the beaches using tourist maps to find their way—a shocking intelligence failure in an island so permeable and close to this country. In fact, some military experts believe the operation revealed serious weaknesses in American defense efforts. This is not to say that Dr. Zakheim is wrong about the "success" of the invasion, but if he wants to prove his case, he must confront rather than ignore the views of serious military critics.

With hindsight, it is clear that the invasion of Grenada might become a neoconservative myth that will blind the United States to the real foreign policy problems it faces. In a commencement address at Yale University in 1962, John F. Kennedy warned that the "great enemy of truth is very often not the lie—deliberate, contrived and dishonest—but the myth—persistent, persuasive and unrealistic."

The Grenada intervention was a minor event in superpower relations. Perhaps it was a net plus for the United States. But if events in Grenada go astray in the months ahead, it might come to be considered a failure. In either case, its impact on American foreign policy will not be shattering. To argue otherwise risks creating the kind of paralyzing myth that President Kennedy warned us about.

GEORGE LISKA

The Grenada Operation and Superpower Relations: A View from the Ivory Tower

In an effort to evaluate the implications of the Grenada intervention on U.S.-Soviet relations, I shall first outline the general principles that underlie my views on American foreign policy. I will then discuss policy implications proceeding from the more specific to the more general aspects of U.S. strategy. If I find myself in the role of the devil's advocate, it is because my perspective does not originate in the Pentagon or Foggy Bottom, and because the case for the prosecution is being made amply and ably by others. The view from the ivory tower has its privileges as well as frustrations and limitations. Even if not persuasive to all, it may be redeemed as intellectually provocative.

I start from the contention that all major powers have forcefully intervened at one time or another in geopolitically delimited spheres of influence against disturbing developments or alien influences. All the pious disclaimers to the contrary notwithstanding, intervention is as much an inalienable right as a common practice in international relations. Actual reasons and artful rationalizations frequently overlap when discussing this practice. Yet the debates surrounding the Grenada intervention and the Soviet invasion of Afghanistan suggest that neither prejudice nor propaganda will permanently obscure their critical features. Were the mode and the scope of these interventions inappropriate, or were they commensurate with implicit provocations? Our judgments on this score will determine whether a given intervention will be viewed as perhaps regrettable, but still an inescapable political necessity—perhaps a requisite of "minimum" world order.

In applying the principle of proportionality to subjective perceptions of local provocation, one must reconcile the right of a "core power" to intervene with its duty to exercise restraint. This balancing act is precarious enough, but it becomes even more so when it is extended to comprise an extraregional great power. It is clear that threats to regional core powers are real, or most real, only if another major power fosters or exploits local disturbances. It is nearly as self-evident that such outside interference is least legitimate if core-power "A" has kept out of the sphere of extraregional power "B." It follows that the right of power "A" to move against a smaller power in its sphere of influence is clearest when the intervention aims at removing the influence and unprovoked interference of an extraregional great power. Such interference is unprovoked when it is not in retaliation for a comparable, prior, or simultaneous interference.

When interference is reciprocal, however, the "right" of a regional power to intervene in its sphere of influence is not nullified. Strategy is not governed by abstract symmetries, significant as the character of the latter might be in interpreting the role of the former. Yet the regional power's right of intervention is somewhat weakened by the extraregional power's right to become involved in "A"'s sphere of influence as part of a bargaining process over the rules of mutual interference, or perhaps mutual abstinence.

In other words, to what extent does past and present U.S. interference in the Soviet sphere of influence "justify" Soviet (and Cuban) interference in the U.S. sphere? The answer will depend on one's point of view regarding other strategic factors such as whether the relevant actors are continental, sea, or insular powers.

The prominent land-based power on the international scene (read, the Soviet Union) invariably seeks direct access to the seas in pursuit of material prosperity and military security. The dominant maritime-mercantile and commonly insular power (read, the United States) will quite naturally oppose this push in the interest of preserving its monopoly of access to sea lanes and uninhibited approaches to land masses. In this respect, the Soviet Union differs no more from the ancient Hittite and Persian empires than from modern Germany, while the United States reenacts the countervailing instincts of imperial Egypt, Athens, and Britain. Land and sea powers have found it difficult, and for the most part impossible to agree on an international equilibrium that would afford each an equal measure of security, material well-being, and status.

When determining "high policy," the issue of overall parity between land and sea powers is inseparable from the issue of reciprocal interference and noninterference between regional core powers that are abstractly symmetrical. In such a two-faceted setting, reciprocal interference tests the durability of the prevailing international system on the one hand, while related bargaining processes revolve around the creation of international equilibrium on the other. The various tendencies of land and sea powers thus verge in the pursuit of equilibrium qualified by the ambiguous concept of parity. These tendencies largely cover the concrete policy problems currently raised by U.S. and Soviet (or Soviet/Cuban) interventions and counterinterventions in the Third World. Another tendency ingrained in the ethos of insular powers facing challenges and opposition from leading land powers is to submerge the dilemmas engendered by the issues of symmetry and parity-in-disparity by denying international equivalence with regard to both physical security and politically significant values.

Who threatens who more by interfering in the other's sphere depends on the relative ease with which land and sea powers project their capabilities and pressure their adversaries. The ability of each type of power to challenge the other in turn depends on how receptive lesser regional powers are to outside influences. This receptivity is contingent on which forms of control are typical for insular-maritime powers as opposed to continental powers. It also depends on the autonomy of such lesser powers as each type of major power is prepared to concede. Current naval technology and international economics also play a role, though these factors usually favor the insular sea power by making it seem more immune than vulnerable. Continental powers, on the other hand, tend to seem more crudely imperialistic because, more often than not, they are not critically imperiled. If, however, the dominant naval power regards itself as threatened, it is because subjective factors have altered its perception of objective conditions. The basic contrast between land- and sea-based naval capabilities (the first eliciting counterpoise and the second having a built-in bias toward one-power superiority) has translated repeatedly into a perceived need for "absolute" security on the part of the insular maritime power.

So sanctified and reinforced by the onset of airborne military power (which changed traditional military-strategic equations), claims to absolute security will be highly sensitive to even minor proximate threats so long as these are even remotely symbolic of the maritime-mercantile power's insecurity. That insecurity is implicit in the fragile bases of its economic superiority, which it feels is crucial to maintaining its political influence. In the blinding heat of domestic controversies concerning national security, it will be often overlooked that the real threat has repeatedly come from other maritime-mercantile powers (e.g., from the English to the Dutch and from the United States to Great Britain). The insular power's fixation on the continental rival or threat is dangerous in that it either distracts attention or dissipates scarce resources.

The advantage of the predominant insular-maritime power over its continental challenger is less pronounced in the age of atomic-powered submarines than it was at the peak of the age of wind-propelled sailing ships. (Equally reduced, if only potentially, is the maritime power's dependence on land bases for support and supply facilities.) The lessening advantage of the principal maritime power is bound to intensify the tendency of privileged insulars to validate normatively their tendency to perceive their security interests as widely threatened. In the aftermath of World War II, it was America's turn to assert not only radical disparity, but claims of the superiority of its political system as well.

When limited to expositions of the excesses of the Soviet system that are superstructural to its geographical-historical base, this claim is plausible. However, such claims also blot out both the lowlands of existential symmetries and the root causes of the value discrepancy between embattled continental powers and powerful mercantile-marine powers. Each type of power is subject to a different evolutionary rhythm and different resource-related threats and attractions.

Distorting the most commonplace perceptions makes it virtually impossible to view the land versus sea power conflict within the conceptual universe of a tragic entanglement—as a mutually destructive contest of values which, while contrary and conflicting, are equally positive or valid in their own terms. Value-based discriminations impede prudent realpolitik to the eventual advantage of third parties in that they emplace an absolutism above a set of relativities. This inhibits the penetration of morally significant existential dilemmas with reference to policies that attempt to encompass the collective emotions of the relevant actors as they press against strategic rationality and attempt to keep passions under control.

When the foregoing general principles are applied to the facts as corroborated by the Grenada documents, it is still possible to hold that the United States was entitled to invade Grenada and entitled to resist Soviet/Cuban involvement in Central America and the Caribbean Basin. This does not mean that being entitled is the same as being well-advised. Moreover, without being annulled, such entitlement is not unaffected by prior or simultaneous U.S. interference in Soviet spheres of interest and concern (i.e., Eastern Europe and Southwest Asia). American interference in these areas to some degree has generated a "right" or incentive to interfere in the Western Hemisphere in order to look for leverages that might serve to constrain such interference, as a part of tacit bargaining process over the reciprocity issue.

America's involvement on the Eurasian continent after World War II was bound to stimulate further the Soviet urge to overseas access as part of its strategy to equalize its position relative to the United States and expand its future options. For the purposes of both analysis and policy responses, this urge should be accounted for with reference to the Soviet Union as the preeminent continental-military (as opposed to communist) power in the world just as the United States should be considered the preeminent insular and industrial (as opposed to imperialist) power.

Furthermore, the Soviet expansionist urge should be seen as both independent of and operationally related to the superpower rivalry. The related values of each nation are only accidentally "communism" and "capitalism," or "democracy" and "totalitarianism." The Soviet Union is eminently capable of exerting its influence both regionally and globally with the aid of economic assets and cultural attraction. These assets have been commonly sufficient either to eschew or disguise physical coercion toward dependents (or dependent elites) willing to trade an often unusable margin of autonomy for substantial material advantage or military security.

Extraordinary social upheavals in dependent countries are necessary before they will asset latent "statist" values (e.g., independence) over the "societal" (e.g., cultural) factors. A shift in alignment from the near regional to the more remote extraregional great power is then likely. As part of this reversal of alliances, past support by the outside power will be rewarded by offers of support from the predominant regional power.[1]

This in turn will lead to a protection-provocation duality that underlies so much of present-day international conflict, but it will restore the dependency to the fold of normal state behavior. More importantly, the reversal of alliances will cause the dependency to assimilate the values of the insular-maritime power. Such events are rather rare, however, as shown by the time elapsed between the Cuban revolution and the Nicaraguan and Grenadian revolutions. The American response to these events diverged from the ideal values and principles of American political culture more than they did from the common Soviet approach to handling revolts. However, a certain similarity of approach reveals itself when one takes into account the possible latitudes for dealing with such events.

Either a detached-olympian or an involved-tragic view will probe beyond procedures and instruments to the realities of power and political instincts. In light of either view, the value systems of land- and sea-based powers are as ideally complementary as they are conflict-aggravating. Differences in habitat and history explain divergent normative thrusts that quicken the operational momentum of rivalry-fostering strategies for dealing with shared dilemmas.

As we leave general principles for the particulars of policy, the dialectic of conflicting rights and values narrow into contention over competing stakes. Inherent tendencies are overlaid by specific attitudes and strategies, and absolute security issues give rise to the problematic relationship between sufficient arms and unnecessary alarms. I will defer here to authoritative assurances that Grenada, the Caribbean Basin, and Central America are strategically important to the United States and potentially vulnerable to Soviet military-strategic designs. It follows that substantially unqualified U.S. control over the Western hemisphere is essential for safeguarding important American interests both in peacetime (e.g., regarding the protection of oil supply routes) and in the event of war when it would be crucial to ensure nuclear weapon deployments, shipments of manpower and material to Europe, and the security of the Panama Canal, etc. I shall limit myself to introducing two caveats.

First, the more that U.S. strategy reduces Soviet warning time concerning nuclear attack, and the greater stress that pundits, planners, and policymakers place on maritime strategy, the greater the countervailing impetus for the Soviets to gain access and assets in overseas areas, not least of all those adjoining North America. Such strategies will give the Soviets all the more reason to increase the very adventurism that U.S. policies are intended to discourage. It is a paradox that the rationale for the implementation of U.S. strategies depend on prior Soviet expansion into grey areas outside the primary Soviet sphere of influence. Thus, for horizontal escalation to work, the Soviets must be present in places where they can be pressed without being provoked into mortal combat. If U.S. strategy is to have a long-term positive versus a short-term preventive thrust, it must be keyed to a prolonged competition that simultaneously expands in scope and subsides in intensity as it becomes routine and ideally generates a shared stake in preventing local conflicts from embroiling the superpowers in unwanted conflict.

Whether competition over crucial areas spirals immediately upward or eventually downward, it is aimed at access to geopolitical softspots. This illustrates the extent to which geopolitical superiority is inseparable from military-technological superiority. The principle of the indivisibility of arms and access is more readily admitted in theory than in practice. It is invalidated when the all-absorbing preoccupation with arms control is disassociated from controlling Soviet forays into the global periphery. As least one would have thought, wrongly it seems, that this was the necessary premise of United States-Soviet détente.

A related caveat concerns the tendency to exaggerate peacetime national security requirements under the influence of mental habits associated with the myth of absolute security. This all-too-common mentality has a way of precipitating developments that eventually cause belligerency. In the event of hostilities, many of the objectives of peacetime security strategy will become secondary. The undifferentiated mental picture of total security is unlikely to be relevant if war breaks out. The battlefront will crystallize into unevenly critical sectors by virtue of gradually clarified priorities and possibilities. The conduct of an actual war is too awesome a task to be governed by peacetime conceptions of national security.

Current alarms regarding Soviet penetration into Central America are reminiscent of earlier American anxieties concerning the presumed scope of German ambitions in the Western hemisphere and the Mexican revolution.[2] Subsequently, American concerns shifted to Asia (most notably to Indochina), and then back to Latin America as U.S. foreign policy waned in intensity and shrank in scope. Later evaluations showed that the objectives of German militarism were overrated. They were almost entirely a function of indigenous (i.e., Mexican) needs and aspirations. American assessments of German motivations were revised, but only after the maximalist perception had done much damage to U.S.-German relations. Regional issues were not decisive in impelling the United States toward participation in World War I, but they were relevant to the land vs. sea power rivalry between Germany and Great Britain.

Mexican and Caribbean strategic assets were far less important regarding U.S.-German differences than they are today. The degree to which these assets are currently perceived as important to the United States and the Soviet Union is unclear, however. The United States might be inclined to exaggerate their importance in order to justify the Grenada intervention, which proved that America retains the ability and will to checkmate the transfer of Soviet power to the Western hemisphere.

Another reason for overemphasizing the strategic threat to the Western Hemisphere has been a revival of the American desire to act as a regional policeman. In the recent past, the regional and global roles of the United States tended to be mutually exclusive. At the height of American empire-building, it took the shock of the emplacement of Soviet missiles in Cuba to end American neglect for Latin America. The current acute concern over Latin America that was also present before World War I should be seen in this light. This newfound concern represents either a desire for retrenchment, or a statesman-like attempt to resolve a new and more assertive foreign policy as represented by the invasion of Grenada. On the other hand, perhaps the Grenada intervention represented a mere flexing of muscles to satisfy public opinion, make up for isolated setbacks in other regions, and signal an end to the Vietnam syndrome.

In either case, the fluctuating dynamic of America's regional and global concerns are important in assessing competing American and Soviet interests in Latin America. It is hazardous to extrapolate present global and regional tendencies to long-term developments in U.S.-Soviet relations. American vacillation between global and regional interests recalls Tsarist Russia's oscillation between European and Asian interests. Both powers in effect strove to create fluid settings for dealing with more stable great power dilemmas. This tendency is present regardless of whether such dilemmas are internal to the respective spheres of influence of the great powers or intrinsic to the intractable key issues of world politics. The question remains, how is it possible to undertake a guarded relaxation of regional predominance without affecting broader global interests?

It would be odd if the priority American policymakers assign to the Western Hemisphere failed to affect U.S.-Soviet relations in general. The physiognomy of regional issues will inevitably alter under different global scenarios. It is a truism that the U.S. approach to countries such as Grenada, Nicaragua, and El Salvador is conditioned by whether they are viewed in a "globalist" East-West context or in terms of local problems subject to pseudo-Marxist or reformist remedies. It should be equally obvious that the present character of U.S.-Soviet relations will determine whether U.S. policymakers are able to adopt an essentially nonmilitary "regionalist" approach without being paralyzed by fears of Soviet/Cuban encroachment.

Critical in this connection are U.S. assumptions about motives and objectives of Soviet involvement in the Western Hemisphere. Do the Soviets seek access and influence in the American sphere as part of a revolutionary strategy of worldwide expansion independent of American policies? Or is Soviet interference a means to gain leverage on U.S. policymaking? If the latter is the case, the Soviets might be seeking to make the United States abstain from challenging Soviet predominance in Eastern Europe or condone more than token Soviet gains in the direction of geopolitical parity outside its primary sphere of influence. Although the immediate time-tables of the two superpowers differ, they are ultimately interrelated. The Soviet objective of geopolitical parity is related to claims to regional predominance both tactically and strategically. The first objective is short-term insofar as even limited gains enhance Soviet standing and permit the cooption of clients into a shared enterprise. The second is long-term insofar as substantial progress toward global parity reduces the Soviet stake in approximating the current American standard of absolute security. With regard to military-strategic security, Soviet objectives and American responses are unavoidably hostage to the ongoing superpower rivalry. They are also dependent on each party's perceived needs and related goals in a narrow military-strategic sense. How comfortable the Soviets feel in the overall geopolitical arena will influence the priority they assign to assets in the Western Hemisphere that they regard as important to worldwide military-strategic parity. Even if their objectives in the Western Hemisphere are primarily military-strategic, they are not impervious to strictly political considerations or the risk of military conflict in the region.

The firmest Soviet intentions cannot withstand the impact of unanticipated developments. Accordingly, Soviet concern with the Western Hemisphere can be reduced by reducing Soviet incentives to retaliation and by augmenting incentives for self-restraint in America's primary sphere of influence. If curtailing retaliatory incentives entails lessened U.S. involvement in Soviet spheres of influence, from the borders of Albania to the battlefields of Afghanistan, then American policymakers should look to expand U.S. involvement in parts of Africa, the Middle East, and Asia that are outside both U.S. and Soviet spheres of vital interest.

The effort to combine mutual self-restraint with a fair sharing of access to the Third World will necessitate bartering arrangements concerning vital and nonvital geostrategic interests. Fortunately, these are flexible categories. An arrangement wherein the Soviets will not observe self-restraint outside their "orbit" but still receive U.S. material and technological benefits is unacceptable. Rather, both superpowers must ease their attempts to outflank each other. Soviet efforts to counter the West in the Middle East and Eastern Africa, America's strategic links with China, and America's insistence on absolute security in the Western Hemisphere should be reconsidered.

Under the most optimistic of assumptions, it remains necessary to test the degree to which Soviet intervention in the Western Hemisphere is self-generating and keyed to objectives independent of American policies. Such testing will require some painful adjustments in current policies that are not immediately or visibly rewarded in the coin of altered Soviet conduct. Such adjustments might include less U.S. interference in places like Poland and Afghanistan (based on a better understanding of Soviet imperial and internal dilemmas), greater reserve in developing the relationship with China (reflecting a keener sense of Soviet anxieties), and a practical acceptance of the Soviet urge toward the oceans (prompted by a realization of the contemporary norms of military-strategic and economic need). The costs and risks of such a "test" can be limited and we should keep in mind that they are reversible so long as the capacity to halt flagrant Soviet abuses remains intact. In the absence of such a test, the debate over Soviet intentions will continue to be stalemated between attempts to read promising trends into the cryptic statements of Soviet officials and affirmations of ominous Soviet goals inferred from often overrated Soviet capabilities. If, as is likely, the perceived importance of Latin America continues to grow while U.S.-

Soviet relations worsen, the actual nature of the Soviet threat and its precise relationship to indigenous factors will never be clearly understood.

The alternative to testing Soviet goals is to postulate a spontaneous Soviet drive for worldwide hegemony as evidenced by support for Grenada-like "national-democratic" or "socialist" revolutions in the Third World. An authentic all-out drive for hegemony must be distinguished from the assertive tendencies of world and regional powers. Historically, the pursuit of hegemony has been as much a response as an initiative for most powers. Hegemonistic powers often responded to manifest structural weaknesses in the international system arising from the decline of leading powers. Typically, the result was a surge in the would-be hegemon's will-to-power backed by technological and organizational innovation. In addition, hegemonistic policies were often expressed in terms of the ascendant power's sense of opportunity and grievance. Both relate to the chronic incoherence of state systems that generate pressures for self-help while limiting such efforts at the same time. This contraction tends to invoke an irresistible urge on the part of the ascendant power to deal with international developments from a position of strength.

The conditions do not seem to be present to justify assuming a Soviet hegemonial drive. Assertions of Soviet hegemony are confused with two wholly normal and intrinsically manageable objects: the assertion of the Soviet Union's status as the preeminent power on the Eurasian land mass, and the ambition to translate military-strategic parity into a corresponding reapportionment of geopolitical access.

Nor is there a sufficiently expansionist impulse inherent in Marxist-Leninist ideology to justify claims of Soviet hegemonism. The intensity of hegemonial drives tend to rise as ascending powers approach and pass their climacteric. Conversely, ideology quickly loses its importance as an impetus to world domination as national power increases. Whether hegemonistic intentions are currently alleged from the outside or is invoked from within, an ideological rationale of Soviet globalism is unconvincing.

Marxist-Leninist ideology has failed to impart to the Soviet state the demonic drive that fascism imparted to the Third Reich. In any case, dire predictions for the loss of the capitalist world are linked to prudent calculations of the "correlation of forces" in Soviet ideology. Ideology also fails to confer on Soviet foreign policy the imperative of accelerating the course of history that Leninism imparts to the vanguard party. Once salient features of Soviet ideology have long since degenerated into scholastic exercises in classifying the "socialist" development of actual or potential Soviet clients. Since communist ideology supplies little or no guidance for action in concrete circumstances, it is redundant to argue that the record of Soviet foreign policy has shown no single instance of a major action at the expense of real political concerns.

The communist creed has failed to generate either the spiritual élan or the innovation that are necessary to fuel a hegemonial drive. The Soviet global impulse is influenced to a certain degree by the foreign policy aims of imperial Russia, but it is also largely subject to that state's traditional handicaps. The result is a growing dependence on the enduring assets of Russian patriotism and nationalism, and an updated reliance on the military-technological sector of the economy. Thus there is little difficulty in deciding whether communism or territorial ambitions are the prime motivating factors behind Soviet behavior. Nevertheless, our conclusions might be dangerous if they bar inquiry into the precise kind of territorial state that the Soviet Union represents. Whether or not we believe that the normal ambitions and frustrations of the Soviet Union are linked to its communist character and an all-out hegemonial drive depends on the opportunities and obstacles it faces in the international arena.

To be sure, even though an ideological rationale is unnecessary for an adequate analysis of Soviet foreign policy, ideological factors contribute to the Soviet world view and the achievement of their international aims. However, an ideologically enhanced ability to relate to indigenous revolutionary trends does not do away with the practical limits on the Soviet Union's global reach. Indeed, Marxist-Leninist ideology is apt to be more useful to local revolutionaries than to their sponsor. Communist ideology is a boon to Third World leaders who are either inveterately self-centered or zealously conformist. It helps them to place a gloss on brute-coercion and provides a vocabulary for explaining and excusing revolutionary violence. But one need not play the role of a superpower to secure links to local revolutionaries. The most conservative powers have always been notoriously promiscuous in taking advantage of upheavals of any kind in their rival's backyard. This was as true of imperial Russia as it was (or is) of any other great power.

Within this general framework, it is probably true that the critical issue for the Soviet regime is how to assess the political and material costs of expansion into the Third World in relation to the issue of regime legitimization. Soviet leaders are also concerned with how to relate the visible costs of expansionism to a still more hypothetical balance between potential material rewards and the ideological risks of relaxing control over the Soviet economy. American leaders, on the other hand, are primarily concerned with determining by trial and error under what conditions the Soviet system might evolve toward normal state behavior—to wit, under what circumstances the Soviets might opt for domestic reforms and a less assertive foreign policy. It is unlikely that any such evolution will take place in the absence of new sources of regime-legitimizing prestige and prosperity that would permit a lessened emphasis on the revolutionary nature of state activity both at home and abroad.

It remains a matter of opinion as to whether acquiescence or opposition to Soviet gains is ultimately more conducive to the evolution of the Soviet Union. Arguing in favor of guarded decompression and against tightened containment is not consistent. In effect, it inverts the proposition that denying external gains to the Soviet regime will coerce it into economic reform. It also ignores a corollary of the just-stated proposition: costly foreign involvements (e.g., Cuba and Vietnam) might economically bankrupt the Soviet system if they accumulate at the present rate. Technical and economic opinions differ on the latter score, yet it seems safe to hold that success abroad is neither a condition for the survival of the Soviet state, nor would it be suicidal, even in the long term. At issue is not the regime's existence but its capacity to change while exhibiting an overall tendency for advancement.

Only a new relationship between the expanded goals of Soviet world policy and increased political tolerance on the part of the United States can produce a shared approach to détente. If such a deal entailed the kind of U.S. contribution to modernizing the Soviet economy that was once futilely offered as a reward for geopolitical self-neutralization, the increased capacity of the Soviet Union to project its economic influence abroad would help move the two powers toward parity and a similarity of methods.

The U.S.-Soviet rivalry will not disappear overnight even in the most favorable of circumstance. Relaxing it might also tend to generate an increase in third party rivalries. However, the currently dangerous superpower conflict would be defused, and the United States would have increasing latitude to deal with Western Hemispheric events on their own merits. Applying instruments proper to the nature of indigenous problems is not a panacea for realizing an ideal foreign policy any more than applying the right concepts and strategies to global problems will facilitate détente. Yet liberal and conservative blueprints for U.S. foreign policy are interdependent if the object is to reduce superpower conflict in the Western Hemisphere, where indigenous problems often seem to exceed the actual global significance of the region.

So long as U.S.-Soviet relations remain what they are, the globalist approach to the Western Hemisphere will be more advantageous for the United States in acute crises than the regionalist approach. Fire has to be fought with fire, and socioeconomic reform has a way of being too slow in producing politically stabilizing results when Third World countries are subject to subversion from either locally engineered or externally supported forces. Put crudely, if one is not prepared to be restrained regarding Poland and Afghanistan, one must be prepared to invade Grenada and make war on Nicaragua. The same is true for the Middle East and may become so for Eastern Africa if the United States continues to tighten its links with China and deny the Soviet Union access to the Third World and American technology. Once they are committed to blending liberal regional and authentically conservative global strategies, it should not be beyond the competence of policymakers to locate the golden mean between acquiescence and opposition to Soviet gains and thus heed one of the major "lessons" of Grenada.

An intermediate U.S. approach would entail extending the strategy of "differentiation" to the "grey areas" of Soviet control and the Western Hemisphere. Such an approach should attempt to exploit the differences between the Soviet Union and its local surrogates such as Cuba. That such differences are important is evident from the varied reactions of the Soviet Union and Cuba to the collapse of the Grenadian revolution. Further differences are illustrated by the fact that Cuba is apt to promote radical sociopolitical movements in the Western Hemisphere as a means to enhance its position *vis-à-vis* the Soviet Union. Thus it seeks to diminish its dependence on the Soviet Union (the extraregional great power) and create a long-term basis for rapprochement with the United States (the regional core power) in return for a demonstrated willingness and capacity to act as an agent for the moderation of regional revolutionary processes.

The global strategy of the Soviet Union does not seek high risk involvements in distant regions. However, it does encourage a diplomatic game with high stakes. Whereas the Cubans would settle for retrenchment rather than lose all to reaction, the Soviets encourage local forces toward radicalism because they cannot lose even if their clients are defeated. They attempt to convert their clients to Soviet-style rule in an effort to mark a step toward geopolitical parity with the United States. Even if such a radicalization compels the United States to intervene, such repression will signal a moral parity or equivalence between the superpowers and produce more tolerance if not legitimacy for the next coercive act in the Soviet sphere of influence. American intervention will also consolidate the Soviet hold on regional accomplices (read, Cuba) by including them in the drive for an all-out Marxist-Leninist solution.

For the United States to be able to exploit divergencies between Soviet and Cuban interests, it must do two things. It must concentrate less on the advantages the Soviets derive from the surrogate-proxy system and more effectively realize the "opportunities" the system presents. The more cautious the Soviets become in backing Third World clients because of fears of American displeasure, the more often they will have to pay the price of conspicuous passivity. This will not do much for their prestige as an authentic world power. By the same token, however cautious the Soviets might be in classifying the "socialist" nature of their allies, any failure to extend assistance in the face of American counteraction is a significant ideological setback. Perhaps the relevant categories will be readjusted as an alternative to blanket support, but the costs of Soviet inaction can still be high in terms of the ideological self-image of the Soviet state.

To further exploit Soviet-client divergencies, U.S. policies should be no more ideologically committed or rigid than those of the Soviet Union—not only with respect to Soviet spheres of interest, but those of America as well. This means displaying greater tolerance for local revolutionary leaders and leftist initiatives pending the eventual and inevitable moderation of radical forces in submission to the facts of life as represented by local penury and American wealth.

In Grenada, greater flexibility and a more permissive stance would have meant more initial tolerance for Bishop's brand of "socialism," and a more alert response to Bishop's tentative rapprochement with the United States. (Appendix A, Document 17) Too much permissiveness, however, would have caused the United States to remain unconcerned about the threatening nature of the Coard faction that came to power just prior to the American intervention. Failing to extend a sufficient benefit of doubt to Bishop's revolution indicates that the United States perceived the establishment of a genuinely Leninist regime that would have moved sharply toward totalitarianism in conditions of terror. This attitude was partially responsible for Bishop's inability to affect a rapprochement with the United States that would have led to a "bourgeois-nationalist" restoration in the view of his opponents.

By failing to be either permissive or patient, the United States gave support to the impression that it was unwilling to countenance any radical change in Grenada or give it the chance to evolve toward moderation under its own steam along either gradualist-evolutionary or violent-revolutionary paths. The incidental loss was to forego the possibility of establishing a tacit U.S.-Cuban understanding as to the scope of change in the Western Hemisphere that the United States would tolerate. Such an understanding might stand a good chance of proving more solid over time than any explicit Soviet/Cuban alliance for promoting revolution by means they can only disagree about because of their differing national interests.

So long as ideologically intransigent and uncompromising U.S. policies are in force, the United States cannot win while defending its irreducible paramountcy in the Western hemisphere. If the United States fails to use military force against its foes in the region in spite of its unqualified opposition to anything smacking of revolutionary change, it stands revealed as impotent. On the other hand, if it intervenes, it stands arraigned as a modern example of a falsely liberal Athens-like tyrant democracy. Thus any immediate gains in America's reputation for either moderation or resolution are liable to erosion. Whatever the United States chooses to do, there is likely to be deepened disaffection in one ideological quarter or the other. Therefore, the United States should seek to create a workable strategy for the Western hemisphere that stands somewhere between permissiveness and intransigence.

NOTES

1. The most interesting single foreign policy document captured in Grenada was the Confidential report on Grenada's Relations with the USSR, from Grenadian Ambassador to Moscow, W. Richard Jacobs, to Foreign Minister Unison Whiteman, Prime Minister Bishop, Deputy Prime Minister Coard, and Politburo Member Ewert Layne, July 11, 1983, Grenada Documents, Log No. W. According to Ambassador Jacobs: "By itself, Granada's distance from the USSR, and its small size would mean that we would figure in a very minute way in the USSR's global relationships. Our revolution has to be viewed as a worldwide process with its original roots in the Great October Revolution. For Grenada to assume a position of increasingly greater importance, we have to be seen as influencing at least regional events. We have to establish ourselves as the authority on events in at least the English-speaking

Caribbean, and be the sponsor of revolutionary activity and progressive developments in this region at least."

"Of all the regional possibilities, the most likely candidate for special attention is Surinam. If we can be an overwhelming influence on Surinam's international behaviour, then our importance in the Soviet scheme of things will be greatly enhanced. To the extent that we can take credit for bringing any other country into the progressive fold, our prestige and influence would be greatly enhanced. Another candidate is Belize." He concluded by noting Grenada's pro-Soviet vote on Afghanistan in the United Nations: "It might be fair to say that their [Soviet] support for us is actually below our support for them."

2. On the Mexican imbroglio, *see* Friedrich Katz, *The Secret War in Mexico* (Chicago: University of Chicago Press, 1981), pp. 166–179.

W. BRUCE WEINROD

Comments

The U.S./OECS intervention in Grenada in October 1983 has been generally accepted or approved of by most observers. What criticism exists has tended to focus on the specific argument that the Grenada operation was an unwise or uncalled for application of U.S. military power. In a thoughtful and interesting (but I believe ultimately unsatisfactory) approach, Professor George Liska has raised questions about the U.S. role in Grenada from a more historical and academic perspective. In the following, I propose to respond to the main points raised by Professor Liska and offer my own conclusions about the implications of the Grenada intervention.

Professor Liska, in my reading, raises three main points. First, Soviet ideology is basically irrelevant to an understanding of Soviet foreign policy behavior, and by implication it need not be taken into account by U.S. policymakers. Second, the moral dimension of U.S. foreign policy is not only irrelevant but might be positively harmful to the conduct of U.S. foreign policy. Finally, the proper approach to analyzing the international competition between the United States and the Soviet Union is to presume a moral symmetry between them—i.e., to posit that both are merely traditional great powers. I disagree with Professor Liska on all three points.

With respect to the role that ideology plays in Soviet foreign policy behavior, it is simply not possible for an outsider to determine with certainty whether Soviet leaders fully believe in their own ideology. Given the complexities of human nature and the constraints and demands of realpolitik, it is likely that Soviet leaders are influenced by factors other than communist ideology. But it is often overlooked that it is not necessary for Soviet rulers to believe in their own ideology for it to have an impact on Soviet foreign policy behavior.

At a minimum, ideology pushes the Soviet leadership toward taking actions that reinforce the legitimacy of its rule, both internally and externally. Often these are actions that a traditional great power might not take. Thus Soviet rulers must portray a highly exaggerated Western "threat" and have new areas come under the influence of Marxism-Leninism and Soviet power in order to demonstrate to populations under their control (both within the borders of the USSR and elsewhere) that communism is the wave of the future. In other words, while some Soviet leaders might not believe in communist ideology, they may well find it useful or necessary for practical reasons to act as if they do.

It is not likely that Soviet leaders consult Marxist-Leninist dogma in determining their each and every move, but this does not mean that ideology cannot serve as a broad "guide" to Soviet strategy. With its long-term historical perspective, communist ideology may well imbue Soviet decision-makers with a confidence, indeed a compulsion, to continually probe for targets of opportunity. In short, communist ideology probably imparts to Soviet rulers a sense of psychological obligation to destabilize Western nations whenever possible and to provide meaningful military assistance to self-proclaimed Marxist-Leninist forces throughout the world. As Zbigniew Brzezinski said in 1962, "The leaders of the Soviet Union possess a sense of compulsive obligation to assist in the spread of communism throughout the world." It is also important to note that the Soviets apparently feel that bordering nations (and others when possible) should have political and economic systems essentially identical to their own. This fact is explained best by communist ideology and its inevitable expansionist side-effects, not by great power theories.

While not directly relevant to Dr. Liska's argument, it is worth noting that whatever its importance to Soviet leaders, communist ideology is clearly very significant to the rulers of other Marxist regimes, especially those in the Third World. The Grenada documents clearly demonstrate that the beliefs and actions of many Grenadian leaders were governed by communist ideological precepts.

The fundamental question is not whether the Soviet Union generally behaves like a great power. Of course it does. In addition, the character and history of imperial Russia is useful in helping us to understand and explain present-day Soviet behavior (although they should not be used to rationalize or excuse it). The question is a matter of whether the behavior of the Soviet Union is any different or more dangerous for the West than it would be if it were not communist. The answer, I believe, is clearly in the affirmative. Soviet ideology significantly shifted the emphasis and rationale for the Russian role in the world. As Lezek Kolakowski has observed:

> Strongly rooted historical patterns of social organization display everywhere a remarkable refractiveness to be sure, and they are capable of sneaking into and surviving profoundly transformed political conditions. On the other hand, the radical change in the principle of ideological legitimacy of power from national, Russian, paternalist, traditional, and religious to internationalist, progressivist, futuristic, truly atheistic, normative (and I would add totalist) was not simply phraseological; it affected all areas of life. It cannot be dismissed as just an adoption of another self-glorifying idiom. (*Encounter*, May 1983)

Finally, Soviet ideology reinforces a crucial asymmetry between the United States and the Soviet Union. U.S. foreign policy is potentially constrained by domestic criticism, whereas there is no equivalent possibility in the Soviet system. By ideological definition, Soviet policy is correct policy; it reflects truth. As Andrei Sakharov has said, "As long as a country has no civil liberty, no freedom of information, and no independent press, then there exists no effective body of public opinion to control the conduct of government."

The second point raised by Dr. Liska is that the moral component of U.S. foreign policy is probably harmful to American interests, and that it would be better all around if the United States were to act solely on the basis of realpolitikal consideration. It is interesting to observe in passing that Dr. Liska downplays the ideological component of Soviet behavior, but appears to believe it plays a significant role in the U.S. foreign policy process (although I am certain he does not find Soviet ideology and U.S. morality to be morally equivalent).

I would contend that the existence of a moral component to American foreign policy is inevitable given the American political tradition. Furthermore, it is necessary in the sense that I do not believe consistent public support for U.S. policies can be sustained otherwise. The moral dimension of U.S. foreign policy also reflects the best of American traditions and values. Finally, if this moral element were dispensed with, I believe the result would be that the United States would move quickly toward a new isolationism as a result of the government's inability to gather public support for an active American role in the world. The ultimate result would be an international power vacuum leading to increased instability. The likelihood that the U.S. would be drawn into a significant military conflict would also increase.

It is true that excessive moralism can be harmful to the ability of policymakers to conduct U.S. foreign policy. But the issue we are addressing here is whether such a moral dimension is appropriate and I believe the answer is in the affirmative. This in no way rules out the usefulness of traditional balance of power approaches to the conduct of U.S. foreign policy. These should remain a part of the global outlook of the United States.

Dr. Liska's point that there exists a moral asymmetry between the United States and the Soviet Union is similar to the sentiment increasingly found in certain Western European circles that there is no real difference between the U.S. and the Soviet Union in international politics; both are basically great powers simply seeking to expand their influence and domination throughout the world.

I strongly disagree with this position when it comes to comparisons between the Soviet intervention in Czechoslovakia (1968) and U.S. involvement in the Dominican Republic (1965) and Grenada (1983). It is true that in recent years, both the United States and the Soviet Union in recent years have sent troops into other nations in order to preserve the status quo. On this level, it can be said that the behavior of both nations is similar. But to leave it at this level is to miss crucial points of difference.

The difference between the invasion of Czechoslovakia and the Grenada intervention is that the Soviet action was aimed at preventing the emergence of a democratic system, whereas the American action preserved the possibility that such a system could exist. Today, Czechoslovakia remains under occupation and without basic freedoms. In comparison, U.S. troops were withdrawn soon after the Dominican intervention, and the Dominican Republic maintains a functioning, viable democracy where political power has been peacefully transferred between parties of the right and left. There is a clear moral distinction between action to preserve a status quo that allows for movement toward liberal democracy, and action to preserve a status quo that denies such movement.

Certain groups have also charged that the relationship between the United States and Western Europe is essentially the same as that between the Soviet Union and Eastern Europe—i.e., merely great power domination. While there is no doubt that occasionally East Europeans are able to take actions the Soviets do not like, the fundamental question is whether they can ever act against fundamental Soviet interests or refuse a Soviet request when the Soviets feel strongly about a matter. This is unlikely as compared to the situation with respect to the United States and Western Europe. Thus the American position in Western Europe is fundamentally different from the Soviet role in Eastern Europe.

The Grenada intervention has had the following effects on the Soviet Union.

Reassessment of Tactics. It is likely that the Soviet Union has reassessed its revolutionary role in the world, particularly in Central America and the most developing nations. On the other hand, undoubtedly the Soviets will take a long-term view of Central America. Moscow understands that the United States usually views events in a short-term perspective. Given U.S. presidential elections every four years, they realize that new administrations sometimes adopt different perspectives than their predecessors. They can afford to wait, fall back for a short time, and move again at a propitious moment.

Clarification of Limits to Soviet Involvement in the Western Hemisphere. The nature of the Soviet response to the Grenada intervention consisted entirely of rhetorical denunciations of the U.S. and attempts to make Europe fear a "trigger-happy" United States. This indicates that Moscow will not risk confrontation with the United States in the Western Hemisphere over marginal stakes. There was little doubt on this score even prior to Grenada, and the same can be applied to Nicaragua. The Grenada intervention also lessens the likelihood of Soviet miscalculations concerning probable U.S. responses to Soviet interference in Central America.

Reduction in Marxist Confidence. Marxist forces and regimes, especially those in the Western Hemisphere, now have less confidence as a result of the Grenada action. It is only common sense that such forces, at least for a time, will not exhibit such confidence about the "inevitability" of a "progressive" triumph. Certainly, they are much less likely to believe that Cuba or the Soviet Union will come to their assistance in the event of open conflict with the United States.

Positive Boost for Anti-Marxist Forces. In the aftermath of the Grenada intervention, there has been a very modest but positive impact on anti-Marxist insurgencies in the Western hemisphere and elsewhere. While UNITA in Angola and the Islamic rebels in Afghanistan are quite distant from Grenada, they no doubt felt that the Grenada events were a gain for the overall cause for which they have struggled. In demonstrating that a quasi-consolidated communist regime could be undone, the Grenada intervention was a positive development for these groups.

Shift in European Perceptions. The Grenada intervention has reinforced a shift away from sympathy for Marxist forces in the Western Hemisphere. There has been a growing perception—not just tied to Grenada, but also tied to the democratic evolution of El Salvador and the movement toward Marxist dictatorship in Nicaragua—that generally speaking, radical forces in Central America and the Caribbean are not genuine democrats, but committed totalitarians. The Grenada documents (especially those revealing Grenadian attempts to manipulate the Socialist International) (Appendix A, Document 24) have demonstrated to Europe that Marxist forces in the Western Hemisphere are not just Social Democrats with rifles.

Increased U.S. Flexibility. The Grenada action has given increased political leeway for the future American use of force in roughly analogous situations, especially in the Western hemisphere. U.S. military actions against Marxist forces in territories close to the United States are likely to be politically acceptable and popular if swift and successful. The Grenada intervention tends to reinforce the argument that it is best—i.e., less costly and more effective—to respond to Marxist takeovers early on. The Grenada intervention also makes it less likely that a U.S.-Soviet conflict might develop in Central America or the Caribbean. For example, the Sandinistas might choose to deploy Soviet fighters and bombers. If this were to happen, there appears to be a consensus of conservatives and liberals that the United States would have to respond. Clearly, such a scenario is avoidable if the Nicaraguans and Soviets exercise sufficient restraint in light of the resolve displayed by the United States in Grenada.

Improved Understanding of Marxist Tactics. The release of the Grenada documents has created a better understanding of how Marxist forces and their allies attempt to manipulate public opinion in the United States and in the West in general.

Strengthened Interest in Unconventional Warfare. The success of the Grenada operation has served to increase further the renewed U.S. interest in so-called "low-intensity conflict" strategies. This interest is reflected in policy debates, military allocations, and efforts to improve the capabilities of security forces in the Eastern Caribbean.

Changed Perception of Regional Marxists. Caribbean Marxists are no longer perceived as carefree, relaxed, and rather indolent; rather, as Howard Wiarda has said, they are "deadly serious revolutionaries committed unequivocably to causing embarrassment to the U.S. and strengthening ties with Cuba and the Soviet Union."

Restores a Measure of Unpredictability. After the American withdrawal from Vietnam in 1975, the world concluded that the United States would shrink from any significant use of force, except perhaps in a clear-cut case of overt aggression. The U.S. response to events in Grenada has forced the world to realize that the United States will respond to a continuum of circumstances.

The "Warnings" Were Correct. The Grenada documents confirm that the so-called "alarmists"—those who painted a fairly dark picture of the situation in Grenada prior to the U.S./OECS intervention—were certainly more correct than those who saw the Grenadian revolution as a benign local event. This tends to reinforce the credibility and authority of those who perceive a significant East-West dimension to events in Latin America.

Vulnerability of Small Nations. The Grenadian revolution epitomizes the vulnerability of many developing nations to a modest application of force by small, disciplined radical groups determined to seize power. This bolsters the argument in favor of a strong counterweight by the United States and other Western nations in these situations.

The Grenada events have presented the U.S. and others with the difficult but crucial task of assisting in the reconstitution of established authority and consolidation of democratic institutions in Grenada. This is not an easy task, and the long-term outcome is far from certain. Attention and resources should be devoted to this problem. Both governmental and private institutions should be involved in this effort as Grenada represents a challenge that the United States might be faced with again in the future. While exact conditions are different in every situation, lessons can be learned from the rebuilding of political authority in a country whose Marxist regime was displaced. It is important that this experiment should continue.

The Grenada documents shed light on the longstanding controversy over whether U.S. policies or the predilections of the new rulers lead emergent Marxist regimes in the Western Hemisphere to embrace the Soviet Union, as occurred in Cuba, Nicaragua, and Grenada. The Grenada documents reinforce the proposition that there is nothing much the United States could have done to alter the policies of determined Marxists who took control in Grenada. Similar conclusions are warranted regarding Cuba and Nicaragua, but in Grenada there is proof. Parenthetically, towards the end of his rule, Prime Minister Bishop seemed to be moving slightly toward a rapprochement with the United States. (Appendix A, Document 17) Since the United States pursued a very tough policy toward Grenada, this leads to the conclusion that tough U.S. policies do not necessarily drive revolutionary regimes into the Soviet camp, and they do not act as an impenetrable barrier to improved relations.

In summary, Professor Liska has offered a stimulating and thoughtful paper. However, it is of little real guidance to those who must actually decide and implement U.S. foreign policy. Aside from misinterpreting the relationship between ideology and Soviet foreign policy behavior, Dr. Liska approaches policy issues from the perspective of the historian. While history is a crucial element in understanding contemporary events and historical awareness is important in policymaking, an overly historical approach can lead to a pessimistic fatalism and passivity regarding world events.

As regards Grenada, a more useful approach would be to analyze the exact roles of the Soviet Union and Cuba in the Grenadian drama, and attempt to understand the internal dynamics of the NJM's attempt to consolidate power. While we lack the benefit of Soviet and Cuban documents (this is why Grenadian statements as to Soviet and Cuban positions must be weighed carefully), there is a wealth of information in the Grenada documents that allows us to understand what occurred in Grenada from 1979–1983, both from an internal and an international perspective.

Grenada was but a single element in a continuing struggle. For the foreseeable future, the United States must anticipate that the Soviets and Cubans will continue to probe the developing nations for opportunities to gain strategic allies and impose Marxism wherever possible. The Grenada documents enlighten us as to the nature of this struggle and confirm that U.S. action was necessary in Grenada.

Ultimately, Grenada highlights one of the most important and continuing sources of tension between the United States and the Soviet Union. Whatever their motivations, the Soviets have continually sought to expand their area of control around the world. As noted, we cannot be certain of the exact role of ideology in Soviet foreign policy. But whether the Soviets are expansionist because of their ideology or use their ideology to rationalize their expansionism, it is still necessary for the United States to resist such expansionism whenever it manifests itself.

It is theoretically possible for the United States and the Soviet Union to exist together in a world of reduced tensions. However, this cannot happen until the Soviet Union makes a fundamental decision to shift its international policies away from the systematic destabilization of noncommunist nations, especially in the Western Hemisphere. Should such a shift occur, a more positive and productive relationship between the United States and the Soviet Union can be achieved.

MARGARET DALY HAYES

Girding for the Long Run: Recommendations and Options for Coping with Soviet/Cuban Strategy in the Caribbean Basin

In 1979, Prime Minister Eric Gairy of Grenada was ousted in an unresisted coup perpetrated by a handful of armed People's Revolutionary Forces, members of the opposition New Jewel Movement (NJM). There was no resistance. Grenadians were tired of Gairy, an eccentric who had ruled Grenada for the 12 years since the island gained full independence from the United Kingdom. Maurice Bishop, leader of the NJM was a popular and articulate politician. In 1979, the prevailing sentiment among the population seemed to be that Bishop deserved a chance.

The New Jewel Movement's violent accession to power in the democratic Eastern Caribbean gave rise to concern among the leaders of the region. The foreign ministers of the region made emergency arrangements to meet in Barbados to discuss "reactions to the first leftist regime to seize power in the Caribbean since the Cuban revolution."[1] After more than a week, Caribbean leaders finally began to recognize the new regime. Jamaica was the first country to approach the new Grenadian government. The Jamaican envoy called on Grenadians to "struggle for socialism as the only answer to the Caribbean's problems."[2] Guyana and Barbados followed, but the leaders of other small Caribbean island states hesitated. Milton Cato, leader of Grenada's nearest neighbor, St. Vincent, called for a British force to oust the Bishop regime. Other leaders promised not to intervene, but determined among themselves to set up a regional police force to defend themselves against "armed and trained revolutionaries."[3]

The NJM established its rule over an island with a population of 100,000–110,000 whose principal sources of income were cacao, nutmeg, bananas, and tourism. Grenada's GNP was about $100 million in 1979, and its per capita income was about $850 per year, making it one of the poorest Eastern Caribbean islands. GNP had been declining throughout the 1970s because of chronic problems, and according to one account, Prime Minister Gairy had been "living almost from month-to-month."[4]

Grenada's was not the only revolution in 1979. In July of that year, the Sandinista National Liberation Front (FSLN), which had been waging a guerrilla war against the Somoza dictatorship in Nicaragua for nearly 20 years, succeeded in routing the Nicaraguan National Guard. In October, reform-minded young military officers in El Salvador overthrew the right-wing military dictatorship of that country and sought to undertake needed reforms. In early 1980, almost without protest or notice, the democratic government of Suriname fell in a putsch by 16 sergeants. In each of these countries revolutionary change was accepted and even welcomed by people who were fed up with government inefficiency and corruption. Few who examined political and economic conditions in the Caribbean Basin could deny that conditions were ripe for revolution throughout the region.

In October 1983, the Grenadian revolution turned upon itself as Maurice Bishop and his friends were brutally murdered in an internal power play. Ideological extremists within the NJM assumed power at gun point. (Appendix A, Document 16) The Grenada revolution was terminated on October 25, 1984 in a combined effort of the Organization of Eastern Caribbean States (OECS), Barbados, Jamaica, and the United States. Grenadians hailed the U.S./OECS mission as a "rescue" sent by God.[5] The invading forces found six warehouses full of Soviet bloc supplied arms, ammunition, quartermaster supplies, and spare parts. In the following three weeks, 800 Cubans, 49 Soviets, 15 North Koreans, 17 Libyans, 10 East Germans, and 3 Bulgarians were repatriated.[6]

At the time of the intervention, Grenadians were certainly no better off than they had been under Gairy. The economy was stretched thin and kept afloat by public spending on construction projects, the most notable of which was the Point Salines airport. The current account deficit was one-third of the total gross domestic product. Unemployment approached 40 percent. Political prisoners numbered 103, and opposition press groups and political parties had been suppressed.

The Grenada experience should be sobering to analysts of other revolutionary situations such as those in Suriname and Nicaragua. Both of these countries demonstrated fundamental political and economic weaknesses that led to the collapse of their former governments followed by easy revolutionary takeovers. In each country the population either worked openly with the revolutionaries (as in Nicaragua) or silently accepted revolutionary change because they had little stake in the fallen system (as in Grenada and Suriname). Yet in none of these countries have the extremists, once in power, dramatically improved the quality of life. In most cases, conditions are more desperate today than they were at the time of the revolution. Persistent international economic circumstances are partially responsible for this state of affairs, but revolutionary mismanagement bears the greatest responsibility for deteriorated economic conditions in Grenada, Suriname, and Nicaragua. Except in El Salvador, where the revolution has taken a different course, revolutionary regimes in the Caribbean that came into power in 1979 and 1980 have tended to adopt anti-Western foreign policies, engage in anti-American rhetoric, and look toward the Soviet bloc for development models and economic and military assistance. In doing so they have challenged U.S. security interests.[7]

U.S. INTERESTS AND CONCERNS REGARDING REVOLUTIONARY CHANGE IN THE WESTERN HEMISPHERE

It is clearly in the American interest to avoid, resist, and perhaps prohibit future Grenadas in the Caribbean Basin. Elsewhere I have sought to develop a formulation of the U.S. national interest in Latin America and the Caribbean Basin. Ignoring that one or another administration may not pursue the following policies, I propose that "it is in the U.S. interest to promote "stable, friendly, prosperous states that permit the free movement of goods and services throughout the region; that respect the political integrity of their neighbors; and that offer no support to the United States' global political rivals."[8] American foreign policy is often, and always should be, crafted to pursue these goals.

If it is to achieve such goals, the United States will have few choices as to its involvement in the Caribbean Basin. Noninvolvement is not an option. The United States is too profoundly involved in the region for such a policy to work. At the most elementary level, the United States depends on the sea lanes of the region for its commerce and military security.[9] Global security interests are closely linked to regional security and political stability. In the five years since the Grenadian revolution, two administrations have felt it was necessary to reestablish a military presence in the Caribbean Basin, to increase the number and size of military exercises in the region, and to commit manpower to a region that was once considered quiescent and secure. The more threatened the situation becomes for the governments of the Caribbean, the more likely it is that the United States will become involved in the region's internal affairs; the more likely it is that the United States will be called upon by the countries of the region to become involved as it was in October 1983.

As Anthony P. Maingot argues in this volume that the countries of the Caribbean Basin look to the United States. Since Britain's departure from the region and virtual abdication of responsibility for its former colonies, the United States has been the nearest power with which the Caribbean states share some tradition. Millions of Caribbean citizens reside permanently in the United States. Other hundreds of thousands are illegal aliens. Still more aspire to come to the United States. Trade and tourism link economies of the region to the United States. In short, the U.S. stake in the Caribbean is considerable. However, most people do not understand or appreciate the

U.S. interest in the region. Few people appreciate the nature of East-West rivalries in the region, or elsewhere for that matter. Fewer still appreciate the complexities and interrelationships of regional problems that need to be tackled, or the slow pace at which change can be effected. Even fewer appreciate the costs of such changes, or the scarcity of the resources available to address the problem countries of the Eastern Caribbean.

Therefore, the question is not whether the United States should be involved, but in what manner it will be involved. The answers to this question are dictated by the nature of the problems facing the region and the skill of those U.S. policymakers who must select and then promote various policy options.

FRAMEWORK FOR U.S. POLICY IN THE POST-GRENADA CARIBBEAN BASIN

The dilemmas of the Eastern Caribbean are problems of economic size on the one hand, and political, social, and economic institutional strength on the other. By comparison, the problems of Central America have less to do with economic size, though this factor plays a role. Central America's problems clearly stem from deficiencies in political, economic, and social institutional strength. Institutional weaknesses are among the principal factors contributing to the entire region's political instability. Given these institutional weaknesses, the region was bound to have encountered growth and development related problems. However, the day of reckoning was advanced by the prolonged world economic crisis that followed the 1973 oil price shock. Problems of rising import costs and declining prices for major export products have been exacerbated by economic mismanagement (which was profound in Jamaica in the 1970s) and corruption. In addition, inherent problems are difficult to resolve because of a lack of political will to find solutions, or a political inability to impose solutions on difficult problems.[10]

The economic situation throughout the region is largely one of unrealized potential, but the political spectrum is somewhat more varied. In Central America, governments are weak, with no tradition of stability, organization, or institutionalization. In the Eastern Caribbean the traditions of parliamentarism are strong, but political parties do not seem to have had much success in imposing or implementing far-reaching policies.[11] Communist penetration of weak institutions, whether by Soviet, Cuban, or other design, has increased over time. The New Jewel Movement is not the only Marxist movement to challenge the elected governments of the Caribbean island states. Because of their ineffectiveness, governments have become vulnerable to challenge. Too many citizens of the region are prone to give revolutionaries a chance because incumbent governments have not done much good. Too often the same people are surprised by developments once the radicals are in office, and too often there has been nothing they could do to change that situation.

Events in Grenada over the past four years demand that the leaders of the United States and the developing countries of the Caribbean Basin find a more effective way to make the democratic pluralist process that all inherited function in the complex political and economic environment of the late 20th century. One of the key frustrations of the present political situation in the Caribbean Basin is the attractiveness that Marxism-Leninism still holds for young political leaders. I do not know how to counter this appeal to the disenchanted youth of the region in the short-term. For the long-term, I suggest that the only way to avoid future Grenadas is to work aggressively to realize the political, economic, and social institutional development of the Caribbean Basin. If democratic institutions were stronger and more effective, the Leninist model might not be so attractive. More importantly, the people of the region would not become so tired of their governments that they would be willing to accept armed coups by small cadres of zealots.

Making the democratic pluralist model work means strengthening existing institutions and creating new ones that can accomplish the task of coping with societal demands. To accomplish such a massive and challenging effort will require a rather substantial change in attitude on the part of both North Americans and residents of the Caribbean Basin. In the first place, it will be accomplished only by a long-term commitment of human and financial resources led by the United States. Second, it will not be accomplished unless the people—especially political and civic leaders—are caught up enthusiastically in the effort. Indeed, local leaders must assume the lead. Finally, it will not be accomplished unless there is strong domestic support in the United States for a significant commitment of resources. But strong domestic support will not be forthcoming without some agreement on the nature of the threat that challenges the United States in the Caribbean Basin region.

The policymaking community has already recognized that U.S. interests are deeply engaged in the Caribbean Basin and that a much more active policy is required. However, until there is a widespread public recognition of U.S. interests and the nature of the threat to those interests, it will be difficult to implement necessary policies.[12] American interests will continue to be challenged from the outside in the hope that the collective "nerve" of the United States will falter and permit a major revolutionary breakthrough in the region.

To develop a consensus on which to build a policy aimed at preempting potentially revolutionary situations, several issues must be sorted out. These include (1) an understanding of the nature of the Soviet (Marxist-Leninist) threat in the region and the need to reinforce the longstanding U.S. policy of "no more Cubas," (2) a recognition of the urgency for economic growth, (3) an acknowledgement of the institutional weaknesses of the region, and (4) an acceptance of U.S. roles and responsibilities as the dominant power in the region.

THE NATURE OF THE "SOVIET THREAT"

There are tendencies in this country both to exaggerate and downplay Soviet intentions and activities in the Third World, especially in the Caribbean. On the one hand, the Soviets are seen as following a well thought out plan in which they are directly involved in fomenting and installing revolutionary governments everywhere. The spectre of Soviet military authority backing Soviet puppet states is emphasized to capture attention and to impress the public with the seriousness of the challenge to American security interests. The argument is then discredited when the villain fails to appear.

On the other hand, sometimes the Soviets are seen as benign observers of revolutionary situations with little vested interest in the outcome of regional conflicts or insurgencies that challenge "reactionary" regimes. Their interest in the Western hemisphere is often seen as too limited for Soviet leaders to permit risking a confrontation with the United States.[13] But neither of these views of Soviet behavior is adequate; both ignore the more subtle and debilitating consequences of a Soviet policy bent on constraining U.S. options in areas of U.S. interest. Both reflect a fundamental misunderstanding (or at least misstatement) of the nature of the political threat posed by Soviet cultivation of Third World leaders and the obvious challenge that this presents to U.S. security.

The United States has a profound interest in the political alignment of the countries of the Western hemisphere. It is in the United States national interest that the countries of the region do not provide support for the global rivals of the United States. The United States is a global power, and the global balance of power is of vital interest to the United States. Consistent with this interest, one of the cornerstones of U.S. foreign policy has been to insist that the political and ideological balance shall not shift against the West or the Western value system in Latin America and the Caribbean Basin. This principle governed U.S. attitudes toward European adventures in the region even before World War II. President Kennedy insisted that the United States would not interfere with Castro's Cuba if Cuba in turn would not interfere in the internal politics of the countries of the region. Cuban, Soviet, and indigenous revolutionary activities in the Western Hemisphere are understood by U.S. policymakers in terms of the precept that there can be no more Cubas in the region. The threat to the United States posed by the Soviet Union is too often dismissed as a military threat alone. Too often "other Cubas" are regarded simply as revolutionary countries that do not sympathize with the United States. However, these threats need to be understood as considerably more subtle and difficult to cope with.

The reality is that the Soviet Union is not going to "adventure militarily" into the Western hemisphere in any foreseeable scenario. To do so would provoke conflict with the United States. Moreover, the Soviet Union does not need to "colonize" the region to threaten the United States. By continuing to encourage groups whose goals are to weaken support for the United States, the Soviets accomplish their goal of building constraints on the United States in order to neutralize or counterbalance American power.[14] Ambassador William H. Luers reminded the National Bipartisan Commission on Central America that the threat to the Caribbean Basin posed by the coming to power of additional Marxist-Leninist revolutionary states would come not from a Soviet military adventure, or even from the establishment of military ties or bases, but rather from the "dramatic polarization and probable militarization of the region" caused by the "shrinkage of the political center and the failure of confidence of the region's struggling democrats."[15] Thus the real threat to the United States, and to the citizens of the region, is from the generalized destabilization that would result from upsetting the ideological status quo in the region.

To appreciate the threat that rival ideologies might pose to the United States, it is useful to reflect on the role of ideology in the Soviet Union's Leninist system because ideology for Leninists is very different from ideology for democratic pluralists. As Charles H. Fairbanks, Jr. notes in this volume, the Grenada documents demonstrate that Grenada's revolutionaries were concerned about the ideological appearance of things, and thought that such appearances were very important to the Soviet Union. (Appendix A, Document 16) The ideology that they sought to adopt was an amalgam of Marxist-Leninist precepts and various foreign policies wholly consistent with traditional imperial Russian power considerations. Thus, according to Jack Matlock, Marxist-Leninist ideology as elaborated by the Soviets has become a convenient justification for the aims of Soviet foreign policy; it provides legitimacy for Soviet involvement overseas and shapes Soviet thinking about the world.

Leninist ideology is a convenient instrument of Soviet foreign policy in the Third World that provides radicals with a "textbook" for organizing revolutionary societies with doctrinal legitimation for the exercise of exclusive state authority, and with norms for imposing order on unstable, postrevolutionary internal conditions. The Soviet preference for vanguard parties as opposed to charismatic leaders who may have their own agendas provides assurance that Soviet clients will continue to be sympathetic to Soviet views. This assures that Soviet allies will remain in power and reinforces the myth of "irreversibility" of Marxist-Leninist revolutions.

In short, Leninism is an ideology that is particularly useful to Third World leaders having trouble staying in power. It demands the creation of a "vanguard" party and a bureaucracy dependent on the party. It provides for control over the military and the economy, and it justifies the exclusion of competing power centers. It should be noted that this set of concerns is precisely what contending Nicaraguan elites have been arguing over with respect to the postrevolutionary direction of that country. The distinction between Marxist and Leninist revolutionaries made by Jiri and Virginia Valenta in this volume is important to understand.

To deal more effectively with Soviet challenges in the Third World and especially the Caribbean Basin, the United States needs to develop better access to information about Soviet activities aimed at cultivating new generations of political leaders. The Soviet Union is considerably more dedicated to winning the hearts and minds of future Third World leaders than the United States and other Western nations. In particular, the Soviets seek out and cultivate the ambitious disgruntled youth of the Third World. The United States and its allies are desperately in need of better, and better-integrated, intelligence on political personalities in the Third World. Much more detailed information is needed on the background and political contacts of revolutionary leaders to gain a better understanding of how the Soviets and Cubans cultivate ideological fellow travellers. It is also relevant to know how much time they spend in Cuba, the Soviet Union, or with the PLO. A greater appreciation of the long-term implications of East bloc boarding schools for Third World elites is required as well. The Soviet Union, Cuba, and their allies annually provide some 100,000 scholarships to Third World youths. It is unlikely that these are provided simply out of concern for the lack of opportunity available to poor but bright children in the Third World. It is necessary to achieve a better understanding of these programs for the attitudes they are likely to instill in the next generation of Third World leadership.

The United States must also upgrade its diplomatic presence in the Caribbean region. An enhanced presence is necessary to carry out an expanded aid program. Equally important, an enhanced presence is necessary in order to understand the region better. Under the Carter administration, the United States erred in not permitting its ambassadors to establish close contacts with the Bishop government in Grenada. It erred in not having a first-class intelligence operation in a country that it immediately preceived to be heading in a dangerous direction. The sharp reduction in intelligence gathering capabilities in Central America in the 1970s contributed to political and diplomatic failures throughout the period, but especially in the confused period beginning in 1978 when the Somoza regime began to be successfully challenged. American responses to the challenge to Somoza, his fall, and the installation of the Sandinista government were based as much on wishful thinking as on a clear understanding of the internal political dynamics of Nicaragua. As a world power, the United States must be well-informed about what is going on. Critics of U.S. policy around the world have correctly complained (if sometimes too stridently) that U.S. officials are acquainted only with friendly elements in their countries. The maxim "know thy enemy" is timeless and applies to all states.

The only solution envisaged regarding to the political challenge posed by Leninist designs on the Western hemisphere is to strengthen regional non-Marxist institutions so that utopian promises have little or no appeal. The United States must work both bilaterally and multilaterally to strengthen the institutional capacity of regional governments and societies to manage and (where possible) overcome their problems. Such an effort should be coordinated on both political and economic levels, and it must combine the energies of both government and private institutions.

Coordinating Economic Development

It is absolutely vital that regional economic development should be restimulated on an urgent basis. American efforts in the region should be coordinated with other bilateral efforts and various international organizations. However, it should be understood that the U.S. effort will have to be the greatest. Of the major bilateral donors, only the United States has a national security interest in the region. The economics of World Bank project assistance to the region does not facilitate major investments. The World Bank's soft loan window, the International Development Agency (IDA), is focused on Africa. On a purely cost-benefit basis, the Eastern Caribbean only qualifies for a miniscule share of World Bank or Inter-American Development Bank funding. As a consequence, it is left to the more limited resources of its own regional banks. Only a significant U.S. contribution and presence is likely to bring other donors and institutions into the region. Equally important, only a major effort on the part of indigenous entrepreneurs and governments will bring in significant amounts of government or private capital. The first step must come locally. It is impossible to strengthen institutions that do not care to be strengthened.

The Caribbean Basin region, excluding major countries like Venezuela, Colombia, and Mexico, presently has an average per capita income of about $1,000. Unemployment ranges from 20–40%, and 40–50% of the population is under 15 years of age. If economic growth cannot be restimulated, these trends themselves will lead to political instability and crisis. The current economic situation in the region is marked by severe balance of payments problems, heavy government debt burdens, stagnant to negative growth, decapitalization of human and financial resources, and a lack of new investments, etc. These circumstances should be attacked by direct government assistance and private sector initiatives that must be encouraged by local governments.

The record of Central American economic growth in the late 1960s and early 1970s is impressive and demonstrates that when circumstances are propitious, the region can expand and benefits can be channeled to the poor. The experience of the Eastern Caribbean is less promising, in part because it has not yet benefited from any large-scale coordinated development effort, and in part because it has unique problems stemming from its size and geography. Historically, Trinidad and Tobago and Jamaica have received the bulk of investment, and the smaller islands (which obviously suffer most from problems of scale) have received the least. Mechanisms should be found to change this balance, for the small islands can create political problems as severe as the larger ones—as the Grenada experience has shown.

A mix of public and private initiatives is necessary for a number of reasons. The U.S. Government has relatively few instruments through which it can provide assistance. Economic support funds, or short-term balance of payments and security support assistance, Agency for International Development (AID) assistance, PL-480 (Food for Peace) support, and transfers to multilateral lending institutions are the most important mechanisms. Unfortunately, these resources are in short supply and hotly contested.

The creative energy and long-term commitment to development must come from the private sector—particularly from the private sectors of the developing countries themselves. Unless local private individuals demonstrate their commitment to economic development by investing their own money and supporting changes in local law to encourage both domestic and foreign investment, no external capital will be forthcoming. The United States cannot order unwilling investment in the Caribbean Basin even though the region is a high national security interest.

The United States has undertaken some policies designed to encourage both public and private sector involvement in the region. Most notably, the Caribbean Basin Initiative (CBI) has created a 12-year one way free zone for the Caribbean Basin. The purpose of the CBI is to provide incentives to entrepreneurs and planners in the region to invest in nontraditional export products and take advantage of the world's largest market to prime the pump. As Jamaican Prime Minister Edward Seaga noted in endorsing the CBI, one simply cannot live next door to the richest market in the world and remain poor. Something is amiss if one does, but nevertheless it will be several years before one sees the real impact of the CBI's incentive mechanism. Unfortunately, problems have emerged during the course of negotiating the CBI. One problem is a lack of expertise on the part of regional producers in dealing with the U.S. market system. Another is the lack of information within the region about the various capabilities of each country.

Another key to regional recovery in the Caribbean Basin is further and accelerated regional integration. Political differences over the past several years have nearly destroyed the rocky integration movement of the English-speaking Caribbean. The Dominican Republic and Haiti have been offered access to these regional institutions only recently. The Central American Common Market (CACM) has languished for years, but a framework remains and there is a renewed recognition that multinational approaches are the most promising route to economic recovery. The problems of regional integration need to be discussed more openly throughout the region. This is an area in which the United States should take a leading role.

Coaxing Political Development

The rules for promoting economic development are uncertain, but the most promising ways to foster political development are all but unknown. The greatest American contribution to political development in the Caribbean Basin region can be in an area which (for lack of a better word) I will call "civism." Civism is active private citizen participation in political life, holding government responsible for its actions, and following through with similar responsibility in private life. The absence of civism is a key problem for the governments of Central America and most of Latin America. Until governments can be held responsible before their constituencies, they will not be sufficiently strong to resist the random winds of adventurous revolutionaries.

The recently inaugurated National Endowment for Democracy represents an effort to provide a permanent forum for communicating the virtues of civism and political organization, especially at the grass roots level. The organization is far from perfect, but it constitutes a step in a direction that has not been tried before. Furthermore, European political institutions can play an important political training role in Latin America and the English-speaking Caribbean. The United States must be prepared to cooperate and not compete with these organizations.

The United States should use its renewed presence in the region to encourage a much greater intraregional dialogue about political and economic problems. The OECS, CARICOM, the World Bank's Caribbean Group, the Central American Development Organization (CADO) as proposed by the Bipartisan National Commission on Central America, and the Contadora group all offer forums for such a dialogue. It is alarming that CARICOM should be near collapse at this crucial point in time because it remains one of the few institutions able to provide a framework for a common approach to regional problem solving. The Caribbean Group at the World Bank has provided a useful forum for debate on economic problems. Similar meetings should begin to offer a venue for discussing political problems.

On a more practical level, the United States must also consider the domestic security capabilities of the Eastern Caribbean. Responding in part to needs recognized as a result of the Grenada crisis, the United States is currently engaged in police and Coast Guard training in the region. Similar activities can be carried out in Costa Rica which has no army. However, some of the worst internal security problems occur in countries like El Salvador, which under present law cannot receive training. While the excesses of the police forces of many Latin American countries should not be tolerated or excused, it is not likely that such behavior will change unless institutional values are changed. This cannot be accomplished by avoiding contacts.

A policy of institution-building does not assure success. Though the Grenada experience has deterred some, there will still be challenges to the political systems of the Western hemisphere from both dedicated revolutionaries and high-minded reformists. The United States will have to deal adeptly with such challenges, reacting on the basis of better information and pursuing a more active diplomacy. Recent crises in the region require action from both the United States and regional organizations. If diplomacy fails, the United States must be prepared to take decisive action—to use force if need be—as a last resort to assure that the interests of the United States and its allies are defended. The United States must assert—perhaps regretfully—that force is a policy option in any circumstance where it is required. Like war, the use of force is a continuation of politics by other means. Because the United States is a superpower, there must never be any doubt that it is able to use its military might to guarantee its interests.

Moreover, the point at which the United States feels compelled to take military action should not be specifically defined lest it is challenged.

A credible argument is made by some that in the 1970s Latin American revolutionaries, especially those in Cuba, became more adventurous and confident in challenging the United States because of a pervasive sense that the United States would not use its military power in the Third World. Leurs attributes recent Cuban and Soviet actions in the Western hemisphere to the conviction that the correlation of forces, including the weakening of U.S. resolve, turned in favor of Marxism-Leninism.[16] Other authors such as Legvold and Zagoria see a similar pattern in other regions of the world. Leftists have intensively lobbied the United States Congress, intensively seeking assurance and reassurance that American military power would be constrained. The general reticence of most political leaders to engage in big stick diplomacy lured some into believing that the United States would not react to events in Central America. As a consequence, they were encouraged to take greater risks in the region. But the overwhelming public reaction to the Grenada intervention reflected the American public's frustration at inactivity in the face of challenges to the United States. Many Latin Americans criticized the Grenada intervention, but as many privately congratulated the United States for its decisive action in defense of democracy.

Given the Soviet Union's great power interests and the ideological justifications of Marxism-Leninism, it is wishful thinking to believe that the Soviets and the Cubans will not continue to challenge the United States in as many places as opportunity permits. A key to managing these challenges is to make clear the boundaries of acceptable challenge and to show that the United States is ready to act if those boundaries are transgressed as was the case in Grenada.

NOTES

1. *Latin America Political Report*, March 23, 1979.

2. Ibid.

3. *Latin America Political Report*, March 30, 1979.

4. *Latin America Economic Report*, April 6, 1979.

5. Testimony by distinguished Grenadian journalist Alistair Hughes in U.S. Congress, House, Committee on Foreign Affairs, *Grenada: Implications for U.S. Policy in the Eastern Caribbean, Hearings before the Subcommittees on International Security and Scientific Affairs and on Western Hemisphere Affairs of the Committee on Foreign Affairs*, 99th Congress, 2nd Session, 1984.

6. See *Grenada: A Preliminary Report*, U.S. Department of State and Department of Defense, December 16, 1983.

7. I have developed more detailed explications of U.S. security interests in the Western hemisphere in "United States Policy toward Latin America: A Prospectus," prepared for the International Peace Academy, March 1984; and "Security in the Western Hemisphere" in Kevin Middlebrook and Carlos Rico (eds.), *U.S.-Latin*

American Relations in the 1980s: Papers of the Inter-American Dialogue (forthcoming 1985).

8. Margaret Daly Hayes, "United States Policy toward Latin America: A Prospectus," op. cit.

9. Margaret Daly Hayes, "Security to the South: U.S. Interests in Latin America," *International Security*, Summer 1980, pp. 130–152.

10. This point was made forcefully by Ambassador Sally Shelton who, in commenting on this paper, observed that there is another provocation for revolutionary change in the Caribbean that might be labeled institutional corruption, or the weaknesses, or ability of existing political, economic and security systems to manage the challenges with which they are confronted. "In this connection, the challenges faced by most of the smaller countries in the Caribbean (except Grenada) derive less from economic deterioration or Soviet/Cuban adventurism than from various "nontraditional" sources. For example, Dominica has suffered three attempted coups in as many years from a combination of the Ku Klux Klan, modern-day adventurers or mercenaries, and organized North American criminal elements. Modern-day buccaneers twice attempted to overthrow the government of Barbados. St. Vincent and other countries in the region have faced similar types of threats. These challenges have little or nothing to do with Cuba, the Soviet Union, or economic deterioration. They have everything to do with elements not willing to work within the system to affect change—elements simply determined to take over the governments of the East Caribbean to run them for their own political or financial benefit."

11. U.S. and Caribbean observers disagree somewhat about the strength of parliamentarism in the region. Ambassador Shelton and others have remarked on the institutional weakness and inability to manage the political and economic challenges confronting the governments of the region. Anthony Maingot has stressed the strength of parliamentary spirit and tradition in the English-speaking Caribbean. He argues that in Grenada, Eric Gairy fell precisely because he abused the parliamentary system. Resistance to the heavy-handed Leninist Bishop and Coard regimes was a foregone conclusion according to Maingot. Leninism would never have "taken" in Grenada unless imposed by force.

12. There are some indicators that suggest that this recognition may be changing. The Salvadoran elections of March and May 1984 finally seem to have persuaded a majority that Salvadorans want an elected government. Guerrilla failures to win wide support in the Salvadoran population are beginning to be recognized, and the political direction being taken by the Sandinistas in Nicaragua is beginning to alarm even the most sanguine observers. Hopefully the Grenada documents, when fully analyzed, will provide further insight into both the activities of Soviets and Cubans in fostering Leninist revolution in the region and the vicissitudes of a "just revolutionary situation" turned awry.

13. Soviet strategies in the Third World, though not in the Western hemisphere, are discussed in Robert Legvold, "The Super Rivals: Conflict in the Third World," *Foreign Affairs*, Spring 1979, pp. 755–778; and Donald S. Zagoria, "Into the Breach: New Soviet Alliances in the Third World," *Foreign Affairs*, Spring 1979, pp. 733–754.

14. See Legvold, op. cit.

15. See William H. Luers, "U.S. Interests in Central America," *American Enterprise Institute Foreign Policy and Defense Review (U.S. Policy in Central America-Consultant Papers for the Kissinger Commission)*, Vol. 5:1 (1984), pp. 26–36.
16. Op. cit.

The views expressed in this paper are the author's and should not be construed as representing positions of the members of the Council of the Americas.

CHARLES H. FAIRBANKS, JR.

Notes on Grenada, Soviet Proxies, and U.S. Policy

THE PLACE OF THE PERIPHERY IN EAST-WEST RELATIONS

In seeking to improve relations with the Soviet Union, to moderate its behavior, and to relax international tensions, we have a tendency to look for answers in a bilateral context. We also tend to assume that negotiations must be commenced when relations are unsatisfactory. A more sophisticated view sees formal negotiations as part of a continuum of diplomatic contacts with the Soviet Union, many of which are quite hidden. This is consistent with the view that arms control talks and agreements are not only important, but the very key to East-West relations and the preservation of peace. This view is intuitively plausible, but it is highly misleading. It contains only an element of truth, and overlooks the fact that U.S.-Soviet relations do not assume their character solely from U.S. actions toward the Soviet Union. Soviet conduct is a result of opportunities and limits that confront the Soviet state at any given moment. Part of these opportunities and limits become visible in American policy or contacts, but they also become visible elsewhere.

Just as American policy toward the Soviet Union is shaped substantially by existing conditions in Western Europe, China, the Middle East, and Central America, the foreign policy of the Soviet Union arises in large measure from the realities it confronts in the same regions. The implication is that, to a large degree, Soviet conduct takes its character from American policy toward third parties—i.e., the Third World. American policy toward the Third World in effect creates the "facts" within which Soviet policy must operate. More so than their American counterparts, Soviet officials emphasize that facts of this type, which they call the "correlation of forces" in the world, are an essential determinant of their policy. In fact, it is likely that U.S. policy toward the Third World is more important in structuring Soviet behavior than its direct relations with the Soviet Union itself.

The intuitive view that sees East-West relations as shaped by bilateral relations with the Soviet Union is taken over whole from our experience with balance of power politics prior to 1945. In a multipower international system, there existed the possibility of a power transfer from one center to another (e.g., Britain between 1903 and 1907, Italy after 1935, and the Soviet Union in 1939). Short of war, such shifts accounted for the most decisive transformations of the international system that could take place, and they could not have taken place without direct negotiations founded upon preexisting bilateral relations.

This intuitive assumption was correct until the end of World War II. But in 1945, an enduring bipolar system emerged for the first time in the modern era. This shift from multipolarity to bipolarity comprehensively changed the conditions of diplomacy. One of the changes was to make major shifts between the superpowers highly unlikely. While competition between the superpowers may be managed or diminished, competition is an enduring fact of the postwar world. Thus, the foreign policies of the superpowers have come to be defined by facts that they confront throughout the world. In turn, these facts are created by mutual policies toward third parties, or by local realities. The most sensitive areas of course are those developing nations that tend to exhibit the greatest possibilities for change. Thus, the small island of Grenada had significance for East-West relations.

If developing countries are vitally important in structuring the foreign policies of the superpowers, they are also the focus of the greatest danger in U.S.-Soviet relations. At present, this view is not dominant either on the "left" or the "right" of the foreign policy spectrum. Critics of the Reagan administration tend to focus on potential dangers to peace in the arms race or some failure to negotiate seriously with the Soviets.

Richard Pipes offers a different view in his article, "How to Cope with the Soviet Threat."[1] The article covers the military balance, domestic divisions in Western democracies, the state of the NATO alliance, the issue of East-West trade, and it largely omits the issue of East-West conflict in developing areas. With regard to possible war between East and West, Pipes argues that "Germany occupies a location of unique importance in that any military conflict on the continent is certain to begin on its territory, and there to find its decision."

However, conflict is most likely to arise where opportunities are greatest, risks at a minimum, and commitments and stakes are unclear. If this is true, a military conflict that ends on the European Continent is more likely to begin in Turkey than in West Germany, or in Iran rather than in Turkey. Armed conflict on the Central European front (which would instantly raise the question of a general nuclear war) is imaginable today only in the midst of a deep political crisis such as that of the 1930s. Such a crisis would be most likely to be triggered by events in a highly unstable area with ample opportunities and risks for Soviet or Western intervention.

The major components of détente (such as *Ostpolitik* and SALT) affected the "central" facets of U.S.-Soviet-European relations under the assumption that they would pacify the entire East-West relationship. This expectation was proven false by events in Angola, Ethiopia, Afghanistan, Nicaragua, and El Salvador. In retrospect, it seems that détente stabilized the "central" U.S.-Soviet relationship to a significant degree, but not to the extent anticipated.

Détente failed to pacify the East-West conflict with regard to the Third World. In terms of the development of Soviet power-projection capabilities, détente in a sense may have "liberated" the possibilities for conflict. Indeed, it is possible that the emergence of nuclear deterrence as a factor in international politics may itself tend to "sublimate" superpower conflict—to channel it from direct to indirect modes.[2]

PRECONDITIONS OF SOVIET ADVANCES IN DEVELOPING COUNTRIES

In the developing world, there are several characteristics of present-day international politics that dampen the expansion of Soviet influence. The internal instability of many Third World countries generates opportunities for the Soviet Union. Soviet foreign policy differs from U.S. foreign policy in its more vigorous exploitation of such opportunities. Two examples will substantiate this point.

In Grenada, the emergence of the ideologically Leninist New Jewel Movement (NJM) was an indigenous development that owed little to Cuban or Soviet encouragement. Once the NJM was in power, however, Cuba and the Soviet Union (as well as several Soviet allies and proxies) vigorously moved to exploit the opportunity presented by the Grenadian revolution. Second, in the Horn of Africa, during the mid- and late 1970s, a new political reality was created by the revolution against Haile Selassie in Ethiopia. This development posed both opportunities and risks for the Soviet Union. There was an opportunity to gain predominant influence over a large and strategically placed country, but there was also the risk that the Ethiopian empire would disintegrate, leaving the Soviet Union with a shambles. The Soviet Union moved quickly to exploit the opportunity by forming close relations with Ethiopia, supplying arms, and airlifting Cuban troops to contain the risks. At that time, the United States did not move to take advantage of the chaotic situation on the Horn of Africa.

The relatively small size of most states and societies in the Third World should be kept in mind when discussing the exploitation of opportunities. This small scale makes it relatively easy for countries the size of Cuba or South Yemen to influence and destabilize states in their respective regions. Again, Grenada provides a striking example. Eric Gairy and his army of 65 had become unpopular in the small area coextensive with Grenada, and he was easily overthrown. The finite scale of Grenadian society facilitated control by a small group of intellectuals who utilized Grenada for the foreign policy and security purposes of Cuba and the Soviet Union. In countries the size of Angola or Ethiopia, the process of communization is more difficult and competing power groups tend to force radical governments into compromise. However, there are many developing countries whose size is similar to Grenada's.

Another factor influencing the exploitation of opportunities is the opening that exists for Soviet ideology in many areas of the developing world. This was one of the surprises revealed by the Grenada experience. Before the intervention, those who knew anything at all about the NJM probably regarded it as leftist and pro-Soviet, but not communist. The minutes and resolutions of NJM Politburo and Central Committee meetings that were captured during the invasion (especially those of September-October 1983 (Appendix A, Documents 4 and 16) are striking in that they reveal the leaders of the NJM as serious communists by their own understanding. Spokesmen of the two contending factions of the NJM constantly used Leninist political concepts such as "democratic centralism," "proletarian internationalism," "right opportunism," to define their positions and delegitimize the positions of their opponents. They constantly referred to the experiences of other communist states (even unpopular ones such as the German Democratic Republic or Afghanistan) as models for their political development. (Appendix A, Document 16) Strangely enough, while engaged in a concrete and ruthless power struggle, they displayed the touching belief that practical difficulties of ruling Grenada could be resolved by forming study groups and holding seminars on Leninist ideology. It is astonishing to see the debate between Zhdanov and Malenkov about the roles of economic efficiency, ideology, and organization repeated in Grenada in the debate between supporters of Bernard Coard and George Louison in the September 14–16, 1983, Extraordinary Meeting of the Central Committee of the NJM. (Appendix A, Document 16)

IDEOLOGY AS AN EFFECTIVE INSTRUMENT OF SOVIET FOREIGN POLICY

The West has tended to discount ideology as an instrument of Soviet foreign policy because generally it is discounted—perhaps correctly—as a motive for Soviet foreign policy. Such a conclusion does not follow. Leninist ideology is a valuable instrument in that it enables the Soviet Union to accomplish certain goals more easily than it could without ideological inputs. The following factors appear to account for the utility of ideology.

Ideology retains a strong appeal in many areas of the developing world despite its decreasing appeal in the West, the Soviet Union, and Eastern Europe since 1956. It appeals simultaneously to two opposed groups within many developing countries. First, it offers convenient legitimizing and organizing principles to those rebelling against established authority. This dynamic is encouraged by the unwillingness of many Westerners to support opposition movements directed against governments in power, thus causing developing nations to turn to Leninist ideology to define their course. They tend to see the West as always supporting the status quo.

Moreover, Leninist ideology is attractive to some Third World leaders because it helps them to deal with the insecure and illegitimate situation in which they often find themselves. When established institutions are not well-developed and there is no unified society or culture that supports the state, a higher premium is placed on the doctrinal legitimization of state authority. Since the decline of the belief in the state of nature and the social contract in Western society, the West no longer offers a legitimizing ideology as clear, simple, and nominally confident as Leninism.

Once a revolutionary group accepts Leninist ideology, an element of political continuity is created that enables both local leaders and the Soviet Union to hold on to any gains that have been made. Soviet gains in developing countries result from instability. However, there is a corresponding danger that what is gained through instability can be lost through instability. This is what happened to the Soviets in Ghana and in Sukarno's Indonesia. Fluctuations in domestic politics removed rulers friendly to the Soviet Union and cancelled out earlier gains. As a rule, the structures and norms brought about by Leninist political structures, inter-party relations, and international contacts contribute to the stabilization of unstable internal environments.

Present Soviet policies are reminiscent of the foreign policies of imperial Russia. Like the Soviet Union, imperial Russia fed on indigenous instabilities as a means of establishing client states. However, most of these proved difficult to hold on to them. In one such example, Russia occupied the area that is now Bulgaria after the Russo-Turkish War (1877–1878). It succeeded in electing Prince Alexander, the Tsar's nephew, to rule under the dominant influence of the Russian Consul General. To control anti-Russian movements, Bulgarian ministers had to be replaced with Russian officials. Eventually Tzar Alexander had to be deposed, Russia was unable to influence the election of its candidate, and the Balkan rival Prince Ferdinand was made king in 1887. Bulgaria's period as a Russian client state ended at that point. Although Russia continued to attempt to exert influence over Bulgaria's foreign policy, it was never again able to establish control over internal Bulgarian affairs. In the long-term, Russian policy backfired and Bulgaria joined the coalition against Russia in World War I.

But as the Grenada documents clearly indicate, ideology is an extremely important tool for manipulating distant states that often share no obvious security or political interests with the Soviet Union. Similarly, Leninist ideology has not been entirely successful in maintaining control over Soviet client states as demonstrated by events in China, Albania, Yugoslavia, and Somalia.

THE SOVIET PROXY SYSTEM

The Soviet use of Third World proxies is not well understood in the United States. Various writers identify a wider or smaller list of proxies, generally including Cuba, Libya, Ethiopia, Vietnam, and South Yemen.

Nicaragua is sometimes considered a proxy as well. Countries or groups that benefit from the efforts of proxy states—such as Grenada, the South West African People's Organization (SWAPO), and the Salvadoran guerrillas—also act as proxies at times.

The term proxy is useful because it implies that the states in question are not necessarily controlled or guided by the Soviet Union. Their foreign policies are generally nationalist in orientation, but their actions are generally "parallel" to those of the Soviet Union. For example, although Vietnam, South Yemen, and Ethiopia are active in their respective regions, they do not consider themselves proxies because they use Soviet support only in the furtherance of their own goals.

There are also several states whose actions are guided by the Soviet Union to a significant degree. The close coordination of Cuban and Soviet activities and resources in Angola, for example, shows that Cuban actions are not merely parallel to those of the Soviet Union.

Finally, some proxy states seem to be dependent on Soviet, Cuban, or East European support to remain in power. The Eastern European type of dependence is a relatively new phenomenon not apparent in other Soviet client states. Nassar's Egypt, Ghana, Guinea, and Somalia did not depend on Soviet strength, but Angola probably does, and Ethiopia did for some time.

Proxies under direct control are the most flexible instruments of the Soviet Union. But those who merely undertake parallel actions are extremely useful as well. Soviet losses resulting from the destabilization of the international communist movement after 1956 were mitigated to some degree by the actions of certain Soviet proxies, most notably Cuba.

WHY PROXIES ARE DANGEROUS TO U.S. INTERESTS

There is a tendency to regard the Soviet Union as the greatest danger to international peace and to ignore Soviet client states as minor additional dangers. This is a serious mistake, for proxies are particularly dangerous in ways that are only beginning to be understood.

The activities of proxy states can diverge from those of the Soviet Union, but as shown by the Grenada documents independent or semi-independent actions by proxies sometimes serve to reinforce the activities of the Soviet Union through multiple channels of influence. The Grenada documents explain this phenomenon in great detail. Prime Minister Bishop was particularly close to Cuba, while the Coard faction gained favor with the Soviet Union. Regardless of who won the internal struggle, the outcome would be more or less favorable to the Soviet Union. This would not have been the case if Cuba was rigidly guided by the Soviet Union in its every policy regarding Grenada.

A somewhat similar situation exists in South Yemen where a pro-Soviet faction is struggling against an even more pro-Soviet faction. But it is unlikely that South Yemen will end its relationship with the Soviet bloc regardless of who wins. In Ethiopia, the channels of Soviet bloc influence include Cuban troops, Soviet arms, and the emergence of a communist party organization that was formed at Soviet insistence. If any of these channels of access should fail, others will remain and the Soviet Union will not lose all in Ethiopia. For the Soviets, multiple channels of influence are the solution to reversals such as those that occurred in Egypt and Ghana.

Although Soviet proxies tend to act according to parallel interests, the activities of various proxies reinforce one another. In a sense, there exists something of a "proxy system" with many complexities and epicycles. Thus it is dangerous that Soviet proxies are not understood to be clients of the Soviet Union by a large sector of the international community. Although one of the Soviet Union's most active proxies, Cuba is prominent in the nonaligned movement. In reality, few countries are as involved as Cuba in Soviet designs. Grenada provides a striking example. Grenadian cooperation with Cuba and the Soviet Union was extremely close across a broad range of foreign policy issues, yet most interested international observers saw Grenada as a socialist (not communist) country prior to the U.S./OECS intervention of October 1983.

Even more fundamental is the fact that because proxies are not understood to be acting on behalf of the Soviet Union, they can carry out actions against U.S. interests that the Soviets themselves could not. Two examples will illustrate this. Had there been thousands of Soviet troops in Angola and Ethiopia, strong reaction would have been forthcoming. Yet the Soviet airlift of thousands of Cuban troops to these countries had no such impact. In addition, Libya was able recently to bomb the capital of the Sudan without provoking any retaliation. But without a doubt the event would have been far more dramatic if a Soviet bomber had attacked Khartoum. Thus proxies increase the global reach of Soviet power and reduce the risks of Soviet involvement. They enable the Soviets to damage or threaten Western interests in a manner otherwise impossible. In short, Soviet proxies pose a great problem for American foreign policy.

One should note, however, that if important proxy states pursue independent international activities parallel to Soviet interests, they may draw the Soviets into unwanted conflicts with the United States. Strong local interests, intimate local knowledge, and greater immunity from world reaction may lead Soviet proxies in directions that the Soviet Union does not wish to go. Nevertheless, the Soviets might feel impelled to follow. This is not merely a theoretical consideration as Grenada clearly demonstrates.

Grenada was a clear case where Cuban policy led Soviet policy. Maurice Bishop was originally a Cuban "find." The chronology of Soviet bloc involvement with Grenada shows that Grenada was not taken seriously at first, but was later given more credence due to Cuban initiatives. A similar process may have occurred in more momentous situations. There is some evidence that Cuban initiatives led Soviet policy in Angola, and to some extent in the Horn of Africa before the Soviet Union became heavily engaged. In addition, Soviet bloc support for the Sandinistas was originally a Cuban initiative in consonance with the historic Cuban preference for armed struggle in Latin America. The Soviet Union was not converted to a strategy of armed struggle elsewhere in Central America until the Sandinista accession to power in 1979. The result is the present Central American crisis—a crisis in which the Soviet Union can inflict losses on the United States disproportionate to the resources it commits to the region.

GLOBAL PROXIES

Soviet proxies are most dangerous to American interests are those that take on a global role. In 1959, Cuba was regarded by most Americans as an obscure "banana republic," unimportant in the Latin American context and negligible in the world balance. But Cuba has become a major problem for the United States, and a worldwide problem as well. Cuba is currently playing a larger international role than any Latin American country in history.

Libya is another such global proxy. Colonel Qadhafi has been active against American interests in the Western Sahara, Tunisia, Egypt, Sudan, Somalia, Lebanon, Iran, Chad, Uganda, Grenada, Nicaragua, St. Lucia, Antigua, and many other nations.

Some proxy states such as South Yemen, Angola, and Ethiopia pursue predominantly local interests under Soviet protection. It can be argued that these countries gain more from their relations with the Soviet Union than vice versa, and that the local nature of their activity limits the damage they can inflict on U.S. interests. Vietnam and Ethiopia pursue predominantly local interests, but the Vietnamese have sent arms to the guerrillas in El Salvador, and Ethiopia is now active in destabilizing the Southern Sudan—an area traditionally outside Ethiopian imperial ambitions. Global proxies, such as Cuba and Libya are particularly damaging to Western interests because they undertake "anti-imperialist" activities in several areas simultaneously and because their global role allows them to harmonize their interests with Soviet interests.

Two factors assure that the activities of the Soviet Union and its global proxies coincide. The first is ideology, and the other is merely a matter of ambition—i.e., worldwide ambition. Libya lacks Leninist ideology, but the universalistic character of Islam substitutes to some degree. A proxy whose expansionist tendencies are primarily local will tend to pursue its own national interests which are traditionally limited. As soon as a proxy takes on a global role, it is compelled to generalize its interests on a worldwide scale. (Cuba, South Yemen, and Grenada are prime examples of this tendency.) Most likely, the resulting void will be filled by anti-Americanism or the substitution of Soviet world interests.

Something in the nature of the proxy system seems to encourage a global role for Soviet clients. For instance, what were Cuba's interests in Angola? If such interest existed, they likely approximated Soviet interest.

Once again, the Grenada documents expose the process by which Soviet proxy interests are generalized and approximated to Soviet interests. One such document was a List of Countries with which Grenada Does Not Wish to Develop Close Relations.[3] (Appendix A, Document No. 19) The second country listed was the Comoro Islands. What could Grenada's interest have been in the Comoro Islands?

Cuba and Libya have emerged as regional powers whose activities have a global scope. If the United States and the Soviet Union are major world powers and France and China are secondary world powers, perhaps Cuba and Libya should be classed as tertiary world powers? This is not meant to imply that they are more powerful than many countries whose political and military relationships are predominantly local, but it recognizes the peculiar reach of Cuban and Libyan ambitions and interests.

FOCUSING AMERICAN POLICY ON THE PROXY PROBLEM

The Soviet proxy system poses a particularly difficult problem for American foreign policymakers. Perhaps the most important feature of the Grenadian revolution was that it highlighted the proxy problem. At this point, U.S. policymakers must develop a fuller understanding of the proxy problem and formulate a strategy to limit its potential to inflict damage on U.S. security interests.

The Carter administration apparently did not regard Soviet proxies as a distinct problem exacerbating the challenge posed by the Soviet Union. It is now well-known that a number of American allies have proposed vigorous U.S. action against Soviet proxies. The late President Anwar Sadat, for example, proposed military action against Libya. However, the United States did not respond to these requests and thus allowed Soviet clients to continue to act with impunity against Western interests. American inaction preserved an atmosphere wherein the nature of proxy behavior was not recognized for the purpose it served.

The Reagan administration broke with this tradition by exhibiting a willingness to undertake actions against Soviet proxies. These were directed primarily against those proxies that created the greatest problems for the United States—Cuba and Libya. American sanctions against Libya and the Gulf of Sidre incident showed Colonel Qadhafi the United States would not tolerate Libyan behavior without opposition. As a result, Libya's neighbors can hope for American protection in the event they become the target of Libyan subversion or aggression.

The Grenada intervention demonstrated that if countries in the region are threatened by Cuban activity, the U.S. will cooperate and engage Cuban forces under certain circumstances. Thus the intervention demonstrated a willingness and ability to respond quickly to available opportunities. Furthermore, it had had significant implications for restraining and limiting Cuban and Soviet expansionism in the Western hemisphere. Some of the effects of the intervention included the expulsion of Cuban advisors by Suriname, and the removal of Surinamese students from Cuba. Another direct consequence was an increased fear of an American invasion in Nicaragua. This resulted in a limited reduction of Cuban advisors and El Salvadoran guerrillas in Managua and a substantial (although temporary) improvement in civil liberties. It can be assumed that there were other less visible consequences of the Grenada intervention. In short, the record suggests that a vigorous strategy against Soviet proxies could have a substantial effect in limiting the consequences of their activity.

To deal effectively with the proxy problem, the United States should familiarize the American public with the nature of the proxy problem. However, a fundamental barrier to this goal is the tendency to separate the problems of the "South" from those of the "North." This has the effect of insulating the security problems of developing nations from their relation to East-West issues. One often hears the argument that Third World conflicts are rooted in indigenous economic and social conditions, not Soviet foreign policy. Whereas this argument contains a degree of truth, the conclusion that indigenous conflicts never affect East-West relations does not follow.

Since 1980, there has been a heightened awareness of the Soviet threat to U.S. security interests. Curiously, however, this has served to hide the proxy problem. Even those highly conscious of the need to oppose Soviet expansionism are not aware that proxies are perhaps the most dangerous means by which such expansion is achieved. In the final analysis, it is clear that U.S. actions to restrain proxy activity have progressed faster than public awareness of the nature of the threat.

NOTES

1. Richard Pipes, "How to Cope with the Soviet Threat," *Commentary*, August 1984.

2. See papers by Richard Betts, pp. 18 and 30; and Charles H. Fairbanks, Jr., pp. 4–6, presented at Conference on Nuclear Weapons and the Nature of Politics, University of Chicago, June 8–10, 1981; Foreign Relations Report and List of Countries with which Grenada Does Not Wish to Develop Close Relations, undated (but probably published in 1981), Grenada Documents, Log No. 105757.

3. Ibid.

SALLY A. SHELTON

Comments

I would like to raise the issue of the origins of revolutionary change in the Caribbean Basin. This is a discussion that seems to be absent from most analyses of the area. Traditionally, liberals attribute the origins of revolutionary change to economic deterioration stemming from a lack of resources, inadequate infrastructure, increases in oil prices, stagnant commodity prices, and the recession in the 1970s. On the other hand, conservative analysts tend to focus on the Soviet/Cuban threat. Certainly elements of both are present in terms of stimulating changes that have occurred in the Caribbean, but there are other elements which may be of considerably greater importance. I am specifically referring to what one might call institutional fragility, i.e., the inability of existing political, economic, and security systems to manage the challenges they are confronted with.

In this connection, the challenges faced by most of the smaller countries of the Caribbean (except Grenada) derive less from economic deterioration or Soviet/Cuban adventurism than from various "nontraditional" sources. For example, Dominica has suffered three attempted coups in as many years from a combination of the Ku Klux Klan, modern-day adventurers or mercenaries, and organized North American criminal elements. Modern-day buccaneers twice attempted to overthrow the government of Barbados. St. Vincent, as well as other countries in the region, have faced similar types of threats. These challenges have little or nothing to do with Cuba, the Soviet Union, or economic deterioration. They have everything to do with political elements not willing to work within the system to affect change—elements simply determined to take over the governments of the Eastern Caribbean to run them for their own political or financial benefit. Given the limited security capabilities of almost all these tiny islands, efforts to revise the status quo in the Caribbean by extra-constitutional means have a reasonable chance of succeeding.

How strongly rooted are democratic processes, Western orientations, and free enterprise systems in the Eastern Caribbean? The general consensus of most analysts is that they are deeply entrenched. However, I suggest this might not be the case. There has been little serious evaluation of the issue, and little attention has been paid to the orientation of the region's young people who have not been through the colonial experience of preceding generations. Both scholars and political analysts should examine these issues in more depth.

A great deal of information has been presented in recent years about American security interests in the Caribbean Basin. However, it should be pointed out that quite apart from the U.S. interest in seeing that the Caribbean is run by stable, democratic, friendly governments, the United States has economic interests in the region as well. There is a considerable degree of U.S. investment in the Caribbean, and there are certain strategic minerals that the United States must maintain access to (e.g., bauxite and petroleum products). In addition, important sea lanes and communication lines in the region must be kept open to ensure our ability to resupply U.S. NATO forces in the event of the outbreak of war in Europe. This ability is largely dependent on Gulf Coast military bases.

I would also point out that the number of Caribbean countries becoming independent seems to be multiplying. This is important to members of the U.S. Government who must worry about close votes and regional issues that are particularly sensitive, such as the Puerto Rican question.

I agree with those who argue that the region would have inevitably encountered problems regardless of the Grenadian revolution because of economic deterioration, growing Soviet/Cuban activities in the area, and increased institutional corruption. Throughout the Caribbean, governments are tempted to bend the spirit, if not actually the letter, of constitutionality. At the same time, there is a lack of clear commitment to the kinds of economic and political policies required to ensure stability in the region. Some islands are literally living off U.S. aid, Canadian aid, and multilateral lending institutions without carrying out tough structural reforms that are desperately needed.

On the political side, some governments are inclined to bend legal and constitutional procedures to ensure the survival of their rule. The long-term danger of this practice (whether in Grenada under Gairy, Dominica under Patrick John, or Guyana under Forbes Burnham) is that once constitutional procedures are bent, they become even easier to bend the next time. The moral highground is lost, and the system itself is called into question. Thus the major task for policymakers is how to strengthen democratic institutions and systems in the Eastern Caribbean. That is easy to say, but how does one go about doing so in terms of specific policy?

I would like to outline several policies that the United States is carrying out (and should continue to carry out), as well as a few policy suggestions. I agree that there is a need for more and better information regarding events in the Western hemisphere. Grenada is a case in point. The existence of this unfriendly government argues all the more strongly for better access to intelligence information. In addition, there has been a tendency on the part of American diplomats to relate just to like-minded foreign leaders.

This is very shortsighted. A stronger effort must be made to cultivate both the left and right in Caribbean governments and the opposition parties of the region through all the various means at our disposal—diplomatic exchanges, scholarly exchanges, and private visits, etc.

When I arrived as Ambassador to St. Lucia, I presented my credentials, talked extensively with government officials, and then went to call on the opposition. Much to my surprise, they told me that they had never before met with the U.S. Ambassador, yet this was an established democratic opposition party. Four weeks later elections were called and this group took office posing a series of problems for the United States in a variety of areas. The point is, the United States cannot afford to be uninformed about political movements in the Caribbean Basin, especially when they have sharp differences of opinion with the United States.

This is exactly what happened in Grenada, where information on the New Jewel Movement (NJM) was dated and sketchy at the time of the revolution. This was because the NJM was not taken seriously, and little effort had been given toward developing systematic channels of information about Grenada. We ignore these political actors of the region—be they on the right or the left—at our own peril.

The United States should also upgrade and expand the quality and quantity of its diplomatic representation in the Caribbean Basin. It is a travesty not to have a U.S. embassy or consulate on each of the independent islands of the Caribbean, perhaps even in the nonindependent isles. One cannot develop good information or a feel for what is happening unless one is physically present. The financial cost of such a network to the United States would be nominal. We should take a cue from the British who maintain such a system.

The extent to which institution-building can be supported in the Eastern Caribbean is a very tricky question. Some would argue that because of the historical baggage we bring to the conduct of policy in Latin America and the Caribbean, the United States simply cannot accomplish such a task. I reject this argument for there are various ways in which we can succeed. Pumping in a lot of money is not the only answer. The level of funding that the United States commits the Caribbean—the second or third highest in the world on a per capita basis after Egypt and Israel—might be at the outer limits of the Caribbean's absorptive capabilities. What is needed is the development of a technical infrastructure that can use the money effectively. Technical assistance is not a sexy idea to sell to bureaucracies, governments, or the American public. However, over the long-term, such assistance might be more significant than just the number of dollars that are being spent. Moreover, economic planning capabilities in the region must be improved. It is shocking that up until a couple of years ago there was no planning or budgeting capability on most of the smaller islands. One island acquired its first economist just two years ago.

Unfortunately, each new U.S. administration promptly tries to undo what its predecessor has done in the attempt to find a new "angle." U.S.

administrations should recognize the dangers of such inconsistency and attempt to avoid it. What is needed in the Caribbean is neither an exclusively private sector approach, nor an exclusively public sector approach. Indeed, in many countries in the region, there is no private sector. Thus a balance between public and private sector approaches is needed to solve the problems of the region.

Congress now tends to place high priority on basic human needs while the tendency in the 1960s and 1970s was to focus on infrastructure. The problem is that the basic human needs approach ignores many serious and pressing infrastructural needs both in the Caribbean Basin and Central America. Again, a balance is needed.

A heavy focus on either regional or bilateral programs is not the correct way to shape policy. Both are required. Bilateral programs are needed because they are politically more visible and much faster dispersing. Yet regional programs are also necessary because regional cooperation movements in the Caribbean are breaking down very much as the Central American Common Market has broken down. The key to economic recovery and growth is partially a matter of strengthened regional integration. In short, the United States must couple its regional and bilateral approaches with a much higher level of technical assistance.

The United States must recognize that the Eastern Caribbean will never achieve self-sustained economic growth. It will continue to be economically dependent on U.S. and Canadian aid. We must recognize that our political interests are a priority of our policy toward the region. However, the governments of the Eastern Caribbean must be encouraged to carry out the kinds of economic and political reforms that will enable them to manage successfully the serious challenges they are facing.

With regard to the security of the Caribbean Basin, the section of the Foreign Assistance Act that prohibits police training should be amended for countries where there is respect for human rights and a need for strengthening constabulary forces. This is the case on most Caribbean islands. In addition, we should work more effectively with the countries of the region as regards intelligence-gathering. The intelligence capability of these islands is virtually nonexistent. Moreover, we need to build up an appropriate policy toward the Eastern Caribbean Regional Security Force, and we need to provide concessional loans and credits to the nations of the region.

Finally, one of the ways in which we can help the Caribbean is through the National Endowment for Democracy (NED). This organization has the potential to carry out institution-building programs that the U.S. Government might have difficulty implementing. If the NED can survive the U.S. Congress and acquire support from groups knowledgeable about the region, it can assist in building the kinds of free institutions that are the underpinnings of democratic systems.

Part IV
Findings and Recommendations

JIRI VALENTA

Findings and Recommendations

THE GRENADA DOCUMENTS

The Grenada documents provide an unprecedented glimpse into the inner workings of an aspiring Third World Leninist regime and its relations with more established Leninist regimes elsewhere. It is true that the documents are not comprehensive. They are highly uneven, and it might be that the most sensational were destroyed by the defenders of the island. Moreover, they are primarily Grenadian, as few documents from Soviet sources were discovered. Despite these shortcomings, this unique set of documents possesses an extraordinary historical value comparable to the Soviet documents Professor Merle Fainsod had at his disposal when writing the seminal *How Russia Is Ruled.*[1] Another such windfall was the internal documents of the Central Committee of the Czechoslovak Communist Party dealing with the crisis of 1968 which have been analyzed by Gordon Skilling, Galia Golan, and Jiri Valenta.[2]

Unfortunately, some of the Grenada documents are incomplete, and others are illegible. Furthermore, not all of the documents had become available to the public by the time of the conference "Soviet/Cuban Strategy in the Third World after Grenada" (August 1984). The volume of documents is enormous, and many still have not been properly catalogued and sorted. However, as a senior U.S. Government official attending the conference noted, none of the Grenada documents have been classified and the vast majority[3] will be made available to the public as soon as they are processed. According to the same source, it has been agreed among U.S. and Grenadian officials that upon completion of processing, all documents will be returned to Grenada.

Notwithstanding their limitations, the Grenada documents can be very useful in analyzing strategies and tactics employed by the Soviet Union and Cuba. The documents allow cross-reference and comparison between New Jewel Movement (NJM) perceptions and assessments and those drawn from open sources in the Soviet Union, Cuba, and other communist and radical developing countries. Such comparisons were used extensively by most of the scholars who were asked to write papers for the conference, or to serve as discussants. Their contributions represent a significant step in the ongoing effort to better understand Soviet and Cuban strategies and tactics in the Third World.

LENINISM IN GRENADA

It is important to consider how the Grenada documents shed light on the NJM and its ties with the USSR, Cuba, and the latter's allies. The prevailing view in this volume is that the revolution in Grenada was much more Leninist-oriented than originally anticipated. Admittedly, there remains the conceptual problem of how to characterize accurately the ideological and political orientation of the NJM and similar radical Third World movements. Analysts refer to them alternately as Marxist, Marxist-Leninist, or even Stalinist. Perhaps the most appropriate label for a party in a Third World country that is building an elitist-vanguard party and pursuing a pro-Soviet foreign policy is Leninist. Despite the obvious shortcomings of this classification, it would appear more appropriate than the term provided by the Soviet vocabulary—Marxist-Leninist. This is because it was Lenin, not Marx, who developed the concept of a vanguard party dictatorship of the proletariat that, combined with proletarian internationalism, forms the core of the political system adhered to and propagated by the Soviet Union.

Current Soviet ideology has very little to do with Marxism, and almost everything to do with Leninism, as illustrated by the Grenada events. Although reasonable analysts differ over the degree to which Leninism had been established in Grenada and how sucessful it was, no one can deny the violent drive of Bernard Coard's faction toward an absolute Leninist transformation of the NJM and Grenada. (Appendix A, Document 16) This process was richly documented in the voluminous, sometimes classified, files discovered on the island. Ultimately, it was the Coard faction's emphasis on ideological mobilization, economic control, democratic centralism, and "Bolshevik staunchness" that produced the factional bloodshed in Grenada during October 1983. The ongoing development of Grenada along Leninist lines was a significant phenomenon for the Soviets. After a period of cautious appraisal, Soviet officials began to describe Grenada publicly as socialist-oriented, while privately they classified the NJM as a "fraternal party"—the most elevated step in the Soviet ideological hierarchy. (Appendix A, Documents 6 and 7) This level of relations was reflected in a CPSU and NJM party-to-party agreement on ideological cooperation. (Appendix A, Document 8) To be sure, the elevation of Grenada to a higher political category (that included Angola, Afghanistan, Ethiopia, South Yemen, and Nicaragua) depended in part on ideological considerations.

Obviously, Grenada was not officially recognized by the Soviet Union as a communist state, and as shown by the Grenada documents, it was not very high on the Soviet list of priorities. (Appendix A, Document 6) This was for a variety of reasons, though mainly because of its minuscule size and geographical remoteness. Nevertheless, Soviet officials appeared to hope that in due time, given its strategic importance and a projected change in the correlation of forces, Grenada would become a valuable ally. The documents provide no conclusive evidence that Grenada had become a depot of Soviet arms for future use in the region, nor were there any Soviet or Cuban military bases or facilities at the time of the U.S./OECS intervention aside from the controversial airport, which also had clear-cut civilian purposes. (The military nature of the airport is suggested by circumstantial evidence. Grenadians reportedly were prohibited from approaching certain areas of the construction project, and the fuel storage tanks were considerably larger than similar airport facilities in the region.)

It is true that the Soviets and their allies made a significant but guarded commitment to Grenada by according it a special revolutionary status. They concluded several top-secret arms transfer agreements and sent a considerable number of weapons and dozens of advisors as part of a comprehensive military assistance package. (Appendix A, Documents 12 and 13) It is possible that Grenada might have become a component in Soviet military planning as well as a bridge to revolutionary forces in the English-speaking Caribbean, thereby following the Cuban example of the last quarter-century. The documents clearly suggest that this prospect was attractive to some NJM officials who considered their compliance essential to obtain continued and improved Soviet support. (Appendix A, Document 6)

The Grenada case, together with the analyses of leading Soviet Third World experts (e.g., Karen Brutents),[4] suggests that in the Soviet mind there are at least two types of socialist-oriented countries in the Third World. Type-I countries have no vanguard party, and only a vaguely defined Leninist ideology. These countries are typically led by a charismatic leader (e.g., Mali, Ghana, Indonesia, Egypt, and Somalia of the 1960s and 1970s). Type-II countries have an incipient Leninist vanguard party, together with other structures built around Lenin's principle of democratic centralism. Because of previous experiences with Yugoslavia, China, and a number of socialist-oriented Third World regimes, the Soviets tend to distrust charismatic leaders of communist and radical regimes, although they might consider such leaders useful in paving the way toward proper Leninist societies.

This is demonstrated by the case of Cuba, where the Soviets worked with Fidel Castro to build a more advanced, Type-II socialist oriented government from a Type-I structure. The final stage in this long and arduous evolution was the Soviet recognition of Cuba as a proper communist state in the 1970s. During this process, Cuban leaders had to establish their communist credentials by building a vanguard party and holding regular party congresses, etc.

The events in the Grenadian situation illustrate that in the 1980s the Soviets have preferred to deal with Leninist-oriented parties that have Soviet-trained cadres or is well-connected with Soviet bureaucracies. The Soviets also tend to deal more readily with Leninist apparatchik types (like Bernard Coard) than with charismatic and unpredictable leaders (like Maurice Bishop).

The evidence does not conclusively support Soviet backing of Coard in the October coup in Grenada, but there is circumstantial evidence to suggest possible Soviet displeasure with Bishop. Bishop and U.S. officials had agreed prior to the coup to avoid antagonistic rhetoric as a "confidence building" measure in U.S.-Grenadian relations. For several months, Bishop kept his promise, hoping for substantial talks with the United States, while apparently displeasing the Soviets by failing to brief Moscow. (Appendix A, Document 6)

According to the Soviets, the stability and reliability of any socialist-oriented country in the Third World should not depend so much on a leader' s popularity as on the leading role of a bureaucratic vanguard party. At the moment, the most advanced existing socialist-oriented countries appear to be Afghanistan and Ethiopia. In September 1984, with Soviet ideological backing, Ethiopia established a communist party, the Workers' Party of Ethiopia. Grenada was about to become a part of that select grouping, and very likely would have had Coard's coalition prevailed. It is no wonder that Coard and his supporters studied Karen Brutents so intensively. [5] (Appendix A, Document 16)

THE NJM AND SOVIET/CUBAN STRATEGY

The Grenada Documents reveal a certain degree of tentativeness and ambiguity in Soviet policies *vis-à-vis* Third World nations. First, they show that the USSR does not necessarily seek to create Communist regimes at any cost. Second, the Soviet Union seems in many instances to prefer that its allies (Cuba in Africa and Latin America, and Vietnam in Southeast Asia) micromanage–that is, play a primary role in–the initial development of new relationships with aspiring Leninist forces. As used here, a Soviet ally is not necessarily a state controlled by the USSR, nor a Leninist state, although some Soviet allies do conform to these qualifications. They might be more appropriately characterized as junior Soviet partners. Cuba, for example, using Soviet military and economic aid, pursues policies that benefit Soviet strategic objectives. Its shrewd move in sending black diplomats and military advisors to both Africa and the Caribbean helped the Soviets gain friends in radical circles.

Finally, the Soviet Union rarely gives explicit instructions or assigns tactical missions to socialist-oriented states in the Third World. (Afghanistan is an exception because of its special conditions, its geographical location on the Soviet border, and the direct engagement of Soviet armed forces.) Instead, aspiring Leninist leaders in the Third World are usually at liberty to use their own imagination (with Cuba often acting as a broker) to cultivate ties with the Soviets and explore basic Soviet strategic objectives and limits of tolerance. (Appendix A, Documents 5, 6, and 7) Thus, in the first years after the revolutionary coup of 1979, the primary task of Grenadian leaders was to demonstrate their usefulness to the Soviet leadership.

As the leaders of revolutionary regimes consolidate internal power, the Soviets gradually become interested in strengthening ties with them. Ultimately, the Soviet Union aims to assert control over Cuba's brokerage role and develop direct relations with socialist-oriented regimes. This strategy became apparent in Angola in 1977, and it may have been a factor in the internal leadership conflict in Grenada in October 1983. A similar trend may evolve in Nicaragua.

The Grenada documents suggest that although Soviet leaders are initially cautious about assigning tactical missions, they have implicit long-term strategic objectives in the Third World. This is indicated by the 1983 remarks of former Chlef of the Soviet General Staff, Marshall Nikolai Ogarkov, regarding the growing struggle of anti-American progressive forces in the Western Hemisphere: "Over two decades ago there was only Cuba in Latin America; today there are Nicaragua and Grenada, and a serious battle is going on in El Salvador."[6] (Appendix A, Document 11)

Over the last few decades there has been a remarkable continuity in Soviet strategy and tactics concerning communist parties and radical forces in developing nations. At the same time, there has been a noticeable increase in the sophistication of methods used by the Soviets. As seen in Grenada (also in Angola, Ethiopia, South Yemen, Mozambique, and Nicaragua), the Soviets have expanded the scope of their policy instruments, particularly the auxiliary capacity provided by foreign communist parties and radical Third World movements.

In the last ten years, the Soviets have made expert use of military security aid via junior allies who at times act as proxies. To be sure, the Soviet ally phenomenon is complex, and the use of the term does not necessarily imply that the USSR is directing the foreign policy of allied or friendly nations. In some instances, the contrary might be more true. Thus the Soviet Union might be perceived at times as a proxy of quasi-independent Cuba in Africa (Angola) and the Caribbean Basin (Nicaragua, Grenada, and El Salvador). As an actor having a great interest in and knowledge of the Caribbean Basin region, it was Cuba that discovered the revolutionary opportunities in both Nicaragua and Grenada. It could be argued that Cuba drew the Soviet Union into the region, much as Vietnam helped to deepen Soviet involvement in Southeast Asia. In the final analysis, however, the Soviets exercise leverage, if not control, over the key decisions of their allies. Moreover, the Soviets also benefit from autonomous Cuban and Vietnamese ventures in strategic areas of the Third World, and one might add from the activities of Libya and North Korea. East European involvement, both in Africa and in the Caribbean Basin, has been much more limited than that of Cuba and Libya.

As illustrated by the Grenadian experience, the intensity and scope of Soviet allied involvement in the Third World varies from state to state, even among Warsaw Treaty Organization (WTO) nations. This depends upon the general nature of each nation's alliance with the USSR, internal conditions and interests, and particularly the need to reinforce the regime's legitimacy. (Among the most involved countries have been East Germany, Czechoslovakia, and Bulgaria; Poland and Hungary have been less involved; and for the most part, Romania has pursued autonomous policies.) (Appendix A, Documents 20–23)

The strategic objectives of some junior Soviet allies such as Cuba are formulated independently, but must win the approval of the Soviets, who provide substantial military and economic assistance. In spite of occasional tactical disagreements such as those witnessed in Grenada in October 1983, the division of labor among Soviet allies ultimately favors Soviet global interests. By employing Cuban personnel, the Soviets avoid damage to their reputation in the international community, do not directly provoke the U.S., and are able to blame others for errors and reversals.

THE IMPACT OF GRENADA

The impact of the Grenada intervention on the Soviets and their allies in radical Third World countries should be neither exaggerated nor underestimated. The intervention was a watershed in the history of the Caribbean Basin. (The last such significant event appears to have been during the 1950s when Western labor movements won over the pro-Soviet labor movement.) The failure of Leninism in Grenada can be interpreted as a general failure of Leninist temptation in an environment such as the East Caribbean where the prevailing political culture is democratic and parliamentarian.

The decline of Leninism in Grenada sent reverberations throughout the Soviet alliance system. The intervention came as a surprise in the Soviet Union, where it was taken as an important signal that America may be recovering from the Vietnam syndrome and again might be prepared (as in the 1950s and 1960s) to use military force to defend its interests. In the months following the Grenada intervention, the Soviets appeared to be reassessing the costs and benefits of their support for revolutionary forces in the Caribbean Basin. Although the intervention added a dimension to the policymaking process in Moscow, it did not trigger a wholesale reappraisal of Soviet foreign policy. The operation was too small and too simple to be compared with what Vietnam demanded, or what Nicaragua could require. Among other things, the long-term impact will depend on the policies of the second-term Reagan administration concerning aspiring Leninist forces in the Third World in general, and in the Caribbean Basin in particular.

Grenada also had an impact on the perceptions of other Communist and radical Third World leaders. The intervention indicated that Soviet allies outside the immediate Soviet periphery were not automatically assured of Moscow's protection, even when faced with a mortal challenge from imperialism. These are troubling implications for socialist-oriented Nicaragua Angola, Ethiopia, and even communist Cuba. The Soviet failure to protect Grenada is yet another example that helps to explain to communists and their socialist-oriented allies why the USSR has avoided contracting military alliances and implicit military commitments with the more vulnerable communist states—Albania, North Korea, and Vietnam (before 1978).

Fidel Castro now might be even more greatly concerned about the ambiguous Soviet commitment to Cuba in the case of direct conflict with the United States. Unlike their behavior in their own periphery (or even in remote regions of Africa), Soviet leaders are less able or willing to support pro-Soviet regimes in America's backyard, particularly when Washington is willing to protect its interests with military force. After Grenada, the Caribbean might have a lower priority on Castro's agenda, and he may rededicate his efforts to expand Cuban influence in Central America.

Initially, the intervention in Grenada had a considerable impact on Nicaragua, where the Sandinistas had earlier anticipated a "Grenada-style" intervention. American pressure in the form of military exercises in the Caribbean and Central America, U.S. sponsorship of anti-FSLN revolutionary activities in the region, and the Grenada intervention have created a bunker mentality in Nicaragua and demonstrated to the Sandinistas that there is a limit to U.S. patience. Despite this sobering effect on Managua, the impact of Grenada on Nicaragua should not be overestimated. The intervention contributed to a noticeable weakening of Nicaraguan support for guerrillas in El Salvador, and increased the pressures toward negotiations with the Duarte government. However, it sharpened Managua's obstinance and played into the hands of hard-liners such as Minister of the Interior Tomas Borge. For him, the intervention served as proof of a forthcoming U.S. intervention in Nicaragua.

Some residual effects of the intervention were evident elsewhere in the Caribbean Basin, particularly in Suriname. Under pressure from Brazil, but also because of events in Grenada, Suriname expelled Cuban advisors only hours after the U.S. intervention, and subsequently reduced diplomatic ties to a minimum. The expulsion decision appeared to have been made after the October 19 coup for which the Cubans were held responsible, but the U.S. intervention might have accelerated the disengagement. However, recent developments such as improved relations between Nicaragua and Suriname suggest that the impact of the intervention has dissipated somewhat.

It is not surprising that in Asia and Africa (particularly in Angola and Ethiopia) the effects of the U.S. intervention were not as profound as they were in the Caribbean Basin. However, even the leaders of Ethiopia and Angola probably were surprised by Soviet and Cuban inability to support Grenada. It cannot be dismissed that the partial withdrawal of Cuban troops from Ethiopia, announced officially by the Cuban Government in July 1984, stemmed in part from the "Grenada syndrome." The action in Grenada conveyed a message about American resolve, which may bolster the U.S. "constructive engagement" strategy in Southern Africa. The intervention was viewed as a positive sign by Angolan guerrilla forces opposed to the Popular Movement for the Liberation of Angola (MPLA). The most important of these is the National Union for the Total Liberation of Angola (UNITA), which in the fall of 1984 increased the scope of its activities to include the capital of Luanda. It also sounded a positive note among Afghan freedom fighters.

While the Grenada intervention raised the costs of Soviet and Cuban support for revolutionary activities in geographically remote regions, its effect upon Third World revolutionary regimes is still unclear. If followed by a long-term U.S. strategy to curb Soviet/Cuban influence in the Third World, and the successful stabilization of Grenada and the Caribbean Basin as a whole, the impact of the intervention may be more lasting than some observers anticipated.

RECOMMENDATIONS FOR U.S. POLICYMAKERS

Most conferees agreed that the U.S./OECS intervention was an extraordinary yet necessary measure. Although the detrimental consequences of the intervention to U.S. relations with Western Europe and some Third World countries were acknowledged, most conferees agreed that in the long run, U.S. inaction in Grenada threatened grave consequences for the security of the United States and East Caribbean nations. For example, U.S. inaction could have led to demoralization of friendly nations in the Caribbean region, and elsewhere. The extraordinary circumstances preceding the U.S. decision to intervene (such as the killing of a popular Prime Minister and several Cabinet members, the subsequent reign of terror, the uncertain status of American students, and the urgent request for help by East Caribbean nations) made intervention a pragmatic option for U.S. policymakers.

There was no conclusive evidence of an immediate, direct threat to U.S. security interests due to conditions in Grenada. Had Grenada continued its military buildup, a threat to U. S. security interests could have become a reality, and it would have been more difficult to effect a reversal. However, the prevailing consensus among members of the OECS in 1983 was that Grenada's military buildup had threatening implications for the region. There is no doubt that President Reagan's decision to intervene prevented the consolidation of a more brutal Leninist and pro-Soviet regime.

It is imperative that U.S. policymakers pursue a vigorous and sustained program of political and economic stabilization in Grenada. Even after the December 1984 Grenadian election that brought to power a democratic government, Grenada continues to be a challenging test of American resolve and commitment to democratic values. The United States must continue to do its utmost by democratic means to prevent a return of Eric Gairy or another NJM dictatorship for such an occurrance would shatter U.S. credibility.

The successful military action in Grenada must be followed by long-term economic assistance. By political and economic means, the United States must continuously seek to strengthen truly to restore the democratic process in Grenada. In this effort, the National Endowment for Democracy should develop educational and research institutions to study the causes and

NJM poster printed prior to the December 1984 election in Grenada. It was intended to depict the U.S./OECS intervention; however, many Grenadians incorrectly interpreted its symbolism as the U.S. eagle protecting the island from the NJM, the USSR, and Cuba. (Poster courtesy of Jiri and Virginia Valenta.)

to the democratic education of future generations of Grenada and other Caribbean countries. The lure of oppressive rule to the power-hungry of both right and left is a lesson that should not be forgotten, as it is applicable to the region as a whole.

Since the late 1950s, superpower competition in the Third World (with the potential for igniting global conflict) has been a central issue for U.S.

the potential for igniting global conflict) has been a central issue for U.S. policymakers. As always, prevention of superpower confrontation and escalation of conflict in the Third World should be given highest priority in U.S. strategic planning.

An understanding and appreciation of the Third World's historical, political, economic, and social diversity is essential for a successful and sensitive U.S. policy toward the Caribbean Basin. It is simplistic to attribute the source of conflict solely to Soviet and Cuban policies. Equally naive is the notion that poverty is the cause of the problem. What is undeniable is that the USSR, its allies, and its proxies often take effective advantage of economic, social, and political instability or crises in developing nations. This has been particularly true over the last decade during which the Soviets invaded Afghanistan, and along with Cuba and other proxies, became active in Angola, Ethiopia, and South Yemen. Meanwhile, the Soviets and Cubans provided substantial security aid (weapons and advisors) to revolutionary forces in Nicaragua, El Salvador, and Grenada.

Given the centrality of the Soviet-American competition in Third World areas, U. S. policymakers must abandon short-term strategies that address short-term crises. Instead, they must develop consistent long-term strategies designed to avoid conflict and manage future crises effectively.

The Caribbean Basin is especially important to the United States because of its geographic proximity. The Caribbean Basin constitutes a vital passageway for petroleum and other important raw materials, and would assume critical strategic importance if the United States were to be involved in an overseas conventional war. In that event, a growing Soviet/Cuban military presence in the Caribbean could endanger U.S. logistical support for NATO forces in Europe, as well as the delivery of strategic materials to the United States. The United States also has compelling economic interests in the Caribbean by virtue of its large private business investments there. Domestic stability and the safeguarding of U.S. interests in the region require the prevention of abrupt economic dislocations, massive immigration, and hostile radicalization of Caribbean political life.

The Reagan administration has recognized the importance of Central America and the Caribbean Basin to the United States, and has directed attention to this long-neglected region. Formation of the National Bipartisan Commission on Central America (chaired by Dr. Henry Kissinger) was a significant step toward devising long-term viable policies. U.S. officials should be much more visible in their support and implementation of legislation that is based on the recommendations of the Bipartisan Commission report.

Moreover, there is an urgent need to anticipate long-term challenges to the United States, not only in Central America (the only region dealt with by the Bipartisan Commission), but also in the Caribbean Basin, South America, and other parts of the Third World. An analysis of NJM strategy in Grenada suggests linkages among the revolutionary forces of Central America, the Caribbean, and South America. These perceived linkages are very much part of Soviet and Cuban strategic thinking, and must not be neglected or overlooked by U.S. policymakers.

There is an equally urgent need to study the dynamics of political and economic challenges in Peru, Argentina, Brazil, Uruguay, and the volatile situation in Chile. Of vital importance is the possible political and economic destabilization of Mexico. It is also necessary to study the strategies and tactics of communist and radical Third World regimes that affect these Central and South American countries, and to examine the latter's ties with the USSR and Cuba. Given the revolutionary experience in Grenada and elsewhere in the Third World, Soviet and Cuban perceptions and policies deserve special attention by U. S. policymakers.

We should be better prepared to anticipate and prevent crises in the Third World and manage those that are unavoidable. Policymakers need to substitute ideological rigidity for a resilient frame of mind in order to understand radical Third World regimes. They should avoid indiscriminant labeling of all radical forces as Marxist or Marxist-Leninist, since these terms tend to confuse the political and ideological orientation of these groups. It is ludicrous to call Suriname's Lt. Colonel Daysie Bouterse a Marxist. Careless usage of the Marxist-Leninist label (even in documents such as the distinguished report of the National Bipartisan Commission on Central America) belies a misreading of the complexity and differences existing among communist and radical Third World parties. National communist parties such as those of China and Yugoslavia fear Soviet imperialist ambitions, while others such as Italy's Eurocommunist Party and Yugoslavia's party are of pluralist or semipluralist orientation and refuse the Leninist label. Some radical regimes in the Third World are not Leninist-oriented. As suggested by the Grenada documents, radically nationalist forces can coexist or struggle with Leninist factions within radical Third World regimes. The distinction between Leninist and non-Leninist forces should not be blurred. Because "Leninist-oriented" clearly means having both a vanguard party and a pro-Soviet foreign policy, U.S. policymakers and their advisors should avoid stereotyping and classifying Third World radical parties.

Politically, U. S. policymakers must support democratic processes in Third World countries, particularly in Central America and the Caribbean Basin, that resist oppression, be it of the left or right. We must continue to exercise greater pressure on El Salvador than we did before the 1984 election to curb and eliminate right wing death squads. However, experience indicates that the extreme left cannot be defeated by wiping out the political center; nor can we endorse the guerrillas' violent approach. Moreover, we must avoid creating a double standard by insisting on progress toward democracy in El Salvador, but not in Nicaragua, where the Sandinistas are establishing a regime similar to that which existed in Grenada.

Political and economic aid should be extended to friendly Third World regimes dependent on their observance of basic human rights and in amounts that each nation can absorb effectively. The most prudent way to prevent a future Grenada is to strengthen existing ties and encourage more capable democratic institutions in developing nations. In the Caribbean Basin in particular, we must help democratic forces resist attempts by the parties in power to subvert legal and constitutional procedures, as in Grenada under Eric Gairy and Guyana under Forbes Burnham. The projected work of the National Endowment for Democracy is an important step toward these goals. However, we need to go beyond this framework to develop new and imaginative ways to accomplish the establishment of capable and responsible democratic institutions in developing nations.

In terms of politics, the U.S. should promote friendly political ties with Third World radical regimes, excluding only those aligned with the USSR and its allies. Meanwhile, through diplomatic exchange programs, we should attempt to cultivate political ties with opposition parties of various persuasions, while becoming better acquainted and more knowledgeable about their leaderships. The Carter administration erred by failing to do this in 1979 in Grenada. It is imperative that we understand various elites and counter-elites in radical Third World nations. Heeding the British example, we must upgrade and expand our diplomatic personnel through permanent representation in each of the developing nations, no matter how minuscule their size.

Inadequate U.S. intelligence concerning the developments in Grenada points out that intelligence gathering and evaluating activities in the area must be upgraded. According to East Caribbean sources, in 1980 there were no experts on Grenada in the U.S. intelligence community. Within U.S. Government structures, efforts must be made to strengthen and disseminate appropriate intelligence evaluations. Moreover, we must train and prepare credible and dynamic diplomatic personnel with adequate linguistic abilities to cope with new challenges in radical areas of the Third World.

The economic situation throughout Central America is appalling. We need to allocate greater resources to encourage economic development in emerging nations, particularly in those on the periphery of the United States. The Caribbean Basin Initiative and the Central American Project are new programs urgently needed to formulate economic assistance packages and improve the flow of credit and investment in Central America and the Caribbean Islands. Immediate economic aid, from both the private and public sectors, is imperative—even before political solutions are found.[7]

Immediate emergency aid should be followed by five-year economic assistance programs as recommended by the Bipartisan Commission. The success of this approach will require not only American resources, but also bipartisan public support, and above all, patience, as there will be no quick fix. However, financial aid alone is not the answer to all the problems of the Caribbean Basin. In fact, economic assistance to some Caribbean islands is relatively high at present, and may be at the upper limit of what these nations can absorb for the time being. Other more urgent needs include concentrated assistance in developing a technical infrastructure (roads, ports, communications, etc.), advice on planning and budgeting programs, and the education of economic and financial experts. We should utilize both private and public sector approaches to provide this assistance.

The United States must not entertain unrealistic expectations for Central America and the Caribbean Basin. We must recognize that despite the best efforts, at least some of the Caribbean nations may never achieve self-sustained economic growth, and therefore will continue to depend on economic aid from the United States, Canada, and other industrialized nations.

U.S. security assistance must be an integral part of U.S. strategy *vis-à-vis* Third World nations. Whereas security threats in some parts of Asia and most of Africa tend not to affect vital U.S. interests, threats in the Caribbean Basin do. In the Caribbean Basin, threats to a given nation's stability might not always be caused by deteriorating socioeconomic conditions, or by the USSR and Cuba, but by coup attempts organized by North American gangsters (Dominica), or by bands of modern-day buccaneers (Barbados).

Therefore, we must not separate diplomacy and force in the Caribbean Basin. Although exact recommendations cannot be given as to how or under what circumstances force should be used, it should be remembered that direct use of American force should be employed only under extraordinary circumstances such as those that existed in Grenada in October 1983.

The indirect application of force (military exercises, for example) is the preferred approach. The Grenada intervention—in conjunction with expanding U.S. naval deployments in the Caribbean and military exercises in Honduras—have had a sobering effect on Havana and Managua. Whenever prudent, in peacetime the U.S. should continue to use indirect military force to further its foreign policy objectives, particularly by conducting regular and irregular bilateral and multilateral exercises in the Caribbean Basin and Central America. To be effective, joint military exercises and other forms of military activities in the Caribbean Basin and elsewhere, require sensitivity and consideration regarding our allies' national pride and self-respect.

Responsible arms transfers and other forms of security aid to friendly Third World nations (taking into account the reasonable security needs of each country and each country's record on human rights) are another option. In this respect, Congress should repeal Section 660 of the Foreign Assistance Act that prohibits the use of U.S. foreign assistance funds for training national police in developing nations. Surely such training should be permitted in countries having Westminster parliamentarian political cultures such as those found in the Caribbean. We should also help strengthen coast guards, internal security organizations, and the intelligence gathering capabilities of friendly countries in the Caribbean and the democratic nations of Central America such as Costa Rica.

The Grenada experience suggests that one of the most complex challenges facing the United States is to counter the activities of Soviet junior partners such as Cuba, Vietnam, North Korea, and some of the East European countries. This has been the most serious security problem faced by the United States in the last decade. An important lesson emanating from the Grenada experience is the recognition of the need for the United States to develop an effective counterstrategy which would multiply and intensify the constraints on the Soviets and their allies in strategic regions of the Third World.

Inducements and pressures need to be exercised upon the USSR, Cuba, Libya, the WTO nations, and other countries whose Third World policies purposely serve Soviet security and political interests. The indebtedness and otherwise serious economic problems facing nations such as Cuba and Nicaragua provide the United States with some excellent opportunities to employ negative incentives to curb their activities. The U.S. Government should do its utmost to coordinate Western credit policies toward Cuba, Nicaragua, and other Soviet junior partners.

In addition to various forms of pressure, and indirect use of force, the United States should not discourage allies (such as former Egyptian President Anwar Sadat) from actively pursuing policies aimed at hampering the activities of Soviet allies. While exerting pressure on Soviet allies, we should not discount proposals for negotiation when offered by regimes such as those in Nicaragua and Cuba. However, we should guard against naiveté. Given the Cuban and Nicaraguan expressed commitment to revolution, any negotiated solution must be based on reciprocity, verifiable agreements, and careful monitoring. Soviet and Cuban military ties with Nicaragua should be unacceptable, and therefore nonnegotiable.

The Grenada documents reveal some tactical differences between the Soviet Union and Cuba, as well as between various competing factions in radical, socialist-oriented regimes. Using new and imaginative tactics, the United States can act upon those existing and future tactical differences to undermine Soviet partnership policies. In some cases, we might consider the option of furnishing aid to insurgents fighting against recognized oppressive governments. Other means can be devised to coopt non-Leninist insurgents who might otherwise develop close ties with the USSR via Leninist elements in the region, such as Coard's group in Grenada or the Communist Party of El Salvador led by First Secretary Shafik Handel. Such a strategy might have been quite effective in both Nicaragua and Grenada prior to 1979.

The experience of Grenada should have dispelled any preexisting misperceptions regarding Third World revolutions. We should neither exaggerate nor underestimate the ties of some of these revolutionaries with the Soviet Union and its allies. Each revolution must be judged independently, and we should distinguish between Soviet/Cuban-fomented strife in the Third World and revolutionary situations indigenous to developing countries.

No American foreign policy can be successful without the bipartisan support of the American people. Implementing policy over a period of time is difficult in the American political system. Effective implementation of policies recommended by the Bipartisan National Commission on Central America will require strong domestic support and an enduring commitment, as will any effective U. S. counterstrategy to Soviet/Cuban involvement in the Third World.

It is very encouraging that the issue of Soviet/Cuban involvement in the Caribbean Basin and the Grenadian intervention did not become a subject of controversy during the 1984 presidential election. In fact, the intervention in Grenada was supported by the Democratic candidate, Walter Mondale, who declared that if he had been president, he too would have used military force "to go there and protect U.S. lives."[8]

Regardless of who resides in the White House, every effort should be made to develop long-term policies for coping with the Soviet/Cuban threat to revolutionary regimes and U.S. security interests. The Soviets and their allies place great importance on reaching, and even influencing, public opinion in the United States. Indeed, one of the captured documents in Grenada was a telephone book listing sympathetic media contacts and other useful persons in the United States.

Much has been written about the need to educate the American public concerning Soviet-American arms control and the strategic balance, but little has been done to generate public interest in revolutionary situations in the Third World and Soviet/Cuban attempts to exploit them. It is up to U. S. Government agencies and private organizations to foster more research and increase public awareness about Third World revolutions as they relate to Soviet, Cuban, and allied proxy strategies and tactics.

There is likewise a great need to educate the American people about Soviet efforts to reduce the U.S. capacity to respond to and challenge Soviet strategy. This reduced capacity has been achieved not only by the impressive Soviet military buildup of the last decade, but also by indirect political maneuvering and propagandizing. These latter efforts are aimed at distorting the nature of local Third World conflicts, presenting each as a new Vietnam and a menacing prelude to general war.

More funding should be made available for East-West and Third World specialists to study these problems, for experts from both groups often have differing perspectives. A divided foreign policy establishment and a divided community of foreign policy specialists seriously inhibits efforts to formulate and gain support for U.S. foreign policy. We do ourselves a great disservice in speaking of liberal versus conservative positions regarding Soviet power and the Third World. We should put all such ideological stereotypes behind us, and work toward a national consensus in support of realistic and effective long-term policies. These efforts should not be sponsored only by a few elitist institutions; they must tap the talent of a broad cross-section of educational and research institutions and the public in general.

Funding should be provided to produce a first-rate series of television documentaries for sustained and expanded coverage of the activities of radical Third World regimes. National Public Radio should broadcast aspects of Soviet and Cuban activities in the Third World. There should be more extensive interaction on these subjects among U.S. Government agencies and academic and research institutions. New research centers dealing with Soviet involvement in the Third World should be funded, and the U.S. Government should take a more active role in bringing about the interaction of Soviet and Third World experts in a number of short- and long-term projects.

An extensive effort must be made to bridge existing divisions on these issues through the education of the American public. This will promote significantly the consensus building needed to implement and sustain long-term foreign policies intended to counter deletorious Soviet/Cuban strategy in the Third World.

NOTES

1. Merle Fainsod, *How Russia Is Ruled*, (Cambridge: Harvard University Press, 1963).

2. Gordon Skilling, *Czechoslovakia's Interrupted Revolution* (Princeton, NJ: Princeton University Press, 1976); Galia Golan, *The Czechoslovakian Reform Movement: Communism in Crisis, 1962–1968* (Cambridge University Press, 1971); and Jiri Valenta, *Soviet Intervention in Czechoslovakia, 1968: Anatomy of a Decision* (Baltimore, MD: Johns Hopkins University Press, 1979).

3. A handful of documents, perhaps ten, appear to affect the privacy of U.S. citizens. These will not be available for public scrutiny.

4. Karen Brutents, *The Newly Free Countries in the Seventies*, (Moscow: Progress Publishers, 1979).

5. Jiri Valenta and Virginia Valenta, "Leninism in Grenada," *Problems of Communism*, July-August 1984, p. 18.

6. Ibid., p. 11.

7. For a more substantial discussion, see William H. Bolin "Central America's Real Economic Help Is Wanted Now," *Foreign Affairs*, Summer 1984, pp. 1096–1108.

8. *The Washington Post*, September 19, 1984.

Appendix A
Selected Grenada Documents

7.	Memo from Comrade Bernard Bourne [Minister-Councillor of the Grenadian Embassy in Moscow] to Comrade Maurice Bishop, Chairman of the Central Committee of the New Jewel Movement, June 30, 1982. Also listed as Log No. 104262.	109242	315
8.	Agreement on Cooperation between the New Jewel Movement and the Communist Party of the Soviet Union, July 27, 1982. Also in Russian.	102318	319
9.	List of NJM Students and, Report of Meeting with Acting Rector of the CPSU Party School, Gaidum, Oleg P. (by W. Richard Jacobs), May 23, 1983.	103672	321
10.	Secret Cooperation and Exchange Plan between the Communist Party of Cuba and the New Jewel Movement of Grenada for the 1983 Period, June 29, 1983. Also listed as Log No. 103919.	100016	323
11.	Memorandum of Meeting between Chiefs of General Staff of Soviet Armed Forces and People's Revolutionary Armed Forces of Grenada [Marshal Nikolay V. Ogarkov and Major Einstein Louison], March 10, 1983.	100008	331
12.	Top Secret Agreement between the Government of Grenada and the Government of the Union of Soviet Socialist Republics on Deliveries from the Union of SSR to Grenada of Special and Other Equipment, October 27, 1980. Also in Russian.	000190	336
13.	Top Secret Agreement between the Government of Grenada and the Government of the Union of Soviet Socialist Republics on Deliveries from the Union of SSR to Grenada of Special and Other Equipment, July 27, 1982. Also in Russian.		348
14.	Secret Protocol of the Military Collaboration between the Government of the Republic of Cuba and the People's Revolutionary Government of Grenada, undated.	000194	385
15.	Summary of Prime Minister's Meeting with Soviet Ambassador, May 24, 1983. Also listed as Log No. 000017.	103913	392
16.	Minutes of the Extraordinary Meeting of the Central Committee, NJM, September 14–16 and 17, 1983.	000123	397
17.	Briefing Notes on Meeting with Judge William Clarke, Chair of the N.S.C., undated.	105300	444
18.	Letter from Fidel Castro Ruz to the Central Committee, New Jewel Movement, October 15, 1983.	T	447

19.	Foreign Relations Report and List of Countries with which Grenada Does Not Wish to Develop Close Relations, undated, but probably published in 1981.	105757	449
20.	Bill of Lading from Czechoslovak Ocean Shipping for 1,250 Cases of Explosive Ammunition (Warheads, Rockets) on Order of Grenadian Embassy in Havana, undated.	102951	464
21.	Agreement for Cooperation between the Bulgarian Communist Party and the New Jewel Movement of Grenada for the Period 1982–1983, undated.	103676	465
22.	Meeting with [East German] Deputy Minister of Foreign Affairs (Latin America and Caribbean) V. Neugebanck, May 18, 1983.	102855	468
23.	Agreement on Cooperation between the New Jewel Movement of Grenada and the Socialist Unity Party of Germany for the Years 1982 to 1985, June 10, 1982, and Working Plan . . . for 1982–83, June 10, 1982.	103896	474
24.	Report on Meeting of Secret Regional Caucus of SI [Socialist International] Held in Managua, January 6–7, 1983.	100046	479
25.	Letter from Nicaraguan Minister of Defense Humberto Ortego Saavedra to Comrade Maurice Bishop, February 19, 1981.	X	485

Since April 1984, the U.S. Government has released several series of documents captured in Grenada. Each series, consisting of NJM Political Bureau and Central Committee minutes, secret agreements with communist countries, letters, diaries, personal papers, reports from the Grenadian embassy in Moscow, etc., is made public as it is processed. The documents reproduced here come from these series and were selected for this volume to give the reader a sample of the material that provided much of the documentation for the chapters in this book. All of the documents released to date may be inspected at the U.S. National Archives in Washington, D.C.

Document 1

CONFIDENTIAL

LINE OF MARCH FOR THE PARTY

PRESENTED BY

COMRADE MAURICE BISHOP

CHAIRMAN, CENTRAL COMMITTEE

TO

GENERAL MEETING

OF

PARTY

ON

MONDAY 13th SEPTEMBER 1982

Comrades of the Political Bureau and Central Committee of the Party, Comrades of the Party.

I will like to join with Comrade Strachan to say on behalf of the Central Committee that we are very happy to have all the comrades here this afternoon. As Comrade Selwyn has pointed out, essentially what we want to do today is to deal with the proposed line of march as examined by the C.C. of the Party in the last few weeks.

In our view the line of march needs to take into account four specific features:-

Firstly, the present character and stage of the Revolution. We regard that as fundamentally important. We must decide what exactly is a correct characterisation of the present stage of the Revolution.

Secondly, the line of march must address in a serious way the question of the main tasks facing the Party and Revolution at this time.

Thirdly, we must determine a correct prioritisation of those tasks; we must establish priorities bearing in mind particularly, the comments, criticisms, suggestions, proposals etc. which have been made by Party members and, of course, taking into account the totality of the objective and subjective situation.

The fourth and final factor is the need to emphasise the further development of the subjective factor, the need to place great emphasis and importance on the further development of the subjective factor, that is to say, the Party. In other words, we must look at the Party itself, review the history of the Party very briefly and deal with the question of criteria for membership into the Party and for remaining as members of the Party.

2..........

-2-

Comrades, in terms of the character of the Revolution, the first aspect to the line of march, we believe it is important for us to look at this question at this time for several reasons.

Firstly and obviously, because we must as a Party know where we are. As Party members, candidate members and applicants we have to face the broad masses out there; we have to answer questions about where we are, what we are trying to do and so on and therefore we must be able to answer those questions in precise terms. We believe further that there is some confusion on this question, that it has not been sufficiently dealt with in the past and therefore we want today to look at it that much more carefully. It is extremely important for us to get a better understanding of where we are, of what we are trying to build and of how we will be able to build it. That is why we feel that this whole question of what exactly is the present stage is so important.

Before looking at that, a few words on the question of where we have come from, in other words, the inheritance of the Revolution. All comrades know of course that we inherited a backward, undeveloped economy, with a very low level - one can say in fact, a primitive level, of technological and economic development in the country. There was a very low level, and there is still a low level of development of the productive forces, that is, of living human labour, objects of labour and instruments of labour. This low level of development of the productive forces in turn resulted in very underdeveloped class formations.

3........

-3-

What we have in Grenada primarily of course, is a very large pet.t bourgeoisie, particularly a large peasantry- the rural petit bourgeoisie - small farmers who own small means of production and who must therefore work as they cannot live off their own plot of land alone. Some of them employ labour; some do not. So a large peasantry or bulk of our rural petit bourgeoisie. Then there is the urban petit bourgeoisie in terms of shopkeepers, garage owners, craftsmen, small restaurant owners and such like. The whole range of the petit bourgeoisie in our country. That of course is by far the largest class formation in the country.

We also have a working class which is very small and made up of agricultural workers based mainly in the rural areas, transport and communication workers on the docks, in telephone, electricity, etc., manufacturing and industrial workers (the smallest section of all) who produce garments, cokes, beer, that sort of thing. Some sections of the working class are employed by Government - garbagemen, the lowest clerical workers, the daily paid workers and so on. And of course we also have the commercial workers. Some of these comrades of the working class are also small owners of the means of production, but do not rely on that to support themselves - at least not as their main means of support.

In terms of the inheritance I also want to emphasise the low cultural level of our population at large as part of that inheritance and in particular the lack of technical skills and technical expertise of the working people. We must emphasise also the 19th century type of capitalist that we have in the country, capitalists

4/ engaged.......

-4-

engaged primarily in comprador activity, in other words largely in the importation and thereafter distribution of goods. This is a particularly parasitic type of capitalist in the full time service of international capitalism on which they must depend for the manufactured goods which give them their profits. They produce nothing and the vast majority of them engage in no form of manufacturing or industrial activity at all.

As part of the inheritance too, we must also note the very low level of infrastructural development of our country. Further, very backward agricultural development is also part of our inheritance and has relevance to the present stage of the Revolution. This inheritance of ours does have negative implications for the road that we are travelling on, for our objective to build Socialism in our country.

First of all, having a small working class is a very very serious disadvantage because only the working class can build Socialism. We know this is so because the working class is the class that is always growing; in fact, it has been historically, and it still is part of capitalist development that the working class gets larger and larger. Again, it is the working class that is most prepared for organisation and discipline because of having to work every day, having to arrive on time, having to engage in collective organisation and collective bargaining in their trade unions and so on. The working class too owns no means of production, in fact owns nothing except their labour and therefore they are the ones who most of all have to fight to end the oppression that comes about as a result of the private ownership of the means of production which of

5/ course......

-5-

course enslaves them and ensures that their own development is stultified and, finally the working class does have the key role in building socialism because of their role in production.

This inheritance is a problem also because of the large p[illegible] bourgeoisie that it has left us. We of course have that number of petit bourgeoisie in our country precisely because of economic under-development, precisely because capitalist production was so undeveloped that they did not need much labour and therefore people were by large forced to try to make a living however they could and wherever they could. But because the petit bourgeoisie is a vaci[illegible] class it is more difficult to build Socialism when there is such a large amount of petit bourgeoisie in the country, precisely because they are in the middle and you have to fight hard to win them. Many of them of course have bourgeois aspirations, many more are deluded and [illegible] by bourgeois ideology and propaganda and therefore the struggle to win the petit bourgeoisie has historically been a very serious intense struggle in all countries that have embarked upon a path of Socialist transformation.

The question we must now pose comrades is whether a society such as ours with their primitiveness, with so little infrastructure, with so little development of productive forces, with such a small working class can really build socialism. This is a question that many other countries before us have posed and many other countries in the future will continue to pose. Of course, this question arises because socialism requires a good level of development of the productive forces, it requires infrastructural development, it

6/ requires........

requires agricultural development, it requires industrialisation, it requires a high level of cultural development of the people, it requires an even higher level of political development and political consciousness, it requires central planning of the economy and society as a whole, it requires a serious Marxist Leninist vanguard Party leading, guiding and directing the whole process. All of these things are prerequisites for the building of Socialism, and, of course, the vast majority of these either do not exist at all or are at a very low level of development, at this time. Nonetheless, the answer is yes, it is possible for a country like ours to build Socialism. That of course we all know. It is possible, but the question is how and we think that this can be seen if we examine some of the possibilities or models for economic development in our country.

We believe that there are four main possibilities for economic development of Grenada and countries like Grenada. The first of these is a total private sector free enterprise system of economic development, your Seaga of Jamaica or your Puerto Rico model of development, where free enterprise is given full rein, where the private sector is able to rule uncontrolled. The second model is a total state sector approach where just about anything important is owned by the State, where the State owns virtually everything that matters. The third type is a mixed economy, but with a private sector dominant, and of course, that is the model that we have chosen in Grenada, the mixed economy - state sector dominant type model. But even after having said that, there are still questions of why

7/ we have.......

-7-

we have chosen that form and the question of precisely how will that form assist us to build socialism are two such questions that come to mind. Obviously, if we are speaking of building Socialism and we are, then it is clear that our objective as Marxist-Leninist must in the first instance be to construct socialism as rapidly, but scientifically as possible. That being so, clearly we cannot choose the path of capitalism. We cannot choose the path of a total private sector free enterprise model because that will be inconsistant with what we believe in and what we have been and are struggling for. We could not likewise choose that path of the mixed economy, with the private sector dominant because that will have tremendous dangers for the successful construction of Socialism and will have us without the effective possibility of guiding and regulating economic development through the imposition of taxes, the granting of credits and concessions and the use of all arms of the State apparatus. This must necessarily be so because it is, as we know, the objective material basis of the economy that determines and directs the political, social and cultural development of the society as a whole.

Equally, we cannot opt for the total state sector model as the state does not have the necessary material of financial resources, management and skills resources, access to markets, international contacts and so on. All of this should be obvious, but for those who have any doubts, please reflect on the tremendous difficulties that we have in finding the dollars necessary to pay the downpayment to the British Company - Plessey's - that will be installing the

8/ radar......

-8-

radar, communications and navigational equipment for our new international airport, or reflect on how difficult it has been to find guaranteed markets for our primary products and our agro-industrial products, or how difficult it is to find engineers or architects or science teachers or managers - and note I did not even say good managers, I just said managers. No, it would be impossible at this time for the state on its own to build Grenada.

That, of course, means that an alliance is necessary, an alliance in the first place between the working class and the petty bourgeoisie, in particular the rural peasantry, and in the second place an alliance with those elements of the upper petty bourgeoisie and the national bourgeoisie who, for different reasons, are willing to be involved in building the economy and the country at this time.

9/..............

TASKS OF THE NATIONAL DEMOCRATIC STAGE

Comrades, the tasks of this national democratic stage can perhaps be summarised in ten points; and I want to just quickly list them.

(1) Ensure the leading role of the working class through its Marxist/Leninist Party backed by

33/some

-33-

some form of the dictatorship of the proletariat. But please note that I said <u>some form</u> of the dictatorship of the proletariat, because obviously at this stage we cannot have the dictatorship of the proletariat or the working class, but the form we would have at this first stage is the dictatorship of the working people.

(2) Build the alliance between the working class and mass of the working people; in other words, the alliance between the working class and the urban and rural bourgeoisie. At the same time, we must also build an alliance with those patriotic sections of the upper petty bourgeoisie and national bourgeoisie who are willing to help develop the country.

(3) Ensure over a period, public ownership of the means of production. In other words, build the state sector.

(4) Work towards the gradual transformation of agriculture along socialist lines through development of voluntary co-operative farms and state farms.

(5) Plan the development of the economy in order to lay the basis for the building of socialism and to raise living standards.

(6) Begin the implementation of the cultural revolution. And this cultural revolution, as all of us know, is one of the four revolutions we are building at the same time - the political, economic, scientific and technological and the cultural. And in the context of the cultural revolution, I want to emphasise three main points - the spreading of the socialist ideology, the wiping out of illiteracy and the building of a new patriotic and revolutionary-

34/democratic.......

democratic intelligentsia!

(7) Build the defence capacity of the country so as to protect it and to protect the revolution from internal and external enemies. Comrades, the applicants on Saturday in one of the six workshops came back reporting that they were very concerned about the fact that there were so many non-party comrades who were leading the militia; and that is an area of concern that we share very strongly. We have to get more party comrades into the leadership of the militia. Just in terms of the means that we have here right now, we are short by over one fifth of the comrades that we need to operate them. Just in terms of what we have, I am not talking about what is to come. So if comrades are not prepared to come out and learn to use those means, then it means that other comrades out there, hopefully supporters and strong sympathisers would be the ones using them, which means that at the appropriate time we won't even have the guarantee that the guns can't be turned back on us. So I really hope comrades will take that comment from the workshop seriously.

(8) Develop proletarian internationalism. As representatives of the working class in Grenada, we have to ensure that our working class and the working people always demonstrate maximum solidarity with all international working class struggles. That is a fundamental responsibility.

(9) Develop equal and friendly relations with all governments in the world, except the fascist military dictatorship and apartheid types. That is why comrades, we have been making trips to different countries in Latin America like Mexico,

35/ Venezuela....

-35-

Venezuela, Ecuador, Panama and so on. That is why in a few days time we leave for France to another state visit. We must develop relations with all different kinds of countries - some of them revolutionary-democratic, some of them social-democratic, some of them, like in the case of many in CARICOM, straight pro-capitalist and pro-imperialist in outlook.

(10) Build rapidly our links with the Socialist World, especially the Soviet Union. And here I should hardly need to say more; we have just come back from an important visit to the land of Lenin, the Soviets in the last two days have arrived, nine of them including the Ambassador and their Embassy is about to be opened and so on. So these links and relations are building reasonably satisfactory.

TASKS FOR THE PRESENT PERIOD

Coming out of all of this comrades, what are the tasks as seen by the Central Committee?

The first task is sinking the ideas of Marxism/Leninism among the working class and the working people. The main vehicle for this comrades is socialism classes. The Central Committee feels very strongly that this is the Number One task. And of course, there can be only one Number One task, and this the Central Committee regards as Number One - sinking the ideas of Marxism - Leninism among the working class and the working people. The fact of the matter is that a national democratic revolution can be turned back easily. For example in the case of Nasser's Egypt, not withstanding the years of hard work put in by Nasser and his party into trying to build the national democratic revolution in Egypt, After his death it took only a few years to roll back

36/ all that......

all that had been accomplished. And there were several reasons. One, the party was not in fact built along Leninist vanguard lines and secondly, because the ideas of Marxism/Leninism had not taken root, there was no deep class consciousness in Egypt. We know that in many of these national democratic revolutions - in Iraq, Somalia, Algeria and so on - the fact is that the ideas of Marxism/Leninism were and are not being spread. And therefore, with the ideological work being weak, at a certain point it becomes easy for forces opposed to revolutionary transformation to overturn what had been accomplished.

2. The second task, comrades, the organisation of the working class and the working people through their trade unions, their organs for popular power, their mass organisations and through sports and culture - the Organisation of th working class and the working people.

3. Thirdly, comrades, strengthening the Leninist character of the party by bringing in the best elements of the working people and in particular the working class, and through building the internal organisation of the Party.

4. Fourthly comrades, building the economy along the path of socialist orientation, thus providing more material benefits for the masses and laying the basis for the construction of socialism.

5. The fifth task, developing the defence capacity of the country through building the militia both quantitatively and qualitatively by strengthening the influence of the Party in the militia.

We believe very firmly, comrades, that the tasks have been put in the correct order of priority by the Central Committee. Unless the party as a whole feels very strongly

37/ about

-37-

about this, and we decide to change this [illegible]ritisation, these priorities in the order outlined will stand as 1.2.3.4. and 5. You can[illegible]e two number ones and you can't [illegible]ve three number twos. One is one and two is two. So we have to look at our workplans and committees and look at the programmes that we are into and revise them to make sure that they are in line with the line of march set by the Central Committee. One is one, Two is two, Three is three, Four is four and Fivo is five. Because, comrades, as you know another historic weakness of ours has been to set priorities one day and then the very next day to break the priorities that we have set; so we really need this time to take a very strong and firm position on this question.

THE SUBJECTIVE FACTOR - THE PARTY

Comrades I want to close, but what I want to close by saying will take another fifteen minutes or so. I want to close by going into the question of the subjective factor, in other words the party, a very brief history of the party's development and the criteria for Party membership at this time.

Over the past nine and a half years, our Party has passed through many stages of development; all of us know that. We have analysed recently that there have been six major stages that the Party has gone through. The first stage began on the 11th March, 1973, with the merger, when came NJM out of JEWEL and MAP led by [illegible] [illegible]ntsia and rural petty-bourgeoisie. The Strategy adopted was one of mass mobilisation with seizure of power coming through mass mobilisation, general strike, street marches and thereafter insurrection. Mistakes were made, a deep class approach was not taken, no attempt was made to build

38/ a Leninist Party.......

-38-

a Leninist Party, there was an over-reliance on spontaneity and the possibilities of crowd politics. That period, comrades, March '73 to April '74 is the period of mass mobilisation in action. Using the issue of Gairy's incorrect approach to the question of independence as a base we went around the country agitating the masses for popular insurrection. During that same period in fact, within the first two months of the Party being formed, we liberated 51 rifles from Gairy. It is true we did not hold them for as long as we would have liked; we had them for one year and then Belmar took them back, but in fact we stole 51 rifles as part of that preparation.

During this period of mass mobilisation, we held the People's Convention on Independence and the massively attended People's Congress where five historic, but nonetheless ultra-leftist, decisions were taken. You remember the decisions? Firstly, we tried Gairy, found him guilty of 27 crimes and gave him two weeks to resign. We suggested that a National Unity Council should be elected and a National Unity Council was elected and we said it would have the task of supervising the orderly transition to power of the new regime. We also decided that the people would take steps to remove the Gairy dictatorship if he did not resign within 2 weeks. So undoubtedly, this was ultra-leftism in action. Nonetheless the major weakness of this period was the subjective factor, the fact that a Leninist approach to pary building and to strategy and tactics were not adopted; and this is notwithstanding the notable achievements of the period, including the publication of our Manifesto.

After the defeat in January '74 the Party held its first major evaluation in April 1974, we were then

39/ exactly.......

exactly one year and one month old. We spent a few days, a whole week-end, looking at the Party and trying to decide where we went wrong and what corrective action was needed. That is when we decided in theory and in principle that we should build a Leninist Party. That decision was taken in April '74 but in practice that decision was not implemented for many years. In fact, there was a constant struggle within the Party to get Leninist principles, in practice and in a concrete way going but it was always an uphill struggle, particularly on the need for collective study. In this second period, that is from April '74 to June '77, the Party was very much going through its period of early childhood, though our contesting of the 1976 General Elections and our policy on Alliances were evidence of a developing political and ideological maturity.

In the time period, July '77 to August '78, the party did make a qualitative leap forward in terms of Leninist standards and principles. That is the period when we stepped up our work among the working class, the work was not sufficiently deep, but at least it was starting. We tried to organise the agricultural working class but did not get very far because of Gairy's use of repression in protecting his base among the agricultural working class. But we did some work during that period with the urban working class and with sections of the rural petty bourgeoisie - the farmers and the fishermen. That is the period too when the Organising Committee of the Party was formed, thus taking some of the strain off the Political Bureau and leaving matters of discipline, party organisation and so on, for the Organising Committee to handle - a critical step forward.

40/ And then........

And then we came to the next period, the fourth period from August '78 to March '79, when the Party really moved into top gear. The timing was fortuitous for us because at the exact moment that a revolutionary situation was developing a number of key work committees of the Party began to function. Inner party democracy was also being strengthened; party study was going on, and a mass scientific approach to organisation was beginning to develop.

And from March '79 to this period, the fifth (5th) we have had a lot of mass activity. It is the period when we broadened and deepended our links with the working people and the masses in general, through the mass organisations - women, youth, pioneers-; through the organs of popular power - workers, parish and zonal councils-; through the socialism classes, very critically and also through our greatly expanded work in the trade unions. In this period, we have considerably deepened, broadened and expanded our links with the working people and the broad masses in general. This is the period too when the Party began to develop a number of critical new structures and committees, including the C.C. itself, PCB's and a Committee on the economy for the first time. They have not all done well as we would have liked but the fact is that important new structures have been set up and have begun to function.

During this period too, the Party has also been involved in supervising many aspects of the State Apparatus and in running the state generally. The party is involved in all the key programmes of the Revolution, the Centre for Popular Education Programme, the Land Reform Programme, Youth Employment Programme, and recently in the

41/discussions......

-41-

discussions around the Budget and the Economy. So this is a period that has seen a number of new mechanisms, new structures and new work committees and greatly expanded work in dozens of different areas at the same time.

But we believe very strongly, comrades, that as from now, September '82 the Party is definitely entering a new stage of the revolution and of our Party's development. We feel that because of the growing internal and external complexity of this period, because of the growing quantity of work required of the Party and in order to cope with the new complexities that once again we have to change gears and step up the pace. This year we have a major role to play in the development of the Economy because this is the essential basis for progressing on our path of socialist orientation. Furthermore, the question of the Armed Forces, especially the militia and of the Party assuming leadership of the key positions there is something that we have to be involved in a lot more this year. The question of increasing the quantity and quality of our socialism classes, as our priorities demand is also, something that we must take much more seriously. <u>The CPE Programme, in its second phase, must also get a lot of attention this year.</u> The Youth Employment Programme and the Land Reform Programme are central to agricultural and overall Economic development.

In other words, we are required to work on a dozen critical fronts at the same time, and that is going to require a lot more application of Leninist standards of discipline, consistency and seriousness. All of this, comrades, means that our ideological and organisational level as a Party will have to rise considerably. It is clear that if we had not insisted

42/ on higher.....

higher standards we would not have reached where we have reached. But it is equally clear, comrades, that holding power is much more difficult than taking power. There is no doubt that the Party can be built more rapidly on the basis of lower standards but this will mean that the tasks we have set ourselves, including our historical task of building socialism, would not be accomplished. As Lenin told us a long time ago "better fewer but better". Immortal words that we must never forget.

During the Party's history, there are members who have dropped out; some for opportunist reasons; others because they were not willing to make the sacrifices required in the particular period; in other cases, as the Party's ideological outlook developed, they came to realise that they did not share the desire to develop socialism; some others just could not take the level of discipline, of organisation, of strain, of hard work, of sacrifice. But no one is a member for life in the serious Leninist Party and, at this point, the Central Committee would like to enumerate the criteria for party membership and to go into some details as to the qualities required for promotion in the Party.

REQUIREMENTS FOR MEMBERSHIP

The four basic requirements for party membership are:-

(1) Regular collective ideological study organised by the Party.

(2) Engage in consistent political work under the guidance of an organ of the Party.

(3) Consistent payment of party dues fixed at 5% of gross salary. And comrades, gross means gross, it doesn't mean net - after you pay tax, or after you take out money to give to some member of the family.

43/ So, if.....

-43-

So, if your salary is $800 per month and you are paying $60 tax, that is not the Party's business; it is 5% of the $800, so you have to pay $40. Unemployed comrades and students must pay $1.00 a month. I don't know how many unemployed comrades the Party has left, but we certainly have students.

(4) Understanding, accepting and implementing the principles and programme of the Party. This last requirement includes a complete willingness to accept Party discipline in many, many areas of one's personal life, not just political life. To fully accept and really implement the principles and programme of the party requires you to let the Party decide <u>when</u> you can get vacation and sometimes even what kind of activities you can be involved in. In other words, even our personal life is under security to some extent.

<u>POTENTIAL APPLICANTS</u>

Comrades, we developed a new category called Potential Applicants after the Revolution, so as to ensure that opportunists, careerists, self-seekers and other elements like that who want to come into the Party because it seems easy, or because the new conditions mean that they don't have to get "bull-pistle" if they join the Party now or because the Party seems like a badge and passport to fame and prestige, are not allowed to enter the Party as applicants before they go through a tight screening process. And what we have been trying to do in choosing Potential Applicants is essentially to look for people with four main qualities and characteristics. Firstly, comrades with a genuinely revolutionary democratic outlook; secondly, comrades who engage in disciplined political work in a particular area; thirdly, comrades who are basically honest and not opportunist in character; and fourthly

44/ comrades whose...

Comrades whose relations to private property do not involve them in the exploitation of labour.

POTENTIAL APPLICANTS TO APPLICANTS

From our experience, comrades, these are the people who are most likely to move to Marxism/Leninism. These comrades are then invited to join classes where they are tested to see whether they are hostile to, or accepting of the ideas of Marxism Leninism. If they are not anti-communist, and if they continue to work well and show an honest approach, they are admitted as Applicants. And as all comrades know the period of applicancy is one year. That gives both the Party and the applicant the time to judge whether the applicant really accepts the science of Marxism/Leninism and is willing to make the sacrifices necessary to become a Party member.

APPLICANTS TO CANDIDATE MEMBERS

When assessing an applicant for promotion to Candidate Member the following five points are looked at:-

(1) Whether the applicant accepts the principles of Marxism Leninism and shows willingness to continue to develop.

(2) Whether the applicant has been working consistently and effectively in his/her of political work and developing in terms of organisational skills.

(3) Whether the applicant has in practice accepted party discipline, in practice.

(4) Whether the applicant has good relations with the masses, including party members and non-party members with whom he he works in his Union, Mass Organisation, Army, Workplace etc.

43/ Whether.......

(5) Whether the Applicant continues to be of good character so as to present an example to the masses he/she comes in contact with; whether certain petty bourgeois traits such as individualism, hostility to criticism, arrogance, indiscipline and so on are being eroded; and whether proletarian qualities such as respect for the working class, co-operativeness and co-operation, discipline, modesty, self criticism are being built. If accepted as a Candidate member, another year would now elapse before the comrade is eligible for consideration for full membership.

CANDIDATE MEMBERS TO MEMBERS

At this stage, the stage of moving from Candidate Member to Member, the Party looks for the fullest possible development of six factors.

(1) Ideological development as seen in a development of the ability to analyse and cope well with many different situations and to correctly apply strategy and tactics - the essence of correct Marxism/Leninism Leadership.

(2) The development of correct leadership. A professional approach to his/her political work, expressing Leninist organisational standards in all aspects of the work.

(3) The development of an ability to supervise and guide the work of junior party comrades.

(4) The removal of petty bourgeois character faults and the development of a character which provides

46/ an.......

an outstanding example to other party comrades and the masses alike.

(5) The development of very good relations with the masses and other party comrades.

(6) The development of the technical and professional skills needed by the comrade in his or her job.

Comrades, some comrades feel that it takes too long to become a full member in our Party. Some comrades feel it is rough enough to have applicants, then candidate members and then members so that on top of that to have Potential Applicants is really just pushing the pace too much. And yet the truth is that some comrades in the Party are right now proposing another new category of not just Potential Applicants but of Prospective Potential Applicant, to make it even more difficult to gain entry. The fact is, comrades, that we feel it is correct in our situation for us to have this long process of what, at one level, can be seen as probation before comrades can become full members. We think it is important now because at the level of party leadership we want to keep the number down; in fact at the level of the Central Committee of the Party, our anxiety and concern is to see the Party lifted in terms of quantity and quality in the shortest possible time. But we also know from experience that this whole question of coming to accept full membership in the party and really internationalism and operationalising in a serious way party discipline and party duties is something that does take time to really sink home. Sometimes comrades might last two or three years but then on a certain issue when the class struggle is really heightened they break and then leave the Party.

The truth is that it is not really a case of the Party Leadership laying down harsh conditions; it is real

47/ life........

life and the demand of the struggle that make it necessary for us to have these difficult conditions and for us to ensure that comrades who are full members, and also candidate members, are truly the finest representatives of the working class and the most steeled in struggle, in discipline, in dedication, in commitment and in total commitment for the working class and their interests. That is not the C.C. laying laws down, that is real life laying the laws down. And that is why comrades, we feel very strongly that these criteria are critical and necessary.

We believe it must become more and more difficult for comrades to become full members and candidate members and it must become more difficult for new comrades to remain as members and candidate members;.and those who are unwilling to live up to the demands of this membership would have to be moved. We believe comrades that this stage of our process requires this. Being a Communist, comrades meansbecoming a different kind of person. Our society is deeply petty bourgeois and this means the majority of our people are deeply individualistic, ill-disciplined, disorganised, un-proletarian, hostile to criticism and so on. Many in the middle strata and intelligentsia often find it difficult to relate as equals with the working people while at the same time many working people lack confidence in dealing with certain types of people. It takes time for a new proletarian person to be built. It takes time for a Communist to be built. So in reality, comrades, promotion is not decided on by the Party but by the development of comrades themselves.

On behalf of the Central Committee of our Party, I want to congratulate all the comrades who have been

48/ recently.......

recently promoted from applicants to candidate members who are here with us today for the first time in that capacity, and who as a result of that new status have assumed new rights, duties and responsibilities. I also want to congratulate in advance those comrades in this room who will shortly be promoted from candidate members to full members. Comrades now know the basis on which they have been promoted. Those comrades who have not been promoted at this time will also, we hope, understand and accept the reasons why they have not been promoted.

We believe comrades, that this line of march will equipt us to go into the field and to move rapidly to ensure that this first stage of the path we are on - the socialist orientation stage - is rapidly built. We believe that we have correctly defined the new tasks required to handle the new situation that has developed. We believe that as Party, individually and collectively, we must now develop ourselves into becoming more professional, more disciplined, more Leninist so that we would be able to meet the demands of this period. We also believe firmly that the path we have chosen is the <u>ONLY</u> correct one. We believe that this path would <u>certainly</u> bring us to our second major historical objective to seeing socialism, of seeing socialist construction achieved in our country, thus ensuring that the working class in Grenada would assume their rightful role and become fully emancipated for the first time.

LONG LIVE THE NEW JEWEL MOVEMENT!

LONG LIVE THE MEMBERS, CANDIDATE MEMBERS AND APPLICANTS OF OUR PARTY!

LONG LIVE THE REVOLUTIONARY HISTORY OF OUR PARTY!
LONG LIVE THE WORKING CLASS OF GRENADA!
LONG LIVE THE INTERNATIONAL WORKING CLASS!
LONG LIVE PROLETARIAN INTERNATIONALISM!
LONG LIVE THE GRENADA REVOLUTION!
FORWARD FROM SOCIALIST ORIENTATION TO SOCIALIST CONSTRUCTION!

FORWARD EVER! BACKWARD NEVER!

**** ____ ****

Document 2

RESTRICTED

REPORT OF THE DELEGATION SENT TO GRENADA BY THE AMERICA DEPARTMENT WITH THE AIM OF STARTING THE GATHERING OF SOURCES FOR THE CHARACTERIZATION OF THE RELIGIOUS SITUATION IN THE COUNTRY, AND THE CONTACTS FOR FURTHER COOPERATION BETWEEN THE PCC AND THE NJM REGARDING THE QUESTION.

DELEGATION: Cde. Aurelio Alonso Tejada

DATE: August 13-24, 1982

This report was handed in on October 14, 1982,

"YEAR 24 OF THE REVOLUTION"

INTRODUCTORY NOTE

This report is the result of an initial ten days stay which, as it coincided with holidays, could not be used to the greatest advantage.

Two more difficulties must be taken into account: firstly, the total lack of informative or unofficial documentation by the NJM* comrades, which resulted in the need to find sources through our visit to the public library, the national museum, and religious bookstores; secondly, the absence of Judy Williams, the most important person among the Christian lay people that actively cooperate with the NJM who, in addition to her personal testimonies, should have arranged our contacts with other positive elements within the laity. This situation caused our interviews to be limited to representatives of the ecclesiastical institutions.

In spite of these difficulties, it can be considered that the work showed useful results so that the thought-out objectives were satisfactorily reached.

We received a decisive support by the revolutionary leadership through Cde. Selwyn Strachan, member of the Political Bureau of the NJM and Minister of National Mobilization, whom we met on three occasions. During the first interview, Cde. Strachan summarized the recent aggressive positions adopted by the Church against the revolutionary leadership and we, on our part, explained the concrete aims we had set for the visit. Cde. Strachan showed interest in receiving a written version. After working out a detailed project starting from the general plan we had thought out, we handed it in at a second meeting. On this occasion, arrangements were made for the interviews. At the same time, we had begun to work in the tracking down of written sources. We met Minister Strachan again at the end of our stay and gave him a brief account of the results of the contacts and tracking down of sources (some of which were supplied to him) and expressed our concerns about the educational

* New Jewel Movement

reform issue and about the mechanisms of response to the recent summons to the Church. We told Cde. Strachan that the report on the visit would be sent to him not before the second fortnight of September.

The constant, efficient, diligent support by Cde. Gastón Díaz, our Embassy's First Secretary who at the time was head of the Mission, played an important role in the positive results we might have achieved in this visit. We left him in charge of finding and sending two important informative sources: the Handbook of Caribbean Churches, 1982, to be bought in Barbados, and the book written by Raymund Devas in 1932, which in case of not being obtained from F. Martin Simmonds, efforts should be made to borrow it from the public library so as to photocopy it.

The documents that make up the report are ordered in the following way:

* CONCLUSIONS
* RECOMMENDATIONS
* REVIEW OF THE RELIGIOUS SITUATION IN GRENADA
  1. Characterization of the churches and religiosity in Grenada.
  2. Positions of the Church in the face of the revolutionary transformation.
* ANNEXES:
  I.- Outline for the study of religion in Grenada.
  II.- Summaries of interviews held and of observation carried out at the curches in St. George's.
  III.- Articles from Caribbean Contact, August and September, 1982.
  IV.- Bibliography

CONCLUSIONS

The religious situation in Grenada shows a series of characteristics which can be summarised as follows:

1) Since the revolutionary triumph in 1979, the diocese showed signs of reservation and started to insist on the holding of elections. During the three years of revolutionary government, the Catholic hierarchy has added to its electoral claim a position of mediation in favor of the 1979 pro-Gairy prisoners and of advocate of the "freedom of the press" in the face of governmental measures to stop counterrevolutionary propaganda. The emphasis of the Church is in harmony with the campaigns carried out by the reactionary governments in the Caribbean against Grenada's PRG* and now has an institutional argument formalized in the pastoral of the Caribbean Catholic bishops in February this year. This pastoral marks a new reference, which goes backward in comparison with that of 1975, and starting from it, political sectors in the area have promoted the summons to the Church for a confrontation of forces with the PRG of Grenada.

2) For the Grenadian Church (particularly the Catholic one) the moment can be described as one of definitions. It cannot be said yet (in our opinion) that the hierarchy has decided on an open confrontation. Although the pressure from the reactionary forces in the region within and outside the Church is aimed at confrontation, the position of the diocese seems to lean towards a combination of the pastoral attacks with repeated reference to the disposition to dialogue and the insistence upon the fact that their position towards the PRG is not uncompromising.

3) There are reasons to think that there is a potential contradiction between the foreign clergy (mainly the British and the Irish) and the West Indian minority. That majority, whom the vicar of the cathedral himself think is alien and inadaptable to the local realities, is at

* People's Revolutionary Government of Grenada.

first sight the most active counterpart of the oppositionist dynamics brought about by the February pastoral and by the provocations of reactionary forces in the region.

4) There are no signs of systematic progressive projections within the Grenadian clergy. It seems that within the institution there is not a trend in the theological and social line sympathetic to the revolutionary project, and there are no indications of a community organization of this kind at the grass roots. However, some believers belonging to Catholic organizations, who gather around the Pope Paul Camp (with whom we could not get in touch during this visit) and who actively collaborate with the NJM, can constitute a ferment in this direction.

5) The strong point of the Grenadian churches (both the Catholic and traditional Protestant ones) regarding their social influence is the educational sector. The religious schools are, at a very high percent, in charge of elementary and secondary education because throughout the colonial period the State traditionally neglected this sector. The PRG does not have a public educational system. In our opinion, the teaching centers are the stronghold of the ecclesiastical institutions and the possibility of a reform that should bring about their exclusion is their main concern.

6) The incorporation of the Catholic churches of the Caribbean to the Conference of Caribbean Churches (CCC), which also includes over 20 Protestant churches since its creation in 1973, besides being an exceptional characteristic of ecumenism, establishes an associational link among the Christian institutions that admits a game of influences in their projection: the Grenada Catholic diocese is a member of the Conference of Churches of Grenada (CCG) and with its positions it can influence on the the Protestant churches, and the other way around; at the same time, the fact that the Catholic Church belongs to the CCC means a similar game of influences at the regional level. In this interaction, the most positive positions of the CCC act as a restraining factor to the behaviour of the Catholic Church at the local (and regional) level. However, the CCC is not a homogeneous body and the

possibility of a reversal of its positions should no be underestimated, which would be in harmony with the tone of the criticisms to the PRG by the Grenadian churches (see diagram in page 4).

7) The estimated believing population is over 80 percent, made up mainly by Catholics (59 percent), Protestant from the historical churches (Anglicans, Presbyterians and Methodists), and a number of sects among which the Rastafarians seem to be widely disseminated. The level of participation observed in the Sunday service is high. There does not seem to exist a significant difference in the degree of religiosity among Protestants and Catholics. The Charismatic Catholic movement has expanded and it is thought to reach no less than a quarter of Catholics. The African roots and their possible syncretic expressions should be studied.

8) The Catholic Church is organized in a diocese with 20 parish churches. It has one Bishop and 22 priests, with a rate of one priest for every 2,950 Catholics (baptized). Sixteen of the priests are religious and 6 are diocesan; 16 are English, Irish, and American; 4 are from other West Indian countries and 2 from Grenada; 15 are white and 7 are mestizo or black. Thus, because of their origin and race this is a clergy with characteritics that alienate them from the problems of the Island.

9) The diocese is suffragan to the archdiocese of Castries (St. Lucia) and belongs to the Episcopal Conference of the West Indies, whose main seats are Jamaica and Trinidad-Tobago. Thus the ecclesiastical organization takes on a supranational character and the projection of the Grenadian Church is linked to the strategy carried out by the West Indian body. (Regarding the framework of institutional relationship of dependence, see the following diagram.)

DIAGRAM OF RELATIONS OF DEPENDENCE AND ASSOCIATION IN THE RELIGIOUS INSTITUTIONS OF GRENADA

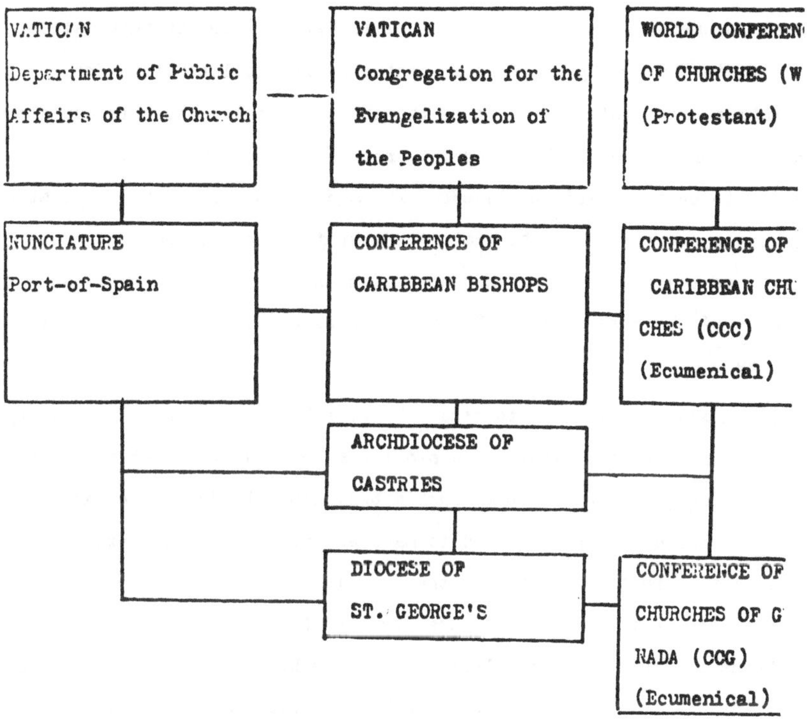

RECOMMENDATIONS

1. We underline the importance of the fact that a comrade responsible for the attention to the religious problems be appointed by the New Jewel Movement: This activity would basically include the information work at the beginning and regular contacts with collaborators from Christian organizations. If it is thought to be relevant, this can also include contacts with the clergy. We repeat the recommendation that the person to be appointed should spend 15-20 days in Cuba so as to be able to know our experiences, be trained in the tasks of systematic information on the subject, and exchange ideas on the most controversial aspects of the work. Comrade Strachan expressed his agreement on this proposal.

2. It would be advisable to study the possibility of formally creating a Register of Associations (or a similar mechanism) attached to the corresponding governmental body. Such a body could be legally established on the basis of the public need to make an inventory of the existing associations in the country and their activities (this would not only include the religious institutions, but the Chamber of Commerce, associations of professionals, clubs such as the Rotarians, the Lions, etc.). This would enable the counting of members, posts, premises, etc., the knowledge on special and regular activities, the means of financing of activities , etc. Both the terms of the resolution or law and the concrete contents of the register and modus operandi would be defined according to the specific conditions. This proposal is based on the need to regularize the access by the PRG to systematic factual information on the religious institutions and their activities. Our recommendation does not dismiss the fact that the resposibility regarding the register could be closely linked to the above-mentioned proposal.

3. To promote contacts among clergymen and members of the laity from Nicaragua and other Latin American circles linked to the theology of liberation and, in general, to the idea of a church committed to the

revolutionary positions, and the Christian sectors in Grenada through the Pope Paul Camp and maybe through talks with religious clergymen from a same order, particularly the Dominicans. These contacts should positively influence the Christian sectors of Grenada.

4. To consider the possibility of the Matanzas Evangelical Seminary inviting pastors from the Grenadian Protestant churches belonging to the Conference of Caribbean Churches (CCC), of which the Conference of Evangelical Churches of Cuba is a member, to short or annual courses. The language problem would be solved here.

5. To promote the invitation of Grenadian members of the laity and clergymen, through the appropriate channels, to visit Cuba. In my opinion, it would be useful to immediately invite F. Cyril Lamontagne, Vicar of the Cathedral of St. George's (second figure in the diocese), who in our interview expressed his willingness to visit Cuba and was interested in knowing how he could be invited. Afterwards, I think arrangements should be made for a visit of F. Martin Simmonds, superior of the Order of the Dominicans in the British West Indies, in case the trip he told us he was planning to make to Havana from Jamaica early next October would not take place. In case he would travel in October, we should be kept informed on his visit so as to organize activities that should help to positively influence his positions. F. Simmonds is the only clergyman who, in spite of his institutional responsibility, enjoys a positive reputation in the revolutionary circles of the Island. I think that after a new inquiry in Grenada we should assess the advisability of continuing this program of visits with other West Indian priests of the diocese.

6. The result of this visit ratifies an existing proposal in the sense of regularizing a reciprocal information link and an exchange of criteria on the strategy and tactics of the Church and the mechanisms of prevention and response. The action of the Church – particularly the Catholic one – has its origin in the policy of the Vatican towards

Central America and the Caribbean, and therefore, entails the existence of mechanisms of combined action within the institution. The exchange on our part should comprise two levels: a regular one with a NJM-PCC bilateral character, and another one with a trilateral character in which the FSLN of Nicaragua would also participate.

7. I think it is indispensable to make a second brief visit within a short time (if possible within the present year) with a view to widen and deepen the gathering of testimonial information and to carry out tasks of observation which were not possible to undertake during the first visit and that are essential both to complete the characterization of the phenomenon and to propose effective measures. I summarize below the main concrete aims which have been left for a second visit:

a) Interviews with Christian collaborators with the NJM (initially, Judy Williams, Annette Campbell and Susan Berkley) and visits to the Pope Paul Camp.

b) Interviews with Mons. Sidney Charles, Catholic Bishop; Rev. John Withington, Superintendent of the Methodist Church; and Rev. Hoskins Huggins, Archdeacon of the Anglican Church. According to the first contacts established, these interviews seem feasible and would result in direct assessments by the local hierarchies.

c) Visit to Catholic communities with F. Martin Simmonds, This was proposed by F. Simmonds during the interview with him, and it would give us a series of worthy elements.

d) Interview with officials of the PRG and leaders of the NJM who could contribute with criteria on the religious phenomenon in Grenada.

e) To keep active the contacts with F. Lamontagne and Deacon Lucky Bernard, for whose optimum preparation there are good possibilities.

NOTE:

We repeat what was stated in the outline presented to Cde. Strachan (Annex 1) regarding the provisional character both of the conclusions and recommendations of the present report.

Document 3

MINISTRY OF INTERIOR,
BUTLER HOUSE,
ST. GEORGE'S.

PLAN OF C.I. OPERATIONS *Ministry of Interior*

Setting up of command post ~~comprising~~ Major Keith Roberts, Cpt. H. Romain, Lt. B. Pivotte.

Responsible for analysing all information that are coming in, in order to pass on to members of the Central Committee.

- Also, one Comrade who we can send to verify situations and incidents that have been reported.
- Recorder of all the information coming into the Centre.

MONITORING REGIONALLY - ST. GEORGE'S

City - three (3) Officers

Dock, Carenage - one (1) Officer

St. Paul's - two (2) Officers

ST. JOHN'S

One (1) Officer plus Party Cadres - Valdon

ST. PATRICK'S

eports from Jan

T. ANDREW'S

wo (2) Officers plus Party Cadres - Mc Gill

egular hourly report from all officers and Party Cadres being ed for this purpose.

[illegible]

Monitoring of all [illegible]ssies and Diplomats in this period

-2-

(ii) To control the movements of all diplomats, with the purpose of revealing the links with possible counter elements.

(iii) Stop any possibility of them actively using this period to create distrubances and confusion and a major counter-actions.

(iv) Monitoring of all visitors who have been in Granada over four weeks and more.

(v) Study the incoming visitors of the various counters to see the composition of visitors.

(vi) Checking and controlling the key middle class elements who have links with diplomats, and influence in some section of the society.

(vii) Check the hotels to see if visitors are leaving before their scheduled time or the booking question.

MEDICAL SCHOOL

Monitor all students during this period.
Check the mood and movements of the school hirachy and professors during this period.

CHURCH

Monitor all sermons by the various parish priests and preachers in the society.
The controlling of all hirachy meeting of the church in particular the Catholic and Anglicans.
Controlling all elements of the society that pay visits to the hirachy.
Tapping of the Hirachy of all the leading counter churches phones.

ESSENTIAL SERVICES

Physical protection of the key installations against sabotage.
[illegible] of confidence people xx to ensure that any signs of [illegible] may be identified.

-3-

Getting a general operative picture of the area in which the key installations are located.
Checking of mails of dangerous elements.
Tapping and disconnection of dangerous elements phones.
Check all Heads of Ministries to see if they have any important documents which needs to be secured.
Special control over technicians who are not very firm and cannot be replaced.

COAST GUARD

Establish communication with watch towers.
Boat patrols on a nightly basis.

Documentation of all telephone calls and security reports from various regions.

Document 4

RESOLUTION OF THE PEOPLE'S REVOLUTIONARY ARMED FORCES BRANCH OF THE NEW JEWEL MOVEMENT

We, the members of the People's Revolutionary Armed Forces Branch of the New JEWEL Movement gathered this day 12th October 1983 unswervingly support the analysis and decisions of the New JEWEL Movement Central Committee at its Extraordinary Plenary meeting of September 14th - 17th 1983.

We share with deep concern the analysis of the Central Committee on the deep seated crisis and danger which exist in our country and party and therefore wholeheartedly stand by the Central Committee decision to officially establish Joint Leadership in our Party as the correct scientific mode of leadership of our Party, as a decisive step in pulling our Party and Revolution out of its present danger. This decision of the Central Committee was unanimously accepted by all members and candidates of our Party. However, a few opportunist elements in our party are now unashamedly spreading vicious lying rumours to obstruct the implementation of the Central Committee decision.

We recognise and uphold that based on the fundamental Leninist principle of democratic centralism that decision of our Party's Central Committee have the force of law and form the basis of the a activity and conduct of all party bodies and of every single party member, candidate member and applicant regardless of their services and posts. We further unswervingly hold high the principles of criticism and self-criticism and collective leadership in our Party as the firm guarantee that our Party will always stay in the correct course and exercise correct leadership and guidance of our Revolution as we struggle to build socialism. Never would we allow cultism, egoism, the unreasonable and unprincipled desires of one man or a minority to be imposed on our Party thus stiffling inner party democrac and endangering the party and revolution and holding our country to ransom. We demand an immediate end to this and the restoration of Leninist norms of party life and their strict observance by all as the key for the normal functioning of the party.

We, the members of the People's Revolutionary Armed Forces Branch of the NJM. uphold as the only reasonable basis for party unity the truth spoken by Comrade Lenin when he said, "Discussing the problem, expressing and hearing different opinions, ascertaining the views of the majority of the organised Marxists, expressing these views in the form of decisions adopted by delegates and carring them out conscientiously, this is what reasonable people all over the world call unity."

We clearly understand that party discipline is nothing less than the active struggle for the implementation of collectively adopted decisions, such as the decision of the Central Committee on Joint Leadership which was ratified by our entire membership. Therefore we call on the Central Committee and the entire party to expel from the Party's ranks all elements who do not submit to, uphold and implement in practice the decision of the Central Committee and party membership but are bent on holding up the party's work and spreading anti-party propaganda.

The People's Revolutionary Armed Forces Branch of NJM. awaits the decision and orders of the Central Committee!

LONG LIVE THE NJM CENTRAL COMMITTEE - the highest body and authority of our Party and Revolution!

LONG LIVE THE PARTY - NJM!

LONG LIVE LENINISM!

LONG LIVE OUR PEOPLE'S REVOLUTION!

FORWARD EVER BACKWARD NEVER!

Document 5

1R
Deputy PM
Foreign Minsiter
Chairman of Grginixing Committ

CONFIDENTIAL

EMBASSY OF GRENADA IN THE USSR

YEAR OF POLITICAL AND ACADEMIC EDUCATION

Dobryninskaya Ulitsa 7
Apartment 221
Moscow
USSR

Telephone:
237-25-41
237-99-05

Relations with the CPSU

Formal relations with the CPSU statred, as far as I can ascertain, iinJune of 1980 with the visit of Comrade Coard to the USSR and the signing of a Party to Party agreement - which I have never seen.

The Soviet side has said that part of that agreement was an undertakingnon the part of NJM to send some students to the Party School here. Another part of the agreement was for the Soviet side to send some literature to NJM. The xxxxx CPSU also undertook to assist substantially in the construction of an NJM Party Headquarters. The Sx CPSU also offered five places for rest and recreation and five more places for a familiarization study tour of the Soviet Union during June and July of 1981. I do not know what other items the agreement contained. I do know however, that real efforts were made on the xxxi CPSU side to implement the familiarization and restand recreation side of the agreement. My recollection is that of the ten people invited only three were actually sent.

When Comrade Hudson Austin visited the USSR in December of 1981, he met with Comrades Chernjaev - alternate member of the CC and Deputy Chief of the International Department of the CC and Nicholai Kostovets - an official of the Office of the CC responsible for USA and Canada. Up to that point in time, there was no section of the CC designated to be in charge of the English-speaking Caribbean. Cuba was being attended to by the Section of the Party dealing with Socialist countries and the Latin American Department covered everywhere xxxxx else in Latin America - except Guyana. Guyana fell under Nicholai principally because it was English-speaking and the Latin American Department was Spanish-speaking. Thus when Grenada came unto the scene, the section dealing with USA and Canada and Guyana, almost naturally took responsibility for Grenada. Up to this date this section of the Party has absolutely no relations with any other ixixxx Party in any other Caribbean island except the WPJ in Jamaica. When for example, I enquired as to which section of the Party has responsibility for Surinam, the amused response was that "no one wants to take responsibility for Surinam". But because we have been in a position to give them some information on Surinam, they seem to be emerging as the people responsible for Surinam.

We are faced with a situation therefore where Grenada has been put in a Department which contains only countries of capitalist orientation and the two big capitalist giants in our region. The CPSU has a valuable relationship with Gus Hall and Company but it is basically a symbolic relationship. The same is true for Canada. As regards Guyana, they have repeatedly expressed cynical attitudes towards the PPP. They see Cheddi as being controlled by Janet and they seriously doubt whether the PPP will ever achieve political power in Guyana. The relationship with PNC is deteriorating and all the prospects are that they will get worse. In the case of Jamaica, they had a pretty good relationship with Manley while he was in power - constantly being aware of the fact that he was a committed SI man. Now they understand that the PNP has taken an anti-communist turn and the relationship is likely to go the way of the PNC. I am not clear as to their views on the WPJ They think of Munroe as a dedicated hard-working communist who, although a bit overoptimistic, may have a future. They have also made the point that the WPJ is "larger" than the CPJ.

So this is the nature of the experience of the Department in which we are placed. This Department has three people working in it - Nicholai Kostovets, Dimitry Muravjev and Sergi Semivolos - in that order of priority. Nicholai is x well known to our Comrades as a brambler. Here, he is regarded as an old loyal CPSU member who has become increasingly less dynamic in his old age. The other two, though having youth on their side, operate in the shadow of Nicholi and this no doubt influences their performance xxxxx and possibly image as well. It is important to note that none of these comrades have any post in the CC. They are described as "officials working in the CC offices". This then, is the character of the officials of this Department in which we are placed. The only Embassy

EMBASSY OF GRENADA IN THE USSR

Dobryninskaya Ulitse 7
Apartment 221
Moscow
USSR

Telephone
237-25-41
237-94-05

that they deal with here in Moscow is Guyana - and they have a very occasional relationship with the Ambassador. They have no experience of dealing with parties of socialist orientation which are in power. This is compounded by the fact that the Caribbean - as they repeatedly state (though often in different contexts) is very distant from them. It is, quite frankly, not one of their priority areas, and this is reinforced by their interest in reducing the areas of conflict with the USA. Furthermore, the CPSU has historically been very cautious in developing relations with parties that are new to them. This is due to their bitter experiences in places like Egypt, Somalia and to a lesser degree Bangladesch and Chile. For all these reasons, if Grenada is to become more central to the CPSU in terms of its thinking and planning we will have to demonstrate:

1. Stability - in terms of policy and line
2. Clear and consistent socialist orientation
3. An interest in developing relations.

Stability - this provides the possibility of predictibility of behaviour. My own view is that we have fulfilled this criterion admirably. Our leadership personnel has been stable and the line enunciated has been consistent. We have developed an international reputation for balance and rationality xxx while at the same time being "perpendicular revolutionaries" as Fidel once described Maurice. Our principled positions are widely admired.

Clear and consistent Socialist Orientation. This manifests itself in the pursuit of state and party policies. The orientation of the economy especially in the areas of - non-capitalist orientation, planning, co-operative development, the profitable development of the state sector - are very important indicators. The structure and development of the xxxx Party is also critical. They were originally concerned about our SI connection. I think that this has been properly and satisfactorily explained. But it is important to keep them informed - if possible ahead of time of any moves that we might make in that forum. The structure of the Party and in particular our links with the mass organizations, is quite satisfactory to them. They need to be more comprehensively informed however about the steps that are being taken to make the NJM a Marxist-Leninist Party. They understand our tactics, but they want to be assured that we are moving in the right direction. These matters need to be discussed at the highest level possible - I would say at the level of Panomarev or at the very least Chernjaev.

As far as our foreign policy is concerned, our clear anti-imperialist stand is indisputable and our consistency on Afganistan in particular xxxxxx must be appreciated although it has never been mentioned to me.

An interest in developing relations. They view the establishment of our Embassy here as the clearest sign of this. It is strange how purely state matters do in fact influence their perceptions on certain matters. Our slowness in taking up the offers made to us in the area of Party education and in the area of these ten comrades who were invited for 1981 has clearly been xxx a mark against us, but the presence of our Party, military and University students here has served to redeem matters a great deal. Also Selwyn's invitation for a "top party delegation" to come to Grenada at the end of February is critical as well as our undertaking to send a delegation of mass organization leaders to the USSR in May. Coming back to the linkage between the state and party on the one hand, xxx and the mass organizations and the party on the same hand, the development of state to x state relations has definitely helped in the development of party to party relations - this is particularly so in the area of planning and trade. Equally, our active participation in the Prague Assembly for Peace in June 1983 is critical. I would recommend that our Peace Council undertakes some mobilizational activity in preparation for this most important event in the 1983 Peace Callender. The links with the Trade Unions, Women and Youth which are growing should be strengthened. All these go into the pot in assessing the nature of our Party and the quality of our relations with the USSR and the CPSU.

The role of the Embassy personnel is critical in this area. We have to xxx

EMBASSY OF GRENADA IN THE USSR

Dobryninskaya Ulitsa
Apartment 221
Moscow
USSR

3

Telephone.
237-25-41
237-99-05

establish ourselves as the point of reference for the English-speaking Caribbean. Even before that we have to establish the Caribbean as an important area of interest for the CPSU. It will not become a priority area in a hurry but we have to impress upon them the importance of the area. This can be done by two methods; ~~xxxx~~ 1. Having regular meetings with the CPSU comrades so as to keep the Caribbean - and in particular Grenada - on their minds. 2. Sharing a deep knowledge of the Caribbean area with them. Point 1. has already been established. Over the last year we have had sufficient material to sustain serious monthly meetings. I anticipate that this will continue in the new year. But it goes without saying that the more Party to Party communication and activity we have the more profoundly will grow the relationships. For this reason, I would recommend that we schedule at least two official party missions - learning tours - to the Soviet Union in 1983 similar to the May mission planned by Mobilization. So far the plans call for the following Party activities this year.

-Late February CPSU party delegation goes to Grenada
-mid May NJM delegation of mass organizations come to the USSR
- Early September NJM Party students arrive in USSR
~~xxxxxx~~ - June/July NJM delegations for rest and recreation and familiarization arrives in the USSR
June/July - CPSU delegation goes to Grenada for rest and recreation.

In addition to this we may have some NJM Comrades coming to learn movie projection and/or management of book store. We may also have a Trade Union delegation coming for May Day. I would strongly recommend that we also programme a Women anf Youth delegation for 1983.

As far as point 2 is concerned, Comrade Coard's visit was critical in giving us an indepth insight into the situation in Surinam. We were able to share this information with the CPSU comrades who appreciated it very much. Comrade Strachan also gave us some deep analysis of the situation in St. Vincent and Surinam which was of great assistance. However, we must develop a more systematic method of keeping us informed of regional developments. I would suggest that a monthly report be prepered by the Party Secretariate for the information of this embassy dealing with Party developments in the region as well as in Grenada. Of course we would like to know as much as possible, but the points of greatest interest would be: Suriname, Belize, Trinidad, Jamaica, Guyana - in that order. Portions of this information could also be used to keep our students informed of developments "back home". I think that this is a feasible and modest proposal that will go a long way towards improving our information and developing the relations between the NJM and the CPSU.

So far all our meetings with the CPSU have been in the nature of business meetings. In the new year we want to schedule a few policy meetings where we would be able to get an appreciation of the CPSU's position on the situation in Poland, Rumania and Hungary for example so as to be able to inform you of these policy orientations. This will dove-tail nicely with the similar meetings we have already arranged for the Foreign Ministry. But it cannot be overstressed that the greatest benefit would come from a policy orientation which cannot be successfully accomplished unless we are fed with the necessary information.

We have been concerned about the fact that even when we have top PB members here, they have been received by relatively low level people. This has been the case with Comrades Austin, Louison and Strachan. In the case of Comrade Strachan, I campaigned extensively to ensure that he was received "at least by an alternate member of the PB" as I insisted at the time. Nicholi and Company clearly have limited pull. I therefore met with the Chief of Protocol who is known to be very close to the leadership here, as well as with the Cuban, Mozambiquan, ~~xxxxxx~~ Ethiopian, Angolan and Nicariguan Ambassadors. As it turned out, they also have had similar problems. From these conversations it emerged that these countries have had many PB visits to the USSR, but the USSR has had very few, if any to their countries. The most persuasive

4

explanation I heard for this experience is that the CPSU leadership is old and cannot do much traveling. All of the comrades however, cautioned that it takes TIME to develop the kind of relationship that would lead to the exchange of PB members. The Kampuchian Ambassador suggested that on the basis of their experience, a Party Congress and fotmal Party Platform and programme is essential before the closest ~~xxxxx~~ PB to PB relations are established. While that might have some credence, I don't put much store in that explanation since we have never ever received any hint of this kind. Recently the Cuban Ambassador came to see me. He told me that he had raised the matter of our Party to Party relations with Carlos Raffael Rodreguez who had said that Cuba had taken fifteen years to establish close PB to PB relations and we must work at it with patience and determination while constantly making the protocol point of PB member receiving our PB member. His basic point is that the whole process takes time, but that time will be shotrened if we press and act appropriately.

As it turned out in the case of Selwyn, he met with the same Alternate ~~xx~~ CC man that George and M.A. had met with before - Chernjaev. The reality is that Chernjaev was able to deal with all the matters that Comrade Strachan raised in a very authoritative manner. Principally these were matters of collaboration - matters that had been raised before and for which we ~~xx~~ were awaiting replies. These are without doubt substantive matters which reflect the nature of the relationship between the NJM and CPSU. But inorder to get to the top people, we have to put our discussions on a policy basis. Here it is cl that time is critical. They need to develop confidence in our alalysis and our own imp For example, I could see us engainig in a policy analysis of the best approach to take to the situation in Jamaica or Surinam. But I think that it would be easier to make an input in relation to the out of power parties, trade unions and other ~~xxxxxxxx~~ associational interest groups. This is why all our activities and contacts are closely inter-related. This is why too, we need to be fed with information of a high analytical character.

The principal recommendations therefore would be:

1. Promote at least one interchange visit per year with each mass organization. The Comrades who come to the USSR on these visits must be propetly briefed in relation to the policies of the NJM and the nature and stage of the revolution. They should at all times pay a visit to the Embassy to be briefed on the very latest developments and to be exposed to some orientation.
2. Promote state to state interchanges especially in the areas of planning and co-operatives.
3. Implement the Party to Party agreement especially in the area of Party Scholarships and Rest and Recreation and Familiarization tours. Here again the Comrades must be properly briefed.
4. Seek to develop policy discussions as frequently as possible. For example,
   1. The relationship with the trade unions in the Caribbean.
   2. The role of the NWC in promoting the Peace programme in the Caribbean.
   3. The potential of the youth movements in the various islands
   4. The character of the Caribbean Press and our role in this.
   5. Assistance to Parties with potential in the Caribbean.
   6. Common policies in relation to particular countries.
5. Institute a programme of providing high level information to the Ambassador a regular monthly basis.

NEW DEVELOPMENTS

There are two new develoments now:

1. Comrade Whiteman will pay a "Working visit"to the USSR on 12th. March
2. A two man team has been named to go to Grenada on 6th. March.

No.1 We have requested that Comrade Whiteman be received by his opposite number - Comrade Gromyko for "high level policy discussions". The Officials in the 1st Latin America Department (this is the state sector that deals with Grenada) of the Ministry of Foreign Affairs has responded that they do not know if Gromyko will be in Moscow at the time. We have said that if Gormyko is not available tyen the Minister will me with his First Deputy. They say that they will try their best, and I believe that th will. The Head of the 1st Latin American Department - Kasimeriov - has far more pull the State level than Nickoli has at the Party level. They have been very helpful to us on a number of matters - the latest of which is arranging the tickets for Comrade Whiteman and intervening with the Ministry of Civil Aviation on our behalf to advance the time of departure of ~~xxxxxxxx~~ the Comrade Minister's plane from Cuba so as to make it possible for him to get the flight to Vietnam - no mean feat!!

5

But even with the best will in the world, they still may not succed in achieving our objectives. In such circumstances, I would recomment that we pitch the discussions at as high a policy level as possible to impress upon them the fact that discussions with a member of the PB of the NJM cannot be dealt with at a low level.

If the meeting takes place at such a low level that the State man cannot deal wit Party matters, it will then be necessary to have a separate meeting with the Party as we Such a meeting should be similarly handled. The details of the implementation of agreeme etc should be left to the Ambassador or other officials while high policy matters should be considered by the PB member.

No.2 Comrade Strachan had specifically requested that a "high party delegation" visit Grenada at the time of maximum mobilizational activity so as to advise the Party leaders on how best to improve planning and organization. The delegation of two which has been selected is of a definite low level. Of the three members of the Section dealing with Grenada, the most junior one - Sergi Semivolos - has been selected. The leader of the team is the Deputy Head of the Department of Science Education - who as far as I could see is one notch below Nicholi - the Head of our Department. I would guess that neither of these dellows have ever met Andropov to speak to. Needless to say both of them are officials in the CC who have no rank in the Party besides - member or Candidate Member!!

Now we are faced with somewhat of a dilemma. We had promised that the high party delegation would meet with our Party leaders for substantive discussions. Now we have a low party delegation how do we treat them? The trouble is that as low as they are, they are the best contact that we have. While in my view they cannot contribute to any dramatic development in Party to Party relations, they can have a negative effect if the produce an unfavourable report. So we have to work to ensure a highly favourable assessm while at the same time not giving them carte blanche access to our leadership. Thus for example, I would restrict them to a short - ½ hour - courtesy call to the Chairman of the EB of the CC. And they should get to know in no uncertain terms that we had expected someone higher than they.

In conclusion, I would say that I have become converted to the concept of [illegible]. It seems to me quite clear that we have to work on the Soviets for some considerable tim before we reach to the stage of relationships that, for example, we have with the Cubans. But I am confident that our objectives will be achieved. The key thing is to make oursel indispensable as the most authoritative and informed people on a critical region of the world...authoritative, informed, reliable and influential!!

Document 6

.MBASSY OF GRENADA IN THE USSR

.olruninskaya Ulitsa 7
partment 221
.oscow
.SSR

Telepho
237-25..
237-99-.

Typed personally by W.Richard Jacobs.
Distribution as follows: Minister Unison Whiteman
PM
Deputy PM Coard
PB Member Ewart Layne who is in the USSR

11th. July 1983

EMBASSY OF GRENADA IN THE USSR

Dobryninskaya Ulitsa 7
Apartment 221
Moscow
USSR

CONFIDENTIAL

Telephone
237-25-41
237 99-05

Grenada's relations with the USSR

Our relations with the USSR are influenced by a number of inter- connecting factors. Among the more important are:
1. Perceived ideological direction of the NJM Party and the PRG.
2. The management of state affairs.
3. The development of state to state relations.
4. Grenada's role in the world (region).
5. Our relationship with other members of the socialist community.
6. Relationship between the NJM and CPSU.
7. Our activity in international organizations.

Perceived ideological direction - ~~kxx~~ PRG

Grenada is regarded as being on the path of socialist orientation. There is a general acceptance among Soviet authorities that we are at the national democratic, anti-imperialist stage of socialist orientation. The USSR assigns a special place to these types of countries in its foreign policy. This is, of course, also the case with other socialist countries. In terms of their priorities, the countries of socialist orientation come right after the socialist community. Therefore, whatever, the internal debate, it is important that we continue to maintain our public assessment of our stage of development as the national democratic, anti-imperialist stage of socialist orientation. After all the PM himself made that assessment when he was here in Moscow as well as during his visit to Berlin. This has recently been reinforced by the Foreign Minister during his visit to Vietnam, Kampuchia and Laos. So it seems to me absolutely necessary that we maintain this line. This is made all the more important by the very high priority that is placed on consistency of analysis here.

- NJM

The Comrades responsible for Grenada in the International Section, have told me that they operate on the basis that the NJM is a "communist party". Given the relatively low level of these comrades (Nicholi etc.) one is not too sure about the authoritativeness of this statement though, I doubt that they would make a statement like that without the necessary authority. In any event, my clear impression is that we are being treated as a fraternal party - ie a M-L Party. My impression too, is that the CPSU delegation that visited in March formed a positive impression of the work of the NJM and have communicated that impression. The CPSU is ~~a~~ in a position to know almost everything about the NJM its size, programme, objectives, orientation etc. and they cannot fail to recognize and accept the authenticity of our credentials. The problem of protocol - the proper level at which our leaders should be met etc. remains. This could perhaps be explained on two levels: 1. They sometimes adopt an over-protective attitude towards us and argue that if we meet at too high a level the USA would use this as an excuse to further squeeze Grenada.(This is one of the explanations floated as to why the PM did not meet with Andropov in April)2. Although we are regarded as a fraternal party we are not in the "inner group" ie members of the socialist community - their highest party officials are reserved for these kinds of encounters. Their answer as to why Nicaragua is treated differently - and at a higher level - would presumably be that Nicaragua is already under direct US attack and it is necessary for them to openly show solidarity. They would like Grenada to avoid that direct attack. The core of the matter however, is that they regard Grenada as a small distant country and they are only prepared to make commitments to the extent of their capacity to fulfill, and if necessary, defend their commitment. (I recall on one occasion explaining the situation in St. Vincent to the Party comrades. Their response was that this is all very interesting but St. Vincent is so far away!!)

2

Recommendations
1. The Soviets have a correct perception of our ideological line both at the Government and Party levels. We should continue along these lines.
2. The problem of "protocol" has to be solved but it must be handled gently. At the diplomatic level, we could keep on insisting that counterparts meet. To the extent that this is not achieved, the principals would mention it in passing - not a substantive point, just in passing. We must not fail to mention the matter to their Ambassador at social activities. Gestures are also important - cutting conversations short with juniof people etc. Receprosity is also important. BP Members should not be easily available to low-ranking Soviet officials on visits. As a rule, the PM in particular, and I would also say the Deputy PM should only entertain courtesy calls not exceeding 15 to 30 minutes.

The management of state affairs
The Soviets have been burnt quite often in the past by giving support to Governments which have either squandered that support, or turned around and become agents of imperialism , or lost power. One is reminded of Egypt, Samolia, Ghana and Peru. They are therefore very careful, and for us sometimes maddingly slow, in making making up their minds about who to support. They have decided to support us for two main reasons. 1. Cuba has strongly championed our cause. 2. They are genuinely impressed with our management of the economy and state affairs in general. They are impressed with our commitment to planning, the absence of corruption, the ethic of hard work among the leadership, the ability of the leadership to spread this ethic among the population, the willingness to sacrifice.They are also impressed with the policy on the communication media, the close links with the masses, the practice of popular democracy and the implementation of the policy of democratic centralism as a guiding principle and not a dogma. Also of importance is the stability of our leadership.
Recommendation
The Soviets are very impressed with our management of state power. We should continue along this line with a continuing emphasis on the "step by step" approach.

Development of State to State Relations
The principal item here is the implementation of the Agreements signed in July 1982. In the area of Trade and Collaboration - this is generally being implemented in accordances with the agreements. Some collaboration agreements however, have been delayed as a result of procrastination on our part.In ~~xxx~~ particular, the sattelite dish agreement has not yet been signed by our side. As far as the Soviets are concerned, this is the centerpiece of our July agreements, the only negotiable items in it are how we house and transport the technicians, and how we pay them in local currency. The other items are fixed. The credit for this project cannot be utezlised for any other project. We really need to get on with this matter. The same holds true for the Fifteen Teachers project. In any event, the reasons for not signing these agreements promptly, sould be routinely communicated to the Embassy. We are not infrequently faced with the question as to what is the state of affairs on this or that project and we are plac in the very embarassing possition of not being able to answer. Meanwhile, our Soviet colleagues who ask these questions often know the answer because their Embassy in Grenada has informed them. But even with these shortcomings, I would say that we are OK in this area of trade and collaboration.

State to state relations are also fundamentally influenced by the development of relations in other fields as well. We have a good record of collaboration at the military and trade union levels. These are positive factors in the development of our state to state relations. A lot more could be done at the NWO and Peace levels. It is important always to remember that plans for visits and interchanges should be made at least one year in advance. The NYO level is developing ~~satisfacto~~ satisfactorily.

One of the most difficult areas is at the University and Technical education levels. As in all the above, the Soviets assess the level of state to state relatic by, among other things, ~~by~~ the extent to which we are willing to share our experiences with them, and learn from their experiences. When trade unionists, youth, women and pioneers come to study in the USSR, we are in effect signaling

3

to them that we recognize that we can learn from their experiences and thereby sending the correct ideological message as well. The same holds true for our University and technical students. The presence of ten of our top planners has made a very favourable impact on the develeopmwnt of our state to state relations. But the same is not true in the area of the University and Technical education. To date we have been offered 80 (eigthy) University or Technical scholarships - 20 in 1981, 20 in 1982 and 40 in 1983. We have accepted eighteen (18) of which two of our students have given up the course. Of the remaining sixteen (16) at least eight (8) do not have the minimum requirements for entry to the level of education they expected to receive upon leaving Grenada. This, it seems to me, is requesting more than we know that we can absorb. It is much better to ask for five scholarships and fill four than to ask for 40 and send only four people. This gives the impression, false as it may be, that our students prefer not to study in the USSR. It introduces a certain question mark and works in a negative way on state to state relations. Of course, it need hardly be mentioned that the behaviour of our students can also have an effect on state to state relations, and we must therefore be careful to select highly motivated students.

The establishment of the Grenada-Soviet Friendship society has a positive effect on our relations. It is now critical that this organization function.

State to state relations are very seriously affected by the use that is made of the aid and assistance rendered to Grenada at the material and technical levels. In the case of technicians, it is important that proper provisions be made for their stay in Grenada and they be fully utilized for the entire time of their stay in Grenada. In general we have received very good feed-back on this aspect and the technicians are full of praise for the enthusiasm and commitment of their Grenadian hosts.

In the case of the use of materials, the feedback has also been generally good. But there have evidently been some lapses, and we must always take care to ensure that we order the correct item with full information and specifications for everything associated with its use. The case of the first set of tractors which arrived without the necessary attachments simply because the Soviets did not know what "attachments" we were talking about; the case of waterpumps going unused because of no hose; and the case of military vehicles without spare-parts in part because of poor specifications on our part - all contribute to a negative impression. There seems to have been some slip-up also in relation to the AN-2. The information needed for certification should certainly have been requested before the completion of the assembly of the plane. The Soviets have serious concerns about the operation and maintenance of the AN-26. We have assured them that we have a suitable stand-by agreement with the Cubans on this one, but it is urgent that we select and despatch as soon as possible ten(10) people - at least - to be trained for the operation and maintenance of this aircraft.

An important aspect of the development of state to state relations is the operation and functioning of the Embassy. All countries use the quality and quantity of personnel assigned as diplomatic staff to particular Embassies as an indication of the nature of a country's priorities in domestic and international affairs. The Soviet Union is no expeption in this regard. Their own Embassy in Grenada is not only an indication of their resource base, but equally a reflection of the fact that they have considerable interest in the development of relations with Grenada.

I have on a previous occasion pointed out that for any Embassy to operate efficiently, the following officers are absolutely essential - Ambassador, Deputy (at the level of 1st. Secretary or above) Secretary to the Ambassador, Accountant. This is emphasized even more in the case of the Embassy in Moscow by the fact that the Ambassador is accredited to nine other countries - GDR, Bulgaria, Checoslovakia, Hungary, Korea, Rumania, Mongolia, Poland, Yougoslavia and Afghanistan - ten in fact - and at least the first five plus the USSR are countries with which we have some serious relations. This means that the job requires a lot of travel. Both inside and outside of the USSR, I would say that about 60% of the Ambassador's work is representational. This responsibility requires two essential elements 1. Information from Grenada 2. Sophisticated analyses of the information available from each country. The first one is lacking but I am confident that a political decision can correct this situation. The second requires a person of high cultural level with some formal training and/or experience in international

4

relations. Equally, we need someone with the appropriate training to undertake the task associated with the maintenance and development of our trading relations with the socialist community. Because of the structure of the diplomatic corps in the USSR both of these people need to be at the level of 1st. Secretary or above. We have a mountain of experience in the proper selection of these people. The fact is that a trained person can absorb and apply the experience to which he exposed in a creative way. An untrained person can be little more than a messenger, and length of service becomes a repetative experience. It is important too, to recognize that particularly in the socialist community, training is highly valued and contributes to the development of the kind of prestige necessar to achieve our objectives.

All members of our leadership with whom I have raised this matter of staffin agree that we need additional staff at the Embassy in Moscow. This matter should be given the most urgent attention. Inadequate staff prevents this Embassy from developing state to state relations to the level necessary to preserve and advanc our interests.

I mentioned earlier about the representational role of the Ambassador and th need for information for this task to be properly performed. I wish to draw on th example of the PM's recent mission to the USA. I was in the GDR at the time of th mission and I happened to hear on VOA a report of the PM's mission just before a meeting with the Foreign Ministry. The PM's mission turned out to be the main item on the agenda. Iwas able to handle the issue because as part of the information package on the March mobilization, the PS (Foreign Affairs) had sent an up-to-date package on our relations with the USA. When I returned to Moscow, the issue was raised by Kazimirov - Director of the First Latin American Department - who handles Grenada's affairs in the Foreign Ministry. Basically, he wanted to know what was the nature of the meeting with Clark. I told him that thus far the results are confidential. He said to me in the usual light vein of t types of conversations that if he were friends with the American Ambassador he could get the information from him!! The basic point that he successfully got ove to me is that in the circumstances of our relations with the USSR and their and our relations with the USA, it would have been courteous to inform them of the intention to visit. I agree with that. The contents of the discussion with Clark is another matter since, among other things, I am certain that the USA could break our code if they wanted to. Kasimirov told me that he first read of the visit in the newupapers and that he first heard that the PM had a meeting with Clark when the Canadian Ambassador,who was on a visit to his office, mentioned it to him. I feel sure that either his Ambassador in Grenada or USA would have informed him of this but the basic point that he is making is that he would have expected the information to come from me.

The other piece of information which is really crucial for our state to stat relations deals with the IMF loan that I understand that we are negotiating or ha signed. Now, when the PM raised the possibility of a US$6million with Gromyko in April he made the point that we could get the money nowhere else. I have been monitoring the response here and the latest thing that they told me is that we may get a reply by mid July. I assume that the IMF loan has nothing to do with th airport project and therefore we are still going ahead with the US$6 million request which is strictly for the airport. But this is only an educated guess on my part, I have no hard information, and it would have been appropriate to let the Soviets know through our Embassy here that we were about to apply for thi loan. Of course, as I understand it, they have no problem with us going to the IMF. But the communication of this kind of information adds to a stable, reliable friendly state to state relations atmosphere. And equally important, it developes an expectation of resoprosity - they will give us information in the future

__Recommendations__

1. We should make every effort to implement all collaboration and personnel-exchange agreements. In the case of personnel exchange, when it is not possible for the Grenada party to fulfill the agreement, the Embassy must be promptly informed. No individual should arrive in the USSR without previously informing the Embassy.

2. Both the Embassy and an appropriate Unit in the Ministry of Trade should monitor the implementation of trade agreements on a monthly basis and exchange this information.The Embassy and the Misnistry of Planning should do the same thi

5

with other collaboration agreements.(I have in the past received such a monitoring report from the Macro-Planning Unit. But only on one occasion.)
3. We should as a matter of principle never request materials and opportunities that we are not in a position to utilize within a defined period.
4. A political decision should be immediately communicated to the International Department of the Party or the PS(Foreign Affairs) to keep the Embassy informed on all important issues.
5. Urgent steps be taken to recruit three new members of the diplomatic staff for the USSR Embassy with the appropriate qualifications.

Grenada's role in the world (region)

By itself, Grenada's distance from the USSR, and its small size, would mean that we would figure in a very minute way in the USSR's global relationships. Our revolution has to be viewed as a world-wide process with its original roots in the Great October Revolution.For Grenada to assume a position of increasingly greater importance, we have to be seen as influencing at least regional events. We have to establish ourselves as the authority on events in at least the English-speaking Caribbean, and be the sponsor of revolutionary activity and progressive developments in this region at least. At the same time, we have to develop and maintain normal state to state relations with our neighbours and concretely operationalise our good-neighbourlyness policy. The twice per year meetings with the progressive and revolutionary parties in the region is therefor critical to the development of closer relations with the USSR. Inorder to keep both the Embassy and the Soviets informed of the outcome of such meetings, perhap a good model would be for a member of the CC to pay a visit to the USSR after each such meeting. The mission of such a person could without difficulty be mixed with other activities. We must ensure though that we become the principal point of access to the USSR for all these groups even to the point of having our Embassy serve as their representative while in the USSR.

Equally important is our relationship with those neighbours who the Soviets regard as our potential adversaries. We have not been making a big deal of the Regional Defence Force but the Soviets never fail to mention that to their mind this is one of the most serious future dangers that we face. It is perhaps possible to use the GG on some kind of good-will mission to the other islands as a prelimilary to the signing of some type of treaty of Friendship and Co-operation with them.It seems to me too, that we need to maintain a high diplomati profile in these islands.

Of all the regional possibilities, the most likely candidate for special attention is Surinam. If we can be an overwhelming influence on Surinam's international behaviour, then our importance in the Soviet ~~xxxxxx~~ scheme of thing will be greatly enhansed. To the extent that we can take credit for bringing any other country into the progressive fold, our prestige and influence would be grea enhansed. Another candidate is Belize.I think that we need to do some more work in that country.

Recommendations

1. Establish a system of informing the Soviets of the outcome of the meetings between NJM and the progressive parties in the region.
2. Maintain these party to party meetings.
3. Examine the possibility of concluding fotmal treaties of Friendship and co-peration with our neighbours.
4. Explore ways and means of influencing the international behaviour (voting at UN etc) of Surinam and Belize.

Our relationship with other members of the socialist community

It is well to remember that there is a constant and very detailed consultatio process that takes place between members of the socialist community. For example, on my recent mission to the GDR (June 1983) they made it very clear to me that they had been briefed on the PM's discussions with Gromyko, and this is to be expected.As a result, our performance in verious aspects of our relations with members of the socialist community directly affects our relations with the USSR - not to mention the fact that it directly determines the relationship between Grena and the country involved.

There have been some positive points that has promoted our image throughout t

6

socialist community. Among the most recent are: 1. The excellent to very good performance of our students who went to the CPSU Party school -this has become generally known. 2. The excellent contribution made by comrade DeRiggs and the generally good impression made by the Grenada delegation at the Berlin Conference on Karl Marx - this is a constant cause of congratulations in various countries. (Incidentally, as a further indication of the communication problem, it is worth noting that I have not yet received a copy of this presentation which I am sure will serve as a good guide of policy.) 3. The fact that I have been presenting credentials and participating in the important occasions of the states involved. But there have also been negative factors. I think chief among them is the very slow process of implementing the agreements signed between Grenada and Bulgaria and GDR. This is very bad for our relations with the countries involved as well as for the USSR because they not only look at the process of implementation of our bi-lateral agreements with them, but also with the rest of the community. In particular, the GDR has floated the view with me that we appear to want to rewrite a solomn agreement agreed to by their President and our PM. (This refers principally to the methodof paying for the bananas.) This, to them, is entirely inconceivable. My own view is that once the agreement is signed at that level, there is no going back and even if it is disadvantageous to us we just have to implement it. It is indescent to be seen as wanting to revisean agreement arrived by the two Heads of Government. I have no evidence that this view ~~xxxxxxxx xxxxxxxxxxxxxx~~ regarding our apparent desire to revise a solomn agreement has been communicated to other members of the community, but I would be very surprised if it has not. In any event, I ~~x~~ have not formed the impression that there is any such generalised view within the commubity and it is of course in our interest to ensure that we retain the reputation as honest brokers who keep their word regardless. It is worth noting also that any effort to revise an agreement signed by the two Heads of Government below the level of Heads of Government will be next to impossible and could only serve to undermine the prestige and authority of the office of the Prime Minister.

~~xxxxxxxxxxxxxxxxxxxxxxxxxxxxxx~~

As far as the relations with the other socialist countries are concerned, it is useful to have our people visit there as frequently as possbile as well as to have state officials visit us as frequently as possible. I think that officials who travel to Eastern Europe should as a matter of policy include on their itinnary, at least one other socialist country in a planned and rotational way so that we get to touch as many bases as possible. If we are informed of such visits atleast ten days in advance, we can get the host country, I am sure, to stand most of the costs. The benefits to us will be very great. As a rule, our officials have made a very ~~xxxxxxxx~~ positive impression on their hosts.

<u>Recommendations</u>

1. Continue high profile, well prepared participation in important events of the socialist community eg Karl Marx Conference and World Peace Council
2. Implement agreements between Grenada and other members of the socialist community promptly and faithfully.
3. Encourage officials to visit at least two countries in Eastern Europe during official missions to this part of the world.

<u>Party to Party Relations</u>

In the socialist community, it has emerged that there is a very close inter-relationship between party to party and state to state relations. Many of the things that the Party was able to arrange in Cuba (eg airline tickets and special considerations of several kinds) are passed on to the state here. Further, as we discovered during the PM's mission and after, there is such an intimate linkage between the party and state at all levels, and notably at the highest levels that the distinctions that we have been inclined to make are not applicable in the socialist community.

One of the direct consequances of this is that the perception of party to party relations is fundamentally influenced by the nature of state to state relations and it is important to constantly keep this in mind.

Of course the implementation of the party to party agreements is paramount. By and large, we have implemented these agreements faithfully. Our first batch of party school students, although they were some two years late, have made a very good impression. Our implementation of the rest and recreation agreements have

7

has been good for our relations. But there are a number of negative points. I think the most telling is the fact that Comrade Strachan undertook during his mission here in December to send a team of party mobilizers to the USSR for a ocuple of weeks in May to experience the Soviet experience. As is known, these people were not sent. This did some damage which could have been minimized if we had received some instrustions to explain to the CPSU comrades that this undertaking was not possible at the moment. As it is, they cancelled it when the time ran out. Another example, has to do with the Public address system. We said that we needed it urgentl for March 13th. 1983. They rushed it down by air to Cuba at the end of January, as promised, and the P.A. system stayed in Cuba far a very long time. I am not even sure if it has arrived as yet. They have brought this matter to our attention on a number of occasions, we have sent messages to Cuba and Grenada to try and co-ordinate our excuses by we have received no response.

We have to insist too that they stick to their agreements. For example, they agreed with Comrade Strachan to send down to Grenada "a high level delegation" - in March 1983 - you know of course, the very low level that was sent. They also agreed to send two people for rest and recreation in 1983, and we must make sure, that they stick by their agreement. They have also fallen down in relation to their undertakings to supply books, magazines, newspapers, films and projection equipment for the political education programme. We have to stick them to their word. I can raise it here at the diplomatic level but it will be twice as effective when it is repeated at the party political level.

The problem of what might be called counterpart protocol remains. That is, we have never been able to meet with our strict counterparts at the party level when we have our leaders here. On 27th. June, I had a very frank and friendly discussion with Boyko Demitrov - the former Bulgarian Ambassador to Grenada who is now Director of International Relations in the Party. He told me that even Bulgaria sometimes faces this problem and that Grenada has to face the reality that it is a question of size, distance and priorities. I think that he is correct. But we then have to deal with these realities. Inorder to elevate our priority in the socialist scheme of things, the recommendations contained in the section dealing with our role in the world (region) becomes all the more relevent. In addition, we have to raise and discuss with the highest authorities, <u>global and regional</u> issues rather than parochial or national issues. In other words, our legitimate begging operations have to be cast in the larger world context. We have in fact done this in the past quite successfully, linking our national requests to a global analysis. What we need to do now, it seems to me, is to become the spokesman for a broader constituency - perhaps the countries of socialist orientation. It is in this context that I have prepared the attached paper dealing with a bank of last resort sponsored by the socialist community for countries for socialist orientation. This will give us an opportunity to dicsuss the highest issues of policy both with the countries of socialist orientation and with the socialist community, lift our profile, and highten our priority. Here we can clearly see the close link between party to party and state to state relations.

All that is said about the CPSU holds true for the other parties as well. We have a very sympathetic hearing in Bulgaria with Boyko Demitrov and we should parhaps draw ever closer to the Bulgarian Party.

In the GDR, we also have made a good impression and there is great sympathy there for the NJM. Four comrades will be coming for rest and recreation in 1983.

I doubt that we will encounter the protocol problems that we have found in the CPSU. But we must at all cost continue to regard relations with the CPSU as the highest priority.

<u>Recommendations</u>

1. Strictly implement all agreements and insist on implementation on the other sides as well.
2. Send prompt explanations when it is not possible to implement an agreement.
3. Seek to become spokesman for the countries of socialist orientation.
4. Develop even stronger relations with the Bulgarian and GDR parties by sending delegations etc.

8

International activity

From the point of view of our relations with the USSR, our international actimity is important from the following perspectives:

1. The consistency of our political line.
2. The influence of Grenada in the international community
3. The degree of support offered to the positions taken by the USSR.

Our performance is assessed at the folling levels:

1. The United Nations and its agencies - UNESCO, UNCTAD ~~ext~~ etc.
2. Organization of American States
3. Non-aligned Movement
4. Missions in various countries (Embassies).

It is very difficult for me to assess their view of our performance in the UN, its agencies and the OAS because, we receive only the minimum of information on our voting and performance ~~tax~~ etc. But during the period of the threats etc. in March 1983, they advised us to play a more active role in the UN ecpecially at the Security Council and spoke approvingly of Nicarigua's performance at the Security Council. But I suspect that we need a bigger staff at the UN to do the kind of job that would impress internationally. The same probably holds true for the OAS. They have however, ~~paxxixxax~~ praised our role in the Zone of Peace resolution and activity.

At the non-aligned movement, they have a high vlauation of our role. You will recall that before the New Delhi Conference they gave me a detailed briefing on their positions and when Comrade Whiteman visited afterwards they expressed admiration for our performance. I think however, that we must insist that we form the inner circle of the advisers to Mrs. Gandhi in line with our leading role in New Delhi especially in regard to the New International Economic Order and the Small States Conference. We have an excellent case - especially since Guyana did not participate when they were invited to in May 1983 in New Delhi. The Guyana Amba sador here tells me that the Foreign Minister decided that the Heads of Mission meeting then taking place in Guyana was more important.

As far as our Embassies are concerned, the most important thing is that they carry the same line on all matters - economic and political, internal and external. To do this successfully, we need to have a common fund of information. Obviously, each mission would have its area of specialty and would have more information on that area than any other Embassy. But a regular series of directives, instructions and information from the Party or the Foreign Ministry would ensure that a common line is maintained throughout.

As far as the role of the mission in the USSR is concerned, the reality of size came to me very early in the game. It therefore became necessary to establish ones influence in the corps by making strategic associations and alliances. Latin America - our natural constituency - lacks cohesiveness and leadership. The Dean of the Latin American group - Venezuela is lazy and uninterested in leadership. The Cuban Ambassador is not very out-going. So I have had to maintain individual relationships especially with Cuba, Nicarigua and Mexico. Ecuador is also a good man. The African group is much more cohesive and influential in Moscow. They have also been very welcoming. My informal inclusion in the group has raised Grenada's profile and influence in the corps as a whole.

The socialist countries to which I am accredited are a ~~natural~~ ^(natural) area of interest. Of these, Bulgaria is the Dean and has little time for socio-political interaction. Checoslovakia, GDR and Rumania have been particularly warm. We have it as a high priority to establish and maintain the closest personal and official relations with these countries. And although the Korean Ambassador for example, is regarded as a recluse, I have ~~x~~ had him over to dinner and he has reciprocated, as is the case with many of the others.

On the whole, I have formed the view that the USSR is satisfied with the degree of support that they receive from Grenada. Indeed, I would say that they have every reason to be satisfied especially if our vote on Afganistan for example, is recognised as one of two Latin American votes (the other being Cuba) in their favour. Considering the risks that we have taken on this and other ~~xx~~ matters, it might be fair to say that their support for us is actually below our support for them. We must therfore work to establish a balance of interests. This might best be done by gentle reminders at critical stages by members of our leadership. We might also seek to develop our links with what has ebeen called the "middle" countries like Yougoslavia and Greece for example and strengthen our links with "off centre" countries like Korea, Rumania, and Hungary. But these calculations have to be done very carefully and in a very sophisticated way. We have to think them out very carefully.

Recommendations

1. Continue our international support for the Soviet line.
2. Strengthen our political efforts in the UN and OAS and their agencies.
3. Seek a more critical role in the non-aligned movement.
4. Examine the desirability, ways and means of developing closer relations with the "middle" and "off centre" countries.
5. Provide all missions with a regular common fund of knowledge so that there can be a guarantee that a common line is being pursued on all matters.

Document 7

EMBASSY OF GRENADA IN THE USSR

Dobryninskaya Ulitsa 7
Apartment 221
Moscow
USSR

Telephone:
237-25-41
237-99-05

TO: COMRADE MAURICE BISHOP, CHAIRMAN OF THE CENTRAL COMMITTEE OF THE NEW JEWEL MOVEMENT.
FROM: COMRADE BERNARD BOURNE

I wish to express my warmest, militant regards to the Central Committee of our Party, the NEW JEWEL MOVEMENT and to you personally.

Allow me comrade, to use this opportunity to raise a matter which, in my opinion, is a necessary and urgent one. This matter concerns my area of work while operating as Minister Counsellor in the Embassy of Grenada in the Soviet Union. The fact that I have been appointed by the Political Bureau of the Central Committee of the New Jewel Movement to be the Minister Counsellor in itself is clear to me, even though I have not received a letter of appointment nor have the guidelines, terms and conditions of work been brought to my attention six months later.

Nevertheless, what concerns me and I wish to add, what bothers me from time to time, is the fact that while in Grenada I considered myself to be a senior member of the Party as I was a member of one of the leading arms of the Party - the Organising Committee and yet, neither the Political Bureau, the Central Committee nor the Secretariat has ever informed me as to whether as part of my diplomatic work I am supposed to be additionally responsible for the co-ordination of the work of the Embassy with the CPSU, KOMSOMOL, TU, etc. etc.

In my view, the diplomatic work is two-fold: STATE TO STATE and PARTY TO PARTY and MASS ORGANISATIONS. I will appreciate it and be gratified if the exact situation is made clear to me as soon as possible and in writing preferably. Additionally, and until such time that a Military Attache is appointed, it is my suggestion that security and military matters should be handled by me.

Furthermore, all that this entails concretely when it comes to the question of reports to Grenada is two reports: one to the Ministry of Foreign Affairs; the other to the Party.

Please comrade, could you or the Party clarify these points for the benefit of the diplomatic staff of the Embassy and for better organisation of our work at the soonest possible time.

In the meantime however, I wish to report on the Party Political work of the Embassy during the last two to three months. In this report, the following points will be discussed:

1. Meetings with North American and English- Speaking Caribbean Department of the CPSU;
2. Upcoming State and Party Visit;
3. Party Work of Party Members;

-2-

1. MEETINGS WITH CPSU

During the last two months comrade Ambassador and myself held three meetings with representatives of the CPSU responsible for our area. The meetings were held on April 22, May 7 and June 9. In the meetings we discussed a wide range of issues, some of which are included in this report. These points are as follows:

i Nature of our Party;
ii 60th Anniversary of the formation of the USSR;
iii Rest and familiarisation;
iv Party School;
v Party Headquaters.

i. During our first meeting the nature of our Party was raised by the Soviet side. They said that in their view NJM is a Communist Party, but what they do not understand clearly is our membership in the Socialist International. We had to point out that NJM's membership in the SI is a tactic which depends on the peculiar conditions faced by Grenada under the Gairy dictatorship and the nature of the governments in the region.

Our assessment is that our Party is not fully known; the Soviet comrades are gathering information about NJM and the peculiar conditions of the region and that is why they are dealing with us cautiously and sometimes skeptically.

However, we think that this matter would be settled during the upcoming STATE and PARTY VISIT.

ii. This year is the 60th anniversary of the formation of the USSR and this occasion will be celebrated in December. The Soviet comrades informed us that NJM would be invited to participate in this big activity. Other parties from the Eastern Caribbean, like JPM, have asked for invitations. The final decision on these invitations will be taken by the CPSU after consultations with NJM via the Embassy.

iii. With referance to an existing agreement between the CPSU and NJM, the comrades have asked us for details from Grenada of Central Committee comrades who will come for rest and familiarisation this year, 1982. It is possible for us under the agreement to send leading members of our MASS ORGANISATIONS for rest and familiarisation.

Additionally, we recommended that the CPSU should create the possibilities for comrades of the Left Parties in the region to enjoy similar facilities. To this the Soviet comrades think that it is necessary and will like to take the final decisions only after getting all necessary information from NJM.

In our assessment, our Embassy will also serve as a bridge between the CPSU and the LEFT PARTIES in the English- Speaking Caribbean. We will be decisive in their work by being able to give details of the situation in each of these countries. In that way, we are certain to develop good working relations and become a trustworthy ally of the CPSU. It goes without saying, therefore, that we will have to be supplied with details of analyses and assessments by the CC NJM and information on developments at home and in the region.

-3-

iv. On the question of attending the CPSU Party School, we were informed that ten (10) of our cadres can attend the school; they are waiting on us. The system is such that if students begin classes in September, the course will be for 9 months. Also, there are three and six months courses which begin in January and it depends on us to decide how we are to utilise the scholarships.

The comrades are pressing us to take up the scholarships. At our last meeting I promised the comrades that as of this September we will take up the offers.

(NOTE: It is my opinion and also that of other comrades that in order for the CPSU to have greater confidence, trust and reassurance in our Party and our process it is absolutely necessary that we should take up these offers and attend the Party School courses. It is important for the image of our Party, the NEW JEWEL MOVEMENT.)

v. This question of Party Headquarters was discussed during our first and second meetings. The comrades were bewildered to learn that no work had began on the construction of our Party Headquarters. Even more so, they were shocked to hear that the Cuban comrades, including PB members, did not know about the agreement to construct NJM Party Headquarters.

The Soviet Ambassadors in Havana and Kingston were to convey the decision to NJM which was done. The present problem lies in the fact that the decision was not conveyed – so it seems – to the Cubans. This is the main problem: the PCC claimed that it was not informed on any decision to provide all materials to Grenada (NJM) which will be compensated for by the CPSU.

Furthermore, the comrades of the CPSU told us that they were ready to send the materials but they hadn't any details from our side. Comrade Jacobs informed them that the details were presented to the Soviet Embassy in Cuba.

On this matter, however, there are two outstanding points to be clarified:

a. That the PCC be contacted on decision;

b. That we follow up details of materials needed to the CPSU.

Finally, in our first meeting with the CPSU, we presented to the comrades a letter from Comrade Chalkie, on behalf of the CC NJM, thanking them for the Literature which they have been sending us. We also gave them the list of materials received then and copies of 'IS FREEDOM WE MAKING', REPORT ON THE 1981 ECONOMY ...' and 'GRENADA IS NOT ALONE.' They were grateful for the little gift.

2. <u>UPCOMING STATE AND PARTY VISIT</u>

- On this subject the document on the proposed agenda for meeting with the CPSU during the visit was handed over to the Chief of the Department for North-America and the English- Speaking Caribbean, comrade Nikolai. With reference to Party to Party collaboration we would have to prepare beforehand written documents and hand over to the CPSU.

Additionally, we conveyed your desire to meet with the General Secretary, Comrade Brezhnev and asked for confirmation on all three occasions. Up to now there is no final word on that score. However, we were told that comrade Boris Ponomaryov will be present during the Party to Party discussions.

3. <u>PARTY WORK OF PARTY MEMBERS</u>

At present, the Grenadian staff of the Embassy are all within the Party. The comrades are Richard Jacobs, Marlene Bourne and Bernard Bourne.

-4-

Today only two of us are working in the Embassy. And in order to organise the work of the Embassy efficiently, we held Party Meetings- only three such meetings were held.

The other area of Party work is STUDY. Other Party cadres who are in Moscow can attend Study sessions which take place on Sundays from 9 to 12 noon. So far five (5) sessions were held, and all during the month of May. The material which we have been studying is the 'REPORT ON THE 1981 ECONOMY AND PROSPECTS FOR 1982.' We chose this material because we did not get a chance to participate in the discussions at home and we believe that it is necessary for us to be familiar with our Economy - 2nd PILLAR OF THE REVOLUTION. Further, we have decided to write up a report, which has some recommendations coming out of our studies. This report is an appendix to this note.

Finally, I wish to reiterate my desire to have greater clarity on my area of responsibility while in Moscow in the nearest future. Maybe, with such clarity, future Party reports will be sent to the relevant structure - the International Department of the Party.

With A FIRM EMBRACE,
Comrade Bernard Bourne
30th June, 1982.

Bernard J. Bourne

Document 8

AGREEMENT

on cooperation between the New JEWEL Movement of Grenada and the Communist Party of the Soviet Union

The Central Committee of the New JEWEL Movement of Grenada and the Central Committee of the Communist Party of the Soviet Union,

guided by the desire to deepen relations between the two parties in a spirit of friendship and solidarity,

noting that common commitment to the ideals of peace, national liberation, democracy and scientific socialism creates favourable opportunities for cooperation,

proceeding from common goals in the struggle against imperialism, neocolonialism, racialism and reaction in all their forms and manifestations,

reasserting their constant striving to render internationalist support to all peoples fighting for their freedom, independence and social progress,

and considering that inter-party cooperation is a most important basis for the development of friendly relations between the peoples of Grenada and the Soviet Union,

have signed the present Agreement under which both parties declare their intention:

1. Steadfastly to extend and deepen their cooperation at all levels.

2. Continuously to exchange experience in party work and party guidance of the social, economic and cultural development of their countries, including regular exchange of information and materials on the aforesaid topics.

3. Regularly to exchange delegations of party workers, to conduct consultations and exchanges of opinion on international matters, problems of the world revolutionary process and present-day social development, and other matters of mutual interest.

4. To promote cooperation in the training of party and government cadres and in furthering their political competence.

5. To develop contacts between the party press and other mass communication media, to inform the public of their countries about the activity of the two parties, and of their home and foreign policy, and resolutely to combat hostile imperialist and reactionary propaganda.

6. To promote all-round development of inter-state relations and ties between mass organisations of their countries.

7. Periodically to coordinate and implement concrete plans of inter-party ties, including initiatives that are not covered by the present Agreement.

FOR THE NEW JEWEL MOVEMENT OF GRENADA

[signature]

FOR THE COMMUNIST PARTY OF THE SOVIET UNION

[signature]

Moscow 27 July 1982

СОГЛАШЕНИЕ

о сотрудничестве между Коммунистической партией Советского Союза и партией Новое движение ДЖУЭЛ Гренады

Центральный Комитет Коммунистической партии Советского Союза и Центральный Комитет партии Новое движение ДЖУЭЛ Гренады,

руководствуясь стремлением углублять отношения между двумя партиями в духе дружбы и солидарности,

отмечая, что общая приверженность идеалам мира, национального освобождения, демократии и научного социализма создает благоприятные возможности для сотрудничества,

исходя из общности целей в борьбе против империализма, неоколониализма, расизма и реакции во всех формах и проявлениях,

подтверждая свое неизменное стремление оказывать интернационалистскую поддержку всем народам, борющимся за свою свободу, независимость и социальный прогресс,

учитывая, что межпартийное сотрудничество является важнейшей основой развития дружественных отношений между народами Советского Союза и Гренады,

подписали настоящее Соглашение, в соответствии с которым обе партии заявляют о своем намерении:

1. Неуклонно расширять и углублять свое сотрудничество на всех уровнях.

2. Постоянно осуществлять обмен опытом партийной работы, партийного руководства социальным, экономическим и культурным развитием своих стран, включая регулярный обмен информацией и материалами по указанным вопросам.

3. Регулярно обмениваться делегациями партийных работников, проводить консультации и обмен мнениями по международным вопросам, проблемам мирового революционного процесса и современного общественного развития и другим вопросам, представляющим взаимный интерес.

4. Содействовать сотрудничеству в области подготовки партийных и государственных кадров и повышения их политического уровня.

5. Развивать контакты между партийной печатью и другими средствами массовой информации, знакомить общественность своих стран с деятельностью обеих партий, их внутренней и внешней политикой, давать решительный отпор враждебной империалистической и реакционной пропаганде.

6. Способствовать всестороннему развитию межгосударственных отношений и связей между массовыми общественными организациями двух стран.

7. Периодически согласовывать и осуществлять конкретные планы межпартийных связей, включая в них и те инициативы, которые не были отражены в настоящем Соглашении.

За Коммунистическую партию Советского Союза

За партию Новое движение ДЖУЭЛ Гренады

[illegible] 1982 года

Document 9

EMBASSY OF GRENADA IN THE USSR

Dobryninskaya Ulitsa 7
Apartment 221
Moscow
USSR

Telephone
237-25-41

<u>Report of meeting with Acting Rector of the CPSU party school Gaidur Oleg K.</u>
<u>23rd. May 1983</u>

This meeting between the Acting Rector and the Ambassador was arranged at the request of the Ambassador to receive a confidential assessment of the performance of our students during the six-month course just completed.

The Acting Rector informed the Ambassador that normally, it is necessary to apply to the International Department of the CPSU inorder to receive an official report of the performance of the students. However, in this case, since this was the first batch of Grenadians students he would be prepared to make available to the Party (NJM) the confidential assessments of their teachers as well as to communicate to the Ambassador in a confidential manner, the general opinion of the teachers regarding the overall performance of our students. The Ambassador thanked the Acting Director for his cooperation in this matter and pointed out that he will also request an official report from the CPSU.

The Acting Director reported that since this was the first group of Grenadians to attend the school, it was the policy of the administrators and teachers to pay very close and careful attention to the performance and behaviour of the students. After a collective assessment of the students, he could inform the Ambassador that he was expressing the unanimous opinion of the teachers and administrators of the school.

The students fully covered the syllabus of the six month course. It was the view of the school however, that the students would have benefited more from a one year course.

As a whole the students were well disciplined and oriented towards collective work. Minor evidences of indicipline were never repeated once they had been identified and explained.

The internal relations of the group were generally good. Friction was kept to a minimum, problems were resolved in time, and due to the excellent leadership of Rita Joseph, the collective maintained a very marked cohesion throughout the course. It is worthy of note that Comrade Joseph was greatly helped in the exercise of her responsibility and authority by the following Comrades: Gordon Raeburn, Ronnie Spooner, Ian Lambert and Fabian Outram.

Comradely relations between members of the group steadily improved over the period of six months.

Attendence at classes was excellent, but punctuality was occasionally weak.

All comrades displayed a conscientious attitude towards their work.

With the sole exception of Fred Burris, our students actively participated in classroom discussions. They always adopted a very serious attitude towards the work, asked relevant questions and all except Burris have been assessed as having achieved good to excellent knowledge. Burris was satisfactory.

All the students made consistent efforts to link up the theoretical points with the tasks to which they have beed assigned by the NJM. This was particularly true of Ian Lambert, Rita Joseph and Roy Cooper.

There was a marked difference in cultural levels of the students as well as in levels of health. Both Fred Burris and Andre Mc Queen (David Gordon) were ill for long periods. A Report on Mc Queen's illness is enclosed.

The group took several good initiatives, and undertook the responsibilities associated with these initiatives. Three exapmles: Celebration of the 10th. Anniversary of the NJM, 4th. Anniversary of the Revolution, Round table solidarity Conference of the Amaricas.

As part of their practical work, the group had a permanent link with the CPSU Party committee of the October factory. They went to the factory on several occasions, participated in voluntary work on two occasions and had a lecture on the cost accounting procedures of the factory. The management of the factory was pleased with the students' performance and the students were satisfied with their

EMBASSY OF GRENADA IN THE USSR

Dobryninskaya Ulitsa 7
Apartment 221
Moscow
USSR

Telephone
237-25-41
237-99-05

experience.

The two most outstanding students were: Rita Joseph and Ian Lambert. The weekest student was Fred Burris. The teachers considered that Burris would be well placed in an area of work requiring inter-personal relations with non-intellectual workers. He can carry out instructions and is very tenacious in his determination to implement agreed procedure, but he is neither an ~~intellectual~~ intellectual nor initiator.

The Acting Rector said that the performance of our students demonstrate a real thirst for knowledge and he recommended that the NJM think very seriously about the establishment of a Party School as a top priority. He pointed out that there were very positive achievements as a result of the establishment of the Party School in Yemen, Afganistan, Angola, Mozambique and very soon Ethiopia. In this context he suggested that the NJM might think of sending students who could qualify as teachers in the future Party School.

In closing the Acting Director said that he would like to emphasize that the teachers and Administrators had come to develop great respect for the abilities of Rita Joseph as a leader. In the beginning they were a bit aprehensive about her ability to manage thirteen men and she was a bit shakey in the beginning, but as time went on, it emerged that it was a wise decision.

W. Richard Jacobs

Document 10

PARTIDO COMUNISTA DE CUBA / COMITE CENTRAL

SECRET

COOPERATION AND EXCHANGE PLAN BETWEEN THE COMMUNIST PARTY OF CUBA AND THE NEW JEWEL MOVEMENT OF GRENADA, FOR THE 1983 PERIOD.

INTRODUCTION

The Communist Party of Cuba and the New Jewel Movement, brotherly united by the same ideals of struggle in their respective countries, as well as of active solidarity in favor of the peoples that struggle for national liberation, and likewise, sharing the same convictions against imperialism, colonialism, neocolonialism, Zionism, and racism, become aware of the need to unite efforts and coordinate actions of cooperation in the different activities within their scope.

Both Parties, on agreeing that the many-sided relations of cooperation be governed by the widest and justest spirit of cooperation, solidarity, and internationalism, reach agreement on the following:

CHAPTER I

a) The CPC and the NJM will exchange delegations for the mutual study of the experiences in the different fields of Party work, according to agreements and needs that will be established between the parties. To this end, they will carry out regular meetings and exchange of experiences between the different departments and secretaries of both Parties, whose agreements and commitments will be annexed to this protocol.

PARTIDO COMUNISTA DE CUBA / COMITE CENTRAL

SECRET

2.

b) The CPC expresses its willingness to send, according to the requests formulated by the NJM in this sense, technical advisers for the organization of public meetings and propaganda of the Party in Grenada.

c) Regarding the political upgrading and professional assistance, the NJM and the CPC express their willingness to receive, at the "Ñico López" School, the NJM cadres that will be decided on mutual agreement.

d) The CPC and the NJM of Grenada will exchange information of mutual interest, both on the field of the development of the two revolutions and their experiences, as well as on the international situation and, fundamentally, that of the Caribbean in its struggle against imperialism, neocolonialism, racism and Zionism. Likewise, they will exchange information on the liberation movements as well as coordinate actions and positions of mutual interest to be adopted at events, conferences, and other Party activities of an international character, with special emphasis on the problems in the Caribbean.

e) Both organizations, vanguard of the peoples of Cuba and Grenada, express their mutual solidarity in the struggle against imperialism, and they are committed to struggle and make sure that they develop to the utmost the mutual solidarity and understanding of the International Revolutionary Movement regarding both revolutions.

f) Both [illegible] will exchange information and join efforts in strengthening their relationship with the socialist and

PARTIDO COMUNISTA DE CUBA / COMITE CENTRAL

SECRET

3.

progressive countries, and in favor of the peoples that struggle for their liberation, particularly within the Movement of Non-Aligned Countries.

CHAPTER II

On political and mass organizations:

Both Parties agree on developing to the utmost the cooperation and assistance in the development and strengthening of the mass organizations of Cuba and Grenada.

In this sense, the CPC and the NJM will promote, according to the needs of the NJM and its mass organizations, a work plan of the Workers' Central Union of Cuba, the Cuban Women's Federation, the Association of Small Farmers and the Young Communist Organization, with their counterparts in Grenada, both for the exchange of delegations, advice, and collaboration in their different fields, and for receiving cadres from these Grenadian organizations in the schools and courses of the Cuban organizations which are arranged and agreed to these purposes.

These agreements on cooperation will include exchange of information, publications, and expertise built up by them.

Likewise, they will coordinate their positions at international events and conferences, by mutually advising each other on the common interests of both Parties.

CHAPTER III

On the exchange and cooperation between both Parties:

The CPC and the NJM of Grenada will approve, control, and en-

PARTIDO COMUNISTA DE CUBA / COMITE CENTRAL

SECRET

4.

sure the fulfillment of the understandings and agreements of cooperation and exchange to be established at state level, for which they will create the mechanisms and controls that they consider relevant.

Similarly, both Parties will periodically oversee the development of the cooperation and exchange between both governments, formulating the readjustments that become necessary for practical purposes.

The CPC and the NJM will coordinate the positions of the governments of Cuba and Grenada at international events, conferences, and agencies where they participate, in attention to the political, economic and social interests of both Parties.

Besides, both Parties, through their state apparatus, will propitiate the exchange of information, publications, research, and scientific and propaganda works related to their political interests.

CHAPTER IV

On their fulfillment:

The CPC and the NJM commit themselves to inform the counterpart, in due time, the implementation of the agreed exchange plans. Also, both Parties will aprove the agreements to be established among the above mentioned political and mass organizations, making sure that they are fulfilled.

The agreements adopted in the different fields of Party life, as well as those to be concluded among the Cuban and Grenadian political and mass organizations, will be incorporated as annexes to this protocol [illegible] December 31, 19[illegible].

PARTIDO COMUNISTA DE CUBA / COMITE CENTRAL

SECRET

5.

1983 PLAN

The New Jewel Movement of Grenada and the Communist Party of Cuba, ratified the general lines established in the Coopera- tion and Exchange Plan between both Parties, and pursuant to the spirit of such Agreement, they establish the following plan for 1983:

I. The Cuban Party will recieve in 1983:

a) Five comrades with secondary educational level to study at the "Nico López" School, for one year.

b) Two technicians in drawing for specialization in mak- ing billboards and posters.

c) Two comrades for specialization in sound equipment for public meetings.

d) A press photographer for training in Cuba.

e) Training of a technician in microfilm for the press.

f) A newspaper librarian, for training in Cuba.

g) Training of a press cartoonist.

h) Training of a technician in general graphic arts.

i) Two comrades linked to the work on religion for exchang ing experiences and coordinating regional and interna- tional work.

j) Two comrades linked to the work on the Socialist Inter- national for exchanging experiences and criteria on this aspect.

PARTIDO COMUNISTA DE CUBA / COMITE CENTRAL

SECRET

6.

k) A delegation made up of three comrades of the Ministry of Mobilization who have to do with the work of Foreign Affairs, fundamentally with the Caribbean, for exchanging experiences, criteria, and coordination in the region.

l) A delegation made up of a Member of the Political Bureau and two other persons for exchanging experience on the work of organization, internal education and propaganda of the Party.

m) Two Members of the Political Bureau and two other persons, each one for one week of rest in Cuba.

n) Two Members of the Central Committee for one week of rest in Cuba.

II. The Grenadian party will recieve in 1983:

a) Two technicians in sound equipment for public meetings, to train and increase the level of their counterparts in Grenada.

b) Two technicians in billboards and posters for exchanging experience and increasing the technical level of the Grenadian comrades.

c) A delegation of two comrades from the Department of Organization forexchanging experience on the organization work of the Party.

PARTIDO COMUNISTA DE CUBA / COMITE CENTRAL

SECRET

7.

d) A srecialist in the work with the religious reorle for exchanging exreriences in the work of the Party on this sector.

e) A srecialist in internal education nlans of the Party.

PARTIDO COMUNISTA DE CUBA / COMITE CENTRAL

The Communist Party of Cuba and the New Jewel Movement of Grenada, satisfied by the discussed and agreed aspects, which fully correspond with the fraternal relations between both Parties, underwrite this document in the City of Havana, Cuba, June 29th, 1983.

The Communist Party of Cuba The New Jewel Movement

Document 11

EMBASSY OF GRENADA IN THE USSR

Dobryninskaya Ulitsa 7
Apartment 221
Moscow
USSR

Telephone:
237-25-41
237-99-05

MEETING BETWEEN CHIEFS OF GENERAL STAFF OF SOVIET ARMED FORCES AND PEOPLE'S REVOLUTIONARY ARMED FORCES OF GRENADA

DATE: Thursday 10 March 1983 (4.00pm)

Representing the Soviet side were:

1.Marshal of the Soviet Union Ogarkov N.V. -Chief of Staff
2.Colonel General N.A. Zutov -10th Department
3.LT.-General G.A. Borisov -Foreign relations Department
4.Colonel Soloviev -10th Department
5.Captain M. Globenko -Foreign Relations Department.

Present on the Grenada side were:

1.Major Einstein Louison -Chief of Staff
2.Bernard Bourne -Minister-Counsellor

The meeting commenced promptly by Marshal Ogarkov who extended a warm welcome to Major Louison. In doing so, Marshal Ogarkov enquired whether Major Louison was having any problems with his studies and living conditions.

Major Louison expressed thanks for the words of welcome and explained that he had no difficulty with studies and thought that he was making progress because there was no report to the contrary from the professors at the school.

Speaking about the Grenada Revolution Major Louison pointed out that the economy had grown by 5.5% percent in 1982 and living standards by 3 percent. He explained that the United States continues with its plans to destabilize the revolution, undermine tourism, linking our international airport with military potential and training of mercenaries in Venezuela, in addition

EMBASSY OF GRENADA IN THE USSR

Dobryninskaya Ulitsa 7
Apartment 221
Moscow
USSR

-2-

Telephone:
237-25-41
237-99-05

to the United States itself. Major Louison then emphasised that the Grenada Revolution got around these problems and still continued to make advances. He also informed Marshal Ogarkov that at the Seventh Non-Aligned Summit Grenada was again elected to the coordinating Bureau of the Movement.

At that moment Marshal Ogarkov said that he was glad for the information on Grenada. About the situation in the world Marshal Ogarkov pointed out that the United States would try now and in the future to make things difficult for progressive changes in all regions and continents. The Marshal said that over two decades ago, there was only Cuba in LAtin America, today there are Nicaragua, Grenada and a serious battle is going on in El Salvador. The Marshal of the Soviet Union then stressed that United States imperialism would try to prevent progress but that there were no prospects for imperialism to turn back history.

Moreover, Marshal Ogarkov emphasised that in an aggressive climate the military people have tasks to do. He explained that since Grenada was located close to US imperialism and was not developed militarily the Grenada Revolution would have to be specifically vigilant at all times. Furthermore, the Marshal declared that once the masses have a burning desire for progress the leadership should move ahead decisively and firmly. On that point Marshal Ogarkov assured Major Louison that the plans outlined by Prime Minister Maurice Bishop during his visit to the Soviet Union in 1982 were good and had the support of the Grenadian people.

Further still, the Marshal of the Soviet Union reminded Major Louison that the Soviet Union would contribute to raising the combat readiness and preparedness of the Armed Forces of Grenada.

EMBASSY OF GRENADA IN THE USSR

Dobryninskaya Ulitsa 7
Apartment 221
Moscow
USSR

Telephone:
237-25-41
237-99-05

-3-

He informed the Grenada Chief of Staff that according to the agreement signed in July 1982, one-third of the means for 1983 were already supplied and the rest would be delivered during this year.

In response Major Louison expressed his gratitude for the supplies sent to Grenada and mentioned that he was confident that more deliveries would be sent to Grenada in the future.

However, Major Louison explained that he wished to introduce another matter for discussion which was not included in the protocol. The Chief of Staff of Grenada explained that he was refferring to the text of a letter from Prime Minister Bishop addressed to Prime Minister Tikhonov dated 28th July 1982. Major Louison said that in the letter, Grenada was requesting additional assistance in: food, fuel, spare parts, transportation, engineering kits, uniforms and others. He disclosed that the greatest part of the budget was used for food and fuel and that spare parts were also of serious concern because many vehicles were grounded since the basic spare parts were unavailable.

Marshal Ogarkov replied rather jokingly that students should be concerned with studies, but that Major Lousion who would graduate on 10th May was also concerned about the problems of his soldiers. Nevertheless, the Marshal indicated that he was aware of such requests, but hastened to assure Major Louison that all items contained in the protocol would be delivered. Marshal Ogarkov further assured Major Louison that the requests contained in the letter to P.M. Tikhonov were presently under consideration and that even though they were handled by GKS and Ministry of Foreign Trade, the Ministry of Defence would exercise some control on the solution. He said, with confidence, that his Ministsy would participate in the settlement of these requests.

EMBASSY OF GRENADA IN THE USSR

Dobryninskaya Ulitsa 7
Apartment 221
Moscow
USSR

Telephone:
237-25-41
237-99-05

-4-

Further still, the Marshal disclosed that there was a possibility that some of the main questions would be solved and as soon as a decision was taken, the Ministry of Defence through Col-General Zutov would inform the Embassy.

Additionally, referring to the question of deputation of Soviet specialists to Grenada to conduct studies related to the construction of military projects the Marshal informed the Grenadian side that the team of specialists would be sent in one month's time and that they await an indication from Grenada confirming readiness to accommodate the specialists.

Finally, towards the end of the meeting the Marshal of the Soviet Union and Chief of Staff of the Soviet Armed Forces proposed a toast from the bottom of our hearts in his words- to Major Louison on the eve of the 10th Anniversary of the New JEWEL Movement and the fourth Anniversary of the Grenada Revolution.

In his turn, Major Louison expressed thanks and appreciation to the Marshal for kind words about the Grenada Revolution; Major Louison also expressed thanks for the assitance to the Armed Forces of Grenada and then raised a toast towards the strengthening of relations between the two countries, parties, people's, and their armed forces.

Marshal Ogarkov was thankful for the warm meeting and reinforced both toasts by raising a final toast for the growth and futher strengthening of the relations between the Soviet Armed Forces and the People's Revolutionary Armed Forces of Grenada.

In conclusion, it should be pointed out that the entire meeting was conducted in an atmosphere of warmth, friendliness, simplicity and unpretentiousness.

EMBASSY OF GRENADA IN THE USSR

Dobryninskaya Ulitsa 7
Apartment 221
Moscow
USSR

-3-

Telephone:
237-25-41
237-99-05

The meeting ended with warm embraces.

Bernard Bourne

Bernard L. Bourne

Minister-Counsellor.

Document 12

Top secret

A G R E E M E N T

between the Government of Grenada and the Government of the Union of Soviet Socialist Republics on deliveries from the Union of SSR to Grenada of special and other equipment

The Government of Grenada and the Government of the Union of Soviet Socialist Republics,

guided by aspirations for developing and strengthening friendly relations between both countries on the principles of equality, mutual respect of sovereignty and non-interference into internal affairs,

proceeding from the desire to promote strengthening the independence of Grenada

and in connection with the request of the Government of Grenada

Have agreed upon the following:

Article 1

The Government of the Union of Soviet Socialist Republics shall ensure in 1980-1981 free of charge the delivery to the Government of Grenada of special and other equipment in nomenclature and quantity according to the Annex to the present Agreement to the amount of 4.400.000 Roubles.

- 2 -

Article 2

The delivery of the equipment listed in the Annex to the present Agreement shall be effected by the Soviet Party by sea, at the port of the Republic of Cuba.

The order of the further delivery of the above equipment from the Republic of Cuba shall be agreed upon between the Grenadian and Cuban Parties.

Article 3

The Government of the Union of SSR at the request of the Government of Grenada shall ensure rendering technical assistance in mastering of the equipment delivered under the present Agreement by receiving Grenadian servicemen for training in the USSR.

The Grenadian servicemen shall be deputed for training in the USSR without their families.

The expenses connected with the Grenadian servicemen's training, upkeep, meals, and equipment in the Soviet military educational establishments as well as with their travel fare from Grenada to the USSR and back shall be borne by the Soviet Party.

Article 4

The Government of the Union of SSR shall ensure free of charge the transfer to the Government of Grenada of necessary technical descriptions,instructions and manuals in standard composition on operation of the special equipment delivered under the present Agreement.

- 3 -

Article 5

The appropriate Grenadian and Soviet organizations shall conclude contracts in which there shall be stipulated the detailed terms and conditions of receiving for training Grenadian servicemen and other services connected with the implementation of the present Agreement.

Article 6

The Government of Grenada shall not without the consent of the Government of the Union of Soviet Socialist Republics sell or transfer, formally or actually, the special equipment, delivered under the present Agreement, the relevant documentation and information or give permission to use the equipment and documentation by a third party or any physical or legal persons but the officials and specialists of the citizenship of Grenada being in the service with the Government of Grenada.

The Government of Grenada and the Government of the Union of SSR shall take all the necessary measures to ensure keeping in secret the terms and conditions of the deliveries, all the correspondence and information connected with the implementation of the present Agreement.

Article 7

The present Agreement comes into force on the date it is signed on.

The Annex is an integral part of the present Agreement.

Done in Havana on October "27", 1980 in two originals, each in the English and Russian languages, both texts being equally valid.

FOR AND ON BEHALF OF THE GOVERNMENT OF GRENADA	FOR AND ON BEHALF OF THE GOVERNMENT OF THE UNION OF SOVIET SOCIALIST REPUBLICS

Top secret

ANNEX

to Agreement of October "27", 1980

L I S T

of special materiel to be delivered to Grenada from the Soviet Union in 1980-1981 /free of charge/

Description	Unit of measure	Quantity	Years of delivery	
			1980	1981
Artillery and small arms armament				
82-mm mortars, used reconditioned	piece	12	-	12
RPG-7V antitank hand grenade-launchers	piece	24	24	-
Group sets of spare parts /1:9/ to RPG-7V grenade-launchers	set	3	3	-
7,62-mm PKM machine-guns	piece	54	-	54
Group set of spare parts /1:50/ to PKM machine-guns	set	1	-	1
7,62-mm AK submachine-guns, used reconditioned	piece	I000	I000	-
7,62-mm carbines, model 1944, used reconditioned	piece	1500	500	-
Antiaircraft armament				
23-mm ZU-23 antiarcraft mounts	piece	18	6	12
Group sets of spare parts /1:6/ to ZU-23 mounts	set	3	1	2

- 3 -

Description	Unit of measure	Quantity	Years of delivery	
			1980	19[illegible]
with B-32 bullet with steel cartridge case	thous. pieces	27,0	-	27,0
with T-46 bullet	thous. pieces	97,2	-	97,2
7,62-mm cartridges, model 1943, without clips:				
with steel-core bullet	thous. pieces	600,0	200,0	400,0
with tracer bullet	thous. pieces	300,0	100,0	200,0
dummy ~~Logistic equipment~~	thous. pieces	75,0	-	75,0
Soldiers'camp tents for 10 men	piece	20	-	20

Spare parts, auxiliary and training equipment on specifications of the Soviet Party to the amount of up to 400000 Roubles

- 2 -

Description	Unit of measure	Quantity	Years of delivery 1980	1981
Repair set of spare parts /1:18/ to ZU-23 mounts	set	1	-	1
Communication means				
Radio stations:				
R-105M	set	12	12	-
R-108M	set	4	4	-
R-109M	set	4	4	-
Vehicles				
GAZ-66-05 vehicles	piece	28	6	22
UAZ-469B jeeps	piece	5	-	5
Ammunition				
82-mm mortar rounds with fragmentation shell	thous. pieces	4,5	-	4,5
PG-7V rounds to RPG-7V grenade-launchers	thous. pieces	2,4	2,4	-
23-mm rounds to ZU-23 antiaircraft mounts:				
with fragmentation, high explosive, incendiary projectile	thous. pieces	162,0	54,0	108,0
with armour-piercing, incendiary, tracer projectile	thous. pieces	54,0	18,0	36,0
7,62-mm rifle cartridges with steve-core bullet in clips	thous. pieces	675,0	675,0	-
7,62-mm rifle cartridges without clips:				
with steel-core bullet	thous. pieces	416,0	-	416,0
dummy	thous. pieces	75,0	-	75,0

Совершенно секретно

С О Г Л А Ш Е Н И Е

между Правительством Гренады и Правительством Союза Советских Социалистических Республик о поставках из Союза ССР в Гренаду специального и другого имущества

Правительство Гренады и Правительство Союза Советских Социалистических Республик,

руководствуясь стремлением к развитию и укреплению дружественных отношений между обеими странами на основе полного равноправия, взаимного уважения суверенитета и невмешательства во внутренние дела,

исходя из желания содействовать укреплению независимости Гренады,

и в связи с обращением Правительства Гренады,

согласились о нижеследующем:

Статья 1

Правительство Союза Советских Социалистических Республик обеспечит в 1980-1981 годах безвозмездно поставку Правительству Гренады специального и другого имущества в номенклатуре и количестве согласно Приложению к настоящему Соглашению на сумму 4.400.000 рублей.

- 2 -

Статья 2

Поставка перечисленного в Приложении к настоящему Соглашению имущества будет произведена Советской Стороной морем в порт Республики Куба. Порядок дальнейшей доставки указанного имущества из Республики Куба к месту назначения в Гренаде будет согласован между Кубинской и Гренадской Сторонами.

Статья 3

Правительство Союза ССР по просьбе Правительства Гренады обеспечит оказание технического содействия в освоении эксплуатации поставляемого по настоящему Соглашению имущества путем приема на обучение в СССР гренадских военнослужащих.

Гренадские военнослужащие направляются для обучения в СССР без семей.

Расходы, связанные с обучением, содержанием, питанием и обмундированием гренадских военнослужащих в советских военных учебных заведениях, а также с их проездом из Гренады в СССР и обратно, Советская Сторона принимает на себя.

Статья 4

Правительство Союза ССР обеспечит безвозмездно передачу Правительству Гренады в установленной комплектации необходимых технических описаний, инструкций и наставлений по эксплуатации поставляемого по настоящему Соглашению специального имущества.

- 3 -

Статья 5

Соответствующие гренадские и советские организации заключат между собой контракты, в которых будут установлены подробные условия приема на обучение гренадских военнослужащих и других услуг, связанных с выполнением настоящего Соглашения.

Статья 6

Правительство Гренады не будет без согласия Правительства Союза Советских Социалистических Республик продавать или передавать, формально или фактически, поставляемое в связи с настоящим Соглашением специальное имущество, документацию и информацию по ним или разрешать пользоваться этим имуществом и документацией третьей стороне и каким бы то ни было физическим или юридическим лицам, кроме должностных лиц и специалистов из граждан Гренады, находящихся на службе у Правительства Гренады.

Правительство Гренады и Правительство Союза ССР примут все зависящие от них меры, которые обеспечат сохранение в тайне условия поставок, всей переписки и информации, связанных с выполнением настоящего Соглашения.

Статья 7

Настоящее Соглашение вступает в силу со дня его подписания. Приложение к Соглашению является его неотъемлемой частью.

Совершено в Гаване "27" октября 1980 года в двух подлинных экземплярах, каждый на английском и русском языках, причем оба текста имеют одинаковую силу.

ПО УПОЛНОМОЧИЮ
ПРАВИТЕЛЬСТВА ГРЕНАДЫ

ПО УПОЛНОМОЧИЮ
ПРАВИТЕЛЬСТВА СОЮЗА СОВЕТСКИХ СОЦИАЛИСТИЧЕСКИХ РЕСПУБЛИК

Совершенно секретно

ПРИЛОЖЕНИЕ

к Соглашению от "27" октября 1980 года

П Е Р Е Ч Е Н Ь

специального имущества, поставляемого Гренаде из Советского Союза в 1980-1981 годах /безвозмездно/

Наименование	Единица измерения	Количество	Годы поставки	
			1980	1981
<u>Стрелково-артиллерийское вооружение</u>				
82-мм минометы, бывшие в эксплуатации, отремонтированные	штука	12	-	12
Ручные противотанковые гранатометы РПГ-7В	штука	24	24	-
Групповые комплекты ЗИПа к гранатометам РПГ-7В /1:9/	комплект	3	3	-
7,62-мм пулеметы ПКМ	штука	54	-	54
Групповой комплект ЗИПа к пулеметам ПКМ /1:50/	комплект	1	-	1
7,62-мм автоматы АК, бывшие в эксплуатации, отремонтированные	штука	1000	1000	-
7,62-мм карабины образца 1944 г., бывшие в эксплуатации, отремонтированные	штука	1500	1500	-
<u>Зенитное вооружение</u>				
23-мм зенитные установки ЗУ-23	штука	18	6	12
Групповые комплекты ЗИПа к установкам ЗУ-23 /1:6/	комплект	3	1	2

- 2 -

Наименование	Единица измерения	Количество	Годы поставки	
			1980	1981
Ремонтный комплект ЗИПа к установкам ЗУ-23 /1:18/	комплект	1	-	1
Средства связи				
Радиостанции:				
Р-105М	комплект	12	12	-
Р-108М	комплект	4	4	-
Р-109М	комплект	4	4	-
Автомобильная техника				
Автомобили ГАЗ-66-05	штука	28	6	22
Автомобили УАЗ-469Б	штука	5	-	5
Боеприпасы				
82-мм минометные выстрелы с осколочной миной	тыс.штук	4,5	-	4,5
Выстрелы ПГ-7В к гранатометам РПГ-7В	тыс.штук	2,4	2,4	-
23-мм выстрелы к зенитным установкам ЗУ-23:				
с осколочно-фугасно-зажигательным снарядом	тыс.штук	162,0	54,0	108,0
с бронебойно-зажигательно-трассирующим снарядом	тыс.штук	54,0	18,0	36,0
7,62-мм винтовочные патроны с пулей со стальным сердечником в обоймах	тыс.штук	675,0	675,0	-
7,62-мм винтовочные патроны без обойм:				
с пулей со стальным сердечником	тыс.штук	416,0	-	416,0
для холостой стрельбы	тыс.штук	75,0	-	75,0

- 3 -

Наименование	Единица измерения	Количество	Годы поставки	
			1980	1981
с пулей Б-32 со стальной гильзой	тыс.штук	27,0	-	27,0
с пулей Т-46	тыс.штук	97,2	-	97,2
7,62-мм патроны образца 1943г. без обойм:				
с пулей со стальным сердечником	тыс.штук	600,0	200,0	400,0
с трассирующей пулей	тыс.штук	300,0	100,0	200,0
для холостой стрельбы	тыс.штук	75,0	-	75,0
<u>Имущество тыла</u>				
Палатки лагерные солдатские 10-местные	штука	20	-	20

Запасные части, учебное и вспомогательное имущество по спецификациям Советской Стороны на сумму до 400000 рублей

Document 13

Top secret

A G R E E M E N T

between the Government of Grenada and the Government of the Union of Soviet Socialist Republics on deliveries from the Union of SSR to Grenada of special and other equipment

The Government of Grenada and the Government of the Union of Soviet Socialist Republics,

guided by aspirations for developing and strengthening friendly relations between both countries on the principles of equality, mutual respect of sovereignty and non-interference into internal affairs,

proceeding from the desire to promote strengthening the independence of Grenada

and in connection with the request of the Government of Grenada

have agreed upon the following:

Article 1

The Government of the Union of Soviet Socialist Republics shall ensure in 1982-1985 free of charge the delivery to the Government of Grenada of special and civil equipment in nomenclature and quantity according to Annexes 1 and 2 to the present Agreement to the amount of 10.000.000 Roubles.

- 2 -

Article 2

The delivery of the equipment listed in Annexes 1 and 2 to the present Agreement shall be effected by the Soviet Party by sea, at the port of the Republic of Cuba.

The order of the further delivery of the above equipment from the Republic of Cuba shall be agreed upon between the Grenadian and Cuban Parties.

Article 3

The Government of the Union of SSR at the request of the Government of Grenada shall ensure rendering technical assistance in mastering of the equipment under delivery by receiving in the USSR Grenadian servicemen for training in the operation, use and maintenance of the special equipment as well as by sending Soviet specialists to Grenada for these purposes.

The Grenadian servicemen shall be sent to the USSR for training without their families.

The expenses connected with the Grenadian servicemen's training, upkeep, meals in the Soviet military educational establishments as well as with their travel fare from Grenada to the USSR and back shall be borne by the Soviet Party.

The Government of Grenada shall provide at its own expense the Soviet specialists and interpreters with comfortable furnished living accommodation with all the municipal utilities, medical service and transport facilities for the execution of their duties and shall ensure their having meals at reasonable prices at the places of their residense.

The Soviet specialists and interpreters shall not be imposed by any taxes and duties on entering or leaving Grenada and during their stay there. All other expenses connected with deputation of the Soviet specialists to Grenada shall be borne by the Soviet Party.

- 3 -

Article 4

The Soviet Party in periods to be agreed upon between the Parties shall depute a group of Soviet specialists to Grenada to determine expediency, opportunity and scope of rendering technical assistance in the creation of the stationary shop for repair of the special equipment and transport, commanding staff trainer school, training facilifies for Armed Forces as well as the deliveries of missing building materials for construction of the storehouses and road.

The deputation of a group of Soviet specialists shall be effected on the terms and conditions of Article 3 of the present Agreement.

Article 5

The Government of the Union of SSR shall ensure free of charge the transfer to the Government of Grenada of necessary technical descriptions, instructions and manuals in standard composition on operation of the special equipment delivered under the present Agreement.

Article 6

The appropriate Grenadian and Soviet organizations shall conclude contracts in which there shall be stipulated the detailed terms and conditions of deputing Soviet specialists, receiving for training Grenadian servicemen and other services connected with the implementation of the present Agreement.

Article 7

The Government of Grenada shall not without the consent of the Government of the Union of Soviet Socialist Republics sell or transfer, formally or actually, the special equipment, delivered under the present Agreement, the relevant documentation and information or give permission to use the equipment and documentation by a third party or any physical or legal persons but the officials and specialists of the citizenship of Grenada being in the service with the Government of Grenada.

- 4 -

The Government of the Union of SSR and the Government of Grenada shall take all the necessary measures to ensure keeping in secret the terms and conditions of the deliveries, all the correspondence and information connected with the implementation of the present Agreement.

Article 8

The present Agreement comes into force on the date it is signed on.

Annexes 1 and 2 are an integral part of the present Agreement.

Done in Moscow on July "27", 1982 in two originals, each in the English and Russian languages, both texts being equally valid.

FOR AND ON BEHALF	FOR AND ON BEHALF
OF THE GOVERNMENT OF GRENADA	OF THE GOVERNMENT OF THE UNION OF SOVIET SOCIALIST REPUBLICS

Top secret

ANNEX 1

to Agreement of July "27", 1982

LIST

of special equipment to be delivered to the Army of Grenada from the Soviet Union in 1983-1985

Description	Unit of measure	Quantity-total	Years of delivery		
			1983	1984	1985
<u>Armour materiel</u>					
BTR-152V1 armoured personnel carriers, used, repaired	piece	50	-	30	20
7,62-mm rifle cartridges without clips:					
with steel core bullet	thous. pieces	100,5	-	60,3	40,2
with B-32 armour-piercing-incendiary bullet and steel case	thous. pieces	37,5	-	22,5	15,0
with T-46 tracer bullet	thous. pieces	49,5	-	29,7	19,8

- 2 -

Description	Unit of measure	Quantity-total	Years of delivery	
			1983	1984
<u>Artillery armament and ammunition</u>				
76-mm ZIS-3 guns, used, repaired	piece	30	18	12
76-mm rounds:				
with fragmentation and high-explosive-fragmentation grenade	thous. pieces	9,3	5,6	3,7
with armour-piercing-tracer shell	piece	540	330	210
with sub-calibre armour-piercing shell	piece	450	270	180
with hollow charge shell	piece	540	330	210
57-mm ZIS-2 anti-tank guns, used, repaired	piece	30	18	12
57-mm rounds:				
with fragmentation grenade	thous. pieces	5,4	3,2	2,2
with armour-piercing-tracer shell	thous. pieces	4,0	2,4	1,6
with sub-calibre armour-piercing shell	thous. pieces	1,3	0,8	0,5

6

- 3 -

Description	Unit of measure	Quantity-total	Years of delivery		
			1983	1984	1985
"Grad-P" /9P132/ portable launchers	piece	50	20	30	-
Group sets of SPTA /1:4/ for "Grad-P" launchers	set	12	5	7	-
Repair sets of SPTA /1:8/ for "Grad-P" launchers	set	5	2	3	-
122-mm 9M22M fragmentation-high-explosive set projectiles in sets with packs of "Grad-P" launchers	thous. pieces	1,8	0,9	0,9	-
14,5-mm ZGU-1 AA mountain mounts	piece	30	-	30	-
Group sets of SPTA /1:10/ for ZGU-1 mounts	set	3	-	3	-
Repair sets of SPTA /1:50/ for ZGU-1 mounts	set	1	-	1	-
14,5-mm cartridges:					
with B-32 armour-piercing-incendiary bullet	thous. pieces	180,0	-	180,0	-
with BZT armour-piercing-incendiary-tracer bullet	thous. pieces	180,0	-	180,0	-
82-mm BM mortars, used, repaired	piece	60	30	30	-

- 4 -

Description	Unit of measure	Quantity- total	Years of delivery		
			1983	1984	1985
82-mm rounds for DM mortars:					
with fragmentation mine	thous. pieces	21,6	10,8	10,8	-
with inert charge mine	piece	200	100	100	-
<u>Small arms</u>					
RPG-7V light anti-tank grenade launchers	piece	50	-	20	30
Group sets of SPTA /1:9/ for RPG-7V grenade launchers	set	5	-	2	3
Repair sets of SPTA /1:01/ for RPG-7V grenade launchers	set	1	-	-	1
PG-7VM rounds for RPG-7V grenade launchers	thous. pieces	3,0	-	1,2	1,8
7,62-mm PKM machine guns	piece	60	20	20	20
Group set of SPTA /1:50/ for PKM machine guns	set	1	-	1	-
7,62-mm PKMS machine guns	piece	30	-	10	20
Group set of SPTA /1:50/ for PKMS machine guns	set	1	-	-	1

Description	Unit of measure	Quantity-total	Years of delivery		
			1983	1984	1985
7,62-mm DP,DPM machine guns, used, repaired	piece	270	170	100	-
7,62-mm rifle cartridges without clips:					
with steel core bullet	thous. pieces	919,5	432,0	308,7	178,8
with B-32 armour-piercing-incendiary bullet with steel case	thous. pieces	45,4	21,9	14,0	9,5
with T-46 tracer bullet	thous. pieces	213,8	101,6	69,3	42,9
7,62-mm AK sub-machine guns, used, repaired	thous. pieces	2,0	1,0	1,0	-
7,62-mm cartridges of 1943 model without clips:					
with steel core bullet	mill.pieces	1,44	0,7	0,74	-
with T-45 tracer bullet	thous. pieces	324,0	162,0	162,0	-
for blank firing	thous. pieces	120,0	60,0	60,0	-
7,62-mm carbines of 1938/1944 model, used, repaired	thous. pieces	1,0	1,0	-	-
7,62-mm rifle cartridges with steel core bullet in clips	thous. pieces	60,0	60,0	-	-

Top secret

A N N E X 1

to Agreement of July "27", 1982

L I S T

of special equipment to be delivered to the Army of Grenada from the Soviet Union in 1983-1985

Description	Unit of measure	Quantity-total	Years of delivery		
			1983	1984	1985
Armcur materiel					
BTR-152V1 armoured personnel carriers, used, repaired	piece	50	-	30	20
7,62-mm rifle cartridges without clips:					
with steel core bullet	thous. pieces	100,5	-	60,3	40,2
with B-32 armour-piercing-incendiary bullet and steel case	thous. pieces	37,5	-	22,5	15,0
with T-46 tracer bullet	thous. pieces	49,5	-	29,7	19,8

- 2 -

Description	Unit of measure	Quantity-total	Years of delivery	
			1983	1984
Artillery armament and ammunition				
76-mm ZIS-3 guns, used, repaired	piece	30	18	12
76-mm rounds:				
with fragmentation and high-explosive-fragmentation grenade	thous. pieces	9,3	5,6	3,7
with armour-piercing-tracer shell	piece	540	330	210
with sub-calibre armour-piercing shell	piece	450	270	180
with hollow charge shell	piece	540	330	210
57-mm ZIS-2 anti-tank guns, used, repaired	piece	30	18	12
57-mm rounds:				
with fragmentation grenade	thous. pieces	5,4	3,2	2,2
with armour-piercing-tracer shell	thous. pieces	4,0	2,4	1,6
with sub-calibre armour-piercing shell	thous. pieces	1,3	0,8	0,5

- 3 -

Description	Unit of measure	Quantity-total	Years of delivery		
			1983	1984	1985
"Grad-P" /9P132/ portable launchers	piece	50	20	30	-
Group sets of SPTA /1:4/ for "Grad-P" launchers	set	12	5	7	-
Repair sets of SPTA /1:8/ for "Grad-P" launchers	set	5	2	3	-
122-mm 9M22M fragmentation-high-explosive set projectiles in sets with packs of "Grad-P" launchers	thous. pieces	1,8	0,9	0,9	-
14,5-mm ZGU-1 AA mountain mounts	piece	30	-	30	-
Group sets of SPTA /1:10/ for ZGU-1 mounts	set	3	-	3	-
Repair sets of SPTA /1:50/ for ZGU-1 mounts	set	1	-	1	-
14,5-mm cartridges:					
with B-32 armour-piercing-incendiary bullet	thous. pieces	180,0	-	180,0	-
with BZT armour-piercing-incendiary-tracer bullet	thous. pieces	180,0	-	180,0	-
82-mm BM mortars, used, repaired	piece	60	30	30	-

- 4 -

Description	Unit of measure	Quantity-total	Years of delivery		
			1983	1984	1985
82-mm rounds for BM mortars:					
with fragmentation mine	thous. pieces	21,6	10,8	10,8	-
with inert charge mine	piece	200	100	100	-
<u>Small arms</u>					
RPG-7V light anti-tank grenade launchers	piece	50	-	20	30
Group sets of SPTA /1:9/ for RPG-7V grenade launchers	set	5	-	2	3
Repair sets of SPTA /1:01/ for RPG-7V grenade launchers	set	1	-	-	1
PG-7VM rounds for RPG-7V grenade launchers	thous. pieces	3,0	-	1,2	1,8
7,62-mm PKM machine guns	piece	60	20	20	20
Group set of SPTA /1:50/ for PKM machine guns	set	1	-	1	-
7,62-mm PKMS machine guns	piece	30	-	10	20
Group set of SPTA /1:50/ for PKMS machine guns	set	1	-	-	1

Top secret

ANNEX I

to Agreement of July "27", 1982

LIST

of special equipment to be delivered to the Army of Grenada from the Soviet Union in 1983-1985

Description	Unit of measure	Quantity-total	Years of delivery		
			1983	1984	1985
<u>Armcur materiel</u>					
BTR-152V1 armoured personnel carriers, used, repaired	piece	50	-	30	20
7,62-mm rifle cartridges without clips:					
with steel core bullet	thous. pieces	100,5	-	60,3	40,2
with B-32 armour-piercing-incendiary bullet and steel case	thous. pieces	37,5	-	22,5	15,0
with T-46 tracer bullet	thous. pieces	49,5	-	29,7	19,8

- 2 -

Description	Unit of measure	Quantity-total	Years of delivery	
			1983	1984
Artillery armament and ammunition				
76-mm ZIS-3 guns, used, repaired	piece	30	18	12
76-mm rounds:				
with fragmentation and high-explosive-fragmentation grenade	thous. pieces	9,3	5,6	3,7
with armour-piercing-tracer shell	piece	540	330	210
with sub-calibre armour-piercing shell	piece	450	270	180
with hollow charge shell	piece	540	330	210
57-mm ZIS-2 anti-tank guns, used, repaired	piece	30	18	12
57-mm rounds:				
with fragmentation grenade	thous. pieces	5,4	3,2	2,2
with armour-piercing-tracer shell	thous. pieces	4,0	2,4	1,6
with sub-calibre armour-piercing shell	thous. pieces	1,3	0,8	0,5

6

- 3 -

Description	Unit of measure	Quantity-total	Years of delivery		
			1983	1984	1985
"Grad-P" /9P132/ portable launchers	piece	50	20	30	-
Group sets of SPTA /1:4/ for "Grad-P" launchers	set	12	5	7	-
Repair sets of SPTA /1:8/ for "Grad-P" launchers	set	5	2	3	-
122-mm 9M22M fragmentation-high-explosive set projectiles in sets with packs of "Grad-P" launchers	thous. pieces	1,8	0,9	0,9	-
14,5-mm ZGU-1 AA mountain mounts	piece	30	-	30	-
Group sets of SPTA /1:10/ for ZGU-1 mounts	set	3	-	3	-
Repair sets of SPTA /1:50/ for ZGU-1 mounts	set	1	-	1	-
14,5-mm cartridges:					
with B-32 armour-piercing-incendiary bullet	thous. pieces	180,0	-	180,0	-
with BZT armour-piercing-incendiary-tracer bullet	thous. pieces	180,0	-	180,0	-
82-mm BM mortars, used, repaired	piece	60	30	30	-

- 4 -

Description	Unit of measure	Quantity-total	Years of delivery		
			1983	1984	1985
82-mm rounds for BM mortars:					
with fragmentation mine	thous. pieces	21,6	10,8	10,8	-
with inert charge mine	piece	200	100	100	-
Small arms					
RPG-7V light anti-tank grenade launchers	piece	50	-	20	30
Group sets of SPTA /1:9/ for RPG-7V grenade launchers	set	5	-	2	3
Repair sets of SPTA /1:01/ for RPG-7V grenade launchers	set	1	-	-	1
PG-7VM rounds for RPG-7V grenade launchers	thous. pieces	3,0	-	1,2	1,8
7,62-mm PKM machine guns	piece	60	20	20	20
Group set of SPTA /1:50/ for PKM machine guns	set	1	-	1	-
7,62-mm PKMS machine guns	piece	30	-	10	20
Group set of SPTA /1:50/ for PKMS machine guns	set	1	-	-	1

- 5 -

Description	Unit of measure	Quantity-total	Years of delivery		
			1983	1984	1985
7,62-mm DP,DPM machine guns, used, repaired	piece	270	170	100	-
7,62-mm rifle cartridges without clips:					
with steel core bullet	thous. pieces	919,5	432,0	308,7	178,8
with B-32 armour-piercing-incendiary bullet with steel case	thous. pieces	45,4	21,9	14,0	9,5
with T-46 tracer bullet	thous. pieces	213,8	101,6	69,3	42,9
7,62-mm AK sub-machine guns, used, repaired	thous. pieces	2,0	1,0	1,0	-
7,62-mm cartridges of 1943 model without clips:					
with steel core bullet	mill.pieces	1,44	0,7	0,74	-
with T-45 tracer bullet	thous. pieces	324,0	162,0	162,0	-
for blank firing	thous. pieces	120,0	60,0	60,0	-
7,62-mm carbines of 1938/1944 model, used, repaired	thous. pieces	1,0	1,0	-	-
7,62-mm rifle cartridges with steel core bullet in clips	thous. pieces	60,0	60,0	-	-

Top secret

ANNEX 1

to Agreement of July "27", 1982

LIST

of special equipment to be delivered to the Army of Grenada from the Soviet Union in 1983–1985

Description	Unit of measure	Quantity-total	Years of delivery		
			1983	1984	1985
Armour materiel					
BTR-152V1 armoured personnel carriers, used, repaired	piece	50	-	30	20
7,62-mm rifle cartridges without clips:					
with steel core bullet	thous. pieces	100,5	-	60,3	40,2
with B-32 armour-piercing-incendiary bullet and steel case	thous. pieces	37,5	-	22,5	15,0
with T-46 tracer bullet	thous. pieces	49,5	-	29,7	19,8

- 2 -

Description	Unit of measure	Quantity-total	Years of delivery	
			1983	1984
Artillery armament and ammunition				
76-mm ZIS-3 guns, used, repaired	piece	30	18	12
76-mm rounds:				
with fragmentation and high-explosive-fragmentation grenade	thous. pieces	9,3	5,6	3,7
with armour-piercing-tracer shell	piece	540	330	210
with sub-calibre armour-piercing shell	piece	450	270	180
with hollow charge shell	piece	540	330	210
57-mm ZIS-2 anti-tank guns, used, repaired	piece	30	18	12
57-mm rounds:				
with fragmentation grenade	thous. pieces	5,4	3,2	2,2
with armour-piercing-tracer shell	thous. pieces	4,0	2,4	1,6
with sub-calibre armour-piercing shell	thous. pieces	1,3	0,8	0,5

6

- 3 -

Description	Unit of measure	Quantity-total	Years of delivery		
			1983	1984	1985
"Grad-P" /9P132/ portable launchers	piece	50	20	30	-
Group sets of SPTA /1:4/ for "Grad-P" launchers	set	12	5	7	-
Repair sets of SPTA /1:8/ for "Grad-P" launchers	set	5	2	3	-
122-mm 9M22M fragmentation-high-explosive set projectiles in sets with packs of "Grad-P" launchers	thous. pieces	1,8	0,9	0,9	-
14,5-mm ZGU-1 AA mountain mounts	piece	30	-	30	-
Group sets of SPTA /1:10/ for ZGU-1 mounts	set	3	-	3	-
Repair sets of SPTA /1:50/ for ZGU-1 mounts	set	1	-	1	-
14,5-mm cartridges:					
with B-32 armour-piercing-incendiary bullet	thous. pieces	180,0	-	180,0	-
with BZT armour-piercing-incendiary-tracer bullet	thous. pieces	180,0	-	180,0	-
82-mm BM mortars, used, repaired	piece	60	30	30	-

- 4 -

Description	Unit of measure	Quantity-total	Years of delivery		
			1983	1984	1985
82-mm rounds for DM mortars:					
with fragmentation mine	thous. pieces	21,6	10,8	10,8	-
with inert charge mine	piece	200	100	100	-
Small arms					
RPG-7V light anti-tank grenade launchers	piece	50	-	20	30
Group sets of SPTA /1:9/ for RPG-7V grenade launchers	set	5	-	2	3
Repair sets of SPTA /1:01/ for RPG-7V grenade launchers	set	1	-	-	1
PG-7VM rounds for RPG-7V grenade launchers	thous. pieces	3,0	-	1,2	1,8
7,62-mm PKM machine guns	piece	60	20	20	20
Group set of SPTA /1:50/ for PKM machine guns	set	1	-	1	-
7,62-mm PKMS machine guns	piece	30	-	10	20
Group set of SPTA /1:50/ for PKMS machine guns	set	1	-	-	1

- 5 -

Description	Unit of measure	Quantity-total	Years of delivery		
			1983	1984	1985
7,62-mm DP,DPM machine guns, used, repaired	piece	270	170	100	-
7,62-mm rifle cartridges without clips:					
with steel core bullet	thous. pieces	919,5	432,0	308,7	178,8
with B-32 armour-piercing-incendiary bullet with steel case	thous. pieces	45,4	21,9	14,0	9,5
with T-46 tracer bullet	thous. pieces	213,8	101,6	69,3	42,9
7,62-mm AK sub-machine guns, used, repaired	thous. pieces	2,0	1,0	1,0	-
7,62-mm cartridges of 1943 model without clips:					
with steel core bullet	mill.pieces	1,44	0,7	0,74	-
with T-45 tracer bullet	thous. pieces	324,0	162,0	162,0	-
for blank firing	thous. pieces	120,0	60,0	60,0	-
7,62-mm carbines of 1938/1944 model, used, repaired	thous. pieces	1,0	1,0	-	-
7,62-mm rifle cartridges with steel core bullet in clips	thous. pieces	60,0	60,0	-	-

- 6 -

Description	Unit of measure	Quantity-total	Years of delivery		
			1983	1984	1985
7,62-mm SVDN-1 sniper's rifles	piece	10	-	10	-
Group set of SPTA /1:18/ for SVDN-1 sniper's rifles	set	1	-	1	-
7,62-mm sniper's rifles of 1891/1930 model, used, repaired	piece	270	207	-	-
7,62-mm sniper's cartridges without clips	thous. pieces	2,7	-	2,7	-
9-mm PM pistols	piece	150	-	150	-
Group set of SPTA /1:100/ for PM pistols	set	1	-	1	-
9-mm cartridges for PM pistols	thous. pieces	10,8	-	10,8	-
Hand grenades:					
F-1	thous. pieces	10,0	-	10,0	-
RGD-5	thous. pieces	3,0	-	3,0	-
Training grenades with fuzes:					
URG	piece	500	-	500	-
URG-N	piece	500	-	500	-

- 7 -

Description	Unit of measure	Quantity-total	Years of delivery		
			1983	1984	1985
Mines:					
PMN	thous. pieces	5,0	5,0	–	–
TM-57	thous. pieces	2,0	2,0	–	–
Communication means					
Radio stations:					
R-104AM3	set	10	–	–	10
R-105	set	40	–	–	40
R-109M	set	20	–	10	10
TA-57 telephone sets	piece	60	30	30	–
P-193M switchboards	piece	10	5	5	–
P-274M two-wire field cable	kilometre	50	50	–	–
TK-2 reels	piece	100	100	–	–
Engineer materiel and workshops					
TZ-5 refuellers	piece	2	–	2	–

- 8 -

Description	Unit of measure	Quantity-total	Years of delivery		
			1983	1984	1985
OP workshop	set	1	-	1	-
MRS-OR workshop	set	1	-	1	-
ESD-10VS/230 power plant	set	1	-	1	-
<u>Other equipment</u>					
10-place tents	piece	100	-	50	50
Aluminium soldier flasks	thous. pieces	1,5	0,5	0,5	0,5
Flask case	thous. pieces	1,5	0,5	0,5	0,5
Sets of soldier uniform	thous. pieces	1,4[x/]	1,4	-	-
SSh-60 steel helmets	thous. pieces	1,5	0,5	0,5	0,5
BPTs5 8x30 field-glasses	piece	100	50	50	-

Spare parts, auxiliary and training equipment by the specifications of the Soviet Party to the amount of 600000-00 Roubles

---

x/ Set composition: panama - 1, field shirt - 1, trousers - 1, sleeveless cest - 2, shorts - 2, socks - 2 pairs, boots - 1 pair, waist-belt - 1.

Top secret

ANNEX 2

to the Agreement of 27 - July 1982

L I S T

of special materiel and civilian equipment to be supplied for the Ministry of the Interior of Grenada from the Soviet Union in 1982-1985

Description	Unit of measure	Quantity	Years of delivery			
			1982	1983	1984	1985
Small arms						
Light antitank rocket launchers RPG-7V	piece	20	-	-	-	20
Group sets of SPTA /1:9/ to rocket launchers RPG-7V	set	2	-	-	-	2
Repair set of spares /1:81/ to rocket launchers RPG-7V	set	1	-	-	-	1
Rockets PG-7VM to rocket launchers RPG-7V	thous.pieces	1,2	-	-	-	1,2
7,62-mm machine guns PKM	piece	25	-	-	25	-

- 2 -

Description	Unit of measure	Quantity	Years of delivery			
			1982	1983	1984	1985
Group set of SPTA /1:50/ to machine guns PKM	set	1	-	-	1	-
7,62-mm rifle cartridges without clips:						
with steel core bullet	thous.pieces	115,5	-	-	115,5	-
with armour piercing-incendiary bullet B-32 with steel casing	thous.pieces	7,5	-	-	7,5	-
with tracer bullet T-46	thous.pieces	27,0	-	-	27,0	-
7,62-mm submachine guns AK	piece	50x/	-	50	-	-
7,62-mm cartridges, model 1943, without clips:						
with steel core bullet	thous.pieces	40,0	-	40,0	-	-
with tracer bullet T-45	thous.pieces	8,0	-	8,0	-	-
7,62-mm sniper's rifles SVD	piece	13	5x/	8	-	-
Group set of SPTA/1:18/ to SVD rifles	set	1	-	1	-	-
7,62-mm sniper's cartridges to SVD rifles	thous.pieces	6,8	4,4	2,4	-	-
9-mm pistols PM	piece	600	50x/	-	550	-
Group sets of SPTA/1:100/ to PM pistols	set	6	-	-	6	-

x/ Used, repaired.

- 3 -

Description	Unit of measure	Quantity	Years of delivery			
			1982	1983	1984	1985
Repair set of SPTA /1:500/ to PM pistols	set	1	-	-	1	-
9-mm cartridges to PM pistols	thous.pieces	44,7	5,1	-	39,6	-
<u>Special instrumentation</u>						
Items:						
"Pobedit-M"	piece	20	20	-	-	-
R-2	piece	5	5	-	-	-
R-4	piece	5	5	-	-	-
"Moshka-MZ"	set	30	5	15	10	-
"Moshka-MV"	set	20	5	10	5	-
"Rulavka"	set	5	5	-	-	-
"Nylon"	set	10	10	-	-	-
"Nylon-ZU"	set	1	1	-	-	-
Photo cutter to "Nylon"	piece	1	1	-	-	-
Photo cuvette to "Nylon"	piece	1	1	-	-	-

- 4 -

Description	Unit of measure	Quantity	Years of delivery			
			1982	1983	1984	1985
Instrumentation:						
"Luza-2-Lakmus"	set	2	2	-	-	-
"Bridge"	set	2	2	-	-	-
Infrared viewers "Kustarnik"	set	5	5	-	-	-
Step-and-repeat machine ER-11K1	piece	1	-	1	-	-
Signalling systems "Rubin-3"	set	4	-	4	-	-
TV systems "PTU-47"	set	2	-	2	-	-
Equipment of general civilian use						
Videotape recorders "Electronika-video"	set	3	-	3	-	-
Tape recorders "Mayak'	piece	15	-	15	-	-
Photo cameras:						
"Zenit-TTL"	piece	10	-	10	-	-
"Zenit-E"	piece	10	10	-	-	-
Exposure meters "Leningrad-6"	piece	3	3	-	-	-

- 5 -

Description	Unit of measure	Quantity	Years of delivery			
			1982	1983	1984	1985
Photographic enlarger "Neva-3M"	set	2	2	-	-	-
Black-and-white film "FED"	cassette	100	100	-	-	-
Colour reversible film, 35-mm	meter	80	80	-	-	-
Various kinds of photographic paper and chemical agents /developer and fixer/	set	1 x/	1	-	-	-
Safes with key locks	piece	6	-	6	-	-
Metal cabinets	piece	50	-	50	-	-
Single-stand tables	piece	30	-	30	-	-
Clothing and equipment						
Cotton khaki tunics with trousers	set	600	-	600	-	-
Officers' equipment /belts and shoulder straps/	set	1500	-	1500	-	-
Kersey high boots	pair	1500	-	1500	-	-
Khaki kepi	piece	600	-	600	-	-
Officers' capes	piece	500	-	500	-	-

x/ To be supplied to specifications of Soviet Party.

- 6 -

Description	Unit of measure	Quantity	Years of delivery			
			1982	1983	1984	1985
Black cotton socks	pair	1500	-	1500	-	-
Kit-bags	piece	1500	-	1500	-	-
<u>Vehicles</u>						
GAZ-66	piece	4	4	-	-	-
UAZ-469B	piece	6	6	-	-	-
VAZ-2106	piece	3	3	-	-	-
Sets of spares for vehicles:						
GAZ-66	set	1x/	1	-	-	-
UAZ-469D	set	1x/	1	-	-	-
VAZ-2106	set	1x/	1	-	-	-
Spare parts, auxiliary and training equipment to specifications of Soviet Party for a sum up to 100000 roubles						

x/ To be supplied to specifications of Soviet Party.

L.J. S.C.

Совершенно секретно

С О Г Л А Ш Е Н И Е

между Правительством Гренады и Правительством Союза Советских Социалистических Республик о поставках из Союза ССР в Гренаду специального и другого имущества

Правительство Гренады и Правительство Союза Советских Социалистических Республик,

руководствуясь стремлением к развитию и укреплению дружественных отношений между обеими странами на основе полного равноправия, взаимного уважения суверенитета и невмешательства во внутренние дела,

исходя из желания содействовать укреплению независимости Гренады,

и в связи с обращением Правительства Гренады,

согласились о нижеследующем:

Статья I

Правительство Союза Советских Социалистических Республик обеспечит в 1982-1985 годах безвозмездно поставку Правительству Гренады специального имущества и имущества общегражданского назначения в номенклатуре и количестве согласно Приложениям I и 2 к настоящему Соглашению на сумму 10.000.000 рублей.

Статья 2

Поставка перечисленного в Приложениях I и 2 к настоящему Соглашению имущества будет произведена Советской Стороной морем в порт Республики Куба. Порядок дальнейшей поставки указанного имущества из Республики Куба к месту назначения в Гренаде будет согласован между Кубинской и Гренадской Сторонами.

- 2 -

Статья 3

Правительство Союза ССР по просьбе Правительства Гренады обеспечит оказание технического содействия в освоении поставляемого имущества путем приема в Советском Союзе гренадских военнослужащих для обучения эксплуатации, применению и ремонту специального имущества, а также командирование для этих целей советских специалистов в Гренаду.

Гренадские военнослужащие будут направляться на обучение в СССР без семей.

Расходы, связанные с обучением, содержанием, питанием и обмундированием гренадских военнослужащих в советских военных учебных заведениях, а также с их проездом из Гренады в СССР и обратно, Советская Сторона принимает на себя.

Правительство Гренады обеспечит за свой счет советских специалистов и переводчиков благоустроенными меблированными жилыми помещениями, обеспечивающими нормальные условия их проживания, медицинским обслуживанием и транспортными средствами для служебных целей, а также организует предоставление советским специалистам и переводчикам питания за умеренную плату в местах их расположения.

Советские специалисты и переводчики не будут оплачивать какие-либо налоги и сборы при въезде, выезде и во время их пребывания в Гренаде.

Все остальные расходы, связанные с командированием советских специалистов в Гренаду, Советская Сторона принимает на себя.

Статья 4

Советская Сторона в сроки по согласованию Сторон командирует в Гренаду группу советских специалистов для определения целесообразности, возможности и объемов оказания технического содействия в создании стационарной мастерской для ремонта специального имущества и транспортных средств, школы для подготовки командиров и специалистов, учебной базы для Вооруженных Сил, а также поставки недостающих строительных материалов для создания хранилищ и дороги.

Командирование указанной группы советских специалистов будет произведено на условиях статьи 3 настоящего Соглашения.

- 3 -

Статья 5

Правительство Союза ССР обеспечит безвозмездно передачу Правительству Гренады в установленной комплектации необходимых технических описаний, инструкций и наставлений по эксплуатации поставляемого по настоящему Соглашению специального имущества.

Статья 6

Соответствующие гренадские и советские организации заключат между собой контракты, в которых будут установлены подробные условия командирования советских специалистов, приема на обучение гренадских военнослужащих и оказания других услуг, связанных с выполнением настоящего Соглашения.

Статья 7

Правительство Гренады не будет без согласия Правительства Союза Советских Социалистических Республик продавать или передавать, формально или фактически, поставляемое в связи с настоящим Соглашением специальное имущество, документацию и информацию по ним или разрешать пользоваться этим имуществом и документацией третьей стороне и каким бы то ни было физическим или юридическим лицам, кроме должностных лиц и специалистов из граждан Гренады, находящихся на службе у Правительства Гренады.

Правительство Гренады и Правительство Союза ССР примут все зависящие от них меры, которые обеспечат сохранение в тайне условий поставок, всей переписки и информации, связанных с выполнением настоящего Соглашения.

- 4 -

Статья 8

Настоящее Соглашение вступает в силу со дня его подписания. Приложения I и 2 к Соглашению являются его неотъемлемой частью.

Совершено в Москве "27" июля 1982 года в двух подлинных экземплярах, каждый на английском и русском языках, причем оба текста имеют одинаковую силу.

ПО УПОЛНОМОЧИЮ
ПРАВИТЕЛЬСТВА ГРЕНАДЫ

ПО УПОЛНОМОЧИЮ
ПРАВИТЕЛЬСТВА СОЮЗА СОВЕТСКИХ СОЦИАЛИСТИЧЕСКИХ РЕСПУБЛИК

Совершенно секретно

ПРИЛОЖЕНИЕ I

к Соглашению от "27" июля 1982 года

П Е Р Е Ч Е Н Ь

специального имущества, поставляемого для армии Гренады из Советского Союза в 1983-1985 годах

Наименование	Единица измерения	Количество-всего	В том числе по годам		
			1983	1984	1985
Бронетанковая техника					
Бронетранспортеры БТР-152В1, бывшие в эксплуатации, отремонтированные	штука	50	-	30	20
7,62-мм винтовочные патроны без обойм:					
с пулей со стальным сердечником	тыс.штук	100,5	-	60,3	40,2
с бронебойно-зажигательной пулей Б-32 со стальной гильзой	тыс.штук	37,5	-	22,5	15,0
с трассирующей пулей Т-46	тыс.штук	49,5	-	29 7	19,8

- 2 -

Наименов. ие	Единица измерения	Количество всего	В том числе по годам		
			1983	1984	1985
Артиллерийское вооружение и боеприпасы					
76-мм пушки ЗИС-3, бывшие в эксплуатации, отремонтированные	штука	30	I8	I2	-
76-мм выстрелы:					
с осколочной и осколочно-фугасной гранатой	тыс.штук	9,3	5,6	3,7	-
с бронебойно-трассирующим снарядом	штука	540	330	2I0	-
с бронебойно-подкалиберным снарядом	штука	450	270	I80	-
с кумулятивным снарядом	штука	540	330	2I0	-
57-мм противотанковые пушки ЗИС-2, бывшие в эксплуатации, отремонтированные	штука	30	I8	I2	-
57-мм выстрелы:					
с осколочной гранатой	тыс.штук	5,4	3,2	2,2	-
с бронебойно-трассирующим снарядом	тыс.штук	4,0	2,4	I,6	-
с бронебойно-подкалиберным снарядом	тыс.штук	I,3	0,8	0,5	-
Переносные реактивные установки "Град-П" /9П132/	штука	50	20	0	-
Групповые комплекты ЗИПа /I:4/ к установкам "Град-П"	комплект	I2	5	7	-

- 3 -

Наименование	Единица измерения	Количество всего	В том числе по годам		
			1983	1984	1985
Ремонтные комплекты ЗИПа /1:8/ к установкам "Град-П"	комплект	5	2	3	-
122-мм реактивные осколочно-фугасные снаряды 9М22М в комплекте с вьюками к установкам "Град-П"	тыс.штук	1,8	0,9	0,9	-
14,5-мм зенитные горные установки ЗГУ-1	штука	30	-	30	-
Групповые комплекты ЗИПа /1:10/ к установкам ЗГУ-1	комплект	3	-	3	-
Ремонтный комплект ЗИПа /1:50/ к установкам ЗГУ-1	комплект	1	-	1	-
14,5-мм патроны:					
с бронебойно-зажигательной пулей Б-32	тыс.штук	180,0	-	180,0	-
с бронебойно-зажигательно-трассирующей пулей БЗТ	тыс.штук	180,0	-	180,0	-
82-мм минометы БМ, бывшие в эксплуатации, отремонтированные	штука	60	30	30	-
82-мм выстрелы к минометам БМ:					
с осколочной миной	тыс.штук	21,6	10,8	10,8	-
с осколочной миной в инертном снаряжении	штука	200	100	100	-

- 4 -

Наименование	Единица измерения	Количество всего	В том числе по годам		
			1983	1984	1985
Стрелковое вооружение					
Ручные противотанковые гранатометы РПГ-7В	штука	50	-	20	30
Групповые комплекты ЗИПа /I:9/ к гранатометам РПГ-7В	комплект	5	-	2	3
Ремонтный комплект ЗИПа /I:8I/ к гранатометам РПГ-7В	комплект	I	-	-	I
Выстрелы ПГ-7ВМ к гранатометам РПГ-7В	тыс.штук	3,0	-	I,2	I,8
7,62-мм пулеметы ПКМ	штука	60	20	20	20
Групповой комплект ЗИПа /I:50/ к пулеметам ПКМ	комплект	I	-	I	-
7,62-мм пулеметы ПКМС	штука	30	-	I0	20
Групповой комплект ЗИПа /I:50/ к пулеметам ПКМС	комплект	I	-	-	I
7,62-мм пулеметы ДП,ДПМ, бывшие в эксплуатации, отремонтированные	штука	270	I70	I00	-
7,62-мм винтовочные патроны без обойм:					
с пулей со стальным сердечником	тыс.штук	9I9,5	432,0	308,7	I78,8
с бронебойно-зажигательной пулей Б-32 со стальной гильзой	тыс.штук	45,4	2I,9	1[illegible],0	9,5
с трассирующей пулей Т-46	тыс.штук	2I3,8	I0I,6	6[illegible],3	42,9

- 5 -

Наименование	Единица измерения	Количество-всего	В том числе по годам		
			1983	1984	1985
7,62-мм автоматы АК, бывшие в эксплуатации, отремонтированные	тыс.штук	2,0	I,0	I,0	-
7,62-мм патроны образца 1943 года без обойм:					
с пулей со стальным сердечником	млн.штук	I,44	0,7	0,74	-
с трассирующей пулей Т-45	тыс.штук	324,0	I62,0	I62,0	-
для холостой стрельбы	тыс.штук	I20,0	60,0	60,0	-
7,62-мм карабины образца I938, I944 годов, бывшие в эксплуатации, отремонтированные	тыс.штук	I,0	I,0	-	-
7,62-мм винтовочные патроны с пулей со стальным сердечником в обоймах	тыс.штук	60,0	60,0	-	-
7,62-мм снайперские винтовки СВДН-I	штука	I0	-	I0	-
Групповой комплект ЗИПа /I:I8/ к снайперским винтовкам СВДН-I	комплект	I	-	I	-
7,62-мм снайперские винтовки образца I89I/30 годов, бывшие в эксплуатации, отремонтированные	штука	270	270	-	-
7,62-мм снайперские патроны без обойм	тыс.штук	2,7	-	2,7	-
9-мм пистолеты ПМ	штука	I50	-	I50	-

Наименование	Единица измерения	Количество-всего	В том числе по годам		
			1983	1984	1985
Групповой комплект ЗИПа /I:I00/ к пистолетам ПМ	комплект	I	-	I	-
9-мм патроны к пистолетам ПМ	тыс.штук	I0,8	-	I0,8	-
Ручные гранаты:					
Ф-I	тыс.штук	I0,0	-	I0,0	-
РГД-5	тыс.штук	3,0	-	3,0	-
Учебные гранаты в комплекте с запалами:					
УРГ	штука	500	-	500	-
УРГ-Н	штука	500	-	500	-
Мины:					
ПМН	тыс.штук	5,0	5,0	-	-
ТМ-57	тыс.штук	2,0	2,0	-	-
Средства связи					
Радиостанции:					
Р-I04АМ3	комплект	I0	-	-	I0
Р-I05	комплект	40	-	-	40
Р-I09М	комплект	20	-	I0	I0
Телефонные аппараты ТА-57	штука	60	30	30	-

- 7 -

Наименование	Единица измерения	Количество всего	В том числе по годам		
			1983	1984	1985
Телефонные коммутаторы П-193М	штука	10	5	5	-
Кабель полевой П-274М в двухжильном исчислении	километр	50	50	-	-
Катушки ТК-2	штука	100	100	-	-
<u>Инженерное имущество и мастерские</u>					
Топливозаправщики ТЗ-5	штука	2	-	2	-
Мастерская ОП	комплект	I	-	I	-
Мастерская МРС-ОР	комплект	I	-	I	-
Электростанция ЭСД-10ВС/230	комплект	I	-	I	-
<u>Прочее имущество</u>					
Палатки 10-местные	штука	100	-	50	50
Фляги алюминиевые солдатские	тыс.штук	1,5	0,5	0,5	0,5
Чехлы к флягам	тыс.штук	1,5	0,5	0,5	0,5
Комплекты солдатского обмундирования	тыс.комплектов	1,4[x/]	1,4	-	-

Состав комплекта: панама - I, гимнастерка - I, брюки - I, майки - 2, трусы - 2, носки - 2 пары, ботинки - I пара, брючный ремень - I.

Наименование	Единица измерения	Количество-всего	В том числе по годам		
			1983	1984	1985
Шлемы стальные СШ-60	тыс.штук	1,5	0,5	0,5	0,5
Бинокли БПЦ5 8x30	штука	100	50	50	-

Запасные части, учебное и вспомогательное имущество по спецификациям Советской Стороны на сумму до 600000-00 рублей.

L.J.

Л.С.

Совершенно секретно

ПРИЛОЖЕНИЕ 2

к Соглашению от "27" июля 1982 года

П Е Р Е Ч Е Н Ь

специального имущества и имущества общегражданского назначения, поставляемых для Министерства внутренних дел Гренады из Советского Союза в 1982-1985 годах

Наименование	Единица измерения	Количество-всего	В том числе по годам			
			1982	1983	1984	1985
Стрелковое вооружение						
Ручные противотанковые гранатометы РПГ-7В	штука	20	-	-	-	20
Групповые комплекты ЗИПа /1:9/ к гранатометам РПГ-7В	комплект	2	-	-	-	2
Ремонтный комплект ЗИПа /1:81/ к гранатометам РПГ-7В	комплект	1	-	-	-	1
Выстрелы ПГ-7ВМ к гранатометам РПГ-7В	тыс.штук	1,2	-	-	-	1,2
7,62-мм пулеметы ПКМ	штука	25	-	-	25	-

- 2 -

Наименование	Единица измерения	Количество всего	В том числе по годам			
			1982	1983	1984	1985
Групповой комплект ЗИПа /1:50/ к пулеметам ПКМ	комплект	1	-	-	1	-
7,62-мм винтовочные патроны без обоймы:						
с пулей со стальным сердечником	тыс.штук	115,5	-	-	115,5	-
с бронебойно-зажигательной пулей Б-32 со стальной гильзой	тыс.штук	7,5	-	-	7,5	-
с трассирующей пулей Т-46	тыс.штук	27,0	-	-	27,0	-
7,62-мм автоматы АК	штука	50x/	-	50	-	-
7,62-мм патроны образца 1943 года без обойм:						
с пулей со стальным сердечником	тыс.штук	40,0	-	40,0	-	-
с трассирующей пулей Т-45	тыс.штук	8,0	-	8,0	-	-
7,62-мм снайперские винтовки СВД	штука	13	5x/	8	-	-
Групповой комплект ЗИПа /1:18/ к винтовкам СВД	комплект	1	-	1	-	-
7,62-мм снайперские патроны к винтовкам СВД	тыс.штук	6,8	4,4	2,4	-	-
9-мм пистолеты ПМ	штука	600	50x/	-	550	-

x/ Бывшие в эксплуатации, отремонтированные.

- 3 -

Наименование	Единица измерения	Количество-всего	В том числе по годам			
			1982	1983	1984	1985
Групповые комплекты ЗИПа /I:I00/ к пистолетам ПМ	комплект	6	-	-	6	-
Ремонтный комплект ЗИПа /I:500/ к пистолетам ПМ	комплект	I	-	-	I	-
9-мм патроны к пистолетам ПМ	тыс.штук	44,7	5,I	-	39,6	-
Специальная аппаратура						
Изделия:						
"Победит-М"	штука	20	20	-	-	-
В-2	штука	5	5	-	-	-
Б-4	штука	5	5	-	-	-
"Мошка-МЗ"	комплект	30	5	I5	IO	-
"Мошка-МП"	комплект	20	5	IO	5	-
"Булавка"	комплект	5	5	-	-	-
"Найлон"	комплект	IO	IO	-	-	-
"Найлон-ЗУ"	комплект	I	I	-	-	-
Фоторезак к изделию "Найлон"	штука	I	I	-	-	-
Фотобачок к изделию "Найлон"	штука	I	I	-	-	-

- 4 -

Наименование	Единица измерения	Количество-всего	В том числе по годам			
			1982	1983	1984	1985
Аппаратура:						
"Луза-2-Лакмус"	комплект	2	2	-	-	-
"Бридж"	комплект	2	2	-	-	-
Приборы ночного видения "Кустарник"	комплект	5	5	-	-	-
Копировально-множительная машина ЭР-IIКI	штука	I		I	-	-
Системы сигнализации "Рубин-3"	комплект	4	-	4	-	-
Телевизионные системы "ПТУ-47"	комплект	2	-	2	-	-
Имущество общегражданского назначения						
Видеомагнитофоны "Электроника-видео"	комплект	3	-	3	-	-
Магнитофоны "Малк"	штука	I5	-	I5	-	-
Фотоаппараты:						
"Зенит-ТТЛ"	штука	I0	-	I0	-	-
"Зенит-Е"	штука	I0	I0	-	-	-

Наименование	Единица измерения	Количество-всего	В том числе по годам			
			1982	1983	1984	1985
Фотоэкспонометры "Ленинград-6"	штука	3	3	-	-	-
Фотоувеличители "Нева-3М"	комплект	2	2	-	-	-
Фотопленка черно-белая "ФЭД"	кассета	100	100	-	-	-
Фотопленка обращаемая цветная 35-мм	метр	80	80	-	-	-
Фотобумага разная и химические реактивы /проявитель и закрепитель/	комплект	1 x/	1	-	-	-
Сейфы с замками под ключ	штука	6	-	6	-	-
Шкафы металлические	штука	50	-	50	-	-
Однотумбовые столы	штука	30	-	30	-	-
Обмундирование						
Кители с брюками, хлопчатобумажные, защитного цвета	комплект	600	-	600	-	-
Снаряжение офицерское /ремни и портупеи/	комплект	1500	-	1500	-	-

x/ Поставляется по спецификациям Советской Стороны.

- 6 -

Наименование	Единица измерения	Количество всего	В том числе по годам			
			I982	I983	I984	I985
Сапоги кирзовые	пара	I500	-	I500	-	-
Кепи защитного цвета	штука	600	-	600	-	-
Плащ-накидки офицерские	штука	500	-	500	-	-
Носки хлопчатобумажные, черного цвета	пара	I500	-	I500	-	-
Вещевые мешки	штука	I500	-	I500	-	-
Автомобильная техника						
Автомобили:						
ГАЗ-66	штука	4	4	-	-	-
УАЗ-469Б	штука	6	6	-	-	-
ВАЗ-2I06	штука	3	3	-	-	-
Комплекты запасных частей для автомобилей:						
ГАЗ-66	комплект	I[x/]	I	-	-	-

x/ Поставляется по спецификациям Советской Стороны.

- 7 -

Наименование	Единица измерения	Количество-всего	В том числе по годам			
			1982	1983	1984	1985
УАЗ-469Б	комплект	I x/	I	-	-	-
ВАЗ-2106	комплект	I x/	I	-	-	-

Запасные части, учебное и вспомогательное имущество по спецификациям Советской Стороны на сумму до 100000-00 рублей

---

x/ Поставляется по спецификациям Советской Стороны.

L. J

А.С.

Document 14

"SECRET"

Copy No. _____

PROTOCOL

OF THE MILITARY COLLABORATION BETWEEN THE GOVERNMENT OF THE REPUBLIC OF CUBA AND THE PEOPLE'S REVOLUTIONARY GOVERNMENT-OF GRENADA

The Government of the Republic of Cuba and People's Revolutionary Government of Grenada, in full exercise of their sovereign right as free and independent State, based on the fraternal relations existing between both countries with the aim of making a constribution to the strengthening of the defensive capacity of Grenada, have agreed upon the following:

ARTICLE I

The Government of the Republic of Cuba in agreement with the - request formulated by the People's Revolutionary Government of Grenada, will maintain Cuban Military specialists in that country in quantities and specialists established in Annex No. 1 - of this document. (Protocol).

ARTICLE II

The Military specialists from Cuba in behalf of strengthening the military capacity of the Armed Forces will assist grenadian military men on the questions of Organization of the Organic Structure, Organization of the Instruction and combative and campaign training of the troops and staffs in the preparation of cadres and minor specialists, and in the elaboration of the operative and mobilization plans for the defense of the country.

ARTICLE III

The Government of the Republic of Cuba will grant scholarships to military personnel of Grenada in the Military Training Centres of the Revolutionary Armed Forces with the quantities - and specialist with the requirements that will be established in Annex No. 3 which will be elaborated afterwards.

"SECRET"

.. 2

ARTICLE IV

The Government of the Republic of Cuba has the pleasure of reciving during 1982 four delegations of the Armed Forces of up to three members each, of the following specialities:

- Engineering, (the fourth-thre months period)
- Communication, (the first three-months period)
- Logistics, (the first three-month period)
- Exploration, (the fourth three-month period)

The dates in which these delegations should travel to Cuba will be communicated to the grenadian side, by the cuban side twenty days in advance.

ARTICLE V

In order to lead the activities of the Cuban Military Specialists, the post of chief of the Cuban Military Specialists is established who will develop functions in the Ministry of Defense.

ARTICLE VI

The Cuban side according to the plans approved by its governments will carry out the systematic change of Cuban Military-specialists in the quantities foreseen in the present Protocol.

ARTICLE VII

The People's Revolutionary Government of Grenada will give facilities to the chief of the Cuban Military specialists in the work places and for using the communication means existing in the country in order to assure the direction of his activities of Technical Military assistance to the Armed Forces.

ARTICLE VIII

The Cuban and grenadian Military specialists who in virtue of the present Protocol are in the Republic of Cuba or in Grenada will respect the sovereignty and costums and will observe the laws.

"SECRET"

.. 3

ARTICLE IX

The People's Revolutionary Government will give facilities to the Ministry of the Revolutionary Armed Forces of the Republic of Cuba to check the work of the Cuban Military Specialists.

ARTICLE X

The medical, technical and material assurance and the expenses as a result of the permanency of the Cuban Military Specialists on the Granadian territory will be implemented according to the time period established in Annex No. 2 of this Protocol.

ARTICLE XI

The People's Revolutionary Government will pay the expenses of the Custom-House and fees of the mems sent to the Cuban Milita ry specialists, by sea and by air.

ARTICLE XII

The Government of the Republic of Cuba and the People's Revolu tionary Government of Grenada, will take all measures depending on them in order to assure the secrecy of the permanency of the military personnel in both states and the character of the ac- tivities, as well as the mail and information related to the - present Protocol.

ARTICLE XIII

Any kind of situation that comes out in respect to the present Protocol or its accomplishment, it will be solved by friendly converrations between representatives of both sides in Havana City or in the City St. George's.

Any charges or additions to the Present Protocol will only be effective in case they are elaborated in a written way and signed by authorized personnel of both sides.

ARTICLE XIV

Annex No. 3 of the Protocol of Military Collaboration on schols

"SECRET"

4

ships to the People's Revolutionary Government of Grenada will be included in the present Protocol, by means of a written request through the chief of the Group of Military Specialists - after having finished the studies that will be carried out.

ARTICLE XV

The Present Protocol will be put into effect from the date of signature and it will be effective until Dicember 31st, 1984.

The Annexes No. 1, 2 and 3 are part of this Protocol.

Written up in two copies, original, in spanich and english, -- both texts are valid and signed in the City of ____________ on the ______ days of ________ of 19____

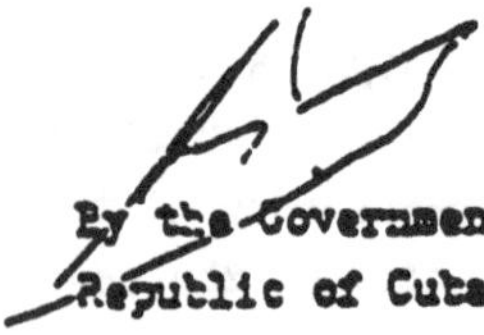

By the Government of the Republic of Cuba

By the People's Revolutionary Government of Grenada

"SECRET"
Copy No. ___

ANNEX No. 1

PROTOCOL OF THE MILITARY COLLABORATION ABOUT THE LEVELS OF WORK OF THE CUBAN MILITARY SPECIALISTS IN THE PERMANENT AR MED FORCES.

The Government of the Republic of Cuba will maintain military specialists in Grenada whose composition will be as follows:

1.- Permanent Specialists

a) In the General Staff of the Armed Forces.

- Chief of the Military Specialists ———— 1
- Specialists ———— 8

b) In the Military Region.

- Specialists ———— 3

c) In the Permanent Company.

- Specialist ———— 1

d) Internal Assurance Groups of the Military Specia - lists.

- Officers, Sergeants and soldiers ———— 16

TOTAL 27

2.- Specialists for short periods and for 2-4 month periods

a) In the General Staff.

- Specialists ———— 6

b) In the assurance units.

- Techinicians ———— 3

c) Transport Repairing Brigades ———— 3-4

TOTAL 12-13

"SECRET"
Copy No. ____

ANNEX No.2

PROTOCOL OF THE MILITARY COLLABORATION ABOUT THE MATERIAL MEANS, SERVICE AND ASSURING PERSONNEL.

The Government of the Republic of Cuba and the People's Revolutionary Government of Grenada agree to guarantee the material, technical and medical assurance of the Cuban Military Specialists according to the time period mentioned below:

CLAUSE No. 1

The People's Revolutionary Government of Grenada will guarantee the material means, equipments and the following services:

a) Maintainance of furniture and properties sent and constructed by Cuba and those given by the country to the Cuban military personnel.

b) Equipment and office material for the usage of the Cuban military specialists.

c) Fresh food-stuff for the feeding of the Cuban Military personnel.

d) The necessary transport means for the develpment of their functions inside the Armed Forces, guaranteeing the fuel and lubricants, its maintainance and repair.

e) Armament and ammunition for the Cuban Military specialists.

f) Qualifield medical assistance in the Hospital of the country as well as the necessary medicines for desease prevention and the maintainance of health of the Cuban Military Specialists.

g) Means of personnel hygiene of every kind.

h) National transportation required for the accomplishment of the service activities.

i) Public Services (water, electricity, telephones and others)

j) A small stipendium for the personal expenses of every members Equivalent to (30) U.S. Dollars.

"SECRET"
.. 2

k) Entrance visa and Identification Documents which accredit them for the civilian and military authorities of the — country.

l) Personnel that guarantee the driving and usage of the trans port Technique, the elaboration of food, washing ang ironing of the clothes, the cleaning of furniture and properties and the security of the house.

ll) Other means and services non-specified which are required - for the development of the work of the Cuban Military perso nell.

CLAUSE No. 2

The Government of the Republic of Cuba will guarantee the means equipment and services we mention as follows:

a) The sending of technical personnel, material means and nece-ssary furnitures for the construction of the necessary ins-tallation for the living conditions and work of the Cuban - Military Personnel.

b) Dried foodstuff of every kind for the feeding of the Cuban-Military Personnel.

c) The trip clothes of the Cuban Military Specialists.

d) The necessary consultive material for the execution of the functions of the Cuban Military Specialists.

e) The salary in Cuba of the Military Personnel.

Document 15

SUMMARY OF PRIME MINISTER'S MEETING WITH SOVIET AMBASSADOR - 24TH MAY, 1983

The Ambassador reported that on his last trip to Venezuela, he met with the Ambassadors from the Socialist Community and raised with them the fact that, since his eight month stay in Trinidad, none of them had visited.

He explained that h had spoken with the General Secretary of the Venezuelan Communist Party and among other things, had raised the question of the level of counter-revolutionary activities in Venezuela. The General Secretary explained that there was, he thought, contact between the Venezuelan Government and the counter-revolutionaries and thought, but wasn't sure, that the President knew of it. The Ambassador asked him to work on it and send more precise information.

The Prime Minister thanked him and pointed out that the General Secretary had never been to Grenada   kept contact with the Grenada Embassy in Caracas.

The Ambassador added that the International Relations Secretary of the Venezuelan Communist Party said he is coming to Grenada.

The Ambassador gave to the Prime Minister, copies of articles on Grenada published in the Soviet press.

The Ambassador reported that special equipment, 2 Coast Guard patrol boats and foodstuff were being sent direct to Grenada. This included 3,000 military uniforms in 1984 and 2,000 spades in 1985.

ITEM	1983	1984	1985	TOTAL
Flour	440	660	770	1870
Grains	88	132	154	374
Canned Meat	82	124	144	350
Canned Fish	73	110	128	311
Sugar	48	72	83	203
Salt	23	31	38	91
Vegetable Oil	14	21	25	60

-2-

ITEM	1983	1984	1985	TOTAL
Gasolene	240	300	370	910
Lubricants	500	400	200	1,200
Army Type Pick Up UAZ 21	18	6	-	24
Military Jeeps UAZ	25	15	-	40
Trucks GAZ	15	35	-	50
Fire Engines	5	-	-	5

The Ambassador indicated that the supply of the vehicles and the fire-engines was based on the inter-governmental protocol of 11th July, 1980. The conditions were:

(1) 15% within 1 year of date of delivery;
(2) 85% over 10 years from date of delivery in equal half-yearly payments with the first to be made 3 years after date of delivery,
(3) 4% interest rate.

This, the Ambassador said are the most favourable conditions given to any body by the Foreign Trade Division of the U.S.S.R.

Talks and agreements can be conducted and signed in Moscow.

Prime Minister promised reply before the Ambassador leaves on 1st June, 1983 for vacation in Moscow.

Ambassador informed that General Chief of Staff, Ogarkov, will like appointment with Gde. Hudson Austin. He reported that 10,000 roubles supply of 14.5mm shells for anti aircraft [illegible] delivered to Cuba in January 1983. Another 30,000 will be supplied this year through Havana. 35,000 roubles in spare parts can be delivered in the 3rd quarter of 1983 after letter of credit comes from Grenada. Soviet trade representative now in Grenada, can discuss this. [illegible] promised to have someone contact him.

Ambassador said agreement reached to exchange 2,000 pairs of boots for larger sizes (40-45); Grenada to follow up with the Cubans who have already been contacted and agreed to principle.

-5-

10 copies of Soviet Military Review coming in May 1983.

Cde. Layne had made requests on those two things and R.... is to check him to follow up.

C.C. of C.P.S.U. has agreed to receive 5 members of Leadership for rest and treatment; Cde. Strachan had given name of Cde. Board, wife and three kids.

On P.M.'s request, Ambassador will clarify whether this will account for the five places. However, Ambassador explained that in event of necessity, a request can still be made.

Aircraft to be supplied to Grenada will be delivered to Cuba. Can seat 39 paratroopers and hold 6 tons of cargo. Has 4,000 flight hours capacity and 4,000 landings. If used [illegible] can last four years without repair. Can be assembled in [illegible] days and will be done in Cuba. Has been designed with Sofa and can [illegible] accommodate 10-12 under those conditions.

P.M. explained that plane can be used for a dual purpose with the other being a Grenada/Cuba weekly run. He explained that the car will not be used as it can have negative political repercussion. He also pointed out that the kind of plane, a military make, can pose problems landing in the more reactionary countries in the region as civilian make craft will not have those problems.

Fifteen specialist will travel from Moscow to Havana to work on the aircrafts. An additional engine and spare parts enough for five planes will be attached. All spare parts will be left in Cuba under supervision of specialists from the U.S.S.R. who will do all warranty services.

The Ambassador said that they will prefer Cubans pilot to use it. Electrical equipment for starting the engine will be supplied to Grenada. Grenada must indicate what colours, emblems, service number are to be put on the plane.

The Ambassador pointed out that technician can be sent to help develop the socio-economic plan for 198[illegible]-8[illegible]. Two specialists and and one interpreter can arrive September/October for three months.

He reported that equipment had been sent to G.I.S. from TASS Agency.

-4-

The Ambassador provided the P.M. with an overview of Venezuela's Foreign Minister, Zambrano's, visit to Moscow 25-30.4.83 and gave him a document on it.

The Ambassador informed that some projects for assistance to Grenada had been drafted but were done without taking into consideration the specific conditions on Grenada, therefore, he needs to know Grenada's position on these. They included:

(a) Technical and economic feasibility for sea-port project;

(b) Fifteen teachers coming to Grenada.

The P.M. pointed out he was glad the Ambassador raised this as he was going to raise a number of things:

(1) more sales of nutmeg and cocoa,

(2) gratuitous supply of 20,000 tons of fertiliser over 5 years (4,000 per year); (Ambassador explained that fertiliser is only product never granted - will still explore the possibility);

(3) Cement Plant;

(4) Satellite Station;

(5) East Coast Harbour;

(6) I.F.E.

(7) Steel.

The P.M. suggested the Ambassador meet with Cde. Strachan or Cde. Louison before departing.

The Ambassador pointed that they have received no names from the Ministry of Education for scholarships granted - 20 per year.

The P.M. reminded the Ambassador about a request made to the Cde. Lronyks for EC$15M for International Airport; Ambassador promised to raise again.

The P.M. then gave the Ambassador, on request, an overview on the situation of the imperialist threat to Grenada.

The Ambassador thus pointed out that the state section was strengthening; he was concerned about the newspaper not being published for three weeks and about the level of propaganda and ideological activity by the mass media.

He offered to consider assistance to the media and requested an outline of what the problems were and what assistance was required.

-5-

The P.M. told him about the imminent closing down of [illegible] and explained that the problem was the Transmitter which could no longer be repaired and a new one could not be bought. The Ambassador promised to arrange to have the media get the outline of the problems and assistance need to the Ambassador before leaving.

The Ambassador indicated that Specialist can come to look at the problems of the [illegible].

The P.M. asked the Ambassador to express his greetings to Cdes. Andropov, Tichonov, Ponomarev and the [illegible] of the [illegible] and to indicate his satisfaction on the progress in the development of the relation and anticipation for even more deepened relations.

FOLLOW UP

(1) Supply of special equipment, foodstuff, [illegible], cartridges. Talks and agreement possible from the Soviet side this year in Moscow. Promised reply to Ambassador before he leaves - 1.6.83.

(2) Delegate someone to meet with Soviet Trade Representative now in Grenada re spare parts for 35,000 roubles to be delivered third quarter in 1983.

(3) Check Cde. Ewart Layne re (i) exchange of [illegible] for larger sizes through [illegible], and (ii) 10 copies of Soviet Military Review coming for May 1. [illegible].

(4) Inform Cde. Strachan to clear with Ambassador question of whether Cde. Coard's five (wife and [illegible] and himself) takes care of five agreed to for rest and treatment or just one place.

(5) Decide what colours, emblem and service [illegible] should be placed on plane.

(6) Read document on Ambassador's visit to [illegible] of Contadora group position on Central America as part of [illegible] for [illegible] trip.

(7) Ensure Grenada's position on project for [illegible] USSR is prepared in time for [illegible] by Soviet [illegible].

(8) Speak to Minister of Education re scholarships [illegible] - 20 per year but no names have been given.

(9) Arrange for Cde. Strachan or Louison to meet with the Ambassador before he leave and give answer on question.

(10) Arrange for comrades in the media to prepare outline of their department's problems and assistance necessary and provide same to Ambassador before he leaves.

Document 16

EXTRAORDINARY MEETING OF THE CENTRAL COMMITTEE NJM

14 - 16 SEPTEMBER, 1983

MEETING STARTED 1.00 P.M

COMRADES PRESENT

Maurice Bishop
Selwyn Strachan
George Louison
Unison Whiteman
Liam James
Chalkie Ventour
Ewart Layne

Phyllis Coard
Leon Cornwall
Kemau Mc Barnette
Tan Bartholomew
Fitzroy Bain
Chris Deriggs

COMRADES ABSENT

Hudson Austin - (out of country)
Ian St, Bernard - (sick)

The proposed agenda by Cde. Maurice Bishop was circulated to Cdes for comments.

PROPOSED AGENDA

14TH SEPTEMBER

1. Minutes (7.00 - 1.10 p.m)
2. Levels of preparation (1.10 - 1.20 p.m)
3. Feed back from members work Committees and masses (1.20 - 2.30 p.m)
4. Evaluation of Feed back (2.30 - 2.45 p.m)
5. Evaluation of C.C (i) Collective role/collective work (2.45 - 6.00 p.m)

   Break at (4.00 - 4.15 p.m)

2/..............

- 2 -

<u>SEPTEMBER 15TH</u>

5. Evaluation of C.C

(ii)	Individual assessment	(8.00a.m - 6.00 p.m
	Break	(10.30a.m -10.45 a.m
	Lunch	(1.00p.m - 2.00 p.m.
	Break	(4.00p.m - 4.15 p m

Procedures - main	5 minutes
Assessment by 13 other Cdes	13x2 = 26 minutes
15 Cdes at 31 minutes per person	465 minutes

6. Key areas of implimentation of C.C conclusions

(i) Regional work/new P.C.B chiefs (5.15 - 6.00 p.m)

<u>SEPTEMBER 16TH</u>

6. Key areas of implimentation of C.C Conclusions

(i)	Regional Work/PCB Chiefs	(8.00 - 8.30 a.m)
(ii)	C.P.E	(8.30 - 9.30 a.m)
	Militia	(9.30 -10.30 a.m)
	Break	(10.30 -10.45 a.m)

7. (a) Proposed new responsibilities of C.C Cdes
   (b) Proposed responsibilities of C.C Secretariat
   (c) New decisions of C.C
   (d) Proposed meetings/dates and agenda of C.C
   (e) Report to the Party on this meeting
   a.b,c,d,e (10.45a.m - 1.00 p.m)

<u>REPORTS AVAILABLE</u>

1. Minutes of Last Emergency C.C
2. Reports from St. George's P.C.B (1)
3. Report from West Coast P.C.B (1)
4. Report from St. Andrew's P.C.B (1)
5. Report from St.David's P.C.B (2)
6. Report from St. Patrick's P.C.B (2)
7. Report from Carriacou P.C.B (1)
8. Report from West Coast G.M (1)
9. Recommendations from Fedon's and Marryshow seminars
10. Document on internal party development
11. Recommendations from Chris DeBriggs C.M Class
12. Present Political Situation Document.

- 3 -

13. Worker Education class August '83 report

14. Workers Committee balance of forces document 9th September 1983.

15. Report from Workers Committee on Socialism Classes July - August 4th 1983.

16. Workers Committee analysis of the Working Class for the Month of August.

<u>COMMENTS ON THE AGENDA</u>

Cde. Liam James said the proposed agenda is lacking in focus. It is not consistent with what was agreed in the emergency meeting of the C.C.

Cde Ventour said that the agenda should be:(

(1) Analysis of the present state of the party and revolution

(2) Analysis of the C.C main problems.

(3) The way forward.

Cde. Layne said the main purpose of this meeting is to discuss the state of the party and revolution and the work of the Central Committee.

Cde. Strachan said that item number six (6) can be taken in the overall assessment of the work.

Cde. James said that he would like the meeting to assess the degree of the state of the rut in the party and to look at the C.C and the way forward in that context.

Cde. Strachan said that item one, assessment of the party and revolution (2)/the C.C line formulation will make the analysis look to mechanistic.

Cde. Bishop said he had no problem with charging the agenda, his main concern is the time limit of the analysis.

Cde. Layne however, felt that the C.C should take all the time necessary to do the analysis given the state of the work. When we have exhasusted the discussion on the item we can move on Sister Coard agreed.

The C.C agreed to follow the approach suggested by Cde. Chalkie Ventour.

(1) Analysis of the party and revolution
(2) Analysis of the C.C (main Problem)
(3) The way forward.

- 4 -

(1) ANALYSIS OF THE PRESENT STATE OF THE PARTY AND REVOLUTION

Cde. Ewart Layne lead off in the discussion. He said that had received minutes of the last C.C plenary, all documents and report from the P.B and C.C. Therefore his assessment is based on these reports and feed back from the ground he had picked up during his short time home.

The situation is that the revolution now faces the greatest danger since 1979. There is great dispiritiveness and disatisfaction among the people. Though not in an open way it can be recognised. The state of the party at present is the lowest it had ever been. The ineternational prestige of the party and revolution is compromised e.g the C.C delegation visit to the S.U.

We are faced with the tasks of Managing the state sector in great economic difficulties, to build the economy in the face of tremendous pressure from imperialism. Politically, to raise the consciousness of the working class and working people in the face of resistance from imperialism and to build the party into a Marxist Leninist vanguard in a country that is dorminantly pettit bourgeoise and to carry the proposed constitution to the people in two years time.

Militarily, to organise the defence of the revolution in the face of a qualitatively stepped up agression from imperialism who for years has attempted to carry out its policy of become more and more into a "gun Boat" policy. The small Caribbean islands are being drawn into an allience against Grenada and all the left organisations in the region.

We have to develop an army with more complicated means. Tighten our relations with the World Socialist Movement especeilly Cuba, S.U, G.D.R, of which relations are becoming more and more complex. To steer off isolation but not at the extent of departing from the correct path, and to carry out all tasks of social development.

In the face of all these tasks the party is crumbling, all mass organisations are to the ground, organs of people's democracy is about to collapse. The internal state of the party is very dread. There is wide protest against the higher organs, prestige has fallen in the eyes of the party members and the masses. The C.C has proven its inability to give leadership to the process e.g this time the C.C cannot determine the stage the revolution is at. The style of the C.C is becoming more and more formalistic. The growth and carrying of working class elements into the party is low. The style of leadership is carried out by directives (members says that democracy is dead in the party). Decision making is characterised by spontainety.

The C.C is on a path of right opportunism and is very dish... to its members e.g in the conclusions of the July plenary was reported that C.C has advanced, every single committee mass orgs were criticise except the C.C and P.B. The failure to match up with incentives to the participants in C.P.E was not criticised. When Cdes have failed to accomplish

- 5 -

tasks and accuses others for this it very serious. For soon ideological justifications will be found for these mistakes.

The C.C criticised the NYO for their short comings, at the same time Cde. Tan Bartholomew has been given additional responsibility of C.P.E and St. Patrick's P.C.B. He said that the tasks given to the NYO in this period are giant tasks which is impossible to accomplish in the end it will only lead to the fustration of the Cdes in this area.

In his view the main problem is the C.C. The C.C has diverted from the correct path. This will lead to the total disintegration of the party and the collapse of the revolution; at the same time when the work on the economic, military and international fronts becomes much more difficult.

The C.C needs to take a serious view, frankly criticise itself inorder to move out of this serious dangers in the interest of the masses and the revolution.

Cde. Ventour supported the points made by Cde. Layne. He said that the party is facing disintegration. Cdes are complaining of the amount of tasks, some are showing signs of resignation, Cdes are afraid to speak up, they show timidity and fear to express their positions. He said that this can make the C.C lose a lot of prestige. Cdes do not agree with the C.C conclusions of July. They also raised that the months have passed and there is no implimentation of the conclusions. There is a serious drift away from the party by the key supporters of the revolution, the vocal Cdes are now passive, they are not prepared to fight the reactionary lines on the ground. Community work is not going as was expected, he graded it as poor to fair. The militia is non existent. In some respects the masses have gone backwards ideologically using the present positions on the Korean plane incident and comparing it with the position of the masses on the Afghanistan in the early days of the revolution. He said that people are getting their lines from VOA.

Cde. Leon Cornwall also agreed with the analysis made by Cde. Layne. He said that the honey moon period of the revolution is over. In the past 4½ years progress was seen in many areas and the masses were on a high, now the work is becoming much more difficult and complex. The C.C has failed to develop a perspective on how the revolution must develop. The C.C has given too much unrealistic tasks and in pushing Cdes to accomplish it they become fustrated. A striking feature in this period is the absence of the masses in the activities of the revolution because of the deep fustrations which exists. He said that there is confusion among the party masses, we do not know how we are going to come out of this situation because the party has not develop a prospective. We tend to push things down Cdes throat and fustrate them.

All areas of mass organisation work has fallen, which is related to our lack of prospective on how to impliment solutions. The serious economic difficulties we face is also affecting the people.

6/.........

- 6 -

He said that Cuba had similar problems in their development but they were able to develop a militant mass base because of the strength of the party in developing a perspective and its work

There is a lot of confusion structurally in the party. There is no clear system of subordination. Structures are created without having a perspective to them. Too much shifting around of Cdes. We have failed to develop Cdes, we also make too much mistakes in who we send to train abroad e.g the Cdes of the Youth Organisations are bitter because training abroad is seen as a passport to transfer them into other areas of work. In some cases we send Cdes to train only to fill the places offered to us.

As a party we are not playing a leading role in the process. Inner party democracy is being down played this is a result of our style of leadership and work, also how we seek to deal with the young Cdes is damagaing the dignity of the party and its membership.

He also agreed that the C.C is on a right opportunist path referring to the conclusions of the July plenary. He continued to say that if the C.C is to gain any respect we must move away from this path. He said that this problem is as a result of the low ideological level of the C.C and the party in general. Cdes see the conclusions of July as a set of administrative measures. There is no system to ensure that Cdes understand the lines of the party. No persective on the development of the G,M's. He thinks that the solution is an ideologically clear and steeled C,C and party which can explain the lines of the party and can impliment it in all areas.

Cde. Fitzroy Bain agreed with the position of the Cdes. He said that the strongest supporters of the revolution are demoralised the party has set too much high standards for the people, we had expected social benefits to do the work for us. Cdes who leave the army are spreading unfavourable lines which is difficult to fight back, it is affecting the credibility of the army in the eyes of the people. There is presently a very low surface mood among the masses which will soon affect their basic mood.

Party Cdes bramble the masses, a small amount of our firmest supporters are leaving the country. The mood of the party is also lower than the masses at this time, there exist a level of mistrust, resentment and fustration among party Cdes. They are not convinced on the lines given by the C.C on Cde. Coard and Cde. Radix. Cdes see double standards in the party e.g when Cdes of the C.C do not do any house to house Cdes do not have any respect for the D.C, they also show a willingness to resign. Cdes of the Workers Committee are saying that their [illegible] is at stake, they attend too many meetings, they have no time to visit workplaces and given very little time to address the tr[illegible] union work. Cdes refer to the case of Sydney Francis and Valentino Sawney who were disciplined recently in saying that Cde. Austin committed a similar offence and he was not discipl[illegible] Party Cdes are just going through motions, they lack the spirit to fight on the ground. They criticise the supervision of the C.C, they say that communication from the C C is weak. They refer to the July Conclusion saying that meetings were held with M's and C.M's no meetings were held with A's but at the

- 7 -

same time A's are expected to carry out the decisions and task from the July Plenary.

Cde. Bartholomew agreed with all the points made so far saying that the C.C has not been giving leadership to the process. The party has been dishonest with its members on a number of issues which has shaken the confidence of the party masses. The C.C does not report frankly, the flow or information is a major problem, internal party democracy has been destroyed and decisions are handed down without involving the full members

Timidity is a major problem in the party, Cdes are afraid to speak out frankly because when they do they are termed in different ways. Members and C.M do not understand basic norms of party life. Cdes were not consulted when the three Cdes of the C.C was brought onto the P.B. Cdes do not know the members of the Central Committee. The D.C has not played the role it had been assigned to do, it has developed a very arrogant attitude towards Cdes, it has not developed ways of assisting Cdes that come before the D.C. The masses have lost confidence in the party, irregularities takes too much time before it is solved, e.g water and electricity problems Police and soldiers who left the army are going to Trinidad. They complain about the condition in the army. The economic problems are not explained to the people and the Church has grabed a number of people in this situation. He also reported an incident of Militia Cdes guarding a Church in this period. He said, that the party has not yet developed a ploicy for dealing with the Church. The revolution has lost its ability to manners counter who are very active. He refered to the 300 turn out in the indoor rally in Sauteurs as a very weak turnout in the context of the amount of mobilisation done. Mobilisers were actually chased in some areas.

Cdes complain of the lack of stability in the leadership of the NYO. He accused the party of bleeding the youth movement. The best Cadres are pulled out at a time when the youth movement is in problems. Leading Party Cdes have contributed to the discrediting of the youth Cdes terrorise the youth calling NYO "Not yet organise". We are not yet clear on the relation of the party and the mass organisation. He referred to occasion where the party is guilty of the above as the O.C ordered to run all youth from the Tivoli court, Cdes of the NYO do not get enough support from the party, Cdes complain that the O.C is not giving them adequate guidance. When members of the party are tied up for NYO activities they do not turn up and failed to give any excuse. He continued to say that the international prestige of the NYO is very poor there is the possibility of loosing seat on the Bureau of W.F.DY. He raised the problems experienced by the G.D.R Cdes now in Grenada. His view is that Cde. Goddard is given too much work as a result he cannot focus on the youth work in St. George's.

He said that the main problem is in the C.C. The C.C need to make frank decisions and communicate to its members frankly.

8/.................

Cde. Chris De Riggs registering his agreement with the points made referred to the 19 characteristics of pettit bourgeois party that party identified in the weekend of the fedons group seminar highlighting the points on(1) inconsistency (2) insufficient planning (3) vascillation (4) agreement in principle windbagism in practice (5) inadequate vision of the future (6) crisis management (7) poor attitude towards criticism (8) lack of a perspective of the future. He said that all these points characterise the New Jewel Movement at this time. He pointed to the fact that the C.C has failed to accept the failure for the work which in his view is very dishonest. This attitude has discouraged Cdes from criticising the higher organs, the reason being that Cdes were not encouraged to think critically of the higher organs. He also refered to the line of march document pointing out that no criticism were made of the higher organs He said that there has always been a tendency for the party to pay very little attention to the economy which has relevance to the question of social benefits and the overall development of the revolution. The C.C needs to prepare lines of educating the people on the present situation with I.M.F and the present sal. negotiations. The C.C lack a perspective for the development of the armed forces, the social problem still remains. There is a serious lack of C.P.E and ideological work in the Armed Forc

The work in the geographic regions is handled unsatisfactoril using the St. Andrew's issue as evidence. He also raised his concern over the C.P.E programme. He said that in a context when the party faces disintegration the C.C has failed miserably. He concluded that if we continue in this way the p rty will soon loose state power.

He went on to say that he has tremendous faith in the C.C. The C.C is comprised of the best Cdes the party can produce at this time, but we have failed to march up collectively to a growing complex situation.

Cde. Mc Barnette said that so far this meetings gives a clear indication of how far the C.C is from the rest of the membership of the party. He felt that the issues raised have been bubbling for quite a long time but the C.C had failed to rest it s finger on the pulse. The structures are there but the C.C has failed to provide the correct atmosphere for Cdes to perform. The lack of a prospective shows itself in may ways e.g community work, failure to deal with the spontaneous work of the masses. Though the conclusion is that C.P.E is the priority there had been no structures in the party for C.P.E up to a few weeks ago.

The revolution is suffering from a serious fall of its active supporters. The party must seek to consolidate. The church has capitalise on our weaknesses using the tactics and strategies of the party. Cdes at this time shows deep fear to criticise the party. The basis must be laid for frank and open criticism in the party.

Sister Phyllis Coard said that we have recognise that the situation is very serious. The mood of the party members can be graded as one (1) or lower. The mood of the masses can be graded as 1.5. The work of the P.C.B can be described as un-successful though there have been slight improvements in St. George's, St. David's and West Coast, it is till very bad in St. Andrew's and Carriacou. All programmes of the Revolution

- 9 -

are in a very weak condition, while propaganda work is still very bad. The mass organisations are showing less participation in the political work. During the months May to August strenuous efforts were made to revive the work but only a mordest 5% improvement was recorded. She analyse the situation as the failure of leadership of the Committees and failure of the C.C to exercise leadership.

As a result of the C.C failure to deal with the problems in NYO there arise a detoriation and pettit bourgeois behaviour resulting in the removal of key sisters in the work. The guidance of the Wormen's Committee work is now in the hands of a non-party member; Sister Claudette Pitt is now considering resigning, (she also know of 8 Cdes who express a willingness to resign from the party at this time). There is no alternative leader to Claudette because Cdes identied expressed their unwillingness to join the party. The C.C has displayed idealism on the question of women in the party, they cannot cope with the demands of the party at this time. She said that she also notice that the older Cdes are getting tired and sick.

There is a need for the party to assist the NYO in long and short term strategy, their role in the state etc.

The militia is non existent, the army is demoralise the Cdes have genuining complains, growth in militarisation and deep economic problems.

No long and short term goals are set for the propaganda Committee and the masses are moving backward politically.

The Poor quality and low moral of the party is communicated to the masses because party Cdes live and work among the masses, they also display a harsh attitude to the masses. The masses are demoralise because of the party's failure to manners the situation. Party members cannot beat back the reactionary lines on the ground. There are also varing trends among party members, at the level of committees there is dog fight going on. The pettit bourgeois elements are using the situation to excuse themselves from criticism. However, some members have become more proletarian in their approach. Members, are demoralise by having to carry out unrealistic tasks and decisions. The C.C has failed to analyse the problems correctly and come up with a long term plan development. Cdes sees the July conclusions as being very dishonest.

The question of the ideological development of the C.C is an issue that we need to make a decision on. If this is allowed to continue the party will disintegrate in a matter of 5-6 months with Cdes resigning, applicants cannot make, workers do not want to join the party as a result the few remaining members will become over burdened, & fustrated the party will collapse and the revolution cannot continue without the party. The revolution can be turned back within one year. The international support of the working class is lessening. The party need to put the interest of the working people first and foremost.

Cde. Bishop said that in some ways Cdes contributions have began to address tomorrows agenda.

He said that he is struck by the levels of thought and preparation of Cdes as evident in their various contributions Though some conclusions are a bit pre mature, they are however, correct he agreed that the main problems lies in the C.C, in his view it have to do with two main factors.

(1) Low ideological levels, insufficient knowledge and awareness

(3) The lack of perspective as evident in a number of C.C meetings e.g 16th July. However, points are coming out more sharply today.

The lack of proper application of strategy and tactics has led to our party paying no significant attention to the views of the party and the masses; there is clearly no channels for communications which has lead to a breakdown of collective leadership. He said that it was premature to move from monthly meetings, wholistic pleanry. The C.C has not been able to receive oral and written reports from the party. Decision were taken outside of the C.C, we have not set up systems for implimentation and verification. The C.C is very adhoc in its approach to the work. The consistent over ruling of decision leads to a lack of clarity regarding the role of the higher organs, and inability for the C.C to provide guidance monitoring and supervision of the work.. This is as a result of the increasing complexity of the work.

The C.C has not been able to rise to the challenge of the increasing complexity this has led it to take a number of unrealistic decisions.

The C.C has made a number of mistakes over the past 18 months because of the weak links with the masses we became bureauractic and too formalistic in our approach. Visits to work places have disappeared, increasing non attendance at zonal councils and parish meetings, visit to communities to meet people at an informal level, decrease in the number of discussion and meetings with people in all areas of work, failure to participate in public activities, village meetings have disappeared. We have not paid sufficient regards to the material base in the country. Changes in the economy, changes in social wages and the predominant P.B Charcter of the masses and society as a whole our propaganda positions have consistently fed economism. We have failed to point out to the masses that this period requires a number of sacrafices and if we are not prepared to build the economy through hard work we will not make it. We have to take the blame for the over economic expectations of the people. We need to develop proper lines on these questions for the people.

He said the mood among the farmers is very low they criticise and attack workers for not producing.

- 11 - -

The mood of the agricultural workers is also very low pointing to his last visit to one of the state farms.

His understanding of the criticism and complain from the party has to do with the lack of channels of communications for the membership to raise their complains and grievances which we need to address. He agreed that a lot of criticisms have developed of leading Cdes in the party. He shares the overall concerns that Cdes have arrived at.

Cde. James agreed that there is a serious crisis in the party. There are signs of the beginning of disentegration, in the party, drop in confidence and prestige of the C.C. If the situation is not rescued there will be no hope for the future of the party and its ability to hold state power.

The work of the party among the masses has been badly affected by the mood of the party masses. At present the mood of the masses is low. We also have to conclude that counter revolution will seek to exploit the situation that we face. It is also clear that our ability to hold state power has also decreased. The problem however, lies in the Central Committee which is the main link in solving the situation. The C.C will have to take an honest cold blooded and scientific approach to save the party and revolution.

Cde. Louison said that he was shocked on his arrival in the country to see the state of the roads which is in the worst state it has ever been since the revolution. This he said is because of the continued decline of the work of the party. He also pointed out to a split in the P.F.U Executive as evidence of the present situation. He said that having listen to a number of Cdes he agree that there is a lot of problems in the leadership. He also pointed to the low ideological level of the C.C and the continued slow rate of development of a number of Comrades on the C.C. There is also a clear lack of contact with the masses among some of the C.C Comrades. He feels however, that sufficeint weight has not been given to the objective situations and the problems in the economy which we have failed to explain to the masses. He also pointed to the fact that while we are locsing links with the masses the middle class types have been coming to the revolution for jobs. He said that this is due to the lack of propaganda work to reach the masses. He said that he is still to be convince that the ideological levils of the masses have gone backwards. Some Cdes gives a panicky impression in the way they make their points.

He feels that the C.C is still capable of leading what is missing is the ideological level and collective leadership. The main feature of the July plenary is still correct. The revolution is deficient in facing the problems squarely and putting things in place.

Cde. Whiteman said that he is shocked at the mood in the country. He pointed to the failure of the two indoor rallies in St. George's as an indication of the present situation. He said that there is not enough two way communications in the party, too much directives is given regardless of Cdes work plans and schedules and unrealistic targets are set especially in C.P.E. The propaganda work has been too idealistic especially on the economy. He has never seen the road in such a bad condition before. We

/..........

- 12 -

have not been able to detect how the enemy operates he feels that there must be some counter revolutionary network in the country. Too much time is spent on small issues instead of fundamental issues e.g the church. He said that we do not fully grasp how the church is working at this time and what tactics and strategy must be employed to counter them. We do not fully know how the masses think and the house to house is not effective in achieving this. His view is that the leadership must spend more time in house to house in order to know what the people are thinking, we also need to think of how to build and substain the mass organisations in the face of economic difficulties.

He described the directive to remove all party Cdes children to public schools as a wrong approach, he said that the decision battle has not come yet, we have to focus on the major contradictions instead of these minor points. He suggested a second leadership structure that can read and summarise reports, he feels that the Leadership spends too much time reading reports.

Cde. Strachan said that he party is now 10 years and 6 months old, though the period we have met on several occasions to look at the work, the problem is that there has been a constant struggle to get the work done, he do not know how long this thing would continue for. The situation the party faces is even at the level of applicants. It is clear that a rebellion has started, it can burst out if it is not solved in a serious way, This is because the C.C have not lived up to expectations.

There is a lot of confusion and unclarity, Cdes are complaining that a large percentage of the party is not working, Cdes are complaining of being over burdened. The party do not give any attention to the economic and social problem of the party members, Cdes have not internalised the channels for communications and use them and even when some of their problems are solved the party do not double check to ensure. There is no system to assess the performance of the C.C members. The C.C is very far from the general membership and the D.C is not playing the role, it helps to demoralise Cdes. A hard look must be taken as to how the D.C must function.

The weekend seminars have shown that there is potential for building a serious M.L party. The sessions brought out both the positive and negative sides of cdes. However, the negative sides was given too much weight. The last rounds of seminar showed a qualitative difference in Cdes discipline. There was an incredible level of thought and participation, these things are happening at the same time when complains are coming up.

The level of attention to internal party development is not given as needed. We accept this in principle but in practice we have been different. The problem we face is in the style and method of our work. He said that a very high level of complacency exist at the level of the C.C. He pointed to the October crisis when the C.C met and took a number of decisions to take the party out of the rut. Cdes began to attend studies on time, prepared and attended meetings on time. However, the fundamental issues were placed aside.

13/......

- 13 -

CC Cdes have not been taking a global look at the work, instead they only emphesise on their narrow area of work. He said that we are maintaining the revolution and not leadi[illegible] it. Our style of work shows a tendecny to platformism as opposed to doing the hard slobbing work. He also refered t[illegible] the points made in the Fedon group seminar to cahcracterise the party. Busy busy action, temporization and vasillation in taking hard decisions is eveident in the C.C and more to Political Bureau e.g the St. Andrew's task force situation. He said that whenever we postpone a decision we are the one loose because imperialism is not waiting on us.

He said that in his view a great majority of Cdes love the party and express a willingness to work in the party but are not aware of what they should do, using example of Gloria Hastick who expressed her willingness to remain in the party but she has been having many problems. He said that the C.C has not tried to appreciate the prcolems that Cdes experienced from time to time. He said that Cdes have used the rules as a form of resistance refering to the no of holiday leaves, excuse from community work etc.

He sa d that if we agree that the role of the party is/to build the revolution and if we believe that an ML party can build what we want then we have to put the party on a M.L footing. He questioned whether we want to build socialism or just chanting sologans? Do we have a vision of the future. He is concern over the fact that the process is without a Leninist Vanguard. He pointed that in October it was agreed to review sister Phyl in regards to her membership on the Bureau but it was never raised in the July plenary. The C.C must now find out what are the essential qualities of a M.L. party.

BRAOD CONCLUSIONS PROPOSED BY CDE. MAURICE BISHOP

1. There is a state of deep crisis in the party and revolution.

2. The main reason for these weaknesses is the functioni[illegible] of the C.C.

3. The crisis has also become a major contributing factor to the Crisis in the country and revolution and the low mood of the masses.

4. The crisis have also been compounded by the weakness in the material base, electricial block cuts, bad roads, retrenchments and jobs as an issue.

To correct this situation the following must be done:

1. Find methods of improving the work and individual and collective leadership of the C.C

2. The need to develop a prospective based on M.L criteria to guide the work in the coming period.

3. Urgently find creative ways of deepening the links with and out work among the masses.

14/......

- 14 -

4. To establish meaningful channels of communications between the leadership and the membership and to formally re-rational ise the work among party Comrades, bearing in mind the ground sewll of complains of over work and lack of of inner party democracy.

5. The C.C need to develop structures for accountability bearing in mind that Cdes are now demanding accounts from the party.

COLLECTIVE AND INDIVIDUAL ANALYSIS OF THE C.C

Cde. Liam James leading off said that this si the last chance for the C.C to pull the party out of this crisis and on a firm M.L path. This crisis is not only among the masses but in the party membership as well. Over the past few months one could have seen that the party and the C.C was not moving forward. The way forward is to take an honest, cold blooded, objective and scientific approach to the situation.

Within the C.C there are many problems all Cdes must be criticise for the lvds of disorganisation, low ideologfcal level and failure to put the party on a firm M.L footing. These weaknesses are so evident that party Cdes are saying that certain Cdes must be chopped from the C.C. It is clear that party Cdes have lost their level of respect for the C.C The removeal of Cdes from the C.C will no way solved the problem in his view all the Cdes of the C.C are by far the best Cdes in the party, what is needed is firm Leninism. He pointed out that the most fundamental problem is the quality of leadership of the Central Committee and the party provided by Cde. Maurice Bishop. In his view the Cdes has great strength, his ability to inspire and develop Cdes, his ability to raise the regional and international respect for the party and revolution; he has the chrisma to build the confidence of the people both in and out of the country, and to put forward clearly the postions of the party. Today these strengths alone cannot put the party any further in this period. The qualities he lacks is what is needed to push the revolution forward at this time:

(1) A Leninist level of organisation and discipline.

(2) Great depth in ideological clarity.

(3) Brilliance in strategy and tactics.
These qualities which are essential for M.L leadership has prove to be lacking in the Cde. at this time.

Cde. Layne said that based on all analysis, discussions and conclusions it is quite clear that the C.C has not been able to give ideological leadership to the process. If we are to be honest and frank througho ut the crisis we go through more and more Cdes coming to realise that we face a real possibility of the revolution being turned back..

15

It is clear that Cde. Bishop lacks theses qualities put forward by Cde. James. Despite his strengths, the strengths that he lacks is vitally needed to steer the revolution off the dangers and to come out of the crisis. The salvation of the revolution calls for us to take a mature proletarian decision to save and carry the revolution forward.

Cde. Ventour agreed with the two cdes that the type of leadership that is neeessary to pull us out of the crisis is lacking in the Cde. Leader. These criticisms were made to him on more than one occasion which he accepted. He shows that he do not have the quality to put the party on a firm M.L footing.

He also criticise the C.C for not criticising the Cde. for areas of work e.g Armed Forces and Propaganda. However, he thinks that the main fetter is that the Cde. do not have these qualities

Cde. Cornwall agreeing with all the Cdes who spoke so far. He said that we have studied O.P.P. Seven points were made one of which was a Leninist C.C as a principle for the building of a M.L. party. He agreed that the root cause is the C.C. For quite some time we have been seeing the problem, The chairmanship and leadership of the C.C appears very weak. He said that there are great strength in the Cde. Leader that have carried the process, but as the complexities grows these qualities alone is proving inadequate. He also added that the Cde. Leader ability to supervise and stay ontop of the work is also lacking. These weaknesses creates a fetter on how we organise to carry the work forward. Instead we move from one crisis to another and the frequency of crisis becoming more and more frequent. If we fail to transform the party we will loose state power, lives will be lost, history has placed a great responsibility on our shoulders which we must seek to deal with in the correct and scientific way.

Cde. De Riggs said that he has been giving the work some deep thought over the past months. He agreed that the situation is favourable for counter revolution in this time, state power can be easily over thrown. The low mood of the party and the masses is also very clear to him. He said that the C.C has failed to match up ideologically to the situation. The removal of any Cde. on the C.C will not help this situation.

The main problem is the question of leadership. There is immidiate need for the reorganisation of the C.C in order to re build the confidence of the membership and masses in the party. In solving this problem. The interest of the party and revolution must be taken first, he pointed that he agreed with all the points made by Cde. James.

Cde. Bartholomew agreed with what he called very frank and open analysis by the Cdes. He said that he had never realsed any criticism of the C.C and Leadership though he was dissatisfied with the quality of the leadership. He agreed with all thepoints points made on the strengths of the Cde. Leader. He continued to say that his weaknesses were known all the while, but Cdes were hesitant to raise them. Though he had accepted earlier criticisms of this, he had never fulfil them in practice. The quality of the C.C has deteriated very badly, there is too much

16/..........

6

vascillation by the Cde. Leader. The M.L quality is becoming even more critical as the revolution develops.

Cde. Kamau said that since the last C.C meeting he has been giving deep thought to the work of the C.C. Overall the C.C is very weak, disorganised and haphazzard in its approach to the work. His personal work is still disorganise and weak which is true to say of most C.C Cdes, there is also a serious absence of deep thought and study. He said that the Cde. Leader has shown great strengths and remained in the positive qualities mentioned by Cde. James. However, the main problem remains the role of Cde. Bishop as the leader of the C.C. He said that the C.C continue to be loose and disorganise and unfocus, he said that the Cde. Leader lacks the quality to leade the C.C as spelled out by Cde. James. He agreed that removal of Cdes from the C.C cannot solve the problem until we deal with the question of leadership of the C.C

Sister Phyllis Coard commented that when she read the minutes of the C.C in July she was very shocked. From the beginning of the year she had began to prepare herself more for study though she had not been doing broad reading. However, she feels that the Central Committee cannot move forward unless it is involve in more indepth studies. As things began to get more complex the C.C have not met seriously to deal with the fundamental problems and in the absence of the C,C the P.B have not done any better.

She said that she had identified a number of questions for the C.C to deal with in order to move forward, being that we now have to decide what perspective to use and how to develop political education, strategic long term and short term goals for propaganda. The best way to coordinate media propaganda with the propaganda work of the party, how do we develop our lines quickly to the party members, how to structure the C.P.E programme to encourage more participation, the level of party participation in C.P.E, what amount of programmes can the party substain and maintain, qualities to look for in the selection of new party Cdes, how do we improve communications from the higher organs to the lower organs, how to structure the Secretariat, should the NYO become a semi vanguard, how to direct political education, how to organise community work successfully, how to overcome militarisation in the army, how to organise militia to ensure maximum participation, what is the long term future of the zonal councils and how do we sacrafice quantity for quality.

She said that neither the P.B nor the C.C have analyse these fundamental questions that is why these problems exist today, and even when it is done it is limited and vasillation follows. She agreed that the leaders of the party has failed to provide the necessary leadership to the party. She commented that the main problem of the C.C is idealism, volunteerism, failure to face up to hard decisions, illness as a result of phycological pressures in this context the Cde. leader has not taken the responsibility, not given the necessary guidance, even in areas where he is directly in charge of the guidance is not adequate, C.C is disorganised very often, avoid responsibilities for dealing with with critical areas of work e.g study class. She criticised

17/........

- 17 -

the C.C for not criticising him in the past, some time ago he pointed out that he was not capable but the C.C ignored him. Some Cdes are scared to criticise him because he had been hostile to criticism.

The P.B and C.C leaned on the O.C to take decisions that they should have taken. Cde. Strachan has taken the full responsibility to hold the party together when the C.C and P.B had failed to provide the necessary political guidance under this pressure he had taken, bound away decisions, shown hostility to criticisms, though she had seen some improvement of this in the past two weeks, the Cde must be complimented for the proletarian qualities which he display. A number of C.C Cdes are demoralise because their work has fallen. We also need to consider whether the C.C will be stronger or weaker if Cdes are chopped, in her view it will be weaker. She agreed to changes in the composition of the C.C. She concluded that the C.C will have to take the hard decisions that will improve the quality and levels of the C.C in terms of ideological and organisational directions..

Cde. Bain said that the analysis is difficult for him in the given circumstances, problems in work, health and a number of Cdes being out of the country. The ideological levels of the C.C is definitely a great concern e.g we are not sharp in determining the main feature of the period of July plenary, which he was worried about particularly when the revolution is 4½ years old. He said that another feature is that we come up with hasty decision as a result of pre mature thinking. Cdes are able to identify that the C.C collectively is weak, he agreed with the points made by Cde. James and added that it is greater demanding the leader to give more guide-ance to the process at this time. ....

S.M.

Cdes are looking to the C.C for this quality, it is dangerous if leading Cdes cannot show these qualities. He said that he would have preferred is the Cdes had named the C.C Cdes that the membership was doubtful of. He said that if this concensus is wide spread and the party do not take action on it it can lead to more problems, how will these members respond and what will be the C.C 's answer to it. He feels that whatever decision must be taken should be given the greatest thought, not only for now but throughout the future.

Cde. Lousion said that the no. one problem is the quality of leadership given the process by Cde. Bishop. He loses focus and spend too much time on details. The points made by Cde. James and Cornwall have really cristalised the problem which we have to find ways and means of solving. He said though that the C.C have not been able to assist the Cde, in developing these strengths.

He said that the names of C.C Cdes mentioned by the member-ship as doubtful were "H.A., Uni. Fitzy, Kamau and St. B. Though in his view reduction or expansion of the C.C cannot solve the problem. He suggested a cross system for developing the work, how to find a methodology for helping and forcing C.C Cdes to develop ideologically. This problem is a funda-mental problem we have been extremely week, the criticisms

- 18 -

are correct we have to come up with a solution quick and ensure that it is communicated to the party within hours. He added that we need to spend much more time doing preperation for study and rigourously execute the tasks. We also have to get rid of trivial issues.

Cde. Strachan said that one of the most striking thing is that he .. never heard any member of the C.C ask for a report from the Political Bureau on its week to week functioning. The P.B is a committee of the C.C and at no point in time was a report summoned. The CC Cdes do no get any minutes or report from the P.B. This is very serious, becaase the P.B is left to do thei own thing.

He pointed that he is in total agreement with the points made by Cde. James he again referred to the Fedon study seminar making the point that Cdes always wait for someone else to take the lead, which is one of the reason for this rut. We now have to take the responsibility of demanding higher qualities from the Cde. Leader. The Cde. should have dealt with him every time he slipped in the past. He recognise the brillance of the Cde. but agreed that this is not enough to carry the process forward and to build a serious M.L party. He used the example of Cde. Fidel who is always reflecting and thinking saying that these are the qualities that a M.L leader must have. He said this is the time when we have to deal with the main problems of the C.C.

Cde. Unison Whiteman said that the weaknesses mention of the Cde. Leader are correct. Since October there have been some improvements in scheduling and study but these improvements are not fundamental enough. He said that the Cde. Leader had not set enough time to the fundamental but we have to be careful that we don't shift too much blame from the the C.C collectively. We need to have a commitment on the C.C to new norms, prioritisation greater reflection, better style of work, we have to build up Comrades, e.g Cde. Leader, we have to assist on higher standards from him which he is capable of.

Cde. Leader thanked the Cdes for their frankness in their criticisms. He said that Cdes in the past have given serious thought to the question of leadership and failed to raise it for diplomatic reasons which was not good. He is disatisfied over the fact that C.C Cdes have not raised these points before with him frankly, though a couple non C.C Cdes have done it. He picked up an overwhelming sentiment that the qualities required are not possessed in him. He agreed that the points are correct especially correct application of strategy and tactics which cannot be achieved except the other qualities are fulfil. He had found difficulties of finding a relevant material to study the question of the functioning of the P.B and C.C which reflects a weakness, he don't think that he had given adequate leadership to bodies. He had several problems over the years especially the style that entails consensus, and unity at all costs which can result in blunting class struggle. He had tried to keep a certain kind of relationship with Cdes even though it is not what it used to be before. He also questioned his approach as regards to collective leadership, he said that

19/......

- 19 -

there is not enough participation and discussions. Too much decisions are taken by smaller and smaller organs which effects collective leadership.

On the question of crisis and problems it is correct as the maximum leader to take the full responsibilities. He needs time to think of his own role and to give a more precise response to the problem addressed which he thinks is a correct approach.

After lunch Cde. Ventour took the opportunity to explain to the C.C that his illness was to a large extent more phycological than physical. Since he came back the situation had affected him which reflects a P.B character of lack of steaunchness. -He said that he would try his best to pull himself out of this situation and to serve the party and revolution in the best way he could.

Cde. Bartholomew also pointed to the health Problem he experienced and the question of his low ideological level of which he is not satisfied with. He said that he is not capable of taking the ideological C.M class. Both himself and sister Phyllis Coard had requested to be personally assessed because of the fact that they were not in the July plenary, the Cdes were told that they were not present at the meeting therefore they could not have been assessed, especially Cde. Tan who was ill and as a result could not have function. Cdes agreed that it was incorrect to do it now because of the focus.

THE ROLE OF THE C.C.

Cde. Bishop said that on many occasion we have tried to look at the role of the C.C. He referred to the documents of June '81 and subsequent minutes of the C.C that dealt with its role.

He proposed that the C.C move to meetings once per month and to have three wholistic plenary, each year.

He said that the montly meetings must be seen as a medium of analysis, exchanging information of various sections, and pre-schedules should cover special areas of party and state work. He sees that at the end of October the main topic being C.P.E, in November the study commission will also have to determine the role of the C.C/secretariat is key in operationalising the sub committee in terms of reports from various bodies etc. Also getting to the party guidelines on major issues ensuring conclusion and resolutions are drawn up after our delebration and be circulated to the membership.

To develop and maintain links with the masses the leadership must personally get on the ground among the people, step up participation in zonal and parish councils, visits schools, monitor and push production. The role of the C.C must be worked out in this regard. Develop mechanism for accountability, and to review constant feedback from the membership and to ensure channels of communications with them.

20/.........

- 20 -

The C.C must do a constant evaluation of the progress made by members, receive reports from C.C on the rationalisation of the work, prioritise the work of Cdes on the C.C and set targets to be achieved on a weekly monthly and yearly basis.

Cde. Kamau Mc Barnette said that the C.C needs to explain the criterior for membership on the C.C and by what mechanism are Cdes work on the C.C are judge. Ensure the right atmosphere are convened for free and frank discussions. The party must be honest and frank with its members and for the last time explain the truth about Cde. Radix.

Cde. Leon Cornwall said that the C.C must have a propsective on its role. We need to work out the framework for the kind of party we would like to build so when Cdes are recruited we will know what structure we must put them in. The commission that is travrlling to Cuba and S.U should know what should be done on their return., They should know how we are going to build the party, drawing the experience of other countries. We also need to start working on a party constitution in a concrete way. We must develop commission for different areas of work. These are concepts that we need to start. The work on how we are going to build people's power. A conference should be set up to look at the submission from the commissions/take decisions and develop the line of march.

Cde. Layne said that he share the views of Cde. Cornwall. He said that the crisis cannot be solved immediately. There are a number of fundamental question that the party need to look at over a period of time. The Party has a very unscientific approach to the work, we rush to do things without deep analysis which further push us into problems. The NJM does not face a problem of commitment. We need to find the root of the contradiction or we will continue to face problems.

When Cdes are working hard without any rest it leads to fustration and demoralisation. We have taken an incorrect position in terms of what is necessary to build the party. He pointed to the fact that Cde. Strachan commission visit to Cuba was not dealt with seriously. He pointed that there are committees but no structures, there is no clear role for the function and future of the V.C.B.& we do not have a C.C Secretariat. We have to make the question of supervision a profession. The O.C has been successful in carrying us to power, the tasks it faces now is enormous. Cdes quality on the C.C has gone down, Cdes cannot supervise the work effectively, good ideas are accepted in principle. However, he complimented the new approach by the O.C, he said that the O.C has been good but we are asking the Cdes to take too much heavy ideological and political decisions in the absence of the functioning of the C.C and P.B.

He made reference to the Etophian Party and the method they took to develop their party, he said that even though their method cannot be applied immediately so that it can be develop in the future, we need to have a policy for the development of Cdes in the party, we have to develop the professional levels of Cdes in the party, Cdes will make mistakes but they will be helped and pulled forward.

21/..........

- 21 -

He said that the struggle for socialism is won, lost or divided in the army. The party must now be organise in the work places. Cdes with state post must be prepared to carry out the lines of the party in the work places. We have experience in mobilising the masses but we do not know how to build the party. We have to lay the basis for taking a strategic approach for the building of a M.L party learning from the experience of other parties.

Cde. James agreed with the postions of Cde. Cornwall and Cde. Layne, he made the following proposals:-

1. The C.C must become fully accountable to the members, so that Cdes can evaluate the work of the C.C on a whole and the C.C members.

2. All C C Cdes must be based in the country at this time until the situation is resolved.

3. The C.C and party must study Brutens.

4. Recall the conclusions of the July Plenary.

5. Proposed a modle of joint leadership, marrying the strengths of Cdes Bishop and Coard. He went to define the responsibilities of the two Cdes.

CDE. MAURICE BISHOP

(i) Direct work among the masses, focus on production and propaganda.

(ii) Particular attention to the organs of popular democracy, working class, youth masses, visits to urban and rural work places.

(iii) Militia mobilisation

(iv) Regional and International work

CDE. BERNARD COARD

(i) Party organisation work
Chairman of the O.C

(ii) Party organisational development and formation of Cdes.

(iii) Strategy and tactics.

The C.C must discuss and ratify all proposals and decisions sought by the Cdes.

22/..........

- 22 -

C.C meetings must be monthly, chaired by Cde. Maurice Bishop. P.B weekly chaired by Cde. Bernard Coard. The bothe Cdes will write quarterly reports to the C.C for review. The membership must be told of this decision.

Cde. Deriggs commented on the brillance of the contributions of Cdes Layne, James and Cornwall and supported their positi

He proposed that:

(1) Cde. George Louison be placed to head the St. Andrew's work while maintaining the teachers, farmers and the Ministry of Agriculture work

(2) Cde. Strachan to head C.I.E and propaganda work,

(3) Cde. Bartholomew responsible for Youth and St. Patrick's

(4) Cde. Austin - Construction.

(5) Cde. Layne chief of the Armed Forces with Cde. Cornwall chief of political and academic work.

(6) Cde. Whiteman, Foreign Affairs and Chief of I.R.D of the Party.

(7) Fitzroy Bain - Rural workers work

(8) Cde. Chalkie Ventour Urban Working Class

(9) Sis. Phyllis Coard, St. George's PCB and NWC.

(10) Cde. St. Bernard, West Coast and Carriacou

(11) Cde. Mc Barnette, St. David's P.C.B.

(12) Cde. DeRiggs -.Health

(13) Cde. Liam James Ministry of Interior.

Cde. Ventour agreed with Cde. Chris especially with the posit on Cde. George Louison. He proposed that Cde. Strachan remai as Deputy chairman of the O.C. He do not agree with the postion on H.A. Because he feels that there is great admiration and respect for the Cde. in the Armed Forces. However, he should also retain his position in Construction.

Cde. Mc Barnette agreed with the positions of the Cdes, he complimented Cdes Cornwall, Layne and James for the depth of their contribution. He took the opportunity to put out his interest in propaganda work.

Cde. Layne agreed with the position of Cde. James on the question of Cde. Coard's return to the C.C and P.B. He said that Cde. Bishop qualities are still necessary, but as Cde. James said these qualities cannot push the process forward. The only Cde. who have these qualities is Cde. Bernard Coard

23/.........

- 23 -

and if one look at the situation in practice he has been giving ideological and organisational leadership, and elaborating strategy and tactics even outside of the C.C e.g the land question. The reason why these qualities are lacking on the C.C and P.B is because Cde. Coard has been out of the partys leadership. He sees Cde. James modle as the best hope of pulling the party out of the crisis. He also feels that Cde. Austin should remain in the army because of his qualities and prestige there.

Cde. Louison said that the scope of the issues raised is very thorough because it put the work into prospective. He disagree with the joint leadership proposal, he feels that this modle cannot solve the problem of Cde. Maurice Bishop. He welcomes a postion of Cde. Coard being back on the C.C and P.B and Chairman of the O.C. He is also not sure that the theoretical postion put forward for joint leadership is correct. He said the qualities missing have two dimensions. The level of effort of personel discipline and struggle that he is able to put in towrds making the change, and the level of collective mannersing from the C.C to ensure that he build these qualities, if he fails then it may be necessary to remove the Cde. in the future. He did not agree with the basing of all C.C Comrades in the country. He said that there is need to have a C.C Comrade as Ambassador to Cuba, and Cde. Layne have only five weeks to complete his course of which he should be allowed to, if he complete the training it will bear more fruits in future He agreed to the monthly meetings of the C.C. He commented that his personel choice is to work in St. Andrew's, but he feels his role in the production sector is key and if he is to be given any additional tasks it should be in this area, He felt that Cdes are underplaying the role of the material base. He also agreed that Cde. Austin should remain in the Armed Forces.

Cde. James said that his proposals is first of all to deal with the problem that we face. His view is that the fullest proletarian type support of the C.C can help the Cde. Leader in developing these qualities, Cde. Bernard is the only Cde. that have the necessary qualities to merge with the Cde. leader's strength for leading the process at this time.

On Cde. Layne and Cornwall, we all agree that the Army is in a state of rut and demoralisation along with a serious ideological drift the army needs at this time Leninist Leadership in that of Cde. Layne and the political and Academic work in that of Cde. Cornwall. He agreed with Cde. DeRiggs proposals, in his view there is no other choice, especially with the position on St. Andrew's work, the state enterprise work is too much for Cde. Lousion.

Cde. Bartholomew said that he is very frightened of the level of ideological drift in the army, Cdes are saying that we are talking of imperialism too much, when there so much problems in the camps. Ministers are buying new cars when soldier cannot get food to eat. They are also saying that the army is a bourgeois army making referances of

24/.........

- 24 -

... standards.

The masses have lost confidence in the Army's capability to defend the revolution. The political work in the Armed Forces have not been very good. He felt that Cde. Layne and Cde. Cornwall are critical in the army at this time, and that we cannot afford to have a C.C Comrade as Ambassador to Cuba, inspite the importance of the relations.

He also agreed that Cde. Louison should be sent to do political work in St. Andrew's because of the problems in the parish and the importance of having a P.B Cde. there. He should remain in N.Y.O and St. Patrick's. He said that he is not capable of handling C.P.E. He agreed that Cde. Coard should be back o the C.C and P.B in a process of joint leadership.

He expressed his concern on the Ministry of Interior. He said that this area is very critical in this period, Cde. James as leader should not be allowed to travel because of the need to sit on top of the work. This excessive travelling does not allow him to effectively supervise the work. P.B minutes should be circulated to the C.C because the C.C is overall responsible for the work.

Cde. Cornwall said that we have two outstanding Cdes in our party being Cdes Bishop and Coard, we have suffered because of the the absence of Cde. Coard in the leadership, what is proposed is joint leadership with specific responsibilities and tasks. He has no problem with the points raised by Cde. George but not as reasons to solve the fundamental problem in the party, therefore he strongly supports the points made by Cde. James.

On the Armed forces he said that no one can deny that Cuba is the most important country to the Grenadian process, but he feels that his time is seriously wasted as Ambassador to Cuba because the work is carried out inspite of him. A good party Cde. can carry out the work while he is used more effectively at home. He suggested that Cde. Mc Phail remain to brief Cde. James Parke who will be going up there soon. Cde. Mitchell has improved tremendously and can do quite a lot of work. Therefore it is quite easy for both himself and Cde. Layne to sit on top of the Army to ensure that it develops.

Cde. Bain felt that the proposals made by Cde. James is a compromise though it is joining strengths of the two Cdes. together. He is confused on how this will work. He would like it to be spelled out clearly, he has problems to conception-lise it especially when one Cde. will chair the C.C and the other chair the P.B. He will need to give this more thought. He isin agreement that the C.C and P.B have suffered with the absence of Cde. Coard. He also don't know how Cde. Coard is going to accept the formula, he said that some structure should be put in place to allow Cde. Layne to complete his course. However, Cde. Cornwall should remain in the Armed Forces. The C.C has shown too much vasillation on the St. Andrew's issue, Cde. George in his view is the best person for this area. Cde. Austin should not be removed from the Armed forces. Cde. Chalkie Ventour is the best person to work

25/.............

- 25 -

... the Urban Working Class but given his present health conditions he should be given a personal assistant. He also agreed with Cde. Bartholomew's point on Cde. James in the Ministry of Interior. He concluded by saying that there is need for the C.C to be more on the ground.

Cde. Layne was shocked by the points raised by Cde. Bartholomew on the Armed Forces in this context, he agreed that himself and Cde. Cornwall should remain to begin work in the Army. The explanation to the Cdes in Cuba and S.U can be handled tactically

Cde. Louison felt that Cde. Cornwall is taking an emotional approach to the question, his purpose in Cuba should be seen in the context of the overall international work for the Revolution The Cde. approach shows a degreed of panic in his view.

Cde. Strachan supported the proposals made by Cde. James in joint leadership. It has been able to recognise the strengths of the two Cdes due to years of experience of working with them. The Cde. Leader can unite all classes and strata which is vitally needed. Cde. Coard has the qualities that he is lacking therefore a creative way must be used to fuse these qualities to move the process forward. It is clear that Cde. Coard's absence is felt over the years. In order to build a Leninist party we must have a Leninist C.C, therefore he supports the proposals of Cde. James and DeRiggs. He do not feel that Cde. Austin should be removed from the Army, he firmly supports the view that both Cdes Layne and Cornwall should be placed to work in the Armed Forces immediately, a strong position can be put to the Cdes of S.U and Cuba so they will understand the situation He suggested that Merle Collins or Joe Charter can function as Ambassador to Cuba. The contributions made by Cdes Cornwall, James and Layne impressed him, all spoken openly and frankly with great clarity, genuin' proposals were made for the transformation of the party which will also help to transform the Cde. Leader into a Marxist L eninist and to Leninise the C.C. We also have to see out ideological development as key to the development of the party.

Cde. Whiteman agreed with the position on Cde. Cornwall and Layne. Cde. Coard should return to the P.B and C.C he do not agree with joint leadership, he feels that Cde. Coard should be given specific functions as deputy leader. Agreed that Cde. Louison should function in St. Andrew's temporarily but should return to the economy. Considering the fact that Cde. Austin will remain in the Army Cde. Layne should be allowed to complete his course. Cde. Cornwall should not be removed from Cuba because it is not correct to remove the three top officials from any country at the same time. The proposal to put Cde. Strachan in C.P.E is correct.

He is not sure whether he should be made head of the I.R.D of the party because both areas requires a great deal of travelling and to do work among the left in the region from a party standpoint can lead to problems at state to state levels. He proposed that his travelling be cut by half.

26/...........

- 26 -

Sis. Phyllis Coard expressed her agreement with Cde. DeRiggs except on the point of Cde. Austin, Cde. Strachan as Deputy chief of the O.C and responsible for C.P.E - She is happy to hear that Cde. Kojo has considered health as an area of political work because health is a social programme around which the masses can be motilised. She predicted that when the international Airport is opened there will be serious demoralisation and counter revolution in St. Andrew's as a result she supported the idea of Cde. Louison being placed to work in the parish. She also pointed to the split in the P.F.U Executive in order to emphasise this need and the fact that the revolution is built on the alliance of workers and peasants She said that there is no Cdes in the party who can do what Cde. Louison is capable of in St. Andrew's.

She also agreed that both Cdes Layne and Cornwall should begin to function immediately in the Army. It is clear that the soldiers are disatisfied. The party should be blamed for what has happened to Cde. Bogo in Cuba.

She suggested that measures should be taken to limit C.C Cdes travelling, Cdes who can adequately represent the party should be identified for the purpose. She hunderstood the situation for Cde. Unison to guide the party's International work and not to impliment it. She agrees that the whole party should study Brutens and that the C.C must study the work of the P.B and E.B, she also proposed that this minutes should be studied by the membership because the stage we are at the membership will not believe what they hear from the C.C. She agreed with dual leadership not only for a short time but on a long term basis.

Cde. Louison said that the decision re Cdes Layne and Cornwall will be hard to sell to the Cdes, they will not be convinced and it will give a note of instability, on Cuba he feels it is a mistake that will further strain the relation between the two countries.

He reminded Cdes of his personal choice to do the St. Andrew's work, but in his view the two component parts that develop the revolution is the political work and the rise of the material base of the revolution . On the material base we have made little or no progress over the years. It we do not work to put these things in place the revolution will suffer over the years to come. To him the work in the Ministry of State enterprise is more important that the St. Andrew's work.

Cde. Strachan reminded him that the long term plan for St. Andrew's is industralisation.

Cde. George responded by saying that St.Andrew's requires maximum attention for at least one year to revive the work. The social and economic problems are very deep , he don't think that the Agricultural development work can suffer without him and his work in the Ministry of State Enterprise can have a great impact on the work in St. Andrew's than he being there.

27/...............

- 07 -

He don't see joint leadership as a solution to the fundamental proble. He can't see the theoretical basis for it, he is not convinced sufficiently that it can work and will not help to develop the strengths in the Cde. Leader. If we convinced that he is not developing despite all attempts to help him then we will have to remove him after his best efforts and his best intentions.

Cde. Whiteman addressing the army problems said that we have to find a moderate increase of salary for the soldiers and a food aid package at the end of every month for the soldiers. He belives that no amount of political work can move them without the material aids.

Cde DeRiggs reflecting on the points made by Cde. Louison said that St. Andrews represent a mutiplicity of problems all programmes there are the weakest in the country, it is possible that the people of St. Andrew's can be a constant resistant to the revolution, the extent of the rut is deep pointing to the problems of youth and marijuana smoking in the parish. He is not arguing that the state enterprises work is more important than St. Andrew's but at this pointing time it is critical and urgent for the party to resume contol of the situation.

The proposals of joint leadership is to solve the problem that exist the collective mannersing and the Cde. Leader's personal efforts will solve his problem collective leadership is important and critical.

Cde. Ventour said that since the July Plenary he had the impression that Cde. Louison was the best person to head the St. Andrew's work. The work in the parish requires P.B guidance if we do not report this in the G.M Cdes will raise concern. In his view, Cde. Louison cannot do the state Enterprise work at this time along with Teachers and P.F.U.

Cde. Liam James for the purpose of Cde. Hudson Austin who attended the meeting on the 16th because of flight problems, went on to explain all his reasons for his proposals on joint leadership basically making all the points he had made earlier in the meeting saying that if we fail to take these measures we will be guilty of right opportunism. ...... He do not see why C.C members should run away from reality he also gave examples of countries where there are more than one leader of the process e.g Nicaragua.

Cde. Louison questioned whether Cdes are saying that he cannot do the Ministry of State Enterprise work or whether St. Andrew's work is more important or a long term strategy or is it tactical for him to be in St. Andrew's for a period then move into the State Enterprise.

Cde. Cornwall in response said that he do not see the party work in St. Andrew's as a question of tactics, he thinks that this is of strategic importance to the revoltuion. He is firm that Cde. Louison should go to St. Andrew's because he thinks the Cde have the necessary tools and confidence to do the work.

08/....

- 28 -

On the question of joint leadership he also remain very firm because of the situation that we face. He referred to Nicaragua saying that a situation of joint leadership came about because of the objective situation they faced. Our situation requires tactical objective strategy.

He also addressed the Cuban Ambassador problems saying that because of the problem we face. He said th t we must explain our problems to our fraternal parties because they already know the problems that we experience now ,if not they will see us as jokers. The problem of they accusing us of instability will be solved if we explain things to these Comrades.

On the question of he going back to Cuba, he said that there is a relation between the internal work and the international work. The key responsibility for him is to build and strengthen our process.

He supported the view Cde. Whiteman should lead the IRD of the party.

Sister Phyllis view is that we have to decide whether George Louison will be in the economy or in politics. She felt that the Cde. cannot do the state enterprise along, agriculture, P.F.U and teachers. T he present split in P.FU is because of the lack of political work among the farmers, she also pointed to his recent failure in O.C tasks as a sign of over work. The S t. Andrew's work is both tactically and strategically important, it will also facilitate his teachers and P.F.U work. She recommended that some one should assist him in the technical work in the Ministry and Cde. George should focus on political work for next few years.

Cde. Layne highlighted Sister Phyllis point on the problems that will develop in St. Andrew's after the International Airport is completed. The work in this parish is a strategic question from all points of view. He went on to say that all the problems in the country cannot be solved immediately. The strength of our country is in the economy our international prestige is because of our economic performance. Therefore St. Andrew's work is both strategic and immediate because according to Sis. Phyl we can face a problem of counter revolution anytime.

On the question of joint leadership, he said that the starting point is the concrete situation that we face. We do not have a M.L party or a Leninist C.C. The situation existed when Cde. Coard lead in ideology, organisation and strategy and tactics for years. All parties must be able to work out their political lines. This is absent in our party because of the absence of Cde. Coard. We have to be able to organise the party and masses in order to develop a political line. Cde. Bishop is the best person to inspire the masses on the line of the party. In this situation the C.C is called upon to accept what is the reality.

29/

Cde. Bishop complimented Cdes Layne and Cornwall for their contributions which reflected ideological growth.

He said his honest view is that the party must utilise all strengths and talents of Cdes in the party. The greater the strength of Cdes is the greater responsibility, will be given to them. Leadership, power, authority and prestige that goes with leadership goes with rights. He has never had any problem with sharing power, or even a bad attitude to criticisms. He had worked very well with Cde. Bernard over the years from school days, they share a lot of policy decisions, they both wrote the manifesto, the peoples Congress enditement of Gairy. He referred to 1977 when Cde. Bernard was accused for aggressiveness and wanting to grab power, he had defended him. His postiion is that he or anybody has the right to be leader for life, he favours cooperation over competition. He feels that Bernard can come back to the P.B because of his skills and intelligence. Cde. James breakdown of responsibility is very useful, however, his concerns is the operationalisation of strategy and tactics. His own idea of his role falls into what Cde. James h d outlined. He feels that school visits should have been included under his responsibilities.

He would like to know what is Cde. Bernard's view of the situation and response, if he do not agree what will be the views of the C.C. He need to get some answers on the operationalisation. We have to decide how we will articulate this to the party and masses of which a clear position must be drawn up. His personal concerns are; image of Leadership, power struggle, imminent collapse of the revolution.

The formuldtion of Cdes criticisms have indicated a clear note of no confidence. He said that there are a two way flow he cannot inspire the masses when he have to look over his back or feel that he does not have the full confidence of the Comrades.

He agreed that Cde. Louison should go to St. Andrew's than to experiment in the State Enterprise Ministry, Cde. Austin must remain in the Army. He agreed with Cde. Whiteman's position on the linking of state and party IRD work. He felt that Cde. Coard should be called in to discuss the postion before the final decision is taken.

Cdes felt however, that the C.C should conclude on the decision before Cde. Bernard is spoken to.

Cde. Louison continued to raise his concern in that how will the joint leadership develop the four points in Cde. Bishop.

Cde. James said this proposal will pull us out of the period of crisis and push the party forward along with the full support of the C.C and the best efforts of the Cde. Leader will develop these qualities.

30/.........

Cde. Louison was not satisfied with the answer.

Cde. James "in the close working together of Cde. Bishop and C oard, the Leader will learn from a working experience. Cde. James brought to the attention of the C.C that Cde. Louison is seeking to disturb the proceedings of the meeting for opportunist reasons.

Cde. George also expressed a willingness to leave the meeting.

Cde. James went on to address the point saying that Cde. Bishop will be Prime Minister and Commander in Chief, he will sign all documents of the C.C. We also have to take a look at how we announce this matter, his view is that this matter must be put forward in a firm and principle way, we also have to decide how we are going to formulate it The key factor however, is how these two Cdes relate.

On the point of strategy and tactics, is that over the years Cde. Bernard Coard has been able to give guidance to the C.C, this does not mean that he will decide strategy and tactics all by himself. However, he will chair all commissions to determine strategy and tactics. The C.C will discuss and ratify all proposals brought forward. Also in real life the Cde. has developed strategy and tactics for the party.

CDE. Layne addressing the point on vote of no confidence made by Cde. Bishop said he do not agree with this positon he felt that the criticisms were made by all Comrades in the spirit of love for the party, ideological clarity and wanting to build a genuining M.L party, and to build the working class. He sees this as the best way to build the party. Cdes were very frank, the criticised themselves for not being brave enough to do so before. This frankness is critical for the development of an M.L party. It will be sad if the meeting concluded that this was a vote of no confidence. This was done in the insterst of the party and revolution what we are solving here is a problem that we experienced for years.

He used the example of the joining of two parties in G.D.R and their difficulties to say that it is only joining the strengths of two Cdes in the same party. It is our historical duty to solve all problems in our party. He also suggestes that the minutes of this discussions should be studied by members of the party.

Cde. Louison apposed the fact that he was puttin his position for narrow oppportunist reasons, he is genuining seeking clarity on the issue.

Cde. James said that he had spoken of Cde. Louison behaviour and he maintain that position.

- 31 -

Sister Phyllis Coard said the most striking thing about this meeting is that Cdes have spoken in an open and frank way if there was any thought of removing the leader Cdes would have said so frankly. The Cde. Leader will have to accept the spitit of the criticisms. She would not like to feel that it was taken by him as a vote of no confidence, this will just discourage Cdes and made them hold back their frankness.

Cde. DeRiggs "the meeting was one of unprecidented frankness and boldness by all Cdes, it was done through the spirit of great love for the revolution and Cde. Leader.

Cornwall. "He had spoken frankly and put forward his position bluntly. If this is the impression, it will hold back Cdes from speaking frankly. They have spotted the weaknesses and strengths and sought to identify a creative solution. The C.C is disposed to asist the Cde. Leader in all areas, if we fail to do so it will hinder the development of the process.

Cde. Strachan said that while he respect the Cde. Leader's position he feels that the points made were frank, open n and genuine. All Cdes spoke with deep sincerity and profound feelings, Cdes have given a lot of thought to the situation and genuiningly wants to come out of the crisis. These points cannot be seen as a vote of no confilence in the leadership. He also complimented the C.C for their frankness. It is extremely important to address the concern raised by the Cde. Leader. He agreed that Cde. Bishop must remain Prime Minister and sign all party and state documents. We also have to ensure that the masses and the counters understand that the party is a united party and there must be no signs of inner fighting. He agreed that we should conclude on /and the issue to speak to Cde. Bernard Coard.

Cde. Mc Barnette said that the exercise has brought to the floor two questions (i) How we are willing to accept our weaknesses and deal with them. (ii) how much we are willing to move forward.

He agreed that the minutes must be brought to full membership. He pointed that the criticisms have not shattered his confidence in the Cde. Leader. He said that we need to ensure that this type of criticisms is applied to every one of the C.C if the idea of no confidence is c it will degenerate the C.C.

Ian Bartholomew said that it took him a lot of guts to made his points. He think that the C.C have very great respect for Cde. Bishop, there is no doubt that the Cde. will remain Prime Minister in the country. He agreed that the minutes should be studied by the membership. We cannot convince the impression that there is a leadership problem, the most important thing is how the Cdes get along.

32/.........

[illegible] Ventour agreed with the positions of Layne and James [illegible] view is joint leadership can work and will work. It is important to give the minutes to the membership because th[illegible] have accused the C.C or being dishonest. Agreed with points made by Cdes on the vote of no confidence, both the Cde's strength and weakness were pointed out, and pointed to a cre[illegible] way forward. He pointed that Tan and Kamau spoke openly for the first time an attitude like this can make them become timid once again.

Sister Phyllis suggested two separate meetings to announce to the membership one for M's and C.M's and one for applicant

Cde. Louison said that the more the discussions is stretched out at theoretical and tactical levels he becomes more worried He said that Cdes of the party were analysed into three sec[illegible] those who can be moulded into communist, those who have to further develop and those who are weak or this basis he cannot see the minutes into the hands of all cross section of the party. He proposed that a summary of the main points should be brought before the membership.

On the question of joint leadership he said that he would like to know what is the intention of the C.C, if they will like to build the qualities or make a leader through joint leadership and at what stage will the prop be taken off. As an aspiring M.L he cannot accept joint leadership, he don't know of any situation of such. He cannot see the dialectics unfold, he is not sure of the evolution of this thing, he cannot see joint leadership helping us. He sees a clear leadership in once embodyment He had never understood the science to mean anything different, he is not convinced that the joint leadership will remain for any length of time without causing any problem.

Cde. Cornwall felt that the Cde. is confuse because he is posing in his mind the wrong question. We are saying that fundamentally the revolution is at stake and that there is a modle that will help to strengthen the process, or will it hamper the Revolution. He pointed to a situation where a Cde. use to be Minister and deputy Minister. This was tactically correct because of the objective situation. He feels that Cde. Louison is posing the wrong question, as a result will come up with wrong conclusion.

Cde. Lousion said that the joint leadership would not strength[illegible] the Revolution. How will it evolve? What would it eveolve to? Is it a temporary feature or permanent feature.

Cde. De Riggs disagreed with the context and spirit in which Cde. Louison made his contribution. He feels the scientific and theoretical basis as put forward by Cde. James has been established. We are seeking to find creative ways to solve the question of leadership of the C.C and the building of a M.L party for building Socialism. The C.C in its present form cannot take the country to socialism which is the long term strategy. We have to safeguard

- 33 -

the Revolution - build socialism. The question of leadership can also be dealt with sometime in the future. He also expressed his disappointment in Cde. Louison.

Cde. Layne said this is a question of fundamental importance. We are called to take decisions to correct the situation the time of manouvering is over. The form of leadership is scientifically decided, based on the situation we face. He used the e,g of the USSR Army where the concept of the Political Commissar and Militarty Leadership had developed and worked. They also defeated the counter revolution and 14 other imperialist powers. The concrete situation we face; the unfolding of the dialectics is the combining the two qualities to strengthen the leadership in a Leninist way for the building of Socialism in Grenade. The attempt to draw the C.C in a personality discussion is a P.B childish attitude.

Cde. George objected. "He has the right to put forward his postion no one can accuse him of opportunism in his struggle over the years in the party. He raise his points seeking clarity in a genuine way. He regarded Cde. Laynes comments as "shit".

Sister Phyllis Coard said that it is unfair of Cde. Louison to think that there have been demogagry in the meeting. She feels that Cdes have been frank. There has been less demogagry than ever before.

Cde. Layne said that he had been frank and fair. The Cde. is trying to provoke the C.C into a discussion that no Cde. has raised. Cde. George object to the point that this has never been his intention.

Cde. Bishop pointed to the struggles and difficulties of the RSDLP to point to the fact that Cdes are overbending too quickly to brand lables to each other in the discussion, which we have to be very careful about, because he cannot see how the meeting can proceed. He raised his concerns, that if the minutes of the C.C is given to the membership to study it will be the best way to create disunity and turn back the Revolution. He said that the response to his no confidence point, that he is not interested in the Cdes comment. The point is that he alone can solve the problem. He expressed his difficulty in chairing the meeting because of the flying of brands etc.

Cde. Liam James said that he can hold the meeting if he speak up and reign in more on Comrades contributions, and to list all the concerns raise and ask Comrades to comment.

Sister Phyllis Coard said that the other three concerns raised can be taken one by one in order to move forward.

Cde. Layne said that if we take each concern Cdes speak on them if they have opposing positions of anything to add may do so.

34/...............

- 34 -

The following postions were voted on:

1. On Cde. James proposals

For	-	9
Obstain	-	2
Against	-	2

2. Formalisation of Joint Leadership:

For	-	9
Opposed	-	1
Abstain	-	3

Cde. Austin abstained because he was not present for the full discussion for the greater part of the meeting.

3. How to inform the Membership:

(A) Tell members only through minutes

For	-	10
Against	-	1
Abstain	-	2

(B) Tell all three categories in one meeting:

Against	-	11
Abstain	-	2

(C) Tell all categories in two meetings M's and C.M's the A.'s

For	-	9
Against	-	2
Abstain	-	2

(d) Informing the masses:

Against	-	9
Abstain	-	3

Cde. George Louison - non participate.

-35-

Cde. Kamau moved a motion that these notes should be taken ... a decision. It was agreed to put it to a vote.

(4) On Cde. Kamau's Proposals

For - 9
Against - 0
Absta in - 3
Non participate 1

Cde. Layne proposed a formal vote on the conclusion of the July Plenary. Cde.

Cde. Louison said that there are aspects of the conclusion that can applied to the way forward. We can criticise certain aspects e.g the section on C.C and P.B was incorrect The conclusion failed on these particular issues.

Cde. Layne said that he has further problems with the overall decision of the July Plenary is not inkeeping with the reality therefore he agree with Cde. James to revoke the document and include the correct conclusion in the new document.

Sister Coard agreed with the revoking of the document. She said for the purpose for the history of the party, we have to disassociate ourselves from the document. She suggested a committee to extract the correct conclusions from the document.

Cde. Lousion said that a complete job must be brought before the members. Revoke the document and at the same time put correct position forward we cannot take a propaganda approach.

Cde. James supported Sister Phyllis, he had difficulty in understanding Cde. Louison position.

Cde. Louison said that if we withdrew the document and promis fail to give the Cdes the postions later it will/give the membership clarity.

Cde. Strachan said that if we are not able to extract the correct conclusions for the G.M, it is correct to tell the G.M that the conclusion will come to them in the future.

Cde. James fully supported Cde. Strachan's postion, he c don't see how the membership will not accept the postion. They will be happy to hear that the document is revoked.

Cde. Louison said the July conclusions had a multitude of administrative decision, if we say that we revoke the conclusions without putting forward a clear positions at the same time, it can lead to further redecule from the membership. He felt that we should point to the good and bad aspect of the document and put forward a new document, including the conclusions of July that is relevant to the building of the Revolution.

36/.......

- 36 -

He felts that we should go to the membership with a full document - giving the Committee a tasks to extract the relevant conclusion within a certain time in order to present the new document.

The sub committee agreed on were Cdes Cornwall, James and Layne. The time is to be taken at the end of the meeting.

Cde. Mc Barnette proposed that we use a break to ask Cde, Coard to come to the meeting for decision to be put to him.

This was seconded by Cdes Cornwall and Layne. Cde. Maurice opposed it because of the fact that he has to make a persona... reflection on the issue. He proposed that the C.C. meet with Cde. Coard in his absence. He felt that modle would be counter productive. He suggested that the C.C meet Cde. Bern... tomorrow while he will be leaving for St. Kitts. He think that this will be in the ineterst of the C.C.

Cde. James had difficulties with the position, he felt that Cde. Bishop should stand up and face the situation because he is part of the Central Committee, he thinks that it can and will affect Cde. Bernard's position on the issue.

Cde. Bishop said that it is difficult for him to understand the question of joint leadership and his own role and function in this modle.

Cde. Layne pointed out that he also had difficulties with Cde. Bishop position on the ground that it will be difficult to put this to Cde. Bernard when Cde. Bishop is not present; because the conclusion will be quite natural as to reasons why he is not present. A pre condition for this thing to work is a correct attitude on both sides.

Cde. Bishop said that it will be purly artificial based on his personal postion to sit down for productive discussion, it will have no usefulness, it will be counter productive and mechanistic.

Cde. Strachan asked if after the reflection, he will attend the meeting with Bernard. He said that he has no problem with that. He said that he do not think that the meeting will be useful with Bernard when he is present. He said that two things that is critical for him is time for him to reflect and Bernard's position at this time. This will even help him in his own reflection.

Cde. Layne said that he agree that the Cde, Leader would need time to reflect. However, if he is absent, conseptually the Cde. will think that he opposed. He felt that it is the right of the C.C to demand of Cde. Bishop that he be present for the sake of the future of the revolution.

37/...............

37

Cde. Bishop said on the question of the minutes to the membership, that the membership are not at the level. It is ideal... and devorced from reality to give C.C minutes to members. Cde. Layne disagree.

Cde. Bishop said that the minutes of the C.C cannot be disturbed to the membership because he has not seen that in any party. He feels that the party is not at the stage to provide all points and argument in the meeting.

Cde. Layne said we have much more to loos if we hold back the minutes of the C.C including the basis for arriving to the conclusions. T he lack of frankness have brought the party to a near collapse.

Cde. James said that this is one of the factors that cause the party to reach to this stage. The failure to give the members clear indication of the meeting will lead to further lack of confidence of the membership in the C.C. The Cdes are not nieve as we think they are.

Cde. Cornwall said that the absence of frankness and dealing with things squarely can lead to more tabay..sm in the party.

Cde. Bishop proposed adjustment of the meeting which was supported by Cde. Whiteman

Cde. Layne then points to the incident when himself and Cde. Cornwall were suspended for serious acts of illdisciplin in the army. He felt that the response had strengthen the prestige and standard of the party along with both himself and Cde. Cornwall

Sister Phyllis Coard then questioned what will the C.C say to Cde. Bernard in the absence of Cde. Bishop. This however, was not addressed.

Cde. James suggested that the C.C meet the following day in the absence of Cde. Maurice to put the decision to Cde Coard then work out the packages of measures.

Cde. Strachan opposed on the grounds that this will be too exploratary.

It was finally agreed to meet at 1.00 p.m. on Saturday 17th Cde. Coard.

38/.........

SATURDAY 17TH SEPTEMBER. 1983

Cdes Present

Selwyn Strachan	Phyllis Coard
Hudson Austin	Kamau Mc Barnette
Liam James	Chris De Riggs
Ewart Layne	Leon Cornwall
Chalkie Ventour	

Cdes Absent

Maurice Bishop	- out of country
George Lousion	- out of country
Unison Whiteman	- out of country
Tan Bartholomew	- Sick
Fitzroy Bain	- Sick
Ian St. Bernard	- Sick

The meeting started 1.30 p.m. Cde. Bernard Coard attended.

Cde. Strachan addressing Cde. Coard said that the C.C have been meeting to look at the state of the party and revolution and to look at the way the process have been developing over the past four years. It is quite clear that there are great concerns from the G.M of the party.

Following the emergency C.C all C.C members were called in to discuss ways and means of pulling ourselves out of this rut.

The revolution is in deep crisis, it faces the dangers of being turned back, while the C.C is not operating in a ... Lenin way. In identifying the root of the problem, it was found that the C.C is not leading the process and has to take the full blame. The reason is the weak leadership exercise by Cde. Maurice Bishop. In trying to find concrete ways of reviving the situation and to put the party of a firm M.L base, it was pointed that while these fundamental weaknesses exists the Cde. Has tremendous strength that will be needed ... ever. But the qualities that are missing are decisive qualities to put us on a correct path. Pointing to the four points referred to by Cdes James and Cornwall and agreeing that these qualities exist in Cde. Bernard Coard the C.C felt that Cde. Coard was the only Cde. who had demonstrated practice these qualities over the years.

As a result a proposal for merging these two strengths through joint leadership between Cdes Bishop and Coard was put forward by Cde. James and supported by the majority of Cdes. The area of responsibility was outlined for the two Cdes, all C.C meetings will be chaired by Cde. Bishop and P.B will be chair by Cde. Coard. C.C meetings will resume monthly. Cdes felt that this modle can help Cde. Bishop in building the qualities missing. This proposal was voted with a majority in favour.

- 39 -

The Cdes will write quarterly reports to the C.C, and on all fundamental questions the C.C will be involved. Other proposals were made but they could not be tackeled because of the need to settle the fundamental issue.

Cdes also outlined the operationalisation of the modle of joint leadership.

Cde. Cornwall said that they also look at the experienced of other countries and how the question of leadership is based on the objective situation that exist.

Cde. Kamau pointed to the fact that everyone spoke with frankness and openess.

Cdes also agreed that the conclusion of the last plenary must be revoked, because it lack content and dishonest, However, applicable sections will be attached as an appenxix to the conclusions of the meeting.

Cde. Ventour pointed that the party was on a right opportunist path.

Cde. Strachan said that it is the first time he has seen M.L position being put forward by the Cdes consistantly and supported by the majority.

Cde. Bernard Coard raised four points being:

1. He would like to see the minutes of the meeting .
2. The position of those opposed or abstain and what are the reasons.
3. Were other options examine, what were these options and why were they rejected.
4. Why was not this meeting schedule so that Cde. Bishop could be present.

Cde. Austin said, it was only right that he abstain because he arrived late in the meeting. When he arrived he askedf for the agenda.

Cde. Louison told him that it is:

(1) analysis of the state of the party and revolution

(2) feedback from the membership and

(3) the way forward. He pointed out that Cde. Bishop said that he had no problem to joint leadership. Therefore he could not understand why members who were here for the whole meeting and could not have taken a postion on this or why it is that members should vote against. He would like to know what were their argument for this.

40/...........

Cde. De Riggs said that Cde. Louison had problems with the s... or theoretical and operational with joint leadership. He felt these weaknesses cannot be solved by a modle of joint leadership. The operationalisation of the proposals will cause difficulties, he do not agree that the minutes should be studied by the membership, he is not clear on how the dialectics will unfold. He said that he has not seen it any where in the science. He supported the idea of tapping the strength of Cdes Bernard Coard, but felt that the joint leadership cannot strengthen Cde. Maurice Bishop's weaknesses, this is not done in any M.L Party. He continued to say that Cde. Whiteman said that we must not seek to shift the blame from oneselve collectively and that the objective situation must be considered. Cde. Bain was not clear on how the joint leadership will work he wanted clarity on the operationalisation.

Cde. Layne said that Cde. Louison said that in some party's that one person heads the state and the other heads the party. but the head of state is subbordinate to the head ofthe party.

Cde. Strachan said that Cde. Louison said that if we agree that the quality missing in the Cde. Leader is possessed in another Cde. why not take the M.L line and change the Cde.

Cde. James recalled his proposals saying that we need to find the scientific solution to get us out of the crisis to put us on the way forward. The scientific solution is based on the objective situation that exist.

The nine man directorate of Nicaragua was also mentioned because of the heated debate.

Cde. Bishop abstained on voting , though in his presentation he agreed to joint leadership. He placed his concern that he needs clarity on before he vote. He also needed a feed back from Cde. Bernard and some time to reflect on the issue.

Cde. Bernard Coard asked whether Cde. Bishop had agreed in principle.

Cde. Austin said that he gathered from Cde. Maurice that he was conscious of the crisis and that he did not have the necessary qualities, he also pointed that NJM had joint coordination and made references to thehistoric working relation with himself and Cde. Bernard. He said he cannot understand how two senior Cdes in the party opposed and abstain from this decision.

Cde. De Riggs said that Cde. Maurice in his presentation said that the point made amounts to a vote of no confidence in him, he sees this as a moral crisis on which he need to reflect. Cdes pointed that the points was made from a standpoint of love and deep respect for the Cde. Leader.

41.............

- 41 -

Cde. Layne said that this is the first time that Cdes spoke so frankly, which must be encouraged if Cde. Bishop was to see it as a vote of no confidence it will intimidate Cdes and harm the Leninist advancement of the Comrades in the party.

Cde. Cornwall said that conceptually Cde. Bishop had no problem with the concept of the joint leadership, he even agreed with the proposed responsibilities, however, when t he came to the point of no confidence he placed it out of the hands of the C.C by saying that he alone can solved this problem.

Cde. Austin said how he heard Cde. Bishop spoke he felt that some of the criticism was incorrect.

Cde. DeRiggs said that Cde. Bishop said he is not sure that he is the main fetter on the C.C.

Cde. James said that in his criticism he said we are now in a serious crisis, is the last chance for the party. In pulling the party out of the rut we have to be scientific cold blooded and objective.

All C.C Comrades must be criticised. Some Cdes have failed consistantly to the extent that membrs are calling for the removal of some Cdes, but he felt that this is not and will not strengthen the party. The main fetter is that of the leadership provided by the leader of the C.C. He pointed out to the great strength of the Cde. Leader, but said that these strengths cannot carry the struggle forward. He pointed to the quality lacking in the leader which is critical for carrying the process forward, he said that the Cde with this quality is Cde. Bernard Coard. On this basis he proposed the marriage of the strengths of the two Cdes to push the struggle forward out of this period of crisis.

Sister Coard said that as a result of the weakness of the leader there have been indeciciveness in solving crisis and we loos confidence in the measure we use to get us out of the crisisis and the frequence of the crisis is getting very frequent.

Cde. Deriggs said that Cde. Maurice response were to thank Cdes for the criticism. That the sense of overwhelming centiment / the what is required for a M.L leader is found in Cde. Coard. He had difficulties in finding reading materials on how the C.C and P.B should function. He had depended too much on unity and and consensus and collective leadership. That he had not prepared himself for that kind of approach because this was not his intention of how the meeting should go.

OTHER RESPONSE WERE: he gave a history of working relation between himself and Cde. Coard.

- he did not agree that he is the main fetter on the C.C.
- his did not agree that he has bad attitude to criticism
- he said his style of leadership may have cutted necessary debate and that he is not clear of strategy and ta ctics as assigned to Cde. Coard

42/........

- 42 -

- he would like to know Cde. Coard's position on the issue how it will operationalise and seek clarity on the concerns raised.

Four options for leadership were identified in the earlier proceedings:-

(1) Remove Cde. Bishop
(2) Joint Leadership :
(3) Have the deputy to play the role that is required.

(4) Remove Cdes from the C.C

On option three (3) Cde. De Riggs said that his own reading is that Cde. George put forward in a general way is that he does not oppose the return of Cde. Coard to the P.B and C.C. Though it was not discussed. It was put forward weakly by Cde. Whiteman as part of the response, it was not done as a concrete proposal. He made it as a response to the fundamental proposal.

Cde. James said that these qualities take years to develop in a Cde. therefore, the Cde. Leader will not be able to lead in this area. Cde. Coard have been leading in this area over the years. We are now recognising in formally and that failure to accept will be right opportunism.

We will not be M.L/ if we have joint leadership in practice and pretend that we have something else.

On point four (4) Cde. Strachan said that the view was expressed that we should take decision on the proposals and call in Comrade Coard. Cde. Bishop said that given that he needs time to reflect and that he need a position from Cde. Coard he will not be able to participate. He is prepared to do so later. He felt that the meeting should go ahead in his absence. Cdes did not agree with the position, they felt that both Cdes should be present in the meeting. The October '82 crisis was alio discussed in this light.

Cde. Austin said one of Cde. Austin said one of Cde. Bishop concern is that he would like to know what is Cde. Bernard's disposition on the issue and whether anyone had spoken to Cde. Bernard on the issue before.

Cde. Strachan said that this meeting should give an indication of Cde. Bernard's postion which will be key for his reflection.

Cde. Layne said that another key issue is that the minutes going to the membership. Cde. Bishop opposed

The Cde. Leaders had strongly opposed to it though he abstained in the voting on the issue. He said he did not understand how Cdes cannot see that this is the surest way of breaking unity in the country undermining his authority, pointing to the level of taybayism in the country.

43/..........

-43 -

C q. Coard said at every single level in the party there are lots of bi-laterals beating the party for dishonesty even to the extent of the study classes.

Cde. Austin said that he was confuse because the C.C was discussing what members were discussing; he want to know how it is possible to report to G,M without submitting the minutes to the meeting.

Cde. Coard sait that his feelings of the present situation are that within six months the party will disintegrate totally unless a fundamental package of measures aredone. He had thought it would take 12 months . given the : . of disgust, the disintegration of the party masses that the lost of state powere is only a few months away. While all of this is happening imperialism has step up its range of attacks laying the basis for direct intervention in Central America. They have set up their troops and using the Korean incident as a basis. American troops are meters away from Nicaragua.

This is happening at a time when the militia is dis-integrate the Army is demoralise, we don't have the capacity of defendi. the revolution.

The party have never had. such weak links and low ... with the masses. The image of the party has deteriated in the eyes of the masses. .

The mood of the party Comrades is at th . lowest, it has ever been. He used the example of the number of Cdes sick.

He is opposed to solving the problem by replacing members of the C.C. All the C.C Comrades have important qualities and strengths to add to the C.C. Cdes knew their weaknesses which he has been always frank with them about. He pointed to the need for vrification using examples of Kamau, Unison, H.A and Kojo. He also pointed out that it is incorrect to think that Cdes in State work is not doing political work Cdes should not see their state work as non political work. He said that Cde. Strachan in an effort to hold the situation together diverted irrationalisation arnachy etc. accused him of idealism.

He raised the issue of his resignation from the O.C and C.C and reminded Cdes of his reasons for resigning last year which he had told Cdes. The C.C had agreed with him for not attending the C.C meeting because he wanted the issue to discuss. He said that he was tired and sick of being the only hatchet man and critique. The failure of C.C Comrades was to speak up freely, as a result he concluded that he was the main fetter to the development of the C.C because everyone was depending on him for everything especially in the area of the economy.

In July he left the O.C off for many months before he was reflecting on the party, the problem was the total absence of making decisive decisiins e.g torchlight and the gang of 26, e.g Cde. Layne and Einstein on the Army, on when the postion was taken to put Layne over Einstein.

44/..........

He said that he had detect a feeling of wanting him to undermine the Comrade Leader's position.

He would not like to return to the C.C and P.B, any tasks given to him he will do it.

He even used the struggle of the formation of the O.C, Cdes Louison, Strachan and himself was accused for organising another seat of power in the party. He felt that when this h reached critical persons on the P.B it was very bad.

He said finally in July last year the C.C unanimously directed the O.C to hold meetings with leaders of committees for rationalisation of Cdes work, as a result extended O.C meeting was held, while this meeting was heppening other .. decisions were taken contrary to the C.C decisions so that the O.C could not have the mandate given.

He was seriously affected by the accusation of wanting to undermine the leadership so he resigned from the O.C. He said the Cde. Leader found himself vasillating between the M.L trend/and the pettit bourgeois trend in the party. This worsened as the C.C was not aware what was going on and the situation was slipping, and because Comrades were not thinking, therefore the severe of drift and disintegration was not seen, He said that the party and revolution will disintegrate within 24 months. He had reached to a stage where he realise that his ability to influence the process was no longer possible.

The bureau took a thousand easy decision that the O.C had to impliment and failed to take hard decisions. For some periods of time the P.B was not functioning, no agenda, no recording of decisions, he found that he could not take these long meetings: for no reason at all.

He had a system for the Bureau to meet three hours for once a week and O.C three hours per week, so that Cdes can spend more time in the field. But Cdes have to be more prepared. Before he was asked to form the idea elaborate these ideas and impliment them, at the same time he had a number of talks behind his back. He would like to operate as he is presently for ever. He said that it will be an emotional strain for him to be back on the C.C under any modle.

The aspect that he had over the years was that he was an ordinary member he would have manners the Cde. Leader years ago, because of his position as deputy Leader and the extent that Cdes will think that he is figthing for leadership, if he comes back and Cde. Bishop falter he would be afraid to criticise him and will resign again. For it to be left for him to manners the leader, he is not prepared to deal with this. He admit that this is a P.B conduct.

However, he had tried to give the party his best support in strategy and tactics he would prefer to operate as in the past year. He also is prepared to take all responsibilities that the C.C offers him but off the C.C. He cannot take emotional

- 46 -

Comrade Coard continued to question whether the points taken on operationalisation will satisfy Cde. Leader concern. Whether he sees the criticisms as a vote of no confidence of the joint leadership lead to a vote of confidence. If on this basis he refused to accept the decision of the C.C on these models what will be the decision of the C.C.

Cde. Deriggs said that when this situation was dealt with the decision was taken based on strategy.. The basic concern is t' character of the C.C.

He said that the only way forward is Cde. Bernard's membership on the C.C. We must take no action to sacrafice the revolution and building the revolution and to build the situation. If joint leadership is decided and one Cde. Comrad don't want to comply the leadership will be decided. Cdes have to be firm and resolute.

Cde. Bernard Coard also questioned the time frame and propsepective in terms of informing the membership and to start the work internally and hitting the ground scientifically and organisationally.

Cde. Starach said that the hold up is based on Cde. Bishop time for reflection.

Cde. Cornwall felt that this cannot be dragged on indefinitely. Cdes felt too that the report should not hold out any longer than next Monday and the C.C should continue to meet with Cde. Coard to work out the package for the way forward. A date was fixed to meet with Cde. Bishop on Friday. In the meantime the G.M will be informed of the meetings.

The C.C agreed that three mmeetings would be held to discuss the minutes with M's, C.M's and A's, it was agreed to cancell the Fedon's week-end seminar and the members will meet on Sunday 25th in Bolunge from 9.00 a.m - 10.00 p.m. Breakfast will be served from 8-9a.m. The C.M's will meet on Monday 27th in Butler House from 5.00 p.m. - 11.00 p.m. and the following Monday 3rd October from 5.00 p.m. - 8.00 p.m in Butler house for A.'s. Transportation and a light snack would be provided. On September 30th and October 1st the weekend of Butler seminar the Fedon and Butler group will stugy the package of measures and the Marryshow group will use their schedule seminar to discuss the package.

Cde. Layne then suggested that the C.C break to use Sunday to sought out positions, then meet from Monday to Friday from 8.00 a.m - 12.00 noon to work out the package of measures.

Cde. Phyllis Coard suggested that Cde. Bishop be informed of th meetings that he can join but he should come on Friday to put forward his positon. She also suggested a system of Comrades sharing their notes with other Cdes who were absent in the meeting and Cdes should assist Cde. Boldeau in preparing the minutes.

5

conflict situation that saps his energies. He wants this to be clearly put to the party.

Unless the C.C is prepared to manners all pettit bourgeois response he will re-draw.

The issue is to start collective leadership of the C.C.. The lack of frank and bluntness has seriously affected the party.

The C.C has never been accountable to any one the Bureau had things from the C.C and the C.C hid things from the membershi

He said that he have problems with any modle of coming back the C.C and P.B unless he is forced to.

There are two trends on the C.C Pettit bourgeois Revolutionar, Democratic trend and M.L trend. As the struggle gets toughe and the taking of decisions becomes harder the level of vasillation and indecisiveness grows, and the crisis becomes deeper. The contradiction will become greater, his emotional strain will also become greater. He has noted a Pettit Bourgeois Revolutionary trend has becoming greater in Cde. Louison over the last year. He has planned to raised it with him. Whatever the decision the C.C take he will have to ordered because there will be much more taybay behind his back. He also think that the situation will worsened.

There is no signs in the last 1½ years where the C.C has consistantly crushed pettit bourgeois characteristics and tr as soon as it rise.

Cde. Cornwall said that in this meeting he had seen very firm sought out positions taken, it gives the idea of what the C.C is capable of doing, he thinks that this is important to recognise. However, we have not been consistent in this area. He said that with-out the consistency the party will rut again.

Cde. Bernard proposed that for the next six months the Bureau should meet as a bureau with all members of the C.C as alternate Bureau members so that the monthly meetings will be to take stock. The Bureau meeting will meet to take decisions on the daily organisation of the work. The Bureau should meet three hours once a week.

Cde. Strachan felt that these meetings should take place in the operations room of Fort Rupert.

Cde. Coard further proposed that there should be absolutely no interuption in the meeting.

Cdes also proposed no smoking in meetings.

46/............

- 47 -

Cde. Mc Barnette was asked to assist Cde. Bain

Cde. Cornwall will assist Cde. St. Bernard.

Cde. Layne will brief Cde. Austin.

Cde. Strachan will brief Cde. Bishop

Cde. Cornwall will supervise the writing of the minutes.

Document 17

BRIEFING NOTES ON MEETING WITH JUDGE WILLIAM CLARKE, CHAIR OF THE N.S.C.

Section 1: Background on the N.S.C.:

Originally the N.S.C. had been an advisory body on Foreign Policy. However under Nixon (with Kissinger as Chairman of the N.S.C.) and Carter (with Brezinski as Chairman of the N.S.C.) and now Reagan the council has become a key body in the formulation of U.S. foreign policy

Indeed it is now widely felt (certainly in the Washington Post and Time Magazine) that the N.S.C. under Clarke has become the chief formulator of U.S. foreign policy. Certainly this is evident in recent U.S. foreign policy decisions in Central America where it is widely felt that the removal of Enders (under Secretary of State for Latin American Affairs) and Hinton (Ambassador to El Salvador) is linked directly to Clarke's recommendations. Significantly it is also widely felt that Clarke (together with Jane Kirkpatick at the U.N.) is the real formulator of policy in Latin America and the Caribbean.

While this is an apparent reality it should be noted that Clarke has absolutely no background in foreign affairs at all. His only credential is his close friendship to Reagan. Moreover that friendship is based on a shared hard line right wing approach on everything including his limited knowledge on foreign affairs.

This dichotomy of control and limited knowledge has led to much conflict between the N.S.C. and the State Department where more real knowle on foreign affairs exists. Nevertheless it is clear that for now the National Security Council under Clarke is calling most if not all of the shots on foreign policy, particularly in regards to central America and

- 2 -

Caribbean.

Section II: Talking Notes

1. Comrade Bishop must clearly in practice and also been seen to take the initiative, even perhaps the offensive in the meeting. Two main reasons:

1. We asked for the meeting, so we must demonstrate that we have issues topics, an agenda.
2. The psycological struggle will be fience, but, of course, very sophisticated. We must definitely win that struggle.

Section III: Suggested proposals;

Concretely propose the following:

1. Our two countries must exchange Ambassadors this year, 1983.
2. The United States Government must end its economic aggression and propaganda destablization against Grenada without delay.

Later These two points will be added:

1. Miami-based agents of destabilization
2. Cease your support for countries - those opposed to PRG and extradite Gairy.

- 3 -

<u>Section IV</u>: Background on Grenada's Position:

For over three (3) years, Grenada's PRG has been saying we want to normalize diplomatic relations with the United States:

- Bernard Coard to Pete Vaky, Carter's Assistant Secretary of States for Inter-American Affairs.
- In almost every multilateral forum e.g. OAS, CARICOM, UN.
- Cde. Whiteman has also made the point on all of his visits here

At the same time the U.S. has refused to respond to many of our overtures.

Document 18

EMBASSY OF THE REPUBLIC OF CUBA
GRENADA

The Central Committee
New Jewel Movement
St. George's

Esteemed Comrades:

I send you this message motivated by certain references which, in their conversations with our Ambassador, have been made by several Grenadian leaders in relation to Cuba.

The supposed notion that on passing through our country Bishop had informed me of the problems inside the Party is a miserable piece of slander. Bishop did not mention a single word to me, nor did he make the slightest allusion to the matter. Completely the opposite. He expressed to me in general terms and with great modesty that there were deficiencies in his work which he thought he would overcome in the next few months.

In reality, I am grateful to Bishop for that discretion, and for the respect he showed to his Party and to Cuba by not touching on such matters.

We are indignant at the very thought that some of you would have considered us capable of meddling in any way in the internal questions of your Party. We are people of principle, not vulgar schemers or adventurers.

....

EMBASSY OF THE REPUBLIC OF CUBA
GRENADA

......2

Everything which happened was for us a surprise, and disagreeable. In our country, the Grenadian Revolution and Comrade Bishop as its central figure were the object of great sympathies and respect. Even explaining the eventx to our people will not be easy.

In my opinion, the divisions and problems which have emerged will result in considerable damage to the image of the Grenadian Revolution, as much within as outside the country.

Cuba, faithful to its moral values and its international policy, will pay strictest attention to the principle of not interfering in the slightest in the internal affairs of Grenada, fulfilling the promises made in the field of cooperation. Our promises are not to men. They are to the peoples and to principle.

History and developments yet to come will judge what has happened in these last few days.

I wish for you the greatest wisdom, serenity, loyalty to principles, and generosity in this difficult moment through which the Grenadian Revolution is passing.

Cordially,

Commander-in-Chief
Fidel Castro Ruz

15 October, 1983

Document 19

FOREIGN RELATIONS REPORT

THEORETICAL PERSPECTIVE OF FOREIGN POLICY

Foreign policy is the extension internationally of domestic policy. It is the projection on the international scene of the national policy line pursued on the homefront.

This does not mean that a country's domestic policy can be simply shifted to and imposed on the international scene. What it means is that the foreign policy of a country has to be rooted in its domestic situation; in its politics, its philosophy,its economy, its geography - these factors are the main determinants of a country's foreign policy.

While the major determinants of a country's foreign policy are of a domestic nature, external factors also impact upon the foreign policy line. Therefore, the foreign policy must always be sensitive and alert to the dynamic regional and international situations and must be cognizant at all times of the world's constellation and array of forces. Foreign policy has to be flexible enough to respond to changes in these situations and in the international status quo.

GRENADA'S FOREIGN POLICY

Grenada's Foreign Policy reposes on the scientific ideological foundation irreconcilably opposed to the exploitation and domination of nation by nation. This is consistent with Grenada's domestic policy which is opposed to the exploitation of man to man. Thus, Grenada's foreign policy is inevitably manifested through non-alignment, anti-imperialism and peaceful co-existence.

(See "Grenada's Foreign Policy" Annex)

/ Needs ......

NEEDS AND GOALS OF GRENADA'S FOREIGN RELATIONS

Arising out of its domestic situation a country's foreign relations is geared to fulfilling certain concrete needs and accomplishing clearly defined goals. For Grenada twelve such needs and goals have been outlined:

(1) grants; (2) soft loans; (3) lines of credit;
(4) machinery and equipment (either through loans or gifts;
(5) technical assistance; (6) markets - guaranteed longterm;
(7) tourism; (8) diplomatic support; (9) moral and political support; (10) military and security consideration; (11) material support; (12) electoral support.

These needs and goals are grounded in Grenada's domestic reality of underdevelopment and economic backwardness. Another significant determinant is Grenada's geographic reality as a small island state lacking vital economic endowments such as: (i) a viable infrastructure; (ii) human resources (especially skilled and trained personnel); (iii) a resilient resource base; (iv) a large market; (v) financial resources; (vi) a diversified economy; (vii) natural resources.

The accent on support in Grenada's foreign relations is determined not only by domestic factors but is significantly influenced by the regional and international situation. The Grenada Revolution, the supreme factor delineating Grenada's reality, is confronted by the hostility and might of U.S. imperialism. As a small country Grenada requires extensive and intensive international support to combat successfully U.S. imperialism. The foreign relations must reflect this need for support. Grenada's foreign relations must be the front line of the defence of the Glorious March 13th Revolution.

ISSUES AND CONCERNS OF GRENADA'S FOREIGN POLICY

Grenada's foreign policy has been consistent. The major themes are constantly reflected in the foreign policy statements,

' in ....

- 3 -

in the speeches by the Foreign Minister and other Ministers both in international forums and before the assemblies of Grenadian people.

Common themes are (1) the call for world peace; (2) the question of detente; (3) disarmament; (4) the resumption of the SALT II talks; (5) peaceful coexistence. Also, on the question of peace Grenada has pioneered and continues to champion the concept of the Caribbean as a zone of peace. On this Grenada was able to have a Resolution adopted by the Organization of American States (OAS) at its Assembly in La Paz, Bolivia in 1979.

Central also to Grenada's foreign policy pronouncements and positions are the hallowed principles of non-alignment - anti-imperialism, anti-racism, anti-zionism, anti-colonialism, anti-neo-colonialism, anti-fascism as well as irreconcilable opposition to the hosting of military bases.

The principles of national sovereignty, respect for the territorial integrity of states, the legal equality of states, the right to develop one's own politico-socio-economic process free from outside interference, non-intervention in the domestic affairs of states and ideological pluralism are consistently stated in and defended by Grenada's foreign policy.

Revolutionary Grenada has steadfastly supported the call for a New International Economic Order (NIEO) and for the democratisation of the international economic system especially the international monetary system. Along with this call Grenada has advocated the widening and strengthening of South-South Cooperation, Economic and Technical Cooperation among Developing Countries (ECDC) (TCDC).

Beginning with the Commonwealth Heads of Government Meeting in Lusaka, Zambia, August 1979, Revolutionary Grenada has led

/ the ....

- 4 -

the call for special consideration and assistance for small island states, a category of states facing particular problems. At the meeting of Foreign Ministers of the Non Aligned Movement, New Delhi, India 9-13 February, 1981 Grenada was able to have the movement recommend that the problems of small island states be particularly considered.

(For more on Grenada's position on small island states see the Prime Minister's speech in Aruba in Annex)

In sum then Grenada's foreign policy is very active. It addresses itself to the international situation and issues of the day reflects the national interest and concerns.

CONSTRUCT OF THE WORLD

The world, as the Ministry of External Affairs has it, is divided into seven (7) geopolitical regions. They are (1) the Americas; (2) Eastern Europe; (3) the Middle East; (4) Western Europe; (5) The Caribbean; (6) Africa; (7) the Far East.

Of course these geopolitical regions satisfy Grenada's foreign policy needs and interests to different extents and levels. Therefore, the degree of closeness in the relationship between Grenada and each of the regions is not uniformed. This also holds for Grenada's relations with individual countries.

GRENADA DIPLOMATIC MISSIONS

Grenada currently maintains seven (7) embassies abroad. These are in Cuba, Venezuela, the United Kingdom, Belgium (the EEC), Canada, the OAS/USA Mission and the United Nations Mission in the United States.

Plans are fully in train to establish an Embassy in Iraq. Grenada's Ambassador designate to Iraq is Mr. O. Benjamin.

The possibility of setting up an Embassy in the Union of Soviet Socialist Republic (USSR) is also being actively explored and should be realised before the end of 1981.

/Grenada ....

- 5 -

GRENADA AND THE AMERICAS

As can be perceived from the fact that Grenada maintains five missions in the Americas, this is a region of importance to Grenada. For one, many of Grenada's nationals reside in the U.S.A., Canada, and Venezuela. The missions in these countries have the high responsibility of looking after the interests of these nationals abroad. Secondly, many of these nationals are able and are willing to assist the revolutionary process unfolding in Grenada economically, financially and politically. The missions have the task of mobilising the nationals abroad to that end. In this regard the missions have done good work particularly the OAS and UN Missions.

Since Grenada seeks to develop very close relations with the Latin American countries despite the language difference our relations with this region shows Grenada as involved in many organisations and groupings which bring together the countries of the region. SELA, ECLA, OLADE, the OAS, IICA, are examples of groupings in which Grenada develops relations with the Latin American countries. Grenada has diplomatic relations with 11 of the Latin American Countries (See Annex) but has ambassadors accredited to only two countries. This will be improved shortly as Cde. Richard Jacobs, Ambassador to Cuba, is Ambassador designate to Panama, Nicaragua and Mexico while Cde. Matthew William, Ambassador to Venezuela, is Ambassador designate to Colombia and Ecuador. Cde. Vernon Simon is the Ambassador designate to Surinam and should present his letters of credence in June 1981. Five Latin American countries have ambassadors accredited to Grenada; only two are resident.

Grenada's most remarkable foreign policy initiative in Latin America was to pioneer the concept of the Caribbean Sea as a Zone of Peace and to have the OAS Assembly in 1979 adopt a positive Resoultion on this in La Paz, Bolivia. Other countries have recently attempted to pretend to be the pioneers and supreme champions of the concept. Grenada must not allow this farce to be

/ successful ......

- 6 -

successful and must tighten up its definition of Caribbean and the Zone of Peace concept and take it into other forums such as the United Nations, the Non-Aligned Movement and CARICOM.

On the El Salvador question Grenada's position is clear and irrevocable: the Junta in El Salvador is a genocidal regime backed solely by U.S. imperialism and devoid of any internal base and consequently any legitimacy. The rtue and authentic representative of the Salvadoroan people in the Frente Democratico Revolucionario (FDR).

Grenada has excellent, relations with the Revolutionary Governments, people and countries of Nicaragua and Cuba. Grenada desires the closest relations with those two countries. Grenada has several agreement with Cuba and receives tremendous and invaluable assistance from Cuba in numerous areas - the New International Airport, Fisheries, Education, Military, Agriculture, Health. Cuba has also consistently supported and defended Grenada in international forums.

Nicaragua has also supported Grenada internationally and Grenada has received technical assistance, in the form of military uniforms, from Nicaragua. Grenada in return has supported and defended Nicaragua internationally being the second country to recognise the Provisional Government of National Reconstruction in 1979 and Grenada sent two teachers to assist the Nicamaguans in their literacy programme in 1980.

Grenada has elos received technical assistance from Panama (training of policemen), Mexico (scholarships in sports), Argentina (1,000 tins of wheat in 1980) and Venezuela. The Venezuelans have given assistance in several areas: Health, Communication (a new beacon for Pearls Airport), Sports, Energy. A technical assistance agreement between Venezuela and Grenada exists and covers areas like raods. Brazil has extended to Grenada a line of credit for the new people's plane chartered by LIAT.

/ In ....

- 7 -

In addition the above Grenada will soon be holding discussions with Brazil and Mexico to explore and arrange areas for technical assistance and cooperation. A delegation from Grenada is due to visit Mexico for this purpose in June. Already a delegation headed by Lyden Ramdhanny, member of the P.R.G. has visited Brazil for similar discussions. Out of these discussions the plane emerged.

Grenada's relations with Latin America has been active at many levels. One thinks though that there is room to intensify and widen these relations. For one, Argentina, like Brazil, Mexico and Venezuela, is among the most developed countries in region. Perhaps the same initiative pursued in regards to intensive discussions with Mexico, Brazil and Venesuela for technical assistance and cooperation agreements can be pursued with Argentina who has indicated strong interest in the Caribbean countries of course the domestic policies of repression, the links with South Africa and Israel, the part she played in the Bolivian Coup, and the rumours of her interest in the South Atlantic Treaty Organisation (SATO), are factors which have to be considered and weighed before moving to close to Argentina. However, the possibility should at least be considered.

EASTERN EUROPE

Grenada now has diplomatic relations with all Eastern European Countries. However, Grenada has no diplomatic representation in Eastern Europ nor does she have any ambassador accredited to any Eastern European Country on a non-resident basis. The U.S.S.R., the G.D.R., Bulgaria, Hungary and Czechoslovakia all have ambassadors accredited to Grenada on a non-resident basis.

Despite the lack of representation Grenada's relations with the Eastern European countries is substantial. Grenada has Trade agreements and Scientific and Technical agreements with the USSR, Hungary, Bulgaria, Czechoslovakia, the GDR and Poland. Under these agreements and the many Protocols attached to some of them

/ Grenada ......

Grenada has received material assistance from Eastern Europe - means of transport, scholarships and assistance in agriculture among other areas.

Grenada's relations with Eastern Europe was significantly developed and began to bear fruit after two visits to that region by Deputy Prime Minister Cde. Bernard Coard in 1979 and 1980. The Cde. Deputy Prime Minister also attended the 26 CPSU Congress in 1981 and further developed Grenada's relations with the USSR.

Grenada perceives the key role the Socialist Community has played in defending the developing countries and is consolidating the hard won independence of these countries. Also, the support National Liberation Movement have had from the Socialist Community has been tremendous and often decisive. Thus, for Grenada the Eastern European Countries can be a real source of political and diplomatic support apart from the vast potential they have for technical and economic assistance. For these two reasons Grenada must continue intensifying its relations with Eastern Europe. Therefore, the possibility of establishing an Embassy in Moscow must be seriously and positively explored.

Another initiative in Eastern Europe which must be considered is a visit to Romania. At the recent meeting of Grenada's Heads of Missions in March 1981, Butler House, Belmont, St. George's, Grenada, High Commissioner to Canada, Cde. Jimmy Emmanuel, reported that the Romanians had approached him expressing interest in having the Cde. Prime Minister visit Romania.

THE MIDDLE EAST

Grenada recognises that the Middle East with its petro wealth offers great scope for:

(i) technical and economic assistance and cooperation;

(ii) Economic Cooperation among Developing Countries (ECDC) - South-South Cooperation;

(iii) a stronger role for the developing countries in the world economy.

Thus, Grenada's foreign relations with the Middle East has been guided by the recognition as well as by Grenada's principles of anti-zionism and anti-imperialism. Grenada has developed close relations with Algeria, Libya, Syria and Iraq. Today it has technical assistance arrangements with Libya, Algeria, Syria and Iraq and has received substantial assistance from these countries. Algeria is providing all the oil, gas, used by the machines employed in the construction of the New International Airport for 1981.

Grenada's relations with these Middle East countries was strengthened and developed after Prime Minister Maurice Bishop visited them in 1980. The Prime Minister brough back over EC$21m. in grants. The possibility of a visit to other Middle East countries such as the United Arab Emirates (UAE) and Kuwait is currently being explored.

Mr. Ashley Taylor, Legal Adviser to the Minister of External Affairs, visited Algeria and Libya in April 1981 as part of the mobilisation for the recently concluded Co-financing Conference for the international airport held in Brussels, Belgium in mid April 1981. Also, it is likely that the Deputy Prime Minister will pay a visit to Libya, Algeria and Iraq this May 1981.

Thus, Grenada has pursued an active policy in the Middle East designed mainly to harness the immense potential the region has for grants, lines of credit, soft loans, technical assistance and energy. However, Grenada's Middle East policy is also geared to develop close relations with the anit-imperialist, anti-sionist forces in the region and to support the Just Struggle of the Palestinian people. Thus, Grenada has recognised the PLO as the legitimate representative of the Palestinian people and remains unswerving in its conviction that no settlement can take place without the involvement of the PLO. Therefore, Grenada has taken a position irreconcilably opposed to the Camp David Agreement.

On the Iraq-Iran war Grenada supports the initiatives taken by the Non-Aligned Movement to mediate between the two countries and bring a Just solution to the conflict. The war between two anti-imperialist countries, tow members of the Non-Aligned Movement, two members of OPEC, two anti-zionist countries is fundamentally regrettable particularly as it consumes tremendous energy and resources which could have been gainfully utilised in the anti-imperialist, anti-zionist struggle.

It must be pointed out here that despite the invaluable assistance Grenada has received from the Mid East, finance, energy, patrol boats from Libya, Grenada has no diplomatic representation in the region. Grenada has diplomatic relations with seven (7) countries in the Middle East but has not even a non-resident ambassador accredited to any of the countries. It is therefore key that Grenada implements the decision to send Mr. O. Benjamin to Iraq as Ambassador

WESTERN EUROPE

Grenada has two missions in Western Europe:

(i) the High Commission to the United Kingdom;

(ii) the mission to the EEC located in Brussels, Belgium.*

Diplomatic relations have been established with 14 West European countries and ambassador accredited to eight.

As a source of tourism and as a market Western Europe is of importance to Grenada. Also, in the United Kingdom are many of Grenada's reinforced its anti-imperialist, anti-colonialist character.

Reciprocally the Non-Aligned countries as a movement have expressed firm support for the Grenada Revolution. Statements to that effect were adopted by both the Havana Summit, 1979, and the Foreign Ministers' Meeting, New Delhi, February 1981. This moral and political support is indispensable for Grenada confronted as it is by U.S. imperialism; the point is that Grenada's membership in the Non-Aligned Movement is a weapon in the struggle against alien domination.

Grenada's membership in the Movement has earned it the respect and material support of many countries. It was through attendance of the Havana Summit that Prime Minister Maurice Bishop made the vital contact with the Middle East countries and was able to visit Algeria, Iraq, Libya and Syria subsequently and obtained tremendous financial and other assistance.

So far Grenada has not yet been very actively involved in the Coordinating Groups of the Movement; that is the groups of countries responsible for particular areas such as tourism, fisheries, women, housing, etc. Cde. Kendrick Radix recently attended the Fisheries Meeting in Cuba and it is expected that Sis. Phyllis Coard will attend the Women's Meeting Cuba this May 1981. Attendance of the Meeting on Tourism in Cyprus, June 1981 should be actively explored. These Coordinating Groups can enhance Grenada's prestige and also bring concrete gains for Grenada.

THE UNITED NATIONS

Grenada has used the United Nations to maintain contact with the many countries in which it has no representation. This adds importance to Grenada's membership in the United Nations.

In that Organisation too Grenada has been able to show support for liberation movements, support initiatives for peace and disarmament and has been able to explain the Grenada Revolution. Grenada has not so far initiated any action in the U.N.

16/...

Membership in the United Nations has allowed Grenada to benefit from U.N. Agencies such as UNESCO, The United Nations Development Programme (UNDP) and The Economic Commission for Latin America (ECLA).

In 1979 Cde. Maurice Bishop addressed the 34th General Assembly of the United Nations while Cde. Selwyn Strachan addressed the 35th General Assembly in 1980.

SOCIALIST INTERNATIONAL

In the Socialist International Grenada has been able to show organised support for peace, peaceful co-existence, disarmament, detenté, cooperation between nations and for the national liberation struggles. Grenada's relations with the SI, developed through the attendance of its meetings by Cde. Unison Whiteman, has earned for Grenada statements of solidarity with the Grenada Revolution. These statements are of vital diplomatic and political importance.

Membership in the SI has also permitted Grenada to develop relations with progressive parties and sectors of Western Europe. Cde. Maurice Bishop's recent attendance of the SI Meeting in Holland served to make good contact with the leading personalities and parties of the SI.

THE COMMONWEALTH

Grenada's main interaction with this grouping was the attendance of the Heads of Governments Meeting in Lusaka, Zambia in 1979. In that meeting Grenada's main initiative in the Commonwealth was made; that is, the advocation of the need for special consideration and assistance for small island states. The Cde. Prime Minister lucidly presented a paper on small island states outlining clearly the severe constraints which those countries must surmount.

FOREIGN POLICY SUCCESSES AND ACHIEVEMENTS

Grenada has scored some successes in its foreign relations. Among these can be cited

(i) promotion of the special situation of small island states - through its determined efforts Grenada has been able to

17/...

have a wide cross-section of the international community recognise the particular problems confronting small island states;

(ii) pioneering and championing of the concept of the Caribbean Sea as a Zone of Peace - the OAS has recognised it as such when in 1979, La Paz, Bolivia, Grenada tabled a resolution which was subsequently passed;

(iii) being the second state to recognise the Provisional Government of National Reconstruction in Nicaragua, June 1979. This move consolidated the revolutionary process in Nicaragua and accelerated Somoza's fall;

(iv) being the first state in the Western Hemisphere to recognise the Saharan Arab Democratic Republic;

(v) giving material support, EC$50,000 to SWAPO;

(vi) the tremendous, invaluable economic, financial and technical assistance received from external sources.

BALANCE OF FORCES IN THE WORLD

Grenada's foreign policy, as can be perceived from the above information, is highly active. It is rooted in Grenada's domestic situation and is guided by Grenada's principles of non-alignment and anti-imperialism. However, any successful foreign policy must be aware of and respond to the international conjuncture.

One of the main characteristics of the present international conjuncture is the changing balance of forces. Previously imperialism led by the U.S.A. held unchallenged sway over mankind. Now the socialist community is strong and growing still. The U.S.S.R. is the equal, at least, of the U.S.A. Other poles of power have developed through the ability of the OPEC countries to exact from the rapacious West adequate compensation for their natural resource: petroleum.

Thus, today when the U.S. imperialism launches economic aggression against Revolutionary Nicaragua and Mozambique, refusing to sell them

18/...

wheat, the U.S.S.R. can supply the two countries with the necessary wheat. When the U.S.A. refuses to loan money to Nicaragua, Libya provides the money. When the CIA destabilises Angola and sends in mercenaries against the popular MPLA, Cuba moves to assist Angola militarily and successfully. When the U.S.A. tries to stop Grenada building an international airport other countries assist Grenada in the construction of the airport.

The point is that U.S. imperialism no longer holds sway over mankind. Though it remains powerful U.S. imperialism is on the decline. Today as oil rich Saudi Arabia increases its contribution to the International Monetary Fund and its voting power increases the basis for the U.S.A. veto control of the international monetary system is being eroded. Doubtless other oil-rich countries will follow the example of Saudi Arabia.

Thus, Grenada's foreign policy must be cognizant of and reflect this change in the balance of forces. A foreign policy which is not mindful of the international conjuncture is doomed to failure. As a country embarked on the construction of a revolution, the change in the world's balance of forces is for Grenada a positive factor.

LIST OF COUNTRIES WITH WHICH GRENADA
DOES NOT WISH TO DEVELOP CLOSE RELATIONS

(i) BOLIVIA

(ii) COMORO ISLANDS

(iii) CHILE

(iv) CHINA

(v) EGYPT

(vi) EL SALVADOR

(vii) HAITI

(viii) HONDURAS

(ix) ISRAEL

(x) GUATEMALA

(xi) PARAGUAY

(xii) SOUTH KOREA

(xiii) TAIWAN

(xiv) SOUTH AFRICA

(xv) URUGUAY

(xvi) ZAIRE

Document 20

4

FEDERAL MINISTRY OF FOREIGN TRADE
T.D.PRAHA

B/L No: 6.-

ORIGINAL

ORDER OF AMBAJADA DE GRANADA 5 AVENIDA
No.8409 MIRAMAR LA HABANA C U B A

CZECHOSLOVAK OCEAN SHIPPING

"SITNO"
KARDELJEVO
HAVANA
FREIGHT PREPAID
THREE/3/

2110054/D 1.25o CASES EXPLOSIVE AMMUNITION (WARHEADS,ROCKET) 32.500 72,292

1.25o/1-1.25o

ČECHOFRACHT PRAHA
Ref:144/80664

FEDERAL MINISTRY OF FOREIGN
TRADE T.D.PRAHA
Ref:121/0859

KARDELJEVO,

22 - 2

Document 21

A G R E E M E N T

for cooperation between the Bulgarian Communist Party and the New JEWEL Movement of Grenada for the period 1982 - 1983

The Bulgarian Communist Party (BCP) and the New JEWEL Movement (NJM) guided by their mutual desire for strengthening and enhancing the links of friendship and cooperation between them, for promoting the friendly relations between the Bulgarian and the Grenada peoples, between the People's Republic of Bulgaria and Grenada, in the interest of the unity and cohesion of all progressive and anti-imperialist forces in the world in the struggle against imperialism, for peace, democrac and social progress, have reached agreement on the following plan for cooperation for the period 1982 - 1983 :

I.

<u>The Bulgarian Communist Party shall receive:</u>

<u>A. In 1982:</u>

1. A two-member delegation of the New JEWEL Movement for seven days, to become acquainted with the experience of the BCP on issues of interest to the Party.

Term: second half of the year

- 2 -

In 1983:

1. A two-member delegation of the NJM for seven days, to become acquainted with the experience of the BCP on issues of interest to the Party.

Term: second half of the year

The New JEWEL Movement shall receive:

A. In 1982:

1. A two-member delegation of the BCP for seven days, to become acquainted with the experience of the NJM on issues proposed by the BCP.

Term: second half of the year

B. In 1983:

1. A two-member delegation of the BCP for seven days, to become acquainted with the experience of the NJM on issues proposed by the BCP.

Term: second half of the year

II.

1. The Bulgarian Communist Party shall grant the New JEWEL Movement yearly, 10 allowances for training cadres in the ten-month specialized courses at the Academy of Social Sciences and Management at the Central Committee of the Bulgarian Communist Party.

- 3 -

2. The Bulgarian Communist Party and the New JEWEL Movement shall exchange delegations which shall participate in the congresses, conferences and other major events organized by them.

3. The Bulgarian Communist Party and the New JEWEL Movement shall assist in the promotion of more intensive cooperation between the public and mass organisations in the People's Republic of Bulgaria and Grenada.

4. The Bulgarian Communist Party and the New JEWEL Movement shall carry out mutual consultations and shall exchange regularly publications, bulletins, films and other materials related to the activities of the two parties.

5. The Bulgarian Communist Party and the New JEWEL Movement may reach agreement on initiatives which have not been included in the present Agreement and which, in their opinion, would help to further strengthen and enhance the relations of friendship between the Bulgarian Communist Party and the New JEWEL Movement, between the People's Republic of Bulgaria and Grenada.

III.

The present Agreement is drawn up in two copies, each in Bulgarian and in English, both texts of equal validity.

FOR THE BULGARIAN COMMUNIST PARTY :

FOR THE NEW JEWEL MOVEMENT:

Document 22

EMBASSY OF GRENADA IN THE USSR

YEAR OF POLITICAL AND ACADEMIC EDUCATION

Dobryninskaya Ulitsa 7
Apartment 221
Moscow
USSR

[illegible]

MEETING WITH DEPUTY MINISTER OF FOREIGN AFFAIRS (LATIN AMERICA AND CARIBBEAN) V. [illegible] 18/5/83 at [illegible]

The Minister welcomed the Ambassador on behalf of the Government of the GDR and said that he was happy to [illegible] that "at long last" we were in a position to present Credentials.

The Ambassador thanked the Minister for the warm welcome to the GDR and apologised for the delay in the presentation of Credentials which was due to factors beyond our control.

The Minister extended an invitation to Ambassador Jacobs and his wife to participate from 11th to 13th June in the excursion and informal exchange of views of Ambassadors with Foreign Minister Fischer for the diplomatic corps accredited to the GDR. The Ambassador thanked the Minister for the invitation and indicated that he would make every effort to attend with his wife.

The Minister said that he had been briefed about the "very fruitful talks" that were held between the Ambassador and the Director of L.A. and Caribbean Affairs Department earlier and he was particularly pleased at the proposal for the establishment of a Joint Marketing Agency. He recommended that this be taken up with the Minister of Trade and Foreign Affairs as well as President Honecker.

He said that he had very fruitful talks with Foreign Affairs Minister Whiteman at the Law of the Sea Convention in Jamaica and the GDR Government was very satisfied with the developments in Grenada. They regarded the situation in Grenada as stable and overall developments were very good.

/cont./

nationals; this adds importance to relations with Britain particularly as the British Nationality Bill is so topical. However, the Thatcher led government of Britain has adopted a hostile posture to Grenada and there has been very little bilateral contact between the two countries.

Grenada's more fruitful relations with Western Europe has been through the EEC Commission. The EEC has funded projects in Grenada including the building of community centres and the supply of milk.

The best known foreign relations initiative Grenada has made in Western Europe was the recent staging of the Co-financing Conference to mobilise funds for the International Airport.

Grenada has also sought through the Socialist International to develop strong relations withethe Social Democratic Parties of Western Europe some of which are in power in their countries. This is a policy which has tremendous potential for realising material assistance for Grenada. Also, through the Socialist International Grenada can make its contribution to detente disarmament and peace in Europe,

With France Grenada has a programme for Technical Cooperation. This includes road communication, energy bio gas, agriculture, mineral water and the training of teachers in French. These areas were raised by Grenada during the visit of the French Technical and Cultural Mission headed by one Mr. André in October, 1979. The victory of Francois Mitterand of the Socialist Party, a member of the Socialist International, in the recent presidential elections should permit closer cooperation with France.

---

*The EEC Mission covers many countries. See Annex

THE CARIBBEAN

Most of Grenada's relations with the C ribbean has been through the regional institutions: CARICOM and its Ministerial Committees, WISA (soon to be the Organisation of East Caribbean States (OECS). Grenada has been consistent in its attendance of most of the meetings, seminars and workshops organised by regional bodies.

The more important ones are the CARICOM Council of Ministers Meetings, the WISA Council of Ministers M etings and the Meetings of the Standing Committee of Ministers Responsible for Foreign Affairs. In these forums, Grenada seeks to cooperate closely with its Caribbean counterparts while not sacrificing national goals and principles.

Grenada has agreed with the other Eastern Caribbean Countries on the transformation of the West Indies Associated States Council (WISA) into the Organisation of East Caribbean States (OECS). The OECS should come into being on 4th July. Gren da has agreed in principle but the proposed treaty must be carefully studied.

Despite the hostility of some Caribbean countries Grenada has displayed its good neighbourliness on several occasions; for one, after the Union Island uprising and the apprehension on on its territory of Bumba Charles, Grenada returned the latter to the Government of St. Vincent; again Grenada has offered, despite its weak economy, scholarships to the other countries in its Fisheries Training School.

In order to stronghten and promote its relations with the Caribbean, Grenada has designated a High Commissioner to CARICOM. Already St. Lucia and the Bahamas have agreed to Grenada's request to the Caribbean. St. Vincent has refused arguing to the effect that the relations should be on a multilateral basis; that is, through the regional institutions.

AFRICA

Grenada's main foreign policy concern in Africa thus far has been the situation in Southern Africa. In all international forums Grenada

13/...

has been very consistent in its condemnation of South Africa's apartheid and racism, its illegal occupation of Namibia, its genocidal repression of the South African and Namibian people and its military aggression and acts of destabilisation against the Front Line States.

As a concrete manifestation of its commitment to the liberation struggle in South Africa Grenada in February 1981 gave EC$50,000 to the Namibian Liberation Fund set up by the Organisation of African Unity. (OAU)

Due to the acute state of underdevelopment of the economies of the African countries Grenada does not view Africa as a source of financial and economic assistance. However, individual countries such as Nigeria with its booming oil economy can provide substantial assistance. As a matter of fact Grenada received a grant of some EC$117,000 from Nigeria for banana rehabilitation in 1981. The potential for intensifying relations with Nigeria exists and is being developed.

Africa can be a source of great diplomatic moral and political support. When the imperialist sponsored bomb went off on June 19, 1980 several African countries came out condemning the vicious attack. Also, when U.S. imperialism attempted to sabotage the Co-financing Conference held in Brussels recently the African countries of the ACP all came out with a strong resolution condemning the manoeuvres of the U.S.A.

Therefore, Grenada must intensify its diplomatic relations with the African countries. Presently Grenada has relations only with less than one half of the African countries and does not have an ambassador accredited to any. Moves have been made to accredit Cde. Fennis Augustine to the Front Line States. Grenada has recognised and has established diplomatic relations with the Saharan Arab Democratic Republic showing once again its support of just liberation struggles.

14/..

- 14 -

FAR EAST

In Asia Grenada has developed close relations with very few countries. Diplomatic relations exists with nine countries and four have ambassadors accredited to Grenada while Grenada has none accredited.

Grenada has been critical of the South Korean fascists and has developed healthy relations with the Democratic People's Republic of Korea (DPRK)(North Korea). Cde. Selwyn Strachan's visit to the DPRK significantly firmed up relations while Korean trade and cultural delegations have visited Grenada. Also, the non-resident Ambassador Mr. Li Jung Ok has made several trips to Grenada. A technical and economic cooperation agreement between Grenada and the DPRK has been discussed and negotiated. One of the areas is an irrigation scheme on the Paradise Estate.

With India Grenada has discussed the possibility of technical assistance. This involves a cotton ginnery for Carriacou. Nothing definite has yet emerged from the discussions.

A Grenada delegation is scheduled to visit Mongolia and Vietnam very shortly. This visit should really widen and deepen Grenada's relations with those two countries of the Far East.

MEMBERSHIP IN INTERNATIONAL ORGANISATIONS

Grenada enjoys membership in several international organisations*. This reflects Grenada's active foreign policy geared to promote peace and cooperation among the members of the international community.

THE MOVEMENT OF NON-ALIGNED COUNTRIES

This international organisation is key to Grenada's foreign policy. Grenada joined the Movement in 1979 and was immediately made a member of the Coordinating Bureau. In the Movement Grenada has expressed organised support for the liberation struggles the world over and has

* See Annex

15/...

-2-

He said that it was the policy of the GDR to concentrate its attention on Grenada, Nicaragua and Cuba and the Government of the GDR will do everything within its capacity to assist in the development and consolidation of the Grenada revolution.

The Ambassador thanked the Minister for this and said that the Government of Grenada was conscious of its responsibility in the development of these bilateral relations. We see also our responsibility in lifting the consciousness of our people and the Caribbean people as a whole about the question of Peace in Europe. The Deputy Minister said that 1983 was a critical year for Europe in so far as this was the deadline for the stationing of Cruise Missiles in West Germany and if this were to happen there would be great tension in Europe as a whole He said that the tension was building and the attitude of the NATO countries was hardening. He noted the anti-communist position of France, Britain and West Germany and said that the situation is likely to get worse as the year drew to a close.

Document 23

Agreement

on cooperation between the New JEWEL Movement of Grenada and the Socialist Unity Party of Germany for the years 1982 to 1985

Guided by the desire

to deepen the friendly relations between the New JEWEL Movement of Grenada and the Socialist Unity Party of Germany in the spirit of anti-imperialist solidarity and proletarian internationalism;

to mutually exchange information on the development of national and social liberation in Grenada and the construction of the advanced socialist society in the German Democratic Republic, and

to conduct a constant exchange of views on the international situation and the foreign policy of both Parties,

both sides agree on the following fields of cooperation for the period up to 1985:

2

1. The New JEWEL Movement and the Socialist Unity Party of Germany attach great importance to the mutual study of their experiences of the revolutionary struggle. Both Parties shall exchange material on the political, social, economic and cultural development of their countries.

2. The Socialist Unity Party of Germany declares its readiness to assist the New JEWEL Movement in the training and political qualification of its cadres. The Socialist Unity Party of Germany will aid the drawing up of a study programme for the acquisition of a knowledge of scientific socialism.

3. The New JEWEL Movement and the Socialist Unity Party of Germany shall exchange information of mutual interest on the development and lessons of the revolutionary process in both countries and also on international questions.

4. Both Parties proclaim their reciprocal solidarity in the struggle against imperialism and reaction and declare their readiness to promote understanding for both revolutions within the world revolutionary movement.

5. Both Parties shall promote the development of cooperation between the mass organizations of their countries.

6. The central organs of the New JEWEL Movement and the Socialist Unity Party of Germany shall enter into a mutual exchange of experiences and shall support each other in their journalistic activity.

7. Both Parties shall promote and support the development of friendly relations between the Governments and peoples of the German Democratic Republic and Grenada.

The New JEWEL Movement and the Socialist Unity Party of Germany shall further concretize these measures by means of annual working plans which shall be drawn up and agreed upon by authorized representatives of both Parties.

For the New JEWEL Movement of Grenada

George Louison
Member of the Political Bureau of the Central Committee of the New JEWEL Movement

For the Socialist Unity Party of Germany

Hermann Axen
Member of the Political Bureau and Secretary of the Central Committee of the Socialist Unity Party of Germany

Berlin, 10 June 1982

Working Plan

for cooperation between the New JEWEL Movement of Grenada and the Socialist Unity Party of Germany for the years 1982/1983

On the basis of the long-term Agreement on Cooperation between the New JEWEL Movement and the Socialist Unity Party of Germany, the following measures are laid down for the years 1982/1983:

I

The Socialist Unity Party of Germany shall receive:

1. a study delegation of the New JEWEL Movement consisting of two comrades who shall acquaint themselves with the experiences of the Socialist Unity Party of Germany.

2. in 1982 two comrades and in 1983 five comrades of the New JEWEL Movement to study at the Karl Marx party college

3. two representatives of the New JEWEL Movement each year for a holiday visit to the German Democratic Republic.

II

The New JEWEL Movement of Grenada shall receive:

1. a study delegation of the Socialist Unity Party of Germany consisting of two comrades for a period of ten days to study the political work of the New JEWEL Movement in 1983.

2. in line with its wish, a temporary adviser from the Socialist Unity Party of Germany on questions of building up the Party (duration of stay to be agreed).

3. annually two representatives of the Socialist Unity Party of Germany for a holiday visit to Grenada.

Both Parties shall inform each other in good time on the dates, the subject matters and the respective representatives responsible for the fulfilment of these tasks and others which may be agreed.

III

The Socialist Unity Party of Germany shall continue to assist in the operation of the New JEWEL Movement's printing press and the training of personnel in this area.

Document 24

REPORT ON MEETING OF SECRET REGIONAL CAUCUS OF
HELD IN MANAGUA FROM 6TH-7TH JANUARY, 1983

The following Organizations were represented:-

F.S.L.N.	- Nicaragua	- Antonio Marguin
M.N.R.	- El Salvador	- Hector Oqueli
R.P.	- Chile	- Freda
P.N.P.	- Jamaica	- Paul Miller
P.C.C.	- Cuba	- Silva
N.J.M.	- Grenada	- Chris DeRiggs

The following items constituted the agenda:

(I) An analysis of the balance of forces within the Socialist International -
- the Regional situation.
- the International situation.

(2) Initiatives to be taken to strengthen the position of progressive forces of Latin America and the Caribbean within the organization.

(3) Initiatives to neutralize forces within S.I. that are against us.

(4) Upcoming activities of S.I. - Regionally and Internationally.

(5) Activities of Copaal - combining S.I. work with Copaal work.

(6) Conference on non-intervention and peace in Central America.

(7) Political character of projected growth of S.I.
- Conference of African S.I.

(8) Structure of S.I.

- Chairmanship of Regional Committees.
- Proposed Regional Executive Secretary.

- 2 -

(9) Proposed Institute of Economic and Political studies.

(IO) ALDHO.- Latin American Human Rights Organization.

(II) Work of Social Democracy in the Region.

The meeting was organized for the purpose of deepening the process of co-ordination among the most progressive S.I. forces of Latin America and the Caribbean with a view towards expanding the influence of the Region as a whole in the Organization and outlining a number of concrete initiatives related to the upcoming Congress of S.I. in Sydney, Australia.

The meeting was chaired by Antonio Harguin of the International Relations department of the F.S.L.N.

I. ANALYSIS

i) Regional Situation - the progressive forces are in control.

a) There are fourteen members of the S.I. Committee for Latin America and the Caribbean.

Of these fourteen, there are seven parties that are generally progressive and some within a Marxist-Lennist trend.

There are three (3) new parties that have recently gained consultative observer status in S.I. They are:

(i) Puerto Rico.
(ii) W.P.A. - Guyana
(iii) P.L.P. - St. Lucia

The presence of these parties will help to strengthen the influence of the progressive forces within the Regional Committee. These parties can, in effect, function like full members of the organization. We must always consult with them and keep them informed.

2. EUROPE IN RELATION TO LATIN AMERICA

a) There are sharp divisions among the European parties in their outlook on Latin America.

- 3 -

b Our friends in this area are prepared to accept the Latin American Revolutionary process as being palatable if restricted to the Latin American context.

c) There is a great amount of misunderstanding about Latin America both among our friends and our enemies - some amount of fear and uncertainty.

d) Many of the European S.I. parties expect us to understand the concept of "the Soviet Menace".

e) Some European parties are concerned that, by the Latin American presence in S.I., they have let in a

f) Many European Parties are willing to hold discussions with us at levels which indicate the contradictions among themselves -
- the difference between Kryski of Austria and Braudl of Germany on the P.L.O. question.

g) Our strongest allies in Europe are the Nordic S.I. parties and that of Holland. There is also good potential with the U.D.P. of Canada.

h) Our principal enemies are to be found among the parties of Soares and Horgo in Portugal and Italy respectively - the Social Democrats of the U.S.A. are also our sworn enemies.

i) The reason why the European parties did not allow W.P.A. and P.L.P. to get beyond the consultative membership status is because of their fear of the growth of membership with parties that they do not control.

j) A Mission to Europe comprising of our most trusted forces in Latin America and the Caribbean can be strategically valuable before the Sydney Congress. It can help to assure our friends and confuse our enemies.

DECISIONS

The next meeting of the Broad Latin America Region S.I. Committee will be in any one of the following places:-

- 4 -

Las Paz - Bolivia
Mexico
Caracas
Canada

Michael Manley of P.N.P. and Auselmo Sule of P.R. will co-ordinate with B. Carlson of the S.I. Secretariat on this matter. Member parties will be informed according.y.

2. A broad resolution on the Latin American and Caribbean situation will be passed at the meeting of the Regional Committee.

Agenda for this meeting will include:

a) Analysis of current political situation.
b) Attitudes to S.I. in Latin America.
c) Issues for Sydney:
   i) New situation
   ii) Expansion of S.I.
d) S.I. Latin America Committee:
   i) Structure
   ii) Staff
   iii) Officers
e) Christian Democracy in Latin America.
f) Actions to strengthen ALDHU.
g) Sydney Resolutions.

3. Hector Oquel of M.N.R. of El Salvador will draft a Resolution on Latin America and the Caribbean by 31st January, 1983. This Resolution will be specifically for the Sydney Congress and will address only the most major issues.

The following guidelines will be the basis for the Resolution:-

(a) The Basle Resolution - including such themes like Peace and Non-Intervention, Anti-Militarisation in the Region, Anti-dictatorship, the settlement of disputes, etc.
(b) Solidarity with Nicaragua, Grenada and the F.D.R., F.M.L.F. and M.N.R. of El Salvador.
(c) A limited number of other key issues in the Region.

- 5 -

(d) The creation of a platform and frame of reference in S.I. for the approach on the Latin America and Caribbean Region until the next Congress in Belgium (in the subsequent 2 years).

4. Subject to the approval of N.J.M., the next meeting of the Secret Regional Caucus of progressive S.I. parties will be in Grenada around the I3th and I4th March. This meeting will have strategic value in that it will provide the opportunity to:
   i) Assess the results of the tour of Europe by the selected parties, and
   ii) Conduct a final assessment on issues related to the Sydney Congress - questions of tactics and levels of co-ordiantion can also be discussed.

6. Grenada should consider inviting a few key S.I. personalities to March I3th celebrations.

7. Bilaterals will be held with new Regional S.I. forces before Congress - Grenada will speak with W.P.A. and P.L.P.

8. In the meeting in Grenada, we are going to consider what initiatives can be taken to support Surinam. If the Surinam Government wishes, an unofficial familiarization visit can be organized subsequent to proposed Grenada meeting. This, it is felt, may have value in preparing members of the Regional Caucus to be able to speak with authority if the question of Surinam is raised in Sydney. If a decision is made to go ahead with this, the team can comprise:

   Radical Party of Chile
   F.S.L.N.
   P.N.P.
   N.D.P.

N.J.M. will establish contact with Surinam and guide the Regional Secret Caucus accordingly.

At the meeting of the S.I. Resolution Committee and Finance Committee in Madrid and Italy respectively during the middle of February, Regional parties should try to have the possible presence.

- 6 -

Subsequent to the Madrid and Italy meetings, a tour of Europe should be organized to hold Bilaterials with all European parties who belong to S.I.

The participants of this mission should include:

Ungo of M.N.R.
Oquel of M.N.R.
Sule of P.R.
Manley of P.N.P.
Miller of P.N.P.
A senior representative of N.J.M.

This mission will seek to counter the forces of Portugal, Italy and the U.S.A.

Seek to spreak discussion within hostile European parties.

Work of the expulsion of the (C.I.A.) U.S.A. Social Democratic Party.

9. Progressive S.I. forces in the Region should seek to attend COPAAL meeting scheduled for Brazil in March and secure reinforcement of Sydney S.I.L.A. Resolution.

10. To push ahead and implement the proposal for the establishment of a Regional Institute for Political and Economic Research.

- Paul Miller of Jamaica as Director
- Open bank account in the Bahamas with signatures of Miller and Hector Oquel.

Maintain the Secret Regional Caucus with periodic and special meetings.

Review membership in the future.

Submitted by.
CDE. CHRIS DE RIGGS.

Document 25

Managua, Nicaragua
February 19, 1981
AÑO DE LA DEFENSA Y LA PRODUCCION.

Comrade
Maurice Bishop
Prime Minister
General Secretary New Jewell Movemet
Grenada.

Dear Comrade:

We acknowledge receipt of your letter, and we thank your for your invitation to our National Direction of the F.S.L.N., through my persom, to attend at your commemoration.

Unfortenatly is not going to be possible for me to attend be-cause of the task that I already have been programed, spe-cially to a particular mission that I have undertake, based on the security and the defense of Nicaragua.

Our National Direction well aware of the importance of this event, therefor has nominated in my place, our brother Sandinista, Comandant of the Revolution Luis Carrión, Vice-Minister of Interior. He will travel with Father Miguel D'Escoto and Father Ernesto Cardenal.

With refference to your needs of uniforms and fabric, we are doing our best. We are going to send you 2,000 uniforms, before March 13th., later on, we are going to send you fabric for another two thousand.

Once upon my return. I will do my best to concret, my wishes to visit your country.

At that time, we will have the opportunity to discurs important matters and also, the Regional situation. That I am sure will help to strength our mutual bonds.

With my best wishes for your people and your Party.

Yours truly,

HUMBERTO ORTEGA SAAVEDRA
MINISTRO DE DEFENSA
COMANDANTE EN JEFE DEL EJERCITO POPULAR SANDINISTA

PATRIA LIBRE O MORIR

Appendix B
Biographical Data

VERNON V. ASPATURIAN

Dr. Vernon V. Aspaturian received his B.A. and Ph.D. from UCLA. Dr. Aspaturian is an Evan Pugh Professor of Political Science and Director of the Slavic and Soviet Language and Area Center at Pennsylvania State University. He has served six years as Distinguished Visiting Professor during summer sessions at the Naval Postgraduate School, Monterey, California. Dr. Aspaturian is the author and coeditor of several books on Soviet foreign policy and comparative communism including, among others, *The Soviet Union in the World Communist System; Process and Power in Soviet Foreign Policy; Eurocommunism between East and West;* and *The Union Republics in Soviet Diplomacy.* He is a frequent consultant to U.S. policymakers such as former Secretary of State Alexander Haig.

MICHAEL CLOUGH

Michael Clough is an Assistant Professor of National Security Affairs at the U.S. Naval Postgraduate School in Monterey, California. He was a Research Fellow at The Brookings Institution in Washington, D.C. before joining the Naval Postgraduate School faculty in 1980. His articles on Zimbabwe, Mozambique, and U.S. policy in Southern Africa have been published in a range of journals over the past five years. He has lectured on U.S. policy toward Africa in Yugoslavia, Portugal, Tanzania, Botswana, Malawi, South Africa, Namibia, Liberia, Zimbabwe, Uganda, Lesotho, Mauritius, and Madagascar. Dr. Clough was the editor of and a major contributor to *Changing Realities in Southern Africa: Implications for American Policy* (Berkeley, California: Institute of International Studies, University of California, 1982). He is currently completing a book on U.S. policy regarding revolutionary conflict in Southern Africa, and he is beginning research on the foreign policies of radical regimes in the Third World.

JORGE I. DOMINGUEZ

Jorge I. Dominguez is a Professor in the Department of Government at Harvard University. He has edited and authored numerous books including *Economic Issues and Political Conflict: US-Latin American Relations; Cuba: Internal and International Affairs; Mexico's Political Economy: Challenges at Home and Abroad; Insurrection or Loyalty: The Breakdown of the Spanish American Empire;* and *Cuba: Order and Revolution.* Dr. Dominguez is a member of several editorial boards including *Cuban Studies, Political Science Quarterly,* and the *Journal of Inter-American Studies and World Affairs.*

CHARLES H. FAIRBANKS, Jr.

Dr. Charles H. Fairbanks, Jr. is presently Deputy Assistant Secretary for Human Rights at the U.S. Department of State. A member of the Policy Planning Staff, U.S. Department of State, from February 1981 to March 1982, Dr. Fairbanks also served as Associate Professor and Assistant Professor in the Department of Political Science at Yale University. He has published numerous articles and publications and the following books: *Arms Races and the Problem of Arms Control: The Soviet Bureaucratic Process* and *The Stalin Regime and Autocratic Politics.* Dr. Fairbanks has held many consulting positions and has served as an advisor to Governor Ronald Reagan, the Department of Defense, and the Rand Corporation.

MARK FALCOFF

Mark Falcoff is a Resident Fellow at the American Enterprise Institute for Public Policy Research, Washington, D.C. He was a Fellow at the Hoover Institution on War, Revolution, and Peace, Stanford University, 1979–1980, and recently served as a senior consultant to the National Bipartisan Commission on Central America, chaired by former Secretary of State Henry Kissinger. Dr. Falcoff's books include (with Ronald H. Dolkart) *Prologue to Peron: Argentina in Depression and War, 1930–43* (1975); (with Federick B. Pike) *The Spanish Civil War, 1936–39: American Hemispheric Perspectives* (1982); and (with Robert Royal) *Crisis and Opportunity: U.S. Policy in Central America and the Caribbean.*

GEORGES A. FAURIOL

Dr. Georges A. Fauriol is presently a Fellow, Caribbean Studies, Senior Research Staff at the Center for Strategic and International Studies, Georgetown University. His past positions have included work at the Naval War College the U.S. International Communications Agency, and the Foreign

Policy Research Institute. Dr. Fauriol has written on a wide variey of topics. His most recent article is entitled, "The Politics of Oil: Belize and Washington," published in *The Times* (Jordon).

CHARLES GATI

Charles Gati is a Professor of Political Science at Union College. Since 1972 he has served as a visiting professor of political science at Colombia University and a Senior Fellow at Colombia's Research Institute on International Change. Dr. Gati is the author, coauthor, editor, and coeditor of numerous books including *The International Politics of Eastern Europe; Caging the Bear: Containment and the Cold War; The Debate Over Détente;* and *The Politics of Modernization in Eastern Europe.* His articles have appeared in *Foreign Affairs, Foreign Policy, World Politics, Problems of Communism, Slavic Review,* and other journals. He has also written for the Op-Ed pages of *The New York Times* and the *Baltimore Sun,* and for the outlook section of *The Washington Post.* Dr. Gati is a member of the Board of the American Association for the Advancement of Slavic Studies and a member of the Council on Foreign Relations. He is presently completing a book entitled, *Democracy in the Soviet Shadow,* a long excerpt of which appeared in the Summer 1984 issue of *Survey* (London).

MARGARET DALY HAYES

Margaret Daly Hayes served as a Professional Staff Member of the U.S. Senate Committee on Foreign Relations with responsibility for Western Hemispheric Affairs. She is currently the Director of the Washington, D.C. office of the Council of the Americas, Washington, D.C. She is a political scientist with special expertise in the Latin American region, United States-Latin American relations, and inter-American Security issues. Prior to coming to the Foreign Relations Committee, Dr. Hayes was Associate Director of the Center of Brazilian Studies at The Johns Hopkins School of Advanced International Studies (1978–1980) and Executive Director of the Commission on United States-Brazil Relations (1979–1980). Dr. Hayes has been a consultant to the Foreign Service Institute of the Department of State, and has directed research projects for the United States Information Agency. She has written extensively on Central American and Caribbean security questions including *Latin America and the U.S. National Interest: A Basis for Foreign Policy.* Dr. Hayes was lead consultant on security issues for the National Bipartisan Commission on Central America. In addition to an active writing agenda, she is a frequent speaker on U.S.-Latin American issues.

COLIN LEGUM

Colin Legum was educated in South Africa, and was active in journalism and politics until 1949. He joined *The Observer* (London) in 1949 as Africa and Commonwealth correspondent, and served as an associate editor until 1981. Mr. Legum also has served as editor of the *Africa Contemporary Record* since 1968 and coeditor of the *Middle East Contemporary Survey* since 1977. He is the author of more than a score of books and has contributed chapters to many other books for American and European universities. A forthcoming book is entitled *The Approaching End of Apartheid.* He has lectured extensively in universities in North America, Europe, Africa, China, and India. Mr. Legum is a regular lecturer at military colleges in Britain, the United States, Holland, the NATO Defense College in Rome, and he has lectured for the New York Council of Foreign Affairs, and for Business International, among others.

GEORGE LISKA

Dr. George Liska is a Professor at the Johns Hopkins University and the School of Advanced International Studies (joint appointment), as well as at the Foreign Policy Institute, Washington, D.C. Dr. Liska has served as a member of the Czechoslovak Ministry of Foreign Affairs (1945–1948), and has held several university teaching positions in the United States. His publications include *International Equilibrium; Nations in Alliance; Imperial America; Alliances in the Third World; Beyond Kissinger: Ways of Conservative Statecraft;* and *Russia and the Road to Appeasement.*

ANTHONY P. MAINGOT

Dr. Anthony P. Maingot del Barco is presently a tenured Professor of Sociology/Anthropology and Director of the graduate program in International Studies at Florida International University. Dr. Maingot has also served as Professor of International Relations at the Institute of International Relations, University of the West Indies, Trinidad, and as Assistant Professor at Yale University. His outside activities include serving as Associate Editor of the *Caribbean Review,* and he is a member of the Executive Committee of the New England Latin American Studies Association. His publications are numerous, the most recent being "Perceptions as Realities: The USA, Venezuela and Cuba in the Caribbean" and "Ethnic Bargaining and the Non-Citizen: Cubans and Haitians in Miami" in John Stack (ed.), *Ethnicity: The Transnational Dimension.*

JACK F. MATLOCK, Jr.

Jack F. Matlock, Jr. is Special Assistant to the President for National Security Affairs and Senior Director of European and Soviet Affairs on the National Security Council staff. He is a career Foreign Service Officer with extensive experience in Europe and Africa. Before assuming his present duties, he was United States Ambassador to Czechoslovakia since November 1981. He earlier served three tours of duty at the American Embassy in Moscow: in 1981 as Chargé d'Affaires; from 1974–1978 as Deputy Chief of Mission; and from 1961–1963 as Consular Officer and Political Officer specializing in Soviet internal affairs. He was also Director of the Office of Soviet Union Affairs in the Department of State from 1971 to 1974. He is the author of a handbook to the 13-volume Russian edition of Stalin's *Collected Works* (Washington, 1966, New York, 1971). He has published articles on Soviet foreign policy, Soviet government, and Russian literature.

CHARLES W. MAYNES

Charles W. Maynes entered the Foreign Service in 1962, and in 1970 became a Congressional Fellow, initially working for Congressman Bradford Morse and subsequently for Senator Fred R. Harris, whom he later served as Senior Legislative Assistant. He worked on Sargent Shriver's issues staff during the 1972 presidential campaign. Mr. Maynes began work for the Carnegie Endowment for International Peace in 1972 as Director of the International Organization Program, and in 1973 became the institution's Secretary. Mr. Maynes became Assistant Secretary of State for Internaional Organization Affairs in January 1977 with responsibility for U.S. Policy in the United Nations and its Specialized Agencies. Since April 1980 he has served as editor of *Foreign Policy*. Mr. Maynes is a member of the Council on Foreign Relations and the United Nations' Association.

RICHARD L. MILLETT

Dr. Richard L. Millett is a Professor of History at Southern Illinois University, Edwardsville. Dr. Millett has also been a Fulbright Professor at National University, Javeriana University, Universidad de Los Andes, Universidad del Valle, Colombia, and Visiting Professor of International Relations at the Air War College, Montgomery, Alabama. Among Dr. Millett's many publications are *The Restless Caribbean: Changing Patterns of International Relations*, *Guardianes de la dinestia*, and *Guardians of the Dynasty*. His most recent articles include "Practorians or Patriots? The Central American Military," in Robert Leiken, (ed.), *Central America: Anatomy of Conflict*, and "Central America," in Jon Black (ed.), *Contemporary Latin America*.

RICHARD PIPES

Dr. Richard Pipes has been a member of the faculty of Harvard University since 1950. He has been Professor of History (1963–1975), Director of the Russian Research Center (1965–1973), and he is currently the Frank B. Baird Professor of History (1975-Present). Dr. Pipes was Director of East European and Soviet Affairs at the National Security Council from 1981–1982, and he served on the Reagan Transition Team at the Department of State in 1980. He has received numerous awards including the Guggenheim Fellow and Member, Council on Foreign Relations. His major works include *Formation of the Soviet Union; Karamzin's Memoir on Ancient and Modern Russia; Social Democracy and the Soviet Petersberg Labor Movement; Europe Since 1815; Russia Under the Old Regime;* and *U.S. Soviet Relations in the Era of Détente.*

CONDOLEEZA RICE

Condoleeza Rice is an Assistant Professor of Political Science and Assistant Director of the Center for International Security and Arms Control at Stanford University. Professor Rice is a specialist in East European foreign policy, defense policy, and international security policy. She is the author of a book on Soviet-East European military relations entitled, *Uncertain Allegiance: The Soviet Union and the Czechoslovak Army.* Her publications include numerous articles on the Warsaw Pact and the Soviet military. Dr. Rice is a consultant to the Rand Corporation and Science Applications, Inc.

SALLY A. SHELTON

Ambassador Sally A. Shelton has spent several years in government service and academia. She served from 1979 to 1981 as the U.S. Ambassador to Barbados, Grenada, and eight other Caribbean nations and territories (Anguilla, Antigua, the British Virgin Islands, Dominica, Montserrat, St. Kitts-Nevis, St. Lucia, and St. Vincent). Before assuming her ambassadorial post, she was Deputy Assistant Secretary of State for Inter-American Affairs, served on the U.S. Mission to the United Nations, and was Legislative Assistant for International Affairs to Senator Lloyd Bentsen of Texas. She was also Senior Consultant to the Vice President of the World Bank. Ambassador Shelton was a Fulbright Scholar at the Institut des Sciences Politiques in Paris, and she is a member of the Council on Foreign Relations.

JIRI VALENTA

Professor Jiri Valenta is Academic Associate and Coordinator of Soviet and East European Studies at the Naval Postgraduate School, Monterey,

California. He was recently appointed Professor of Political Science and Director of Soviet Studies at the Graduate School of International Studies, University of Miami, Coral Gables, Florida. He has been a Fellow at Woodrow Wilson International Center for Scholars, the Brookings Institution, the Council on Foreign Relations, and the Rockefeller Foundation. He is author of *Soviet Intervention in Czechoslovakia, 1968: Anatomy of a Decision,* coeditor of and contributor to *Eurocommunism between East and West,* and more recently, *Soviet Decisionmaking for National Security.* His articles have appeared in *Foreign Policy, International Security, Problems of Communism, Comparative Politics,* and the Op-Ed pages of the *New York Times* and *The Baltimore Sun.* He has directed a Council on Foreign Relations group on the Polish Crisis of 1981–1982, chaired by Lt. General Brent Scowcroft (USAF, Ret.). He has also testified before the Kissinger Bipartisan Commission and in Congressional Hearings on Soviet policy in Latin America. He is a member of the Council on Foreign Relations.

VIRGINIA VALENTA

Virginia Valenta received an M.A. in Romance Languages from the University of Missouri, Columbia. She has written several articles on Soviet and Cuban policies in Latin America, and is coauthor of *Soviet Strategy in the Caribbean Basin* (forthcoming) and "Leninism in Grenada," *Problems of Communism,* July-August 1983. She has lectured in China at the Latin American Institute of the Chinese Academy of Sciences, Peking, People's Republic of China, and she has conducted extensive research in several Latin American nations on the Caribbean Basin.

BRUCE WEINROD

Bruce Weinrod is Director of Foreign Policy and Defense Studies at the Heritage Foundation, a public policy research organization based in Washington, D.C. Dr. Weinrod served with the U.S. Army in the Panama Canal Zone for 18 months. He has served as a Latin American specialist at the Foreign Policy Research Institute in Philadelphia, and has published numerous articles on Latin American matters. Prior to joining the Heritage Foundation, he served on the Writing and Research staff at the White House and as Legislative Director to Senator John Heinz of Pennsylvania. He is a member of the International Institute for Strategic Studies. Most recently, Dr. Weinrod returned from a fact-finding visit to Central America, and was an observer to the first round of the 1983 presidential election in El Salvador.

HOWARD J. WIARDA

Howard J. Wiarda is a Resident Scholar and Director of the Center for Hemispheric Studies at the American Enterprise Institute for Public Policy

Research in Washington, D.C. He is Professor of Political Science and Adjunct Professor of Comparative Labor Relations at the University of Massachusetts in Amherst. Dr. Wiarda was a consultant to the National Bipartisan Commission on Central America and has held grants from the Rockefeller Foundation, Fulbright Program, Mershon Center, the Social Science Research Council, American Philosophical Society, National Endowment for the Humanities, and National Institute of Health. His most recent books include *In Search of Policy: The United States and Latin America; Rift and Revolution; The Central American Imbroglio;* and *Politics and Social Change in Latin America.*

DOV S. ZAKHEIM

Prior to entering service with the Department of Defense, Dr. Dov S. Zakheim was a Principal Analyst with the Security and International Affairs Division of the Congressional Budget Office, where he served as team leader for policy and program analyses of naval, mobility, and intervention force issues. Dr. Zakheim is currently Assistant Under Secretary of Defense for Policy/Resources. Among other responsibilities, he serves as Program and Budget Review Manager, and as Defense Systems Acquisition Review Manager for the Under Secretary of Defense for Policy/Resources. In addition, Dr. Zakheim coordinates the Under Secretary's production of the Policy section of the Annual Report of the Secretary of Defense. He has also led, or has been a member of, high-level teams that have successfully negotiated agreements with a number of European nations.

Appendix C

CONFERENCE PARTICIPANTS

Dr. Vernon V. Aspaturian
Director of Slavic and Soviet Language Studies
Pennsylvania State University

Mr. John Blacken
Deputy Coordinator for Public Diplomacy for Latin America
U.S. Department of State

Dr. Sherman Blandin
Chair
Department of National Security Affairs
Naval Postgraduate School

Col. Brian J. Bosch, USA
Defense Intelligence Officer for Latin America
Defense Intelligence Agency

Mr. Richard C. Brown
Deputy Assistant Secretary for the Caribbean
U.S. Department of State

Dr. Michael Clough
Coordinator of African Studies
Department of National Security Affairs
Naval Postgraduate School

Mr. Charles E. Courtney
Associate Director
Bureau of Programs
United States Information Agency

Mr. Edward Desmond
Correspondent
Time

Dr. Jorge I. Dominguez
Department of Government
Harvard University

Dr. Herbert J. Ellison
Secretary
Kennan Institute for Advanced Russian Studies
Woodrow Wilson International Center for Scholars

Dr. Charles H. Fairbanks, Jr.
Fellow
Woodrow Wilson International Center for Scholars
and former Deputy Assistant Secretary for Human Rights
Department of State

Dr. Mark Falcoff
Resident Fellow
American Enterprise Institute

Dr. Tom J. Farer
Distinguished Professor
Rutgers School of Law
and former Chair of the Inter-American
Committee on Human Rights (OAS)

Dr. Georges Fauriol
Senior Research Staff—Caribbean Studies
Center for Strategic and International Studies
Georgetown University

Dr. Charles Gati
Department of Political Science
Columbia University and Union College

Dr. Toby T. Gati
Vice President for Policy Studies
United Nations Association

Dr. Alexander George
Deparment of Political Science
Stanford University

Dr. Margaret Daly Hayes
Director
Council of the Americas, Washington, D.C.
and former Professional Staff Member
U.S. Senate Committee on Foreign Relations

Mr. John Helgerson
Director
Office of African and Latin American Analysis
Central Intelligence Agency

Dr. Jerry Hough
Senior Fellow
The Brookings Institution
and the Kennan Institute for Advanced Russian Studies

Mr. Karel Jezdinsky
Radio Free Europe/Radio Liberty, Inc.

Mr. Bradford P. Johnson, Esq.
Kennan Institute for Advanced Russian Studies
Woodrow Wilson International Center for Scholars

Dr. Stephen S. Kaplan
Central Intelligence Agency

Dr. Andrzej Korbonski
Political Science Department
University of California at Los Angeles

Mr. Colin Legum
Senior Editor
The London Observer

Dr. George Liska
School of Advanced International Studies
and Department of Political Science
The Johns Hopkins University

Mr. Winston Lord
President
Council on Foreign Relations

CDR William Lyda
United States Navy

COL James McDevitt, USA
National Defense University
Strategic Concepts Development Center

Dr. Anthony P. Maingot del Barco
Professor of Sociology and Anthropology
Florida International University

Dean Kneale Marshall
Naval Postgraduate School

Mr. Michael Massing
Atlantic Monthly

Hon. Jack F. Matlock, Jr.
Special Assistant to the President
and Senior Director for European and Soviet Affairs
National Security Council

Dr. Charles W. Maynes
Editor
Foreign Policy

Dr. Constantine Menges
Special Assistant to the President
and Senior Director for Latin American Affairs
National Security Council

Dr. Richard L. Millet
Director of History
Southern Illinois University

Dr. Richard Pipes
Department of History
Harvard University

Dr. Susan Purcell
Senior Fellow
Council on Foreign Relations

Dr. Condeleeza Rice
Department of Political Science
Stanford University

Hon. Gilbert A. Robinson
Special Advisor to the Secretary of State for Public Diplomacy
U.S. Department of State

Hon. Edward Rowny
Chair
U.S. START Committee
Arms Control and Disarmament Agency

Mr. Nestor D. Sanchez
Deputy Assistant Secretary of Defense for Inter-American Affairs

Provost David Schrady
Naval Postgraduate School

Ms. Kate Senerad
Assistant Administrator
Agency for International Development

Lt. Frederick F. Shaheen
Naval Postgraduate School

Hon. Sally A. Shelton
International Business Government Counselors

RADM Robert H. Shumaker, USN
Superintendent
Naval Postgraduate School

Ms. Sonia Sluzar
Senior Editor
Problems of Communism
United States Information Agency

Mr. Dan Southerland
Christian Science Monitor

COMO Robert Steele, USN
Director
Military Policy and Current Plans Division
U.S. Department of Defense

Ms. Kay Stevenson
Policy Support Programs
Office of the Secretary of Defense

Dr. Dana Sweet
Cuba-Caribbean Section
Defense Intelligence Agency

COL George Thompson, USAF
Deputy Director

Policy Support Programs
Office of the Secretary of Defense

Dr. Jiri Valenta
Coordinator, Soviet and East European Studies
Department of National Security Affairs
Naval Postgraduate School, 1985–86
Professor of Political Science and
Director of Soviet, East European
and Strategic Studies
Graduate School of International Studies
University of Miami

Mrs. Virginia Valenta
Monterey, California

Hon. Vernon Walters
Ambassador to the United Nations
U.S. Department of State

Mr. W. Bruce Weinrod
Director of Foreign Policy and Defense Studies
The Heritage Foundation

Dr. Robert Wesson
Senior Fellow
Hoover Institution
Stanford University

Dr. Howard J. Wiarda
Director of Hemispheric Studies
American Enterprise Institute
Professor of Political Science
Amherst College

Dr. Walter Max Woods
Dean of Educational Development
and Executive Director
Office of Continuing Education
Naval Postgraduate School

Dr. Dov Zakheim
Assistant Under Secretary of Defense for Policy/Resources
U.S. Department of Defense

Index